NUCLEAR
POLITICS

NUCLEAR

POLITICS

Towards a Safer World

Satyabrata Rai Chowdhuri

NEW DAWN PRESS, INC.
USA • UK • INDIA

NEW DAWN PRESS GROUP

Published by New Dawn Press Group
New Dawn Press, Inc., 244 South Randall Rd # 90, Elgin, IL 60123
e-mail: sales@newdawnpress.com

New Dawn Press, 2 Tintern Close, Slough, Berkshire, SL1-2TB, UK
e-mail : ndpuk@mail.newdawnpress.com

New Dawn Press (An Imprint of Sterling Publishers (P) Ltd.)
A-59, Okhla Industrial Area, Phase-II, New Delhi-110020
e-mail: sales@sterlingpublishers.com
ghai@nde.vsnl.net.in

Nuclear Politics: Towards a Safer World
Copyright © 2004 by Satyabrata Rai Chowdhuri
ISBN 1 932705 02 3

PRINTED IN INDIA

In Memory of Bela
with love, admiration
& gratitude

FOREWORD

The past few years have witnessed a number of remarkable developments in the field of nuclear arms control and non-proliferation. The United States and the Soviet Union (now Russia) signed the START I and II agreements, which promised to reduce the nuclear arsenals of the two countries by two-thirds, to approximately 3,000 nuclear warheads each by the year 2003. President Bush's announcement on September 27, 1991 of a nuclear "stand-down" resulted in the removal of all US ground-based tactical nuclear weapons from overseas and halting the deployment of such weapons at sea. Similarly, Russia has removed all its tactical nuclear weapons from ships and has gathered in those tactical nuclear weapons that had been based in Belarus, Ukraine and Kazakhstan. With respect to non-proliferation efforts, France and China signed the Non-Proliferation Treaty (NPT) in August 1991 and March 1992, respectively. North Korea finally signed a safeguards agreement with the International Atomic Energy Agency (IAEA) in January 1992, providing some measure of confidence that Pyongyang's nuclear ambitions could be moderated. South Africa signed the NPT and placed all its nuclear facilities under safeguards. Thirty-three states of Latin America and the Caribbean, including Cuba, have already signed the Treaty of Tlatelolco which was ratified on March 20, 1995. They have also acceded to the NPT. These positive developments have not been matched in South Asia, where the nuclear programmes of India and Pakistan still cause great concern to many countries. While Pakistan's nuclear programme has been frozen at its 1989 level, India has not. Along with Delhi's refusal to discuss nuclear issues in the proposed Five Power Talks, India's ongoing efforts in the nuclear field seem quite at odds with the prevailing trend towards "new thinking" in international affairs.

Before new thinking on these issues is possible, however, it is imperative to have a comprehensive understanding of "old thinking", namely, an appreciation of the history of the nuclear arms race and efforts to control it. Professor Chowdhuri's book, *Nuclear Politics: Towards a Safer World*, provides a comprehensive examination of the history of nuclear weapons. He has condensed a remarkable amount of information and presented it in a coherent and readable manner. His emphasis on the politics of nuclear weapons is exactly right, as the decisions to develop and refine a country's nuclear arsenals are inherently political.

While I do not agree with Prof. Chowdhuri on all points – I am more optimistic about the NPT and its future, more positive about regional stability, and more appreciative of the real accomplishment of recent arms control agreements – his book is full of accurate and provocative insights. The study makes a contribution to the growing literature in India on these important subjects. That this study was compiled by an Indian scholar should also ensure that it receives a wide reading outside of South Asia.

Mitchell Reiss
Woodrow Wilson International
Center for Scholars
Washington D.C.

ACKNOWLEDGEMENT

I owe a debt of deep gratitude to Dr Mitchell Reiss, Guest Professor at Woodrow Wilson International Center for Scholars, Washington D.C., for taking keen interest in this work and going through the manuscript over and over again with unfailing patience. Although he did not agree with all my views expressed here, my discussions with him, his suggestions and criticisms were illuminating and full of insights. In my times of despair, I found in him a fount of unwavering inspiration. His words of encouragement redounded to my hope that this work might, in some way make a humble contribution to the growing literature on a host of issues relating to nuclear politics.

This work is based upon the belief that serious effort and integrated forethought can contribute – indeed, are indispensable – to progress in the coming decades towards a more humane, peaceful, productive, and just world. And it rests upon the hope that readers of this work – whether or not they agree with my point of view – may be helped to think more informedly about the opportunities and the dangers that lie ahead and the consequences of various courses of future action.

CONTENTS

Foreword   vii
Acknowledgement   ix

1. Prologue   1

2. Nuclear Politics   51

3. Megatonomania   113

4. Nuclear Regimes   175

5. IAEA Safeguards: New Challenges   264

6. Post-Soviet Nuclear Politics   321

7. Epilogue   372

   Appendices   483

   Glossary   615

   Abbreviations   622

   Bibliography   626

   Index   651

PROLOGUE

"The time has come," the Walrus said, "to talk of many things: of shoes – and ships – and sealing wax – of cabbages and kings - and why the sea is boiling hot – and whether pigs have wings."

Lewis Carroll, Through the Looking Glass

The meaning of life has puzzled men's minds ever since the first appearance of our planet, of the puzzle we call the mind of man. The question as usually posed has no answer. The reason has to do with the meaning of "meaning".

Nothing new under the sun – book, picture, or symphony, rock, flower, or butterfly – has any meaning to any of us unless and until it stirs some feeling or thought derived from past experience. Meaning in the mind, and corresponding action in dealing with the world, is ever a business of defining each day's challenge to our senses and our wits, by reference to what has already been built into our organisms through earlier "education", of our own and that of our ancestors. Life is like a dictionary: each word means other words; the relationship to other bits of experience, then the whole experience, i.e., the "meaning of life", is literally meaningless save in terms of the connections among the segments or in terms of the mind of God – whose wisdom and will mere mortal men and women can comprehend only dimly.

We shall be concerned in these pages not with all experience but with that fraction of our shared experience known as "politics" and, more particularly, with that area of politics in which nations encounter nations. These contacts are often dramatic. They are also disturbing. Contemporary mankind seems somehow to have so mismanaged the relations among nations as to confront us all with their peril and, often, bitter tragedy. But we are unlikely to learn much that is useful about these matters, or how to act relevantly in the service of our purposes, unless we first try to examine international politics from afar, in the widest possible perspective, rather than limit our view to this evening's news broadcasts and tomorrow morning's headlines.

People think about, and act upon, each day's events only in terms of what they know about past events and about the things the events remind them. In politics, as in all spheres of life, what people "know" largely determines what they see, hear and feel, and how they think and act. In looking at world affairs and the acts of other men, all men see what is not but not what is, because all of us are inevitably prisoners of our past and interpret what we look at in terms of what we want to see or what is easiest to see because we presume we have seen it before. The difficulties of freeing ourselves from this thralldom were well put more than two thousand years ago by an astute psychologist, philosopher, and political scientist named Plato (428 - 348 B.C.) "Behold! Human beings living in an underground den ... here they have been from their childhood, and have their legs chained so that they cannot move, and can only see before them ... Above and behind them a fire is blazing at a distance, and between the fire and the prisoners there is a low wall built along the way, like the screen which marionette players have in front of them, over which they show the puppets."

"I see."

"And do you see men passing along the wall carrying all sorts of vessels and statues and figures of animals made of wood and stone and various materials, which appear over the wall? Some of them are talking, others silent."

"You have shown me a strange image, and they are strange prisoners."

"Like ourselves, and they see only their own shadows, or the shadows of one another which the fire throws on the opposite wall of the cave."

"True. How could they see anything but the shadows if they were never allowed to move their heads?"

"Yes."

"And of the objects which are being carried in a likewise manner they would only see the shadows?"

"Yes."

"And if they were able to converse with one another, would they not suppose that they were naming what was actually before them?"

"Very true."

"And suppose further that the prison had an echo which came from the other side, would they not be sure to fancy when one of the passersby spoke that the voice which they heard came from the passing shadow?"

"No question."

"To them the truth would be literally nothing but the shadows of the images."

(*The Republic*, Book VII; Jowett's translation.)

Plato goes on to discuss the wonderment of such bondsmen if they were suddenly liberated and brought out into the sunshine, and their reluctance to accept the "real truth" in place of what they supposed was the truth. Here, undoubtedly is the central difficulty in all life, and most markedly in all politics – as to both its study and its practice. Why it is central was well explained a generation ago by Walter Lippmann in his *Public Opinion*: "What each man does is based not on direct and certain knowledge, but on pictures made by himself or given to him. If his atlas tells him that the world is flat he will not sail near what he believes to be the edge of our planet for fear of falling off. If his maps include a fountain of eternal youth, a Ponce de Leon will go in quest of it. If someone digs up yellow dirt that looks like gold, he will for a time act exactly as if he had found gold. The way in which the world is imagined determines at any particular moment what men will do ... The world that we have to deal with politically is out of reach, out of sight, out of mind. It has to be explored, reported, and imagined. Man is no Aristotelian God contemplating all existence at one glance. He is the creature of an evolution, who can just about span a sufficient portion of reality to manage his survival, and snatch what on the scale of time are but a few moments of insight and happiness ... Each of us lives and works on a small part of the earth's surface, moves in a small circle, and of these acquaintances knows only a few intimately ... Inevitably our opinions cover a bigger space, a longer reach of time, a greater number of things, than we can directly observe. They have, therefore, to be pieced together out of what others have reported and what we can imagine."

In this process of piecing together, Lippmann points out that we see the world through our "stereotypes" – i.e., through the pictures-in-our-heads that others have called habits or configurations (Gestalten) or "conditioned responses". This way of looking at, and thinking about and responding to the world is useful and necessary and is, indeed, the only way we have. But if we are unaware of its nature and its imperatives, we are easily deceived rather than helped to fit our image to reality. For every stereotype has its "blind spot" which close our eyes to everything which does not fit into the pattern to which we have become accustomed.

Everyone who studies or teaches or writes about world affairs is bound (try as he will to escape) to spend some time considering shadows-on-the-wall as if they were real. And as for politicians, diplomats, strategists, lawmakers, and ordinary citizens who do little studying, their vision is blurred and their judgement twisted, more often than not, by lenses which magnify or reduce or otherwise distort. This is chiefly due to the fact that our views of politics, and especially of international politics, are coloured not only by our past perceptions but also by our loyalties.

This again is quite inevitable and even necessary and desirable. A man without loyalties is a man without a country, without a faith, without the shared beliefs and hopes which make life livable. But if we would study world politics "objectively" and "scientifically", in the expectation that new wisdom may be acquired thereby, and if we would read printed pages critically (including those you are reading now), then we need to take account of the loyalties of man as a source of prejudice and error as well as of fellowship and faith.

All loyalties are designed for organizing love, fear and hate. Every human baby responds with "rage" or hatred to restraint and deprivation, with "fear" to loud noise and loss of support, and with "love" to food and petting. He soon learns to love mamma and papa and to fear and hate a great variety of things and persons, often including, ambivalently, mamma or papa or both. He later learns, as his universe enlarges, to transfer these feelings to creeds and fatherlands, churches and states, and the belief systems and value patterns we have come to call "ideologies". In the buzzing, booming world of great society of modern civilization, old loyalties to home and neighbourhood, town and province, guild and parish have been merged in newer allegiances to larger communities, and these in turn have been mingled with diverse devotions to symbols of loves and fears and hates, transcending physical frontiers e.g., Democracy, Fascism, Communism, Atlantic Union, United Europe, the Free World, the Dictatorship of the Proletariat, Free Enterprise, the New International Economic Order.

Through such glasses, various groups of human beings, or the same groups at different times, observe the passing skin and act upon what they see. Since all thinking is thus conditioned, people think differently and act divergently. Often they act combatively against those labeled as enemies, traitors, heretics, or infidels. Most people unite more readily against what they fear and hate than in dedication to what they love. "Orthodoxy", commented Carlyle, "is my doxy and heterodoxy is your doxy." We each tend to regard our faith as the only faith, our picture of the world as the true picture. Fearing and scoffing and sneering at others is a temptation resisted only by those well skilled in tolerance.

All of the vast literature of international relations bears upon its face the sundry beliefs, values, and hopes of its many authors – with a rigid "line" of political conformism enforced in contemporary totalitarian societies and a fruitful variety of divergent views still permitted in democracies. Much of this literature act as special pleading "for" or "against" specific nations or statesmen or particular creeds or cults. Some of it, including the works commonly regarded as most useful in institutions of higher learning in the Free World, aspires to be "scholarly" and "unprejudiced".

With respect to the problem of how people think about world affairs, two ways of classifying such works are perhaps more illuminating than others i.e., by the field of learning which each writer most carefully cultivate and by the focus of attention of each writer as he tries to interpret the kaleidoscope of international relations.

Historians tell a tale of human events through time. Without accurate and documented accounts of foreign politics, wherein are wars, negotiations, and treaties, no knowledge of world politics is possible. Equally indispensable are the contributions of the geographers and geologists who are concerned with relations of space: landways, seaways, gateways, barriers, climates, resource and other aspects of man's earthly home. The economist views the adventure in terms of the production, exchange, and consumption of goods and services and the distribution of wealth and income. The political scientist looks at government – the absence of government, approximations to government, and aspirations toward government in the community of nations. His chief concern may be law or administration or political theory or political processes and public opinion, or some combination of these. Psychologists, sociologists, and anthropologists, among other specialists, each supply data and area relevant to some phases of the spectacle.

The "science" of international relations is clearly not a single compartment of knowledge but is rather an eclectic interdepartmental discipline. Each of the social sciences and the humanities and the biological and physical sciences as well, has gifts to bring to the banquet. But if the diners are not to suffer indigestion or die of a surfeit, the various contributions to the repast must somehow be carefully chosen, skillfully blended, and well cooked and flavored – an arduous but appetizing task which is now only barely begun.

As for the question of what each writer "sees" in what he tries to look at, perceptions are many and varied. Some see the community of nations as an enterprise in law and order. Many of these seers, despite disappointments, envisage a sequence of struggles toward the world in which all sovereignties will ultimately abide by the rules of law, settle their disputes peacefully, and build a growing structure of collective security collaboration. A few see a trend towards world government, and doubt whether law and order among states is possible without a merging of sovereignties into some supranational pattern of power. Others see a global area of power politics in which the "Powers" incessantly compete, by trickery and force, for advantages over their rivals. Still others see in these striving a combat between good and evil. Many other ways of looking at world affairs are available to those still free to choose among differing perspectives.

Since there is no one "correct" way to view the world for those who still enjoy the blessings of liberty, these quarrels are confusing. But they can recall the Hindu legend of the blind men who felt the elephant. One described the creature as like a snake (he had grabbed the tail); another as like a wall (he had touched the flank); a third as like a tree (he had seized the trunk); a fourth as like a sword (the tusk), etc. All these conclusions were "true". But each was incorrect unless balanced by the others. The problem is even more difficult with world affairs, for the elephants of international relations are less tangible than the physical elephant's anatomy. Most observers see some aspect of reality. But they see little if they see only that which interests or excites them most.

To see the world truly, one must see it steadily and see it whole. Citizens, teachers, students and text writers, even in highly literate and free communities, cannot hope to achieve full success in this endeavour. The most learned of savants have not yet learned the trick. But the crises of our era summon each of us to try and make whatever contributions we can to insight and foresight through discriminating selections and combinations among the various orientations offered for our guidance. No one can do more. To do less is to betray that faith in human rationality and in the salvation of mankind through wisdom and virtue which we have all alike inherited from the philosophers, prophets, and saints of times gone by.

This then is our enterprise. It is, thus, never ending. Pursuit of truth is a continuing adventure. But understanding is a process, not a destination. It is to be found only in the course of the journey and not at the end. Before we set forth on our travels, however, we shall do well to explore where we are and whence we have come – by way of a backward glance of the route by which humanity has slowly entered the dangers and opportunities of the thermonuclear era.

In the perspective of the long centuries during which the Western state system emerged in Europe and evolved into a global constellation of sovereignties, World War II represents a formidable attempt to achieve the political unification of the world community by violence. Here, as before, the powers aspiring for universal domination were ultimately crushed by a superior coalition of powers raised up against them by their own ambitions. The final result was the preservation of the existence and independence of the victors and the restoration of the state system as a congeries of separate sovereignties. And here, as before, the triumphant allies drifted apart and became rivals for power among themselves.

Despite the persistence of this antique design for anarchy, some novel features of the new time are noteworthy. One was the scheme since 1917 between the New Russia and the Atlantic Powers, the former viewing the latter as a foul matrix of bourgeois decadence, capitalist exploitation, imperialistic sin, and wicked plots to attack and destroy the proletarian paradise; and the latter viewing the former as a hideous citadel of tyranny, slavery, godlessness, and viciously subversive conspiracy to destroy property, piety, and popular rule throughout the world. Another is the subsequent emergence of Fascist totalitarianism in three great powers, dedicated in the name of anti-Communism, anti-Liberalism, and anti-Capitalism to the conquest of the globe, followed by crushing defeat and the reduction of these states to powers of second or third rank, along with a comparable reduction in the status of the impoverished western European democracies. The result of the victory of the United Nations was to give the United States effective influence over Eurafrica and the Atlantic and Pacific areas and over Eurasia to the Soviet Union. Today, the scenario has undergone a sea-change, but the world of 1950s was a divided and bipolar world of two colossal Super Powers, with the rest as their allies or prisoners except for the few non-aligned countries.

· The fascinating problem of "measuring" the relative power of the giants is scarcely worth pursuing, since the decisive elements of imperial power are beyond measurement. Military science is more than ever the wildest guesswork, with each wholly incalculable and irresponsible move in diplomacy and war being dignified and rendered plausible by being called "a calculated risk". We may more usefully conclude our survey of power by noting some of the efforts, largely futile but occasionally suggestive, on the part of the serious students of world affairs to find some key or clue to the conclusions and paradoxes of a strange new world.

The focus of professional and public attention has shifted from point to point as each new source of power or weapon of battle has impressed itself most vividly on men's minds. The practices of governmental control of business activity i.e., mercantilism, neo-mercantilism, and, more recently, "economic planning", have led some to develop the thesis that national power rests primarily on wise and masterly regulation of the national economy by the state e.g., Alexander Hamilton, Friedrich List, Walter Rathenau and Barnard Baruch, among others. Military writers have urged anew the merits of the swift offensive e.g., H. von Moltke, Alfred von Schlieffen, Ferdinand Foch, Charles de Gaulle; or the relative impregnability of modern defence – Magonot, Gamelin, Liddle Hart. The cult of the decisiveness of sea power was first popularised at the turn of the century by Adm. Alfred Thayer Mahan, who was echoed by various British, Continental, and Japanese writers. The contention that contemporary wars are won through air power was first developed in 1921 by Gen. Giulio Douhet of Italy and later propounded in the United States by Gen. William Mitchell and Alexander de Seversky. In recent times, literature on missile warfare, biological warfare, chemical warfare, and nuclear warfare has been growing at a rapid pace.

The most impressive single effort thus far to correlate and synthesise these various approaches and to link them with new concepts of global geography is that of the "geopoliticians". This movement, curiously enough, stems in a sense from the "wheel maps" of the Middle Ages, which depicted Jerusalem as the "centre" of the world, with the precise spot marked on the floor of the Church of the Holy Sepulchre. This quaint notion is absurd to anyone who pictures the world in terms of the familiar "Macerator's projection", with the American continents in the middle and the northernmost land masses of the planet vastly inflated by virtue of converting a sphere into a cylinder. A glance at a globe, however, reveals that the Holy Land does, in fact, lie near the midpoint of the great Eurasian-African landmass.

In 1904, the English geographer, Sir Halford J. Mackinder, delivered a lecture in London on "The Geographical Pivot of History", in which he pointed out the peculiar role of the "Fertile Crescent" extending from Palestine to the Persian Gulf. In his *Democratic Ideals and Reality* (1919) he developed the concepts of the "World Island", i.e., Asia-Europe-Africa, and the "Heartland", i.e., the north central Eurasian plains whose waters drain into the Arctic or inland seas. He suggested that the holders of the Heartland, while able to threaten peripheral areas, are secure against the sea power of the Atlantic and Pacific coastal states, and that land-based air power might well prove superior to naval might. His moral was: "Who rules East Europe commands the Heartland; who rules the Heartland commands the World Island; who rules the World Island commands the world".

Meanwhile, the German geographer and Major General, Karl Haushofer (who prior to 1914 had visited and written about the Far East and the "Indo-Pacific sphere"), interested himself in Mackinder's formulations; pursued the studies suggested by his predecessor Friedrich Ratzel (1844-1904) at the University of Munich; and borrowed the term *geopolitik* from the writings of the Swedish scholar, Rudolf Kjellen. In 1922, Haushofer founded in Munich the Institute of Geopolitics, which published the *Zeitschrift fur Geopolitik* and became a large research organisation. He predicted approvingly the Japanese programme of Greater East Asia and as early as 1923 asserted: "Italy and Japan are the future allies of Germany." He published *Macht und Erde* (1927), *Wehrgeopolitik* (1932), *Welpolitik von Heute* (1934), and innumerable monographs and articles. His aide-de-camp in World War I was Rudolf Hess, through whom he first met Hitler in 1924. Since *der Fuhrer* and his co-conspirators found much of value for their purpose in Haushofer's "new science", they made much of him after 1933, permitting him to keep his Jewish wife, proclaiming his two sons "honorary Aryans", and expanding the Institute as a centre of geopolitical planning for world conquest.

But this marriage of the new science to the new barbarism came to an evil end. Haushofer fully shared the patriotic, Pan-German expansionist ambitions of the Nazi leaders and was equally concerned with making the Reich a "World Power" over the ruins of the British Empire. But he favoured a German-Russian-Japanese bloc and warned that any Japanese frontal attack on China or any German frontal attack on Russia would get bogged down in the vast reaches of Eurasia and end in disaster. When his advice was ignored and his predictions were not realised, he fell from grace. His eldest son, Albrecht, was arrested for plotting against Hitler, imprisoned, and finally murdered on the eve of the fall of Berlin. Haushofer himself was sent to the Dachau concentration camp in 1944. His younger son, Heinz, suffered a similar fate. Both were liberated at the end of the war. He returned to Munich, a bitter and broken old man. On March 10, 1946, he and his faithful wife committed suicide.

To extract the wheat of science from the chaff of nonsense and mysticism in the still burgeoning literature of *geopolitik* is no simple task. There is no past or present evidence to support Sir Halford's original political and strategic generalisations about the Heartland (as he himself conceded in his last days), even though some aspects of Anglo-American policy toward Russia since 1945 suggested acceptance of the error in high places. Haushofer's views of China and Russia have been vindicated by events, along with the emphasis placed on the Near East by all the exponents of this school. The late Nicholas Spykman, outstanding disciple of geopolitics in the USA, applied many of its concepts brilliantly and fruitfully to the problems of the American continents. He reformulated Mackinder's original dictum: If any power or bloc of powers bring the "Rimlands" or coastal plains of Eurasia, under unified control, it could command the World Island and threaten the security of both the Heartland Powers (Russia and China) and the Island Powers (Britain and America). Just as Allied victory in World War II was contingent upon effective cooperation among the USA, UK and USSR, so enduring peace depends upon a stable balance and concert among them to the end that the Rimlands shall not be used by either against the other and shall not again fall under the control of any other power or coalition.

It is not uncharitable, nor is it a denial of the value of much of the literature in this field, to suggest that these and other valid conclusions can be reached by routes less devious than those taken by the geopoliticians. This discipline or pseudo science views the data of world geography in terms of the struggle for global power among giant sovereignties. Since the outcome of such struggles depends always on unpredictable factors of morals and on incalculable "happenstances" in peace and war, along with consideration of space, position, material, and national purpose, a truly "scientific" formula for victory or even for survival is, in the nature of the case, impossible. Diplomacy and war, like bridge, boxing, chess and hockey, have their rules, principles, and techniques derived from practice or custom. But none of them makes possible any reliable prediction as to which player will win in any given contest. It is certain, however, that, as long as the struggle continues, the contestants will rationalise their purpose in plausible jargon, seize eagerly upon every new weapon and strategic plan, and always grasp some principle or hypothesis which promises successes. If the effort almost invariably ends in frustration, the cause may lie in the circumstances, that the game itself, under the conditions of the 20th century, is a self-defeating enterprise.

A slowly dawning realisation of this fact during the 1950s promoted frustration, confusion, desperation, a reversion to old formulas of warfare, and a grouping effort to evolve new ones on the part of the diplomats and strategists of the power politics. All the generalisations and precepts here are applicable to power politics in the Western state system, and in all its precursors, during the long millennia when the art of weaponry advanced from sticks and stones through bows and spears to heavy artillery, tanks, and booming planes. A new era opened in 1945 when scientist gave statesman and generals a simple device to wipe out whole cities, whole nations, and possibly the human race itself. The advent of atomic and thermonuclear weapons obviously meant that "total war" among the Great Powers, and indeed all "power politics" premised on the assumption of force, was now obsolete if civilisation was to avoid suicide. But men are creatures of habit; statesmen, therefore, continued the age-old game, hoping that somehow ways could be found to prevent it from eventuating in the self-destruction of the species.

The various formulae designed to reconcile ancient ways with the formidable hazards of a new time need not survive here, for all were futile. Communist power-holders, while secretly fabricating all kinds of weapons of mass destruction, publicly appealed to mankind to espouse the abolition of nuclear weapons. So did the Americans. American policy-makers, while engaging in comparable operations, toyed publicly with the baffling problem of preparing for war under conditions which appear to mean that any general and total conflict would spell the co-annihilation of the belligerents – not in the sense of total defeat, but in the sense of the physical extermination via blast, fire, and radiation sickness of many or most of the inhabitants of the warring nations.

No plausible "solution" and strategy of conflict resolution was arrived at as long as the Cold War continued between the two power blocs. The US Strategic Air Command, like its counterpart in the erstwhile USSR, devoted itself to elaborate plans for the atomic destruction of the foe. In both countries, civil defence authorities strove through ceremonial exercises and mock drills against simulated atomic attack to device ways and means, through planned evacuation of cities and fantastically expensive projects for shelters, to reduce anticipated casualties – with everybody understanding, privately if not publicly, that all such plans were absurd, and that the "next war" would spell total chaos and universal death. West Europeans, members of the North Atlantic Treaty Organisation (NATO) and Asians, however, indulged in no such nonsensical rituals. In Washington, advisers to the Pentagon, the National Security Council, and the State Department struggled vainly to resolve the dilemma with the doubtful aid of sundry unofficial commentators.

None of the formulae propounded in official circles or in the media was compatible with common sense. Some contended that the threat of "massive retaliation" via atomic weapons would "deter" any aggression, forgetting that the suspected "aggressor" had comparable capacity to inflict total destruction and that no war has ever been avoided through prior contemplation of its horrors. Others sought to revive an old concept of "limited war" in which atomic weapons would not be used unless national survival were at stake. Among these, some urged the need of substantial conventional forces to cope with localised or "brush-fire" wars, with atomic attack reserved for all-out global conflicts. Still others strove to develop a new military doctrine whereby "tactical" or small-scale atomic weapons would be used in future wars only against "military" targets, with the great urban centres being spared from nuclear annihilation, although no such centres accessible to any belligerent had been so spared from aerial bombardment in World War I or II.

It is possible, the optimists said, that out of these endeavours there may yet emerge a new "military science" which may facilitate the perpetuation of warfare in the Nuclear Age without risking the mutual incineration of the belligerents, the demise of human civilisation, i.e., the prospective doom of the human race for many thousands of years to come ... However, it seemed far more probable that no such dispensation was obtainable. The strange imperatives of history would seem to be irreversible. In a century of "total wars" in which the antagonists were invariably bent upon the "annihilation" or at least "unconditional surrender" of the enemy, it seemed unlikely that a return to the 18th century practice of "limited war", fought by limited means for limited ends, could be made effective in the minds and motives of national policy-makers or of their highly patriotic constituents.

To the degree to which this prognosis was valid, it was universally realised that a future war between the Great Powers spelled suicide and a reversion to barbarism by the miserable survivors, if any. "In the thermonuclear age," said President Eisenhower in the fall of 1954, "there is no alternative to peace." Statesmen and citizens must, therefore, renounce war or invite irreparable disaster. Their choice as rational human beings could not be in doubt except for the fact that all human beings were prisoners of the past and were often nonrational, and sometimes irrational. Mankind is forever called upon to choose between alternatives. During the Cold War, the choice was grim and possibly final. There was much reason at that time to hope that the choice would be conducive to life rather than death. But the time-honoured ways of power politics, far older than Western civilisation, offered no basis for complacent optimism regarding the future fortunes of mankind.

This grim realisation led to some serious thinking about "conflict resolution" among politicians, decision-makers, strategists, arms control negotiators and students of international relations. Study in this field underscored the fact that how states live together and on what terms, is the product of diplomacy or bargaining, which decides "who gets what, when and how". Bargaining encompasses three tasks: defining a state's interests; communicating to the party or parties with whom conflicting interests are to be negotiated; and conducting the actual process of negotiation. Such negotiations may be conducted by chiefs of governments at summit meetings, professional diplomats, or, on certain occasions, military officers or special emissaries. They may be bilateral, between two states, or multilateral, among three or more states. They may be carried on publicly in an open forum and in the glare of constant publicity and media exposure, or secretly and privately (although in democracies the results will be made public and will usually need public approval). Finally, such negotiations may be formal, and include the officials who are trying to negotiate a compromise between conflicting positions using face-to-face meetings or messages transmitted between governments by ambassadors. Or they may be tacit, that is, when governments talk to one another indirectly, sending each other signals about how vital an issue is to them and frequently informing an adversary not to interfere (such as by calling up the reserves or placing troops on alert or moving them to another country or even fighting). Thus, bargaining goes on between states not only when diplomats gather and talk to one another but also when no formal meetings take place.

An example of formal negotiations was the Reagan Administration's bargaining over intermediate nuclear forces (INF) in the early 1980s. A few years earlier, the Soviets had deployed SS-20 nuclear missiles within the Soviet Union to cover targets in

Western Europe. Then, during the Carter years, the countries in
Western Europe asked the United States for a similar deployment
of US missiles to neutralise the SS-20s, which they perceived to be
a means of political intimidation. One of the proposed American
missiles, the Pershing II, were capable of reaching Soviet territory.
Moscow vehemently opposed such a counter-deployment, arguing
that an overall military, including nuclear, balance already existed
in Europe when British and French nuclear forces were counted,
and that the American missiles would upset this balance. Subsequent
negotiations failed, however, because the Soviets insisted that only
they could deploy modern INF; they would not accept even a single
American missile as they, despite their claim of an existing European
balance, continued to emplace more SS-20s. Moreover, they
threatened a series of reprisals if the United States deployed any
missiles, most notably, to break off all arms control negotiations.

Many Europeans, already nervous about talk from Washington
on "nuclear war fighting" instead of deterrence, and some of the
harshest denunciations of the Soviet Union and Communism since
the Cold War began, took to the streets in mass demonstrations
against the plans of the US and West European Governments to
balance the Soviet missiles. The fear of a new Cold War, even nuclear
war, was high and the Soviets sought to exploit these fears. In the
United States, the Reagan Administration was faced with the anti-
nuclear freeze movement. When the first US missiles were deployed,
nevertheless, the Soviets walked out of the arms control negotiations,
saying they would not return until all US missiles were withdrawn.
Thus, the Soviets raised the pressure on the United States and its
allies, testing NATO's will and waiting to see whether the western
allies would change their position and accept the Soviet one, as
European governments continued to face huge mass demonstrations
opposing the NATO position.

But the United States and its allies persisted. The position of
the Reagan Administration, initially rather hostile to arms control
negotiations, and bent on launching a huge unilateral programme,
was that if Moscow wished to avoid the deployment of US INF,
neither super power should deploy these. It did not expect Moscow

to accept its "0-0" proposal, however, because it meant the elimination of Soviet missiles that the US had not yet matched. But with 0-0, it was hoped, it would calm the protests and place the blame for the deployment on the Soviets. If they had accepted 0-0, the US reaction would not have been necessary. Two developments led the Soviets to eventually change their minds, however, and accept not only 0-0 but also the elimination of all intermediate and short-range missiles on a global basis. One was Mikhail Gorbachev's accession to power and his priority of reforming the Soviet economy. The other was his desire to relax heightened tensions with the United States, and to avoid a new potentially expansive arms race in space stemming from the additional Reagan plan for a Strategic Defence Initiative (SDI). Not only did the Soviets return to all arms control negotiations, but they accepted virtually the entire range of US proposals on INF.

The Administration had "hung tough". Initially, probably not even caring about making a deal, it had avoided any appearance of eagerness. Then it had insisted on the US deployment in Europe and had strengthened the US bargaining position in two ways: first, by deploying, Pershing II, among other missiles; and second, by announcing SDI. That really worried the Soviets because not only would a new arms race divert enormous resources needed domestically, but they lagged behind in the very technology at issue. Thus, the Reagan style of bargaining – more traditionally a Soviet characteristic – created assets that the Soviets considered threatening, thereby giving them the incentive to be more compromising and to settle on terms favourable to the United States. SDI was particularly instrumental in bringing Moscow back to the bargaining table. Moscow was eager to conclude an INF agreement as a first step toward a strategic arms reduction in which it would offer a radical reduction in the Soviet forces that worried Washington, in return for a deal on SDI. Thus, hard bargaining, patience, a refusal to bow to public pressure to be more conciliatory, deployment of weapons (just like Moscow) for political bargaining – not military use – and use of SDI as a potentially powerful bargaining chip for a future trade-off in strategic arms negotiations (except that Reagan liked SDI and refused to trade) paid handsome dividends.

An example of tacit diplomacy occurred in 1965 when the United States intervened in Vietnam to prevent the takeover of South Vietnam by North Vietnam. By destroying the enemy forces, or at least by inflicting heavy and sustained casualties on the enemy, the United States hoped to weaken the Communist side and strengthen South Vietnam. Then either the North Vietnamese would finally call off the war or, if negotiations took place, the United States and South Vietnam would have more leverage. Thus, the fighting itself was the bargaining. And although there was no visible or explicit negotiation – US diplomats did not meet with North Vietnamese diplomats at some neutral spot in Switzerland – negotiations were going on constantly. North Vietnam had already stated its expectation of unifying Vietnam. Any solution short of taking over the South was unacceptable. The United States rejected that solution; it intervened massively to prevent unification as the South Vietnamese army had failed. It expected an improved position on the battlefield to be reflected in the terms of any final statement. Formal talks are only a minor part of such tacit negotiations, if they occur at all. The issue for Washington was not that of peace; it could have had peace at any time – on North Vietnam's terms. The critical issue was peace on what terms. Determined to protect South Vietnam, it decided to fight. The fighting was not an alternative to peace time diplomacy; it was a violent continuation of the bargaining process.

Whether diplomacy is explicit or tacit, resolution of a conflict does not necessarily always take the form of compromise. In fact, there are at least four kinds of conflict resolution: (1) that in which both states lose; (2) that in which neither state wins; (3) that in which one state wins everything; and (4) that in which both states are partial winners and partial losers in an agreement based on compromise.

The best example of the first kind of conflict resolution is the concept of deterrence. The deterring side seeks to prevent an adversary from initiating the use of force by making such action much more costly in the calculations of the would-be aggressor than any possible benefits. In the context of the US-Soviet conflict and their possession of nuclear weapons, the deterrer seeks to prevent the opponent from attacking by announcing, in effect, "You may kill me if you attack me, but I will kill you before I die." Thus, deterrence is based on the ability to retaliate even after the enemy's first strike. Mutual deterrence is said to be equivalent to mutual suicide. The United States even calls its capacity to destroy the Soviet Union an "assured destruction" capability. The reciprocal capacity is called "mutual assured destruction" or MAD – probably not a bad name for a strategy in which everyone loses.

When neither party can win, the conflict resolution is called a *stalemate*. It can occur under a variety of conditions: when both parties have exhausted themselves in the struggle; when both are unwilling to invest greater resources in a struggle that is not critical; when both are unwilling to escalate the conflict because the risks are too great; when a third party intervenes and calls a halt to the conflict; or when new problems and priorities arise.

In the Korean War, the United States, unwilling to escalate the war by attacking China, sought instead to exhaust the Chinese through a war of attrition. In Vietnam, the American strategy of physical attrition was designed to exact such a heavy price, in bombing damage of North Vietnam and battlefield deaths, that at some point the North Vietnamese would stop trying to take over the South. In Korea, a settlement resulted when the battle lines were drawn along the 38th parallel, approximately where the war had started. In Vietnam, however, the American strategy failed.

Probably the most obvious form of conflict resolution is a clear-cut victory for one side. It occurs when one side is much stronger than the other, or the issue no longer seems important enough to cause the other side to take great risks to defend its position. Diplomatically, a complete victory for one side is relatively rare. The Munich settlement of 1938 is one of the most infamous examples. Germany won a total victory over Britain and France by threatening war. The American victory over the Soviet Union in the Cuban missile crisis of 1962 is another example. President

Kennedy did not overtly threaten war – the possibility was inherent in the confrontation. A war time illustration is the Allied victory over Germany, Italy, and Japan in World War II. Other examples include the Soviet interventions to crush the Hungarian rebellion in 1956 and the Czechoslovakian uprising of 1968; and the Vietnamese Communists' defeat of France in 1954 and of the United States two decades later.

Compromise is probably the most common form of conflict resolution. Both states win part of what they want and give up part of what they want. The two sides may "split the difference", or one side may gain more than the other. The settlement is likely to reflect the perceived power relationship of the two states, their respective willingness to take risks and make sacrifices, or the importance each attaches to the issue in dispute. A compromise may be easier to achieve among states friendly to one another than among adversaries; a higher degree of mutual trust may be the critical ingredient.

The search for compromise, specially among adversaries, may be prompted by the use of force (as in the Egyptian-Syrian attack on Israel in 1973), the threat of force (as in the conflict between the United States and the Soviet Union over Berlin in 1948-1949), the offer of rewards (as when the United States, in 1973, offered North Vietnam the withdrawal of American forces, continued Communist control of captured areas in South Vietnam, and US economic aid for post-war reconstruction), or a mixture of the proverbial carrot and stick.

In fact, in these years we find ourselves in the midst of a historic shift in understanding how nations relate. As a result of this shift, new concepts are slowly coming into focus that are steadily changing how governments and citizens will play their roles in relationships among nations. The changes will not be complete, quick, or neat, but the process has already began, and the sooner the participants are clear about how they can play their roles legitimately and creatively, the more resourceful and constructive those relationships can become.

One characteristic of our changing world is the widening influence of private citizens in national policy-making and in the conduct of international relationships. To be sure, that may be more a phenomenon of the industrialised nations than of the developing ones today, but it is not limited to the Northern Hemisphere. Admittedly, nation-states still have institutional lives of their own, but, more and more, people are demanding that their institutions reflect human needs and values. Of course, some systems still minimise the role of people in the design and conduct of policy and see international relations as a strategic chess game among powerful state leaders. But the cost of ignoring the larger role of people came home vividly in 1989 to leaders from Tiananmen to Timisoara – not to mention US leaders struggling to respond with the full human and intellectual resources of the United States.

The differences between official behaviour and the behaviour of private citizens may not be entirely explained by their governmental or non-governmental status. These differences may be fully explained only by the fact that some citizens are already acting – at least instinctively – from a shifting perception of how nations relate, for they can sense that a new way of thinking is needed to reflect accurately what the world is becoming. As officials also widen their views, the behaviour of the two groups may come closer. Real differences will remain, but one hopes that more complementary behaviour may replace the regrettable suspicion and antagonism of the past between the rulers and the ruled. So great has the distrust between governments and citizens become that it is essential for them to reassess openly what they expect of each other. Governments see "citizen diplomats" as dangerous meddlers – sometimes with reason. Citizens see governments as paralysed in dealing with vital issues of war and peace – sometimes with reason.

As the numbers and kinds of participants in relationships among nations multiply in a changing world, all need to understand the context in which they play roles. All need to consider afresh what each can and cannot effectively or properly do – what strengthens a relationship and what does not. The following examples make, but do not exhaust, the point.

First, the lenses through which officials or citizens see a problem partly determine how effectively they communicate. This may seem an unnecessary point, for one would assume that leaders will communicate effectively. However, that is not the case in normal human relationships, and it is no more the case among human beings who are leaders. Sitting in on conversations among leaders reveals dramatically how they are not immune to the normal human frailties of speaking imprecisely from self-centred positions and not showing interest or really hearing another's concerns. If they simply state positions, they can be easily misunderstood. But if they attempt to explore problems together, misunderstanding is less likely.

Second, it makes a difference whether those engaging in dialogue simply presume what the conflicting interests of an adversary are or even the declared interests of a friend are or whether they develop a relationship within which they can probe for the real fears, concerns, and feelings underlying stated interests.

Only when persons feel safe in expressing real concerns, even though doing so may increase vulnerability, do they begin to share what really moves them. Understanding those real concerns is a first step in shaping workable courses of action.

If one defines interests as including psychological as well as physical needs, one must create a setting in which these can be gently probed. To date, that kind of understanding has been more possible in non-official dialogues, where participants act as the human beings they are, than in official exchanges, where the persons involved often speak as though they are the titles they hold. That difference can be diminished, even though some limits would still restrict official dialogue.

Third, it makes a difference whether officials or citizens paper over divergent interests or explore them honestly. Acting self-consciously to develop and sustain a relationship requires honesty about each party's limits of tolerance – those points at which the balance of interests becomes too one-sided to accept. Unless that balance is redressed, it threatens to break down the relationship itself.

Fourth, it makes a difference whether two nations simply deal with problems as they arise or constantly nourish and tend a relationship that can cope with whatever comes up. A relationship nurtured over time acquires value and interests of its own. In making policy, two parties will then think not just of their own interests and political problems but also of shared interests and the other side's sensitivities. An effective relationship enables identification and exploration of a wide range of alternative solutions and approaches since the tolerance and respect engendered reduce the fear of being exploited for throwing out unorthodox ideas of conflict resolution.

If nations and leaders are working in the context of a relationship to deal with a commonly defined problem, they will be more likely to develop courses of action that take into account each other's political needs and constituencies. They will not come immediately to the battlefield or negotiating table with their separate positions based solely on an analysis of their own immediate interests; they will have explored whether they can resolve their differences through political steps that take into account their common as well as unique interests.

Fifth, it makes a difference whether two nations interact through a linear sequence of action and reaction or engage in a dynamic political interaction on many levels simultaneously. Conducting a relationship involves consciousness of the continuous process of interaction by which the interdependence of needs and interests is defined, developed and nurtured over time to become the basis of action.

If we see relationships among nations as a political process of complex and continuous interaction, we are not using "relationship" as a static word or a word connoting structures. Human relationships can be described in part by statistics; but even more important, they reflect the dynamic or "chemistry" of the interaction. In international affairs, the structures of national policy-making differ markedly and shape policy, but the policies, actions, and politics of one side continuously affect the politics of policy-making of the other. Within that political process of interaction often lie the real obstacles or opportunities in building or strengthening a relationship or changing a situation.

What is important here is that, even during periods when recognition of common interests has been minimal, some individuals have found ways to talk – whether articulated as such or not – that have preserved the essence of a relationship. After the Cold War developed, some Americans and Soviets, for instance, in government and outside of it, preserved a dialogue to understand the stakes in situations ranging from the Cuban missile crisis to developing a common ground for arms control. They attempted to understand fundamental differences so as to begin working through them to find a limited, common, political ground.

The idea of building problem-solving relationships as a foreign policy objective is not new, but the interdependencies in today's world may give new importance to that objective. The growth of the European and Atlantic communities reflected an early move in this direction. Political leaders have long recognised that what two nations can achieve together will depend heavily on understanding the political environments, both at home and abroad, in which they work. New experiences in the world require that political leaders now give as much attention to the interaction among nations as they formerly gave to the practice of statecraft and balance of power politics.

To understand where one fits in the conduct of relationships among nations, one needs to recognise the opportunities offered by different ways of thinking, talking, and acting. A first step is to identify the range of participants and activities involved in a relationship. It is wiser to see a spectrum than to try to develop rigid lines to differentiate participants and activities. For simplicity's sake, one can identify six points in that spectrum.

First, *governments* support leaders, but they have structures, methods, continuity, and instruments of their own that sometimes operate in ways not entirely consistent with leaders' aims. Governments negotiate arrangements that facilitate a wide variety òf transactions and exchanges between their nations, and governments deploy armies. Sometimes at the margins of formal processes, government officials see the need for informal exchanges; thus, we have pictures of diplomats "walking in the woods" for private exchanges of ideas or the so-called back-channel discussions between officials and diplomats. A lot more of this takes place than government officials are normally given credit for.

Second, *national leaders* operate from a broader political base than the institutions of government. Their statements and actions project the intentions and characters of their own bodies politic to people in other bodies politic. Political leaders think and often talk about their political bases and about the constraints and permissions that come from their political arenas in dealing with each other. They can try to broaden that political base, but they take risks if they try to operate far beyond it for long. Again, in varying degrees, that political framework states the limits of their authority.

Third, moving outside of government, we find a number of private citizens engaged in what has been called *supplemental diplomacy* or Track II diplomacy. These are individuals who, one way or another, participate in dialogue outside official channels on the same policy problems that governments struggle with. These groups may discuss elements of the overall political relationship, solutions to arms control problems, resolution of regional conflicts, issues of trade policy, or other areas of competition. What distinguishes these efforts from those by governments that deal with the same issues is that citizens speak without authority to commit their governments. They may identify causes and underlying purposes and even design ways of dealing with problems, but they normally do not have the resources, let alone the political authority, to make solutions happen.

Fourth is a range of participants *who do business of one sort or another*. They do have certain resources and programming capacity within specific areas of competence, and within those areas they can reach and implement agreements that produce concrete results. Transnational or trading corporations are the most familiar example, and one with historic roots. Others would include academic and professional organisations that have some specific purpose which they organise themselves to accomplish together. It may be common research; it may be organising student exchange; or it may be arranging sister-city relationships.

Fifth are groups or individuals whose purpose, one way or another, is the *pursuit, exchange, and accumulation of knowledge*. One range of activities in this group may be the institutionalised and highly visible work of journalists. Their purpose is to acquire and disseminate knowledge through academic enquiry or in the interest of advancing general research. The governing purpose is the exchange and development of knowledge rather than problem solving.

Sixth is a range of participants whose purpose may best be described as *people-to-people diplomacy* or "getting to know the other side". The aim in people-to-people exchange may be simply to learn through sharing common pleasures such as an interest in athletics, music, art, or other activities that illuminate different ways of life. Student and citizen exchanges, and visits of peace and friendship groups are common examples. The experience can advance personal knowledge, or it can build a sense of common humanity. These activities are distinguished from others by their focus on probing the personal experience of another person rather than on using that knowledge to design solutions to particular problems or turn out a concrete product. The insights gained may provide valuable clues as to underlying causes of fear and behaviour and equip a person for participation in other areas later; the immediate aim is personal learning and experience rather than the resolution of problems in the near term.

The underlying idea behind all these is to develop a conceptual framework for understanding international relationships that provide room for as many insights of political leaders as possible and to create common ground for the widest possible dialogue between a broad range of scholars and policy-makers. In other words, supplemental diplomacy can provide opportunities for bringing into play insights not always used or even tested in governmental exchanges.

The Dartmouth Conference – one of the oldest bilateral, non-official dialogues between American and Soviet citizens – has been one of the most intensive exchanges of this kind. After the breakdown of the Eisenhower-Khrushchev Summit in 1959, President Eisenhower discussed with Norman Cousins, then editor of *The Saturday Review*, whether he could organise a citizen dialogues to maintain US-Soviet communication when official relations soured. He took the idea to Moscow, and the first group met at Dartmouth College in October 1960. The third meeting happened to take place during the Cuban missile crisis, and the participants left persuaded more than ever of the value of such dialogue.

Certain characteristics and principles became prominent in the Dartmouth Conference: First, it was non-official but policy related. Participants spoke only for themselves, and none had authority to represent governments or to negotiate. But, since the dialogue was policy related, the participants discussed issues of concern in the relationship between their nations.

Second, a conscious sense of continuing relationship and the cumulative dialogue – "the next meeting begins where the last left off" – developed. In the early 1980s, participants consciously experimented with approaches that would enhance understanding of the overall US-Soviet relationship, regardless of the particular subject discussed. The effort to assure that these meetings were not one-time discussions but would build toward a cumulative achievement distinguished Dartmouth from many other meetings. At a minimum, the phrase "Dartmouth process" refers to this continuous communication and discussion that produces a sense of relationship with a life and value of its own.

Third, major efforts were made – with considerable success since the early 1970s – to talk analytically and without polemic. Increasingly, it was possible to approach problems as common problems and to develop a shared analytical framework for understanding them, and even political scenarios that could change the political environment and pave the way for moving toward solutions.

Fourth, one characteristic was critical from the start — joint ownership. Since the late 1960s, Dartmouth was sponsored in the United States by the Kettering Foundation and in the Soviet Union by the Soviet Peace Committee and the Institute of USA/Canada Affairs. As David Mathews, president of the Kettering Foundation, said, "I can refuse to go to your meeting but joint ownership means that I won't refuse to go to my own meeting."

Dartmouth changed with times, both in format and essence. The changes, especially in the early 1980s, reflected markedly an increased attention to the US-Soviet relationship as itself a political process between significant elements of the two bodies politic – not just the actions and reactions of state institutions. Dartmouth was seen as a microcosm of that relationship.

It is now recognised that in a nuclear world, citizens in non-official dialogue have more opportunity to ask questions, develop alternative definitions of problems, and explore policy options in their discussions than do official representatives operating within instructions reflecting established policy. In fact, both officials and the increasing number of informed private citizens involved in international relations may find it useful to give new attention to thoughts about how the world really works today. Government officials may find it useful to listen to citizens saying that the world has changed and that policy-makers need to be informed of the new insights. Citizens may become more effective if they stop to educate themselves in policy thinking. Both may find it useful to understand the complementary roles that governmental and non-governmental individuals and organisations can play. Both may find it useful to study the function to be fulfilled in developing and tending relationships among nations and then to focus on the particular points in the process of developing and conducting relationships when intervention may be most constructive. The issue is not whether the proliferation of relationships is good or bad but how to understand what is involved and how to build relationships that put the spectre of nuclear war behind us, to establish relationships of genuine peace. "In the present state of international relations," says Harold H. Saunders, "the Dartmouth process can alone pave the way for conflict resolution among nations with nuclear power and with apparently irreconcilable positions."

Thus, the advent of the nuclear age and the fear of MAD brought about fundamental changes in the strategies of conflict resolution. Similar changes also came about in the concepts of military planning and strategic doctrines.

A nation's military strength is an important component of its power, for, as E.H. Carr wrote: "War lurks in the background of international politics just as a revolution lurks in the background of domestic policies." Ironically, democracy, which was expected to abolish war, multiplied the importance of this component many times over. One democratic assumption used to be that only irresponsible rulers were belligerents; for them wars were merely an enjoyable and profitable "blood sport." In this view, it was the people who paid the price of wars with their lives and their taxes. If peace-loving people could hold their rulers accountable, wars would be culminated and peace secured. Democracy would then bring an era of goodwill – of individual freedom and social justice at home, of peace and harmony abroad. The world would be safe for democracy because it would be democratic. Government by the people, of the people, and for the people would ensure perpetual peace.

Instead, democracy became tied to nationalism, and the two gave birth to the "nation in arms". Once people were freed from feudal bondage and granted the right to some form of self-government, they came to equate their own well-being with that of their nation, and it seemed only reasonable that the nation should be able to call on them, the citizens, for defence. Not surprisingly, it was the 1789 French Revolution that brought people into contact with the nation-state. One result was the first system of universal military service. When the supreme loyalty of the citizens was to the nation, the nation in arms followed logically. Democracy and nationalism, thus, enabled France to mobilise fully for total war and destroy its opponents completely.

This change was one reason why the Congress of Vienna in 1815 reacted with such horror to the revolution, which had unleashed mass passions and all-out war. Previous wars had been restrained because men had identified not with nations but with smaller units such as towns or manors, or with universal entities such as embodied in the Roman Catholic Church. The armies of the *ancient regime* were composed largely of mercenaries and lowly elements of society such as vagrants and criminals – men who were animated neither by love of country nor by hatred of the enemy, but who fought because they were paid or compelled to do so. States lacked sufficient economic resources to maintain sizeable armies. Indeed their tactics were determined by the need to limit expenses.

And to keep casualties low, the emphasis was on manoeuvre rather than pitched battle. The revolution enlisted popular support, however, and mass armies aroused by nationalism began to fight in defence of their countries. Frenchmen Bertrand de Jouvenel described this "new era in military history" as "the era of cannon fodder".

It remained only for the Industrial Revolution to produce the instruments that enabled men to kill one another in greater numbers. Modern military technology brought total war to its fullest realisation. Mass armies were equipped with mass produced weapons that were ever more destructive, making it possible for nations to inflict progressively greater damage on one another in shorter and shorter periods. In the 17th century, it took thirty years for the states of central Western Europe to slaughter half the population of central Europe. In the second decade of the 20th century, it took only four years for them to bleed one another into a state of exhaustion and, for some, collapse. But the atomic bomb, and especially the hydrogen bomb, made it possible to inflict catastrophic damage in minutes, or at most hours, that previously had taken years, and this catastrophic damage was tantamount to near annihilation.

With the ascendancy of strategic air power and nuclear weapons, human beings had then the means with which to accomplish their own extermination. Cities – indeed, whole nations – could be laid waste in a matter of hours, if not minutes. The effectiveness of that kind of strategic air power against a highly urbanised and industrialised society is no longer a matter of dispute.

Nuclear bombs are so destructive that they make World War II bombing attacks appear trivial by comparison. Atomic bombs, such as those dropped on Hiroshima and Nagasaki, were surpassed in destructive power within a few years by the new hydrogen bombs. Kilotons were replaced by megatons (one megaton equals one million tons of TNT). A single US Strategic Air Command B-52 bomber can carry 25 megatons of explosive power or 12.5 times the explosive power of all bombs dropped during World War II, including the two atomic bombs.

A nuclear explosion has four physical effects: blast, fire, immediate radiation and long-term radiation. The blast or shock wave is the almost solid wall of air pressure produced by an explosion, creating a hurricane-type wind. The blast from a low-altitude bomb exploding in a city will collapse all wooden buildings within six miles of ground zero for a 1-megaton bomb, within fourteen miles for a 10-megaton bomb, and within thirty miles for a 100-megaton bomb. For brick buildings, the figures for the same bombs are four, nine and eighteen miles respectively, and for sturdier buildings, the distance ranges from three to twelve miles.

The thermal impact of a bomb can be heightened by a higher altitude explosion or airburst. The heat generated by a 1-megaton bomb is tremendous, producing second-degree burns of the skin up to nine miles from ground zero; a 10-megaton bomb has the same effect up to twenty-four miles; a 100-megaton bomb up to seventy miles.

Furthermore, the heat in most instances would ignite wooden houses and other combustible objects – from plastics and furniture in homes to gas lines and furnaces – over the same range. World War II demonstrated that the real danger from fire, even when started with ordinary incendiary bombs, is the firestorm. In a firestorm, the intense heat from the fire rises, heating the air in turn. As the difference in pressure between the hot and colder air sucks in fresh oxygen to feed the hungry flames, the process builds in intensity. Air rushes in at ever greater speeds until wind velocity surpasses gale force. The flames, whipped up by the wind and fed further by the gas, oil, and other incendiary materials of the homes and streets of the burning city, leap upward, stabbing high into the air, enveloping the stricken area. Everything burns in this tomb of heat and flame. There is no escape. Those who have not yet been crushed in their shelters are asphyxiated by lack of oxygen or by carbon monoxide poisoning; if they seek to escape into the burning streets, their lungs are seared, and their bodies exposed to the intense heat, burst into flame. During the 1943 attack on Humburg, the firestorm caused a ground temperature of 1,400 degrees Fahrenheit. Indeed, near the centre of a firestorm, the temperature exceeds 2,220 degrees Fahrenheit.

The third and fourth effects of a nuclear explosion, the radiation impact, can be maximised by the surface burst or a low-altitude explosion. The resulting fireball – a large, rapidly expanding sphere of hot gases that produces intense heat – scoops up debris and converts it into radioactive material. The fireball of a 10-megaton bomb has a diameter of' six miles. The heavier particles of debris fall back to earth within the first few hours. Besides the immediate radiation in the area of explosion, long-term, lighter particles "fall out" during the following days and weeks over the area, the size of which depends on the magnitude of the explosion, the surface over which the explosion occurs, and meteorological conditions. The American 15-megaton thermonuclear explosion of 1954 in the Pacific Ocean caused substantial contamination over an area of 7,000 square miles. Under more "favourable" conditions, the fallout could have covered an area of 10,000 square miles.

Fallout can emit radiation for days, months, and even years. The power of this radiation depends on the amount absorbed by humans and animals. A dose of 100-200 roentgens causes radiation sickness, a combination of weakness, nausea, and vomiting that is not fatal, although it can result in disability. At 200 roentgens, radiation becomes very dangerous: disability is certain, and death can come within a month. The possibility of death increases, at 500 roentgens and it is certain for 50 per cent of those exposed to the radiation. Above 600 roentgens, the number of deaths continues to mount, and deaths occur more rapidly. Radiation also has two other effects: cancer and genetic transmutations that may affect subsequent generations.

Considering the overwhelmingly destructive character of a single nuclear weapon and the large number of them in the possession of the United States and the Soviet Union, a coordinated nuclear attack on either power's major urban and industrial centres would be catastrophic, reducing everything to rubble and leaving the population dead or injured, with little hope of help. Most hospitals, doctors, nurses, drugs, and blood plasma would be destroyed, as would the machinery for the processing and refrigeration of food and the purification of water. Medical "disaster planning" for a nuclear war is meaningless. Not surprisingly, nuclear

war has been called "the last epidemic". In addition, there would be
no transportation left to take survivors out of the smouldering ruins
and into the countryside; most, if not all, of the fuel would have
burned up. Estimates of casualties in such a coordinated urban strike
range from 30 to 90 per cent of the population, depending upon
the yield of the bombs, the heights at which they were exploded,
the weather, civilian protection, and preparations for coping with
the aftermath of such an attack.

If cities are the main targets in a nuclear war, Nikita
Khrushchev's remark that survivors would envy the dead appears
all too true. A 1977 US Department of Defence study estimated
that 155 to 165 million Americans would be killed if all explosions
were detonated at ground level and no civil defence measures existed.
If half the explosions were airbursts, the casualties would be reduced
to 122 million. Other studies show equally high figures, although
some differ by 20 million fatalities or so. Even "low" figures such as
55 million dead are staggering and unprecedented in the history of
human existence, particularly when it is recalled that these are only
the casualties that will occur immediately and within thirty days of
the attack (see Figure 1). Deaths occurring afterward from injury,
radiation, starvation, and general economic chaos are not included.
Total fatality figures would be much higher.

Today, we are more aware of some of the side effects of nuclear
explosions. In 1983, some scientists issued a warning that nuclear
war may destroy the ozone layer in the stratosphere. This layer
protects all living things from ultraviolet solar radiation which
destroys protein molecules. In addition to death, destruction, and
radiation, extensive ozone depletion could destroy the food chain
of plants and animals upon which humans and animal life depends
for survival. As if this were not sufficient, these scientists also
concluded that fires from large-scale attacks on Soviet and American
cities in a nuclear war would create so much smoke that it would
filter out sunlight, thereby creating a "nuclear winter". The Northern
hemisphere would be plunged into darkness by plumes of dust and
soot suspended in the stratosphere; this would cause extensive
freezing of the earth's surface, including lakes and rivers, even during
the summer, leading to the extinction of a major portion of plant

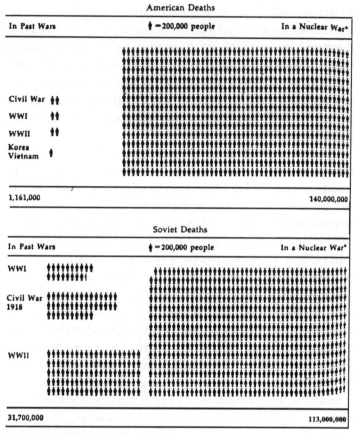

American Deaths

In Past Wars	✝ = 200,000 people	In a Nuclear War*

Civil War
WWI
WWII
Korea
Vietnam

1,161,000   140,000,000

Soviet Deaths

In Past Wars	✝ = 200,000 people	In a Nuclear War*

WWI

Civil War
1918

WWII

31,700,000   113,000,000

*Estimate by U.S. National Security Council

Fig. 1: American and Soviet deaths in past wars and in a projected nuclear war

and animal life. Such a freeze might last weeks, months, possibly even years. The implications of a nuclear winter are two fold: first, even if the initiator of a nuclear war could launch a surprise attack and destroy most of the opponent's retaliatory capability, the first-strike state would be the victor only briefly because the nuclear winter would soon cripple it as well; second, because the nuclear winter would spread from Northern to the Southern hemisphere, the human race could become extinct. Scientists continue to debate whether in fact nuclear war would unleash such a deep freeze and how long it would last. But clearly the environmental effects of a nuclear war can no longer be considered secondary to the results of blast, fire and radiation.

The psychological impact upon the survivors will be as devastating as the physical destruction. The elimination of a nation's largest cities, the deaths of more than 100 million of its citizens, and the wrecking of industries, communications, and transportation all would undermine the confidence of those who survived. A nation in ruins is not likely to retain its *élan vital* or entertain optimistic expectations for the future. It took Europe, especially France, more than forty years to recover from the psychological wounds of World War I and the loss of a generation on the battlefields. A quicker recovery after World War II was brought about primarily by extensive infusions of American economic aid. European losses then are minor compared with those incurred in a nuclear attack. Not only cities but the very fabric of social life would be destroyed. Henry Kissinger noted in the late 1950s: "Any society operates through confidence in an orderly succession of events, either natural or social." A catastrophe is an interruption in what has come to be considered natural. The panic it often produces is the reflection of an inability to react to an unexpected situation and the attempt to flee as rapidly as possible into a familiar and, therefore, predictable environment, but some confidence can be restored. Most natural catastrophes can be dealt with because they affect only a very small geographic area or a very small proportion of the population. The remainder of the society can utilise its machinery or cooperative effort to come to the assistance of the striken area. Indeed, such action tends to reinforce the cohesiveness of a society, because it becomes a symbol of its value and efficiency. The essence of the catastrophe produced by an all-out thermonuclear war, however, is the depth of the dislocation it produces and the consequent impossibility of escaping into familiar relationships. When all relationships, or even most relationships, have to reconstitute, society as we know it today will have been fundamentally transformed.

The impact of this awesome power on the conduct of international politics has been revolutionary. Before 1945, war was still considered a rational instrument of policy, despite the rapidly

increasing costs of modern warfare. States usually preferred to accept
these costs rather than submit. Nuclear weapons however endanger
the very substance of national life. Rather than helping to preserve
civilisation, the new instruments of violence promise to destroy it
through the "assured destruction" of society. What possible goal
could be "worth" the cost of self-immolation? How could a nation
defend its political independence and territorial integrity if, in the
very act of defence, it could be sacrificing itself? Nuclear war can
know no victors; all the contestants will be losers. Total wars may
have been compatible with weapons of limited destructive capacity,
but they are incompatible with the "absolute weapons".

The conclusion to be drawn from this general principle is that
the main function of strategic military strength in the nuclear age
is *deterrence* of an all-out attack. Deterrence protects a nation's
security by preventing an attack rather than by defending the nation
after an attack. The opponent is threatened with such massive
retaliation that it dare not attack. The assumption is that, faced
with the risk of virtual suicide, the enemy will desist. Mutual
deterrence between two states, each seeking to protect its own
security interests, thus, becomes a matter of conflict resolution. "I
won't destroy you if you don't destroy me" is the offer of each side
to the other. "We shall both lose if you attack me because I shall
retaliate" is the answer.

In this extraordinary situation, the role of nuclear power is that
it is not to be used. Its primary value is in peace time. If war erupts,
it will have failed. The decisive test of arms is no longer vanquishing
the enemy in battle; it is not having to fight at all. Furthermore,
deterrence must be perpetual. There can be no margin for error.
The frequency of war throughout history suggests how often
deterrence failed. But because no weapon was so destructive that
failure spelled extinction, such mistakes were not irreparable. The
critical issue for the military was not whether it could prevent the
outbreak of hostilities but whether it could win on the battlefield.
This is no longer true. The nuclear powers today possess
overwhelming power yet are completely vulnerable to attack and
destruction. Thus, modern nuclear warfare would be irrational.
Nuclear technology has so vastly augmented the scope of violence

and destruction that total war can destroy the very nation that wages it and can do so in a matter of hours, not years.

In sum, the balancing of power historically has had two purposes: protection of individual states and protection of the state system as a whole. Peace has not been the chief aim. When states have been secure, peace has followed; when states have not been secure, they have gone to war. The philosophy of "peace at any cost" has been rejected by states. But nuclear weapons have changed all that; security can no longer be given priority over peace. Security and peace have become virtually identical. The deterrent function of the balance has therefore, become supreme. To fight a war – a total war – is no longer feasible.

No wonder, defence planners and strategists have been very much put about by the frightening consequences of a nuclear war. "I am a dedicated believer in putting all the talent and vigor and patience and persistence that our storehouse has to offer in controlling the arms race. If it is not somewhat brought under control, atomic arms will sooner or later be used." This warning was given by General Bruce K. Holloway, retired chief of the US Air Force Strategic Air Command and consultant to the Pentagon's Director of Defence Research and Engineering. The Strategic Air Command operates some 500 strategic bombers. This intercontinental bomber fleet can produce unimaginable devastation wrought by a nuclear explosive power equivalent to more than one ton of TNT for each person on earth. Small wonder that, with his intimate knowledge of this awesome force, the General should add his voice to those calling for a halt to the madness of the nuclear arms race.

Since the early seventies, much has been said about the need to preserve "mutual deterrence" as the strategic relationship between the USA and the Soviet Union. We are told that until nuclear weapons are abolished, the two powers must preserve their nuclear arsenals at very high levels and continually improve the quality of their nuclear weapons. "Retaliation" to a nuclear attack – particularly a sudden attack – is the stated reason for maintaining nuclear arsenals, and this retaliation must be as swift and as massive as possible. And, of course, both sides must have the ability to threaten retaliation so that "deterrence" is "stabilised" because it is "mutual". The hostages for this deterrence and the threat underlying it are the enemy's citizens. The prevention of nuclear war according to this doctrine requires, therefore, the threat of deliberate mass killing on a scale hitherto unheard of. Assured genocide is the keystone of today's nuclear strategists.

Today's deterrence strategists do not concern themselves with what happens after a retaliatory nuclear strike nor do they comment on the rationality of such a strike. Rather, if challenged, they argue that nuclear weapons are not actually to be used but are simply to "threaten retaliation" to see us through those moments when otherwise rational political leaders may be tempted to act in a less than rational way. But their strategy does not cope with the problem of truly "irrational" opponents nor with accidental war. The Strategic Arms Limitation Talks (SALT) agreements imply that both the USA and the Soviet Union have officially adopted the strategy of mutual deterrence – a perilous basis for protection from nuclear catastrophe brought on by irrationality, accident, or miscalculation.

For over forty years now, negotiations to abolish nuclear weapons have taken place in all conceivable forums, ranging from the UN General Assembly down to bilateral talks between the USA and the Soviet Union. But, despite this continuity of effort, no nuclear disarmament has yet been achieved. Meanwhile, the destructive power of existing nuclear arsenals has increased many thousand-fold and knowledge of, and experience in, nuclear technology has become so widespread that the number of nuclear-weapon powers is likely to increase continuously.

Surprisingly, knowledge of the catastrophic destructiveness of nuclear war has sunk so deep into man's consciousness as to remove the great anguish once caused by the ever-present danger that nuclear war would, in an instant, end our lives and our society. Who would have thought, more than fifty years ago, after the annihilation of two Japanese cities by the only nuclear weapons then existing, that man would rest easy knowing that tens of thousands of weapons capable of delivering thermonuclear warheads are kept on continuous alert? Can we now really believe that the political leaders of the nuclear-weapon powers will always behave so responsibly that these weapons, with their almost incomprehensible destructive power, will never be used? We certainly act as though we do. Do we now dismiss totally the possibility of nuclear annihilation by miscalculation, madness, or accident, once thought to be a very real danger? Or will it take the emergence of many new, possibly less responsible, nuclear-weapon powers to reactivate public concern about the danger of nuclear war? Must this wait until a limited nuclear war shocks us into action, assuming, of course, that this limited war will not escalate into a general nuclear war, destroying us all?

Since the beginning of the Cold War, the nuclear arms race between the USA and the Soviet Union was, undoubtedly, the greatest single threat to man's survival. Although the Soviet Union has disintegrated, halting the nuclear arms race, even among smaller powers, is proving to be as difficult as reversing it. The past many years of active negotiations have produced seven major multilateral treaties and a number of bilateral agreements between the USA and the Soviet Union, but the dangerous momentum of the proliferation of nuclear weapons has hardly been slowed.

In the late 1950s, the decision was made to shelve plans for general and complete disarmament (GCD) and to tackle the problem by partial measures, the so-called arms control approach. This decision was made in spite of the fact that several concrete GCD proposals had been put forward, in particular by Khrushchev, Selwyn Lloyd and Kennedy, which differed mainly in the timing of each successive phase of disarmament. The moves to bury these excellent comprehensive draft treaties were so successful that there has been no real discussion of GCD in the past fifteen years. During this time, all efforts have been concentrated on partial arms control measures, mainly at the Conference of the Committee on Disarmament (CCD) in Geneva. The theory is that instead of directly tackling disarmament as a whole, it would be more "productive" to take small steps, one at a time, toward disarmament. What then has been achieved so far by this piecemeal approach?

The first arms control treaty to be negotiated was the Antarctic Treaty (1959) which prohibits the militarisation of Antarctica. The veteran disarmament expert Philip Noel-Baker commented, "While disarming Antarctica, we put 7,000 nuclear weapons in Europe. We should have disarmed Europe and put those weapons in Antarctica." But the Antarctica Treaty was only the first of a series of arms control measures which merely banned weapons from environments in which there is no military interest. Another treaty of this type is the Outer Space Treaty (1967) which controls military activity in space. Who, though, wants to conduct military manoeuvres on the moon or to establish an orbiting military base? And then there is the Seabed Treaty (1971) which rules out the seabed for the emplacement of nuclear weapons, an activity no one has even seriously suggested.

The intention of the Treaty of Tlatelolco (1967), to make Latin America a nuclear-free zone was a good venture. The two countries in the region most likely to acquire nuclear weapons, Brazil and Argentina, along with thirty-three stages of Latin America and the Carribean, including Cuba, have already signed the Treaty which was ratified on March 20, 1995. They have also acceded to the NPT.

Most apologists for the arms control approach regard the Partial Test Ban Treaty (1963) as a singular success. It is true that in the international climate at the time, the treaty was a political watershed. But, in retrospect, it can be seen that the treaty has not significantly slowed the nuclear arms race. It has, however, reduced the radioactive contamination of the atmosphere. No one doubts that our environment would now be considerably more contaminated with radioactive material if the USA, the Soviet Union and the UK had continued testing nuclear weapons in the atmosphere and under water. Although France and China have not stopped conducting nuclear tests in the atmosphere, they have done so at much less frequency than did the other three powers. The treaty may also have prevented India, who has ratified it, from detonating its nuclear device above ground.

After the treaty, the USA, the Soviet Union and the UK continued testing nuclear weapons underground at about the same rate as they tested nuclear weapons before 1963. The Partial Test Ban Treaty has not, therefore, significantly slowed down the nuclear arms race. If it has had any effect at all, it was to limit the further development of very large thermonuclear weapons. On the other hand, since 1963, very substantial progress was made by underground testing in the following areas: improving the yield-to-weight ratio of nuclear warheads and, thus, developing, for example, very small nuclear weapons; hardening weapons against anti-ballistic missiles (ABM); developing multiple independently targetable re-entry vehicle (MIRV) and ABM warheads; improving delivery systems; and so on.

There is little doubt that public concern over the radioactive contamination of man's environment was the main factor which stimulated the USA, the Soviet Union and the UK to agree to discontinue tests in the atmosphere, in outer space, and under water. Public opinion had been aroused by a series of dramatic nuclear events prior to 1963, such as the severe radioactive contamination of a boatload of Japanese fishermen by an American thermonuclear explosion in 1954 in the Pacific, and the Soviet explosion in the atmosphere at Novaya Zemlja in October 1961 of the largest nuclear device ever exploded in the world – a 58-megaton thermonuclear weapon. The fact that the force of public opinion overcame the strong objections to a partial test ban of those groups in the nuclear-weapon powers with vested interests in nuclear testing is an object lesson. It demonstrates that if successfully mobilised again, public opinion could compel reluctant politicians to move toward nuclear disarmament. This may be the best, if not the only, hope of achieving disarmament.

The other two existing arms control measures are the Non-Proliferation Treaty (1970), which is a very fragile treaty indeed, and the convention prohibiting the production of biological weapons (1972). The latter is the only one of the seven arms control treaties actually to contain an element of disarmament. The parties to it are obligated to destroy any stocks of biological weapons which they may have accumulated. There is, however, little military regard for biological weapons and so this sacrifice is a minor one.

The most obvious best measures for arms control are a ban on chemical weapons and a Comprehensive Test Ban Treaty (CTBT). Verification is said to be the main stumbling block in the negotiation of both these measures but history shows that once the political will to obtain an agreement exists, verification problems are easily dealt with. Such was the experience with, for example, the biological convention and the SALT agreements.

The real reason for the delay in banning chemical weapons is that they are of much greater military interest than are biological weapons. Meanwhile, binary chemical weapons are being developed. These weapons contain chemicals which although relatively harmless on their own, produce poisonous compounds when mixed. Mixing occurs either when the munition is fired or when it impacts. The deployment of binary weapons will make the negotiation of a comprehensive ban on chemical weapons considerably more complicated. And a ban which did not include binaries would be ineffective.

There is also considerable military interest in the further development of low-yield nuclear weapons, particularly for tactical purposes. Therefore, a comprehensive test ban, prohibiting all nuclear weapon tests, has still not been negotiated, in spite of the legal commitment made nearly two decades ago in the Partial Test Ban Treaty to do so.

The treaty on the limitation of underground nuclear weapon tests, agreed on during the 1974 Nixon-Brezhnev talks, was not as promising as it might seem. The very high threshold of 150-kilotons was not in practice, even a significant limitation since most US and Soviet tests during those years had, in any case, been under the threshold. The treaty would, therefore, hardly affect the continuing development of nuclear warheads and the two great powers gave up practically nothing. The commitment to limit the number of underground nuclear tests was too loose to be meaningful. And the fact that the "limitation" was effective only from March 31, 1976, was bound to raise the suspicion that the powers had deliberately left themselves a free hand to test nuclear weapons of any size in the interim. Presumably the second generation of Soviet MIRV warheads was the main issue here.

Verification of the treaty was to be by unspecified national means. Countries other than the USA and the Soviet Union were not even invited to accede. Not only did the treaty appear valueless for disarmament, it would probably indefinitely delay a comprehensive ban.

Peaceful nuclear explosions were to be regulated by a separate agreement which might involve the presence of observers from the two superpowers. If on-site inspection was really implemented (for the first time), it would have been a big step forward, with far-reaching ramifications for future arms control and disarmament measures.

In addition to the treaty on the limitation of underground nuclear weapon tests and the SALT agreements, a number of other bilateral arms control treaties had been negotiated. The first of these agreements between the USA and the Soviet Union established a direct communications link between Washington and Moscow – the "hot line" – and came into force in June 1963, after the events of the 1962 Cuban missile crisis. A second hot-line agreement came into force in 1971, to improve the reliability of the link by the use of communications satellites. The hot-line, intended for the exchange of messages in times of emergency, was first used by the two great powers for serious business in the 1967 Middle East War to reassure each other of their mutual desire to avoid direct confrontation. Similar uses occurred in 1970, again during a Middle East crisis, and yet again in the 1973 Middle East War.

A rapid communications link between the great powers was undoubtedly of value in clarifying their intentions at times of severe crisis and, thus, minimising the risk of unintended war between these powers. Other American-Soviet bilateral agreements were on measures to reduce the risk of the outbreak of nuclear war between the two powers (1971); on the prevention of incidents on and over the high seas (1972); and on the prevention of nuclear war (1973). The first of these agreements provided for immediate notification in the event of an accidental, unauthorised incident involving the possible detonation of a nuclear weapon; the detection by missile-warning systems of unidentified objects; or signs of interference with these systems.

The most significant provision in the agreement on the prevention of nuclear war was that if at any time relations between the USA and the Soviet Union appeared to involve the risk of nuclear war between them, then the two powers would immediately enter into consultations with each other and make every effort to avert the risk. The fact that the USA put its forces on nuclear alert during the 1973 Middle East War justified the grave doubts about the effectiveness of the agreement.

In October 1973, negotiators from nineteen NATO and WTO (Warsaw Treaty Organisation) countries met in Vienna to discuss the mutual reduction of forces and armaments in Europe. These Mutual Force Reduction (MFR) talks were expected to go on for several years, but no significant result was obtained because the first round of talks ended in a deadlock.

The lack of progress at the MFR talks disappointed many who had pinned great hopes on these discussions. Also disappointed were those who thought that the entry of China into the United Nations would have far-reaching consequences for future disarmament negotiations. China was, in fact, unwilling to commit itself to partial arms control measures because those were considered detrimental to its interests, strategically and politically, vis-a-vis the USA and the Soviet Union. It was for this reason that a nuclear test ban had been dismissed by China as implying a threat to its security.

In summary, the arms control efforts – multilateral and bilateral – totally failed to produce any nuclear disarmament. On the contrary, the nuclear arms race between the two great powers continued unabated throughout at period. Moreover, arms races in other regions of the world had accelerated and had sprung up even among some nations of the Third World who had acquired, at least theoretically, the capability to produce nuclear weapons. Thus, increased military expenditures and ever-increasing trade in armaments continued to militarise all regions of the world.

The general lack of progress at the CCD, at SALT, and at the MFR negotiations in Vienna renewed interest in other approaches to the problem of reducing the role of military force in international affairs. One such approach was the attempt to prohibit, first, the use of unnecessarily cruel and indiscriminate weapons and, second, acts of warfare directed against civilian populations. While these efforts should not be allowed to divert attention from the main issue of the abolition of weapons of mass destruction, they did address a serious problem.

The Hague Convention of 1899 prohibits, for example, the use of Dum Dum bullets and the Geneva Protocol of 1925 prohibits the use of asphyxiating, poisonous, and other gases and chemical agents' bacteriological elements. However, since these early treaties, enormous improvements have been made in the effectiveness of a variety of inhuman weapons. Initiatives are now being taken to modernise the humanitarian law of war to take into account these advances in military technology.

The laws of war do not recognise in belligerents an unlimited power in the adoption of means of injuring the enemy. The means of combat are restricted in two ways: weapons should not cause "superfluous injuries", nor should they be employed indiscriminately against non-combatants. These principles are being undermined by current methods of warfare. Some modern weapons cause injuries similar to those caused by weapons that are already prohibited, but their mode of action is not specifically covered by the formulations of the existing international law. It is necessary to define these weapons and effectively ban their use.

The massive firepower of modern weapon systems, the use of chemical sprays, area weapons delayed action fuses, and a variety of means of environmental destruction undermine those regulations intended to offer civilian populations some measure of protection from the exigencies of armed conflict. These regulations must be reaffirmed and developed.

Among the so-called conventional weapons being given serious consideration at the United Nations and in the International Committee of the Red Cross for possible prohibitive measures are napalm, white phosphorous, and other incendiary weapons, hyper velocity rifles, and anti-personnel bombs. Napalm and other incendiary weapons may well be the first candidates for prohibition. The amount of napalm used in major wars is roughly as follows: World War II (1943-1945): 14,000 tons; Korea (1950-1953): 32,000 tons; Indochina (1963-1975): 372,000 tons. These figures exclude napalm used in the strategic bombing of cities during World War

II, and the napalm used in flame-throwers, mines, grenades, and shells. Wounds received from incendiary weapons are particularly horrifying. Burn wounds are not only intensely painful, but to treat them on a large scale, require enormous medical resources, far beyond the capacity of most countries. Fire has the ability to propagate rapidly and, therefore, it is likely to be indiscriminate in its effects. Indeed, in World War II and in the Korean War, incendiary weapons had all the characteristics of weapons of mass destruction. More people died in Tokyo and Dresden, for example, from the effects of a single night's incendiary bombing than from the nuclear weapon bombardment of Hiroshima and Nagasaki. And the heat and fire were the major causes of death resulting from the nuclear bombardment.

Two parameters related to the wounding power of penetrating projectiles were exploited in the war in Indochina. The first is the velocity of the projectile. At low velocity, the wound created by a bullet is of a diameter similar to that of the bullet. But at high velocity (for example, over 800 metres per second) a conical wound tract can be produced which may have a diameter many times that of the bullet. These effects are increased if the projectile is made to tumble by ballistic instability, creating a wound just as devastating as that caused by the prohibited Dum Dum bullet. So far, the US M-16 rifle is the only widely used weapon which fires high velocity bullets of this type, but prototypes have been produced in Switzerland, Belgium, Germany, Italy, Israel and some WTO countries. There is, therefore, an immediate prospect of the rapid proliferation of these weapons.

The second parameter is the number of projectiles. The greater the number of small projectiles, the larger the number of wounds inflicted and, consequently, the greater the lethal effect and the higher the number of casualties produced. This principle has led to the development of anti-personnel cluster bombs that can distribute as many as 192,000 steel bombs over an area of up to 1.0 x 0.3 kilometres. Weapons such as these have been developed in the USA, the UK, France and Germany. Prohibition of these and other inhumane and indiscriminate weapons is urgently needed to prevent the complete erosion of human rights in armed conflicts.

Another approach to the problem of reducing the role of military force in international affairs is a reduction of the resources devoted to military purposes. This could take the form of cutting military expenditures directly without specifying the type of weapons or other costs involved. The world military expenditure is currently running at about $300 billion per year – over 6 per cent of the Gross National Product (GNP) of the countries of the world. The military expenditure of those countries which provide development aid is approximately 6.7 per cent of their GNP, or nearly thirty times greater than the official development aid they provide. The transfer of resources from military to peaceful uses could significantly raise standards of living and promote faster growth.

In this connection, the enormous resources devoted to military research and development (R & D) should be mentioned. The $25 billion per year spent on military R & D is about one-third of the entire world expenditure on all R & D. The use of these resources for appropriate R & D for peaceful purposes could contribute enormously to progress and development in the underdeveloped parts of the world.

The dangers inherent in the present situation, particularly in the consequences of the onward rush of military technology in which one revolution follows another and including the probability of the proliferation of nuclear weapons, necessitates that achieving effective disarmament must have the highest priority.

It is sometimes argued that in the world as it exists today, disarmament can be achieved only as the end product of a long process. The first stage in this process involves banning weapons of little or no military value, and weapons from environments of little or no military significance. This stage, so it is claimed, will build such a degree of mutual confidence among the negotiating parties and so improve the climate of international relations that, in due course, far-reaching disarmament will be possible. History shows that this first stage will indeed be a lengthy one. In the meantime, it is said that we must learn to live with nuclear weapons.

At first sight, this argument appears convincing. Yet military technology is advancing extremely rapidly. Weapons are being developed and deployed that produce periods of considerable instability. As time goes on, the intensity of instability increases. Sooner or later, a period of instability may occur, for example, at a time of severe international tension and also possibly when one or more of the relevant states is led by an irresponsible leader. The extreme dangers inherent in such a combination of events is obvious. There is an ever-present risk that any major conflict, even a limited non-nuclear war, will escalate to a general nuclear war. Moreover, the possibility of a nuclear war by accident or miscalculation is always with us. The dangers of this situation are increased by advances in nuclear-weapon technology. They will also be multiplied if new nuclear-weapon powers continue to emerge. And the likelihood is that new nuclear weapons will continue to emerge if no substantial progress in nuclear disarmament takes place.

The catastrophic consequences of a general nuclear war demand either that the probability of any war be reduced to an acceptable level (most reasonable men would say that this would have to be zero) or that nuclear weapons ultimately be abolished as part of a comprehensive programme of disarmament. Even though we do not underestimate the difficulties of the latter, we believe its achievement to be a simpler task than the former. There may always be wars; but must they be nuclear wars?

Conflict and war historically have been the chief characteristics of international politics and now threaten the end of civilisation. In fact, the destructiveness of war has grown so enormously as a result of nationalism, industrialisation, and technological innovation that the world may be living in the "Indian summer" of its existence, to be followed by a "nuclear winter", which will end the history of the human race. This possibility was apparent as early as World War I. When the carnage of that war ended in 1918, Winston Churchill wrote: "Mankind has got into its hands for the first time the tools by which it can unfailingly accomplish its own extermination ... Death stands at attention, obedient, expectant, ready, if called on, to pulverise, without hope of repair, what is left of civilisation. He awaits only the word of command. He awaits it from a frail, bewildered being, long his victim, now – for one occasion only – his Master."

Although war, not surprisingly, is often regarded as somehow abnormal – at best an awful error, at worst a criminal undertaking – the fact is that the history of war is as old as human history. In this century, the brutality of war has greatly influenced thinking about international politics.

Long before the nuclear weapon, war had already become so costly that questions about its usability were widespread. Instead of the short and not very costly conflict that the diplomats, soldiers, and others had expected, the long and extremely costly Great War was the first modern war to raise the issue of the legitimacy and rationality of warfare as an instrument for advancing a nation's purposes. After 1945 and six years of fighting in which the loss of life, military and civilian, exceeded that of World War I, the futility of another total war became obvious to all. World War II had ended with the dropping of two atomic bombs, each of which had caused a heavy loss of life and widespread destruction. The bomb was quickly called the "absolute weapon". What was the point of defending one's way of life if, in the process, that way of life was utterly destroyed? In the nuclear age total war had become irrational; the costs of such a war completely exceeded any conceivable gains. One knew that without even having to fight. Had the leaders of Europe, who went to war in 1914, been able to look into a crystal ball and foresee what the costs would be, they might have chosen a different course. Today, we have that crystal ball.

The enormity of the threat of nuclear war increases year by year as rapid advances in military technology are incorporated into weaponry. No means have yet been found even to control the onward rush of military technology, let alone stop it. As time goes on, increasingly sophisticated weapons become available to more and more countries. All nations seem bent on acquiring more abundant and more lethal armaments, and nuclear weapon powers are likely to emerge continuously.

Unless effective steps are soon taken to halt these processes, it would be extremely foolhardy and totally unrealistic to imagine that they can end in anything short of disaster. But, it is often asked, what can the individual do to affect this situation? Clearly the primary responsibility of the conscientious citizen is to inform himself, and if, after an objective assessment of the facts, many people judge that action must be taken to avert disaster, sufficient pressure will be brought to bear on political leaders to achieve this end. It is hoped that this book will assist the dissemination of this essential information.

2

NUCLEAR POLITICS

When the news of President Roosevelt's death reached Moscow, in the middle of the night of April 12-13, 1945, Vyacheslav Molotov at once went to the American Embassy to pay his respects. Stalin wrote to Mrs. Roosevelt, referring to her husband "as the leader in the cause of ensuring the security of the whole world". In a separate message to President Harry S. Truman, Stalin said: "The American people and the United Nations have lost in Franklin Roosevelt a great politician of world significance and a pioneer in the organization of the peace and security after the war. The Government of the Soviet Union expresses sincere sympathy to the American people in their great loss and their conviction that the policy of friendship between the great powers who are shouldering the main burden of the war against the common enemy will continue in the future."

The Associated Press reported from Moscow that the Russians were firmly convinced by Roosevelt's election to the fourth term that the American people desired close relations with the Soviet Union in building peace and security after the war. They would look for every sign that his programme would be continued without interruption.

The New York Times correspondent in Moscow reported that the sorrow for Roosevelt was profound and unprecedented.[1] People felt it both in a political way and in a personal sense, from the highest official to the lowest man in the street. Since early morning the President's death had been the single topic of conversation everywhere. Condolences were delivered to Americans all day as if a close personal relation had died. Not even Pearl Harbour of the Second Front had made the first page in the Soviet press, and pictures seldom appeared there. On that day, all newspapers were late, having been made over to carry black-bordered pictures of Roosevelt on the front page.

The next day, the official black-fringed red banner of national mourning was raised over Marshal Stalin's residence, the Kremlin, all government and many private buildings. No foreigner had ever received such honour in the history of the Soviet Union. People in the subway were still talking about what Roosevelt had meant. Many were still weeping. Attendance at the cinemas and theatres fell off noticeably. Many Russians cancelled private parties. Extra telephone operators had to be put on at the American Embassy and hundreds of Russians begged for the privilege of an invitation to the memorial service in Averill Harriman's residence. The government used all possible means to encourage the people to honour the memory of their friend.[2]

On the day of Roosevelt's funeral, workmen stood weeping at their benches in all parts of the Soviet Union. Indeed, mourning for him was more widespread in the Soviet Union than in his own country, where so many influential people hated him.[3]

The London *Times* representative in Moscow summarised the newspaper tributes as emphasising Roosevelt's preeminent part in establishing good relations between the two nations "and his long and resolute struggle against the forces of reaction, in the domestic and international fields, in his country." But, more than anything else, the President's work for the post-war organisation of peace was emphasised, and determination was expressed that the cause to which he gave so much of his strength must prevail. The same note was struck in an unprecedented tribute to Roosevelt by the Supreme Soviet of the USSR on April 22. Before the Assembly rose in tribute to him, a declaration was read out saying that the Soviet people would always honour him. It closed with the sentence, "let us ensure that in future the friendship between our peoples will stand as a memorial."[4]

It does not follow that if Roosevelt had lived and retained his vigour during the next three years, there would have been no serious problems between the Soviet Union and the West. There were serious problems but at the worst, they would have caused severe strain. The shock of Roosevelt's death caused the Soviet leaders to feel their need of his friendship, and the UNO, more keenly. Nevertheless, the presumption must remain that the knowledge of his proven friendship would have been a powerful influence in Moscow during the critical years which immediately followed.

It was Roosevelt who had fused the war time coalition together. Roosevelt and Cordell Hull had convinced the Soviet leaders that they meant to give their country a square deal. They had prevented the formation of an Anglo-American front against the Soviet Union. When they were gone, there was no one left to hold the scales evenly, no one who could mediate between Churchill and Stalin and strive to find common goals for the two worlds.

Of course, Roosevelt's effort to make peace in cooperation with his allies, one of which had been at odds with the West and rejected by it for twenty years prior to the Grand Alliance, had history against it. Victorious coalitions had traditionally fallen apart soon after the victory, rapidly becoming rivals and enemies. That is inherent in the egocentric nature of national governments, all trying to exercise their sovereign wills. Yet, in history, the business of great power struggle ending the world wars had come to a dead end. No more could be endured. In 1945 and thereafter, no man who did not understand this, was qualified to control the destinies of any great power.

Roosevelt was everlastingly right in his gallant, sustained effort to break out of the ancient cycle of national rivalries arms race — and war. He saw that there were no objective reasons for the United States and the Soviet Union to fall out immediately and fight for mastery of the world. Till his last days and hours he attempted to prevent that, and succeeded in it up to the moment of his passing. It was not Roosevelt who failed; it was his successors who were unable to make peace.

Roosevelt died believing that he would be able to build a structure of cooperation with the Soviet Union on the foundations which he had laboured so hard to lay. There had been disquieting developments after Yalta, leading to sharp words on both sides, but Roosevelt did not believe that they indicated the beginning of any basic rift. Most of the problems would get straightened out, "and our course thus far is correct".

Cordell Hull has also recorded his conviction that Roosevelt did not believe any rift was imminent when he died, saying: "On the occasions when the President came to see me at the hospital after my resignation, including his last visit only a few days before his death, he said nothing about any fears he might have that Russia would abandon our cooperative movement for peace or would block or destroy it."[5]

It is frequently said that Roosevelt knew during his last weeks that his strategy had failed. If so, he would not have failed to mention it to Hull. But he also talked with Edgar Snow about Russia, on March 3, 1945, and said positively that at his last meeting with Stalin they "had got close to speaking the same language." Many points had been disputed between Stalin and Churchill, "but Stalin," said Roosevelt, "agreed to every single suggestion I made". "I am convinced that we are going to get along," the President said emphatically.

"His optimism was so contagious," Snow wrote, "that it dispelled most of my fears. He spoke with absolute conviction of his ability to get along with the Russians. Some have said his disputes with Stalin over the Polish question disillusioned him, but it is incredible to me that Roosevelt could have permitted one incident to cause him to abandon overnight a purpose for which he had worked so ardently throughout the war."

Snow's judgement is well based. It would indeed have been incredible if Roosevelt had allowed one incident or a series of them in the hectic atmosphere of ending a world war, to deflect him from the urgent necessity of working with Russia in the post-war world. This was a need so desperately evident that any layman could grasp it. To Roosevelt, great world politician that he was, there could be no other rational policy. When Edgar Snow saw him in

May 1944, Snow had just read the series of articles in the *Saturday Evening Post* by Forrest Davis, "The Great Design", in which Roosevelt's purpose "to remove Russia's historic fear of encirclement and exclusion from Europe" was discussed. Roosevelt agreed that Davis correctly interpreted his views, but demurred at the phrase "The Great Gamble", used to describe "our policy of working with Russia." "Gamble" was not the right word, the President said, when there was no real alternative to working with Russia except to begin preparations right then for World War III. "I am all for trying to make a durable peace after this war, a world we can live in together," he added.

It has been said innumerable times that even Roosevelt could not have worked with the Russians and averted the Cold War. This is an article of faith for cold warriors. "Surely he could not have stood for the way they broke their Yalta promises to him." Yet it is altogether probable that if Roosevelt had been able to finish his fourth term in the White House there would have been no Cold War.

"But what about Eastern Europe? Wouldn't he have broken with the Russians about that?" Of course, this is the key question, but there is no evidence that Roosevelt would have plunged the world into decades of a futile and sterile Cold War on this score. In his March 1945 interview with Snow, he said: "Obviously the Russians are going to do things their own way in areas they occupy. But they won't set up a separate administration independent of the Allied Control Commission to rival any arrangement made for all Germany."[6]

"Aside from the accuracy of his prediction about Germany," writes Fleming, "this understanding of what the Russians would, and from their standpoint, must, do in the areas they occupied was indispensable to peace in the post-war world, and without that understanding in the White House, there could and would be no peace. The fate of nations is always in the hands of a few men at the top, and everything too often depends upon their point of view. Roosevelt was clear about the overriding necessity of making the peace in cooperation with the Soviets. It was his purpose to be firm with them and to *minimise* the inevitable post-war disagreements.

As we shall soon see, his successor was quick to say, *maximise* the difficulties and be tough with the Russians. He was soon engaged in doing what would have been inconceivable to Roosevelt – an attempt to 'contain' and encircle the Soviet Union with arms, alliances and bases around her frontiers." [7]

II

On August 6, 1945, Anglo-American officialdom announced the destruction of Hiroshima, the result of the test of July 16, and the advent of the atomic epoch. Three days later, on August 9, another Japanese city, Nagasaki, was destroyed. President Truman's statement spoke of "a harnessing of the basic power of the universe". Secretary Stimson reviewed the history of the enterprise. Churchill reported to the House of Commons. They all emphasised, in the interest of "security", the need of secrecy regarding details of production and use of the atomic bomb. Chancellor Hutchins opined that world government was now essential and the fear of the bomb might move mankind into taking steps towards that goal. General Groves, however, insisted that "this weapon must be kept under control of the United States until all other nations of the world are as anxious for peace as we are". Secretary of Commerce Henry A. Wallace urged the "sharing of the secret" with the Soviets, but President Truman emphatically stated that he alone would decide what the Administration policy should be. In October, J. R. Oppenheimer, supported by Robert Wilson and H. J. Curtis, warned that the "secret" was "no secret at all"; that no nation could "win" an atomic arms race, since only a few bombs would be necessary to put an enemy "out of action," regardless of the size of his own stockpile; and that nothing short of effective international control could meet the issue. On October 26, Einstein urged that America and Britain invite Russia to join them in establishing a world government, to which all possible information regarding the bomb should be transmitted.

Not until mid-November 1945, were any steps taken at the top level to evolve an international *programme* for coping with the menace of the bomb. On November 10, Prime Minister Attlee and

Mackenzie King began a series of conferences with President Truman in Washington. Attlee was reported to have urged the "sharing of the secret, subject to satisfactory assurances of good intent from Russia, with the members of the Security Council, which should devise and administer a system of controls. The Joint Declaration issued on November 15 recognised that the bomb constituted "a means of destruction hitherto unknown, against which there can be no single nation, that can in fact have a monopoly … We are aware that the only complete protection for the civilized world from the destructive use of scientific knowledge lies in the prevention of war." Exchange of scientific information "for peaceful purposes" was espoused, but the "spreading of specialized information regarding the practical application of atomic energy, before it is possible to devise effective, reciprocal, and enforceable safeguards acceptable to all nations," was eschewed as not constituting a contribution "to a constructive solution of the problem of the atomic bomb." A reciprocal exchange of information "concerning the practical industrial application of atomic energy" was favoured, "just as soon as effective, enforceable safeguards against its use for destructive purposes can be devised. Despite this ambiguous and evasive phraseology, the declaration concluded hopefully with a proposal that the United Nations should set up a Commission to make recommendations: "The Commission should be instructed to proceed with the utmost dispatch and should be authorized to submit recommendations from time to time dealing with separate phases of its work. In particular, the Commission should make specific proposals (a) for exchanging between all nations the basic scientific information for peaceful ends; (b) for control of atomic energy to the extent necessary to ensure its use only for peaceful purposes; (c) for the elimination from national armaments of atomic weapons and of all other major weapons adaptable to mass destruction; and (d) for effective safeguards by way of inspection and other means to protect complying states against the hazards of violations and evasions.

"The work of the Commission should proceed by separate stages, the successful completion of each one of which will develop the necessary confidence of the world before the next stage is undertaken. Specifically, it is considered that the Commission might well develop its attention first to the wide exchange of scientists and scientific information, and as a second stage to the development of full knowledge concerning natural resources of raw materials.

"Faced with the terrible realities of the application of science to destruction, every nation will realise more urgently than before the overwhelming need to maintain the rule of law among nations and to banish the scourge of war from the earth. This can only be brought about by giving whole-hearted support to the United Nations Organisation, and by consolidating and extending its authority, thus creating conditions of mutual trust in which all peoples will be free to devote themselves to the arts of peace. It is our firm resolve to work without reservation to achieve these ends."[8]

This formula solved no problems but opened a way toward a solution. That no solution had been arrived at more than a decade later was a consequence of circumstances generally deemed extraneous to the problem but actually inseparable from it. The prospects were not unfavourable in the fall of 1945. In his Charleston address of November 16, James F. Byrnes was forthright: "The civilized world cannot survive an atomic war. This is the challenge to our generation. To meet it we must let our minds be bold." On November 22, Attlee declared in the Commons that "where there is no mutual confidence, no system will be effective ... We wish to establish between all nations (just) such confidence." Anthony Eden commented: "For the life of me, I am unable to see any final solution that will make the world safe from atomic power other than that we all abate our present ideas of sovereignty."[9]

At Moscow in December, 1945, the Foreign Ministers of the "Big Three" achieved agreement on preparation of peace treaties with Italy and lesser enemy states on the administration of Japan; on Korea, China, Romania and Bulgaria; and, as a result, on a procedure for dealing with atomic energy. The communiqué of December 26 proposed a resolution, to be submitted to the General Assembly, for the establishment of a UN Commission on Atomic Energy to make proposals for the four purposes quoted above. It was stipulated that the Commission should consist of delegates of the states in the Security Council, plus Canada, and should "submit its reports and recommendations to", and "be accountable for its work to", the Security Council, which should "issue directives to the Commission in matters affecting security."[10]

Meanwhile, Truman and Byrnes were obliged to assure Congress that no "secrets" would be revealed to the Soviet Union until Congress was satisfied regarding the efficacy of the system of inspection and control. On 24 January, the General Assembly of the United Nations adopted a resolution reiterating the language of the Moscow Declaration. Despite the UN injunction to "proceed with the utmost urgency", the Commission did not meet for another six months. On 18 March, President Truman named multi-millionaire Bernard M. Baruch as the US representative, to be assisted by John Hancock (a Wall Street banker), Ferninand Eberstadt (a Wall Street banker), Herbert Bayard Swope (a publisher), and Fred Searles (a mining engineer and businessman).[11] Whether a group so constituted was best calculated to promote a viable Soviet-American accord and to deal boldly with a challenge having no precedents in the vocational experience of bankers and stock speculators remained to be demonstrated.

A bright hope dawned on March 16, 1946, with the release of the Lilienthal-Acheson proposals: "A Report on the International Control of Atomic Energy", prepared by Chester I. Barnard, J.R. Oppenheimer, Charles A. Thomas, Harry A. Winne, and David E. Lilienthal (Chairman), as consultants to the Secretary of State's Committee on Atomic Energy, consisting of Undersecretary Dean Acheson, Vannevar Bush, James B. Conant, Leslie R. Groves, and John D. McCloy.[12] This masterpiece of unanswerable logic admits of no brief summary. It should be read and reread by all who are seriously concerned with the fate of human civilisation. It distinguishes between "safe" and "dangerous" operations in the use of atomic power. The mining of uranium and thorium, the maintenance of reactors for making and separating plutonium, and all research and production in atomic explosives are designated as "dangerous" under all conditions when left to exclusively national exploitation. The "solution" proposed is a UN Atomic Development

Authority, which, under the direction of the Security Council, will own and operate all uranium and thorium mines throughout the world, as well as laboratories and plants using fissionable materials in their dangerous form, and will conduct all activities all over the earth in atomic research, inspection, licensing, and leasing – for the double purpose of making impossible the production of atomic bombs and making available atomic power and its by-products for the good of mankind.

But the tragic fact was that while the Lilienthal-Acheson report was being prepared, the animus between Washington and Moscow was growing rapidly. The mounting enmity between the two super powers was less a consequence than a cause of failure to agree about the bomb. Assessment of responsibility for lack of concord was almost academic in the light of the appalling fact of discord. Soviet policy in Iran and in the Balkans in the winter of 1945-46 evoked fear in Washington and London. The Byrnes-Bevin Doctrine evoked anxiety in Moscow. The Soviet Union and its satellites had already been placed in the position of an obnoxious minority in the United Nations. On March 5, 1946, in Fultong, M.O., Churchill, applauded by Truman, called for an Anglo-American alliance against the Soviet Union. Truman, apparently astonished that the spectacle should have provoked anger in the Soviet Union, sought to mend matters by inviting Stalin on 5 April, to cross the sea aboard the *U.S.S. Missouri* and deliver an address, in Truman's presence, in Columbia, M.O. Stalin politely declined, as any Chief Executive of a Great Power would necessarily have declined so naive and humiliating a proposal.[13]

In this context, all hopes of an accord were foredoomed. The USA continued to produce atomic bombs at the war time rate. Moscow accused the United States of "brandishing the atomic weapons for purposes which have little in common with the peace and security of nations."[14] The result, wilfully or unwittingly, was that the USA proposed a plan for the control of atomic energy which its leaders knew the Soviet Union would never accept, while the Soviet Union proposed a plan which its leaders knew the United States would never accept.

When the UN Atomic Energy Commission (UNAEC) finally met on June 14, 1946, Bernard Baruch put forward the American proposals and said:

> We are here to make a choice between the quick and the dead. That is our business. Behind the black portent of the new atomic age lies a hope which, seized upon with faith, can work our salvation. If we fail, then we have damned every man to be the slave of fear. Let us not deceive ourselves. We must elect world peace or world destruction.[15]

Baruch went on to endorse the goal of a global Atomic Development Authority (ADA). But he offered no assurance that his government would discontinue the manufacture and stock-piling of atomic bombs or share relevant information with others, until it should be satisfied, at some remote and unspecified date, that the successive stages of international control were operating effectively – during which indeterminate interval, other nations (i.e., the USSR) would, by implication, be precluded from producing atomic bombs. His major motive, however, was reversion to irrelevant conceptions. Despite his comment that "our solution lies in the elimination of war", he proposed that atomic obligations should be enforced through the threat of war – i.e., the coercion of states by states. He demanded that in all atomic matters the great powers must renounce the central principle of the UN Charter and agree to the abolition of the "veto" on coercion, thereby presumably agreeing in advance that others might legitimately wage war upon it if a simple majority in the Security Council should hold an accused state guilty of violating its obligations. "We must provide immediate, swift and sure punishment of those who violate the agreements that are reached by the nations. Penalization is essential ... Condign punishment must be set up for violations of the rules of control, which are to be stigmatized as international crimes ... It would be a deception, to which I am unwilling to lend myself, were I not to say to you, and to all peoples, that the matter of punishment lies at the very heart of our present security system. It might as well be admitted, here and now, that the subject goes straight to the veto power contained in the Charter of the UN so far as it relates to the field of atomic energy ... There must be no veto to protect those who violate their solemn agreements." [16]

On June 19, 1946, without referring to Baruch's proposal, Andrei Gromyko of the Soviet Union proposed a wholly different procedure. All states should agree by treaty to forbid the production and use of atomic weapons and to destroy all stockpiles within three months. They should further agree to set up a UN committee for the exchange of scientific information and another committee to propose measures of inspection and control. "Efforts made toward undermining the activity of the Security Council, including efforts directed toward undermining the unanimity of the members upon questions of substance, are incompatible with the interests of the United Nations. Such attempts should be resisted." Gromyko later indicated that the Soviet Union would never accept the Baruch proposal, in whole or in part.

The deadlock was never broken. The Soviet proposal for "outlawing the bomb" could not reasonably be expected to meet the exigencies of the problem unless accompanied by a programme for global legislation in the field of atomic energy that was capable of being enforced effectively on individuals. Without this, the treaty urged by Moscow would become another scrap of paper. Since Washington also rejected any federalist solution and relied for safety upon agreements for war by states against states, the American proposals were also tragically irrelevant to the needs of a new time. Each government, moreover, knew that its programme had no chance of acceptance by the other. In both capitals, therefore, some policy-makers may be presumed to have reconciled themselves from the outset to an atomic arms race, doubtless on the assumption that "our" side could win. "I pray God," said Senator MacKeller on February 17, 1947, "we will never have an agreement."

Prior to his statement of June 14, 1946, Baruch was vainly urged by Lilienthal and Barnard not to introduce the "veto" question on the ground that it was meaningless and would lead into a "blind alley."[17] After the predicted impasse was reached, Secretary of Commerce, Wallace, in a letter to the President on 23 July, and in his public address on 12 September, declared the veto question to be "entirely irrelevant and accused Baruch of promoting an atomic-armament race by ignoring the legitimate anxieties of the security needs of the Soviet Union. The ensuing exchange of public recriminations early in October produced more heat than light.

In this context, the diplomacy of nuclear fission stumbled dolefully towards its doom.[18] Within the USA, control of bomb making was taken out of military hands and placed in those of a civilian Atomic Energy Commission headed by Lilienthal – in the face of stout and almost successful senatorial opposition.[19] But in the United Nations, the principles championed by the USA and the USSR admitted of no compromise. On 27 December, Baruch asserted: "It has been said that if a great nation does not have the right to release itself from its obligations by veto, the result will be war. I agree. I believe that a clear realization of this would be the greatest step towards peace that has been taken in history ..." On 30 December, the UNAEC voted approval of a programme based on the Baruch approach. The USSR and Poland abstained. Baruch resigned on January 4, 1947. Warren R. Austin and Frederick H. Osborn carried on, with no change of US policy. Gromyko continued to restate Soviet policy, also without change.

By June, Osborn was calling the Soviet proposals "a fraud on the people of the world," while Gromyko insisted anew on outlawing of atomic weapons and immediate establishment of a limited inspection and control system on this premise. At the end of June, the Emergency Committee of Atomic Scientists issued a solemn warning: "The American people should understand that ... the creation of a supranational government, with powers adequate to the responsibility of maintaining the peace, is necessary. Is this realistic? We believe that nothing less is realistic ... Men must understand that the times demand a higher realism."

All in vain. By August, Osborn was declaring the new Soviet proposals "wholly unacceptable". Gromyko replied that the American proposals were designed to secure for the USA "a position of monopoly in the field of atomic energy. The Soviet Union cannot agree to accept such proposals." Efforts by other governments, most of which sided with the USA, to promote a change in the American and Soviet positions, or to achieve a compromise between them, all failed. Efforts by physicists and other anxious observers to impress politicians and public opinion with the desperate urgency of a solution were also without result. On April 5, 1948, the Working Committee of the UNAEC reported that the Soviet proposals for limited international control were inadequate, unworkable, and unacceptable. In May, the Commission announced that it had "reached an impasse" and, on the initiative of the USA, Britain, and France, suspended further discussion in an admission of complete failure.

The rest of the tale is all of a piece. Its intricacies were meaningless, since neither side at any time had any intention of compromising. Moscow, determined to acquire atomic energy for its own purposes, adhered to its proposals for outlawry of atomic weapons by treaty, knowing that the USA would never agree. Washington – equally determined to prolong the American monopoly, to secure absolute safety and, if possible, to prevent any other power from acquiring the bomb – adhered to its proposals for "international" ownership and management and for abolition of the "veto", knowing that the USSR would never agree. The UNAEC voted to suspend its work on July 29, 1949. Subsequent "negotiations" led to a report of continued deadlock on October 24, 1949.

Moscow conceded that a convention for control of atomic energy should be signed simultaneously with a convention for outlawry and destruction of stockpiles and that the veto should not apply to the day-to-day operations of any ADA or international control commission. Washington conceded that national quotas of atomic facilities should be written into the control treaty. But these "concessions" were amply gestures. Trygve Lie asserted in January 1950: "There has been no real negotiation."

The advent of the Soviet bomb effected no modifications in the positions already taken.[20] Acheson: "This event makes no change in our policy." Tass: "The Soviet Government adopts, and intends adopting in the future, its former position." In fact, the Soviet bomb had prospective strategic consequences of the utmost importance. Churchill's view that Soviet seizure of Western Europe had been prevented only by the American monopoly of the bomb was now invalidated, if it ever had validity. American policy-makers hastened to project the rearmament of Germany and Western Europe as a whole as a kind of counterweight to the Soviet bomb. But since the crowded urban centres of the Continent and the British Isles were far more vulnerable to atomic bombing than any areas of Marxland, the Soviet bomb might well be regarded as having reduced, to doubtful efficacy, the concept of building locally in Western Europe a structure of military power commensurate with that of the Soviet Union and its allies – just as the vulnerability of Japan rendered doubtful the similar American project in the Far East. Says Frederick L. Schuman:

> But it is of the essence to the issue we are considering that modern mankind is here, more than ever, a victim of 'cultural lag'. The bomb renders all power politics obsolete, since the 'victors' in the atomic war will, in all probability, be as miserable and barbarized as the 'vanquished'. Nuclear fission therefore calls, by all reason and logic among men who prefer life to death, for radical new departures in political thought and action looking either toward world government or toward a new diplomacy dedicated irrevocably to peace. But statesman, strategists, and patriots continue to deal with every new weapon as they have always in the past dealt with every new weapon. [21]

III

Clearly, a chain of dramatic events had taken place since Hiroshima and Nagasaki were destroyed in August 1945. The destruction of Hiroshima in a single blow climaxed the greatest single coordinated effort the American scientific, engineering and industrial genius ever made. Since the Germans had first split the atom in 1938, Americans feared they would perfect atomic bombs during the war. Actually, the Germans had given up the effort as unattainable in their time, but the Allies did not know that.[22]

By the time Germany was knocked out, success in creating an atomic bomb seemed assured, though the first one was tested at Alamogordo, New Mexico, only on July 16, when Japan was obviously very groggy. Before that, however, the advisability of using the bomb on Japan had been canvassed and the decision was made to do so, if the test succeeded.

Afterwards, controversy arose as to the wisdom of this decision. Some suspected that the reasons were political, that the A-bomb was used to knock Japan out of the war before Russia could enter it, if possible, and, in any event, to restrict Russia's gains and voice in the Far East. Is there any foundation for this charge?

In his report on the Potsdam Conference, on August 9, President Truman said: "The world will note that the first atomic bomb was dropped on Hiroshima, a military base. That was because we wished to avoid, in so far as possible, the killing of civilians. But the attack is only a warning of things to come. If Japan does not surrender, bombs will have to be dropped on her war industries, and unfortunately thousands of civilian lives will be lost." The bomb was used, he added, "to shorten the agony of war, in order to save the lives of thousands of young Americans".

It is true that Hiroshima was the military headquarters of southern Japan, and it contained several thousand troops at the time of the A-bomb attack. Yet it was not at these troops that the bomb was aimed at. In order to have any effect in knocking Japan out of the war, it had to be aimed at the Japanese people and it had to kill a huge number of them. In the words of the *US Strategic Bombing Survey*, "Hiroshima and Nagasaki were chosen as targets because of their concentration of activities and population."[23]

After Hiroshima, the United States' highest military authorities agreed that the use of the A-bomb had not been essential. General Henry H. Arnold, the head of the Army Air Force, wrote that "the fact is that the Japanese could not have held out long, because they had lost control of the air."[24] Fleet Admiral William F. Halsey, Jr. also stated that "the first atomic bomb was an unnecessary experiment. It was a mistake to ever drop it. Why reveal a weapon like that to the world when it was not necessary?" Explaining that the Japanese Navy was already finished, Halsey blamed the use of the bomb on the scientists.[25] The US *Strategic Bombing Survey* also concluded: "Based on a detailed investigation of all the facts, and supported by the testimony of the surviving Japanese leaders involved, it is the Survey's opinion that certainly prior to December 31, 1945, Japan would have surrendered, even if the atomic bombs had not been dropped, even if Russia had not entered the war, and even if no invasion had been planned or contemplated."[26] Secretary of State Byrnes also stated that the bomb did not end the war, that Japan was beaten and suing for peace when it was dropped.[27]

There was, however, a very strong domestic political reason for the use of the bomb. The USA was determined to settle accounts with Japan, but it had had enough of war and yearned to see the end of it. This desire was especially deep because of the geography involved. Most of the army veterans of the European war who were being re-deployed to the Far East, were in the USA, on furloughs. This was, doubtless, necessary but it was extremely difficult to ask those same men to go half way around the world again to finish another war. They would do it, but the prospect was so infinitely distasteful to them that any administration would grasp at almost any means which would avoid that painful necessity.[28]

A further incentive was bound to motivate strongly some of the military men who had been responsible for the administration of the vast atomic project — the desire to show the world and the American taxpayers that the stupendous effort had paid off. The whole undertaking had been sensational, but secret. Now news of it would soon begin to spread, and what more effective announcement of results could there be than the mightiest explosion in history? This was a natural impulse in men who had been closely associated with the saga, one so powerful that it was by no means an inconsequential element in the decision to use the bomb. The urge to demonstrate in the most striking manner, the great "invention" ever made, was certain to be compelling. The expenditure had been huge, the anxiety about success had been great, and finally it had come. How else could it be announced so effectively as by using the bomb?

Unquestionably, strong psychological forces worked for an early use of the bomb. Yet two considerations remain to be explored: (a) were there long-term reasons for avoiding the military use of the bomb? and (b) if not, when was the best time for its employment?[29]

One group of Americans had done some deep thinking on the problem which would arise. Several memoranda prepared by scientists who had worked on the atomic energy project crystallised in the report of a "Committee on Social and Political Implications" to the Director of the Metallurgical Laboratory in Chicago, which was forwarded to the Secretary of War on June 11, 1945. The committee was headed by James Franck.

The Franck Report is the first important document looking towards international control of atomic energy. It warned that in Russia the basic facts and implications of nuclear power were well understood in 1940, and that the experience of Russian scientists was "entirely sufficient to enable them to retrace our steps in a few years." The report also warned that a nuclear arms race could not be avoided, either by keeping "our advance steps secret or by cornering raw materials. Evaluating our own vulnerability, Russia and China were the only great nations which could survive an atomic attack."

For these reasons the Franck Committee urged that the first use of the bomb should be a test demonstration in a desert or a barren island, at which representatives of all the United Nations would be present. Stressing that new and imaginative methods were required to handle so momentous a development, the committee asked "the highest political leadership of this country to consider what the effects would be if the bomb were first used without warning as a military weapon." The committee added:

> Russia, and even allied countries which bear less mistrust of our ways and intentions, as well as neutral countries may be deeply shocked by this step. It may be very difficult to persuade the world that a nation which was capable of secretly preparing and suddenly releasing a new weapon, as indiscriminately as the rocket bomb and a thousand times more destructive, is to be trusted in its proclaimed desire of having such weapons abolished by international agreement.

They felt that "it is not at all certain that American public opinion, if it could be enlightened as to the offset of atomic explosives, would approve of our own country being the first to introduce such an indiscriminate method of wholesale destruction of civilian life." The saving of American lives might be outweighed by "a wave of horror and revulsion sweeping over the rest of the world and perhaps even dividing public opinion at home."

Altogether, "if the United States were to be the first to release this new means of indiscriminate destruction upon mankind, she would sacrifice public support throughout the world, precipitate the race for armaments and prejudice the possibility of reaching an international agreement on the future control of such weapons.[30]

In addition to the Franck Committee, which forwarded its report on June 11, two individuals made strong efforts to avert the routine use of the A-bomb on Japan. One member of the Interim Committee, Ralph A. Bard, Undersecretary of the Navy, at first assented to its report, being entirely new to the subject, but on further consideration, he wrote to Secretary Stimson urging that two or three days' warning be given to Japan. On July 1, to make his dissent emphatic, he secured an interview with President Truman and, knowing that Japan was already securely bottled up, he urged that an all-out American invasion would not be necessary.[31]

One of the atomic scientists, Leo Szilard, who had been instrumental in initiating the atomic project, did his utmost to bring to the attention of the President the effect that the atomic bomb would have on America's relations with the Soviet Union. Some time in March 1945, he drew up a memorandum which by implication warned against the use of the bomb against Japan. President Roosevelt's death prevented him from presenting it to Roosevelt. Then he tried to reach President Truman and was advised to go down to South Carolina and see the President's personal advisor, James F. Byrnes. He did this on May 28, accompanied by Walter Bartkyt, Associate Dean of the Physical Sciences at the University of Chicago. This attempt to reach the President directly, which greatly disturbed General Leslie Groves, was unproductive.[32]

The issue had been decided by Secretary Stimson's memorandum to the President on July 2, in which he listed the evidence that the Japanese were nearly knocked out, along with his conviction that they would fight forever, in very rugged terrain, if the Americans set foot on the larger islands. Surrender, he thought, could be arranged through the Emperor, if a very impressive warning were first given, outlining assurances for Japan's future and warning of "the inevitable and completeness of the destruction" which "the varied and overwhelming" force at America's disposal would bring about.

The President promptly accepted this programme and the discussion at once turned to the timing of the warning to Japan which would precede the use of S-1, the atomic bomb. In the end, the decision was made by President Truman, who ruled that the warning should be solemnly issued at the Potsdam Conference, in the name of the United States, Great Britain and China, so that it would be plain, in Stimson's words, that "all of Japan's principal enemies were in entire unity.[33] In other words, it was decided to try to force Japan's surrender by an A-bomb attack before Russia's entry into the war on August 8. Writes Fleming:

> We do not, however, need this evidence to dispose of the suggestion that our policy makers simply forgot about the date of Russia's entry. Everyone in high authority in Washington, and many others, knew that Russia was due to enter the war on that date. It had been known, since the Moscow Conference of 1943, when Stalin volunteered the information to Hull, that Russia would enter the war against Japan when Germany was defeated. It had been one of our very first objectives at Yalta to secure the fixing of the date and there was great satisfaction when Stalin advanced it from six months after VE day to three months. Since VE day fell on May 8, August 8 at once became a key date in all the thirty-four principal allied capitals.[34]

When Russia did declare war on Japan, on August 8, the Moscow correspondent of the *New York Times* cabled that he had heard months ago that Russia would enter the war three months after VE day, and both the military expert of the *Times* and the editor stated plainly, on August 9, that they knew about the Yalta Agreement. Churchill also testified in his address of August 16 that he knew Russia's entry was due on August 8.

Nor was it possible for American officials to forget so momentous a date. Stimson's memorandum of July 2 on warning Japan raised the question by suggesting "if, then a belligerent, Russia should be included in the warning." At the close of the memo, he added: "If Russia is a part of the threat, the Russian attack, if actual, must not have progressed too far."

In other words, effective use of the bomb depended either on dropping it before Russia's entry into the war or immediately afterwards. A dramatic warning was to be issued from Potsdam by "*all* of Japan's principal enemies." Actually, this term included Russia since she was pledged to war with Japan, but technically and legally, she could be ignored and the warning issued without her knowledge.

For the Russians, this cataract of events was extremely embarrassing. The Washington correspondent of the *New York Times* reported on August 9, "It was learned on high authority that although Russia had been told by President Truman that a new explosive was about to be brought into play in the Pacific war, nothing of its destructive potential was revealed." This is confirmed by Byrnes' statement that after one of the Potsdam sessions, on July 24, the President walked around the table and told Stalin that after long experimentation "we have developed a bomb far exceeding any known in destructiveness and we plan to use it very soon unless Japan surrendered." Stalin merely replied that he was glad to hear about the bomb and that he hoped it would be used.[35] The whole episode was brief and casual. There is no evidence that the Russians understood that an epochal event was about to occur. They displayed no curiosity whatever after the conversation.

It would have been strange if the Russians had not ascribed the Western post-Hiroshima diplomatic offensive – particularly in the Balkans. The A-bomb had supplied a counter to the great strength of the Red Army, and, whether mentioned or not, would be a factor in all future balance of power moves. Churchill was the first to indicate publicly that the A-bomb should be used as an instrument of power politics. In a speech in the House of Commons on August 16, 1945, he had attacked Russian policies in East Europe and pleaded that the atomic bomb be kept an American-British monopoly. The great plants necessary to produce atomic bombs could not be built in less than three or four years. In the meantime, the United States stood at the summit of the world, and he rejoiced that it was so.

Describing the feelings of the Anglo-American leaders at Potsdam when the news of the successful test of the bomb arrived, he said: "We were in the presence of a new factor in human affairs. We possessed powers which were irresistible." From that moment "our outlook on the future was transformed." [36]

Comments McGeorge Bundy:

In the decades since Hiroshima a number of writers have asserted a quite different connection between the American thinking on the bomb and the Soviet Union – namely, that a desire to impress the Russians with the power of the bomb was a major factor in the decision to use it. This assertion is false, and the evidence to support it rests on inferences stretched as to be a discredit both to the judgement of those who have argued in this fashion and the credulity of those who have accepted such arguments. There is literally no evidence whatever that the timetable for the attack was ever affected by anything except technical and military considerations; there is no evidence that anyone in the direct chain of command from Truman to Stimson to Marshall to Groves ever heard or made any suggestion that either the decision itself or the timing of its execution should be governed by any consideration of its effect on the Soviet Union.[37]

Bundy argues that what is true, and important, is that these same decision-makers were full of hope that the bomb would put new strength into the American power position. They were in some confusion as to how this "master card" (Stimson's term) should be played, but they would have been most unusual men if they had thought it irrelevant. It is also true that Byrnes in particular was eager to get the war in Japan over before the Russians came in, thinking quite wrongly that their moves on the mainland might thus be forestalled. He also argued with Leo Azilard on the question of whether the use of the bomb in Japan would make the Soviet Union harder or easier to deal with – but this was merely an argument with a scientist who was presenting a contrary view, not a statement of basic reasons for the decision. That decision stayed, by all the accepted practices of wartime Washington, in the hands of the Commander in Chief and the Pentagon; Byrnes supported it, but he did not originate it or modify it in any way. At the most, the opinions of Byrnes deprived Truman of the different advice that he might have heard from a different Secretary of State. But the name of a man who would have been ready and able to sway Truman from the course so powerfully supported by Stimson and Marshall, and so deeply consonant with the wartime attitudes of the American people and with his own, does not come to mind. Ending the war in complete victory; as far as possible, was the totally dominant motive in its own right. The preemptive purpose, along with the compulsive secrecy of the whole business, certainly made men slow to attend to other considerations, one of which could well have been a more thoughtful look at the real effect the use of the bomb would have on Moscow. But this is a totally different point well made by later and more careful critics.[38]

Each of the realities, adds Bundy, "that produced the Japanese surrender was purposely concealed from Japan, and each of these concealments was governed on the American side by the conviction that for use against Japan, the bomb was indeed *a military weapon like any other*, if more so. Keep the value of surprise and do not give warning; use it to bring your enemy to the very brink of surrender *before* you make a concession on the emperor that might otherwise seem weak or embarrass you at home, and use it right on schedule if its use can help to minimize the role of an increasingly troubled ally."[39]

There are several tantalising hints that Roosevelt was troubled about the basic question of using the weapon against Japan in a way that his successor never was. In a most secret private memorandum that no other senior American saw until after he was dead, Roosevelt agreed with Churchill, at Hyde Park on September 18 or 19, 1944, that "when a 'bomb' is finally available, it might perhaps, after mature consideration, be used against the Japanese." Four days later, he asked Vennevar Bush, his chief of defence research, in a long and general exchange, whether the bomb should actually be used against the Japanese or tested and held as a threat. The two men agreed that the question should be carefully discussed, but Roosevelt also accepted Bush's argument that it could be "postponed for quite a time" in view of the fact that "certainly it would be inadvisable to make a threat unless we are distinctly in a position to follow it up if necessary." So twice in less than a week, Roosevelt thought about *whether* and *how* to use the bomb.[40]

Six weeks later, in a fireside chat on the eve of the election, he made his one public reference to the bomb. It was cryptic and not much noticed at the time, but its meaning is plain enough now. Speaking of the need to put a lasting end to "the agony of war", he warned of terrible new weapons: "Another war would be bound to bring even more devilish and powerful instruments of destruction to wipe out civilian populations. No coastal defences, however strong, could prevent these silent missiles of death, fired perhaps from planes or ships at sea, from the crashing deep within the United States itself."[41]

The records at Hyde Park shows that this extraordinary forecast was the product of the President's own changes in the speech writer's draft, and it takes no great leap of imagination to suppose that a man facing a decision on the use of just such a "devilish" device would have thought about it pretty hard. Yet, in the same speech, Roosevelt called it an all-important goal to win the war "at the earliest moment." In 1944, he said to his secretary, Grace Tully, without telling her what the Manhattan Project was about, that "if it works, and pray God it does, it will save many American lives." He also told his son, James, in January 1945, that there was a new weapon coming along that would make an invasion of Japan unnecessary. It would, therefore, be wrong to conclude that Roosevelt would not have used the bomb *in some fashion.* Nevertheless, the joint memorandum with Churchill and the conversation with Bush do give the impression that the question of actually dropping an atomic bomb on a Japanese target was for Roosevelt a real question as it was not for Truman, or indeed for Byrnes. The men at the top, when the time came had the rapid ending of the war as their wholly dominant purpose.[42]

There remain two questions of morality, one specific and one general: even if Hiroshima was necessary, or at least defensible, what of Nagasaki? Long before Alamogordo and Potsdam, it was agreed to seek authority for more than one attack in a single decision, and Truman accepted that arrangement. This decision was defended later on the ground that it was not one bomb or even two, but the prospect of many, that was decisive.[43]

But Hiroshima alone was enough to bring the Russians in; these two events together brought the crucial imperial decision for surrender, just *before* the second bomb was dropped. The news of Nagasaki arrived during a meeting that had been called by Prime

Minister Suzuki Kantaro after the Emperor had told him expressly that he wanted prompt surrender on whatever terms were necessary. There can be little doubt that the news of a second terrible attack strengthened the peace party and further shook the diehards, but the degree of this effect cannot be gauged. It is hard to see that much could have been lost if there had been more time between the two bombs. If the matter had not been settled long since, in a time when victory seemed much less close than it did on August 7, or if the authority to order the second attack had simply been retained in Washington, one guesses that the attack on Nagasaki would have been delayed for some days; the bomb in actual use was a shock in Washington too.[44]

More broadly, what if the notion of dropping the bomb on a city was simply wrong – not just hasty because there should have been warning, or gratuitous because assurance to the Emperor could have done the job, or excessive because a smaller target could have been used just as well, or even dangerous because of its impact on the Russians – but just plain wrong? This fundamental question has been addressed most powerfully by Michael Walzer, and his argument deserves respectful attention, although – or perhaps because – no one put it forward before Hiroshima.[45]

All of the alternatives that were proposed or considered to surprise attack on a city by anyone who knew about the bomb, in 1944-45, were put forward in terms that allowed for such possible use if other alternatives failed. Roosevelt asked Bush about a demonstration and a threat, but he recognised in the same conversation that you do not make a threat you are not able to carry out if necessary. The Franck Committee proposed a demonstration, and George Marshall at one point considered a uniquely military installation, as distinct from a city full of such installations, but both recognised that it might be necessary to go on to urban targets. Bard, with all his desire for a complex diplomatic demarche, never argued against using the bomb if the demarche failed, nor did McCloy. No one ever went beyond the argument that the United States should use up other forms of action – warnings, demonstrations, or diplomacy – before an urban attack. Szilard came closest; in a petition which Truman almost surely never saw – he was already at Potsdam when it was signed on July 17 – Szilard and sixty-seven colleagues asked Truman not to decide on use "without seriously considering the moral responsibilities which were involved". Yet even this petition conceded that "the war has to be brought to a successful conclusion and attacks by atomic bombs may very well be an effective method of warfare". No one ever said simply, do not use it on a city at all.

That is what Walzer says, and he says it powerfully. To underline the strength of this conviction, he accepts in its strongest form the contention, that the bomb was less terrible than the kinds of warfare it helped to end. His reply is that the attack on Hiroshima was still wrong, because it violated a fundamental rule of war – that the rights of non-combatants must be respected. The citizens of Hiroshima had done nothing that justified the terrible fate that overtook them on August 6; to kill them by tens of thousands merely in order to shock their government into surrender was a violation of the great tradition of civilised warfare under which "the destruction of the innocent, whatever its purposes, is a kind of blasphemy against our deepest moral commitments."[46]

Walzer's is a powerful argument, but it runs as forcefully against incendiaries as against nuclear bombs. His moral argument against the use of the bomb required an equal moral opposition to the whole long, brutal tendency of modern war makers to accept, and sometimes even to seek, the suffering of civilians in the search for victory. He may well be deeply right, but there is enormous distance between this view of war making and what Americans actually thought in 1945. To reject the climatic act as immoral, Walzer must reject so much else that his judgement becomes historically irrelevant. The change in strategy and tactics required by his argument is one that no political leader could then have imposed. By requiring too much, he proves too little.

There remains a final question: was not the nuclear weapon, in and of itself, morally or politically different from firebombs and blockades and in ways that should have required that it not be used? Cannot Walzer's argument be amended and strengthened, by remarking that even these "primitive" nuclear weapons were so terrible, not only in their explosive and incendiary effect but also in their radiation, that it was morally wrong to be the first to use them? And especially because the American effort had uncovered, as early as 1942, the still more terrible prospect of thermonuclear weapons, was there not also a political imperative to set an example of restraint? Although none of them ever presented such an argument in categorical terms, thoughts like these were strong among men like Franck, Szilard, and Bard. But since they all agreed that the bomb might be used on an inhabited target if all else failed to bring surrender, they accepted the terms of the debate that in fact were followed. When their proposals were judged unlikely to end the war as quickly as direct military use, they could not fall back on a claim that there was a moral or political imperative against killing civilians in this new and terrible way. Even the doubters were in some measure prisoners of the overriding objective of early victory.

Yet it is right for us to ponder on these more absolute questions. Bundy does not find Hiroshima more immoral than Tokyo or Dresden, but he finds the political question more difficult. "The nuclear world," he says, "as we now know it, is grimly dangerous; might it be less dangerous if Hiroshima and Nagasaki had never happened? If so, a stretch out of the anguish of war might have been a small price to pay. No one can make such an assessment with certainty; as we move on to later events, we shall encounter evidence that weighs on both sides. All that we can say here is that the Americans who took part in the decisions of 1945 were overwhelmingly governed by the immediate and not the distant prospect. This dominance of clear present purpose over uncertain future consequences is a phenomenon we shall meet again." [47]

Historically almost predestined by the manner of its birth and its development, made doubly dramatic by the fateful coincidence that it was ready just when it might be decisive, and not headed off by any carefully designed alternative – of threat, assurance, demonstration, or all of them together – the bomb dropped on Hiroshima surely helped to end a fearful war. It was also the fierce announcement of the age of nuclear weapons. To the men who made and used it, or at least to many of them much of the time, this double meaning of what they were doing was evident, and we shall soon be looking at what they did and did not do about its import for the future. In the summer of 1945 their overriding present purpose was to shorten the war, and in that they succeeded.

Given this overriding purpose, it was natural for most of them to accept the argument for using the new weapons by surprise just as soon and just as impressively as possible. The President, with doubts, never acted on them or set others free to work them through. The President without such doubts never looked behind the assumptions of April, the recommendations of June, and the final approvals of July, nor did anyone close to him ever press him to do so. Whether broader and more extended deliberations would have yielded a less destructive result we shall never know. Yet one must regret that no such effort was made.

IV

On July 14, 1949, there was a very secret meeting of key members of the Congressional Joint Committee on Atomic Energy with the President at Blair House, to discuss the desire of Britain and Canada for a larger share in the atomic energy programme. Since they had added very notably in the original Oak Ridge project, and since they supplied most of the uranium essential for its continuance, they felt that the tight American monopoly of the atom should be loosened for their benefit.

Soon afterwards, members of the Joint Committee began to make public statements attacking any proposal to share atomic bomb secrets. Senator Knowland threatened "intense" opposition if any information was given to the British without Congressional approval. Legislators who believed themselves to be clutching the atomic secrets had no intention of letting them get away.

On July 19, a second meeting was held behind closed doors, "and with window-blinds drawn, in an isolated room just under the edge of the Capitol's great dome". The Joint Committee was meeting with top level executive officials, behind a special guard of

Capitol policemen. The official reporter was excluded, and even the porter with ice water was not allowed to come in. The result of the meeting was not made known until July 26, when Secretary Acheson assured Congress in effect that there would be no exchange of atomic weapon information with America's Allies without the full knowledge and approval of Congress. Senator Bouke B. Hichenlooper was "greatly relieved" and Senator Knowland appeared satisfied.[48]

Two months later, on September 23, President Truman issued his epochal announcement that the Russians had achieved an atomic explosion.[49] His announcement stated that nearly four years earlier he had pointed out that "scientific opinion appears to be practically unanimous that the essential theoretical knowledge upon which the discovery is based is already widely known. There is also substantial agreement that foreign research can come abreast of our present theoretical knowledge in time."

The President did not add that the scientists had almost unanimously warned that American monopoly would be short-lived. Thus, in December 1945, Harrison Brown had written that "three years can be considered a reasonable period for other nations to produce their first atomic bombs," and he warned that this would probably be an upper limit. [50]

The Soviet news agency *Tass* issued a statement on September 25 recalling that Molotov had claimed possession of the secret of the atomic bomb on November 6, 1947, and asserting that it was now being used in large scale blasting work. The Soviet press was filled with quotations from the West to develop three themes: that the need for some sort of agreement between the Soviet and the United States was more urgent than ever; that the end of the American atomic monopoly was a "blow against warmongers and strengthens the cause of peace"; and that Soviet production of atomic energy was proof of the "strength of the Socialist system of society." Harrison Salisbury reported that the general atmosphere of comment published by the Soviet press was "sober and serious and fully recognized the great tasks which lie ahead." [51]

Four months later, on January 31, 1950, President Truman announced that the United States would proceed with the development of "the so-called hydrogen or super bomb". His announcement was only 125 words long, and he refused to go one word beyond it in public until the very end of his presidency. This decision is second in importance only to Roosevelt's commitment of October 1941; it led straight on, with no second thoughts by the President, to the world's first full-scale thermonuclear explosion, on November 1, 1952. For the human race there was now no turning back. The first Soviet device was tested less than a year later.[52]

Let us note at the outset that Truman's decision was only half of what produced this result. There was a parallel decision by Stalin, and the Soviet decision probably came first. Certainly, there is no evidence of any delay by anyone on the Soviet side; Soviet accounts give no hint of any debate or dissent over thermonuclear development, and the impression left by both official accounts and the recollections of such a crucially important scientist as Andrey Sakharov is that there was a unanimous determination in August 1949 to go forward promptly to the "second stage of the atomic epoch". There is no reason to believe that the Russian effort was caused by Truman's January decision or indeed by any other American action. Nor was there any change in the dreary emptiness of Soviet propaganda for an uninspected ban on all nuclear-weapons, or any sign of even the most modest Soviet effort to find some way of reaching agreement not to go on to the next stage. No one, from Stalin to Sakharov, appears to have harboured any doubt at any time that the right course of action was to get a Russian H-bomb just as fast as possible. The responsibility of this second great step in the nuclear age is, thus, shared by two governments. When Roosevelt told Bush to go ahead in 1941, he was acting out of fear that there was a rival in the race. That rival was a phantom, but Truman in 1950 was choosing to engage in a competition that was entirely real.

The government in Washington that had to consider its response to the Russian bomb was not the government that had faced the question of international control four years earlier. Truman was still President, but nearly all the other leading players had changed or taken new roles. The President himself was different. He had now been through decisions that he always considered larger and harder than these: he had launched the Truman Doctrine and the Marshall Plan; he had replaced Byrnes with Marshall, and Marshall with Acheson. Above all, he had fought and won an election in which he beat Henry Wallace and Strom Thurmond as well as Thomas Dewey. He had successfully defended Berlin by airlift, and the blockade of that city had been lifted in May. He correctly estimated himself as stronger and wiser than any of his election opponents, and he was President now in his own right. He thought himself well and truly in command of the executive branch, and one thing he understood clearly about nuclear weapons – they were Presidential business.

The strongest early reactions naturally occurred among those most directly concerned with atomic energy. They were in three places, each interconnected with the other two: among nuclear physicists, in the Atomic Energy Commission, and in the Joint Committee on Atomic Energy. In these small circles, during the weeks immediately after the President's announcement, individuals of ability, energy, and conviction determined that the necessary answer to the Soviet explosion was an all-out effort to develop a thermonuclear weapons, also called a hydrogen bomb, or more simply, the super.

Truman's acceptance of military advice on building more and better bombs was not accompanied by any relaxation of his own determined personal control over questions of custody, deployment, and use. He never departed from his insistence on complete Presidential control of the weapons whose multiplication he supported. After Nagasaki, he never came close to the use of even one against an enemy.

In particular, Truman never came close to the use of nuclear weapons in Korea, where war broke out on June 10, 1950, and continued through his time in office. Once, at the height of the general anxiety over the Chinese advances of November 1950, he seemed to suggest serious consideration of such use in incautious replies to press conference questions. His slip promptly led to such a series of disclaimers and clarifications – complete with a summit visit from Attlee – that the real situation was plainly revealed: this President and his advisers saw no good role for nuclear weapons in Korea. And while the military argument was at least in part that the weapons were too scarce and valuable for use in a secondary theatre, Truman's own view was simpler. In the very answer that caused the furore, he made his view clear and showed in doing so that he now understood the weapon better than he had before Hiroshima:

> The President: We will take whatever steps are necessary to meet the military situation, just as we always have.
>
> Will that include the atomic bomb?
> The President: That includes every weapon that we have.
>
> Mr. President, you said "every weapon that we have". Does that mean that there is active consideration of the use of the atomic bomb?
> The President: There has always been active consideration of its use. I don't want to see it used. It is a terrible weapon, and it should not be used on innocent men, women, and children who have nothing whatever to do with this military aggression. That happens when it is used.[53]

The real meaning of this exchange is in the President's last two sentences. What Truman had thought about using the bomb to end World War II was not what he thought about using it in later years.

As his term drew to an end, Truman showed a much better understanding of the thermonuclear world into which he had led his countrymen. He had been President from before the first explosion through the 10-megaton thermonuclear test that took place on November 1, 1952, at Eniwetok Island in the Pacific. In his final message to the State of the Union, he discussed the nuclear future in a fashion which at once sums up his own hard-earned understanding and sets the stage for an examination of the labours of his successors.

"The stakes in our search for peace are immensely higher than they have ever been before.

"For now we have entered the atomic age, and war has undergone a technological change which makes it a very different thing from what it used to be. War today between the Soviet Empire and the free nations might dig the grave not only of our Stalinist opponents, but of our own society, our world as well as theirs.

"This transformation has been brought to pass in the seven years from Alamogordo to Eniwetok. It is only seven years, but the new force of atomic energy has turned the world into a very different kind of place.

"Science and technology have worked so fast that war's new meaning may not yet be grasped by all the peoples who would be its victims; nor, perhaps, by the rulers in the Kremlin. But I have been President of the United States, these seven years, responsible for the decisions which have brought our science and our engineering to their present place. I know what this development means now. I know something of what it will come to mean in the future ...

"... The war of the future would be one in which man could extinguish millions of lives at one blow, demolish the great cities of the world, wipe out the cultural achievements of our past - and destroy the very structure of a civilization that has been slowly and painfully built up through hundreds of generations.

"Such a war is not a possible policy for rational men."[54]

Truman continued by expressing his doubt that Soviet rulers understood this fundamental truth, along with his belief that once they did, the American response would be warm. But he saw no early prospect of this change, and meanwhile expected "a long, hard test of strength and stamina". This test would take place at levels of conflict well short of nuclear war. The examples Truman cited were those most obvious at the time: the continuing war in Korea, the struggle for political and economic strength in Western Europe, and new patterns of change in the decolonising world of Asia and Africa. And as he left office, the first and the only American President to order the use of nuclear weapons was fully aware that in only seven years, such changes had been wrought that it would now be madness to make nuclear war.

Dwight Eisenhower was the first American President to come to office with significant previous knowledge of nuclear weapons. Indeed, he knew more about them, in every respect except the direct experience of final authority and responsibility, than Truman ever learned. Moreover, something in him had led him to a quick and humane response when, as the victorious Allied Commander in Europe, he first learned about Alamogordo from Henry Stimson at Potsdam, he hoped "we would never have to use such a thing".[55]

As the new President came to consider what he would do, it was inescapable that he should re-examine the possible role of nuclear weapons, and in this study his closest associate would be his Secretary of State, John Foster Dulles. To Eisenhower, general nuclear war would soon be no better than suicide; eventually it would be like that for Dulles too. In broad political terms, the truce in Korea would lead on to a gradual but powerful easement of tension, comforting to the President, troubling to his Secretary of State. A whole set of somewhat separate themes would enter later, when Eisenhower begins to struggle with the unyielding problem of effective arms control. However, the Eisenhower Administration would not be slow to threaten, but it would not be first to act, and between the threat and the act – and also between the desires of subordinates and the decisions of the United States government – would stand the enigmatic but self-commanding President. And it is exactly here that one would find the nuclear meaning of the modifications of American defence policy that were called the "New Look!"

On October 30, 1953, Eisenhower formally approved the following sentence as part of a statement of the basic national security policy of the United States. "In the event of hostilities, the United States will consider nuclear weapons to be as available for use as other munitions." The President authorised this statement with full awareness of its importance; unlike many other parts of the ten-thousand-word document, it was the product of argument in which he had taken a direct part, and its language was what he himself wanted. He also approved an accompanying sentence: "This policy should not be made public without further consideration by the National Security Council." The origins and consequences of these two sentences are the nuclear part of the story of Eisenhower's initial review of the defence posture of the country.

This New Look was not a quick look. Eisenhower had come into office with many ideas of his own about the right military posture for the country; these ideas were generally shared by his senior civilian advisers, but he took his time about putting them into effect. In their first months in office, he and his Secretary of Defence carried out a clean sweep of the Joint Chiefs of Staff and then devoted several months to an effort to obtain military agreement to the change of emphasis which they were planning. The basic national security policy of October 30 (National Security Council the NSC–162/2) was one part of this process, and the decisions on nuclear policy which it embodied were a direct reflection of the views of Eisenhower and his most trusted associates.

Eisenhower's insistence on the central role of strategic nuclear forces was reinforced by his conviction that there would never be another full-scale conventional war. As the man who had commanded the largest American expeditionary force in history, he felt that he was entitled to be his own expert on this question, and he liked to point out what two atom bombs would have done to the two artificial harbours on which the early logistic support of the Normandy landing had been dependent. He was not impressed by military arguments for the maintenance of large forces "ready to sail at a moment's notice".

He found only one respect in which the position was deteriorating, "namely, the forthcoming achievement of atomic plenty and a nuclear balance of power between the US and the USSR". But how, he asked, "were we to prevent the Soviet Union from achieving such a balance of power without going to war with the USSR?"[56]

The man who had a ready-made answer to this question was Dulles, who, on January 12, 1954, announced the decision of NSC 162/2 in a form which became known as the doctrine of massive retaliation. He declared: "... What the Eisenhower administration seeks is a similar international security system ... Local defence will always be important ... but must be reinforced by the further deterrent of massive retaliatory power ... The way to deter aggression is for the free community to be willing and able to respond vigorously at places and with means of its own choosing."

This speech, which caused great commotion, was a curious mixture of Dulles, the individual, and Dulles, the loyal spokesman of Eisenhower. It was Dulles who believed in "a community of security system" and in the homely but ill-judged analogy to deterrent police protection. Dulles was also the author of the phrase "massive retaliatory power", which Eisenhower had disliked when he first came across it in a Dulles paper of 1952. Much more than the President, the Secretary of State believed that there should be no squeamish constraints on nuclear weapons. He had no irresponsible desire for their instant use, but he wanted nothing to inhibit the threat of such use; that inhibition was what Soviet propaganda was trying to achieve, and what Soviet propaganda sought, Dulles reflexively opposed. There is more than a hint of relish in his repeated emphasis on the nuclear threat, and in his warnings that a potential aggressor "must know that he cannot always prescribe battle conditions that suit him".[57]

The first operational test of the Eisenhower Administration's new policy on the use of nuclear weapons came in the climactic months of the French effort to defend against Communist insurgency in Vietnam. When the French Army was put to rout on May 7, 1954, in Dienbionphu, the French Foreign Minister, Georges Bidault, was rebuffed by Eisenhower in his appeals for massive American military intervention in Indochina. London also refused to participate in a joint military intervention. Admiral Arthur W. Radford urged unilateral American action, amid talk of using at least a "baby atomic bomb". Eisenhower, however, opted for a peace of compromise as preferable to the hazards of enlarging a war already lost. Eisenhower kept a strong recollection of his feelings on this occasion. Years later, he told his biographer, Stephen Ambrose, that he had turned on Robert Cutler and said: "You boys must be crazy. We can't use those awful things against Asians for the second time in less than ten years. My God."[58]

The distance between Radford and Eisenhower does not in itself complete the story of the relation between nuclear weapons and Indochina in 1954. A much more subtle but equally important question is that of the relation between nuclear fears and the diplomacy of the powers concerned. To Dulles, for example, it appeared at the time that at least one major friendly government was severely inhibited by the emerging menace of thermonuclear weapons. After visiting Churchill in early May, he reported to Eisenhower that "he found the British, and particularly Churchill, seared to death by the scepter of nuclear bombs in the hands of the Russians."[59]

As Dulles admitted, part of Churchill's concern was caused by Radford's apparent belligerence, but it had deeper origins. Profoundly affected by the 15-megaton American test at Bikini on March 2, the Prime Minister reported to the House of Commons three weeks later that the subject filled his mind "out of all comparison with anything else".[60] This concern was not unreasonable, but it did not take the hydrogen bomb to make Churchill and his colleagues unenthusiastic about supporting the French in Indochina. What Churchill said to Radford was enough: "Since the British people were willing to let India go, they would not be interested in holding Indochina for France."[61]

Twice in Eisenhower's Presidency, in 1954-55 and again in 1958, there were international crises over Chinese attempts to take by force the small offshore island groups of Quemoy and Matsu, and each time Eisenhower had to contend with the possibility of a painful choice between embarrassing defeat and the use of nuclear weapons. The situation was different from the one at Dienbienphu, and the means by which the President successfully avoided the choice are instructive. [62]

Although Dulles spoke of "new and powerful weapons of precision which can utterly destroy military targets without endangering unrelated civilian centres" and warned against the Chinese effort to portray the United States "as being merely a 'paper tiger'" and insisted on US readiness "to stand firm and, if necessary, meet hostile force with the greater force that we posses," the highly dramatised threat of war soon dissolved. Dulles declared that Washington would defend the islands if an attack upon them seemed preparatory to an attack upon Formosa. However, no attack materialised since the power-holders in Beijing had no desire to provoke war with the USA and were convinced that, sooner of later, Formosa would be theirs, whatever Washington might do or threaten to do.

If Eisenhower's resolve not to go to war in Quemoy and Matsu was instructive, so was his restraint during the second Berlin crisis. From 1958 and 1963, under the guiding hand of Nikita Khrushchev, there were more than four years of political tension over the future of Berlin. This long and intermittently acute crisis was closely related to the way in which the interested governments understood and misunderstood the politics of nuclear danger. It began in the time of Eisenhower and ended in that of Kennedy. While the courses followed by the two Presidents were different, and while there was variety also in the flow and ebb of Soviet pressure, the crisis is best examined as a single phenomenon centrally defined by the purposes and choices of Khrushchev. It is for this reason that it is called "Khrushchev's crisis".

Khrushchev's Berlin crisis gives us what is otherwise missing in the nuclear age: a genuine nuclear confrontation in Europe. Governments were forced to ask themselves repeatedly what might make it necessary to fight, and in what measure, and on what terms they must be prepared to use nuclear weapons.

Khrushchev's Berlin crisis began in the autumn of 1958, with his decision to assert that there must be a peace treaty between the war time allies and Germany that would redefine the condition of West Berlin. If such a treaty were not accepted by the West within six months, the Soviet Union would make separate arrangements with East Germany and be free to see these new arrangements imposed on West Berlin, where the existing rights of the British, the French and the American would have expired. The West would face in Berlin a surrounding adversary overwhelmingly superior in local strength, and could be forced to choose between the acceptance of East German authority and a resort to force.

Khrushchev hoped that the nuclear strength achieved by the Soviet Union in the 1950s would persuade the West that it must come to terms. In a sense, he was trying to get concessions that would split the American alliance, and he was exploiting the new prestige of the apparent Soviet lead in missiles announced by *Sputnik*. In this way, the Berlin crisis was a Soviet exercise in atomic diplomacy – an effort to use a new appearance of Soviet nuclear strength to force changes in the centre of Europe. Both the atomic threat and the aim were made explicit in the first formal Soviet note of November 27, 1958. Characteristically, the threat was delivered only after a denunciation of the asserted threats to others:

> Methods of blackmail and reckless threat of force will be least of all appropriate in solving such a problem as the Berlin question. Such methods will not help solve a single question, but can only bring the situation to the danger point. But only madmen can go to the length of unleashing another world war over the preservation of privileges of occupiers in West Berlin. If such madmen should really appear, there is no doubt that strait jackets could be found for them.[63]

The Western governments read Khrushchev's announcement as a demand that there must be a new arrangement, either agreed or imposed. On the very day that the note was delivered, the American response was firm:

> ...the United States will not acquiesce in a unilateral repudiation by the Soviet Union of its obligations and responsibilities formally agreed upon with Britain, France, and the United States in relation to Berlin. Neither will it enter into any agreement with the Soviet Union which, whatever the form, would have the end result of abandoning the people of West Berlin to hostile domination.[64]

What were the reasons for Khrushchev's decision to try for change in Berlin? Many explanations have been offered: an ambition to break the Western alliance by humiliating the Americans, a desire to frustrate the military and political ambitions of the anti-Communist West Germans, a need to shore up his East German friends, a desire to be a better Communist than his Chinese critics, and so on and so forth.[65]

Bundy writes:

> He started a crisis but as the final result made clear, it was built on a bluff. As we look back, we find all sorts of threats, along with intermittent

expressions of goodwill, but we do not find a decisive challenge. For students of the technique called salami slicing – a process of little encroachments not easily resisted by democratic governments because each one in itself seems trivial – the Berlin crisis remains a treasure house of varied examples. But the action that requires either strong response or damaging acceptance does not exist here – with the signal exception of the wall. Except for the wall, Khrushchev never took the actions he so often threatened and never came close to a forcible separation of the free people of West Berlin from their Western friends. What is decisive is that he himself had no intention, at any point, of running a nuclear risk? He hoped that an asserted danger of nuclear disaster would make other governments responsive, but at the same time he was determined that no act of his should result in any risk of nuclear warfare that he couldn't control.[66]

However, there followed four years of intermittent tension, which did not end until after the successful resolution of the Cuban missile crisis of 1962, when it became plain that the Soviet Union would not press the question of Berlin to a final test of will.

The same conclusion applies to the Cuban missile crisis which began on October 14, 1962, when two American U-2 aircraft took pictures over Cuba which conclusively showed that the Soviet Union was installing there nuclear missiles that could reach the United States. After five days of analysis and argument in a small circle of his own selection, President Kennedy decided on October 20 to impose a naval quarantine on the further delivery of offensive weapons to Cuba and to insist on the prompt withdrawal of Soviet missiles already delivered. On the eve of October 22, he announced his decision to the country and the world. There followed a six-day international crisis of unprecedented severity in which the risk of a nuclear war was almost universally believed to be greater than at any time before or since. After negotiations, as complex and serious as they were brief, and military moves and counter-moves in which astonishingly only one life was lost by hostile actions, the acute phase of the crisis was ended on October 28, by a public statement from Khrushchev undertaking to remove the missiles. In fact, Khrushchev recognised that he was in a situation in which he had no better choice. There was no prospect of gain and much to lose in any other course. He knew that the quarantine was effective, that it could be tightened, and that he could not evade it. He knew that the Americans were ready and able to attack Cuba both from the air and from the sea, and that there was no way for him to win those battles either. He had no promising move to make elsewhere. In particular, there was nothing in this crisis that could encourage him to take the steps against West Berlin that he had been carefully avoiding for four years. Everywhere, the political contest had gone against him – in the Organisation of American States (OAS), in the United Nations, in Western Europe, and even in Africa, where non-aligned leaders cancelled landing rights for Soviet planes that might have delivered warheads. Nor did he have anything to gain, in either the political or the military arena, by delay. His letters to Kennedy show that he understood perfectly well these missiles must not be fired if he could prevent it. But the decisive consideration was that in the Caribbean, Khrushchev was in a position of such inferiority at every level of conventional strength that unlike the President, he must have feared not only the unpredictable consequences of an accident, but also the certainty of defeat at every level up to a common catastrophe. If he had been the reckless risk taker whose possible existence we were required to consider on October 27, he might have tried one more roll. But he was prudent; he remained in charge, and he chose to end the crisis. There is no doubt that it was the situation, not the American ultimatum, that was fundamental in the decision.

In the almost six decades since the appearance of nuclear weapons, concern over the dangers these weapons raise has varied markedly. A preoccupation with nuclear weapons has characterised only very few nations, and even among these few, anxiety over the prospects of nuclear war which has not been constant. Beyond the nuclear strategists and a small entourage, the nuclear question has not evoked a steady level of attention, let alone of anxiety. On the contrary, the attention of foreign policy elites, and even more the general public, has swung from one extreme to the other and within a brief period of time.[67] Thus, at the outset of the Kennedy Administration, a preoccupation with the prospect of nuclear war characterised a portion of the foreign policy elites, but hardly the public at large. The preoccupation, in part the product of high and sustained international tension and in part the response to administration calls for measures of civil defences, quickly dissipated in the wake of the Cuban missile crisis. Within the period of scarcely a year, it had virtually disappeared. Yet there had been no significant change in the strategic relationship between the United States and the Soviet Union. Nor had the arms competition between the two powers been significantly altered. Certainly, the 1963 Partial Test Ban Treaty did not alter this competition whether by making it less intense or less dangerous than it had been earlier. But the test ban did signal that the political relationship between the two states had changed modestly for the better and might register still further improvement.

A substantial and even dramatic change in outlook towards the prospects of nuclear war went hand in hand with a changing political relationship. A generation later, the same process only worked in the opposite direction, marking the beginning of the Reagan Administration. On this occasion, an anti-nuclear weapons movement developed that was unprecedented in the breadth of support it appeared to enjoy. In this respect, there is no real comparison between the anti-nuclear movement of a generation ago and that of today. Whereas the movement of yesterday represented little more than the stirring of a few, the movement of the 1980s assumed mass proportions. Even so, the appearance of the later movement was almost as sudden as the disappearance of the earlier one. As late as the winter or 1979-80, there was little to indicate that nuclear weapons would become the critical issue of public life and discourse they became by the summer of 1981. The sudden rise of the anti-nuclear weapons movement and the attendant debate over nuclear strategy must be attributed in the first place to a renewed fear of war with the Soviet Union. By the same token, it also reflects a decline in the faith by which we have come to live in the nuclear age. For we were nearly all believers in deterrence and this despite the different ways in which this faith might be expressed. We are nearly all believers if only for the reason that once we seriously admit nuclear war as a distinct historical possibility, we not only conjure up a very dark landscape but one in which our accepted categories of political and moral thought no longer seem relevant. In the still alien world of nuclear weapons, it is only a faith in deterrence that preserves continuity with a familiar past. The idea of deterrence is, of course, as old as the history of human conflict. But the functions that strategies of nuclear deterrence are expected to serve and the expectations those strategies have raised are as novel as the weapons on which deterrence today rests. If nuclear deterrence is indeed something new under the sun, it is not only because of the expectations it has evoked. The expectations constitute the core of faith and their intensity has invested nuclear deterrence with a reliability that is tantamount, for all practical purposes, to certainty. In turn, faith in the effectiveness of deterrence is largely a function of the consequences generally expected to follow from the use of nuclear weapons.

By a psychological mechanism as simple as it is pervasive, it is assumed that if the results of an act are inconceivable, the act itself must be inconceivable. The death of a nation is an event difficult to conceive, the act itself must be inconceivable and the extinction of humanity far more so. Nor is it all. It is faith in the effectiveness of deterrence that has enabled us -to entertain what otherwise would prove to be irreconcilable convictions: a continued readiness to threaten the use – even the first use – of nuclear weapons to preserve interests deemed vital, but, at the same time, a conviction that nuclear war would in all likelihood destroy the ends for which it is waged; a belief, if not in the moral rectitude, then at least in the moral neutrality of a deterrence strategy, but also a disbelief that the use of nuclear weapons could ever be morally justified; these and other convictions can be reconciled if only the expectations placed in a deterrent strategy are strong enough. With enough faith in deterrence there is no need to torture oneself over the justification for ever employing nuclear weapons; the issues arising from the use of these weapons deal with a contingency that has been virtually excluded from our vision of the future. The faith commonly placed in deterrence has never gone unquestioned. The history of strategic thought in the nuclear age is, after all, a history of the persisting controversy between the deterrence faithfuls and the deterrence sceptics, between those who believe that deterrence follows from the existence of nuclear weapons and those who believe a credible theory of use must be developed if deterrence is to be assured.

The nature of that controversy is often misrepresented, not least of all by the participants themselves. It cannot properly be characterise simply as one "between those who wish to give nuclear-weapons a war deterring and those who want to give them a war-fighting role."[68] Those accused of wishing to give nuclear weapons a war-fighting role have not abandoned deterrence. At least, they have never admitted to doing so. Instead, they insist that the effort to fashion a war-fighting role for nuclear weapons, however precarious and even abortive that effort may ultimately prove, is undertaken in the first instance in order to enhance their role as a deterrent. The deterrence sceptics do not deny deterrence. They do deny a faith that is given, in the manner of all true believers, unconditional expression. To the deterrence faithful, the position of the sceptics has always smacked of apostasy and perhaps never more so than today. To be sure, the faithful no less than the sceptics have regularly warned against the dangers of taking deterrence for granted. Still, there is a world of difference between what the sceptics have understood taking deterrence for granted to mean and what true believers have understood it to mean. To the believer, deterrence is not only an inherent property of nuclear weapons, it is very nearly a self-sufficient property. "The strategy," one of them declares, "is determined by the weapon. The missiles have only to exist and deterrence is the law of their existence." [69] Deterrence is the law of their existence by virtue of their inordinate and uncontrollable destructiveness. Given this destructiveness, the future of deterrence is not the beginning but the end of strategy. This being so, if deterrence fails, the only rational course is to end the conflict as quickly as possible without regard to calculations of relative advantage.

McGeorge Bundy, in a recent elaboration of the concept of "existential deterrence", echoes the well known dictum of Bernard Brodie in declaring that if deterrence ever breaks down "the attention of both sides must be driven toward the literally vital need for ending the nuclear battle if possible, not winning it".[70] The controversy over the necessary and sufficient conditions of deterrence is more intense today than it has ever been. This persisting debate does not, in the end, turn on technical considerations, though the disputants regularly foster that mistaken impression. Instead, what is ultimately at issue are varying judgements about the character and aspirations of the former Soviet regime and, to a lesser extent, the American government. Whether asymmetries in strategic systems have political significances, whether some capacity for war-fighting is a necessary element of deterrence, are not issues that, at bottom, could be resolved by technical considerations but only by one's assessment of the two great adversaries. Among the priesthood of experts, the nuclear debate over nuclear weapons is but a debate over politics. In this debate, both sides shared a common faith; but how they interpreted the conditions of faith depended on what they believed to be the truth about the Soviet-American conflict. Thus, for all their differences, which were surely serious enough, the two sides to this familiar controversy not only believed in deterrence, they also believed broadly in the strategic status quo and were hostile to apocalyptic visions.

By contrast, visions were a hallmark of the anti-nuclear movement that has arisen in recent years. The view that nuclear war had become ever likely in the early 1980s, and that if the Americans continued along their course they would transform it into a probability, was given frequent expression. Jonathan Schell had attributed the "collapse of deterrence" to nothing other than the build-up of nuclear stockpiles. "Possession inevitably implied use," he says, "and use was irremediably senseless." [71] The crisis in deterrence stemmed, at bottom, from nothing more than the "continuing reliance on nuclear arms". George Kennan reached a similar conclusion and attached to it similar urgency. "The clock is ticking, the remaining ticks are numbered: the end of their number is already in sight." [72] We may call this view that of "existential disaster". Nuclear weapons have only to exist in sufficient numbers and destructiveness to render disaster likely. Time is the great nemesis. It is so if only because no social contrivance – of which deterrence is one – can go on indefinitely without a breakdown. As is true of virtually all aspects of the nuclear debate today, this conviction was articulated a generation earlier. In 1961, the novelist and scientist C P Snow wrote: "Within, at the most, ten years, some of these bombs are going off ... *That* is the certainty. On the one side, therefore, we have a finite risk. On the other side, we have a certainty of disaster. Between a risk and a certainty, the same man does not hesitate." [73] Snow's forecast was made in the same spirit and on behalf of the same purpose – far-reaching measures of arms control – that moved Jonathan Schell and George Kennan. But whereas Snow's message could only be directed profitably to a quite restricted audience, Schell and Kennan have a potential audience that is far larger. And while Snow's prophecy was one of limited catastrophe, Schell and Kennan entertain a vision of a nuclear exchange that would put an end to our own species." [74]

In retrospect, what seems remarkable is that for virtually a generation, the issue of nuclear weapons had not been of central concern in public life. Certainly, the years between the Cuban missile crisis and the Soviet Union's invasion of Afghanistan had not been without portentous developments in the spheres that provoked so much anxiety – changes in the strategic balance, the technology of nuclear weaponry and East-West tension. Yet these developments did not provoke a comparable anxiety. In one view, a heightened sensitivity to the dangers of nuclear weapons simply reflected the tightened perils of the competition in arms or the arms race. In the 1983 pastoral letter of the American Catholic bishops, it was written "the dynamic of the arms race has intensified" and that one compelling reason for the letter was the growing dangers this dynamic holds out. [75] The nuclear freeze movement had been largely predicated on the belief that the danger of nuclear war in the late 1980s would be greater than ever before because of weapons systems that, in the words of a movement leader, "will increase the pressure on both sides to use their nuclear weapons in a crisis, rather than risk losing them in a first strike. [76] *The New York Times'* national security correspondent expressed the concern that: "In ten to fifteen years, new technologies now being developed and tested could, if deployed, fundamentally and irretrievably undermine the basic philosophy that has been the center of both sides' nuclear strategy – mutual deterrence."[77] These technological developments promised to lead to ever greater "crisis instability". New weapons of greater accuracy and speed would at once sharpen the fear of preemptive attack while encouraging the hope of undertaking such an attack successfully should this prove necessary. And ever more complex command and control systems would, beyond a certain level of alert, make increasingly difficult the efforts of political leaders to retain effective control over their nuclear forces.[78]

What is crucial to this view is the contention that in certain circumstances the new technologies and the systems for controlling them will prove very dangerous. These circumstances are those of severe crises. In normal circumstances, by contrast, the dangers of the arms race have markedly diminished, when compared to a generation ago. The likelihood of an accidental war is substantially lower today and the prospects of a preventive war, of a nuclear strike from out of the blue, are not seen by most expert observers as measurably enhanced. For the residual uncertainties that attend the use of nuclear weapons are such that a coldly planned attack appears almost certain to remain beyond the purview of rational policy choice. To contend otherwise in the case of the former Soviet U nion requires the assumption that the Soviet leadership would be quite determined to impose its will on the Americans in circumstances that could not reasonably be interpreted as forcing them to do so and despite having to pay a price that would be so high as to be without any real precedent. There is virtually no evidence to support such assumptions. It was, then, only in periods of severe crisis that the effects of the arms race were properly seen as critical.

The case for considering these effects profoundly destabilising could be summarised thus: when command systems that could not be reliably controlled were joined to weapons systems that could not be reliably protected, the stage would be set for the breakdown of deterrence. This view rested on a truism that when it seemed better to strike than to hold back, deterrence would in all likelihood break down. But what were the conditions in which it would be better to strike than to hold back? The critical condition would be the emerging conviction of one or both sides during a crisis that was inevitable, but that something – perhaps even a great deal — could be gained by striking first. Another, though less than critical, condition was the existence of weapons that were believed to enhance the promise of preemption, but because of their vulnerability increased the risk of failing to preempt. We may call these weapons destabilising. But what had brought the crisis to a point where the "destabilising" weapons seemed almost to "take over" and to undermine deterrence was a political process, a process out of which the conviction increasingly grew that war was inevitable. Before weapons systems could impose a necessity of their own, statesmen must have created a situation that enabled them to do so. Whatever their characteristics, weapons as such could not undermine deterrence. To believe otherwise, as many appeared to do, was to dissolve politics into technology. What weapons could do was to require a change in the operation of deterrence. They might do so chiefly by changing the point or the threshold beyond which deterrence breaks down and the conviction then emerged that war was inevitable. It is the statesman who undermines deterrence.

Moreover, he undermines deterrence not so much by permitting the development of the new technologies as by refusing to recognise that these technologies may require corresponding change in the operation of deterrence. If deterrence is in substantial part a function of technology, it must change as technology changes. The contention that the kind of crisis we could have a generation ago over missiles in Cuba would prove much more dangerous today does not mean that deterrence has been partially undermined. It means that the threshold beyond which deterrence is likely to break down has shifted.

One of the tasks of the statesman in the nuclear age, and perhaps his most important task, is to adjust the definition of the nuclear threshold to the conditions that determine it and to bend all efforts to ensure that this threshold is neither crossed nor closely approached. If these considerations had merit, an apparent obsession over the arms race was for the most part an obsession over the reality, largely an anxiety over politics. The great worry over deterrence being undermined by the new weapons is in fact a worry over the wisdom, or lack thereof, of political leaders who are entrusted with the operation of deterrence. Is the lapse of faith in deterrence to be laid largely at the doorstep of the Reagan Administration? A legion of critics insisted that this Administration must bear major responsibility for the movement and debate that might have been avoided by a government with a less ideological and less bellicose outlook. Whereas previous Presidents were sobered by their tragic power to initiate nuclear war, this President was presumably different. He was different because he was in thrall to an ideology that bound him to the terrible dangers of nuclear war.[79] The evidence for this blindness consisted, in part, of statements made about nuclear weapons and nuclear war by Reagan as a private citizen or as a candidate for office. Although betraying no particular sophistication about nuclear matters, none of these statements could reasonably be taken as grounds for coming to an apocalyptic view of the future. In the most quoted of his statements, the President responded to a question about whether he believed in the possibility of a limited nuclear war between the United States and the Soviet Union in these words… "I could see where you could have the exchange of tactical weapons against troops in the field without it bringing either one of the major powers to pushing the button."[80]

Whatever one might think of this response, it scarcely demonstrated the power of ideology in blinding men to the dangers of nuclear war. No doubt, it must arouse those who took as an article of faith that any use of nuclear weapons could only lead to an unlimited nuclear exchange. But there were many people who shared Reagan's scepticism in this matter and who were not, by any reasonable definition, blind ideologues. Whether or not limited nuclear war in Europe was possible was not a matter to be settled by faith or ideology. Nor did the President in his reply indicate otherwise. If anything, his response was far less dogmatic than the vast majority of utterances on the subject. One lesson to be drawn from the Reagan experience is simply the rising sensitivity to any statements about the possible use of nuclear weapons by high public officials, and particularly by the President. Such statements about nuclear weapons or strategy are likely to prove an invitation to trouble. For the public and its elites do not want to be reminded of the basis on which their security ultimately rests. The Reagan Administration badly erred by not taking this aversion sufficiently to heart; instead of glossing over a subject that could not be dealt with at considerable risk, it responded to enquiries that were put to it, and occasionally even offered some gratuitous elaboration. The responses were neither startling for their novelty nor unreasonable in their substance. On balance, they preserved a striking continuity with positions taken by preceding administrations. Still, in the circumstances of the early 1980s, dominated as they had been by growing Soviet-American tension, responses that might otherwise have gone largely unremarked provoked a series of minor political storms. The Reagan Administration not only tended to talk too much about nuclear matters, but to use an idiom that seemed to confirm the dark suspicions held by many about its intentions. Thus, the dismayed and accusatory reaction to the 1982 Defence Guidance statement with its concept of "prevailing" in a protracted nuclear war. American nuclear forces, a critical passage reportedly read, "must prevail and be able to force the Soviet Union to seek earliest possible termination of hostilities on terms favourable to the United States." [81] This document did not break new ground. Its essential features added up to little more than a refinement of the Carter Administration's 1980 Presidential Directive 59, which in turn built on strategic concepts that may be traced back a generation.

From Kennedy to Reagan, no administration had been able to disavow the prospect, however aseptically it might have viewed that prospect, of the controlled use of nuclear weapons and the prospect of emerging from a nuclear conflict with some kind of meaningful victory. Unable to disavow these prospects, no administration had been able to disavow the force structure that might make possible fighting a limited nuclear war. It was America's least bellicose and most sceptical of recent Presidents who declared during his first year in office that the American strategic arsenal "should be strong enough that a possible nuclear war would end on the most favorable terms to the US."[82] At the time, 1977, these words of Jimmy Carter did not provoke noticeable criticism. It is true that they do not go quite as far as the 1982 Defence Guidance paper. Still, the difference between ending a nuclear war "on terms favorable to the US" rather than "on the most favourable terms possible to the US", is scarcely great enough to account for the very different receptions given them. The Reagan Administration had been repeatedly accused of breaking radically from its predecessors in being intent on recapturing the Golden Grail of strategic superiority. This was presumably the meaning of "prevailing", that is, of "concluding hostilities on terms favourable to the US," just as it was the meaning of having a capability that "will ensure that the Soviet leadership, by their own calculations, will determine that the price of aggression outweighs any potential benefits". These words of the Reagan-Weinberger Defence Guidance document did indeed suggest a kind of strategic superiority. But then so did the Carter-Brown PD-59 "countervailing" strategy. The former Secretary of Defence, Harold Brown, defined the countervailing strategy in these terms "...to convince the Soviets that they will be successfully opposed at any level of aggression they choose, and that no plausible outcome at any level of conflict could represent 'success' for them by any reasonable definition of 'success'." [83]

The countervailing strategy did not posit an American victory. Instead, it promised a Soviet defeat. For it "seeks a situation in which the Soviets would always lose more than they could reasonably expect to gain from either beginning or escalating a military conflict".[84] Was this note however, a definition of sorts of victory? Unless it was assumed that American losses, too, were always disproportionate to their gains, in which case there would scarcely be grounds for recommending it, the countervailing strategy did come to hold a promise of victory. The distinction between "countervailing" and "prevailing" was, accordingly, a very thin one. So too, was the difference with respect to the forces required to implement strategy. In fact, neither the Carter nor the Reagan Administration pursued a procurement policy designed to achieve strategic superiority. Yet each had articulated a strategic doctrine that implied a kind of superiority. In part, this apparent anomaly is explained by the need to retain, if only for moral reasons, some semblance of a claim to a theory of victory. In part, however, the explanation must be sought in the American strategic predicament. The root of that predicament was an asymmetry of interests that imposed more difficult and exacting deterrence requirements on the United States than on the Soviet Union. While in the Soviet case, these requirements extended no further than to Eastern Europe, in the American case, they extended beyond its own hemisphere, to Western Europe, Japan and the Persian Gulf. To an extent far greater than for the Soviet Union, deterrence for the United States had always been the extension of deterrence to others than the self. By its very nature, extended deterrence, moreover, could not be fully compensated for by greater conventional forces. Greater conventional forces would raise the threshold of nuclear conflict. Ultimately, compensation must be found either at the strategic nuclear level or nowhere. But it could only be found at the strategic level by forces that were more than simply the equivalent of the Soviet Union's forces. As Americans are now aware, equivalence and no more must subject extended deterrence to pervasive and increasingly corrosive doubt.

Since the late 1960s, strategic doctrines have increasingly assumed the function of bridging the growing gap between the forces for extended deterrence and the forces in being. If the gap could no longer be bridged in fact, it could still be bridged in word. Without claiming strategic superiority – indeed, even while disavowing an interest in seeking superiority – the benefits of superiority were nevertheless salvaged in some measure. Thus, the claim that the Americans might still ensure that the Soviets would always lose more than they could expect to gain from resorting to any kind of armed aggression. Or the claim that in a nuclear conflict, American forces would have the capability of imposing early termination of the conflict on terms favourable to the United States. In proclaiming the strategy of prevailing, the Reagan Administration simply followed an established practice, though perhaps it did so too exuberantly. What is important is that it did so at a time when détente had clearly broken down and tension between the superpowers was rising to a level that had not been experienced since the years of the classic Cold War. In these circumstances, the doctrine of prevailing was subject to a scrutiny it might not, and probably would not, have otherwise received. In the same circumstances, the earlier doctrine of countervailing power was subject to a criticism considerably harsher than the criticism that marked its appearance in 1980.

The real indictment made of the Reagan Administration was not of its military strategy but of its politics. It was not so much what Reagan said about nuclear weapons and their possible use that aroused opponents, but what he said about the Soviet Union. In word and in spirit, though as yet much less so in action, this Administration largely returned to the period of the classic Cold War. It did so, however, in strategic circumstances which were bleak by comparison with those of the earlier period.

The classic Cold War began with an American monopoly of nuclear weapons. It ended, if we take the period immediately following the Cuban missile crisis as marking its end, with the United States still enjoying a position of strategic superiority over the Soviet Union. A nuclear revisionism now contended that, contrary to what had been the conventional wisdom, strategic superiority was useless, in that it could not be translated into diplomatic power or political advantage, and that this inutility was dramatically demonstrated at the time of the Cuban missile crisis. In turn, this view of strategic superiority was part of a larger assessment of the significance of nuclear weapons, an assessment in which these weapons were found to be "totally useless – except only to deter one's opponents from using them." [85]

If nuclear weapons are useful only for deterring the use of nuclear weapons, if strategic superiority cannot be employed to any meaningful advantage, then clearly a good deal of the conventional wisdom respecting the history of the post-war period must be discounted. Neither the American monopoly of nuclear weapons at the start of this period, nor the subsequent American strategic superiority conferred any advantage on them. Indeed, if the revisionist view is to be literally credited, the existence of nuclear weapons and the fear of nuclear war had little to do with the maintenance of peace in Europe.

In the decade or so following the Cuban missile crisis, the loss of strategic superiority had no more than a marginal impact on the Americans' faith in deterrence. Although the Soviet achievement of strategic parity was an event of first-order importance requiring a rethinking of the entire American security position, its effects on the structure of extended deterrence attracted only moderate attention and caused even less anxiety. In contrast to the early 1960s, the early 1970s gave rise to almost no agitation on the body politic over the nuclear issue despite the momentous changes that had taken place.

Vietnam apart, the reason for this extraordinary unconcern was that Americans were in the floodtide of détente. Having developed slowly and unevenly in the course of the 1960s, by the early 1970s, détente had become the centrepiece of the Nixon policy reformulation. In the context of détente, the loss of America's strategic superiority was generally seen as an event without great significance. Instead, far more attention was directed to the Strategic Arms Limitation Talks (SALT), though in retrospect the results of these negotiations, embodied in the 1972 Moscow Accord, appear almost inconsequential in comparison with the Soviet Union's achievement of strategic parity. But the arms control negotiations were considered almost from the outset a litmus test of the overall relationship of the superpowers. If this relationship was relatively good, the possible consequences of the Soviet Union having achieved strategic parity might be taken in stride. Besides, the Soviet achievement did not challenge the predominant view that the preservation of mutual deterrence was best guaranteed by both sides maintaining a retaliatory force with the capability of assured destruction. The Moscow agreements were successfully defended as preserving mutual deterrence while stabilising it by limiting the build up of nuclear forces.

What is immediately apparent in considering the present nuclear debate is its continuity with the past. Although a generation has elapsed since the last major debate over nuclear weapons, the questions raised today are largely the same that were raised then. What are the requirements of deterrence? Can these requirements be met indefinitely and, even if they can, at what political and moral cost? Are they compatible in the long run with the political institutions and moral foundations of a liberal-democratic society? What happens if deterrence fails? Can nuclear weapons be employed to achieve any of the traditional objectives of war? If they can, why has a plausible scenario of a nuclear conflict not been devised? If they cannot, must not the breakdown of deterrence be attended by the determination to stop the ensuing conflict and to do so without regard to consideration of relative advantage? But quite apart from the intrinsic difficulty of crediting a strategy – deterrence – that has only this response to the contingency of its breakdown, does not the quick termination of the conflict depend on the parallel behaviour, if not the agreement, of both sides? If only one side moves to terminate the conflict, however, may it not be placed at a great and perhaps even fatal disadvantage?

It is not only the questions that have remained by and large the same. The answers, too, have remained the same and they seem no more satisfactory than they did on an earlier occasion. None of this should prove surprising. All of our political and moral thought is predicated on the assumption of limits. Nuclear weapons challenge this assumption by virtue of their destructiveness and, of course, their rate of destruction. By introducing a new quantitative dimension into the conduct of war, by holding out the prospect of a war that might escape any meaningful limitation, nuclear weapons take the standards heretofore applied to force and threat to make a hollow mockery of them.

Deterrence escapes these considerations only so long as the possibility of its breakdown is either denied or simply ignored. If the reliability of deterrence arrangements is believed to approach certainty, the only issues that can arise will concern deterrence and not nuclear war. These issues will not challenge the foundation of faith.

Even the champions of pure and simple deterrence have seldom been so indiscreet as to endow deterrent strategies with certainty. No social contrivance can be invested with certainty. All are flawed. All may fail, including deterrence. But once this is acknowledged, the difficulties that a faith in deterrence had managed to exercise reappear, and in acute form. If a deterrent strategy may fail, it is absurd to refuse to consider seriously the possible consequences of failure beyond saying that all effort must be directed to bringing the conflict to an end as quickly as possible and without regard to any other considerations. Equally, if a deterrent strategy may fail, it is absurd to insist upon using and justifying the threat of nuclear war as an instrument of policy but to deny that any meaningful or just purpose could be served by such a war.

Yet, what are the alternatives to these absurdities? One, we have long been told, is frankly to acknowledge nuclear war as a distinct historical possibility. Having done so, though, what is the character of this possibility? We still cannot say with any real assurance. The actual character of nuclear war remains as obscure today as in the 1950s. It may well be, as Lawrence Freedman concludes in his history of nuclear strategy: "The question of what happens if deterrence fails is vital for the intellectual cohesion and credibility of nuclear strategy." Yet Freedman also concludes: "It now seems unlikely that such an answer can be found." [86]

"Nuclear Winter", as it is described, may be regarded as nature's equivalent of the Doomsday Machine. Nuclear Winter appears as the final confirmation of the very idea that the institution of war contains within itself the means for achieving its own disappearance. All it needs do is become sufficiently destructive.

Notes

1. Quoted in Fleming, D.F., *The Cold War and Its Origins* (1917-1960); vol. I, London, George Allen and Unwin Ltd. 1968, p. 216.

2. *The New York Times*, April 13-15, 1945.

3. Fleming, op. cit., p. 217.

4. *Times* (London), April 16, 1945; *The New York Times*, April 25, 1945.

5. Hull, Cordell, *The Memoirs of Cordell Hull*, vol. II, New York, Macmillan Co. 1948, p. 1467.

6. Snow, Edgar, "Stalin Must Have Peace," *Saturday Evening Post*, March 1, 1947, p. 96; *The Monthly Review*, March 19, 1959, pp. 399-403.

7. Fleming, *op. cit.*, p, 216.

8. Blackett, P.M.S., *Fear, War and the Bomb*, New York, McGraw-Hill, 1948, pp. 149-51.

9. Laurence, William L., *The Hell Bomb*, New York, Knopf, 1951, p. 209.

10. *Department of State Bulletin*, December 30, 1945, pp. 1027-1032.

11. See Carter, Field, *Bernard Baruch, Park Bench Statesman*, New York, McGraw-Hill, 1944.

12. *Department of State Document No. 2498.*

13. See Nover, Barnet, *Chicago Daily News* and the *Denver Post*, February 2, 1948.

14. *New Times*, Moscow, March 20, 1946.

15. *The New York Times*, June 14, 1946.

16. See Watler Lippmann's comments in the *Washington Post*, June 20, 1946, pointing out that the Charter, like the US Constitution, does not "Protect" states violating agreements but is silent on the point for the very good reason that the only thing that can be done is to make war. "...I cannot see what Mr Baruch thinks he can gain by binding the US now to fight, not necessarily with its own consent, in the future. What is more, I do not think that he and our Senate today can under our Constitution legally commit a future Congress to war..."

17. *New York Herald Tribune*, March 28, 1948.

18. For details, see *Records of the UN Atomic Energy Commission: International Conciliation Pamphlet No. 430,* April, 1947; *Second Report of the UN Atomic Energy Commission to the Security Council,* September 11, 1947; and *Draft Third Report,* May 7, 1948.

19. Quoted in Hermoot, Peter, *The World Without the Bomb,* New York, Martin Press, 1948, p. 602.

20. The extent to which Soviet development of atomic energy was the result of the work of "atomic spies" rather than of Soviet scientists and engineers admits of no judgement on the basis of available evidence. The trial records of convicted "spies" are inconclusive on this point, though worth studying for other reasons.

21. Schuman, Frederick L., *International Politics,* New York, McGraw-Hill, 1958, pp. 667-8.

22. *The New York Times,* December 7, 1945.

23. *The United States Strategic Bombing Survey: The Effects of Atomic Bombs on Hiroshima and Nagasaki,* Washington, 1946, p. 3.

24. Masters, Dexter, and Way, Katharine, eds., *One World or None,* New York, McGraw-Hill, 1946, p. 28.

25. *New York Herald Tribune,* September 9, 1946.

26. *The United States Strategic Bombing Survey 4: The Summary Report on the Pacific War,* p. 26.

27. Reston, James, *The New York Times,* November 11, 1945.

28. Stimson, Henry L., and Bundy, McGeorge, *On Active Service in Peace and War,* New York, Harper & Brothers, 1948, p. 632.

29. Fleming, op. cit., pp. 298-299.

30. See *The Bulletin of the Atomic Scientists,* Washington, May 1, 1947. Also see Fleming, op. cit., p. 299.

31. Smith, Alice Kumball, *A Peril and a Hope: The Scientists' Movement in America: 1945-47:* Chicago, University of Chicago, 1965, p. 297.

32. Ibid. pp. 293, 296.

33. Stimson, Henry L., "The Decision to Use the Atomic Bomb," *Harper's Magazine*, February, 1947, p. 104.

34. Fleming, *op. cit.* p. 302.

35. Byrnes, James F., *Speaking Frankly*, New York, Harper & Brothers, 1947, p. 263.

36. *The New York Times*, August 17, 1945.

37. Bundy, McGeorge, *Danger and Survival: Choices About Nuclear Policy in the First Fifty Years*, New Delhi, Affiliated East-West Press, p. 88. Also see, for contrary view, Blackett, P.M.S. *Fear, War and the Bomb: Military, and Political Consequences of Atomic Energy*, New York, McGraw-Hill, 1948.

38. See Bernstein, Barton J., "The Atomic Bomb and American Foreign Policy, 1941-45: A Historiographical Controversy," *Peace and Change*, 2, Spring, 1974, pp. 1 - 16.

39. Bundy, op. cit., p. 89.

40. Quoted in Bundy, *op. cit.*, p. 90.

41. *Ibid.*

42. See Roosevelt, Franklin D., *The Public Papers Addresses of Franklin D. Roosevelt, 1944-45*, New York, Random House, p. 412. Burns, James McGregor, *Roosevelt: The Soldier of Freedom*, New York, Harcourt Jovanovich, 1970, p. 456. Roosevelt, James with Bill Libby, *My Parents: A Differing View*, Chicago, Playboy Press, 1976, pp. 169-70.

43. Stimson, Henry L., "The Decision to Use the Atomic Bomb", *Harper's Magazine*, February, 1947, pp. 97-107.

44. Toland, John, *The Rising Sun: The Decline and Fall of the Japanese Empire, 1936-45;* New York, Random House, 1970 pp. 806-7. Butow, Robert J., *Japan's Decision to Surrender*, Stanford, Stanford University Press, 1954, pp. 158-65.

45. Wallace, Henry A., *The Price of Vision: The Diary of Henry A. Wallace*, 1942-1946; Edited by John Morton Blum, Boston, Houghton Miffin Co., 1970, p. 474.

46. Walzer, Michael, *Just and Unjust Wars: A Moral Argument with Historical Illustrations*; New York, Basic Books, 1977, p. 262.

47. *Ibid.* p. 262-63.

48. Bundy, op. cit., pp. 96-97.

49. *The New York Times*, July 28, 1949; See also *Times*, July 21, 1949.

50. Truman, Harry S., *Memoirs by Harry S. Truman*, vol. 2, Garden City, New York, Doubleday & Co. p. 306.

51. Brown, Harrison, *Must Destruction Be Our Destiny?* New York, Simon & Schuster, 1946, p. 25.

52. *The New York Times*, October 2, 1949; *Herald Tribune*, October 12, 1949.

53. Hewlett Richard G., and Duncan, Francis, *Atomic Shield 1947-52*; Vol. 2, University Park, Pa, Pennsylvania State University Press, 1969.

54. Truman, Harry S., *Public Papers of the President of the United States: Harry S., Truman, 1945-1950*; Washington D.C., US Government Printing Office, 1950, p. 727.

55. *Ibid.* pp. 1124-25.

56. Eisenhower, Dwight, D., *Crusade in Europe*, Garden City, New York, Doubleday & Co. 1948, p. 443.

57. *Foreign Relations of the United States, 1952-54.* (FRUS), Washington D.C., US Government Printing Office, 2:789.

58. *Documents on American Foreign Relations*, US Government Printing Office, 1954, pp. 7-15.

59. Ambrose, Stephen F., *Eisenhower*, 2 vols., New York, Simon Schuster, 1983, p. 2:184.

60. *FRUS, 1952-54*; p. 13, 1437.

61. Bell, Coral, *Survey of International Affairs: 1954*, Edited by Nenham, F.C., London, Oxford University Press, 1957, p. 121.

62. *FRUS, 1952-54*, p. 13:1437.

63. See George, Alexander L., and Smoke, Richard, *Deterrence in American Foreign Policy: Theory and Practice,* New York, Columbia University Press, 1974, Chaps. 9 and 12.

64. *Department of State Bulletin,* Washington D.C., January 19, 1959, pp. 81-89.

65. *Department of State Bulletin,* Washington D.C., January 15, 1958, p. 948.

66. See Adomeit, Hannes, *Soviet Risk-Taking and Crisis Behavior; A Theoretical and Empirical, Analysis,* London, George Allen & Unwin, 1982, pp. 183-94.

67. Bundy, op. cit. p. 364.

68. See Kissinger, Henry A., *Nuclear Weapons and Foreign Policy,* New York, Harper & Brothers, 1957, and *Years of Upheaval,* Boston, Little, Brown & Co., 1982.

69. Draper, Theodore, "Nuclear Temptations", *The New York Review of Books,* January 19, 1984, p. 43.

70. Wisseltiers, Leon, *Nuclear War, Nuclear Peace,* New York, Holt, Rinchart & Winston, 1983, p. 38.

71. Bundy, McGeorge, "The Bishops and the Bomb". *The New York Review of Books,* June 10, 1983, p. 4. Also see Brodie, Bernard, "The Development of Nuclear Strategy", *International Security,* Spring, 1978, p. 79.

72. Schill, Jonathan, "Reflections: The Abolition," *The New Yorker,* January 2, 1984, pp. 64-65.

73. Kennan, George, *The Nuclear Delusion,* New York, Pantheon Books, 1983, p. 231.

74. Snow, C.P., "The Moral Un-Neutrality of Science," *Science,* January 27, 1961, p. 259.

75. Schell, *op. cit.,* p. 44.

76. "The Challenge of Peace: God's Promise and Our Response", *Origins,* May 19, 1983, p. 1.

77. Forsberg, Randall, "Call to Halt The Nuclear Arms Race," in Randall Forsberg et al, *Seeds of Promise: The First Real Hearings on the Nuclear Arms Freeze,* Andover, Mass., Bank House Publishing, 1983, p. 197.

78. Gelb, Leslie H., "Is the Nuclear Threat Manageable"? *The New York Times Magazine*, March 4, 1984, p. 26.

79. See Bracken, Paul, *The Command and Control of Nuclear Forces*, New Haven, Yale University Press, 1983.

80. Schlesinger, Arthur Jr., "Foreign Policy and the American Character", *Foreign Affairs*, Fall, 1983, p. 13.

81. Gwertzman, Bernard, "President Says US should Not Waver in Backing Saudis," *The New York Times*, October 18, 1981, p. 1.

82. Cited in Halloran, Richard, "Pentagon Draws Up First Strategy For Fighting a Long Nuclear War", *The New York Times*, May 30, 1982, p. 1.

83. Mohr, Charles, "Carter Orders Steps to Increase Ability to Meet War Threats," *The New York Times*, August 26, 1977, p. A8.

84. Secretary of Defense, *Annual Report to the Congress, Fy 1982*, US Department of Defense, January 19, 1981, p. 40.

85. Brown, Harold, *Thinking About National Security: Defence and Foreign Policy in a Dangerous World*, Boulder (Colo), West View Press, 1983, p. 81.

86. Freedman, Lawrence, *The Evolution of Nuclear Strategy*, St. Martin's Press, 1983, p. 395.

3

MEGATONOMANIA

Considerably less than one half of the present world population remembers the non-nuclear world. The first ever nuclear explosion was carried out on July 16, 1945, by British and American scientists at Alamogordo Desert in New Mexico. The device exploded with a power equivalent to that which would have been obtained from the explosion of about 19,000 tons of TNT (19 kiloton — KT). Shortly afterwards, on August 6 and 9, 1945, two nuclear bombs were dropped on two cities: the first on Hiroshima with a yield of 12.5 KT, the second on Nagasaki with a yield of 22 KT. In spite of the ghastly consequences of these events, the United Nations Organisation proved incapable of preventing the further development and stockpiling of nuclear weapons by nation-states. Instead, a nuclear arms race began between the United States and the Soviet Union, with as great a momentum as technological developments and treaty provisions allowed.

In March 1946, the US Strategic Air Command (SAC) was formed with a fleet of B-17 and B-29 medium bombers of World War II vintage as the first nuclear force. The nuclear capability of the SAC was greatly enhanced in 1948 by the delivery of the first post-war bombers − B-35 heavy long-range bombers and B-50 medium bombers. By then, adequate overseas bases had been obtained in England and the Far East, and the SAC provided an undeniably credible strategic nuclear threat to the Soviet Union. As might be expected, this threat greatly stimulated Soviet efforts in the nuclear field and on August 29, 1949, the Soviet Union exploded its first nuclear weapon near Semipalatinsk in Central Asia. The speed of Soviet nuclear developments shook the world. By this time, the Americans had already exploded eight nuclear devices, with yields up to 50 KT, and had stockpiled in the SAC arsenals a few hundred nuclear weapons with a total yield of about 10,000 KT (10 megatons – MT).

The American reaction to the Soviet nuclear explosion came quickly. The following January, President Truman ordered the full-scale development of a thermonuclear weapon – a major escalatory decision in the nuclear arms race. The American programme was so successful that the first thermonuclear reaction (in which the nuclei of the element tritium were fused together, a reaction accompanied by a relatively enormous release of energy) was achieved in May 1951 at Eniwitok Atoll in the Pacific. Shortly afterward, in November, the first significant US thermonuclear explosion took place on Elugelab Island, Eniwitok Atoll. The yield was about 10 MT. But the Soviets were not lagging far behind, and they exploded a thermonuclear device on August 12, 1963.[1]

By this time, the SAC was operating from a worldwide network of bases with an intercontinental modern bomber fleet (including high-performance B-47 bombers) capable of delivering nuclear weapons on Soviet targets at about 3,000-mile ranges with one air-refuelling.

The first Soviet and American thermonuclear devices were not true deliverable bombs. The first thermonuclear bomb was, in fact, exploded by the Americans in Bikini Atoll on March 1, 1954, giving a yield of about 15 MT. And a comparable Soviet thermonuclear bomb was exploded on November 23, 1955. The first nuclear bombs were 1,000 times more powerful than the largest conventional bombs ever made. And the first thermonuclear bombs were 1,000 times more powerful than the first nuclear bombs. There was, therefore, a million-fold increase in the destructive power of weapons in the space of a decade. A single thermonuclear weapon could now be made so powerful as to exceed in explosive power that of all the explosives used by all the combatants during World War II.

In 1955, the USA began intensively developing long-range strategic missiles with nuclear warheads. Within three years, six missiles programmes were initiated: four in 1955, for the intercontinental ballistic missiles (ICBMs) Atlas and Titan and one for the intermediate range ballistic missiles (IRBMs) Jupiter and Thor; one in 1957, for the Minuteman ICBMs; and one in 1958, for the Polaris submarine-launched ballistic missiles (SLBMs). It was also in 1955 that the B-52 all-jet heavy bomber, a much larger version of the B-47, began to replace the B-36s in the SAC. And in 1955, Soviet long-range bombers, the TU-20 Bear and Mya-4 Bison, entered service. The Soviet Union, however, never built up as large a strategic bomber fleet as the United States. Nor did the Soviets deploy an air-refuelling capability, necessary for intercontinental bomber operations, as sophisticated as the American one.

The year 1957 was a very significant period for the strategic nuclear arms race. In May the first US IRBM, Jupiter, was successfully launched; in August, the Soviet Union achieved the first long-range flight with an ICBM; and on October 4, and November 3, the Soviet Union launched its first two satellites, Sputnik I and II, into orbit. During the year, the SAC reached its peak force of about 2,000 bombers – mainly B-47s.[2]

On January 31, 1958, the USA launched its first satellite, Explorer I, into orbit, but the satellite weighed considerably less (14 kg) than did the first Soviet satellite (83 kg for Sputnik I and 508 kg for Sputnik II). But the following December, the first US ICBM Atlas-A was successfully flight-tested. Atlas-A entered service in 1960, as did the first US nuclear-powered strategic submarine, *USS George Washington*, carrying sixteen Polaris SLBMs. In 1961, the Soviets started to deploy ICBMs. The missile age had really begun. And once it began, it rapidly accelerated.

By the end of 1962, the USA had deployed 54 Titan, 90 Atlas, and 150 Minuteman ICBMs, in addition to its large bomber force and growing SLBM force. At this time, the Soviet Union had about 100 Tu-20 and 90 Mya-4 long-range strategic bombers in service, in addition to 75 ICBMs. But the Soviets did not deploy SLBMs, capable of being fired from a submerged position, on nuclear powered submarines until 1964.[3]

In 1965, the number of missiles in the US strategic nuclear force exceeded for the first time the number of bombers due to the phase out of B-47s and the deployment of new Minuteman ICBMs. However, SAC bombers (630 B-52s) continued to carry about 80 per cent of the megatonnage deployed by the American strategic nuclear forces.

In 1967, the US land-based missile forces stabilised at 1,000 Minuteman ICBMs and 54 Titan II ICBMs and remained at this level for about a decade. But throughout the 1960s the Soviet Union actively continued to deploy ICBMs of various types, including the very large SS-9 capable of delivering a nuclear warhead of up to 30 MT.

A number of other important developments in the strategic nuclear arms race took place in the 1960s. In 1964, the US Polaris A-3 SLBM, with three multiple re-entry vehicles (MRVs), entered service and the development of a multiple independently targetable re-entry vehicle (MIRV) for Poseidon SLBMs was officially approved. With MRVs or MIRVs a single missile could deliver warheads on to a number of separate targets, a development which greatly increased the power of nuclear arsenals. In 1967, the US decision to proceed with a limited anti-ballistic missile (ABM) deployment was announced. An ABM system was designed to detect, intercept, and destroy incoming enemy missiles but no really effective ABM system had yet been devised. Nevertheless, by 1969, the Soviet Union had deployed an operational ABM system around Moscow.

MIRVs were first deployed in 1970 on land-based missiles, when the US Minuteman III entered into service. Each of these ICBMs carried three MIRVed warheads. The following year, the first US nuclear-powered submarine, carrying sixteen MIRVed Poseidon SLBMS, was deployed. And in 1973 the Soviet Union began an extensive flight-test *programme* of MIRVed ICBMs. [4]

Over the past thirty years, many distinguished military and civilian analysts argued that the nuclear arms race had produced arsenals of nuclear weapons in the USSR and the USA which were so large as to be of the order of magnitude in excess of any conceivable rational need, military or political, of either power. In a brief survey, it is impossible to give a real impression of the astonishing variety of forms in which tactical and strategic nuclear weapons were deployed and developed by these powers. The nuclear arsenals of the USA and the USSR contained intermediate-range ballistic missiles, submarine-launched ballistic missiles, depressed-trajectory ballistic missiles, fractional-orbital bombardment systems, free-fall tactical bombs, free-fall strategic bombs, air-to-surface missiles, air-to-surface standoff missiles, air-to-air missiles, army artillery shells, naval artillery shells, howitzer projectiles, torpedoes, rocket torpedoes, depth charges, demolition devices, land mines, sea mines, anti-ballistic missiles, and so on. And many of these devices were produced in a wide range of types. In a public debate, it is the strategic nuclear weapons that usually dominate, but it should not be forgotten that in addition to huge strategic forces, the USA and the Soviet Union deployed tens of thousands of tactical nuclear weapons. In Europe alone, in the late 1960s, there were 7,000 American and 3,500 Soviet tactical nuclear weapons. Nor should it be forgotten that the UK, France and China were deploying and continuously developing nuclear forces. Even though pocket size compared with those of the USA and the Soviet Union, each of them was quite formidable. [5]

The American strategic nuclear force had developed from a small fleet of World War II bombers, land-based missiles and sea-based missiles. Each of the three systems had been continuously improved, one did not replace another, and each was still regarded as an important element of the force. The Soviets, however, seemed to place greatest emphasis on strategic missiles, land-based and sea-based, and up to the early seventies, did not deploy a modern and large strategic bomber fleet.

By the mid-seventies, the US nuclear arsenal contained: 420 B-52 and FB-III strategic bombers; 41 strategic nuclear powered submarines; and 1,054 land-based strategic missiles. The Soviet nuclear arsenal contained: 140 strategic bombers; 42 strategic nuclear-powered submarines and 1,567 land-based strategic missiles. Taking into account multiple warheads on missiles, the US strategic forces were capable of delivering about 6,000 nuclear warheads on the Soviet Union from missiles and about a further 2,000 from bombers – making a total of about 8,000 warheads. The Soviet strategic nuclear forces were capable of delivering about 3,600 nuclear warheads on to the USA from missiles and bombers. The megatonnage carried by these Soviet warheads, however, exceeded those carried by the American warheads even though the number of Soviet warheads was considerably smaller. The reason is that many Soviet warheads were considerably larger than the largest American warhead. But, in spite of the differences in megatonnage and numbers, it was often claimed, usually for political purposes, that both sides were in "parity". Political leaders found it difficult to defend negotiations from a perceived position of weakness.[6]

When it became possible to claim a position of parity, even though ill-defined, the USA and the Soviet Union were more easily able to begin the negotiations, which led, in May 1972, to the strategic arms limitation agreements (commonly called the SALT I agreements), limiting the number of land-based ICBM launchers (but not warheads), modern ballistic missile submarines, and ABM launchers that each side was allowed to deploy. The negotiations leading to these agreements went on over a three-year period, 1969-1972. A new phase of the talks, SALT II, began in 1973. In June 1974, as a result of the Nixon-Brezhnev summit meeting, ABMs were further limited to 100 launchers at one site – Moscow for the Soviet Union and the ICBM site at Grand Forks for the USA.

On November 24, 1974, in Vladivostok, President Ford and General Secretary Brezhnev agreed that the SALT negotiators would work for a new SALT II agreement under which each side would be limited to 2,400 strategic nuclear delivery vehicles (strategic bombers, ICBMs, and SLBMS). Within this number, both sides would be further limited to a total of 1,320 ICBMs and SLBMs equipped with MIRVs. Neither side had deployed these numbers at the time of the accord.

Presumably the reason why the SALT II limit on MIRVed missiles had been set so high was to make planned deployments possible. The latter would mean that the strategic arsenals for the two powers would total about 17,000 independent nuclear warheads on missiles alone, about equally divided between them. In addition, several thousand nuclear warheads would be carried on strategic bombers. Both sides were now much more interested in modernising their nuclear warheads than in significantly increasing the number of their strategic delivery vehicles. The replacement of existing strategic weapons with improved versions was totally unrestricted by the proposed agreement – on the contrary, modernisation was encouraged. For at least a decade, the strategic nuclear forces of the two sides would probably be no different under SALT II than they would have been without it.

What the Ford-Brezhnev accord did, in fact, was not to limit the nuclear arms race but simply to define it. Worse still, the proposed SALT II agreement was to run until 1985. This almost certainly meant that there would be no actual nuclear disarmament, presumably the major objective of SALT, until the end of the 1980s at the earliest.

A major weakness of both the SALT I agreement and the then ongoing SALT II agreement from the disarmament point of view was the total lack of any prohibition on qualitative improvements in nuclear weapons. The nuclear arms race had, in any case, already moved from a race of quantity to a race for quality. A new premium had been placed on military research and development. Because qualitative improvements were unhindered, improvements in nuclear weapons and their delivery systems – for example, accuracy and survivability – had continued, and were continuing unabated. The proposed high limit on MIRVs would result in a substantial increase in the number of warheads deployed on strategic missiles, and, therefore, the SALT agreements would not even impose real quantitative limitations on the number of nuclear warheads deployed.

II

For some, it would be reasonable to assume that while serious negotiations on strategic arms limitation were taking place between the USA and the Soviet Union, both sides would exercise some measure of restraint on the further development of their strategic nuclear forces. As this chapter will show, however, restraint had not been exercised during SALT, even though this was the most significant bilateral attempt to limit the arms race. The total lack of restraint during this period demonstrated just how strong the pressures really were in both the American and Soviet societies to maintain the momentum of the arms race at all times and at any cost. In fact, it had become fashionable to use SALT as an excuse for accelerating certain strategic weapon developments which, so it was said, provided "bargaining chips" in the negotiations.

The most dramatic quantitative change during the period of SALT I was in the total number of offensive strategic missiles deployed by the Soviet Union. Over this period, the Soviets increased their number of deployed ICBMs by about 25 per cent. At the time of the first SALT agreement, the Soviet Union had a land-based ICBM force deployed or under construction of 1,618 launchers – nearly five times the number deployed in 1966. The US land-based ICBM forces, on the other hand, remained constant at 1,054 launchers, the number reached in 1967.[7]

The USA retained its advantage over the Soviet Union in the numbers of SLBMs – 656 missiles as against 450, respectively. But the latter was rapidly closing the gap with the construction of more Soviet Yankee class nuclear-powered ballistic-missiles submarines. These submarines, similar to the US Polaris, could carry sixteen missiles each. The construction rate was six to seven per year. However, the range of the Soviet missiles carried on the Y class submarines was about half that of the Polaris A-3 missiles, and generally the performance of the Soviet nuclear submarines was not as good as that of their US counterparts.

The most significant qualitative advance was in the US strategic nuclear forces, namely, the deployment of MIRVs on both land-based ICBMs and sea-based ballistic missiles. In the simplest multiple warhead system, the MRV, as soon as the warheads were released from the platform carrying them, rails, springs, or small, fixed, solid-propellant rockets provided small velocity movements to the warheads in various directions, causing them to land in a fixed pattern around the target point. But MIRV contained a more sophisticated arrangement to adjust the individual velocity increments so that each re-entry vehicle was caused to follow a trajectory, after release from the platform, to individually selected targets. In the US system MIRVs were carried on a low-thrust final stage called a bus, which had a guidance system. The bus was guided through a series of predetermined velocity changes and after each one a warhead was released from the bus towards a target defined by the velocity change achieved at that time. The targets might be separated by over 100 miles.[8] MIRVs enabled a given number of missiles to cover a large number of targets or, alternatively, deliver more warheads to each target. In other words, MIRVs represented a significant quantitative advance as well as a qualitative one.

The replacement of the US Minuteman I missiles with Minuteman III began in June 1970. Minuteman III, with three MIRV thermonuclear warheads, each of approximately 160 KT, had improved survivability and penetrability, greater range (7,020 nautical miles), and higher accuracy, and was installed in super hardened silos. The installation of 150 Minuteman III missiles at Minot Air Force Base, North Dakota, was completed in December 1971 and the installation of a further 150 at Grand Forks Air Force Base, North Dakota, was under way. The plan was to have a Minuteman force of 550 Minuteman IIIs and 450 single-warhead Minuteman IIs.

The first operational deployment of MIRVed Poseidon missiles took place in February 1971. These missiles carried on the average, ten 40-kiloton warheads and was more accurate than its predecessor, the Polaris A-3.[9] Development work was also under way on the Undersea Long-Range Missile System (ULMS), subsequently called Trident. This follow-on system involved new large "quiet" submarines and longer-range missiles.

The Soviet Union tested MRVs containing three warheads, but had not, at the conclusion of SALT I, tested a MIRV. The development of the Fractional Orbital Bombardment System (FOBS), designed to dispatch warheads against the USA on a South Polar orbit to complicate detection by defence systems, also continued, with tests of the system occurring at a rate of about one or two per year. The Soviet Union also tested out a new missile with a range of about 2,600 nautical miles. This missile would clearly be the follow-on to the 1,530 nautical mile SS N-6 fleet ballistic missiles deployed on Y-class submarines.[10]

The guidance and control systems for ballistic missiles were continuously developed by both the USA and the Soviet Union during SALT I, as were all other aspects of these missiles. While MIRV provided a marked increase in accuracy, the ideal method of directing warheads to their targets was to provide actual terminal guidance for each warhead. Prototype MIRVs were developed and tested in both the USA and the Soviet Union. Such warheads would be able to take evasive action against missile defences, but, above all, they would have pinpoint accuracy, thus, guaranteeing the destruction of the target. In the USA, the development of miniaturised gyroscopes and accelerometers, a major prerequisite for MIRV, was already well advanced. More sophisticated terminal guidance systems were also being investigated, using a combination of lasers and microwave radar.

At the time of SALT I, missiles had circular error probabilities (CEPs) of between 1,500 and 4,500 feet, with the most accurate US missile being at the lower end of this range and the most accurate Soviet missile at the higher end of this range. The CEP was the radius of the circle centred on the target in which half of a large number of ICBM warheads fired at the target would fall. From the developments in guidance technology, considerable improvement in this accuracy could be foreseen. It could also be foreseen that the development of warheads combining high reliability with high accuracy would be effective counterforce, or first strike, weapons against fixed land-based forces.

The effectiveness of US strategic bomber forces had been significantly enhanced by the introduction of the new Short-Range Attack Missile (SRAM) which entered production in mid-1970. This 100 mile range, supersonic, air-to-surface nuclear missile, capable of penetrating advanced enemy defence systems, could be carried by B-52 G/H and FB-III strategic bombers. The medium-range supersonic FB-III entered service with the SAC in 1970. A B-52 could carry twenty SRAMs together with up to four thermonuclear weapons. A FB-III could carry six SRAMs. The planned deployment of some 1,100 SRAMs represented a considerable increase in the number of nuclear weapons deliverable by the US Strategic Air Command.

The Subsonic Cruise Armed Decoys (SCAD), a nuclear-armed electronic countermeasure system, also intended for the B-52, was in the early stage of development.[11]

The development of the B-I advanced, manned intercontinental strategic bomber was initiated in 1970 to replace the B-52s and FB-IIIs. This swing-wing aircraft was designed for Mach 2.2 speeds at high altitudes and high subsonic speed at low altitudes for flying past air defence systems at altitudes below radar acquisition ranges. It would carry a larger payload than the B-52 (about thirty SRAM missiles and thermonuclear bombs) and more sophisticated electronic equipment.

In the Soviet Union, a new variable-geometry bomber (NATO codenamed Backfire), with supersonic speeds at low altitudes had been developed and flown in prototype. The range of those bombers was about the same as the FB-III. There was no known Soviet air-to-surface missile comparable to SRAM.[12]

Programmes to develop survivable satellite communications systems for the command and control of strategic forces following a surprise attack were under way during SALT I. In a US system, for example, direct satellite-to-satellite links would permit global communications between airborne and earth terminals without relying on ground relay. This would eliminate the need for vulnerable overseas earth-relay terminals in the control of strategic nuclear forces. Ultra-high frequencies would be used for earth-to-satellite and satellite-to-earth communications so that airborne and submarine command posts could communicate with the satellites.

The development of new early-warning satellite systems designed to detect an ICBM attack, continued. Such systems were already deployed. In particular, new types of infrared sensors were being evaluated to track ICBM warheads, after the booster phase was cut off, and to feed the information to ABM systems. The early-warning satellites deployed at that time detected the launch of an ICBM from the infrared radiation emitted from its rocket as the missile rose above the earth's atmosphere. It was believed that if enemy ICBMs could be intercepted in mid-trajectory, before they could release decoys and other penetration aids, it would increase the probability of a successful defence. [13]

Both the USA and the Soviet Union were improving their strategic defensive systems against bombers and missiles. In the USA, a proposal for a modernised bomber defence system involved several new developments: an Airborne Warning and Control System (AWACS); the Continental US Over-The-Horizon Back-scatter Radar (CONUSOTHB) and satellite reconnaissance systems; a new nuclear surface-to-air missile (SAM-D); and an improved all-weather "air superiority" interceptor aircraft (F-15). The OTE-B radar was designed to detect enemy aircraft at great range to give maximum possible warning time, and AWACS was designed to track aircraft flying beneath the cover of other radars. With AWACS, command and control of interceptors was put in the air. It was claimed that the CONUSOTHB radar would locate and track enemy aircraft sufficiently accurately to allow AWACS aircraft to be dispatched to the general area in which their conventional long-range airborne radars would take over. [14]

Both the USA and the Soviet Union continued to develop means of defence against ballistic missiles. Extremely sophisticated high-powered solid-state, phased-array radars and very large capability highly complex data-handling equipment for ABM systems were under continuous development.

The Soviet Union was testing an improved ABM missile which could loiter – that is, once fired, it could coast out to a general intercept area, select its target, restrict and restart its engine and manoeuvre to destroy the enemy warheads. In the USA, planning continued on Hardsite, an alternative ABM system to Safeguard which would replace the Safeguard missile-site radars with a large number of smaller radars and use a variant of the Sprint missile anti-ballistic missiles* of very high acceleration – about 200 g – designed to intercept incoming ICBM warheads at low altitude for the terminal defence of Minuteman silos. In addition, Project Upstage, a new anti-ballistic missile with loitering capability and using an advanced propulsion system to give it sufficient manoeuvrability to intercept a manoeuvring re-entry vehicle after its motor had burnt out, was under development. Although this ABM could carry a nuclear warhead, it was claimed that it would be able to destroy a non-manoeuvring re-entry vehicle with a high-explosive warhead. The first test of an Upstage missile occurred in November 1971.

Further developments occurred in anti-satellite warfare. The Soviet Union achieved the first low-altitude satellite interception involving a target at an altitude of less than 160 miles. The Soviet Union appeared to have the capability to destroy low altitude reconnaissance satellites, as well as higher-altitude communications satellites. The verification procedures agreed to in SALT I, however, made it illegal to interfere with "national technical means" of verification, chiefly reconnaissance satellites.[15]

The strategic weapon programmes under way in the USA and the Soviet Union at the end of SALT I (May 1972), and new initiatives taken by both sides since then, now brought the two countries to a critical point in the strategic arms race. The deployment of the next generation of strategic weapons loomed close and new systems were already beginning to take shape in the plans of the weapon designers and in the arguments of the strategists.

As we have seen, the main trend in American and Soviet strategic weapon improvements had been towards qualitative

---

* A Sprint missile is also an anti-ballistic missile. It can be lowered into its underground silo prior to a launch.

improvements rather than quantitative increases. The significant exception was the continuing build-up of the Soviet sea-based force.

Despite the tendency of the number of strategic delivery vehicles to level out, significant quantitative expansions in nuclear forces were continuing, the most important being those which resulted from MIRVed missile warheads. American deployments of new MIRVed missiles (Minuteman III and Poseidon) between 1970 and 1977 produced a five-fold increase, from about 2,000 to about 10,000, in the number of independent nuclear warheads that could be delivered by the missile forces. The deployment of MIRVs had given the USA a very large quantitative lead over the Soviet Union in the number of deliverable nuclear warheads. However, since the Soviet Union was developing MIRV technology and had deployed a large number of land-based missiles, and missiles with a greater "throw-weight", it might close the gap and possibly exceed the USA in numbers of warheads.

But there were several areas of technology in which the USA had long held qualitative advantages that could not easily be incorporated into an overall qualitative comparison of forces. These included five important areas in which continuing advance had been made by the USA since SALT I. The first was missile accuracy, which provided the capability to destroy ICBMs in hardened silos. Minuteman III and Poseidon missiles had an accuracy of about one-quarter of a nautical mile, a two-fold improvement over the previous US land and sea-based missiles. The Soviet ICBMs and SLBMs were said to have an accuracy of about one mile. Programmes for improvements on the US side were clearly within reach, given the existing state of US technology, the latest systems under development in the Soviet Union had not shown any significant improvement in accuracy.[16]

Second, all 1,000 US ICBM silos were "hardened" (reinforced with structures of concrete and steel) to withstand nuclear blast overpressure of about 300 pounds per square inch. These silos were now being upgraded to withstand at least 900 pounds per square inch (psi) and possibly considerably more. In the case of the Soviet Union, only two thirds of the ICBM force was emplaced in silos capable of withstanding 300 psi overpressure: silos of other missiles, including the large SS-9s, were estimated to have a 100 psi resistance or, in the case of the older SS-7s and SS-8s, as little as 5 psi. The 91 latest Soviet silos were believed to have a 500 psi resistance, but there was little evidence of substantially increased hardening of the 1,527 earlier missile silos.

Third, a new US advantage in ICBMs, introduced within a year after SALT I, was the "remote retargeting" of missiles. Even earlier, the USA had some lead in this technology; it could pre-programme Minuteman II missiles with up to eight alternative targets, compared with the one or two targets which could be set in the earliest US ICBMs or in the existing Soviet missiles. For the Minuteman III, the number of alternative targets was essentially unlimited. This capability permitted more rapid and flexible replacement of first round missiles which failed to reach their targets.

Fourth, continuing advances had been made by the USA in strategic bomber range and payload (including advances in the B-I bomber). There had also been improvements in "escape time" and in the resistance of electronic equipment to the effects of radiation, which increased the survivability of the bomber fleet in the event of an attack by Soviet nuclear forces.

Finally, the USA had a considerable lead in the quietness and reliability of its strategic submarines. This increased their invulnerability to ASW operations. Instalment of "submarine quieting" equipment which would further improve the performance of the US strategic submarines was being undertaken at the same time as the fitting of the new MIRVed missile (Poseidon).[17]

A new qualitative advantage on the Soviet side had been observed since 1972. At the end of 1972, the Soviet Union tested its new SS-N8 SLBM with a range of 4,200 nautical miles – a vast improvement over its first ASLBMZ and one which gave the Soviet Union a considerable advantage over the USA in the SLBM range. However, when payload was taken into account, the Soviet advantage was less obvious. The "SS-98 was believed to carry about the same payload as the US Polaris A-3 and the Poseidon C-3, which had the same range as the Polaris A-3 (2,500 nautical miles), weighed three times as much as, and carried twice the payload of, the A-3. But a reduction in the larger payload of the Poseidon would give it an increased range. The potential range of the Poseidon had been kept secret, but published estimates ranged from more than 3,000 to 4,300 nautical miles.

Soviet testing of a new, large MIRVed ICBM with a relatively large number of warheads, four to six, suggested a potential to develop a land-based missile force with first-strike capabilities comparable with those being introduced in the USA. The exploitation of this potential would require the development of greatly improved missile accuracies, as well as the full use of the large potential throw-weight of the missiles. Over the long term, a capability to destroy virtually all of the US ICBM force might be evolved. But the Soviet lag in missile accuracy was such that it would probably require a considerable time to develop this potential, particularly in the view of the super-hardened silos under construction in the U.S.A. The US *programmes* to improve ICBM guidance, warhead yield and warhead numbers would permit a much more rapid US acquisition of the capability to destroy the entire Soviet land-based missile force with a first-strike.

The most dramatic development in US and Soviet strategic forces that had taken place since 1972 was in the land-based missiles, in particular the Soviet tests of three new ICBMs with MIRVed warheads and the proposed US programmes for the accuracy of its Minuteman missiles.

In all, four new ICBMs were observed on the testing grounds in 1973. These had been given the designations of SS-X-16 to SS-X-19. The SS-X-18, which was believed to be a replacement for the very large SS-9, had been tested with either five or six MIRV warheads of about one megaton each. The SS-X-17 and SS-X-19, believed to be competitive potential replacements for the SS-II, had been tested with smaller MIRV warheads – four per missile in the case of the SS-X-17 and six in the case of the SS-X-19. Multiple re-entry vehicle tests of the SS-X-16 had not been observed, although the warhead was believed to be a MIRV "bus". The SS-X-16 resembled the deployed SS-13 and differed from all of the other Soviet ICBMs in that it was powered by a solid rather than a liquid propellant. The advantage with solid propellant was that the ICBM could be launched much more rapidly. The SS-X-16 might, therefore, be a replacement for the SS-13. However, the SS-l3 had been deployed in small numbers (60 out of a total of 1,550 Soviet ICBMs); and the ZZ-X-16 might be a prototype mobile ICBM rather than an SS-13 replacement.

The new Soviet missiles were larger than the deployed ones and were believed to have greater "throw weight". The SS-X-18 was estimated to have 30 per cent more throw-weight than the SS-9, while the SS-X-17 and SS-X-19 were reported to have three to five times the throw-weight of the SS-11. In addition, the SS-X-17 and SS-X-19 were said to have warheads shaped for high-speed atmospheric re-entry, which would permit the development of considerably improved accuracy.

Two Soviet ICBM development programmes under way in late 1973 might indicate the further development and deployment of the new ICBMs, one of which involved MIRVs. Since advanced MIRV technology could provide pinpoint accuracy, this programme increased the likelihood that the new ICBMs would eventually be deployed in versions much more accurate than the existing ones. The second programme involved the development of "pop-up" techniques, in which missiles were ejected from their silos prior to the ignition of their motors. The use of these techniques permitted the emplacements of larger missiles in silos of a given size; and it appeared that the additional volume that could be gained would be more than sufficient to allow backfiring of the new larger ICBMs into existing silos.[18]

In the USA, the major ICBM activity since SALT I had been the continuation of the Minuteman III programme. But a number of specific US programmes were related to the ICBM programmes and performance. These programmes included two new projects to improve ICBM accuracy; the Minuteman III Guidance project and the MIRV accuracy portion of the ABRES (Advanced Ballistic Re-entry System) programme. In addition, the following projects were under way: one to increase the numbers of MIRVs deployment on Minuteman III missiles and another to increase the yield of the individual warheads; continued development of the Missile Performance Measurement System (MPMS), which provided better data on missile operation during testing and, thus, permitted improvements; continuation of work on the general ABRES project, and further development of the evasion capabilities of MIRVs. Moreover, a project to develop a new ICBM had been proposed. If this was approved, both mobile land-based and airborne launching platforms would be considered.

The conversion of thirty-one of the forty-one US strategic submarines from Polaris missiles, with single warheads or three MIRVed warheads, to Poseidon missiles, capable of carrying ten to fourteen MIRVed warheads, had continued. Twenty-four submarines had been converted by early 1974. There had been several postponements in the conversion schedule, which ran to mid-1977. When completed, the number of independently targetable warheads carried by the Polaris/Poseidon fleet would have increased from 656 to an estimated 5,120.[19]

Work on a new SLBM, the C-4 Trident, had been going on and funds for the first Trident submarine, which was to carry twenty-four ballistic missiles, had been approved. It was originally planned that the Trident missile should be initially deployed in existing ballistic submarines (Lafayette class), in advance of the availability of the Trident submarine. However, in the spring of 1973, it was announced that development of the missile could be extended for another year so that the initial operating date, now 1978, would coincide with that of the new submarine and, meanwhile, plans for backfitting SLBM fleet were suspended.

Yet another strategic submarine had been proposed. This vessel would carry sixteen of the new Trident missiles, would be much smaller than the Trident submarine and would have a very quiet water-cooled reactor of a new type developed for the experimental *Narwhal* submarine. With a smaller size and quiet propulsion system, the proposed new submarine would be even quieter than the Trident and, therefore, more invulnerable to the Soviet ASW.[20]

Two other new US SLBM projects had been proposed: one to increase the accuracy of existing SLBMs and the other to develop a MIRV for the Trident missile. A new navigation satellite system called the Global Positioning System (GPS) was under development to provide a highly accurate (within tens of feet) global positioning capability. This system, for which the first launch was to take place in 1977, and limited global capability to be achieved by 1981, would help increase the accuracy of SLBMs.

The major development in Soviet sea-based strategic forces since 1972 was the testing of the new longer-range SS-N8 SLBM, followed by the deployment of this missile in new D class submarines. Construction of the earlier Y class submarines, with sixteen SS-N-6 missiles, as well as the new D class, with twelve SS-N-8s, had continued at the rate of five to six a year, with existing construction apparently devoted entirely to the D class. According to US defence officials, a total of 33 Y class ships had been built. The remaining 18 or 19 vessels launched or under construction were of D class.

The 1974 ABM Treaty restricted the USA and the Soviet Union to 100 ABM launchers at one site, but both powers continued to work on more advanced ABM technology. No new ABM deployments had been observed in the Soviet Union since the time of the SALT I agreements, and the Soviet Union still had 64 ABM launchers located in four groups around Moscow. The USA had continued with the deployment of 100 ABM launchers (30 for the longer-range Spartan missile and 70 for the shorter-range Sprint) around the Grand Forks, North Dakota, Minuteman ICBM sites. The US ABM system was scheduled to be fully operational in June 1975. The alternative ABM system, Hardsite (now called Site Defence) remained under development.

The development of the B-1 strategic bomber was one of the major US strategic weapon projects. If the B-1 was procured, an order of 241 was planned. The development cost of $2.8 billion and projected average unit price of $56 million made it the most expensive military aircraft project ever undertaken. The rationale for the development of the B-1 was to assure penetration of the Soviet air defence system. The number of surface-to-air missiles deployed in the Soviet Union had apparently declined slightly

. but remained very large (on the order of 9,000 to 10,000). The majority of these missiles were standard Soviet anti-aircraft missiles (SA-2 and SA-3) against which the United States had developed effective electronic countermeasures. Several other strategic weapon programmes in addition to the B-1 had, however, also been pursued by the USA as a counter to these defences. Two of these were the SRAM (Short-Range Attack Missile) and the SCAD (Subsonic Cruise Armed Decoy) programmes.[21]

The production of the full complement of 1,500 SRAMs (including about 400 reserve missiles) for B-52 and FB-III bombers was expected to be completed in late 1975. Additional procurement of SRAMs for deployment on the B-1 was expected, if the B-1 was approved for production, and attempts were now being made to find ways of keeping the production line open in the one-to-two-year interval before the B-1 production decision. SRAM was intended for use both as a defence suppression weapon – striking surface-to-air missiles, air-defence radars, and so on, to permit bomber penetration – and as a stand-off weapon, allowing the aircraft to attack targets located near the enemy's border without crossing the air-defence perimeter.

Development of the SCAD, which was also to have been deployed on B-62 bombers, was suddenly terminated in mid-1973. One explanation given was that the projected unit cost of the weapons ($1.2 million) was too high. But it had also been suggested that the increase in the total programme cost (estimated at $1.2 billion) as well as in the capability which this weapon could be expected to add to the B-52 was so great as to jeopardise support for the development of the B-1. The purpose of SCAD a missile with a reported range over 500 kilometres was to divert air-defence forces from the bomber aircraft by simulating the radar characteristics of the aircraft. In addition, armed versions of the missile would attack certain targets.[22]

At the time when the SCAD programme was terminated, increased attention was being given in the USA to the possible development of naval strategic cruise missiles and it was speculated that all future strategic cruise missile development would be ship or submarine launched types. However, support had been requested for an Air Launched Cruise Missile (ALCM) to be delivered by a modified tanker-type aircraft and/or possibly by the B-1, which might be a replacement for SCAD. No significant work on strategic bombers was under way in the Soviet Union. The supersonic bomber Backfire was in series production by early 1974, but it was incapable of intercontinental missions without air refuelling and it did not appear to be intended primarily for a strategic role.

The lack of a significant Soviet strategic bomber force had led to a gradual but steady decline in US air defence systems. The number of fighter-interceptor squadrons committed to continental US air defence declined from 40 in the mid-1964 to 14 in 1970 to 11 in 1972. The figure scheduled for mid-1976 was six. The number of air defence missile batteries had decreased from 107 to 40 to 21, and these batteries were to be entirely phased out by mid-1975. There had also been a slow-down of work on the SAM-D air-defence surface-to-air-missile system, which was now being oriented more towards tactical deployment. And the AWACS was being considered for a tactical as well as a strategic role.

In summary, the strategic nuclear forces of the United States under the SALT II agreement would consist of 450 Minuteman II, 550 Minutemen III, 31 Poseidon submarines, and 10 Trident submarines and a force of B-1 strategic bombers. Each Poseidon submarine would carry 16 MIRVed missiles and each Trident 24 MIRVed missiles, giving the US a total of 1,286 MIRVed missiles capable of delivering nearly 9,000 warheads. The strategic bomber force would almost double this number. The Soviet Union would deploy 300 SS-X-18 and 1,000 SS-X-17 or SS-X-19 missiles, all MIRVed, together with 33 Y class submarines and 27 D class submarines. Each Y class submarine would carry 16 missiles and each D class submarine 12 missiles. If the Soviet Union deploys its SLBMs it would have to deploy fewer land-based MIRVs.[23]

III

Arms control negotiations failed to halt the arms race between the United States and the Soviet Union, let alone lead to nuclear disarmament. It was now realised by all that the pace of arms control negotiations was outstripped by the rate of innovation in military technology and that an approach to disarmament other than a piecemeal approach was needed increasingly. It was believed that an approach in which each measure was part of an agreed plan – a comprehensive approach – might be more successful than the piecemeal arms control approach.

One way of involving all countries in an effort to solve such a comprehensive approach would be through a world disarmament conference. The subject of disarmament and the idea of such a conference had long been considered by the United Nations. But there had been opposition to a world disarmament conference. The Soviet Union strongly opposed a world conference, but some other important countries did not. China, for example, demanded that all nuclear weapon countries, particularly the Soviet Union and the United States, should first pledge that they would never be the first to use nuclear weapons and would never use them against non-nuclear weapon countries and in nuclear free zones. The United States argued that a world disarmament conference might be useful at the right time; but because of political disagreements, it would now hinder rather than assist arms control and disarmament efforts.

Given the opposition to a world conference and given the support of the non-aligned countries for such a conference, UN members opted for a Special Session of the General Assembly on disarmament. The resolution was unanimously adopted on December 24, 1976.

The Soviet Union and the other socialist countries of Eastern Europe did not vote against the resolution as they regarded it as a mere step, albeit an important one, towards a world disarmament conference. The Special Session, these countries rightly argued, provided an opportunity to discuss approaches to disarmament, to identify priorities, and to decide on, and make preparations for an eventual world disarmament conference. Needless to say, nothing came out of the General Assembly's resolution and a world disarmament conference never took place.

Meanwhile, there had been much debate, particularly in Europe, about the consequences of the deployment by NATO of enhanced radiation reduced blast nuclear weapons (the so-called neutron bombs). These very low yield nuclear weapons, normally to be used on the battlefield against men in armoured vehicles, were designed to incapacitate and kill mainly by ionizing radiation, with relative small blast and heat effects. The intense interest of the public in these weapons might have been stimulated by the general feeling of abhorrence towards ionizing radiation.

If enhanced radiation weapons were deployed, however, the greatest significance of this event might be that it was another indication of the growing influence of those who believed that a nuclear war could be fought and won. Another important aspect of the deployment of these weapons was that it might encourage the proliferation of nuclear weapons to countries which did not have them. This danger had been admitted by the White House.[24] In the Arms Control Impact Statement about enhanced radiation weapons, sent to the US Senate by the National Security Council, it was said that some governments might couple a decision to deploy enhanced-radiation weapons with perceptions that US doctrine had changed to make the use of nuclear weapons more likely in a tactical situation. Such a coupling, the statement went on, could have an adverse effect on US efforts to prevent further nuclear proliferation.

The gap between conventional and nuclear weapons in terms of explosive power might be narrowed by the deployment of the new types of conventional weapons. The attention given to nuclear weapons tended to obscure the considerable advances being made in conventional weapons. One such weapon was the fuel-air-explosive (FAE). A typical FAE (as used in Vietnam to detonate mines over areas greater than 700 square metres) contained highly volatile ethylene oxide, which burned spontaneously without oxygen. An FAE bomb produced a cloud of ethylene oxide vapour (typically about 15 metres across and 2 or 3 metres high), which was detonated by a delayed action igniter, normally about 150 milliseconds after impact with the ground.

The blast-wave effect of an FAE like ethylene oxide was equivalent weight for weight, to the explosive effect of several times as much TNT. Efforts were aimed at substantially increasing the TNT equivalent of fuel-air-explosives. They would then make formidable warheads for cruise missiles. For example, if a 100 kg FAE warhead was made equivalent to a ton of TNT, a helicopter-borne dispenser containing, say, 24.50 kg FAE bombs could produce the same blast effects as 12 tons of TNT. Thus, by using FAEs it is quite feasible to produce much larger blast-ware effect.[25]

It was unlikely that Soviet-American efforts to negotiate a SALT II agreement would satisfy the advocates of nuclear disarmament. It was predicted that a new SALT II Treaty would limit the total number of strategic bombers, ICBMs and SLBMs to between 2,160 and 2,250 each for the United States and the Soviet Union respectively. Within this limit, there might be a limit of 1,320 on the total number of ballistic missiles equipped with MIRVs and bombers armed with cruise missiles. The new agreement might limit the number of MIRVed land-based ICBMs and SLBMs to between 1,200 and 1,250. A further limit of 820 might be placed on land-based ICBMs. It seemed that the Soviet Union might be allowed 308 heavy ICBMs of the SS-18 type.

A three-year protocol might limit the range of air-launched cruise missiles to 2,500 kilometres and of ground-and-sea-launched cruise missiles to 600 kilometres. The deployment of mobile ICBM launchers and the flight-testing of ICBMs from such launchers might be banned. And the flight-testing and deployment of new types of ballistic missiles might be limited.[26]

The United States admitted to having 1,710 ballistic missiles (1,054 ICBMs and 656 SLBMs) of which 1,046 (550 ICBMs and 496 SLBMs) were MIRVed. About 300 B-52s were assigned strategic roles (although 478 B-52s existed). As of mid-1977, the Soviet Union was thought to have 2,326 ballistic missiles (1,477 ICBMs and 849 SLBMs) of which up to 230 ICBMs were

MIRVed. Perhaps 140 Soviet long-range bombers were assigned strategic roles. The Soviet Union appeared to be scrapping about 100 old ICBMs (SS-7s and SS-8s).

Although the United States was developing the MX ICBM, it had officially announced no plans to increase the number of its MIRVed ICBMs above the existing level of 550. The first Trident strategic nuclear submarine carrying 24 SLBMs was scheduled to be operational in 1981. Others might become operational at the rate of four every three years.[27] The development of air-launched cruise missiles was planned to begin in 1980, perhaps at the rate of about 35 per month. Therefore, 130 B-52Gs could be armed with 20 missiles each by 1985. The Soviet Union has deployed MIRVs over the past five years at an average rate of about 60 per year, although in a peak year (1974), the number deployed was double this. The Soviet Union might, therefore, find it difficult to increase its MIRVed ICBM force from 230 to 800 by 1985.

According to existing deployment plans, by 1985, the United States, for example, would probably have 550 MIRVed ICBMs, 496 MIRVed SLBMs on 31 Poseidon nuclear submarines, 144 MIRVed SLBMs on six Trident submarines and 130 B-52G bombers each equipped with 20 cruise missiles. These strategic delivery systems could deliver about 10,000 nuclear warheads – 2,600 by cruise missiles, about 1,600 by land-based ICBMs and about 6,400 by SLBMs. Single warhead ICBMs, the remaining SLBMs and the other strategic bombers could deliver an additional 4,000 warheads. American ICBMs, SLBMs and strategic bombers deployed in mid-1977 could deliver about 12,000 US warheads. Thus the total of 14,600 strategic nuclear warheads which might be developed by the mid-1980s still represented an increase in the US nuclear arsenal.

A SALT II Treaty, similar to the one which the United States and the Soviet Union were now reported to be considering, would not significantly affect quantitative increase in the US nuclear arsenal, as was being planned. Similarly, the size of the Soviet nuclear arsenal was likely to increase considerably. But qualitative improvements in nuclear warheads were likely to be more destabilising than quantitative increases in nuclear arsenals. The latter had for a long time been so huge as to make further increases virtually meaningless, at least from the military and strategic points of view. The major test of SALT would, therefore, be its effect on the qualitative aspects of the nuclear arms race.[28]

In this connection, it may be pointed out that the cruise missiles had considerable potential as strategic nuclear delivery systems for smaller countries. Britain and France, for example, might see these missiles as potential cheap replacements for their strategic nuclear weapons as these became obsolete in the 1980s. The Federal Republic of Germany might look to cruise missiles (possibly armed with conventional warheads) as cheap alternatives to combat aircraft. A cruise missile would cost about $750,000; a Tornado combat aircraft would cost about $20 million.[29]

Most industrialised countries (and perhaps some Third World ones too) were technically capable of producing cruise missiles indigenously. But what was often lacking was the precise knowledge of the coordinates of potential targets and accurate information about the flight path to navigate the missiles to these coordinates with the full effectiveness of the missile's guidance system. The need for such information could stimulate a proliferation of military satellite programmes.

The spread of cruise missiles, particularly among NATO countries, could have far-reaching effects. The Soviet Union would probably react strongly to the proliferation of these weapons, particularly if the Federal Republic of Germany was involved. The Soviet Union would also argue that this would make arms control negotiations more difficult, particularly the European mutual force reduction talks and the SALT negotiations. If cruise missiles did proliferate widely, they might turn out to be the most far-reaching military technological development ever. In that case one could expect that improved versions of cruise missiles would be developed in rapid succession.[30]

During 1977, efforts to establish an effective non-proliferation regime continued. Most now realised that the proliferation problem required a political rather than technical solution. In April 1977,

President Carter announced his policy to slow down the rate at which nuclear weapons might spread. This involved deferring indefinitely the commercial reprocessing of spent reactor fuel and the recycling of plutonium. Greater priority was to be given to breeder reactor designs not dependent on plutonium for fuel, and the commercial use of breeders was to be deferred indefinitely. The President hoped that other countries would follow his lead, but some countries that were most advanced in nuclear technology did not support his plan. Many of these countries were interested in using plutonium as a nuclear fuel. Reprocessing plants of a commercial size existed in Belgium, France, the Federal Republic of Germany, India, Japan, the United States and the Soviet Union. New commercial-scale plants were planned by France, the Federal Republic of Germany, Pakistan and Britain. Special facilities for the reprocessing of breeder reactor fuels were in operation in France, the Federal Republic of Germany and Britain, and were planned by India. Four countries – the Federal Republic of Germany, France, the Soviet Union and Britain — operated liquid metal fast-breeder reactors with outputs greater than 20 megawatts (electrical). India, Italy and Japan were also developing the technology.

When a country had a large financial stake in developing a plutonium economy, it was often unwilling to change its policy to cooperate in international efforts to prevent the proliferation of nuclear weapons. Nevertheless, since mid-1975, a group of suppliers (actual and potential) of nuclear equipment and material had been trying to establish a set of rules to minimise the risk of the diversion of imported nuclear material and equipment for weapon purposes. [31]

In September 1977, the "London Club" of nuclear exporters agreed on certain guidelines to be followed in dealing with importers. Some members had adopted a more restrictive nuclear exporting policy than others. Canada and Sweden, among others, would export nuclear equipment, materials and technology only to those countries which either had ratified the Non-Proliferation Treaty (NPT) or agreed to accept safeguards on all their nuclear facilities (whether imported or indigenously constructed). The Club's Guidelines required safeguards only on imported nuclear equipment and materials. This was a major weakness of the guidelines and one which a number of members found very hard to accept.

The fact that countries outside the NPT were subject to less stringent safeguards than those in it was an absurdity. The very existence of the London Club could, however, be seen as an admission of the failure of the NPT as an effective non-proliferation measure. But the London Club Guidelines did include new requirements. Provisions for safeguarding heavy water production facilities and copies of transferred technology for uranium enrichment reactor fuel reprocessing and heavy water production were, for example, included. Members must also agree on levels of physical protection for certain nuclear materials and facilities aimed at preventing the theft of fissionable material. And IAEA (International Atomic Energy Agency) safeguards must be applied to certain nuclear plants built by using design information obtained directly from a member. [32]

It was at the same time, that is, ten years after the first artificial Earth Satellite was launched, that the Outer Space Treaty came into force. Some hoped that this treaty would make outer space a zone of peace. But, in fact, the treaty had done little to check the number of military satellites. About 75 per cent of all satellites launched had military uses. During 1977, 433 satellites were launched, and of these 95 were military satellites (82 belonging to the Soviet Union, 12 to the United States and one to NATO). The number of US satellites was relatively small because they had longer lives than Soviet ones.

Military satellites had also been launched by China, France and Britain. Military satellite missions included reconnaissance, navigation, tactical and strategic communications, geodesy, early warning of attack and meteorology. Interrupter/destructor satellites had probably been tested by the Soviet Union. Methods for "killing" satellites were also being investigated by the United States.

Satellites undoubtedly played a useful role in verifying arms control agreements, such as SALT. And some of their reconnaissance activities might contribute to international security. Reconnaissance satellites might have confirmed, in 1977, preparation by South Africa for a nuclear test, and monitored an area in Zaire being used by the Federal Republic of Germany as a rocket test-and-launch site. Nevertheless, the continuing militarisation of space was a danger to international peace.[33]

In March 1977, the Unites States proposed to the Soviet Union an agreement to ban the arming and destruction of each other's satellites. The Soviet Union appeared to have responded favourably. Although an agreement to this type would eliminate only part of the arms race in space, it was agreed that it would be a step in the right direction. Moreover, if launching of space satellites was stopped, it would save a huge amount of money in both the United States and the Soviet Union. According to SIPRI (Stockholm International Peace Research Institute) estimates, global military spending amounted about $400 billion in a year. Since World War II, the trend had been for military expenditure to double in each decade. If measured in constant prices, to take inflation into account, it doubled in about 20 years. If this trend continued, the world would spend about $10 trillion (one trillion is equal to a million million) by the turn of the century. This sum was about one-half of the US Gross Domestic Product (GDP) and about equal to that of the Soviet Union and Japan put together. For some it was hard to imagine that military spending would really reach that level. But it was equally hard to see what would stop it.

The amount spent worldwide on military activities was so huge, not far off one million dollars a minute, as to be of a magnitude hard to grasp. But a few comparisons might help to put it into perspective. Governments spent half as much on education and twice as much was spent on health. Yet, about 1,500 million people (nearly 10 per cent of the world's population) had no effective medical services; nearly 3,000 million lived in countries which had more than 1,000 inhabitants per doctor; nearly 3,000 million people lacked access to safe water; about 750,000 died each month from water-borne diseases; nearly 1,000 million people were seriously undernourished; nearly 2,000 million had life expectancy of less than 60 years, usually less than 50 years; about 1,000 million are illiterate, including about 70 per cent of the population of Africa, and nearly 550 million children under 14 did not attend school.[34]

World military expenditure was about double the GDP of all of Africa, about equal to that of Latin America, and about three-quarters of that of all of Asia (except Japan). In other words, it was about 40 per cent of the GDP of the Third World in which over 70 per cent of the world's population lived. Perhaps, more significantly, world military spending was about 30 times the total official development assistance given by the developed to the under-developed countries.

An important characteristic of world military spending was that the proportion spent by Third World countries was steadily increasing: the share spent by these countries, excluding China, increased from about 6 per cent in 1967 to about 15 per cent in 1977. The share spent by the developed countries had fallen from 84 per cent in 1967 to 75 per cent in 1977.[35] Within the Third World, there were large variations in per capita military spending between regions. The Middle East, which accounted for about one-third of total military expenditures by the Third World, had tripled its military spending during 1970-77. Africa was another area in which military expenditure was increasing relatively rapidly, though not as rapidly as in the Middle East.

We know too little about the economic and social consequences of these expenditures to make general statements about them. But there cannot be any doubt that a significant reduction in military expenditures could help the development of many individual Third World countries. Moreover, a significant increase in the flow of economic aid from the developed countries to the Third World was unlikely unless the military budgets of the developed countries were reduced. There was usually no other major source of official development funds.

Large military expenditures are said to cause a reduction in world trade and contribute to inflation. By so contributing to the widening of the gap between rich and poor countries, high levels of military spending are likely to erode the very security that they were meant to provide. Many economists forecast that a new and serious economic recession might hit the Western industrialised countries in the 1980s. This recession which could lead to much social unrest, and political turmoil might, so it was said, be avoided (or at least lessened) by sharply reduced military spending.

But the most serious waste of resources might not be the financial waste, serious though it was, but the waste of talent involved in military activities. Talent is man's most valuable resource, particularly as far as development is concerned. The number of scientists employed by the military was especially disturbing. Of the world's physical and engineering scientists who worked in research and development (R & D), more than half worked full-time on military R & D. If these scientists devoted themselves to peaceful rather than military pursuits, there could be a dramatic improvement in global living conditions.[36]

The way in which military money was spent to buy weapons abroad was particularly disturbing. In fact, the worldwide spread of the most modern weapons by the international arms trade was dangerous to world security as was the Soviet-American arms race and the spread of the capability to produce nuclear weapons.

Moreover, nearly all of the conflicts since World War II had been in the Third World and the bulk of the weapons used had been acquired through the arms trade. About 75 per cent of the trade in major weapons – armoured vehicles, aircraft, ships and missiles – was with the Third World. This had increased more than 15 fold between 1960 and 1970. During the 1970s, it had increased at an annual rate of 15 per cent. In the 1950s, the weapons transferred to the Third World countries were mostly second-hand. But since the mid-1960s, any importer willing to pay the price was likely to find a seller of even the most sophisticated weapons. For example, long-range nuclear-capable tactical ground-to-ground missiles like the US Lance and the Soviet Scud, had been sold to the Third World countries.

According to SIPRI valuations, the four main suppliers of major weapons to the Third World were the United States, the Soviet Union, the United Kingdom and France. These countries together supplied about 90 per cent of the major weapons sold to the Third

World between 1970 and 1977. The United States supplied 38 per cent, the Soviet Union 34 per cent, and the United Kingdom and France 9 per cent each. The Middle East was by far the largest importing region; during the 1970s, it received more than half of the major weapons transferred to the Third World. [37]

But some Third World countries were themselves beginning to supply major weapons to other Third World countries. Although the total value of the arms involved was still small, the fact that the trade between these countries was expanding was one more indication that the world was becoming increasingly militarised. The Third World countries which had supplied major weapons were: Abu Dhabi, Argentina, Brazil, Cuba, Chile, Egypt, Ivory Coast, Jordan, Libya, Malaysia, Saudi Arabia, Singapore and South Africa. Other countries which started to supply weapons since the late 1970s were: Gabon, India, Iran, Iraq and Israel.

Limiting the transfer of conventional arms was a difficult problem mainly because of the large profits earned in the defence industries, the ready and expanding market for weapons, the conflicting political interests of the Great Powers in specific regions, and the interests of the allies of the Great Powers. Although no substantial negotiations on controlling the international arms trade had yet begun, some supplier governments were anxious about the effects of this trade. And some importing countries were beginning to regret the consequences of buying sophisticated military equipment, including the need for many military advisers and the use of scarce resources urgently needed for civilian purposes.

Yet another indication of the increasing militarisation of the planet was that more and more countries, particularly in the Third World, were producing their own weapons – indigenously designed under licence, or in cooperation with other countries. Argentina, Brazil, Colombia, Egypt, India, Indonesia, Iran, Israel, North Korea, South Korea, Mexico, Pakistan, Peru, the Philippines, Singapore, South Africa, Taiwan and Venezuela were the Third World countries producing one or more types of major weapons – aircraft, armoured vehicles, missiles and ships. If smaller weapons were included, the list would, of course, be even longer.

The industrialised countries producing major weapons were: Australia, Austria, Belgium, Canada, China, Czechoslovakia, the Democratic Republic of Germany, Denmark, the Federal Republic of Germany, Finland, France, Hungary, Italy, Japan, the Netherlands, New Zealand, Norway, Poland, Romania, the Soviet Union, Spain, Sweden, Switzerland, Turkey, the United Kingdom, the United States and Yugoslavia. The increasing number of countries producing arms might be even more disturbing than the arms trade, although it received far less attention. After all, if weapons were not produced they could not be traded.[38] As regards developing countries, diversion of resources to military purposes seriously impeded their economic and social development.

The UN Special Session on Disarmament was likely to seek links between disarmament and development. Not surprisingly, the enormous gap between the money spent on armaments and that transferred to the Third World as official development assistance had stimulated attempts to find such links. In its crudest (and most naive) form the idea was that if the resources saved by disarmament in the industrialised countries were all given to the Third World, the problem of development would be largely solved, at least in the medium or long term. It was often forgotten that some underdeveloped countries themselves used significant, and often rapidly increasing, resources for military activities. Perhaps these countries should have noted the post-war experience of Japan and the Federal Republic of Germany, among others, which indicated that countries with relatively small military budgets performed better economically than countries which spent a relatively large amount on armaments.

The idea of a link between disarmament and development had been encouraged, for example, by the UN report on the economic and social consequences of the arms race, published in August 1977, which concluded: "The arms race with its economic costs and social and political effects, nationally and internationally, constitutes an important obstacle to effective progress ... (on) the problem of development and the associated task of establishing a new international economic order ... Development at an acceptable rate would be hard, if not impossible, to reconcile with a continuation of the arms race (and) disarmament should be so designed that the close connection between disarmament and development gets full recognition."[39]

According to the report, the transfer to development assistance of just 5 per cent of the existing military budgets of the industrialised countries would provide the target set by the International Development Strategy for the 1970s (0.7 per cent of the GNP).

However, one should be cautious in linking disarmament too strongly with development. For one thing, a situation should not be created in which accelerated development was dependent upon the achievement of disarmament. The prospect of a significant "disarmament dividend" could make even more difficult the initiation of the major effort needed just to prevent a further increase in the per capita income gap between the rich and poor countries, let alone reduce this gap. But, if disarmament and development were to be linked in any systematic way, the first priority must be much more knowledge of the economic and social consequences of armaments and disarmament. We know virtually nothing about these.[40]

Perhaps the biggest single obstacle to disarmament was the popular fear that significant disarmament would cause more unemployment and falling living standards. Thus, the need was clear for a serious study of how the resources used for armaments could be diverted for peaceful purposes, including development.

Negotiations at the Geneva-based Conference of the Committee on Disarmament (CCD), the main international forum for arms control and disarmament discussions, produced no treaties in 1977. Perhaps spurred on by the desirability of presenting some concrete results to the UN Special Session, there were trilateral negotiations among the United States, the Soviet Union and the UK on a ban on chemical weapons. There were also discussions between the United States and the Soviet Union about banning radiological weapons. These weapons had not as yet been produced nor was there any serious interest in them, and, therefore, their prohibition would hardly be significant.

There was a widespread belief that unless the CCD could present a draft treaty banning either nuclear tests or chemical weapons to the Special Session it would have lost its credibility, which was already low, as a negotiating body. And it seemed that a comprehensive test ban was more likely than a chemical weapon treaty.

The trilateral negotiations on a comprehensive test ban, which began in the summer of 1977, had to deal with the problems of verification, peaceful nuclear explosions, and when the treaty should enter into force. It appeared that the problem of verification caused less difficulty than that of peaceful nuclear explosions. But General Secretary Brezhnev indicated in a speech that the Soviet Union would accept a moratorium on peaceful nuclear explosions. Moreover, the Soviet Union now seemed willing to agree that a comprehensive test ban treaty could enter into force without ratification by all five nuclear-weapons powers.

The lack of real progress at the CCD, and the fact that member countries were repeatedly faced with ready-made draft treaties prepared bilaterally by the United States and the Soviet Union – the substance of which they could not significantly influence – were causes of considerable criticism and unrest, especially among the small powers at the CCD.

If the CCD was to function as a truly multinational negotiating body, the superpowers need to stop excluding other members until the late stages of negotiations. The dominating role they played was also emphasised by their co-chairmanship of the CCD. Unless this situation changed France and China were unlikely to participate in the Committee. The absence of these two nuclear weapon powers would seriously weaken the CCD.

The tens of thousands of nuclear weapons in the world's arsenal in the late Seventies probably had a total explosive power equivalent to that of about one million Hiroshima type atomic bombs. If all of these weapons were used, or even a significant fraction of them, the consequences would be unimaginable. Most of the cities of the Northern Hemisphere would be destroyed in a flash, and the bulk of their inhabitants killed instantly. Many of the rural inhabitants would soon die from the effects of radiation from radioactive fallout, as would millions in other regions of the world.

And then there would be the aftereffects of a nuclear world war. These were unpredictable. Nobody knew what global climatic change would be induced by such a war. Nobody knew what damages would be done to the ozone layer, the stratosphere shield which helps to protect life on earth from excess ultraviolet radiation. The long-term consequences of the genetic damage done to the human race by the radiation from the resulting worldwide radioactive fallout were also unknown. The genetic damage could, over many generations, decimate the human race.

A nuclear world war was probably most likely to occur, not as a direct attack of one Great Power on the other, but because of the escalation of a conflict in some other region. It was generally believed that the more nuclear weapon powers there were, the more likely such escalation becomes. The probability of the involvement of the Great Powers in the conflicts of others increased if the countries involved in the fighting depended on these countries for their weapons.

For these reasons, control of nuclear weapons proliferation and of the arms race and trade, was almost, if not equally as urgent, as the control of the Soviet-American nuclear arms race. It was hoped that the UN General Assembly Special Session on Disarmament would really achieve progress in controlling these activities. Failure to do so was likely to set back the prospects for disarmament for a long time to come.

IV

In the mid-1970s, the strategic competition between the United States and the Soviet Union had been somewhat transformed. From a clear American superiority, by all criteria of measurement, the balance had tilted to an increasingly precarious parity. A net American inferiority in all dimensions of capability was projected by 1985. At the same time, the strategic nuclear arsenals of both the Soviet Union and the United States had increased greatly in power, and expenditures on strategic forces and their ancillaries had grown considerably. All these changes had taken place under the aegis of an American strategic policy dominated by arms-control objectives. Clearly something must be very wrong with the pursuit of arms control, especially in the SALT. But what?

Whatever was wrong with arms control, it was not the essential theory, whose logic was perfectly sound.

Imagine a world of two identical countries, X and Y, whose array of forces was also identical. Let X make preparations to build a new weapon, say, a bomber. Faced with an emerging bomber force in X, the leaders of Y could choose between two instruments of strategic state craft – force-building or arms control. The force-building response was defensive; in this case, it would mean developing fighters and anti-aircraft weapons capable of intercepting the new bombers. The other response would be competitive; country Y could build a bomber force of its own (or some other offensive force) to offset whatever political or military gains X hoped to achieve with its new bomber force.

As Y reacted to X and vice versa, an additional and purely mechanical source of tension would arise between the two countries, even if each had good information about the actions of the other – so that surprises and overreactions could be avoided. If, for example, Y's progress in building air defences lagged behind X's bomber effort, Y would be faced with an interval of vulnerability. At worst, it might be tempted to launch a preventive attack to destroy X's nascent bomber force before it became ready to operate. Even less drastic alternatives, such as the accelerated deployment of bombers or other offensive weapons to offset by competition what could not be negated by defence, would open new channels of competition which would unfailingly generate their own instabilities. If the information that each side had about the other was not good, with odd glimpses of truth or falsehood dimly perceived through walls of secrecy, the action and reaction could be altogether more dangerous. But this case was irrelevant here, since without good information, arms control was not feasible either.

Even if no preventive war broke out, the best result that the force-building response could yield, was that the two countries would acquire a matched set of bombers and anti-bomber defence. While they were reaching this new equilibrium, scarce resources would have been expended, new weapons would have come into existence to add to the violence of an eventual war, and the military and military-industrial interests in each country would have been strengthened, thus making it much more likely that there would be yet more military competition between X and Y. And when the new offensive and defensive weapons were fully deployed, neither country would have gained any lasting advantage in physical security or political power. Moreover, any temporary advantage gained by either along the way would have entitled a corresponding risk of conflict, generated precisely by the imbalance which yielded that advantage in the first place.

The force-building approach guaranteed these grim results, while also increasing the risk of war. Arms control, by contrast, offered the possibility of a zero-cost and low-risk solution to the same predicament.

Provided with early information of X's bomber-building intentions, let Y open negotiations. Assuming that the leaders of X were rational, and assuming further that they did not believe that Y would react to their bomber effort with equivalent force-building of their own, the leaders of both X and Y should be able to agree in principle that the best course for both would be to foreclose the new channel of competition. At this point, matters could proceed to detailed technical negotiations, in order to agree on a precise description of the bombers to be prohibited, and to define the means of inspection which would be used by both sides to verify compliance. If the difficulties of drafting could be overcome, and mutually acceptable verification arrangements could be made, both sides could avoid the costs of building new forces, as well as the risks they generated. The two countries would also have averted a further increase in the overall destructive potential of the military force that any war might unleash, and, moreover, they would have prevented an increase in the role of the military and industrial interests of each society.

The same happy result might be achieved without any actual negotiations, through unilateral or tacit arms control. For example, country X might be initiating its bomber programme in reaction to some tentative weapons-building plans being discussed in Y. If so, Y might pursue unilateral arms control by formally renouncing any intention of acquiring weapons being considered, so long as X exercised similar restraint. Or else, to avoid provoking X with an offer of mutual restraint that could easily be misinterpreted as a polite ultimatum, Y might practise tacit as well as unilateral arms control by demonstratively abandoning plans to build the weapons which were triggering X's bomber effort, while leaving the condition of its restraint implicit.

To some ears, unilateral arms control might have defeatist connotations, but whether arms control was negotiated or unilateral, declared or tacit, was in fact of little consequence; the different methods could yield exactly the same beneficial results.

In this elementary and abstract formulation of national strategy, the merits of arms control were compelling. As compared to force-building, it offered a fully equivalent degree of security, and indeed a higher degree of security in many cases, at a much lower risk of instability and war, at no cost, without any increase in the ultimate destructive potential of war arsenals, and also without the deformations of society caused by the artificial growth of military-industrial interests. Whatever was wrong with arms control, then, it was clearly not its logic.

To be sure, this model of the basic theory was highly artificial, assuming, as it did, only two identical countries, with identical weapons-building capabilities and good information. When these artificial assumptions were waived, practical obstacles arose.

For example, once the real world of many powers was accepted into the model, the scope of arms control might diminish. Country X might be deploying its bombers against country Z rather than against country Y; as far as Y was concerned, the threat to its security was real nonetheless, but in this case it could not hope to dispose of the problem by negotiating a bilateral arms-limitation agreement with X, and still less could it hope to dissuade X by unilateral restraint and tacit bargaining. There did remain the possibility of multilateral arms control, with Z being brought in along with X and Y, but that would complicate matters severely, and might fail (even with ample goodwill all around) simply because of the sequence and phasing of the various force-building efforts. If, for instance, X was building its bombers in response to some effort by Z, undertaken by Z in the first place to react against the weapons being deployed by yet another country, by the time Y moved to negotiate limitations, X might be confronting weapons already being produced in country Z, and it in turn might be facing a force already deployed in country A.

And then, of course, countries were not identical and neither were their weapons. In our model, the decisive argument that Y advanced to persuade X to agree to limit bombers was that Y could and would nullify whatever military or political gains X might be hoping to obtain from its new bombers. But if X was richer and more advanced than Y, its leaders might remain unpersuaded, and might calculate instead that Y would not be able to afford the resources needed to nullify their bomber effort. Alternatively, the leaders of X might concede that Y did have the resources needed to make their bomber programme unprofitable, but they might also believe that Y's rulers lacked the political will to react, or that Y's populace might refuse to make the necessary sacrifices. In either case, arms control might be impossible.

Variety in weapons characteristics was as great a problem as variety in the countries that build them. If X was planning to build weapons of a given type, and Y of another, the two countries might disagree about their respective capabilities, thus failing to agree on criteria for reciprocal limitations. It was enormously difficult to find any objective standard to measure the capabilities of dissimilar weapons: strategic bombers might have more payload than strategic missiles, but the performance of the latter might be more reliable, especially if anti-bomber defences were deployed while anti-missile defence were not. Even within the same category of weapons, comparison were very difficult (until quite recently there was disagreement on the capabilities of the new Soviet Backfire bomber even within different agencies of the same US government). In practice, each side might privately believe that its weapons were superior, while arguing the opposite in arms-control negotiations. ("If you are allowed to build fifty of your large payload bombers, then our side must be allowed to build a hundred of our little missiles.")

Even if there was no deliberate manipulation – which the internal politics of arms control did tend to encourage – there was much scope for honest disagreement. Prudent defence planners must be conservative in assessing the performance of their own forces (thus, evaluating downward) while being equally conservative in estimating the enemy's strength (thus, evaluating upward). In their calculations, prudent country Y planners must accordingly assume that all the bombers of country X were fully operational when needed, and that very few would be intercepted by Y's defences, while at the same time, making all due allowance for technical failures, enemy intercepts, and maintenance rotation when estimating the capabilities of their own weapons. And, of course, country planners must make the opposite assumptions. With prudent evaluation on both sides, there was, therefore, a systematic difference in the weight that each side gave to the forces of the other.

Geographic and demographic differences compounded the difficulty of evaluating weapons and forces. If the forward bases of country Y were quite close to the main cities of X, then the two sides might disagree on the definition of a "strategic" weapon. From the X-country point of view, Y's light bombers might as well be heavy since they only had a short way to travel. But it might be very difficult to secure an agreement in which Y's light bombers were counted on the same footing as Y's heavies; any departure from clear-cut parities was likely to meet much resistance. Differences of demographic structure are of particular importance in today's world of nuclear forces aimed at entire national populations. If country X was largely urban, with some high proportion of its population in a few large city areas, while Y's population was significantly more dispersed, then the destructive potential of identical nuclear forces would be correspondingly different. Country X was not likely to agree to a treaty that limited each side to, say, fifty identical missiles, if Y's fifty missiles could kill 70 per cent of X's population while X's identical force could only kill, say, 7 per cent of Y's population. Of course, a formula that equalised vulnerability rather than the forces themselves could be written into a treaty. But, again, as matters were made more complicated, agreement became correspondingly less likely.

And then there was the still greater problem of information. With the technological development, the superpowers had reliable observation satellites, and indeed much of the whole arms control phenomenon had been brought into existence by their development. It was well known that TV and film cameras carried into space by orbiting satellites could produce very precise images of the ground below for immediate transmission, or in a more accurate and secure form, the data could also be recovered on film. (Capsules released from orbiting satellites in space were caught at low altitude in a rather spectacular manner by transport aircraft equipped with nets.) But if satellite observation was available for arms control inspection, it was equally available to find targets for a disarming "counterforce" attack. This provided an automatic incentive to build exactly those types of strategic weapons (mobile and/or concealed) which could not be reliably located by satellite observation, and the qualities which protected against attack must also prevent inspection for arms control.

In retrospect, it seems clear that the advent of satellite observation in the 1960s did not truly abolish strategic secrecy, thus, assuring the information needed for arms control forever after; satellites merely opened a temporary window in the wall of secrecy because of the sheer coincidence that the weapons of the 1960s happened to be large and easily identifiable. Satellite observation came along precisely when the weapons that the cameras could identify and count were being deployed. Nowadays, by contrast, we have new types of weapons, including both cruise and ballistic missiles, which are mobile or small, or both; and, thus, easily concealed from satellite observation. While it was virtually impossible to hide fixed-site ballistic missiles properly housed in their concrete "silos", or the yards in which submarines were built, thousands of cruise missiles could be kept fully concealed quite easily. It was true that the scrutiny of the satellites, and all the incidental knowledge of industry which they provided, would undoubtedly allow us to determine whether or not some large number of mobile missiles had been built, but satellite cameras could not be used to count these weapons with any precision, any more than they could help us to fix their position for a disarming counterforce attack.

This brought to the surface the peculiar paradox of arms control over the cruise missile. The qualities of the cruise missile which subverted the procedures of negotiated limitations were precisely the qualities which also achieved the substantive purposes of arms control. Because cruise missiles were small, inherently mobile, and therefore easily concealed, it was a hopeless task to devise any treaty to limit them that would rest on any serious assurance of verification. But their small size was also the reason that cruise missiles were relatively cheap. Further, since these small and easily concealed weapons were not vulnerable to disarming counterforce attacks, rival cruise-missile forces should be quite stable; neither side could hope to disarm the other in a surprise attack, so that both sides could be secure. Thus not only the costs, but also the risks generated by these weapons, were inherently smaller than those of the fixed-site ballistic missiles deployed. It follows that as far as cruise missiles were concerned, the best form of arms control might be no control at all.

But the nexus between arms control and the information needed to draft treaties and to verify compliance entailed a deeper and ultimately more sinister paradox. If all obstacles were overcome and arms control treaties were duly negotiated to constrain all that could be constrained with adequate verification, the ironical result might be to displace the strategic competition from the large weapons of classic form that were easily identified and counted, to weapons that had neither attribute. In a world of many powers, each with its own distinct internal politics of resource allocation, and each with its own circle of friends and foes, it was entirely unlikely that arms control efforts, however successful, could achieve more than prohibition of the deployment of specific weapons and forces. The hope, sometimes expressed, that arms control might in itself bring the strategic competition to an end was supported neither by the pure logic of arms control nor by the experience of its practice.

Successful arms-control efforts would, therefore, channel the competition for military power into the development of those weapons which were not subject to limitations because they could not be identified and counted. In this way, the very success of arms control might eventually create a situation of the most dangerous instability, in which all sides were working on small and easily concealed weapons which could suddenly appear fully operational to confront unready opponents. With each side knowing that it might be faced by strategic surprise at any time, maximum incentives for competition and for preventive war, would have been created.

It is true that the imponderable results of research efforts conducted in the secrecy of military laboratories entailed a permanent danger of instability. But the large-scale force-building efforts then conducted openly (because arms control was not effective) provided a double guarantee against destabilising surprise. First, the sheer scale of the visible efforts implied a corresponding limitation on the resources flowing into secret force-building activities; second, the large and diversified forces now deployed provided a high degree of insurance that the sudden emergence of any revolutionary new weapon would not undermine stability. This indeed was the logic of American deployments. The land-based missiles, the submarine systems, and the long-range bombers could all be neutralised quite suddenly by the emergence of revolutionary devices. But simultaneous breakthroughs in all the very different scientific areas involved were most unlikely.

Neither guarantee could survive in the wake of prolonged and successful arms-control efforts, through which the forces in place would have been greatly reduced in size and diversification, and through which overt force-building efforts would have been greatly diminished or even eliminated, thus, releasing abundant resources for less visible activities. True, secrecy was much more easily maintained in laboratory research than in engineering development, when weapons were taken out to be tested, but this did not dispose of the problem. Even if the tests of some revolutionary new weapon that threatened to undermine stability were duly observed and properly understood, it might take years for development to catch up, and in the meantime, the prospect of unilateral vulnerability would be an incentive to preventive war. This, then, was the ultimate irony: the inherent limits that information set on the scope of arms control might mean that the final reward of sustained success in arms control would be the utter defeat of its goals.

Still, even when all these practical problems and all these dangers of varying likelihood were taken into account, arms control remained in principle a much more desirable alternative than force-building.

Bilateral arms control was undoubtedly easier to achieve than arms control in a real world of many powers, but then multilateral agreements were scarcely an impossibility, either. Negotiations would be more complicated when many parties were involved, but on the other hand, the existence of alliances might offer solutions denied in the pure bilateral case of country X and country Y. For example, alliances could help to overcome the difficulties that emerged when the artificial assumption of identical countries was waived. Country Y might be too poor, or too irresolute, to effectively discourage X from opening a new channel of competition by building its bombers, but an alliance of Y and Z might dissuade X by convincingly threatening to nullify the gains of its bomber programme through a join force-building effort of their own.

As for differences in weapons characteristics, and the built-in asymmetry caused by conservative evaluations on each side, these certainly created many difficulties, but they were after all of a purely technical character, and patient negotiations by technical experts should in principle be able to overcome such problems.

Much the same goes for geographic and demographic differences between the parties. Given goodwill, or rather a rational appreciation of the mutual advantages of restraint, there was no reason why formulas could not be found to equalise the asymmetries. If Y's light bombers could reach the main cities of X as easily as X's heavy bombers could travel the much greater distance to Y's cities deep inland, then the two physically different forces could be evaluated by their actual effectiveness against their respective targets, and then limited accordingly in a treaty. Similarly, if X was inherently more vulnerable to nuclear bombardment because of its higher population densities, Y's weapons could be more severely restricted so as to yield equality in destructive power under an arms limitation treaty.

Even the paradox of visibility and vulnerability as well as the long-term effects of arms control over the more visible weapons which released resources for more unstable invisible weapons, did not make arms control futile. If cruise missiles inherently achieve the substantive aims of arms control, the negotiations could focus on the many other costly and destabilizing weapons being built. As for the long-term problem, it might well be argued that in the presence of today's luxuriant force-building, the immediate gains of economy and safety that arms control could yield were of much greater consequence than the remote danger which successful arms control might eventually cause in the very long term. Certainly these hypothetical dangers need not deter the modest efforts under way since the mid-1960s.

Whatever was wrong with arms control, therefore, it was not the various practical difficulties, each of which could be overcome, at least in part.

If our arms control model was brought still nearer to reality by substituting the Soviet Union and the United States for X and Y, a new set of difficulties immediately arose. The Soviet Union undoubtedly, lacked the attributes of an ideal partner for arms control; indeed, some might say that it was grotesquely miscast for the part.

The first obstacle was the Soviet negotiating style. If a unilateral concession was made to the Soviet negotiators for the sake of "generating a positive atmosphere", the Soviet side would take what was given but would under no circumstances volunteer a reciprocal concession. It was not that Soviet diplomats were necessarily tougher than Western negotiators or even that their conduct was a symptom of inflexibility. It was merely a question of method. Soviet negotiators insisted on treating each issue quite separately, bargaining where they could in each case. They did not try to smooth the path to agreement by yielding on the lesser points for the sake of the common interest in the outcome of the negotiations as a whole.

There was training, and tradition behind this method; there might also be fear, personal fear. Soviet diplomats must clearly remember what happened to their colleagues during the earlier stages of the purge period under Stalin, when very many were killed or deported on the charge that they had betrayed the Soviet side in international negotiations by making unnecessary concessions. (In the later stages of the great purge, this was no longer the case: mere contact with foreigners was then often sufficient evidence of treason). But whatever the reason, Soviet negotiators invariably sought to make each bargain as specific as possible, and far from trying to create a good "negotiating climate", would sometimes deliberately stage episodes of uncivil conduct as a bargaining tactic to intimidate the other side or just to distract attention.

None of this mattered very much in negotiations where single issues must be decided by straightforward bargaining. One could certainly agree on the price of a shipment of apples with Soviet traders as well as one could with their British or French counterparts. But in trying to negotiate significant arms control measures, one must almost invariably trade across the issues, since the variety of weapons characteristics and all the other asymmetries made issue-by-issue bargaining very difficult.

In the Western diplomatic practice, negotiators often made "goodwill" exchanges to one another to help overcome technical complexities and other intractable obstacles to agreement. If the British and Americans were negotiating on the price of apples today and would move on to determine the price of pears tomorrow and there was sharp disagreement on both, one side might well yield on the price of the apples in the expectation that the other side would feel duty bound to show flexibility when negotiations moved on to the pears. In dealing with Soviet negotiators, by contrast, the full difficulty of resolving the apple issue would have to be confronted; and when the discussions moved on to the pears, the process must begin all over again, with neither side having goodwill points in hand to make an agreement any easier. Given the inherent complexities of arms control negotiations and the great scope for sharp disagreements on hard technical questions, it was evident that issue-by-issue bargaining might sometimes make agreement quite impossible.

A second and more serious obstacle to arms control with the Soviet Union was the very nature of its politics. The logic of arms control depended on the recognition of a common interest in avoiding force-building which could bring no national advantage. In our initial example, country X refrained from building its planned bomber force because it calculated that after Y had duly reacted, it would have gained no net benefit, it being, the country as a whole, rather than just its soldiers and weapons builders. But if country X was the Soviet Union, then the logic might not apply at all.

In American politics, the arms controllers had some political leverage, especially on Capitol Hill, since they employed quite a few constituents (In fact, the arms industry seemed to have more influence than the soft-drink bottlers, though, of course, much less than the dairy farmers). But in the Soviet Union the "metal eaters", as the party leaders who ran the military industries were known, were not just one interest group among many, as in the United States, but rather core members of the major coalition of Soviet politics. The key of the ability of the "metal eaters" to claim such a large proportion of Soviet economic resources seemed to be their alliance with the secret police at one end – whose calls for "vigilance" and whose repressions were justified by the fancied menace of NATO and of the Chinese – and, at the other, with the armed forces, which of course had a direct consumer interest in military production.

The politics of the Kremlin were poorly understood, but virtually all experts agreed that the coalition of the KGB, soldiers, and military-production managers was a major force in shaping policy. It follows that within the Soviet Union, there was powerful and systematic pressure for more force-building – in fact, there was every reason to believe that the coalition only allowed Brezhnev to embark upon the policy of détente on the condition that the military build-up would continue as before, if not actually accelerate. This state of affairs naturally restricted the scope of arms controls since the common interest on which it must be based could not be the Soviet "society-wide" interest in economy and safety. Instead, there was only the much narrower overlap between the general US interest, on the one hand, and the highly specialised interest of the Soviet military-production coalition, on the other. American SALT negotiators were given some idea of the peculiar autonomy, even at the fairly high level in the Soviet government, when a senior Russian delegate privately asked his American counterpart to persuade his colleagues to stop discussing the details of Soviet forces in front of the Soviet Foreign Minister in the delegation.

Another serious obstacle to arms control was the traditional Russian passion for secrecy. Even after many years of supposedly intimate negotiations on strategic forces, the Russians refused to disclose any meaningful information about the characteristics of their weapons and the structure of their forces, let alone about their force-building plans; there was not even any substitute discussion of Soviet strategy and doctrine. It had been reported that in SALT both delegations used only American data, for the Soviet as well as for the American forces; apparently the Soviet delegates had not even disclosed the proper designations of their weapons (that was why the terminology of the 1972 SALT I accords was so vague, with references to "ballistic-missile launchers of older types" and so on, in lieu of any precise designation). Of course, satellite observation could provide a reliable count of strategic weapons, as long as they were fairly large, of classic form, and actually deployed. However, not even the magic of high-resolution cameras, scanning computers and electronic intelligence could reveal weapons until after they had been tested, and sometimes not until they were actually deployed. Unfortunately, the success of arms control often depended on information at the earliest possible stage of the force-building cycle and certainly before production was under way. If country Y found out about X's bombers only when the prototypes began to appear on the testing airstrip, it would usually be too late to negotiate limitations. Within country X, the bomber effort would have acquired momentum, if only because much of the total cost would have been paid already, and Y, on the other hand could not have much confidence in a limitation treaty if X already had developed prototypes, ready for large-scale production at any time. The Soviet refusal to publish future development plans – as the United States did – or, indeed any specifications about its military forces, past, present, or future, therefore restricted the scope of arms control rather seriously.

The Russian passion for secrecy also diminished the scope of arms control by making verification extremely difficult. Satellite observation was once again crucial, but for all the remarkable detail of the photography, and the valuable performance data that could be obtained from electronic intelligence, the information might nevertheless be too ambiguous to give sufficient confidence for proper verification; data which were technically very good might be worthless because Soviet secrecy denied that wider circumstantial knowledge that could give them meaning. When Soviet satellite cameras photographed a missile-like object on some American testing site, Soviet analysts could usually identify the missile quite safely and easily, and they could then consult an abundance of published information on the exact specification of the missile, its particular mission, the number to be built, and so on. By contrast, American analysts provided with a similar photograph could do no better than guess the mission of the weapon and make very tentative estimates of its range and payload.

Usually the numbers to be built could not be estimated; the counting could be done only when the weapons were actually being deployed. Even then, doubts might remain; there could be hundreds of uncounted strategic missiles kept in concealed places other than the characteristic operational launchers easily recognised in satellite photographs. In practice, this meant that in dealing with the Soviet

Union, standards of verification must be relaxed, or else many arms control hopes must be abandoned. In either case, the scope of genuine – that is, properly verified – arms control was considerably restricted. Arms control without high-confidence verification was a contradiction in terms. It did not lessen the risks of conflict but increased them, and it did not diminish incentives in force building but made them stronger. Low-confidence verification was not a substitute for proper inspection procedures, and it was not even a good device to attempt unilateral disarmament.

Another peculiarity of Soviet statecraft which affected arms control or rather the observance of its agreed limitations, was the Soviet penchant for the use of probing tactics. Like the hotel thief who would walk down the corridors trying each door in the hope of finding one carelessly left open, Soviet policy constantly probed such arms limitations as there were, to exploit any gaps in American vigilance, as well as any loopholes in the agreed texts. For example, under the terms of Article IV of the 1967 Outer Space Treaty, no nuclear weapons might be placed in orbit around the earth. The Russians were not known to have sent up weapon satellites equipped with nuclear warheads, but they had continued to test the so-called FOBs version of the SS-9 heavy missiles since signing the treaty; with FOBs delivery, these large nuclear-capable missiles did not quite complete a full orbit around the earth, but rather descended to earth just before doing so. In this way, the Russians had tested a weapon (which might or might not have carried a nuclear warhead) without precisely violating the terms of the agreement, which defined space vehicles as those completing at least one full orbit around the earth.

An altogether more serious probing operation also failed to evoke a firm American reaction. The 1972 ABM Treaty, actually the only really significant arms control measure in force, prohibited not only the deployment but also the development and testing of mobile systems designed to intercept ballistic missiles (Article V). In a "common understanding" appended to the treaty on April 13, 1972, the Soviet Union further agreed that the development and testing of any non-fixed ABM component was forbidden by the treaty. However, there had been persistent reports from authoritative intelligence sources that the Soviet Union had violated the treaty by testing components of mobile ABM systems at the Kapustin Yar and Shary Sagan ranges; it seemed that there had been intermittent American complaints about these tests but no really determined action. It appeared to be diplomatic doctrine that if the injured party did not resist such probing, it was actually giving its tacit consent, so that the violations were thereby virtually legitimised.

There were, no doubt, many observers who would dismiss each of these separate points as trivial, arguing quite simply that the Russians could not be trusted to keep the agreements they signed, least of all important arms control agreements. It was certainly true that the constant duplicity of Soviet public discourse scarcely inspired confidence. The Soviet press, radio and television and all the overseas outlets of Soviet propaganda, did not merely slant the news and distort history, as many others did, but also disseminated a great quantity of outright falsehood, obviously quite deliberately. In the Soviet media, one might read stories full of circumstantial details about secret American cooperation in South African nuclear-weapons efforts, about the Nazi experts who instructed the Israeli General Staff, about CIA payoffs to Soviet dissidents, about West German plots against Czechoslovakia's independence, and so on. At a more prosaic level, there was constant lying in newspaper articles which compared the Soviet and the Western standards of living, and these were lies known to be such by those who wrote them, by the typesetters, the proofreaders, the censors, and all but the most ignorant readers. All governments engage in lying, but in the Soviet Union, deliberate and massive public falsehood was very much a normal circumstance. This naturally inspired doubts about the sincerity of Soviet statements, and about the reliability of Soviet understanding, including those written into the texts of treaties.

Nevertheless, although the Soviet Union had violated many treaty commitments, this mostly occurred in its dealings with the weak. There had been few outright violations of agreements signed with the United States, and of these violations, most had been quite small, in accordance with the slow tempo of Soviet probing tactics. An outright violation was an exception. Article IV of the Agreement on the Prevention of Nuclear War of June 22, 1973, required the Soviet Union to inform the United States of Arab preparations for the 1973 War, about which the Russians clearly knew a great deal. A mere 104 days had passed between the signature of the agreement and its clear-cut violation. Naturally, the Soviet Union did not live up to the "spirit" of international understandings, but there was no duplicity at all in this case because Soviet diplomacy explicitly rejected that concept. In fact, Soviet leaders had been frank in stating that only the actual language of treaties was binding, so that everything not explicitly disallowed would be treated as fair game by them. It had been Western statesmen who had insisted that this or that summit, or treaty, had generated a binding "spirit" of cooperation.

The United States, a nation of lawyers, should hardly be incapable of dealing with this particular problem. The Soviet refusal to accept voluntary inhibitions for the sake of the "spirit" of things merely required that arms-control agreements be drafted very carefully indeed, in all necessary detail. The Soviet position was, in fact, quite traditional. Russians accepted the necessity of fulfilling treaties (*pacta sunt servanda*) but they also maintained the hidden conditional clauses, "so long as conditions do not change" – as did many others who would also break treaties if their interests were no longer served by them. This did not mean that the Soviet Union was not a fit party for arms control by treaty. It merely required the United States to be ready at all times to make violations unprofitable.

None of the other obstacles to effective arms control caused by the peculiarities of Soviet conduct was decisive either. For example, it was true that the Soviet negotiating style, with its refusal to make goodwill exchanges from issue to issue, greatly prolonged the process, but, on the other hand, Soviet negotiators were very patient, and Soviet policy did not lack persistence. There was, therefore, plenty of time to overcome the additional complications created by ferocious haggling on each point. Certainly, it should not have been beyond the tenacity of American diplomats to suffer prolonged bargaining.

The structural obstacle of Soviet party politics was not so easily dismissed. Now that Ustinov, the Defence Minister and former Chief of Military Production, was overtly identified as a top-level leader, it was evident that the coalition of the "metal eaters" with the secret police and the armed forces was more powerful than ever. Even the traditionally optimistic analysts of the CIA conceded that the Soviet Union was allocating between 11 and 13 per cent of its GNP to military purposes, as compared to roughly 5.5 per cent for the United States; other reputable observers rejected the CIA estimates as too low and argued for 15 or even 17 per cent, almost three times the American proportion. All seemed to agree that Soviet defence expenditure had been increasing at a steady rate of roughly 1.5 per cent a year for many years, and this too was much higher than the American rate, which was actually negative between 1968 and 1972 when outlays on strategic weapons had increased, that stood at less than 3 per cent, net of inflation.

The contrast in these figures suggested that the Soviet interest in equitable arms control was bound to be rather limited. But even this obstacle was not insurmountable. First of all, experts on the Soviet Union assured the Americans that the coalition was not entirely dominant in the top echelon of the Soviet leadership. While it was true that the earlier plans for a major expansion of consumer-goods production had been dropped, the existing leadership was making a really huge investment in agriculture and it was steadily increasing the effort going into light industries. Such considerations must have moderated in some degree the claims of the "metal eaters" on Soviet resources, and this in turn suggested that there might be room for successful arms control. Of course, this was only true of weapons systems and forces that were particularly costly – as opposed to those that were particularly destabilising or destructive – but that still left plenty of scope for arms control.

Nor should the obstacle of secrecy be overestimated. True, it was most unfortunate that the Soviet government insisted on denying to its own citizens and to the outside world all manner of information, military or not, even when it gained no possible advantage from doing so. It would be much better for all concerned if the Soviet Union were to adopt the practices of most civilised states and publish its force-building plans in advance. The lack of advance information meant that the huge advantage that came from negotiating over force-building plans, as opposed to actual deployments, was irremediably lost. But the need to wait until weapons were brought out into the open to be tested need not utterly preclude successful arms control. Even if it would be preferable to negotiate before the momentum of such investments had had an opportunity to develop, a rational calculation of mutual advantages should still serve to limit armaments, at least in those cases when further outlays still to be made were sufficiently great, and the likelihood of a determined American response was sufficiently credible.

The effect of Russian secrecy on verification was not decisive either. It must be conceded that the lack of truthful budget data, the lack of a Soviet technical press on military production, and the lack of other sources of circumstantial knowledge made it very difficult to interpret visual and electronic data to verify compliance with arms control agreements. But on the other hand, verification ultimately required positive proof rather than circumstantial evidence. If a violation must be proved to American and world opinion as well as to Soviet delegates in consultative meetings, generic evidence would not suffice in any cause; in fact, usually only the photographs matter.

Nor did the Russian fondness for probing tactics to create gaps in limitation agreements while fully exploiting bonafide loopholes make a stable arms control regime impossible. It did not mean that the United States must expect probing operations to begin as soon as an agreement was signed, and that it must be ready to take firm action to stop violations – any violations, however small – as soon as they were detected. It was, of course, fatal to silence protests and to refrain from sanctions in order to preserve the "atmosphere of détente", and it was quite useless to complain in general terms. Unless appropriate retaliation was convincingly threatened for each specific violation, complaints would simply be ignored. It should be normal American practice, for example, to suspend all US-Soviet negotiations, on all issues, military or not, as soon as there was fully reliable evidence of the deliberate violations on any prior agreements still in force. Failure to do this might harden the Soviet position in general, and it certainly invited further probing unless there was a prompt and forceful reaction; those Soviet officials of moderate views who had counselled prudence in the pre-violation internal policy debate would be undermined, and the hard-line advocates of further probing would be strengthened. Inaction tended to legitimise the prior gains of probing operations while inviting new ones, and since each small step led to the next, any violation, even if quite inconsequential in itself, must be resisted in full force. For example, when the United States failed to react adequately to the visits of Soviet ballistic missiles submarines to Cuban ports, in violation of an executive agreement, these visits were gradually lengthened until the presence of the submarines became commonplace. Next, supporting facilities were established. American protests led to the removal of non-critical crew facilities but technically essential maintenance items remained. This situation had been inherited by the Carter Administration as a reality no longer open to challenge. Similarly, the Russians used probing tactics in implementing the SALT I accords by taking new submarines out for sea trials before scrapping equal numbers of pre-1964 land-based missiles, or converting older submarines, as required by "agreed interpretation" Khrushchev appended to the 1972 "interim agreement". Again, American complaints on the matter were belated and not forceful. It seemed that the Russians blamed the poor weather for the overlap, and that the feeble excuse was accepted. If a new SALT Treaty included similar provisions, "slippages" would no doubt become quite routine.

At a time when the Soviet Union had more that 2,500 nuclear weapons of intercontinental range, it might be difficult for an outsider to understand why its military and civil officials would try so hard to cheat on the rules to deploy a few more weapons here and there, which could add nothing of substance to overall Soviet capabilities. It was hard to resist the impression that, for these men there were rewards, political or bureaucratic, to be had for cheating successfully. All this was, of course, very unpleasant, and also at first quite unsettling for those who came to deal with the Soviet Union from the relatively innocent atmosphere of American academia or even American public life. However, so long as the United States acted correctly, that is, promptly and forcefully, the probing tactics could be defeated, or at least contained so as to make their results insignificant from the arms control viewpoint.

It was, therefore, clear that none of the peculiarities of Soviet conduct was a decisive obstacle to successful arms control. Whatever was wrong with arms control, it was not the fact that dealings with the Soviet Union must loom large in its pursuit. The process of elimination had left only the one possible culprit: the United States.

While arms control could be effective only in limiting specific deployments under specific arrangements, serving thereby as an alternative to force-building, the United States had consistently misused arms control in pursuit of the abstract goal of "strategic parity". When the concept was challenged, it was redefined by the White House as "essential equivalence", which was equally vague. Neither set of words had any meaning in the reality of weapons or forces. Neither set of words could define negotiating objectives.

While arms control could only be effectively pursued if negotiated limitations were defined with extreme precision, the United States had consistently tolerated ambiguities in its urgent pursuit of agreement for its own sake. As a result, a new and entirely artificial source of US-Soviet tensions had been created. Changes in the Soviet strategic forces that would otherwise have passed almost unnoticed, excited suspicion and resentment when in high contrast against the poorly drafted texts of the 1972 Moscow accords. One side benefit of each arms control agreement should be to build confidence for the next, but the tensions creating ambiguities of SALT I had utterly defeated this purpose.

While effective arms control required that high standards of compliance be enforced, the United States had consistently allowed Soviet probing to develop without effective challenge. This permissive stance was a natural consequence of the attempt to use SALT as a general sedative in US-Soviet relations. The attempt had undoubtedly failed, SALT having become, on balance, a further source of friction. But in the process, arms control itself had been discredited, since negotiated agreements had been enforced far too loosely in deference to the atmospherics of détente.

Above, all the United States had misused arms control in the attempt to dampen the strategic competition in itself, as if the growth of strategic arsenals was the cause of Soviet-American rivalry rather than merely one of its symptoms, and incidentally a much less dangerous symptom than the growth of non-nuclear forces whose war-like use was much more likely.

Who were the men in the United States who had brought about these consequences that might yet prove to be catastrophic? Some, including a former Secretary of Defence, were essentially technicians, who had nevertheless been allowed to shape strategic policy as if its essence were technical rather than political. Unable to define the benefits of superior strategic nuclear forces with technical precision, in mathematical terms, entirely unable to comprehend the diffused political meaning of military capabilities, these technicians who imagined themselves to be strategists saw no reason why the United States should strive to keep a strategic superiority which they believed to be meaningless. After all, they could prove with their mathematical models that there was no middle level of capability between the minimum of strike-back deterrence and the unattainable maximum of a disarming counterforce capability. Under attack for having waged war in Indonesia, these men had embraced the cause of multilateral arms control with much enthusiasm; the activity had a pleasant humanitarian connotation and also some intellectual appeal while supposedly entailing no loss in "real" American strength.

Others, sometimes very influential but mostly outside government, advocated arms control because it was a respectable vehicle for an isolationist foreign policy. After all, the logical result of abandoning additional forces and retaining only a strike-back capability was to uncouple American nuclear forces from NATO and the other alliances. The United States would still be able to deter any direct nuclear attack upon its own soil, and only the nuclear protection offer to its allies would be sacrificed.

For still others, by no means devoid of influence, arms control was a substitute for disarmament, which to their regret the American people still entirely reject. More or less convincing arms control arguments could always be invoked, along with technical, economic, and now environmental objections, to oppose any and every strategic weapon that the services wanted to build. Some of these unilateral disarmers camouflaged as arms controllers simply believed that strategic nuclear weapons were so destructive that their use could not ultimately serve any rational purpose, military or political. Some were driven by the passionate desire to change the course of world history, so largely characterised by the dismal consequences of force-building, and they did not accept the prosaic objection that wars were most frequently brought about by the failure to make aggression unprofitable. Others among them opposed American weapons because they were American, and remained quite undisturbed by the huge increase in all forms of Soviet military power; believing America to be an essentially evil force in the affairs of mankind, they necessarily regarded all instruments of American power as instruments of evil. And some arms control advocates shared none of these beliefs but had merely made arms control their profession, having found work in the dozens of anti-Pentagon lobbies which were now active. Seeing themselves in unequal combat with the vast defence bureaucracy and the still greater military bureaucracies, and forced to contend with a public which obstinately continued to believe that the richest country on earth should also be the most powerful, these professional advocates of arms control concentrated their energies on fighting the Pentagon.

Arms control could be no more than a tool of national strategy if it was to be effective. It was an alternative to the other tool, the deployment of weapons, and it could be the superior alternative. But this was only true when its goals were the same, that is, the goals of national strategy to enhance security at the lowest possible cost and risk. In American policy, arms control had usurped the function of strategy and had become an end in itself. The consequences were now manifest: the unilateral arms control pursued by the US since at least 1964, and the bilateral efforts that culminated in the 1973 Moscow agreements, had diminished rather than enhanced American security; they had not contained the growth of the arsenals of both superpowers; they had increased rather than diminished outlays on US strategic forces; and they had now begun to compromise strategic stability, since the increasing obsolescence of an old bomber force and the approaching vulnerability of American land-based missiles would soon leave the submarine-missile force exposed to undivided Soviet counterforce efforts. As a result of these unhappy trends, mankind might be approaching a new period of acute instability in which Americans would be forced to undertake very expensive build-up programmes on a crash basis. One consequence was already with the US: the trust that Allies could place in American nuclear protection had been sharply diminished, the bonds of alliance had been weakened and powerful incentives had been created for nuclear proliferation.

Notes

1. Barnaby, Frank and Huisken, Ronald, *Arms Uncontrolled*, Stockholm International Peace Research Institute (SIPRI), Cambridge, Harvard University Press, 1976, pp. 119-120.

2. *Ibid.* p. 120.

3. Puller, David R., *The Arms Race*, Stanford, Stanford University Press, 1979, pp. 91-93.

4. Hamilton, Lee, *Superpower Rivalry*, New York, Basic Books, 1964, pp. 106-8.

5. Kox, Robert L., *American-Soviet Strategic Relations*, New York, Harder & Harder, 1972, p. 78.

6. Larson, Daniel, *Nuclear Reality*, New York, Harper Row, 1976, p. 91.

7. Potter, James R., *SALT I and After*, Ithaca, N.Y. Cornell University Press, 1974, pp. 51-53.

8. *World Armaments and Disarmament*, SIPRI Year Book 1974, Almgvist and Wiksell, 1974, Chap. 6.

9. Lapp, Ralph Eugenet, *Containing the Arms Race*, Cambridge, Mass., MIT Press, 1976, pp. 68-69.

10. Miller, Ronald B., *The Missile Race*, New York, Stein & Day, 1977, p. 89.

11. Lowell, Stephen, *Whether SALT?* Washington D.C., National Defence University Press, 1974, pp. 113-14.

12. Morrison, Herald, *The Arms Race*, Notre Dame, Ind., University of Notre Dame Press, 1977, p. 71.

13. Stern, Theodore, *Nuclear Power Today*, New York, Vintage Books, 1977, p. 98.

14. Rovere, Hugh, *The Nuclear Balance*, Urbana, University of Illionis Press, 1975, p. 137.

15. Grew, Joseph G., *Political Strategy and Nuclear Arms Race*, Boston, New Books (Beacon Press), 1978, pp. 112-113.

16. Hewlett, John W., *The Great Crusade*, Baltimore, The John Hopkins University Press, 1978, p. 115.

17. Dawer, John W., *Future of SALT*, Chicago, University of Chicago Press, 1978, pp. 213-14.

18. Furniss, Edgar S., *US Nuclear Strategy*, Ithaca Cornell University Press, 1979, pp. 87-98.

19. Drell, Sidney D., *Weapons and Hope*, New York, Viewpoints, 1977, p. 152-53.

20. Feis, Herbert, *End of SALT*, Athens, Ca, The University of Georgia Press, 1977, p. 132.

21. Morrison, Leonard R., *Nuclear Arms Race*, Baltimore, The John Hopkins University Press, 1979, pp. 121-23.

22. Harper, Edgar L., *The Balance of Power*, Boston, Little Brown & Co., 1978, pp. 171-73.

23. Bailey, Sydney R., *The Strategic Arms*, New York, Stein & Day, 1978, pp. 147-49.

24. Galanter, M., *The Pattern of the Arms Race*, Boston, Little Brown & Co., 1979, pp. 120-32.

25. Lowell, Joseph N., *US-Soviet Nuclear Strategy*, Notre Dame, Ind, University of Notre Dame Press, 1979, pp. 107-9.

26. Fuller, J.F.G., *The Grand Strategy*, London, Nicholson & Watson, 1979, pp. 97-99.

27. Carrell, Henry F., *Future of SALT*, London, Casseil & Co. 1979, p. 211.

28. Brown, Peter M., *Why the SALT Failed?* London, Pall Mall Press, 1978, pp. 181-83.

29. Earle, Robert L., *Nature of US Nuclear Strategy*, New York, Double-day Press, pp. 161-62.

30. Brodie, Steil P., *Nuclear Arms and Stability*, London, Kegan Paul & Co. 1979, p. 187.

36. Barnaby, Frank, *World Armament Report*, SIPRI Publication, Stockholm, Almgvist & Wiksell, 1977, pp. 69-72.

37. Barnaby, Frank, *Trade in Arms*, SIPRI Publication, Stockholm, 1978, Almgvist & Wiksell, pp. 122-24.

38. Beaton, Leonard, *Must Arms Spread?* London, Allen Lane, 1978, p. 76.

39. Clarke, Robin, *Defence and Development*, London, Jonathan Cape, 1981, pp. 69-71.

40. Stone, Jeremy K., *Containing the Arms Race*, Cambridge, Mass. MIT Press, 1979, pp. 167-69.

4
NUCLEAR REGIMES

The significance of nuclear weapons is not only confined to the central questions of global war and peace. However, faint the danger of holocaust, nuclear forces policies, plans, and rhetoric can affect – pervasively, if subtly – hierarchy and interaction among nations, perceptions of constraint and opportunity among leaders, and feelings of well-being or fear among peoples. For instance: First, nuclear weapons can earn influence for those countries that ostensibly commit them to bolster the security of other countries. The very presence of American nuclear weapons in Europe and the Far East helps confirm perhaps otherwise dubious defence assurances that evoke deference to Washington on issues of trade, monetary affairs, UN voting, and the like. [1]

Second, quite apart from the military implications of success or failure in efforts to control nuclear arms competition, the direction and pace of such endeavours heavily influence the basic political relationship between those who are competing and negotiating. If the SALT negotiations have not been the leading edge of détente – and most would contend that they have been – they have at least given substance to what might otherwise have been a fleeting experiment in noble intentions. Conversely, failure to maintain demonstrable progress in SALT may signify, if not reinforce, the malaise of détente.

Third, owing to the belief that constructing nuclear weapons is proof of national scientific excellence and industrial depth, the possession of a nuclear arsenal earns respect for the country in the eyes of other capitals and societies. China has become no richer, its scientists no brighter, by conducting nuclear tests; but in the currency of international respect, its stock as a world power has been appreciated considerably since its first such test in 1964.

Fourth, nuclear weapons can increase the national *hubris* and self-confidence of the possessor, thus, emboldening its general international behaviour. France's nuclear force, though minute compared with those of the USA and Russia, restored a measure of French self-respect in the wake of imperial losses and fed the elan with which Charles de Gaulle manoeuvred politically between Washington and Moscow in the 1960s.[2]

Fifth, in the future as in the past, the development and maintenance of nuclear weapons will consume enormous human and financial resources. Annual worldwide investment in nuclear weaponry will probably continue to exceed the level of resources needed to eliminate acute malnutrition on a global scale. To take a more practical example, it might be argued that American conventional military strength will continue to suffer due to budgetary competition with the nuclear forces.[3]

Sixth, "mutual deterrence" – or more graphically, MAD (Mutually Assured Destruction) – has come to be widely accepted as the key to survival in the nuclear age. But the mentality that has formed around this concept, with its emphasis on "credibility" and "retaliation" and "will", may affect the judgements and warp the policies of the national leaders who have custody of the arsenals of mass destruction. To be credible in threatening certain and devastating reprisal for a nuclear attack is to contribute responsibility to the preservation of civilisation; to batter a weak and temporary adversary for the sake of appearing credible is a morbid misapplication of a strategic concept that is best made an exception and not a rule.[5]

And lastly, in the long run, the existence of nuclear weapons could fundamentally alter government-citizen relationships. If, over time, the need of governments to field expensive deterrent forces is not appreciated by citizens who no longer sense a real nuclear threat, popular support for the maintenance of forces could fade – and governments might feel compelled to provide for deterrence without the consent of the governed.

Because of the apparent weight of nuclear weapons in world security and world politics, the thought of dramatic change in the management of these arms summons no less anxiety than the expectation that present conditions will persist. The current situation (in which available explosive power equals roughly 7,000 times the explosive power released in all of World War II) is absurd but stable.[6] The impulse to perfect stability is at least as strong as the impulse to escape absurdity. Attention to esoteric detail (such as how quiet, and, therefore, how safe from detection and destruction, missile-bearing submarines are) is both an imperative of prudent management and an impediment to the contemplation of fundamentally different nuclear futures. Those impressed with the gravity of practical strategic questions and the risks involved in departures from familiar conditions are brand as naive, if not irresponsible, by those whose thoughts are on sweeping change. Those who believe that survival requires radical change – ultimately, if not urgently – despair of the experts' penchant for debating details and fine-tuning war scenarios.

The question of how to manage nuclear weapons has been designed to avoid two pitfalls: preoccupation with the particulars of force posture and arms control issues at the expense of conceiving more basic alternatives to present conditions; and bold prescriptions for dramatic change that leave unattended the specific policy issues most likely, in fact, to form the next decade's nuclear agenda. The approach around which this chapter is organized – in which four distinct nuclear "regimes" are discussed – permits intensive inquiry into each of a diverse set of conceptions of the role and control of nuclear weapons in the decades to come. The purpose is not just to assess any one broad conception, but in fact, to advocate a particular design and to indicate the steps needed to implement that design.

Simply put, a nuclear regime may be thought of as system of international obligations (formal accords, tacit commitments, and informal understandings), national force structures (how many and what kind of weapons), and doctrines (when, where, why, how, and which nuclear weapons ought to be used) that together govern the role of nuclear weapons in war, peace and diplomacy.[7]

Each regime is based on a set of values and goals and on certain premises about the dangers and virtues of nuclear weapons. Each is shaped by certain expectations about the political and technological future. A preference for one regime over others should be based not only upon sympathy with its underlying values, but also upon satisfaction that the specified characteristics of the regime would in fact help deliver those values. Even then, doubts about the feasibility of bringing about the desired conditions may cause one to lean toward a more realistic, if less satisfying, alternative, perhaps in the belief that the second best is a logical and necessary rung on the ladder toward the best.

The discipline, for the present author and the readers, of having to think through the internal consistency of a single vision of how to manage nuclear arms and strategic relationships, has been an important aim in our decision to take the regime approach. The pursuit of contradictory objectives is the mother of policy failure. For instance, one might favour having states with nuclear weapons pledge never to be the first to use them, yet, at the same time, be averse to the removal of all American tactical nuclear weapons from Europe lest such a step weaken Western confidence and encourage Soviet conventional military pressure. Espousal of both these policies would either undermine the value of the tactical nuclear weapons in deterring conventional aggression, vitiate the "no-first-use" pledge, or both.

Existing arms control literature is a cornucopia of concepts, critiques, and proposals; too often, at least of late, there has been little attempt to tie separate strands together, to scrutinise particular objectives in the light of other objectives, and to develop out of a welter of prescriptions a coherent sense of direction. Admittedly, the regimes presented here are abstractions; they have a certain tidiness, a snug fit of all the pieces, that cannot be expected in the complex and protean conditions of the world. But the value of the regime approach is that it requires that proposals be set and judged in a broad context, that assumptions be spelled out, and that priorities be established among competing goals.

A sense of direction about the nuclear future must emanate from a basic philosophy about the meaning of nuclear weapons and how to govern them. In its pure form, the *First Regime* rests on the premise that nuclear weapons of the superpowers, however they offend our intuitive sense of safety and proportionality, have in fact fostered – if not forced – moderation and stability in international politics. This regime advocates, and sees good prospects for, a continuation of the "system" that has prevailed since the Cold War began, a system that has, thus, stood the tests of time and tension. The *Second Regime* is derived from the belief that nuclear weapons are an inescapable burden and that our efforts should be devoted to reducing dependence on them in the conduct of world politics and the maintenance of international security. It would quite explicitly entrust nuclear weapons with one and only one purpose: to deter the use of other nuclear weapons. The availability or use of nuclear weapons for other purposes would be sharply constrained by an assortment of unilateral and multilateral measures. The *Third Regime* does not accept the fate of an eternal nuclear predicament. It sees nuclear weapons not as a manageable burden but as an intolerable menace and, therefore, seeks to ban them. The nuclear system seems stable now, but certain stresses and contradictions may eventually lead to collapse and calamity. This expectation and the belief that it is morally corrosive for peace and stable world politics to depend in perpetuity upon the capacity and expressed willingness of leaders to destroy one another's societies underscore the need to conceive of workable and enforceable arrangements for the abolition of nationally held nuclear weapons. Finally, the *Fourth Regime* anticipates a number of plausible developments in technology and politics over the next ten to fifteen years that could undermine strategic stability, shake world politics, and perhaps increase the chances of nuclear conflict. Specifically, it confronts several adverse possibilities; extensive nuclear proliferation, technological disequilibria, and nuclear imbalance between the superpowers. It looks less at how we can improve conditions than at how we might attenuate the perils of a forbidding nuclear future. In a sense, the implicit link between the

Third Regime and *Fourth Regime* closes the circle, for movement from present conditions to a denuclearised world might be politically possible only if catalysed by a resurgence of nuclear danger. [8]

The full value of the regime approach is realised only if comparisons are made among alternatives along several dimensions of practical policy concern. What do each of these sets of premises imply for such familiar issues as the size of nuclear arsenals, the doctrines that govern their deployment and use, the conventions and institutions that might provide some measure of international control, and the acquisition of nuclear weapons by an increasing number of nations? [9] Beyond these analytical questions, comparison is also essential for judging the worth of each regime. How achievable is each, how durable – that is, how invulnerable to future erosion by the currents of competitive politics and technological change, and how flexible in the event that certain internal features of the regime prove easier to attain and sustain than others? How would each regime meet untoward contingencies – growing distrust, confrontation, war? How would each affect the tone and temper of international politics and the prospects for progress on a variety of other "issue fronts"? Answers to these and other relevant questions may be available if we examine the substance and implications of the four regimes.

The *First Regime* has three principal pillars. The first is *anarchy*. [10] The system of independent nation-states that appeared in Europe in the 17th century now covers all the planet, and this international system has no institutional equivalent to the government of the state in domestic politics. There is no supranational authority with a legitimate monopoly of force to guide and regulate international affairs and to enforce international law. Each member of this anarchic system retains a full complement of sovereign prerogatives, among which a central one is the right to resort to force in whatever way it chooses. Each nation-state has not only the right to make war but also the incentive to be ready to do so, for all other states retain the same right and set their own rules regarding how and when to do so. The principal nuclear states of the current regime not only have few formal restraints on the use of their arsenal, they have declared that they will actually use nuclear weapons under certain conditions and circumstances. Thus, the present international system and the nuclear regime are part of that system in which the weapons, including nuclear weapons, persist, and in which the use of force, even nuclear force, is neither illegal nor unthinkable.

The second pillar is – *nuclear equilibrium* between the principal nuclear powers. Although their arsenals do not correspond in every detail, they are almost equal in the most important category of comparison, the capacity of "assured destruction". Each has a nuclear arsenal that is potent and resilient enough to deal a death blow to the other's society even after absorbing a full-scale attack. Neither can count on disabling the other, even with an all-out surprise attack. The result has been a standoff: the two stalks of the nuclear plant brace one another; the certainty of annihilation has "deterred" each superpower from attacking the other.

The third pillar is *hierarchy*, the uneven, rank-ordered distribution of nuclear might. For four decades, the United States and the Soviet Union owned by far the most significant nuclear arsenals. The vocabulary of politics has drawn on other fields to describe this state of affairs. From the argot of advertising has come the label "superpower", which the two wear with a mixture of pride and anxiety. Physics has contributed the term 'bipolar' to describe how the superpowers act as distinct centres in the international society around which lesser states cluster. But their relationship with each other was best characterised by the economic term "duopoly"; like two giants firms that dominate a single market, they have common and distinctive rights and privileges that they exercise competitively but they also collude with each other to maintain their dominance.

The United States and the Soviet Union do not share an exclusive franchise on nuclear weapons. Three other states have manufactured them, and in 1974, India set off a nuclear explosion, which is tantamount to testing a bomb.[11] But the French and British nuclear stockpiles are relatively small, and the political and geographical circumstances of the two states make their weapons, for most purposes, part of the American strategic force, despite gestures of independence by the French. China is most emphatically part of neither the Soviet nor the American camp, but the Chinese arsenal had not had a profound effect on the international system's nuclear arrangements because it is dwarfed and held in check by the two giant forces. Although the regime is not strictly a bipolar one – the Chinese nuclear force had undoubtedly influenced American and Soviet foreign policies and defence planning – the United States and the Soviet Union remain, overwhelmingly, the two most important nuclear nations.[12]

The First Regime has three closely related achievements to its credit. First, there has been no nuclear war since 1945. Since the end of World War II, nuclear explosions have taken place for experimental purposes only, far from cities, factories, and military bases that would become their targets in a real conflict. Second, within the sphere of greatest interest to the United States and the Soviet Union, which covers the most heavily industrialised parts of the world – Europe, North America, and Japan – there has been no war at all, even of a non-nuclear character, in over four decades. In the first half of the 20th century, by contrast, this "industrial circumference" was ravaged by two of the bloodiest conflicts in history. The third achievement is the way in which nuclear weapons have altered the tides of international politics. Within the industrial circumference, this regime has dampened political conflict. There have been sharp disagreements between the United States and the Soviet Union, but the leaders of these two nations have managed these disagreements with sobriety and caution, taking great care to limit as far as possible the political conflicts that have grown out of them. On occasions, disagreements between the two have threatened to spill over into fighting – such as over Berlin several times and when the Soviet Union placed nuclear-capable missiles in Cuba in 1962 – but crises of such gravity have been relatively rare, and when they have erupted, the two sides have resolved them without going to war. Each superpower has tacitly granted the other a free hand within its own geographic sphere of influence, as when

Soviet forces crushed political uprisings in Hungary in 1956, Czechoslovakia in 1968, and when American troops intervened in the Dominican Republic in 1965.

Within the industrial circumference as a whole, the United States and the Soviet Union have concluded that nuclear weapons are too dangerous to permit unfettered political conflict. However, outside this perimeter, it is too acute, and too difficult for the superpowers to control for there to be a significant role for nuclear weapons in peace and war. The dissolution of the great colonial empires has spawned disputes and wars over who was to control the successor states, where their borders were to be drawn, and what the relationship among the diverse groups within them was to be. But, at least, since the Soviet Union became a full-fledged nuclear power, nuclear weapons have not been caught up in the political turbulence outside the industrial circumference, even where one of the superpowers was involved – with the exception of the Korean peninsula. The war in Vietnam sucked in the United States but the use of nuclear weapons was not seriously contemplated at any stage of the conflict. Politics outside the industrial circumference has remained apart from nuclear weapons for a number of reasons. Most obviously, it has chiefly involved states that do not have nuclear weapons. And the mutual restraint of the United States and the Soviet Union engendered by nuclear weapons has carried over into the two nations' behaviour in these regions: each has had to take care not to provoke a crisis with the other by its actions in the Middle East, in Africa, and in Southeast Asia; neither has wanted or allowed their competition in these regions to take on a nuclear character. Moreover, the political ends that the great nuclear powers seek outside their own particular spheres of interest are neither of the sort nor of the severity to justify the involvement of nuclear arms. So this regime has had the effect of moderating politics among nations within the industrial circumference and keeping weapons of mass destruction apart from the often immoderate and bloody relations among states outside it.[13]

The existence of a connection between the First Regime and the relative political stability of the post-war world cannot be proved. It is possible that the "achievements" of the regime would have come to pass even if human beings had never split the atom. It can be argued that once Europe was divided and the United States and the Soviet Union faced each other heavily armed, they would have found a way to coexist peacefully even without nuclear weapons; weariness with fighting, the considerable destructive power of non-nuclear armaments and a rough military balance between the two camps would have prevented another great war. It is impossible to either prove or disprove this contention, for the history of the last fifty years cannot be rerun leaving out nuclear weapons. But it is plain that those three or four decades have brought with them opportunities for war between the United States and the Soviet Union. And in wrestling with the problems that gave rise to those opportunities, the leaders of the two nations have borne in mind the nuclear devastation that mishandling them could bring about. The destructive power of the non-nuclear weapons that had become available by the end of World War II would have made national leaders reluctant to go to war again. The harnessing of nuclear energy for military purposes dramatically increased the destructive power and, so it is reasonable to assume, stiffened that reluctance. If the examples of Bastogne and Dresden made World War III an extremely unattractive prospect, the vivid images of Hiroshima and Nagasaki made it a horrifying one and have kept it so as the other battles of World War II have faded from memory.

Leaving aside the question of the existence of nuclear weapons, it might be argued that the particular nuclear regime that has evolved since 1945 has not been crucial in maintaining the political calm within the industrial circumference. Perhaps an alternative regime would have performed as well or better. It is conceivable, for example, that the third pillar of the regime, hierarchy, has had nothing to do with this stability, that *any* distribution of nuclear power would have ensured it. The distinct prospect that many more nations that now own them, will have nuclear weapons during the 1990s, and especially during the early years of the present century, means that this proposition may be tested in the years ahead; it is by no means certain that it will be proved true. It is finally possible to concede the importance of nuclear weapons and of their hierarchical distribution for international tranquillity but to doubt that the First Regime's second pillar – equilibrium – has contributed to it; it could be argued that a nuclear arsenal of nearly any size and composition would have deterred each superpower once the other had one. This contention is the heart of the "minimum deterrence" school of nuclear strategy and it is the governing assumption of the French and, perhaps, the Chinese nuclear forces. But against this school stand those who argue that gross differences in the size of the Soviet and American arsenals would be bound to influence global relations between the two states, even if those differences did not give either a "first strike" capability.

What precisely the world would be like without nuclear weapons, nuclear equilibrium, or nuclear hierarchy cannot be deduced. What can be said of the second and third pillars of the first regime is that, like nuclear weapons themselves, they have at least reinforced impulses for stability that would have existed without them but that might not have been strong enough alone to contain the disruptive forces in world politics. So the relationship between the first nuclear regime and international stability is probable, if not provable. And in that relationship lies the regime's value and the reason for preserving it into the present time and beyond. The three pillars are not certain of surviving through the present century in the same form as they existed in the 1970s. Nuclear politics – the discussion and disposition of questions involving nuclear weapons – will revolve around the respective fates of these pillars in the coming years and decades.

The first pillar, anarchy, is not so much a pillar of the present system, in the sense that equilibrium and hierarchy are, as it is the foundation of the first or any other foreseeable nuclear regime. The anarchic nature of the international system is not likely to come to an end in the near future. The system of independent states that made its first recorded appearance in ancient Greece, that came to prevail in Europe in the 17th century, and that has spread over the world in the latter half of the 20th century, will endure. For the states of the world to be fused into a single unit, for some supranational body to emerge to govern them, nuclear issues — and all of international politics — would have to change dramatically. But this is extremely unlikely to occur. The various proposals and high hopes for world government and the vicissitudes of history that have spawned them have never managed to bring such a global order into existence, and there is no reason to suppose that these ideas will be implemented in the future.

In the absence of a world state that would do away with the international anarchy altogether, people and nations have attempted to tame it through the creation of international law. There is no authority to enforce the law of nations, but states often obey it nonetheless, and it does provide guidelines for their behaviour. The anarchy of the First Regime could conceivably be modified in the future by an expansion of international law to include certain nuclear rules of engagement. Whereas, for the last four decades of the 20th century, the United States and the Soviet Union publicly reserved the right to use their nuclear weapons when, where, and how they choose, they could undertake to observe certain limit on these freedoms. The most likely limits are of two sorts.[14]

In the first place, it is within the power of the nuclear powers to remove the ambiguity in their stated policies by officially declaring that they will not be the first to use nuclear weapons – strategic or tactical – under any circumstances. This step has been urged upon them from time to time. The main purpose of a no-first-use declaration is consistent with a principal objective of the First Nuclear Regime: to minimise the chances of a nuclear shot being fired in anger. And such a declaration could serve other goals as well. It could discourage the spread of nuclear weapons to states that do not have them by helping to assuage one fear that must influence the decision to go nuclear: a non-nuclear state would have a pledge that nuclear arms would never be used against it. A no-first-use declaration could also make for smoother relations between the major nuclear powers, whose thousand-mile border ranks near the top of the list of troubled areas where nuclear war could be ignited in the future. But it must be borne in mind that it is possible that decoupling nuclear and conventional war would increase the danger that the worst would occur: restraint on both sides could be so undercut that war will beat out, with the no-first-use pledge abandoned in the heat of the battle and nuclear weapons brought into play.

There is no way of knowing whether a no-first-use avowal would bring disaster in this way. What is certain is that as long as nuclear weapons exist, the policies of states possessing them will have a double edge. The owners of nuclear weapons will always be reluctant to use them, especially if the foe is another nuclear state. But war brings with it extremes of behaviour – confusion, panic, and miscalculation as well as extraordinary courage and self-sacrifice – such that neither side could be certain, once war erupted, that the other would not bring its nuclear arsenal into play no matter what commitments had been undertaken beforehand.

For four decades, both the United States and the Soviet have resolved to respond to a nuclear assault by the other with a nuclear salvo of their own. It is this resolve that deters an initial attack. And it has been assumed that in each case the retaliatory blow would be massive, each side would lay waste as many of the other's cities and as much of its industry as it could. This policy of "mass destruction" has come under some criticism in American strategic circles on two counts and these underscore the second limiting factor. The first criticism is that it is morally wrong to rest the nation's security upon the threat to annihilate millions of people. The second is that it is a strategic blunder to do so. It would, according to the second criticism, be irrational to do what the doctrine of deterrence threatens to do after a first strike had been launched; that is, it would be foolish – an act of spite and revenge, not of policy – to lash out indiscriminately at enemy targets in response to a nuclear attack.

Partly in response to these concerns, former American Secretary of Defence James Schlesinger advocated a policy of "limited retaliation" or "limited counterforce" in 1974. However, this policy did not represent a complete shift in American nuclear arrangements: American missiles had always been aimed at "military" as well as "civilian" targets, and they could be fired selectively. Nor was it a purely doctrinal matter; he asked Congress for new weapons to carry it out and it was announced as an important change in the nation's strategic principles. It was hailed by many as both a more humane way of fighting a nuclear war and a more effective way of deterring one.

However, it is possible that no-first-use, limited retaliation, or any other change in strategic doctrine will not significantly affect the stability of the First Nuclear Regime as its physical properties persist. In the first years of the nuclear age, doctrine had enormous importance: the weapons were new, there were few of them, they seemed to have a several possible purposes, and relations between the United States and the Soviet Union were tense and uncertain; each side needed to know what the other intended to do with its weapons. Now the habits of forty years give a part of the answer to that question, and the high force levels each has achieved supply the other part. Because each side has so many nuclear weapons, neither can attack the other and escape terrible retaliatory damage. Because each side has so many nuclear weapon neither can be confident that the other will refrain from using its stockpile once war breaks out. The future of the regime, therefore, rests less upon the fate of its first pillar, anarchy, than upon that of its second, equilibrium.

Equilibrium, the heart of the First Nuclear Regime, the strategic balance between the United States and the Soviet Union, has attracted more attention, consumed more resources, and provoked wider concern than any other nuclear issue in the last four decades. The central component of this second pillar is the series of agreements that the two superpowers have concluded among themselves. Together, they codify the three principal elements of the equilibrium between the strategic nuclear forces of the two superpowers.

The first element is the doctrine of MAD. In the 1972 SALT I agreements, each superpower abjured extensive networks of missile defences, thereby promising, in effect, to leave its cities exposed to the rockets of the other. By agreeing to curtail the deployment of ABM systems, each effectively committed itself not to strike first by giving the other the assurance of being able, if necessary, to wreck vast destruction in retaliation.

The SALT agreements have also ratified a second important element of nuclear equilibrium – high force levels – by leaving each side with an enormous strategic arsenal. The 1974 Vladivostok protocol permitted each as many as 2,400 "launchers" of nuclear explosives – long-range bombers, submarines, and land-based missiles – and both had approximately that many. [15] Of these, 1,320 could be fitted with multiple warheads. [16] These totals far exceed the firepower necessary to visit immense, "unacceptable" destruction on the two societies. The bomb that struck Hiroshima had an explosive force of about 20,000 tons (20 kilotons) of TNT; both sides now have thousands of bombs that are many times more powerful.

SALT has also codified a third characteristic of the nuclear balance between the United States and the Soviet Union – equality. Numerical equality in strategic weapons delivery systems is a hallmark of the 1974 protocol. Not only can each rain down "unacceptable" damage upon the other even after absorbing an initial blow; not only does each have a nuclear stockpile capable of inflicting far more than unacceptable damage; now the sizes of those stockpiles and, hence, the degrees of destruction they can produce are, by agreement, roughly equal.

These three elements – MAD, huge forces, equality – are like layers wrapped around each other, the outer layers reinforcing the inner ones. Mutual assured destruction is the core of the equilibrium between the United States and the Soviet Union. Even without either high force levels or numerical equality, a handful of submarines armed with nuclear-tipped missiles would give one side or the other an "assured destruction" capacity. But the two outer layers are not without consequence. High force levels anchor the strategic balance by giving each side insurance against changes in the other's arsenal. They also ensure the continuation of hierarchy – the regime's third pillar. And they may help to extend to the fringes of the industrial circumference the caution with which the two Great Powers treat each other in Europe; conceivably one or the other might behave more recklessly outside Europe if only a small strategic force threatened it. Equality is a less important layer than the other two and could be removed without seriously weakening the pillar. But the equality between the two arsenals which the SALT accords have mandated helps both governments resist domestic pressure for more and more sophisticated weapons. And it serves as a reassuring symbol to each Great Power of the other's benign intentions and commitment to restraint. The equilibrium between Washington and Moscow might hold steady on the basis of mutual assured destruction regardless of the relative dimensions of their strategic arsenals, but the three layers together make nuclear equilibrium a stout and sturdy pillar of the First Regime.[17]

Of the three layers of the equilibrium pillar of the First Regime – MAD, high force levels, and equality – the third could most easily be eroded in the future. The consequences of such erosion are extraordinary and extremely difficult to foresee. They depend, in the first instance, upon just what sort of inequalities arise. Additions to one arsenal that threaten the retaliatory capacity of the other will obviously have more serious repercussions than those that do not. But even when the dimensions of the asymmetries are known, their implications will remain problematical. There are different indices by which the two forces can be compared, and the United States may lead the Soviet Union by some, and trail by others. Comparing the two arsenals numerically may not be the best way to determine their relative strategic value, but it is a convenient approach. The erosion of numerical quality would mean the loss of a useful benchmark by which each side can judge the strength and intentions of its adversary. This erosion might conceivably lead to heightened suspicion, an escalation of the arms race, and a greater risk of confrontation in the international arena.

And just as importantly, strategic inequalities could affect the relationship of the central nuclear balance to the rest of international politics. The effect of inequalities would depend upon how the two superpowers and third countries perceived the military balance between them and how these perceptions affected their foreign policies. Even if the inequalities were inconsequential in strictly strategic terms, if they were perceived as significant, they could unsettle the international system. It is the psychological effect of movement away from equality more than strategic significance of the developing inequalities themselves which can, it has been argued, damage the prestige and influence of the country that is "left behind".

Because inequalities could easily appear, because their effects are hard to estimate and because these effects could, some believe, disturb the equilibrium between the superpowers, they are likely to be controversial in the decades to come. So it is worth considering what might conceivably happen should one of the Great Powers find itself in a position to demolish a large fraction of the other's striking force.

There is no doubt that inequality might aggravate crises. Here speculation is particularly difficult, for a crisis is, almost by definition, a time when people and nations do not behave as they ordinarily do, when customary conduct is suspended, and sound judgement sometimes left behind. Here one may be tempted to recall the Cuban missile crisis of 1962. But "the Cuban missile crisis, like the Bible and the works of Lenin, can be cited to prove anything".[19] The "lessons" to be drawn from it are far from fully obvious. First, it was not an unalloyed triumph for the United States; a flurry of negotiation took place between the two sides, out of which the Americans gave a pledge not to invade Cuba and tacitly promised to withdraw some missiles from Turkey in exchange for the Soviet retreat. The record of the crisis does not show any confidence among American officials that a nuclear exchange would have left the United States in a favourable position. And insofar as the missile crisis ended in an American "victory", this was not necessarily due to the strategic balance at the moment; the United States had much more non-nuclear military force in the Caribbean than the Soviets, and this may have been decisive. The missile crisis may demonstrate, finally, not the political productivity of marginal advantages in nuclear weaponry but the tendency of each superpower to act more firmly than the other within its own sphere of direct concern.

Strategic equality between the superpowers is always preferable to inequality between them. If their arsenals match one another, each side will harbour fewer doubts that the other is seeking to undermine the basic conditions of strategic stability (the most important of which is the invulnerability of retaliatory forces) or that it is attempting to garner greater political influence in the global arena through nuclear superiority. The impact of foreseeable strategic inequalities upon international politics cannot be foretold with certainty. But there are at least three reasons for doubting that conceivable inequalities will have any appreciable effect at all.[20]

The first is that the strategic forces of the superpowers will continue to be very large. The larger they are, the greater will be the assurance that a powerful part of them can survive any attack. And the larger they are, the less difference in inequalities in appearance, as distinct from strategic capability, will make. Second, the nuclear inequalities of the past did not have significant political consequences. The historical record is not an infallible guide to the future, but it is a source of evidence in thinking about it; and such evidence as there is does not offer much support for the view that differences between the two principal nuclear forces will crack the major alliances of the international system, convert either Great Power into the international equivalent of a reckless driver, or turn a crisis into a nuclear disaster. The third and final reason is that the political usefulness of all military might has tended to decline in the past four decades. Nuclear force has had a particularly limited utility. It has had a sobering influence, injecting a concentrated dose of caution into the international conduct of the Great Powers – caution that would not be abandoned with the achievement of marginal superiority. In fact, the growth of Great Power nuclear arsenals has reached a point of diminishing returns. There is not much that can be done with 11,000 nuclear weapons that cannot be done with 10,000.

But if the fruits of technological progress in nuclear weaponry seem to offer no cause for alarm, this does not mean that nobody will be alarmed by them. National leaders are likely to continue to believe, or at least to act as if they believe, that nuclear inequalities do matter. The government of neither superpower is likely to allow the other to increase and refine its arsenal without responding in some way. The Soviets, it is true, have some experience in living on the short side of inequalities more pronounced than any that the future decades will see. But the Soviets did seem to place a high value on precisely what was at stake – appearances. And if they became accustomed to nuclear inferiority in the past, they apparently did not enjoy it, since they made such an effort to achieve parity during the sixties and seventies.[21]

Both the superpowers, it may be contended, will be better off if neither feels impelled to add to its already abundant nuclear store. Nuclear weapons, while not ruinously expensive, cost a great deal of money. And neither superpower is without alternative channels for investing the funds they both devote to strategic hardware. In addition, competition in armaments is a source of political friction although it is less a source of direct conflict than a hindrance to cooperation. Neither side could, in practical terms, outbuild the other to the extent that the resultant asymmetries would be of political consequence. But if either tries, the other is likely to follow suit, leaving each of them poorer, more muscular, but no more powerful in relation to the other. Restraining the arms race is, therefore, a worthy project.[22]

The arms race may partly restrain itself in the coming years – particularly after the dismemberment of the Soviet Union. Its pace has shown signs of slowing in the last two decades and may well slow further in the future. Since advances in satellite reconnaissance let each side know what the other has, since neither has as much fear of a revolutionary break – through weapons technology as it did earlier – and since both rest comfortably on cushions of high force levels, neither needs to rush to replace one generation of armaments with the next with the urgency felt during the first years of the nuclear age. And as new weapons become ever more intricate and expensive, they take longer and longer to design, test, produce, and deploy. But even if it does slow down, the arms race will not on its own wind down to dead stop. Rather, like a hardy weed, it will keep growing if left to its own devices.[23]

In all likelihood, the forces that fuel the arms competition between the superpowers will still be potent in the coming years; the competitive dynamics of the anarchic international system will still be at work; however, the hopes or fears, may not persist that further investment in strategic hardware will yield political dividends. Yet research and development will go on; and the politicians, industrialists, and government officials with personal and professional stakes in the continuing manufacture of nuclear weapons – the constituent parts of the "military-industrial complex" – will be at their desks. In the coming years, curbing the arms race that the interaction of these forces encourages, will require a conscious policy of deliberate restraint.

Even if there is such restraint, it does not guarantee that the future will be wholly free of war and crisis. What it does mean is that the nuclear relationship between the superpowers will continue to discourage instability. The sources of instability lie outside the nuclear regime. The nuclear regime cannot prevent all political explosions. What it can do, and has done, is encourage the superpowers to dampen the most explosive spots in the international system and to manage eruptions as prudently as possible when they occur. The second and most important pillar of the First Nuclear Regime – equilibrium – will be firm enough to promote this prudence as effectively in the future as it has in the past. The endurance of the first pillar anarchy – will reinforce this effect by preventing the taking of measures that would formally constrain the use of nuclear weapons and thereby eliminate much of the sobering influence that the fear of nuclear war has had in world politics. The third pillar, hierarchy, is not so hardy.

Hierarchy, the third pillar of the First Nuclear Regime, complements the second pillar, the equilibrium between the superpowers, which has meant that despite temptations to use force against the other, neither Great Power dared to do so. Hierarchy has meant that the superpowers' mutual nuclear restraint has been transposed to the entire international community; as long as the United States and the Soviet Union, effectively the only countries with the option of initiating nuclear war, chose not to do so, nobody could.

Just as the component parts of the First Nuclear Regime's second pillar, superpower equilibrium, are codified in the various SALT accords, so are the main features of the third pillar, hierarchy, built into the Non-Proliferation Treaty (NPT) that was signed in 1968 and went into effect in 1970. The signatories to the NPT that do not have nuclear weapons promise not to acquire them and, to show the world that no weapons development is in progress, they agree to open their peaceful nuclear facilities to international inspection. The nuclear weapons states that sign the NPT, for their part, pledge not to assist any non-nuclear nation in joining what has come to be known as the "club" of nuclear weapon states.

The NPT reflects two important distinctions among nations which together make up the nuclear hierarchy. The first is the obvious, fundamental, and official distinction between those states that possess nuclear weapons and those that do not. The second distinction – unofficial but no less a part of the First Nuclear Regime – is that which separates the two nuclear superpowers from the other nuclear weapon states. The United States and the Soviet Union were the chief architects of the NPT and have taken on the task of coaxing other nations to sign it. Their nuclear forces give them far more political power than the arsenals of the four lesser nuclear nations provide. And the superpowers have, as well, a less equivocal commitment to the nuclear hierarchy itself than do the other four. Three of the four secondary nuclear powers – France, China and India – have had distinctly ambivalent attitudes towards it; while none has given a bomb or the means to make one to another state, all have criticised the NPT as discriminatory against small powers, and none has signed it.

Like SALT and nuclear equilibrium, the NPT not only reflects the two elements of nuclear hierarchy, but is also aimed at confirming and perpetuating one of them – the distinction between nuclear and non-nuclear nations. But there is no guarantee that either hierarchical distinction will last through the 1990s; both might be seriously challenged in the not very distant future. The hierarchical categories are not airtight, and states could move from one to the other in the years ahead. While perhaps not physically possible within a decade, over a longer period, the arsenal of one of the smaller nuclear powers could develop until it rivalled those of the two superpowers or otherwise complicated the problem of managing the current superpower nuclear equilibrium. Or the presently non-nuclear states could join the nuclear club. Either of these two developments could erode the First Regime and jeopardise what it has thus far achieved.

The nuclear hierarchy may be eroded not only by the enlargement of the lesser nuclear arsenals of today's international system but also by the acquisition of nuclear arms by nations that do not now have them. Whether proliferation threatens the relative calm that the First Regime has brought to international politics will depend upon who joins the nuclear club and how fast its membership expands. The greater the number of countries that have nuclear weapons, the greater the statistical probability that one will go off, even if only accidentally. The farther the bombs spreads from the confines of the industrial circumference, the greater are the chances that it could find its way into the hands of persons who would not show the prudence that the guardians of existing nuclear stockpiles have so far displayed. The farther they proliferate, the greater the risk that nuclear weapons will enter areas troubled by political quarrels. And as states begin constructing primitive nuclear arsenals – initially composed only of a few bombs and jet airplanes or simply passenger aircraft to deliver them – their better-armed neighbours or even the superpowers, may feel tempted to attack them in a preemptive strike.

The rate at which the nuclear club expands may also affect whether or not the international system can digest more nuclear states without undue distress. Nuclear weapons could spread very rapidly if a modest nuclear arsenal comes to be as vivid and as obligatory a symbol of national independence and importance as a steel mill or a seat in the UN General Assembly. Such a system-wide impulse can sometimes touch the members of the international community. This happened in the 1880s, when the principal European powers engaged in a "scramble for Africa", each feeling the need to conquer as much of the continent as it could lest its rivals appropriate a larger share of it. Their African rivalry fed the tensions in Europe that exploded in 1914. Nuclear weapons could become a similar touchstone in the years ahead.

Nuclear proliferation is a complicated problem. Or, more properly, it is a complicated series of problems, which are as numerous as the number of potential nuclear weapon states. It is often suggested that a fruitful way to deal with these problems would be to alter the structure of the present nuclear regime to make it less hierarchical. Two particular steps are often proposed. The first is to reduce significantly the forces of the superpowers. This, it is argued, would diminish the perceived importance of nuclear weapons and thereby make them less attractive to currently non-nuclear states. This proposal, however, rests on questionable premises. Anyone with a memory of Hiroshima or an elementary knowledge of Physics understands the power that nuclear weapons can give. Indeed, paring down the two foremost arsenals would more likely *encourage* the acquisition of nuclear weapons, since members of the two major alliances might feel their senior partners less able to protect them, while fledgling nuclear powers would not have quite so far to go to become the nuclear equals of the nuclear superpowers.[25]

The second proposed step to ease pressures for the spread of nuclear weapons is to admit other nations, especially those toying with the idea of obtaining nuclear weapons, to today's principal arms control discussions. However, this has already been tried in the past without fruitful results. Numerous UN forums over the last four decades have brought the great and the small of the world community together to grapple with the problems that nuclear weapons have presented; the more nations that have participated in negotiations, the gloomier the results. Those agreements that many nations have signed, the Limited Test Ban Treaty and the Non-Proliferation Treaty, were worked out by the United States and the Soviet Union, which then coaxed and cajoled others to subscribe to them. Broadening the strictly bilateral SALT negotiations would complicate them; there would be more parties to consult before anything could be agreed to, and more potential snags in the proceedings. These negotiations are difficult enough already, involving, as they do, considerable bargaining within as well as between the superpowers. Nuclear hierarchy cannot be disguised by inviting non-nuclear states to meetings of the superpowers. That hierarchy will remain a glaring feature of international politics for the foreseeable future.

Nor will proliferation be prevented by enacting nominal measures that chip away at the nuclear hierarchy. Indeed, the prospects for curbing the spread of nuclear weapons will only brighten to the extent that the principle of hierarchy is strengthened and the superpowers cooperate to persuade or coerce others not to obtain nuclear armaments. The second is political: ministering to the fears and suppressing or appeasing the aspirations that propel states into the nuclear club. Superpower cooperation would reinforce both approaches. Together the superpowers could regulate with some effect the flow of nuclear technology beyond the industrial circumference. And by cooperating, openly or tacitly, they could do a great deal to guarantee the security of most members of the international system, since the two Great Powers tend to be either the main threat or the main source of reassurance for most of them. But whether the two can work more closely together to inhibit the spread of nuclear weapons remains to be seen; the political barriers to intimate cooperation are high. And an alliance of the two to close the doors of the nuclear club might not be received with good grace by all those left standing outside. The other members of the international community would have to be persuaded that their security was not in jeopardy and that the "condominium" of the Great Powers encompassed only nuclear matters and nothing more.[26]

Like the second pillar of the First Nuclear Regime, the equilibrium between the two superpowers, its third pillar, hierarchy, is threatened with erosion springing from technological change and its political application in the years ahead. There are, however, three important differences between the futures of these two bulwarks of the First Regime. First, the technological challenge in the case of hierarchy comes not from advances in the state-of-the-art of weapons design but from the diffusion of its more elementary techniques. Manufacturing a fission bomb is not a simple operation that can be performed in an average basement, but neither is it an overwhelming or mysterious technical feat. It requires scientists with an understanding of the fundamental precepts of nuclear energy, a cadre of engineers, and a supply of fissionable materials. In the coming decades, more and more nations will come to have all three. Proliferation, therefore, will depend more upon political decisions and less upon technological progress than will the arms race between the Great Powers.[27]

Second, proliferation is more menacing to the First Nuclear Regime than is the arms race between the superpowers. Proliferation increases the chances that nuclear weapons will be fired in anger, whereas the spiral of the arms competition between the superpowers is not very likely to dislodge the constraints against war – the certainty of mutual assured destruction in the event of a nuclear exchange – that both have increasingly felt for four decades.

And third, proliferation will be more difficult to control than the superpower arms competition, for more centres of decision are involved; governments other than those of the superpowers, which are the ones most deeply committed for the First Regime, will have a say in how proliferation proceeds. In the early years of the nuclear age, the United States and the Soviet Union were able to exert more influence on other members of the international community than will be possible in the foreseeable future. Their advantages in wealth and power and their prestige were greater in the past than they will be in the future. The Soviet Union has already disintegrated.

The number of independent nuclear arsenals in the international system in the future will ultimately be determined by political choices that cannot be clearly foreseen. That number and the resultant likelihood of nuclear weapons being used in battle, will depend less on concerted superpower policies and more on the "climate" of international politics than has been true for the first three decades of the nuclear age. The number may not be alarmingly high; many nations have signed the NPT and will not lightly violate it. In fact, the nuclear club may become less, not more, attractive over time. Now regarded as a breach in the dike that had been holding back the waters of proliferation, India may be seen as a cautionary example of the disadvantages of joining the nuclear club. If Pakistan acquires nuclear armaments in response to India's May 1974 explosion, if the maintenance of a respectable strategic force turns out to be an intolerable burden on India's already staggering economy, and if the rest of the world accords New Delhi no greater, and perhaps less, respect than before, India and its potential imitators may conclude that precious resources have been poured into a project that has yielded neither power, prestige, nor security.[28]

And whatever the rate of proliferation in the near future, the First Regime – and its heart, the nuclear equilibrium between the superpowers – will help to cushion the international system from any disruptive effects that proliferation may produce. The First Regime has reduced the incentives for proliferation by calming ancient political disputes and by putting in the hands of each superpower a large and sturdy nuclear umbrella under which many nations can confidently take shelter. And the high force levels that are an integral part of the regime makes the states of the industrial circumference, at least, far less vulnerable to proliferation elsewhere than they would be if these arsenals were much smaller or if they did not exist at all.

It may be argued that the First Regime will contribute to the successful management of a host of new international issues by keeping the issue of nuclear weapons separate from them. Mingling them will be to the benefit of no one; if nuclear weapons grow in importance in international affairs, non-nuclear states will find themselves at a disadvantage. At the same time, the nuclear powers will find their arsenals blunt and unwieldy for achieving many of the goals they are likely to set for themselves in the future. And if nuclear matters become entangled with the budding international questions of the near or distant future, these will be more difficult to resolve. A spirit of egalitarianism pervades contemporary international politics, and it is likely to gather force in the future.

The non-nuclear states will not want to endorse the First Regime, at least not publicly, while the nuclear powers will not want it changed. A joint exercise in reevaluating the regime would lead to stalemate and acrimony. It would sap the world's limited supply of goodwill that is needed to address the international problems that are now emerging. And the world has, as well, a limited amount of attention to bestow on each of its various problems. In the words of Alastair Buchan: "We, the nations, are a little like the members of a committee who have been struggling hard to settle items one to three on the agenda, how to control or eliminate weapons of mass destruction, how to create easier relations between countries of opposing ideologies, how to narrow the gap between the rich and the poor countries, only to find that we must add five, six or seven new and important items to it."[29]

That first question, how to control or eliminate weapons of mass destruction, was the foremost item on the world's agenda in 1945. The First Nuclear Regime had, by the mid-1970s, provided a settlement of sorts for it. Discarding that regime or trying to reform it will only hurt the chances of coping with all the other matters that will be part of the agenda in the years to come.

A historical perspective is instructive. Over forty years ago, the nuclear stalk dominated the garden of international politics. But as the First Nuclear Regime was put into place – in part because it was put into place – other issues blossomed. There is going to be more and more to international affairs than nuclear weapons and the issues they affect. The First Regime helps keep the nuclear plant upright; away from it, other flora are poking through the soil. But the nuclear plant still towers menacingly. Should it crash to the ground, it would destroy everything in its path. The First Nuclear Regime, though awkward, fragile in spots, and far from perfectly designed, remains the best possible prop for it.

II

In designing the Second Nuclear Regime for the time frame of the 1980s, it is assumed that an alliance structure similar to that of the 1970s will persist, but neither that structure nor the relative rank of nations nor the technology of war and peace will be static over the decade. It is also assumed that public officials will generally attempt to act in the national interest as they see it – specifically, that leaders of both the United States and the Soviet Union will be wise enough and strong enough to emphasise national survival over bureaucratic advantage, to recognise the possible conflict between national security and defence industry interests, and to press for national advantage but not at great risk to national survival.

The Second Nuclear Regime is one with continued possession by relatively few nations of weapons of terrible destructive power, but with a reduction in the perceived advantage accruing to the few possessors. Under the Second Regime, the assigned tasks for nuclear weapons are limited strictly to roles they are generally recognised as performing well, namely, deterring or retaliating against other nations' use of nuclear weapons. These attributes would contribute to popular acceptance of the regime and allow a diversion of attention and resources to the important problems confronting individual societies and the world at large, such as the increasing cost of resources, environmental pollution, population explosion, and political and social instability of nations.[30]

Under the Second Regime prescribed here, confining the possession of nuclear weapons to a few states and limiting their utility to possessors would be furthered by the adoption by all possessors of a policy of non-use against non-nuclear weapon states, a restriction of the role of nuclear weapons to deterrence of, or response to, a nuclear attack, and the extension of nuclear deterrence to non-nuclear states confronted by an adversary with nuclear weapons. Taken together, doctrinal and declaratory measures of this sort would reduce the significance of nuclear weapons in world affairs and permit certain reductions in the physical capabilities of nuclear forces which would enhance the stability and, as a result, the legitimacy of the regime.[31]

While characterised by a lesser dependence on nuclear weapons than is true of the First Regime, the Second Regime has other parameters of comparable importance, among them an enhancement of the nature and level of conventional forces to bring about a reduction of the necessity of using nuclear weapons to deter or respond to low-level aggression. Also important for Western countries are a high degree of support by the electorate for the national security policy and the prevalence of hope over despair among the citizenry. Another parameter of the Second Regime is its effect on nuclear proliferation. Burgeoning nuclear forces among the lesser nations of the world would increase the chances of nuclear weapons being stolen or seized in coup d'état, with great potential for escalation and terrorism. As a means of severely limiting the utility of nuclear weapons and providing security guarantees to non-nuclear weapon states, the Second Regime prescribed here would command substantial world support for effective action against nuclear proliferation and, thus, would promote international stability.

It is sometimes argued that the comparative advantage of nuclear weapons lies in visiting destruction upon an enemy's society rather than in directly defending one's own population, territory, or military forces by destroying the enemy's forces. If nuclear weapons and the means for their delivery against enemy cities exist, then it is inconceivable that a nation will not threaten to use them *in extremis*, in order to prevent its effective annihilation. Therefore, a Second Regime would entail the continued existence of nuclear weapons among a relatively few powerful nations to deter the annihilation of these nations or their allies. In other words, under a Second Regime, the principle of MAD that has long served to prevent a nuclear exchange between the superpowers would be preserved.

The benefits of the Second Regime can be obtained to a large extent by the initiative of one side. Therefore, the American views as to the desirability of this regime need not depend on Soviet responses. The prescription for the United States to eschew a silo-killing force does not depend on a similar decision on the part of the Soviet Union. As emphasised above, we would like *least* to have an effective counterforce capability on *both* sides; but stability could be maintained if the Soviets alone had such a force and the Americans did not or vice versa, for there are many feasible countermeasures that the United States could take. For the United

States to respond by building a similar force would only cause serious concern on the other side regarding the probability of a preemptive strike against its strategic forces, a situation that would be as intolerable for Moscow as for Washington.[32]

The easiest way for the United States to offset a Soviet counterforce attack is to maintain a sufficiently large force of SLBMs and airfield-based strategic bombers so that even an extraordinary effective surprise attack in American ICBM silos would not constitute a disarming strike and, hence, would not be undertaken. Furnishing strategic aircraft with a rapid-start capability so that they can be airborne at short warning, and fitting them with long-range air-launched cruise missiles that can be fired at strategic targets from a thousand or more miles away will ensure the survival and effectiveness of the bomber force by minimising its dependence on an airborne tanker fleet in carrying out long-range missions. The advanced technology for strategic cruise missiles will allow cargo-type aircraft to replace many of the more expensive bombers altogether, since there will no longer be a need for planes that can penetrate Soviet air defences. Deploying the 4,000-mile range Trident I missile in place of the shorter-range Poseidon missile on Poseidon submarines will similarly reduce the vulnerability of the sea-based arm of the American deterrent.[33]

As an alternative, or in addition, to greater reliance on the bomber and submarine arms of the "triad", the United States could restructure its land-based ICBM force. A new, smaller ICBM – with a 10,000 pound launch-weight, single 50-kiloton warhead, 1/3 mile accuracy, and hard silo to suit – could be developed as an alternative to the force of Minutemen with MIRVs, with a view to deploying thousands of them and, thus, making a thoroughgoing Soviet silo-killing attack more difficult. The degraded accuracy and lesser total throw-weight would not even reduce the second strike capability. The stability of the Second Regime described here does not depend on the absence of MIRVs, but ensuring against the achievement of a counterforce capability by one side would be easier if, over the years, the MIRVed force on one or both sides were replaced by a large one of small ICBMs.

A less costly and quicker way for the United States to respond to a Soviet counterforce threat would be to modify the Minuteman to a "smart ICBM" – one that would have, in addition to the usual flexible command and control systems, the capability of being armed or disarmed in flight. Developing such a capability and deploying it if necessary would not only deter the Soviets from carrying out a silo-killing strike, but might also discourage them from ever developing or deploying the force capable of doing so. Insofar as it would permit the United States to adopt the following declared limited launch-on-reliable-detection (LORD) options:

1. *Command - arm-in-flight*: On reliable detection of a Soviet attack on American ICBM silos, the United States would launch approximately 50 Minutemen, unarmed – against Soviet cities – the missiles to be armed by secure, redundant radio command after fifteen minutes in flight if most of the unlaunched Minuteman were indeed destroyed in the interim.

2. *Command - disarm-in-flight*: Under the same circumstances, Minutemen would be launched armed, to be *disarmed* by secure, redundant command if the main Minuteman force were *not* destroyed in the interim. In both the options, the radio signals could be relayed from satellites, from special communications rockets, from aircraft, and from land sites.[34]

The purpose of planning and developing these more flexible capabilities would be to demonstrate *in advance*, to the Soviet Union and to the world, the futility of the Soviets' deploying an expensive force of silo-killing ICBMs. Such capabilities should be publicised; if Washington emphasises in official statements that it has developed such capabilities and is able and willing to deploy them, this may reduce the necessity of actually doing so by deterring the Soviets from deploying their new ICBMs.

To the extent that the Soviets were stimulated by such American developments and deployments to create their own limited launch-on-reliable-detection options, strategic stability would be further enhanced without the overall capability for destruction being increased. The two LORD options could be maintained inoperative at Presidential command under normal conditions, when strategic intelligence guarantees that Soviet forces could not possibly destroy the American strategic offensive force to a degree that would vitiate the United States' capability to inflict assured destruction in retaliation. The command-arm-in-flight option would be readied if there was a legitimate concern for force survivability, with the command-disarm-in-flight option held in reserve for use only if the Soviets appeared to have the ability to destroy the redundant radio-arming link.

Giving such a capability to Minuteman would be analogous to having the ability to quickly launch those bombers in the Strategic Air Command on ground alert, and in certain circumstances, maintaining bombers on air alert, until a crisis situation can be clarified. The size of the Minuteman force would be reduced temporarily by 5 per cent with the launch of 50 missiles in a false alarm situation – one ultimately not warranting a nuclear attack on the Soviet Union and so resulting in the destruction in flight of the 50 missiles; these missiles could be replaced in refurbished silos in a matter of weeks.

Still another way for the United States to respond to a Soviet silo-killing capability would be the development of model ABM defences specifically designed for the defence of the hardened, replicated ICBM silos and capable of being deployed at a lower cost and faster pace than a Soviet silo-killing force, but not having a technical capability to protect industry and population. While ABM defence of cities, in view of exaggerated claims of its effectiveness, is destabilising in that it might be seen to threaten the other side's ability to retaliate and, thus, might foster suspicion of a planned first attack ABM systems with a silo-defence-only capability, by increasing the survivability of retaliatory forces, are stabilising. Some are even compatible with the ABM ban of SALT I. Therefore, greater research and development efforts should be devoted to them, as well as to the Minuteman in-flight command arm/disarm system.[35]

The overall force levels resulting from SALT II, while unnecessarily high, would be acceptable in the Second Regime prescribed here. There is no compelling reason to face the problems of negotiating alternative American and Soviet strategic forces that might be more suitable to the regime. Strategic stability is insensitive to minor changes in such high force levels. This is because of the declining marginal utility of additional warheads arising from the finite number of important military, industrial, and civilian targets that a force must be able to destroy with confidence. Therefore, it is important first to move away from the First Regime, with its excessive dependence on nuclear weapons, while retaining these high force levels and to worry about negotiating more desirable force levels until after decreased dependence of the Second Regime has been achieved.

The United States evidently regards the ability to put the SAC bomber force on various levels of alert as a significant political tool. For this reason, it would be useful to put a substantial fraction of the ICBM and SLBM forces into a strategic reserve from which the missiles could not be fired but from which they could be brought into readiness in a matter of weeks or months. The purpose would be not to preserve them from an actual attack (in which they could be more or less vulnerable than the active strategic forces) but to reduce clearly excessive force levels in an easily reversible way. For the ICBMs, some 300 silos could be covered with earth or rock to a depth of perhaps thirty feet, making them useless on a scale of days but available in the unlikely event that continued Soviet force expansion and improvement began to place the effectiveness of the frontline American deterrent in doubt. For the SLBMs, 50 per cent of the Polaris, Poseidon, and Trident submarines could be kept in port on patrol in the southern oceans, well out of missile range of the Soviet Union. While primarily an arms control measure, the submarine strategic reserve would also further enhance SLBM survivability. Unusual communication practices could be employed so that it would be clear to the Soviet Union that these submarines were for out of firing range. Another form of strategic reserve would be an airfield-based strategic force element consisting of a combination advanced tanker/cargo/cruise missile-launching aircraft that in normal circumstances would be used only in its first two capacities.[36]

Assuming that domestic opposition and uneasiness could be overcome, such a posture would make it clear to the world that the United States had confidence in its strategic strength in reserve, indeed in superabundance. Furthermore, the United States would have a ready and immediate response to any new Soviet deployments or to ambiguities in Soviet activities, a response that would provide a visible increase in the American strategic offensive force long before any new procurement could become effective. By voluntarily reducing its ready force – without appreciable cost savings – the United States would provide evidence that smaller numbers do not connote inferiority.

The United States' national security would not depend on the Soviet Union's following suit by placing some of its own forces in strategic reserve, although such actions by Moscow would certainly improve the climate between the two nations. The long-term durability and stability of the Second Regime would benefit from visible signs that the Soviet Union saw its strategic forces in the same light as the United States saw its own forces. As a first step, Washington could put its MIRVs into the reserves, if indeed MIRVs are necessary, only against some future ABM systems, and move a fraction of its submarines to the southern ocean patrol. Unilateral measures such as these would provide a costless test of the readiness of the Soviet Union to establish its own strategic reserve.[37]

A complex defensive systems that is effective against all types of an opponent's strategic weapons, either present or possible, would not be technically feasible, nor would it be so in the foreseeable future. The recommended Second Regime has been conceived on the assumption of the continued dominance of strategic offensive and the consequent desirability of continued controls over the development of strategic defences, as it would be fruitless for the United States and the Soviet Union to deploy partially protective defence against one another – the rationale behind the 1972 treaty limiting ABMs.

However, Washington and Moscow might find it desirable and even possible to construct an effective defence against nations with much smaller strategic capabilities.[38] Although the strategic forces of both the superpowers are at least as effective, if not more so, in deterring Third world as in deterring each other, *second* nuclear powers may well be less able to maintain control over their nuclear weapons, to prevent theft or unauthorised launch, than the superpowers are. Since such nations in general, would not even come close to having strategic destruction capability against the United States and the Soviet Union, defences sufficiently effective to reduce the damage by such nations' nuclear force would be feasible.

However, two problems would arise for both superpowers: First, how to make such a defence clearly ineffective against a retaliatory attack by the principal opponent and not provocative in the sense that it should appear to constitute a base from which effective defence against the principal opponent could subsequently be achieved; second, how to cover the entire territory (since retargeting of even a small offensive force could otherwise restore its limited destructive capability) and defence against a mildly responsive threat, that is, one modified to help penetrate the defence system without threatening the principal adversary. In the case of the United States ABM system, it was argued that a "thin ABM defence against the Chinese ICBM threat" – one not providing a base for a heavy defence – could have been deployed using "perimeter acquisition defence-radar" and Spartan missiles to shoot down a small number of incoming Chinese ICBMs as they approached the United States space.[39] Such a thin ABM system would not require the expensive missile-site radar and short-range Sprint missiles essential to an effective anti-Soviet system and would ostensibly be ineffective against a massive Soviet attack because the radar, the "eyes of the system", could be easily exhausted or destroyed by large numbers of light, inaccurate ICBMs. However, the effectiveness of such a thin ABM system against China or other nuclear powers is dubious, as these states could saturate the perimeter acquisition-radar ready (by the use of lightweight decoys of balloons) almost as easily as the Soviets could.

In any case, the SALT I Treaty includes an agreement by the United States and the Soviet Union not to defend their territories against the ICBM forces of other nations. In view of the overriding importance of each maintaining an assured destruction capability against its major opponent, population defence against ICBM attack by lesser powers and revision of the 1972 treaty should be sought only if the treaty is clearly ineffective against the major opponent, a condition thus far not adequately satisfied by proposed systems, including the thin anti-China ABM. However, if future analyses and experiments provide a means of defending hardened missiles (in their assigned roles) against ICBM attack, a means not effective in defending industry and population, deployment of such defensive system – and revisions of the ABM Treaty, if necessary – would be desirable. This would enhance stability by ensuring the survivability of a retaliatory force without compromising its offensive potential.

Since the 1950s and up to the mid-1980s, the United States has had strategic nuclear weapons-forward-deployed on aircraft carriers, on IRBMs around the perimeter of the Soviet Union, and even on nominally tactical land-based fighters in Europe and East Asia. These forward-based systems were originally intended to supplement the far more expensive United States-based strategic bomber force; their cost (for an aircraft itself or other delivery vehicle) was lower because their required range was less. Forward-deployed strategic weapons also had the virtue of shorter response time; in contrast with the 12 hours or so of the travel time for bombers travelling from the United States, a forward-based aircraft takes only one SLBM, and especially with the formal prohibition of ballistic missile defence, these reasons for forward-basing of nuclear weapons no longer existed. And when the cost of bases was included, forward-based systems became highly expensive. In the 1970s, ICBMs became the dominant choice over forward-based fighters, being cheaper per weapon delivered, more survivable, more reliable and having a response time of only half an hour.[40]

A separate reason for deploying nuclear weapons in Europe was that of alliance strategy. Forward-based nuclear weapons deployed on allied aircraft, piloted and commanded by allied forces, not only contributed to allied military capabilities in the field, it was argued, but also gave NATO forces a mini-strategic force capable of reaching Warsaw Pact capitals on two-way missions and Soviet cities on one-way missions.

Furthermore, and perhaps most importantly, the use of such weapons in a truly tactical, countermilitary role could serve as a bridge, and a guaranteed lever of escalation, to the strategic level, and, hence, a deterrent to Soviet aggression. America's European allies want to be very sure that if their deterrent fails, the United States would come to their aid against invading Soviet or Warsaw Pact forces. The Europeans saw the vulnerability of American forward-based tactical nuclear weapons as an asset, for any Warsaw Pact attack on these forces in the event of theatre hostilities would force the United States itself to respond. Therefore, since an attack on Western Europe would turn into a direct Soviet-American nuclear confrontation, the Soviet bloc would be deterred from making such an attack.

While this argument revealed some of the benefits of tactical nuclear weapons, it ignored their many liabilities, including the possibility of accidental or unauthorised used by local commanders, of capture by the enemy or by the host country, and of theft or terrorism. A further liability of the United States tactical nuclear weapons in Europe was their significant cost in labour and material (on the order of 50,000 people simply to guard and maintain 7,000 weapons). Finally, having tactical nuclear weapons in Europe meant the removal from conventional forces of the aircraft and other systems carrying them, for these systems' ostensibly "dual-capable" role did in fact reflect a nuclear priority. Was there some way to reduce these liabilities while retaining the benefits of deterrence which these weapons conferred on American Allies?[41]

Before the Soviet Union acquired a large number of nuclear weapons, American tactical nuclear weapons certainly had a deterrent effect on a conventional Soviet attack in Europe; given the rather hazy distinction between tactical and strategic nuclear weapons, an American "tactical" nuclear response to a Warsaw Pact offensive would have meant massive destruction for the Soviet Union or its allies. But with the advent of Soviet IRBMs targeted on Western Europe, there was no reason to believe that a Western nuclear response against Warsaw Pact territory would not be answered by a Soviet IRBM counterattack on NATO territory. Nor was there reason to be confident that the use of even very small, clean, and well-controlled tactical nuclear weapons, and NATO only against Warsaw Pact troops in combat, would not be answered by larger, dirtier, and more randomly targeted Warsaw Pact nuclear weapons. Therefore, a strictly tactical role for the United States nuclear weapons in Europe might fail to credibly deter Warsaw Pact aggression. The truly effective deterrent had been the threat to the Soviet Union and East Europe homelands, which could be achieved through a shared targeting and release scheme for United States ICBMs.[42]

Developments in the 1970s in precision-guided munitions and microelectronics, together with the deployment of the Navstar navigation and guidance system (which would provide American and NATO cruise missiles, cannon shells, and bombs with accuracy as great as twenty feet almost all the time, anywhere in the world), had greatly reduced the comparative utility of nuclear weapons in performing tactical missions, that is, in attacking troop concentrations, armoured columns, and the like.[43] The tactical nuclear weapon had always been a major threat to an army on its own territory, but since civilians far outnumber potential combatants in any region, the use of tactical nuclear weapons on American or allied territory had not been looked upon with favour. Recent technological advances have somewhat improved the capability of tactical nuclear weapons, but they have also enhanced the capability of non-nuclear weapons to the point that tactical nuclear weapons no longer have an overall advantage.

Improved accuracy and flexibility of delivery vehicles, advanced homing and fusing technology, new dispenser warheads and minelets, and more capable command and control systems all improve the capability of conventional weapons far more than they improve that of nuclear weapons. Because of the greater variety of conventional weapons and the fewer inhibitions to their use compared with nuclear weapons, a well-conceived non-nuclear force is more capable than a tactical nuclear force. Higher-yield weapons are not tactical at all; their use will be countered or deterred by determined use of strategic nuclear weapons.

Therefore, to the extent that strictly local capabilities are desired, the non-nuclear precision-guided munitions, mines, and the like which have entered the United States inventory in recent years, and which are susceptible to further improvement, are far preferable to the maintenance of nuclear weapons by the thousands in Europe. In fact, not replacing the tactical nuclear weapons with conventional systems of this sort, while it might not be tragic in the European context, could have the unintended side effect of encouraging nuclear proliferation, for it would convey to would-be proliferants the erroneous notion that nuclear weapons are of great utility in theatre warfare.

An important part of any nuclear defence posture is that which is announced about it – within a nation, to other nuclear powers, and to non-nuclear powers. Like the physical force posture it influences the actions of adversaries, allies, and neutrals in building their own nuclear and non-nuclear forces as well as their willingness to use those forces. Both postures should be chosen with this in mind. In other words, the physical posture for nuclear forces in the Second Regime could be largely achieved through the unilateral actions of the United States. This is equally true for the declaratory posture regarding the use of those forces.

With respect to the central confrontation between the United States and the Soviet Union, Washington should be consistent in publicly declaring its readiness to respond to the use of strategic nuclear weapons by the other side with its own nuclear arsenal, either to inflict assured, massive destruction or to use its own strategic weapons more flexibly, that is, in smaller numbers. In other words, it should be made clear that any nuclear provocation will be answered by a nuclear response, that there is an inevitable, near-physical linkage between destruction of the United States and destruction of the Soviet Union. Consistent with this posture, no silo-killing capability should be sought or tested, even if the Soviets deployed some elements of such a force, since the American nuclear force would be intended solely for second-strike retaliatory missions.

While under the Second Regime a nuclear response to a non-nuclear Soviet provocation would not be explicitly ruled out, it would be reduced to an extreme option.[44]

This approach to determining whether and how to respond to Soviet non-nuclear provocations is not vital to a Second Nuclear Regime. However, if it could be put into practice, it would help preserve the deterrent value of nuclear weapons below the level of massive strategic attack without requiring the retention of tactical nuclear weapons, the advancement of counterforce weaponry or the abandonment of the principle of MAD.

The Second Regime would be a posture of restraint – one in which the United States in particular would continue to possess nuclear weapons in a dangerous world but would seek above all to nullify the importance not of its own weapons alone, but of nuclear weapons everywhere. Thus, its nuclear weapons would not only protect the United States against destruction by the Soviet Union, they would also help protect other, even non-aligned, if non-nuclear, nations against a nuclear attack. Continued United States retention of strategic nuclear weapons would become much more acceptable to many nations.

The recommended posture could be achieved by the United States acting alone. By limiting expenditures on its strategic force and limiting the scope of what that force need and can do, the United States would be able to avoid buying excess insurance for a very narrow aspect of its national security. Such excessive emphasis would lead to reduced security and also give the false impression to the world's less favoured nations that the United States felt it had an exclusive right to protect itself against the threat of nuclear destruction. Reduced expenditures of human and material resources on strategic systems might facilitate the achievement of other American goals in both its domestic and foreign policy. Even more important to the attainment of this end would be the introduction of a philosophy of purpose and a sense of proportion in the strategic sphere.

Would the Soviet Union exercise similar restraint in response to American initiatives? Would it join in the proposed agreements? In all likelihood it would, because it is in the Soviets' national security interest to do so. The Second Regime prescribed here would put an end to the situation in which the continuing display of American technical virtuosity – whereby the United States has repeatedly gained putative "advantages" in strategic capabilities – has compelled the Soviets to follow suit, at tremendous cost to the strained Soviet economy, with this imitation by the Soviets, in turn, spurring some in the United States to urge further improvements because the Soviet Union is "catching up". A consistent American policy of restraint would strengthen the hands of those in the Soviet bureaucracy arguing for a similar rationalisation of Soviet strategic programmes and perhaps, of those advocating reductions in Warsaw Pact forces.[45]

Although most of the actions advocated here for maximising American security could be taken by the United States unilaterally, the endurance of the proposed Second Regime depends on the actions of others, particularly with regard to nuclear proliferation. Many people and nations in the world strongly oppose the foreign policy of the United States; they cannot be won over to America's ideology, let alone to America's support.

But others could and would support American actions that advance the goals of order, justice, and equity of opportunity in an imperfect world. Halting nuclear proliferation would further these goals, and it is for this reason that the prescribed regime would downgrade the importance of nuclear weapons in international politics. The Second Regime would make it clearly to the advantage of non-nuclear states not to acquire nuclear weapons. Most nations would come to see the United States and the Soviet Union as antagonists whose declining stocks of nuclear weapons were a burden they bore, somewhat unwillingly, for the benefit of the rest of the world, putting their nuclear weapons at the disposal of others to deter a nuclear attack, but not using them to defend against a non-nuclear attack or to coerce non-nuclear nations.

III

It is now clear that the advocates of the Second Regime based their arguments mainly in terms of the actions and interests of the United States rather than from an international perspective. The exception seems warranted. Richard Garwin, for example, believes that the United States could bring about many desirable conditions unilaterally – in some instances without a need for reciprocity by other actors and, in others with reciprocity desirable but not essential. In still other respects, Garwin quite explicitly calls for international action to facilitate the emergence of the Second Regime. But since he argues that altered American policies would largely suffice, it is appropriate for him to make the case that such policy change is in fact in the American as well as the global interest.[46]

The burden of the Third Regime is this: why should mankind bother to examine nuclear disarmament – a plainly infeasible goal for the near future? First, thinking about the nature of, paths towards, and obstacles to, a world without nuclear weapons compels one to reckon with basic questions that might otherwise escape notice. Second, if denuclearisation is to be a goal for a more distant future, the coming decades could be periods in which certain processes leading towards that goal could be put in train and, of course, in which the interposition of new obstacles must be avoided. If, for example, the difficulty of proscribing nuclear weapons increases due to the number of nations that have nuclear weapons, some progress towards the Third Regime in the coming decades must be imperative, lest proliferation render eventual denuclearisation utterly impossible. Third, since nuclear disarmament is so widely accepted in the abstract as a fundamental goal, it is only prudent to ask more systematically whether such a condition is in fact desirable – or at least what its benefits and drawbacks might be. Last, if the desirability of denuclearisation depends upon what form it takes (its institutions, its safeguards, its attendant changes in politics and attitudes), we had better know, with as much precision as possible, towards what sort of nuclearised world we should steer.[47]

Ever since the invention of nuclear weapons, many strategic and political thinkers have urged that these weapons be removed from national control. Undoubtedly, this attitude towards nuclear weapons rests primarily upon an emotional reaction against the magnitude and horror of the destruction produced by such weapons. This emotional reaction is a crucial political asset supporting the control of nuclear weapons. Yet, even though it has created very strong inhibitions against the use of nuclear weapons, it has not proved strong enough to inhibit a number of nations from possessing them.

Arguments against the possession of nuclear weapons are, therefore, somewhat more subtle. Nuclear weapons have at least four effects that argue for their undesirability or their incompatibility with existing institutions. The first is that the destruction that might accompany even "limited" use of nuclear weapons is disproportionate to the goals that can be obtained through their use. The emergency of nuclear deterrence muted the fears, reflected in the initial Acheson-Lilienthal Plan, that there could be no defence against nuclear weapons. Nevertheless, the dynamics of nuclear deterrence place the lives of enormous numbers of people at risk, and the resulting responsibility – in decisions that must be taken rapidly – has impressed every American and Soviet leader. Although the Soviet-American nuclear relationship has become remarkably stable, the chances of nuclear destruction seem likely to increase as the number of nuclear weapon states rises and the potential of nuclear terrorism grows. One feels that a world structure of national defence policies that imposes such risks is fundamentally irrational.

Second, with the spread of nuclear weapons, the balance-of-power system, the classical way of controlling conflict between autonomous opposed actors, may lose its ability to maintain peace. A successful balance-of-power structure required an ability to shift coalitions to bring a preponderance of power against a potential combatant. This underlying military requirement – that against a single nation, a coalition will deter war that one nation cannot deter - is much less likely to be satisfied when the nations are armed with nuclear weapons. Stable deterrence may be possible between two nations; but any effort to calculate first-strike and reply-strike-force balances with varying coalition possibilities leaves one less confident that stable deterrence is possible among many nations, unless all nuclear forces are deployed unambiguously as strictly retaliatory systems or unless all proliferants are deterred by the mere possibility of nuclear war.

Even if a multipolar nuclear deterrence system is possible, it is likely to be much less flexible and adaptable at the political level than is the traditional balance of power system. Deterrence has made it difficult for the United States and the Soviet Union to meet political conflict except through stalemate. If nuclear weapons spread, one naturally wonders if stable deterrence relationships and multiple regional deterrence relationships would produce a stalemate on problems throughout the international system out of a widespread fear that altering the status quo may be more risky than accepting it. In a proliferated world, problems that might otherwise have been solved, although in some instances with sub-nuclear violence, might instead be frozen. Some would dissipate over time. But others might fester until unrelieved tensions burst, stable relationships broke down, and large-scale violence – now nuclear – erupted.[48]

Third, nuclear weapons are more easily adapted to attacks upon civilians than to attacks upon military forces. This anti-civilian role raises profound moral issues. It also affects the philosophical relationship between government and citizen, for in the nuclear era, a government can defend its own citizens only through threats to attack other nation's citizens or through agreements with other governments, sometimes even designed to leave its own citizens vulnerable. The government's defence function is, in a sense, turned against its citizens, and part of the unity of interest between government and citizen is lost. Perhaps because national governments are now tending to find their central mission an economic one rather than a strategic one, this philosophical separation between government and citizen has not yet become politically significant, but it is hard to visualise this disparity of interest being submerged for much longer at a time when national governments are under attack on so many other grounds.

The force of the last point is intensified by a final point: nuclear weapons give national governments military power that is substantially independent of the contributions and control of the citizenry of the nations. Once the nuclear weapons are built – a process that will become increasingly cheap for all but those engaged in large-scale deterrence competitions – the contemporary government controls its nuclear power independently of the people and husbands it relatively independently of the economic and political factors that shaped conventional military capability. The point holds for all sophisticated weapons but is particularly strong for nuclear weapons, with their relative power, their low personnel requirement, and the special authority that citizens are willing to give to governments in the nuclear area. This independence from moral and institutional constraints means that nuclear forces are relatively unaffected by political changes; one can visualise American and Soviet strategic arms construction going on and on, whether or not there are actual grounds for conflict between the two nations. Military capability is not necessarily like to be proportionate to a regime's ability to solve internal political problems; a weak government's nuclear weapons may deter about as effectively as those of a strong government.[49]

On the domestic side, governments could, thus, lose both their need to maintain public support and part of their basis for public support. Although the economic function of government might remain coupled with the conventional forces that maintain internal security, the nuclear security role could become uncoupled from traditional government. Although some branches of government would continue to face traditional problems, persons who control the nuclear weapons might become little more than warlords, ensuring their own survival through the threat to use nuclear weapons but not compelled to accede to public political desires. The ultimate change in world politics arising from nuclear weapons could be as profound as the transition from feudalism to the nation-state system. In that transition, the application of gunpowder undermined the decisive military role of the mounted knight. Strength in battle was no longer determined by the loyalty of a relatively small number of knights. Instead, infantry, larger armies, and ultimately the Napoleonic nation-in-arms became crucial. Although non-technological factors also played a major role, the effect of gunpowder was thus to support an order in which national power was dependent directly on the citizenry.

This system gave military power as a reward to economic success; it tended to ensure that those governments more successful in nation building would also be more successful in war; and a central government's dependence on the citizenry sometimes favoured the development of democracy. These couplings helped make the nation-state system beneficial with respect to many world goals. The parallel to today's transition is not perfect. Nuclear weapon holders might still be vulnerable to a broadly based revolution or a coup d'état and the economic aspects of feudalism may differ radically from those of nuclear weapons procurement. Nevertheless, the nuclear weapon may tend to undermine precisely those dependencies that made the nation-state system relatively beneficial.

Although the arguments just stated are far from fully probative, they suggest that the nation-state system may find it very difficult to adapt peacefully to the existence of nuclear weapons. The fact of one generation's nuclear peace between the United States and the Soviet Union does not refute this point; the arguments depend on the existence of more than two major nuclear powers and on the emergence of political and cultural responses that may require a generation or two to unfold. More broadly and more strongly, the arguments imply that any system embodying relatively free access to nuclear weapons is likely to be risky, to pose serious moral dilemmas, and to have difficulty in adapting to change without catastrophic conflict. It is, therefore, sensible to examine the proscription of nuclear weapons as a possible rational goal under various assumptions about the future of the nation-state system.[50]

What does it mean to proscribe nuclear weapons? Even the most perfect inspection system could not guarantee that there would never again be nuclear weapons in the world. The limits of possible denuclearisation must, therefore, be defined, because these limits shape the character of military disputes in a denuclearised world.

First, ever since some time in the 1950s, national nuclear-material production capabilities had been so large as to create uncertainties in each nation's intelligence estimate of other nation's production capabilities. Even if a denuclearisation agreement were reached, these uncertainties would prevent an accurate assessment of whether those other nations had actually destroyed their nuclear stockpiles. Significant quantities of weapons or nuclear materials could, thus, be retained and concealed. Although the numbers that can be hidden could perhaps be calculated more precisely using data about intelligence capabilities, it may be assumed that these numbers are of the order of a fraction of a per cent of nuclear inventories preceding denuclearisation. Based on current inventories, the numbers might be in the low hundreds of weapons for the United States and the Soviet Union, and in the tens of weapons for the other nuclear powers. Long-term concealment of nuclear weapons might be more difficult than it sounds: there would probably have to be guards (although guards need not know what they were guarding), there would have to be informed military planners, and there might eventually have to be physical refurbishment of the weapons themselves. Nevertheless, such concealment could perhaps be successful for a time measured in several transitions of authority in the nation's government – from a few decades to a few generations. These weapons could be available for national use within hours; their military role would depend on the delivery vehicles available.

Second, weapons could be constructed from nuclear materials diverted from peaceful nuclear programmes (it is assumed here that a substantial peaceful nuclear programme would remain and spread through the world but be subject to reasonably stringent safeguards). The quantities available this way, even with the best safeguard systems likely to be politically possible, would again be substantial: at least tens of weapons a year from a reasonably sized national nuclear power programme that includes a reprocessing facility. The amount would depend on the reactor type, on the importance attached to obtaining a high-yield weapon, and on the characteristics of international safeguards and the importance attached to avoiding detection. Weapons would not, of course, be immediately available: conversion of the material into weapons would perhaps require several months to a year. Nations with access to experts who had participated in a successful nuclear programme would be able to move more quickly. Nations could also develop and maintain a small stockpile of clandestine, untested weapons in this way in anticipation of a crisis. There would always be some risk of detection, probably greater than the risk that a former nuclear nation's retained stockpile would be detected, because a new weapon building *programme* involves more detectable activity.

Third, so long as there were experts who had participated in a nuclear weapon programme or were able to reconstruct nuclear weapon technology, a nation could initiate a new weapon programme. Depending on the details of safeguards arrangements for the international nuclear industry and on whether the nation had independent access to uranium supplies and its own reprocessing or enrichment facilities, the time lag could range from months to years and the probability of detection from moderate to quite high. Avoiding detection for long would probably be impossible with current technology; it might become possible with the advent of laser enrichment and, thus, enable a closed society to build weapons clandestinely. One also has to assume that any major nation could choose to rebuild nuclear weapons openly under circumstances such as a long conventional war.[51]

Fundamentally, then, the primary meaning that can be given to denuclearisation is that it could increase the time lag before nuclear weapons became available for use. Denuclearisation would replace a deterrence at the military response level with a deterrence at some point closer to production. It would probably be several generations after the proscription of nuclear weapons before one could assume with any safety that all hidden nuclear weapons were gone. But for the current nuclear powers, the number of nuclear weapons immediately available could be drastically decreased, the meaning of 'immediately' stretched from minutes to hours, and through parallel arms control measures, the speed of delivery systems perhaps decreased. Depending on new enrichment and reprocessing technologies and on international safeguards arrangements, other nations could have at the most a small untested stockpile immediately available, and any nation seeking to rebuild substantial nuclear forces might have to do so openly and over a number of years.[52]

The overall concept of a denuclearised world must rest logically on the fact that denuclearisation is possible only in the limited sense just described. For at least several generations, the denuclearised world could never be more than hours to months from a nuclearised world. Some of the political forces of a nuclearised world would, therefore, remain, and almost any major long-lasting war or conflict might lead to renuclearisation. If the world is to remain denuclearised, then, these political forces would have to be accommodated and the long-lasting war or conflict avoided.

By far the most important question related to the design of a denuclearised world is whether the nation-state system remains. Retention of that system would be based on the possibility that national governments would find themselves forced to control, and ultimately to eliminate, nuclear weapons out of recognition that lasting nuclear stability cannot be assured. The difficulty is that the most relevant weakness of the nation-state system in the face of nuclear weapons is a systematic one, the danger of catastrophic war, and not one that exerts a constant and strong pressure upon each individual national government. National leaders assume that a systematic breakdown can always be averted for a few more years. Therefore, an "incremental" pattern for a denuclearised world is most likely to be negotiated in the aftermath of a nuclear war or a narrow escape from such a war. It would presumably involve the minimum change necessary to cope with denuclearisation.

The alternative, or "internationalised", pattern would arise from the accumulation of power and authority at the supranational level due to political processes quite separate from the control of nuclear weapons, from the persistence of nuclear weapons while these processes are under way, and, later on, from the possibility of renuclearisation. As hypothesised above, political forces could tend to divide citizen and government and to weaken the ability of the nation-state system to respond to change. Citizens might transfer their loyalties to more responsive authorities, presumably at the international level. National governments would follow, caught in an evolutionary process over which they would have little leverage. The pressure would operate continuously and the transition would be gradual. It is not inevitable that the transition would be towards international authority rather than towards regional authority or even some form of decentralised feudalism or warlordism. Although such forms are perhaps more likely to emerge, they seem so unlikely to be stable that only the global international pattern will be considered in this discussion.

The traditional sovereignty of the state would necessarily be severely infringed in both cases. But political structures and alliance patterns would differ radically between the two. In the incremental model, popular concerns would continue to be expressed through national governments, and the necessary international organisation would be an ally of these governments, helping them to avert wars and, ultimately, avoid loss of power. The pattern is analogous to that of the centralisation of Prussia – an alliance between the crown and the feudal lords in which the crown gained power at the expense of the population. In the centralised world, in contrast, popular concerns would be expressed to the international organisation directly or through non-national organisations. The nuclear weapon would hopefully become irrelevant to those popular concerns and to the national governments, which would eventually no longer think of acquiring nuclear capabilities than to the states of the United States. The pattern is comparable to that of the centralisation of England – an alliance of Parliament with the bourgeoisie in which power was centralised and democratised at the same time.[53]

The questions of the desirability and the centralisation of a denuclearised world centre on the maintenance of security. Denuclearisation would probably enhance the security of non-nuclear powers and might well be preferable *per se* to widespread proliferation. But its benefits for the nuclear nations, whose security has been relatively great since World War II and who hold a veto against at least the incremental denuclearised world*, are less clear. And all nations might fear clandestine stockpiles or open rearmament. Any evaluation of a denuclearised world, therefore, requires careful analysis of the mechanisms for maintaining security. These mechanisms would, in general, differ between the incremental world** and the internationalised world.

One need not pause very long on the technical issues of verification and control of the international nuclear industry. These issues have been the bread and butter of a stream of nuclear arms control efforts from the Acheson-Lilienthal Plan to the contemporary anti-proliferation debate and are relatively well understood. Careful safeguards would have to be imposed on all peaceful nuclear facilities, and the right to inspect places where clandestine stockpiles were suspected would have to be guaranteed. And as the International Atomic Energy Agency has concluded, safeguards could not be applied effectively unless there were some outside control over the design of nuclear facilities.[54]

The primary security goal of a technical control system would be to provide assurance that the denuclearisation arrangements would be respected. The problems of undetected clandestine stockpiles, of open or detected renuclearisation, and of the appropriate international response in either case would be more political than technical. But the character of these political problems provides a useful organising concept for the control system; to help lengthen the warning time between a nation's decision to renuclearise and the actual availability of militarily significant weapons. Thus, the international supervisory body might seek to locate such sensitive facilities as plutonium stockpiles and enrichment plants in places where their seizure for conversion to nuclear weapons would be relatively unlikely. Various denaturing procedures for nuclear materials might lengthen response times. Control or verification of missiles and perhaps long-range aircraft,

---

* Incremental denuclearised world refers to a world where threshold countries will be deterred from becoming full-fledged nuclear powers.
** Incremental world refers to the 'threshold' nuclear powers which are on the rise.

if consistent with non-nuclear arms control arrangements, could add a few more hours to help delay the use of clandestine stockpiles that would offer the quickest form of reclearisation.

The technical procedures just described would be inadequate to meet severe challenges to denuclearisation: a nation maintaining a large clandestine stockpile, a nation becoming dissatisfied with the system and directly challenging the denuclearisation requirements, and nations or other political groups in such conflict as to create severe temptations towards renuclearisation. These would be the fundamentally political problems of enforcement and of maintaining a relatively stable general peace.

The prevention of war is best considered by dividing forms of war initiation into two types: diplomatic and ideological. *Diplomatic war* is defined here as war decided upon or stumbled into by government leaders in pursuit of foreign policy goals, while *ideological war* is defined as war forced upon government leaders by deeply felt popular beliefs and domestic pressures. World War I, at least in its immediate triggering phase, is an example of diplomatic war; the American Civil War is the example, par excellence, of ideological war. Although it is obvious that most war initiations contain elements of both types, the distinction does point to two different aspects of war initiation: the diplomatic mechanism emphasises the bargaining among sovereign leaders calculating their relative power and ability to influence one another, while the ideological mechanism emphasises the underlying forces that are beyond the control of government leaders but shape the context in which they seek to pursue national goals.

Just as it was possible before nuclear weapons were invented, war deriving from the interplay of different nations' strategic ambitions and from miscalculations in anticipating other nations' reactions to strategic actions would remain possible in an incremental world. Such war would become more likely if escalation to the nuclear level were a more remote possibility. At the same time, such war and even its threat could create temptations towards arms competitions that could lead to retention or reconstruction of nuclear weapons.

Stability, therefore, would depend on keeping the risk of diplomatic war low. A balance-of-power system based on conventional arms might arguably be possible and might be stabilised by non-nuclear arms control. Arms control is likely to be much more effective in preventing diplomatic war than in preventing ideological war. On the other hand, clandestine nuclear stockpiles and rapid nuclear rearmament might be perceived as decisive in a conflict. Although the potential for nuclear rearmament might create a new form of deterrence, nations would perhaps know less about other nations' nuclear capabilities than in today's world.

The result could be diplomatic bargaining less stable than that in today's world, with strong temptations to violate the denuclearisation agreement. The fundamental questions, whose answers require more judgement than logic, are how much arms control and what sort of international force would be adequate to provide reasonable stability, and how that level of stability would contrast with the stability that would be present in the type of nuclear world that is likely to exist in the absence of an international authority.[55]

The problem of intervention against a clandestine stockpile would arise if a former major nuclear power defied the denuclearisation agreement or if a strong conventional power threatened to use a previously clandestine stockpile to intervene in a conflict or to deter international intervention. This problem would be parallel to that of the vulnerability of the United States and the Soviet Union to sanctions under the UN system – they are too powerful to be defeated by a coalition of all other nations. Perhaps such intervention would continue to be impossible, and it might be wisest not to prepare for this situation, just as the framers of the United State's Constitution chose not to resolve questions of nullification and secession; it might be impossible to negotiate a reasonable response in advance, and the problem might never arise.

If a response is to be prepared, one alternative could be to maintain an international force with a number of nuclear weapons comparable to that which can be clandestinely hidden, to defend and disperse the weapons well, and to design a disarming attack using conventional forces, operating under the umbrella of the international nuclear deterrent. The burden of initiating nuclear escalation would, thus, be on the offending nation; depending on prior arms control arrangements, there might be some chance of effective intervention, assuming that clandestine weapons could be located after being announced. If they could not be located, a full-scale conventional war would be the only practical form of intervention. It is hoped, but not necessary, that the possibility of such a war and the existence of an international nuclear force in reserve would be enough to deter violation in the first place.

Alternatively, the intervention force against detected stockpiles could be non-nuclear. Its tactics would be essentially the same, but it would have to work without a deterrent umbrella and might itself be deterred. Nuclear or non-nuclear, however, the force would have to be able to assemble strong conventional capabilities.

The choice between no preparation, a non-nuclear intervention force, and a nuclear intervention force would depend on the probability of effectively deterring violations and on the ability to adequately control the international nuclear force. Nuclear weapons would probably be essential to the international force; otherwise the violator would almost certainly be appeased rather than deterred. Nuclear weapons would also give additional legitimacy to the intervention organisation. Nuclear intervention forces perhaps would provide the only basis upon which non-nuclear nations would accept an incremental world model, for without such a force, the former nuclear nations would retain a permanent diplomatic advantage.

Moreover, the problem of deciding when to use nuclear weapons may be relatively solvable. Intervention itself would be non-nuclear, perhaps even peaceful, and would be occasioned only upon violation of the denuclearisation rules. The intervention force would use nuclear weapons only in response to a prior use of nuclear weapons. Thus, the decision to use nuclear weapons would follow relatively simple rules and depend more heavily on factual determinations than on political judgement, and the use of nuclear weapons in a strictly retaliatory mode would have relatively high innate legitimacy. This would be as favourable a decision-making situation as possible. Moreover, misuse of nuclear weapons could be restricted through geographic dispersal of the forces among a number of nations. Thus, on balance, the intervention force probably should be supported by an international nuclear capability; while there would be a risk that clandestine stockpiles would be retained for protection against the international force, the benefits of an international nuclear deterrent to discourage nations from retaining clandestine nuclear stockpiles for blackmail purposes would appear to outweigh this risk.[56]

The general bias of an incremental denuclearised world would be towards the powerful if there were no broader-purpose intervention force, and towards the status quo if there were such a force. Security for all would probably be greater than in a heavily proliferated world, but the model leaves so little opportunity for readjustment of power relationships that it would not be likely to be stable for a long period. There would be greater danger of a world split in which sides would be willing to ignore the anti-nuclear rules.

Ideological or popular war will be the more dangerous threat to international stability over the next several decades. Mass movements, or at least elite movements acting with mass support, are likely to come into conflict in ways that cannot be controlled by established leaders, particularly if national governments begin to lose their legitimacy. Recent examples of such conflict include the Arab-Israeli conflict, the religious conflict within Lebanon, and the Northern Ireland conflict. The era of conflict over decolonisation may be nearly over, and ideological conflicts are likely to change their character in developing nations as these nations enter a second generation of independence, but nevertheless, conflicts will probably continue to arise from ethnic or religious antagonisms and from concerns about the treatment of communal groups in foreign lands. Economic conflict seems likely to encourage ideological war given the world's inequitable resource and income distribution, as well as global unemployment. New transnational ideological movements analogous to Communism are certainly possible.[57]

These conflicts may often be manipulated by national leaders. They may also capture national leaders and pressure them to build military forces including nuclear weapons. Objectives can be unlimited, unlike those of diplomatic war: persons participating in ethnic and ideological conflict often dehumanise opponents, frequently place a positive value on martyrdom for the sake of the cause, and nearly always support temporary injustice for the sake of a greater future good. They are, thus, relatively likely to use any available nuclear weapons, even in the face of likely retaliation. The nation or international organisation seeking to negotiate a compromise or maintain a temporary truce is itself likely to be seen as being compromised and to become the target of popular movements of terrorist attacks.

Arms control is not a very helpful option in preventing these conflicts, which tend to occur regardless of initial force levels. One must instead devise political ways to prevent the conflicts and, as a second step, establish security systems that discourage escalation of the conflicts to the nuclear level.

In an incremental denuclearised world, prevention of ideological war would require drastic improvement in the diplomatic and political structures through which nations adjust their objectives in deference to the political pressures upon one another. The extent of improvement would have to be enormous because ideological conflict would probably be more difficult to contain than in today's world – though probably easier to contain than in a proliferated nuclear world. In the bipolar nuclear world, the superpowers have it within their power to set limits on the scope of local conflicts, if necessary through intervention; in a proliferated world, the superpowers, out of fear of nuclear complications, would be more wary of playing a conflict-defusing or containing role; in an incremental denuclearised world, the superpowers would find it both more difficult and less exigent to intervene to contain conflict. Nations would be so strongly tempted to build nuclear weapons out of fear of ideological war that the incremental world could be stable only if the potential for widespread ideological conflict were generally believed to be low.

Some of the conflicts could possibly be avoided by new institutions that were basically extensions of the existing ones. For example, those economic issues in which cooperation would be in everyone's interest – such as many global macro-economic problems – would be amenable to solution by more substantial efforts of international organisations. But there are issues, such as resource allocation, which might not be amenable to solution by traditional forms of multilateral diplomacy. At the least, international decision making in these areas would be much more difficult, and the right to withdraw from international organisations might have to be restricted. Truly heroic national commitments to international order would be necessary.

The problem of dealing with nuclear terrorism would seem likely, on balance, to be little changed by the proscription of nuclear weapons. There would be fewer nuclear weapons available for theft, and security arrangements in the nuclear industry would likely to be more effective. In an incremental world, the only really new opportunity for terrorists to obtain nuclear weapons would lie in the possibility that a nation might supply weapons from a clandestine stockpile to terrorists or their convert agents. But the arguments against such supply would be quite strong, resting on both inhibitions against the use of nuclear weapons and fears of the untrustworthiness of the terrorists or even of the agents. Even the use of nuclear weapons by terrorists would pose relatively few new problems. One finds it hard to visualise the need for a nuclear response against a nuclear terrorist; this threat would not require the international authority to possess nuclear weapons. The relevant defences to terrorism would still be the traditional ones: careful police work, maximum physical security around nuclear material, and international accords to deny safe havens to terrorists. One would anticipate greater integration of counterespionage services; this might call for international agreements to protect against abusive actions by those services, although national civil liberties arrangements might suffice.

Non-nuclear terrorism could become a more serious problem in an incremental world than in today's world, if, as national governments began to lose legitimacy and were perceived as weak, citizens became more prone to condone or even support terrorism.

At the cost of still more interference with national structures, one might try to ensure that there were enough outlets for effective political activity to minimise the incentives towards terrorism. The more likely response would be that national governments, learning to cooperate in other areas, would cooperate against their citizens to halt terrorism by forceful means. A repressive police structure marked by substantial exchange of information and responsibility among different national police forces would be a disturbing possibility and could necessitate an international response to protect civil liberties.

The total array of intervention mechanisms that would be needed for the incremental world appears overly elaborate. The design of such mechanisms would reflect the political and military balance of the time when they were created; after a decade or two, these balances might change so significantly that the intervention system would lose credibility. To renegotiate these arrangements successfully, to foresee conflicts accurately, and to resolve them early would require both good luck and continued goodwill on the part of all major powers. And it is not clear what pressures would lead nations to maintain such long-term diplomacy. The pressures and viewpoints would be substantially like those of today's world, a world that, at least in the absence of widespread proliferation, poses many of the same problems.

In the nuclear world, the effect of breakdown is war; in the incremental denuclearised world, the effect would likely be nuclear rearmament in unpredictable and asymmetrical patterns that could lead to war. In either world, the amount of power to be transferred to an international authority is a matter of judgement, for no one can predict quite how much tension the system can accept. An international organisation could resolve crises, but it could also provoke crises because its power balances, reflected in voting schemes, might shift less flexibly than those reflected in conventional diplomacy.

If the incremental denuclearised world worked, it could be a way station to an internationalised world, because the intervention process might help build international legitimacy and attract citizens' pressure to the international organisation. If it failed without war, it could be a way station to repression by a few nations able to act in concert and dominate others in the arenas of both power politics and international organisation. The inflexibility of the incremental model and its risks of instability and repression leave one doubtful that it would be an improvement over any but the most pessimistic projections for a nuclear world.

A denuclearised world would require substantial international inspection and control of the nuclear industry. Conventional war would also have to be substantially restricted in order to weaken incentives towards renuclearisation and to avoid a breakdown whose outcome could be catastrophic, given the chances of clandestine nuclear stockpiles and differential abilities to renuclearise. The two models offer radically different solutions to this problem of conventional war; the international model is designed to make conventional war as obsolete and irrelevant as possible.

The concept of an incremental world rests on the judgement that the nation-state could be preserved when nuclear weapons were essentially eliminated, and the concept's support rests on the perception that the nation-state could be preserved only if nuclear weapons were essentially eliminated. Most political loyalty would continue to be entrusted to nation-states, and stability would depend on the nations' ability to resolve conflicts through careful diplomacy. Substantial new international authorities would nevertheless be necessary, for example, to assist the balancing of power and to deal cooperatively with economic and social problems. Diplomacy would have to forestall conflict at a very early stage, and some of the international organisations would almost certainly require powers far beyond those of current international bodies. The need to prevent conventional war would also require some international intervention arrangements to stabilise borders, to seize incipient national nuclear forces, and to conduct peace-keeping. This force would best have access to nuclear weapons. After the transition, conventional arms procurement would not necessarily have to be limited greatly but the elimination of nuclear guarantees would probably dictate some control of conventional arms during the transitional phase.

Substantial control of conventional arms could be beneficial by reducing the size of the intervention force required to put down non-nuclear war and by reducing the risk of diplomatic war.

The dominant political motivation in the incremental world would be the prevention of conflict through elaborate military and political institutions and careful, traditional diplomacy. The international authorities would necessarily be heavily dependent on, and essentially in alliance with, national governments. International decision-making effort to enforce denuclearisation would be relatively easy, but the effort required to restrain conventional war would be so difficult as to leave one doubtful about long-term stability. As an alliance of national governments, such a world could become repressive in its efforts to contain revolution and ideological war. More likely, it would fail to resolve conflict successfully and collapse as did the elaborate European structures in the 1930s. This would be quite similar to the non-nuclear world that produced the two World Wars – it is doubtful that it could maintain the necessary level of responsibility or that its institutions would hold up in crises. And the rapid renuclearisation that would be likely to mark the collapse of such a world would be exceedingly dangerous, for the nation with even a small head start at rearmament could practise nuclear blackmail with impunity.[58]

The internationalised world would seek to prevent conflict by giving an international political body enough responsibility that it would attract the pressures for change that now operate upon national governments. National governments would, thus, become less and less important foci of the political pressures and aspirations of peoples. For the international body to be effective enough to achieve such a transfer of legitimacy, it would have to have relatively great powers over some traditionally domestic affairs and have a political organ directly responsible to citizens. Diplomatic conflict, it is to be hoped, would become obsolete as a result of this shift in legitimacy, and ideological conflict would take forms less likely to escalate to nuclear warfare. The international organisation would still have to have some military intervention capability, but the need for international nuclear weapons would be less crucial than in an incremental world. Conventional arms could either be controlled at the outset or be left for ultimate limitation in response to political pressures working towards the weakening of national militaries.

The motivating philosophy would be the promotion of local political change through the establishment of an internationalised order. Rather than being in alliance with national governments, the international government would be in alliance with forces within nations, particularly the citizenry. Stability would depend in part on the character of these alliances; one would face a dilemma in choosing between alliances with the powerful forces, which would more likely be helpful in transferring power; and alliances with the weak elements, which would more likely be helpful in promoting international legitimacy and averting long-term conflict. The major dangers for this world would be "seizure" of the international order by special interest groups, its use for either repressive or revolutionary ends, and its break up in a world-level civil war. In fact, the transition period, one of mixed national and international legitimacy, would probably be conducive to ideological war.

The fundamental advantage of an internationalised system over the incremental system would be that the institutions of the former would more likely be self-reinforcing and resilient than those of the latter. If diplomatic war were believed the more likely threat and were judged not difficult to avoid through partial measures, one might choose the incremental system. Likewise, if economic development were an adequate way to prevent ideological war, the incremental system might again be better, at least at first, because individual nations could probably operate more effectively in the economic area than could an inchoate international organisation. However, ideological war is almost certainly the more serious threat in the coming decades, and it can be resolved only through power transfers, which would occur more easily in an internationalised system than in an incremental one. Moreover, combined resource, environmental, and population pressures might ultimately threaten the continued détente necessary to maintain the incremental system's stability. At this point, the internationalised system would be the only practical one. Nation-states might even be eager to cast off some of their responsibility.[59]

The implicit alliance structure would also effect the future of individual freedom. A plausible risk in the incremental model is that national governments might become repressive in an effort to maintain the independence of their international policies and to control ideological war. On the other hand, the centralization imposed through the internationalised system would be one in which the world organisation sought to look past the national governments. The foundation could be laid with individual freedom in mind, but one could not be certain that ideas of freedom and representation would grow along with internationalisation.

IV

The essence of the world's strategic situation as we have known it for the last few decades and as we expect it to persist, is the availability to both the United States and Russia of sufficient deliverable nuclear power to render nuclear war between them improbable in the extreme. Moreover, the magnitude and basic symmetry of these two arsenals are such that this central balance – and the political power relationship it implies – cannot be fundamentally altered by any plausible, near-term quantitative, technological or doctrinal developments. The present nuclear regime is extraordinarily stable. But one should not be surprised if a strategic deterioration takes place in the coming decades.

A strategic deterioration can be defined as a sustained increase in the probability of general nuclear war resulting from changes in the numbers, distribution, and/or qualities of nuclear weapons; the doctrines that govern when, where, and how they might be used; the perceptions and rhetoric about their relevance to war, peace, and diplomacy; the procedures by which they are maintained; or the international norms and agreements that constrain them. To this definition we might attach two assumptions. First, as the probability of general nuclear war increases, the threat, stated or tacit, to resort to nuclear weapons, having become more credible, can exact a higher price in terms of other values, such as territory and resources, sovereignty over domestic affairs, freedom in the conduct of foreign policy, and individuals' perceptions of personal safety. Second, since any incidence of lesser forms of nuclear conflict will stand a good chance of leading to general intercontinental exchange, as the former becomes more likely, the latter can be regarded as more likely also. Accordingly, deterioration may be thought of as a sustained increase in the probability of any form of nuclear combat.

A disintegration of the institutions, norms, formal accords, conventions and common doctrinal bases that have taken root over the past decades and currently govern strategic behaviour might be deemed a third path of deterioration. Such a development might accompany, result from, or stimulate any of the three types of deterioration just identified. It might reflect a perception by the parties to these institutions that long-held assumptions about strategic stability had been invalidated by new weapons systems. It might arise from the sheer unmanageability of a strategic environment in which nuclear weapons were rapidly spreading or in which the technological options open to force planners were multiplying. Or it might result from the intrusion of political conflicts into the management of nuclear stability, conflicts originating in other areas of inter superpower relations less amenable to the pursuit of common interests than in the nuclear area. Whatever the case, the institutional atrophy (such as a growing sterility of SALT, divergence of strategic thinking among the superpowers or a paralysing politicisation of the International Atomic Energy Agency) can be viewed as a fourth avenue of deterioration that could intersect with any of the three direct routes specified above.

While the development of certain technologies has helped to stabilise the superpower balance, the horizontal spread of nuclear technologies is inherently unstable and destabilising. There is no need to recite here the full litany of dangers attending the spread of inexpensive isotope-separation processes, the accumulation of reprocessed plutonium and the diffusion of technology for effective delivery systems, to name but three of the most serious trends. These and other technological and industrial trends will persist in the years to come; the susceptibility of these technologies to effective international control is likely to decrease as their spread proceeds. We face a dilemma: measures to restrict the world market in nuclear technologies invite the production of home-grown facilities and materials, beyond the reach of international safeguards, but trying to preempt the growth of indigenous capabilities by maintaining an active, open market accelerates the diffusion of nuclear technologies under international safeguards that can be revoked or violated without risk or punitive sanction.[60]

Whatever stability exists in the current international distribution of nuclear weapons stems from the fact that certain key states have ratified or are poised to ratify their accession to the NPT. Each important state that ratifies the NPT helps refute the curious, though tenacious, notion that the detonation of a fission device heralds a nation's arrival as a Great Power. Looking just at the politics of proliferation the fulcrum of the problem is the continued refusal of a number of critical states to accede to the NPT. The confirmed or rumoured acquisition of nuclear weapons by any of these states would eclipse the positive effects of ratification by, say, an equal number of other non-nuclear states. Unquestionably, much depends on the nature of the world reaction to further proliferation, but if the two most recent cases (China and India) are thought to be prototypical, the international standing of the next few proliferants will improve in the years following their initial tests. Thus, proliferation to only one or two more nations might well revitalise the belief that possession of nuclear weapons, irrespective of military risk or gain, constitutes an almost unrivalled source of raw political capital.[61]

While the technological aspects of proliferation are inherently unstable, the political aspects are not so yet. But a revived interest in nuclear "prestige" superimposed upon the already unstable technological conditions could create a groundswell of momentum. In fact, the less stable the technological conditions, the harder it will be to keep the politics in order, since the general spread of nuclear resources and skills could lead many governments to conclude that it would be foolhardy to foreclose their own options.

Should a few more critical states acquire nuclear weapons even if only for vague motives of power and prestige, the resultant perceptions of military insecurity at local and regional levels could compound instability. This progression – availability of technology feeding political motivation to acquire nuclear weapons, consequently destabilising regional security conditions – can be brought into focus by considering how the Brazilians and Iranian cases might evolve should these two states go nuclear. As the regional balance of power tilted towards the nuclear state, rival powers (Argentina and Saudi Arabia) would feel increasingly compelled to try to restore some semblance of the political and military *status quo ante*.

This tendency takes on a troubling new dimensions with the recognition that quite apart from the issue of their direct mutual security concerns, American and Soviet leaders may be faced with the serious question of how to respond politically to the nuclearisation of any of a number of chronically tense regions: the Middle East, Southern Africa, South Asia or the Far East. Simply stated, the choice would be to either try to stabilise regional nuclear situations by supplementing the embryonic deterrents of local powers with nuclear commitments by the superpowers or to attempt to insulate the central balance from the chaotic forces of regional nuclear instability and insecurity set loose by proliferation.

An interconnecting of nuclear relationships would permit the superpowers to offset imbalances in regional nuclear match-ups, including cases in which non-nuclear states were confronted by nuclear neighbours with crude but undeterred weapons. To instill caution in the stronger nations and confidence in the weaker one's, the superpowers could transform existing security ties through which local nuclear powers were, in effect, drawn into the central deterrence system. An integrated world nuclear system of this sort might keep regional nuclearisation from upsetting regional stability. But the great danger of concocting an intricate and expandable network of deterrence relationships to accommodate the appearance of new nuclear states would be that nuclear hostilities, if ever ignited, might travel along the very lines of commitment put in place to suppress nuclear conflict in the first place, turning a regional conflict into a global cataclysm. For example, the superpower guarantee to stabilise an otherwise shaky nuclear standoff in South Asia would make the prevention of global nuclear conflict dependent not only upon the avoidance of direct crises between the superpowers but also upon moderation in the potentially more volatile relations among India, Pakistan and China.[62]

Generally speaking, with the spread of nuclear weapons, superpower geostrategic movements would become more restrained, not only out of a reluctance to get directly embroiled with lesser nuclear powers possessing crude and vulnerable forces but, more generally, because only exceedingly high stakes would justify involvement in local disputes in which the outbreak of some form of nuclear conflict was a real possibility. Long accustomed to avoiding confrontation within the central security theatres (Central Europe and the Far East), the superpowers would increasingly show a similar respect for the dangers of local crises in "outlying" areas where moderate behaviour has historically been less exigent. Moreover, as allies acquired their own nuclear weapons, the diminished protective responsibilities of the superpowers would tend to shrink their spheres of influence and security ties. Vital superpower interests would compete less frequently. Relations would mature and might even improve.

A wave of proliferation in the coming decades would almost certainly have harmful effects on international security conditions below the strategic level of the superpowers. These adverse effects would derive mainly from three special features of a proliferating world: the perceived coercive and military value of nuclear weapons to states facing local conflicts or confrontation; the inflamed suspicion, cautious force posturing, reduced predictability of behaviour, and increased risk of miscalculation that would result from the existence or suspected existence of undisclosed nuclear capabilities or of undisclosed quality and quantity; and the unevenness with which nuclear weapons are likely to spread into various regions. These three factors – utility, uncertainty and unevenness – no longer characterise the superpower strategic relationship, their diminution having been a precondition for stability and success in enacting measures of joint control of the central balance. All three factors would flourish below the superpower level in a proliferating world.

States that face local confrontations and disputes are among the most likely to seek nuclear status in the coming years. Such states could become increasingly inclined to conceal the fact, but promote the fear, that they had assembled deliverable nuclear weapons. This element of uncertainty will become increasingly prominent as more and more nations, perhaps with developing civilian nuclear industries, attain a high level of technological sophistication and accumulate enough fissionable material to reduce the step to nuclear weapon status to simply an assembly problem. In addition, the spread of advanced conventional weaponry, particularly surface-to-surface missile systems, could eliminate the construction of delivery systems as a formidable hurdle. Proliferation might lose its drama; *the coup theatre* of the first nuclear test could be increasingly replaced by the quiet, almost casual substitution of conventional missile warheads of fission devices secretly manufactured with relatively insignificant quantities of plutonium from growing stockpiles. By the turn of the century, the nuclear community could consist of, say ten "certain" nuclear states, five more "probables", and ten more that apparently had no nuclear weapons but could acquire one within a matter of weeks or months. The new nuclear states would probably be clustered around areas of traditionally or potentially high tension – the Middle East, Northern Asia, the Persian Gulf, Southern Africa and perhaps Southeast Asia – and would vary markedly in the size and quality of their arsenals and in their willingness to use them.[63]

It is conceivable that the wave of proliferation could spend its energies in the creation of, say, a dozen new nuclear weapon states. Well over a hundred countries would probably resist the tide, because of technological retardation, national poverty, the absence of serious security problems, or sheer political and/or popular pacific will. A dissipation of the pressures for proliferation would begin to relieve the acute security problems generated by the very process of proliferation. Uncertainties regarding the intentions of adversaries would, over time, probably be resolved one way or another. International norms and institutions for controlling nuclear weapons could be resuscitated and reformed to suit the new conditions. Nuclear industries could perhaps expand, unfettered by non-proliferation restraints (though still haunted by the danger of nuclear theft by terrorist groups). All these expectations are, of course, to some extent based on the assumption that the point of exhaustion of a proliferation trend would be recognisable when reached. It is more likely that after a surge in which most middle-power industrialising states would go nuclear, new additions would come with decreasing frequency; perhaps by the turn of the century, the achievement by another state of nuclear status would be as rare an event as it has been to date.

Whether in the throes of accelerating proliferation or in the relative calm of the post-surge phase, a world of many nuclear states would differ fundamentally from a world of five or six nuclear powers. Foremost among the differences, of course, is that nuclear hostilities would be more likely to occur from time to time. As observed above, local conflicts could prove to be breeding grounds for a new generation of nuclear states, just as conflicts (World War II and the Cold War) bred the first generation. And in regions where conflicts were absent or quiescent, the appearance of nuclear weapons could excite new turbulence, especially when uncertainty, unevenness, and perceived military utility characterised the introduction of nuclear weapons. The increase in the number of local conflicts and crises in which one or both sides possessed nuclear weapons would imply a higher probability of their being used.[64]

This statistically higher risk would be amplified by the fact that at least some new proliferants might be less self-controlled and less prudent than the older nuclear states, an unpopular but almost certainly logical expectation. The political systems of the five members of the first nuclear generation are less susceptible – though, of course, not immune – to succumbing to "irrational" leadership than those of many prospective members of the next nuclear generation. Consider the factor of leadership composure in a crisis situation. Some observers would contend that Kennedy behaved somewhat irresponsibly in 1962, that Mao was incautious in 1969 and that Kissinger acted recklessly in 1973 (the "October alert"). How much greater would the chances of nuclear hostilities be if the weapons were in hands of messianic states with messianic leaders or states and regimes threatened with extinction or states and regimes lacking in the considerable non-nuclear military capabilities and options possessed by the old nuclear states? Yet these are the countries whose leaders will be most likely to perceive a need for nuclear weapons – indeed, a pressing need — as proliferation proceeded around them. Nuclear weapons may spread to the very areas where the inherent restraints on their eventual use would be lowest. Many proliferants of the future will probably assemble their nuclear weapons in the heat of conflict. It is sobering to recall that only one of the five original nuclear powers initially produced nuclear weapons during war time and that power promptly incinerated two enemy cities.

The potential for internal turmoil also distinguishes the prospective nuclear young from the old. For example, control over nuclear weapons by a particular military service branch or, in the case of a large proliferant, a regional command, could precipitate or decide a coup d'état or civil conflict. Inexperience in technical safety measures, deployment, and use of doctrine and a lack of reliable command-and-control systems and procedures would amount to what might be called "nuclear immaturity". Each of the existing powers has experienced it, the latest case being that of the Chinese, who only recently seem to have developed a deep understanding that there is, and must be, a quantum difference between full-scale conventional and nuclear war on the spectrum of violence. And if politicians seem slow to grasp the uniqueness of nuclear weapons, professional military officers have been even slower to abandon or modify traditional concepts of war when a nuclear dimension is added.

These probable traits of new proliferants – inexperience, imprudence, internal instability, and involvement in specific situations – mean that a straight-line projection of proliferation could increase exponentially the probability that nuclear weapons would be used in warfare. If "irrationality" were the only problem, one could tender modest hope that the learning experience of living with nuclear danger would bring new proliferants quickly up to the standards of prudence respected by the existing nuclear states. Unfortunately, nuclear weapons would objectively be of some practical utility to future proliferants in the context of regional security problems. Conventional military effectiveness – abundant worldwide – is rampant in most parts of the Third World; the threat to use nuclear weapons to defeat or coerce a neighbour might be credible and therefore, useful in regions where neighbours openly challenge each other's right to exist in the present form. And even in strictly military terms, nuclear weapons can in fact provide the capacity for destroying armies, airfields, dams, industries, and capitals to states whose conventional impotence once placed such tantalising targets beyond reach. It is comforting, and, therefore, popular, to assume that nuclear weapons will be as unusable once widespread as they are today. But this is simply not so. Nuclear hostilities would become more likely with proliferation, if not in the immediate future then after a decade or two.[65]

A high and pervasive expectation that limited nuclear violence might occur would not reduce the political and psychological impact of its actual occurrence. The outbreak of nuclear conflict or even the isolated use in combat or the accidental detonation of a single nuclear weapon would generate a political shock wave affecting nearly every facet of international order and security. It has been suggested above that the spread of nuclear weapons would shrink the geographic scope of the superpowers' interests and moderate their international behaviour but should those weapons actually be used in some corner of the earth, the superpower could be expected to react, especially after the danger of being drawn in had begun to pass. In other words, while neither superpower would consider proliferation itself so insufferable that it need accept or share responsibility for maintaining nuclear peace, nuclear war would not be similarly tolerated. Indeed, in the event of a regional nuclear war or a serious scare, international consensus might shift from support of superpower non-involvement in regional security matters to a demand for superpower peace-keeping. Failure of the international community, under superpower leadership, to react more than rhetorically to nuclear violence might encourage further outbreaks.

In situations in which one superpower had more vital interests than the other, a major unilateral exercise of power could occur in the wake of regional nuclear combat. Intervention in a small nuclear war might have its own nuclear overtones, possibly in the form of a threat to disarm the local use of nuclear weapons. In regions where the superpowers were about equally engaged, local nuclear hostilities could well lead to a severe global crisis and resultant deterioration of mutual superpower trust and restraint. Alternatively, the superpowers might collaborate to disarm by ultimatum and jointly dictate a "solution" conducive to the restoration of nuclear order (and, one would hope, prejudicial to the party that initiated the nuclear exchange). The greater the degree to which nuclear relationships were compartmentalised, the more likely it would be that a direct superpower collision could be avoided but the more difficult it would be for the superpowers jointly to establish their authority in the wake of nuclear hostilities. Ironically, the superpowers would probably engage in enforcing international nuclear security only after it was too late, for the dangers of involvement before it was too late would seem unacceptably high.

So the question remains: what would have to be done to ensure nuclear peace – especially regional peace – in a proliferated world? The international mechanisms that have been developed over the past decades to impede the spread of nuclear weapons would be severely weakened by the cancerous political effects of a period of rapid proliferation. Circumvention, abrogation, and abuse of the withdrawal clause would leave the NPT in shreds. Just as aspiring proliferants would tend to ignore the NPT's proscriptions, so might the superpowers and other established exporters of nuclear technology come to regard observance of their obligations as increasingly costly and naïve.[66]

And if the architects and staunchest defenders of the NPT-IAEA system fail to abide by their treaty commitments, the next nuclear generation would be likely to behave even less cautiously in exporting nuclear material, fuel components, technical assistance, and even assembled explosive devices masquerading as peaceful nuclear explosives. In any case, today's rules and institutions devised to prevent proliferation would seem to be suitable or adaptable for use in controlling the effects of proliferation. Trying to inhibit the use of nuclear weapons is a quite different problem from trying to prevent their acquisition, though, of course, the latter problem could not be dismissed as long as some potential for further proliferation persisted.

If we think of the problem of maintaining nuclear peace in a proliferated world as having three essential components – *uncertainty* as to who possessed what nuclear weapons capabilities and where, when and how they might use them; *unevenness* of the weapons' distribution; and the perceived *utility* of nuclear weapons in regional disputes – it follows that our remedies should be designed to foster certainty, evenness, and decreased utility. Also, we must distinguish these measures pursuant to those goals which should be undertaken at the global level from those which should or must have a regional orientation.

High hopes for success at either level are unwarranted. Efforts at the global level would be hampered by the likely, and desirable, increased compartmentalisation of nuclear relationships and of security patterns in general, which would diminish prospects for fostering a global common interest. And regional efforts would be retarded by the plain fact that it is at this level that the incentives and adverse effects of proliferation would be most salient. Thus, while the superpowers have managed over the years to identify and cultivate a common interest in avoiding nuclear war, we cannot assume that a similar phenomenon would accompany proliferation and serve as the basis for international action, global or regional, to suppress nuclear war outside the domain of the central balance.[67]

Still, it is possible to imagine a rather mixed and messy "regime" of international constraints, institutions, procedures, and, above all, rudimentary acceptance of collective responsibility for nuclear peace to control nuclear weapons in a proliferated world. Any mechanisms that could decrease uncertainties and misinformation about the nuclear production capabilities and weapon systems would help reduce reliance on worst-case assumptions that influence a state's acquisition, development and deployment of nuclear weapons. Rarely does the truth accord with the assumed worst case. And the likelihood of disclosure could inhibit nuclear ambitions. Therefore, it would be desirable to create an international agency to ascertain, evaluate, and disseminate information about states' nuclear programmes. Such an organisation – more appropriately instituted at the global rather than the regional level – could be erected out of the debris of the IAEA which has unique experience in dispatching international scientific teams to crawl around reactors and other sensitive national nuclear facilities.

The ambience of uncertainty regarding nuclear capabilities would probably be sufficiently disconcerting to most governments and a requisite number of them – especially those with nothing to hide – could be motivated to organise a potentially viable international information agency. The problem, of course, would be to involve the key nuclear, non-nuclear, and quasi-nuclear countries that might perceive significant disadvantages to membership in a highly intrusive system offering nothing more than interesting information about others' nuclear capabilities which would, in practice, be readily available to non-members in any case. Therefore, inducement and coercion would be necessary for such an organisation to emerge from incubation.

One of the main purposes of such an organisation would be to disclose and, therefore, possibly deter clandestine deployment of nuclear weapons, particularly by states with an admitted or suspected capability of constructing nuclear explosives. A prohibition against any weapons deployments not announced and publicly justified in advance would serve as a nuclear "confidence-building measure" and might discourage not only covert undertakings but provocative new deployments in general. In the face of effective international information gathering and sharing, governments bent on continued concealment of the existence or scope of a nuclear weapons capability would find it difficult to deploy their devices in any militarily useful way without revealing their nuclear secrets. And governments with a known weapon capability might be more self-conscious about actual deployments if they knew that their neighbours and the rest of the world would promptly learn of them.

Even if such an organisation is instituted, the grave and complex problems of a proliferated world discourage confidence in humanity's ability to adapt its politics and its institutions. By contrast, the task of perpetuating a stable nuclear relationship between the superpowers would seem to require only minimal restraint on the part of the leaders of those countries, restraint that should quite naturally flow from their declared common cause of averting a nuclear catastrophe. The existing central strategic relationship is based on, and equipoise of, two massive arsenals, each being, for now, safely beyond meaningful vulnerability by virtue of size, diversity systems, and the comparative backwardness of strategic defence and damage-limitation technologies. Russian and American leaders of the present generation have, by their actions if not always by their words, exhibited a basic satisfaction – enlightened, pragmatic, or both – with the essential invulnerability of their rival's offensive forces and the vulnerability of their own societies to those forces. The leaders and their arsenals have been, and probably will continue to be, subject to competing pressures for change: on the one hand, to build more and better weapons (including some designed to provide national advantage should deterrence fail and war occur); on the other hand, to reduce their arsenals' size. Neither pressure would seem sufficiently strong to alter the basic equilibrium in the near future. And however strong the pressure may become, they will probably continue to be largely offsetting in terms of their political effects and their capacity to bring about significant changes in actual capabilities.[68]

The strength of these pressures for change and their consequences for strategic stability will be determined by the interaction of future technological and political developments. Innovation in weapons design is only partially driven by political preference, though the incorporation of innovations into actual forces can be tempered by political prudence. Conversely, a technologically stable relationship of nuclear forces will not guarantee moderation in superpower politics, though it may provide some insurance that political deterioration will stop well short of open confrontation and frequent crisis.[69]

The danger is that both technology and politics will evolve in undesirable ways, that neither will be stable enough to arrest erosion of the other, in fact, that degradation of each will accentuate degradation of the other. The appearance of weapon systems designed to reduce retaliatory damage, for example, would be more likely in an atmosphere of political distrust, and the political distrust would, in turn, most likely become increasingly poisonous as such technical capabilities were introduced. There is nothing inherently unstable about present strategic conditions that would preclude the possibility that each leadership might begin seriously to question the other's commitment to mutual deterrence and alter its military posture accordingly. Neither numerical equality nor rough symmetry in the kinds of weapons on each side ensures stability.

There is, admittedly, little danger that the next ten or twenty years will bring so serious an unravelling of the political and technological threads of stability that Soviet-American nuclear conflict will become significantly less "unthinkable". But present conditions and orientations provide no assurance that by, say, 2010, stability as we know it will not have yielded to fragility.

Of all the trends in weapons design that might threaten stability, among the most serious threat is the multiplying of the number of warheads on each missile. The effect of this technology – which the superpowers have mastered – is not unambiguously destabilising, for while it is true that an increase in the number of warheads usable in a first strike would worsen the odds that a given retaliatory weapon could survive the attack, each missile that did survive would, with its own multiple warheads, be that much more potent as an instrument of retaliation. Thus, it might be argued that despite increases in warhead numbers, yield and accuracy, the greater lethality of each surviving retaliatory weapon will ensure that the price of launching a nuclear attack can be kept unacceptably high. Such confidence, however, must be qualified by the recognition that an attacker with multiple-warhead weapons could destroy the enemy's retaliatory vehicles at a faster rate than that at which its own weapons were expended. This could lead to a situation in which the side that had been attacked, though still capable of delivering a devastating response, would be faced with an extremely favourable balance of forces after the enemy's first strike and might, therefore, if rationality prevailed, surrender. Thus, on balance, the multiplication of warheads is destabilising in that it puts the side that initiates nuclear war at a distinct advantage.

It is now being argued that plans for retaliatory strikes against cities, aside from being normally repugnant, in fact, have little relevance to the way a nuclear war ought to, and would probably be, fought. Though the threat of destruction of population centres is useful in maintaining peace, the argument goes, actual launch against cities would be foolish. Rather, after suffering a first strike, retaliating against the attacker's unexpended strategic forces would be eminently more sensible in that a strike against its population would simply encourage similar subsequent targeting by the original attacker and leave intact its ability to do so. Thus, we may be witnessing an evolution towards a more "rationalised" doctrine, one that eliminates the anomaly of threatening population centres.[70]

But a doctrinal rejection of mutual assured destruction could produce an effect that is quite the opposite of what is intended. The forces needed to implement a "rationalised" doctrine – counterforce weapons – would, by and large, be the very force, that enhanced first-strike capabilities. The more doctrines were rationalised to correspond to anticipated or preferred nuclear war scenarios (such as that of limited exchange) and the more capabilities were shaped to correspond to the evolving doctrines, the more vulnerable would retaliatory forces become. To complete the paradox, as counterforce capabilities improved, the plausibility of "controlled" nuclear exchange between the adversaries would decrease. Since retaliatory restraint would invite further depletion of forces, both sides would increase their preparedness should war occur. Presumably, those who argue for a rationalised doctrine as a means of improving the chances of limiting or controlling nuclear war intend the opposite effect. Indeed, the consequences could be worse than self-defeating. Not only would nuclear war be made no more controllable, it would also be made at least marginally more likely by the fact that in a predominantly counterforce world, the penalty for initiating nuclear hostilities would be reduced, and in a severe crisis, the incentives for striking first and striking massively would be higher.[71]

We are accustomed by intuition and education to associating stability with equality and mutuality. Strategic deterioration normally connotes imbalance in forces and asymmetry in constraints and prerogatives. In fact, pursuit of symmetry could aggravate strategic deterioration both by stimulating arms competition and by shaping conditions in which each side perceives a clear advantage in surprise and knows that the other side also sees that advantage.

A crucial question is whether superpower X compensates for the improved war-fighting capabilities of superpower Y by strengthening the invulnerability of its own retaliatory force or imitates the counterforce and defence emphasis of Y. Empirical evidence is ambiguous in this respect. Both powers have displayed a predilection for imitation, but both have also at times found compensation a preferable practice. Still, should either or both powers move to improve war-fighting capabilities over the coming decades, the imitation phenomenon – as a means of establishing bargaining leverage as a hedge against further deterioration, and as a policy to preserve symbolic "equality" – could well develop frightening momentum.

Under today's strategic conditions, it is unimaginable that leaders of the superpowers would regard any competing interests as so vital that they would contemplate launching a first strike. Indeed, no conceivable stakes are high enough to warrant behaviour that might cause a crisis to escalate to the point that a nuclear attack would be thinkable. A decade or so from now, however, superpower estimates of each other's retaliatory capabilities might be lower than today, perhaps considerably lower if some or all of the developments that are likely to take place were to occur. The minimum stakes or costs of inaction or of backing down required to cause serious contemplation of resorting to nuclear weapons in the midst of crisis would then be correspondingly lower. And the inclination of the superpowers to take the sorts of risks that would lead to confrontation might be greater.[72]

In other words, not only might crises be more intense – involving higher stakes for each side and, therefore, a greater willingness to suffer retaliatory destruction but the expected severity of retaliation would itself be diminished. The inability virtually to disarm the adversary would not preclude at least consideration of resorting to nuclear weapons if the stakes of some future crisis dwarfed such issues as the placement of missiles in Cuba or the survival of the Egyptian Third Army.

The point is not that nuclear war might be likely in a deteriorated strategic environment, but that it might be significantly less unlikely. And the danger is not so much that either Russian or American leaders would launch an attack to bring a confrontation to a favourable outcome; rather it is that if war were to begin to appear a strong possibility, both sides would, quite rationally, be sufficiently impressed by the advantages of striking first rather than second, that one or the other would decide to preempt lest it be preempted. In such a situation, the level of retaliatory destruction might be close to what some observers would consider enough to support minimum deterrence.

Moreover, confidence in deterrence must be qualified by the awareness of a potential nuclear aggressor that, irrespective of capabilities, retaliation may in fact not occur because political will is lost or a calculated decision is made, that, once struck, retaliation is irrational. If a large fraction of one's own force were destroyed by a small fraction of the enemy's force, retaliation for a first strike would only ensure that most or all of the enemy's unexpended forces, being vulnerable themselves, would be launched before being struck. In other words, the attacker's remaining forces would deter the victim's deterrence. This consideration might not increase the incentive to launch a nuclear attack, rather it could lower the disincentives.[73]

Perhaps most importantly, arguments about the adequacy of minimum deterrence in a deteriorated strategic environment tell us less about the avoidance of nuclear war. Obviously, the leaders of both superpowers will continue to be aversed to nuclear devastation. But nuclear weapons might come to play a more prominent role in geopolitical competition in the coming years and beyond than they do now. Either power might, from time to time, come to believe that it could convince the other that, given the nature of the stakes and the temporary attainment of a high state of nuclear readiness, it was less fearful of a confrontation than the other was. A political or military initiative taken as a result of such a belief would produce either successful nuclear coercion or a dangerous crisis. More generally, greater emphasis on first-strike forces, doctrines and rhetoric would, apart from its effect on the actual probability of a first strike leave the two governments and the two societies far more suspicious and politically antagonistic than they are today.

It must be admitted that generalising about strategic imbalance is neither easy nor especially enlightening. Still, three general observations should be made. First, looking strictly at the question of the likelihood of nuclear war, imbalance would probably be less dangerous than a mutual, balanced improvement of counterforce and defence capabilities. Given that nuclear war will remain a catastrophic contingency no matter what strategic environment prevails in the future, the most plausible impulse that might trigger a nuclear exchange will continue to be the desire to preempt should the perceived likelihood of the other side initiating a war rise sharply in time of crisis. The impulse to preempt would be stronger in the case of mutually improved first-strike capabilities than in either case of strategic imbalance. In the former situation, each side would have reason to fear that the other, also out of fear, might decide to strike before being struck. In the latter situation, the weaker side would suffer catastrophically whether it struck first or second, and the stronger side, aware of the constraints on the weaker, would sense no need for preemption.

Second, whatever the form of imbalance, Russo-American arms control would be likely to become even more difficult than it is today. However dubious its importance in other respects, rough strategic equality provides a central organising concept for arms control. We have seen in the negotiations on mutual force reduction (MPR) in Central Europe how badly handicapped an arms control effort can be when the participants do not start from a position that both sides recognise, openly or privately, as balanced. In essence, before there can be any hope for progress in actual negotiations, there will have to be at least tacit agreement on one of the following guiding principles: (a) that the imbalance should be rectified; (b) that control should affect each party in proportion to its powers, thus, leaving the imbalance essentially unaffected; (c) or that controls should apply equally in absolute terms, thus, affecting the stronger proportionately less than the weaker. In contrast to the deadlocked MFR negotiations, the SALT experience illustrates the benefits of parity as a basis for arms control, for parity obviates the choice among these three approaches.

Finally, it is important to note that what most analysis warrants is not the nightmare of nuclear hostilities but the effects on the patterns of world politics, if any, of measurable differences in the deterrent and war-fighting potential of the United States and Russia. Such an inquiry must look not just at, but also beyond, the question of the symbolic relevance or irrelevance of strategic imbalance. It must examine the ways in which imbalance might affect the perceived opportunities and constraints, the plans and the rhetoric, of policy makers in Washington, Moscow, and elsewhere. It must examine possible changes in the political functions of nuclear weapons – the increasing extent to which they would define political power relationships and be used "diplomatically" to influence events – that might result from strategic imbalance.[74]

One must be wary of overdrawn, and of overdrawing, estimates of the significance of strategic disparity. Slight but acknowledged inequality would probably not noticeably affect international politics and security conditions, unless too many influential persons were convinced that it would. But significant disparities would matter at least at the margin. And marginal behavioural change by both the weaker and the stronger of the two states that dominate world politics would have important international repercussions.

It is all too easy to say that no rational leader would ever allow even, say, 10 per cent of his or her people to perish, so why worry if it is 30 per cent that is vulnerable one year and only 20 per cent the next, or 20 per cent for one country and 60 per cent for the other. Indeed, our ability to estimate is so poor that we can at best say that national casualties would be, to pick an arbitrary range, certainly higher than 10 per cent but probably no more than 60 per cent, in other words, within a range of twenty to over hundred million Americans or Russians.

But we cannot ignore the danger that a gross difference in expected losses between the two superpowers would encourage the stronger to exploit the more acute fears of the side whose losses would be much greater. And if one side were to retreat from its tacit commitment to expose itself to the full fury of nuclear holocaust, a disturbing and exploitable asymmetry in the expected effects of such a contingency could develop. The problem lies in the question that haunts national leaders, strategists and military planners in both the United States and the Soviet Union: does it make more sense to arrange for maximal losses, in the hope that nuclear war can, thus, be permanently averted, or to prepare to minimise one's own losses – indeed to "win" – on the assumption that nuclear war may occur some day? Translated into forces and doctrine and expectable casualties, there is a massive difference between the two alternatives. If either American or Russian leaders became obsessed with the need to prepare for nuclear war and designed their forces and revised their plans accordingly, would they face that contingency or situations from which the contingency might arise - no differently than would the leaders of a rival that was prepared to deter but not to win?

The two hypothetical cases of strategic disparity outlined above entail what must be considered "significant" differences between the likely effects of nuclear war on the stronger and the likely effects on the weaker. Under such conditions, it would be foolish (if commendable) for the strong not to act more boldly, and reckless (if admirable) for the weak not to act with greater circumspection.

Perhaps more important than static conditions of strategic inequality are perceptions of trends. For instance, when the Chinese express disappointment and concern over Russian strength and American weakness, what they are really worried about is Russian accretion and American decay. Static conditions reflect capabilities; trends reflect intentions, that is, they indicate complacency or strength of will. Static conditions are more easily analysed and estimated, but perceptions of trends, however unrefined, are what drive behaviour.

It is one thing to recommend against any effort by the United States to strive for a strategic advantage and quite another to prescribe a proper course of action for the United States in the face of such an effort by Russia. Since strategic imbalance would matter, and since Russian superiority in particular would have undesirable international consequences, the question is not whether Russian superiority should be resisted, but rather how. The choice would essentially be between compensation and imitation. And the dilemma would be that compensation alone might leave a strong impression of inferiority – disclaiming notwithstanding – with significant international political consequences. Yet imitation would likely lead in the more dangerous direction of mutual improved counterforce and defence capabilities. Both courses would involve considerable expense; neither would be desirable on the basis of budgetary considerations. So for Americans, the choice would come down to the worst or to do the best to ensure that the worst did not occur.[75]

In facing this choice, as the United States, in fact, does today in numerous strategic policy issues, it is worth remembering that the Russians are no less influenced by American actions than vice versa. What to Washington may seem justifiable imitation is likely to be seen as a provocation in Moscow. For example, today many Americans may deem it only prudent to develop a heavy missile in view of the greater yield of Russian weapons. But in view of superior American accuracy, the Russians may ask why the United States must also increase throw-weight. They, in turn, may be dissatisfied with their heavy but inaccurate weapons.

Thus, in acting to preclude a Russian strategic advantage, the United States should develop forces that will both strengthen deterrence and, if copied by Russia, pose no threat to deterrence. With its technological superiority, the United States can and should ensure that nuclear war remains at least as terrifying to the Russians as it is to the American leaders and that any sustained Russian effort to make nuclear war less terrible is offset. If the Russians adhere to a similar policy, there is hope that the arms race will decelerate and that deterioration of the strategic balance will be avoided.

Notes

1. Killian, James R. Jr., *Diplomacy of Power*, Washington: The Brookings Institution, 1981, p. 119.

2. Kull, Steven, *Minds of War - Nuclear Reality*, New York: Basic Books Inc. , 1988, pp. 21-23.

3. Divine, Robert A., *War Without Mercy*, New York: Harper & Brothers, 1976, p. 43.

4. MAD is the relationship whereby both the USA and the Soviet Union possess the ability and espouse the determination to inflict "assured destruction" upon the other in response to a nuclear attack, thereby ensuring that such an attack never occurs. Since about 1974, when US Secretary of Defence Schlesinger openly began to signal American interest in Soviet forces rather than Soviet citizens, a debate has raged in the USA as to whether or not to abandon MAD in favour of a more flexible and selective targeting doctrine. On the Soviet side, while the political leadership and the academic community has emphasized mutual deterrence as the basis of force planning and doctrine, the military establishment has continued to stress the importance of being prepared actually to fight a nuclear war.

5. In *The Time of Illusion*, Alfred A. Knopf, New York, 1976, Jonathan Schell explores the effects of contemporary strategic thinking – notably, the "deterrence 'theory" – on American politics and foreign policy since the US involvement in Vietnam.

6. *Stable* strategic conditions are those in which the certainty of devastating retaliation precludes any advantage to the side that initiates a nuclear attack (crisis stability) and in which expectable additions to or improvements in the forces of one side will not significantly affect the overall balance of forces (arms race stability). It is generally accepted that these conditions prevailed until the end of Cold War.

7. Gomport David C., Mandelbaum, Michael, Garwin, Richard L. and Barton, John H. (eds), *Nuclear Weapons and World Politics*, New York: McGraw-Bill Book Company, 1984, p. 6.

8. *Ibid.* p. 8.

9. Jonathan H. Campbell in *Nuclear Proliferation*, Washington, Ballinger Books, 1982, deals comprehensively with the issue of nuclear proliferation.

10. The term *anarchy* means the absence of a central governing authority. It does not necessarily imply lawlessness or chaos.

11. For India's nuclear-policy, see Sen Gupta, Bhabani, *Nuclear Operations: Policy Options for India*, New Delhi, Sage Publications Pvt. Ltd. 1983; Rao, Rama R. (retd.), "A Nuclear Munich?" in Poulose, T.T. (ed), *Perspectives of India's Nuclear Policy*, New Delhi, Young Asia Publishers, 1978; Bajpai, U.S. (ed), *India's Security; The Politico-Strategic Environment*, New Delhi, Lancers Publishers, 1982; Subramanian, R.R., *Nuclear Pakistan; Atomic Threat to South Asia*, New Delhi, Vision Books, 1980; Kaufman, John S., *India and the Bomb*, New York, Harcourt, Brace, 1979; Schelling, Robert N., *India's Nuclear Choice*, Princeton, Princeton University Press, 1981; *The Hindu*, January 1, 1982; *The Times of India*, January 25, 1982; *The New York Times*, January 24, 1982; Singh, Jasjit, "India's Nuclear Policy: A Perspective," *Strategic Analysis*, Institute for Defence Studies and Analyses, New Delhi,

November 1989, vol. XII no. VIII; "Pressures or Reasons for Proliferation", New York, Houston Institute, 1976, HI 2336/3RR. Dunn and Kahn gave five reasons for India's nuclear explosion: (a) Deterrence of a nuclear rival (China); (b) buttressing the bargaining position; (c) quest for-regional/international status/influence; (d) strengthening military scientific/bureaucratic morale; (e) scientific and technological momentum.

12. For this aspect of China's nuclear policy, see Barnett, Doak A., *The Making of Foreign Policy in China*, Boulder, Co and London: Westview Press, 1985, pp. 57-70; Oberdorfer, Don, "US Analyzes Gorbachev's Bid to China", *The Washington Post*, July 30, 1986, p. 15; Ross, Robert S., "International Bargaining and Domestic Politics: US-China Relations since 1972", *World Politics*, vol. 38, January, 1986; Sutter, Robert G., *China's Nuclear Policy*, New York, St. Martin's Press, 1982. Hollingsworth, Claire, "China and the Bomb" *Wall Street Journal*, June 1978; Southerland, Daniel S., "Chinese Leaders' Offer to Gorbachev," *The Washington Post*, September 7, 1986. p. A21; Asian Studies Center, *Backgrounder*, no. 48, Washington DC: The Heritage Foundation, July 24, 1986 Delhi; Paul F., *China and the Bomb*, Athens, Ga: The University of Georgia Press, 1981, pp. 58-79; *The Military Balance*, 1976-1977; The International Institute of Strategic Studies (IISS), London, pp. 110-119; Dreyr, June Teufl, *Nuclear China*, Stanford, CA, Stanford University Press, 1972, pp. 71-112; Bullard Mont R. and O''Dowd, "Defining China's Nuclear Role," *Asian Survey*, August, 1971.

13. This particular distinction is drawn from Stanley Hoffmann, "Nuclear Proliferation and World Politics", in Buchan, Alastair, (ed), *A World of Nuclear Powers?* Prentice Hall, Englewood Cliffs, N.J, 1996, p. 67. The USA has indicated that it might well defend South Korea and Taiwan with nuclear weapons. These two countries have acquired manufacturing industries in the last quarter-century. They have therefore earned at least corresponding membership in

the industrial circumference. See Kahn, Herman, *On Escalation; Metaphors and Scenarios,* New York, Frederick, A Praeger, 1965, pp. 211-35.

14. See Ullman, Richard H., "No First Use of Nuclear Weapons", *Foreign Affairs,* vol. 50 no. 4, July 1972. pp. 669-689. Also see Brodie, Bernard, *War and Politics,* New York, Macmillan Company, 1973, pp. 91-103.

15. By the best unofficial estimate the USA had, in the mid-1975, 2,152 launchers and in mid-1976, 2,097. The Soviet Union had 2,537 in 1975 and 2,507 in 1976. See *The Military Balance,* 1976-77, IISS, London, 1977, pp. 75. Also see Kaplan, Fred, *The Wizards of Armageddon,* New York, Somin and Schuster, 1983, p. 212. Arneson R. Gordon, "Balance of Armaments" *Saturday Evening Post,* Dec. 1, 1979, p. 13.

16. In 1976 the USA had deployed 1,964 launchers with MIRVs and the Soviet MIRV programme had just begun. See Ikle, Fred Charles, "Nuclear Arms Race", *Atlantic Monthly,* March, 1978, pp. 55-57.

17. Nitze, Paul, "Assuring Strategic Stability", *Foreign Affairs,* vol. 54, no. 2, January, 1976.

18. Lebow, Richard N, "International Security", *New Yorker,* June 12, 1975, pp. 26-30.

19. Ball George W., *Nuclear Diplomacy,* Boston, Little, Brown & Co. , 1981, p. 93.

20. Yager, Joshep A, *Nuclear Stability,* London, Macmillan, 1983, pp. 151-54.

21. Gordon, Bernard K., "National Security Strategy", *International Herald Tribune,* May 16, 1974.

22. Brick, Andrew P., "The Failure of Nuclear Balance?" *World Policy Journal,* vol. 4, no. 2. Fall, 1976, pp. 441 - 46.

23. Phipps, John, "What kind of Stability?", *Pacific Review,* vol. 12, no. 5, March 1981, pp. 21-22.

24. Weiner, Richard, *The United Slates in World Affairs,* New York, The Viking Press, 1973, p. 112.

25. Toland, Henry A., *Men Who Play God*, Cambridge, Harvard University Press, 1986, pp. 90-92.

26. N. Cholas, Ronald R., *Decade of Decision*, New York, St. Martin's Press, 1983, pp. 136-38.

27. Rees, Andrew J., *Myth and Reality in Nuclear Age*, Baltimore, The John Hopkins University Press, 1979, pp. 78-80.

28. Miller, Norman B., *The Essence of Security*, Westport, Greenwood Press, 1976, p. 49.

29. York, Robert K., *Making Weapons: Talking Peace,* Boston Houghton Mtffin Co., 1971, pp. 166-69.

30. Larson, Daniel, *Nuclear Reality*, New York, Harper & Row.

31. Kraft, Harold, *Nuclear Diplomacy,* Boston, Little, Brown & Co., 1972, pp. 191-93.

32. Kevles George B., *Years of Upheaval*, New York, Harper & Brothers, 1978, pp. 301-4.

33. Kinnard, Douglas, *A Study in Defence Policies*, Kentucky University of Kentucky Press, 1977, p. 137-38.

34. Lamont, Eric, *Diplomacy of Power*, Princeton, Princeton University Press, 1975, pp. 88-89.

35. Kase, Robert F., *The Strategy of Peace,* New York, Vintage Books, 1971, pp. 207-9.

36. Kahn, Herman, *On Escalation: Metaphors and Scenarios,* New York, Frederick A. Praegar, 1965 p. 189.

37. Dower, Herbert S., *Arms Control: Issues and Prospects*, New York, W.W. Norton & Co., 1982, p. 321.

38. Duffy, Gloria, *Future of Arms Control,* Cambridge, Ballinger Books, 1988, p. 79-81.

39. Feis, Otto, *Shaping the Defence Program*, New York, St. Martin's Press, 1981, p. 97.

40. Garthoff, Robert L. *Deterrence: Theory and Practice*, New York, Simon & Schuster, 1971, pp. 169-71.

41. Rovere, Warner R., *Nuclear Options Today*, Cambridge, MIT Press, 1979, pp. 221-23.

42. Walker, Richard L., *Strategic Planning*, Washington D.C., National Defense University Press, 1983, p. 285.

43. Howard, Charles R., "Nuclear Strategy Today" *New Yorker*, June 26, 1974, pp. 26-28.

44. Larson, Derek K., *The Strategic Design*, New York, Funk & Wagnalls, 1968, pp. 116-19.

45. Lewis, Wilson K., *Nuclear Deterrence*, Stanford, Stanford University Press, 1973, p. 57.

46. Bottmme, James F., *A World of Nuclear Powers*, Wye Plantation, AIHS, 1981, pp. 49-50.

47. Holloway, Michael R., "US Nuclear Strategy", *The Journal of Strategic Studies*, March, 1983, pp. 27-30.

48. Tatu, Michael, *Power of Kremlin*, New York, The Viking Press, 1969, pp. 311-13.

49. Tyroler, Ferrell, *The World in Crisis*, Chicago, University of Chicago Press, 1973, p. 173.

50. Alsop, Joseph, "Nuclear Grand Strategy", *Peace and Change*, 4, Spring, 1974, pp. 12-16.

51. Bowie, Robert R., "Nuclear Strategy and Atlantic Alliance" *International Security*, 9, Summer, 1984, pp. 132-34.

52. Welch, David A., *Foreign Policy in the Nuclear Age*, Boston Little, Brown & Co., 1979, p. 154.

53. Schelling, Thomas C., *The Strategy of Nuclear Conflict*, New Haven, Yale University Press, 1980, pp. 97-98.

54. Rostow, W.W., *Nuclear Weapons - Strategy and Politics*, Berkeley, University of California Press, 1987, p. 219.

55. Speer, Albert, *Politics of Arms Race*, Toronto, Macmillan Co., 1979, pp. 96-98.

56. Talbot, Lewis L., *Nuclear Strategy Today and Tomorrow*, New York, Alfred A. Knopf, 1984, p. 183.

57. Shea, Glenn T., *Nuclear Politics Today*, Boston, D. Reidel Publishing Co., 1981, p. 302.

58. Martin, John Barlow, *Our Nuclear Dilemma*, New York, McGraw-Hill Books, 1977, pp. 161-63.

59. Nicholas, Steven D., *The strategy of War and Peace,* Boston Little, Brown & Co., 1979, p. 107.

60. Valperin, Morton H., *The Nuclear Fallacy*, Bloomington, Indiana University Press, 1978, p. 164.

61. Groves, Ted, *The Ends of Nuclear Power*, New York, Harder 1978, pp. 77-78.

62. Drell, Anthony, *Nuclear Strategic Planning*, Baltimore, The John Hopkins University Press, 1981, p. 211.

63. Weinberger, Casper W., "Why Offense Needs Defense", *Foreign Policy,* 68, Fall, 1982, p. 18.

64. Teller, Hans, "Superpower Nuclear Stability", *International Security*, 12, Winter, 1987-88, pp. 29,31.

65. Bell, Corad, *Nuclear Strategy: Crucial Issues*, Athens, Ohio University Press, 1972, p. 213.

66. Adams, Graham, *American Defense Policy*, Rutherford, N.J. Dickenson Press, 1984, p. 49.

67. Erickson, John, *Evolution of Nuclear Strategy*, Handen. Conn, The Shoe String Press, p. 252.

68. Morrison, Norman, *Strategic Thought in the Nuclear Age*, Notre Dame, Ind., University of Notre Dame Press, 1980, p. 98.

69. Lowell, Harold, *Patterns of Soviet American Strategic Relations,* New York, Stein & Day, 1982, pp. 179-80.

70. Harderman, Samuel, *Nuclear Weapons in a Changing World*, New York, Harper & Row, 1981, p. 142.

71. Jervis, David, *The Illogic of American Nuclear Strategy*, N.Y., Cornell University Press, 1984, pp. 91-93.

72. Sidey, Henry. F., *Fighting to a Finish,* New York, Harper & Brothers, 1978, p. 82.

73. Burnes, Peter, *Nuclear Balance*, Washington D.C., The Brookings Institution, 1984, pp. 172-74.

74. Blechman, Robert R., "What is Strategic Superiority?", *International Organization*, 19, Summer, 1982, pp. 662-64.

75. Allison, Joseph, *The Essence of Decision,* London, George Allen & Unwin, 1981, pp. 192-93.

5

IAEA SAFEGUARDS: NEW CHALLENGES

There has always been an acute awareness of the fact that some of the materials, technologies and expertises that are relevant for the peaceful uses of nuclear energy can be equally of use for making nuclear weapons. Since the launching of the "Atoms for Peace" programme in 1953, the promotion of the peaceful uses of nuclear energy has, therefore, invariably been linked to policies and measures for preventing the proliferation of nuclear weapons.[1] By and large, this two-pronged approach has been successful. There are now some 450 nuclear power plants and an even larger number of facilities for other applications of nuclear energy (for example, in medicine, agriculture and industry), yet the number of nuclear weapon states has remained limited.

Many different factors account for the relative success of proliferation efforts. One important factor has been the common interest of the five states officially recognised as nuclear-weapon states – China, France, the former Soviet Union, the United Kingdom and the United States – in impeding any further horizontal spread of nuclear weapons, a common interest that transcended their differences during the Cold War. Another factor was that, until recently, most states that were not protected by the nuclear umbrellas of major military alliances were not at a technological level that would make it possible for them to develop nuclear weapons. Yet other factors have been the public aversion to nuclear weapons and the ability to provide verifiable, treaty-based assurances of non-proliferation.

At the present time, in a world moving towards greater détente and nuclear disarmament, and in which a growing number of states may be reaching a technological level that could make it possible for them to construct nuclear weapons, it is fortunate that the non-proliferation precept has become strongly established. In the recent past, three so-called threshold states – Argentina, Brazil and South Africa – have entered into legally binding non-proliferation commitments that are subject to verification, and the subject of a nuclear weapon-free zone has appeared on the agenda of the Middle East peace talks.

Thus, there are some reasons for optimism about the prospects for non-proliferation. However, the case of Iraq has raised several important questions. One of them is how International Atomic Energy Agency (IAEA) safeguards, which are designed to give confidence about respect for non-proliferation commitments, can be strengthened so as to minimise the risk that a clandestine nuclear programmes may go undetected. IAEA safeguards were a radical novelty some years ago when the first on-site inspection took place. They have been instrumental in creating confidence in the peaceful nature of many nuclear programmes and have constituted a *sine quo non* for nuclear trade. Moreover, they have served as a source of inspiration in the wider discussions of arms control.

The case of Iraq was, however, a reminder of some of the limitations of the present safeguards system. It is important, therefore, to examine the evolution of IAEA safeguards and the current efforts to strengthen them.

The Agency was created in 1956 with the twin objective of promoting peaceful uses of nuclear energy and ensuring that assistance provided by it or at its request, or under its supervision or control, was not used in such a way as to further any military purpose.

Under the IAEA statute, safeguards are obligatory for IAEA-related activities. Other nuclear activities can be subject to safeguards, but only at the request of the state or states concerned.

This statutory scheme for the application of safeguards was based on an assumption that nuclear know-how would be confined to a privileged few and that the IAEA would be the centre of most nuclear activities.

By the mid-1960s, with all the permanent members of the Security Council already in possession of nuclear weapons, it became clear that this statutory scheme alone would not prevent the spread of nuclear weapons. Nuclear technology was being acquired by more and more countries and the assumption that the IAEA would be the principal channel for the transfer of nuclear technology had proved incorrect.

A major new approach was taken through the development of what is referred to as the "non-proliferation commitment": the legal obligation not to manufacture or acquire nuclear weapons and to accept the IAEA safeguards on existing and future nuclear activities. This commitment was first embodied in a regional treaty – the 1967 Treaty for the Prohibition of Nuclear Weapons in Latin America, known as the Treaty of Tlatelolco. [2] With the 1968 Treaty and the NPT a universal approach was taken. Under this Treaty, open to all states, non-nuclear weapon states assume an obligation, *inter alia*, not to manufacture or otherwise acquire nuclear weapons or other nuclear explosive devices, and to conclude an agreement with the IAEA for the application of safeguards to all source or special fissionable material in all peaceful nuclear activities, within their territories, under their jurisdiction, or carried out under their control anywhere.

Subsequent regional non-proliferation commitments were embodied in the 1985 South Pacific Nuclear Weapon Free Zone Treaty (the Treaty of Rarotonga) and the 1991 Argentina-Brazil Agreement for the Exclusively Peaceful Uses of Nuclear Energy.[3] Through these treaties, the IAEA safeguards have become obligatory in character and comprehensive in scope for the 146 states parties to one or other of them.

The actual application of safeguards requires the conclusion of an agreement between the IAEA and the state in which the safeguards are to be applied. This is irrespective of whether the application of safeguards follows and fulfils a prior legal obligation to accept safeguards, as in the case of safeguards following adherence to the NPT, or is the result of a separate voluntary undertaking.

The safeguards agreements set out the parties' basic rights and obligations relevant to the application of safeguards. These include the state's basic undertakings, which is to be verified through the application of safeguards, its obligation to maintain a system of accounting and control for all nuclear material subject to safeguards, and its obligation to provide the Agency with all information relevant to the application of safeguards. They also include the obligation to avoid "in doing so", hampering the economic and technological development of the state and its obligation to protect the state's commercial, industrial and other confidential information that comes to the knowledge of the IAEA through the application of safeguards.

Detailed implementation procedures are found in a set of technical subsidiary arrangements of safeguarded facilities. Four categories of safeguards agreements have been entered into by the IAEA.

First, there are agreements with non nuclear-weapon states that have made a binding non-proliferation commitment in a multilateral or a bilateral context. This includes states parties to the NPT, the Treaty of Tlatelolco, the Treaty of Rarotonga, and the Argentina-Brazil Agreement for the Exclusively Peaceful Uses of Nuclear Energy. These safeguards agreements cover all the nuclear activities of the state, present or future.

Secondly, there are agreements with non-nuclear-weapon states that have not made a binding non-proliferation commitment. These agreements are normally entered into upon the conclusion of a project agreement between the IAEA and a member state, upon unilateral submission by a state, or upon the conclusion of a supply agreement between the state and a supplier state requiring the application of IAEA safeguards. Agreements in this category cover only specified facilities, equipment and material. In these cases, assurance by the IAEA are necessarily limited to the facilities, equipment or material submitted to safeguards and do not extend to the totality of the state's nuclear activities. This is the case of

IAEA safeguards in Algeria, Cuba, Israel, India and Pakistan, none of which has accepted safeguards on its entire nuclear programme, present and future.

Thirdly, there are agreements with nuclear-weapon states. All five of the recognised nuclear-weapon states have made declarations, not required by any treaty, to accept the application of safeguards on some or all of their peaceful nuclear activities. As a result, the IAEA has entered into agreements with each of them. The agreements with nuclear-weapon states are obviously not designed to verify non-proliferation. They are meant to broaden the Agency's safeguards experiences, to affirm that nuclear-weapon states are not favoured by being exempt from safeguards on their peaceful activities, and to promote the principle that all peaceful nuclear activities in all states should be subject to safeguards.

Fourthly, there is an agreement with non-nuclear weapon states which have not yet made a non-proliferation commitment but which were ready to make such a commitment as part of the safeguards agreement. This is the safeguards agreement concluded with Albania before it became a party to the NPT.

The IAEA safeguards are technical means of verifying compliance with legal obligations. Their objectives are to assure the international community of the peaceful nature of safeguarded nuclear activities and, through the risk of early detection, to deter the diversion or misuse of safeguarded material or facilities.

Agency safeguards are limited to verifying compliance by a state with its specific undertakings under the safeguards agreement. They are based primarily on information provided by the state as to the existence of nuclear material or equipment that should be subjected to safeguards pursuant to the agreement. Safeguards do not prevent states from acquiring nuclear material, facilities or technology, nor can they assure the physical protection of nuclear material or facilities or, by themselves, prevent a violation of the safeguards agreement. Safeguards cannot read the future intentions of states, but are designed to provide an early warning of a violation by a state, of its undertakings, setting in motion response mechanisms within the IAEA, among states and in the United Nations.

The IAEA safeguards system has three basic elements which, taken together, are designed to verify that no nuclear material is diverted for non-peaceful purposes. These elements are: material accountancy, containment and surveillance measures, and on-site inspections.

Material accountancy establishes the quantities of nuclear material present in the state and the changes that take place in those quantities. Reports on the nuclear material subject to safeguards in the state are provided by the state itself to the IAEA.

Containment and surveillance measures are designed to take advantage of physical barriers such as walls or containers to restrict or control access to, or the movement of, nuclear material or equipment, and to reduce the probability of undetected movements. These measures include the use by the IAEA of seals, automatic cameras and videotape recorders, which would reveal the removal of nuclear material.

On-site inspections are designed to verify the information provided to the IAEA. During an inspection, the inspectors perform a number of functions for example, they check that fuel quantities actually match the reported quantities, they take independent measurements and samples, they verify the functioning and calibration of instruments, and they apply surveillance and containment measures.

The type, intensity and frequency of inspections vary with the kind of facility and the particular circumstances. Verification is concentrated on the stages of the fuel cycle that involve weapons grade nuclear material, such as plutonium and highly enriched uranium.

The Agency carries out ad hoc, routine and special inspections under conditions prescribed in the safeguards agreements. Ad hoc and routine inspections constitute the bulk of inspection activities. During ad hoc and routine inspections, the IAEA has access to the relevant records and to locations where safeguarded nuclear material is declared to be present. The Agency may carry out a certain fraction of routine inspections unannounced.

Special inspections are carried out if the IAEA has concluded, through an initiative taken by the state or on its own, that unusual circumstances as specified in the applicable agreements are evident, the Agency may conduct special inspections to verify information provided by the state in special reports, or if it considers that information made available by the state "is not adequate for it to fulfil its responsibilities". These responsibilities under the comprehensive safeguards agreements include the obligation to ensure that safeguards will be applied on all source or special fissionable material in all peaceful nuclear activities within the territory of the state, or under its jurisdiction or control. In carrying out special inspections under the comprehensive safeguards agreements, the IAEA may obtain access to information or locations additional to those to which it has access to during routine and ad hoc inspections.

The circumstances under which the IAEA might consider that information provided by a state was inadequate for it to fulfil its responsibilities and under which a special inspection was warranted would naturally depend on the particulars of each situation. In all cases, however, the information provided has to be assessed in good faith by the Director General or the Board of Governors, as the case may be.

Safeguards are a set of measures designed to create confidence that states are complying with specific non-proliferation obligations. The continuation of such confidence is essential for the transfer of nuclear technology and for the maintenance and evolution of the non-proliferation regime. For states to accept obligations that are directly related to forgoing a military option, it is essential that they be assured that such obligations are respected by other parties – especially neighbouring parties – to the compact. It is natural, therefore, that states should want safeguards to be subject to periodic evaluation so as to ensure their continuing effectiveness. The latest such evaluation was made during the 2000 Review Conference of the Parties to the NPT. Many recommendations relevant to the strengthening of NPT safeguards in the light of new technological and political developments were discussed at the Conference, and have since been followed up in the IAEA.

Iraq's clandestine enrichment programme in violation of its safeguards agreement with the IAEA has brought out dramatically both the strengths and the weaknesses of the IAEA safeguards system and has prompted efforts to strengthen it.

The fact that for its weaponisation programme Iraq did not use nuclear material which was under safeguards inspection was probably due to the effectiveness of IAEA safeguards. It would have been discovered and triggered an alarm. On the other hand, the ability of Iraq to construct and operate undeclared uranium enrichment facilities without detection highlighted a weakness in the system. The system has worked well in providing assurance with regard to the diversion or other misuses of material and facilities declared by the state, but it was not designed to detect possible undeclared material and facilities.

The IAEA Secretariat and Board of Governors are currently engaged in an effort to close this loophole and to identify other areas where comprehensive safeguards need to be strengthened and streamlined. A number of recommendations are under consideration by the Board of Governors, and others are being prepared. In a recommendation that is currently the focus of attention, the Director General of the IAEA proposes that he activate and make full use of the Agency's right to carry out special inspections. As already indicated, the IAEA has the right and the obligation to *ensure* that safeguards will be *applied* to all nuclear material in peaceful nuclear activities in states with comprehensive safeguards agreements. The agreements do not distinguish between declared and undeclared material. The Agency's obligation is to ensure that *all* material subject to safeguards is, in fact, safeguarded. A way for the IAEA to fulfil that obligation is to exercise its right of special inspection.

The procedures for carrying out special inspections are identical in all comprehensive safeguards agreements. If the IAEA considers that information made available by the state is not sufficient to enable it to fulfil its responsibilities under the agreement, the IAEA shall forthwith consult with the state. In the light of the consultation, the IAEA may request access "in agreement with the state" to additional information or to locations in addition to those declared by the state. Any disagreement concerning the need for such access shall be resolved in accordance with the dispute settlement procedures provided for in the agreements. However, if the Board of Governors determines that action by the state to grant access for the Agency to carry out a special inspection is essential and urgent, the state has to take the required action without delay, irrespective of whether dispute settlement procedures have been invoked.

The actions to be taken by the Board in the event of non-compliance by the state with its safeguards obligation, for example, refusal to allow the access demanded by the Board are provided for in the Agency's Statute and in the Relationship Agreement between the IAEA and the United Nations. Article XIIC of the Statute provides that the "Board shall report the non-compliance to all members of the Security Council and General Assembly of the United Nations." The Relationship Agreement contains a similar provision.

The Agency has, so far, had occasion to carry out special inspections only at locations declared by the states concerned; the special inspection mechanism provided for in the comprehensive safeguards agreements has not been used in order to secure access to undeclared nuclear material or facilities because no sufficiently specific information has come before the IAEA suggesting that such access was called for.

Although the IAEA inspections in Iraq have been carried out pursuant to a Security Council Resolution – Resolution 687 (1991) – under Chapter VII of the United Nation Charter and are not special inspections under a comprehensive safeguards agreement, the lesson learned in Iraq is that three conditions need to be fulfilled in order to make special inspections under the comprehensive safeguards agreements an effective instrument for the detection of undeclared nuclear material.

First, the inspectorate must have access to relevant information. No inspectorate can comb the entire country in a blind search for proscribed facilities or activities. They must have information indicating locations that merit inspection. Apart from information routinely collected in the course of safeguards activities, publicly available information and relevant information in the possession of member states may give such indications. This includes reports on the production, import and export of nuclear material, and sensitive equipment and non-nuclear material. It also includes information that would have to be analysed for its veracity before the Director General of the Board of Governors could decide whether there was any justification for setting in motion the procedures for a special inspection.

Second, the inspectorate must have a right of timely and unrestricted access to any location which, according to credible information, might be an undeclared nuclear installation or contain undeclared nuclear material.

Third, the IAEA must be able to exercise its right – under its Statute and the Relationship Agreement with the United Nations – of access to the Security Council if a state rejects a request for a special inspection or refuses access. Awareness of possible recourse to the Security Council may deter states from failing in their duty under a safeguards agreement.

In another proposal submitted to the Board of Governors of the IAEA it is proposed that the Agency be given design information on nuclear facilities as soon as the decision to construct a facility or to modify an existing one has been taken. The early provision of such information demonstrates an openness that is likely to inspire confidence and facilitate the effective and efficient implementation of safeguards.

Other proposals under consideration deal with: ensuring universal reporting of the production, import and export of nuclear material, sensitive equipment and relevant non-nuclear items in states with comprehensive safeguards agreements; prompt and unhindered access for IAEA inspectors; and effective application of safeguards in states with small, but significant, quantities of nuclear material.

As the IAEA goes through the process of adjusting its safeguards to new technological and political realities, it is important to bear certain facts in mind.

First, safeguards are not a static concept. They have to be constantly adjusted to take account of technological developments. They are aimed at a moving target and always have to be in focus.

Second, safeguards are not a uniform concept. Different models have been developed to deal with different legal commitments and political realities. They vary from safeguards designed to verify specified facilities in countries that have not accepted comprehensive safeguards to those designed to verify the complete nuclear fuel cycle in a state. While certain safeguards models have been developed for application as the only safeguards system, others have been developed to operate in conjunction with other safeguards; this is so in the case of the EURATOM countries and for Argentina and Brazil, where EURATOM (the European Atomic Energy Community) and ABACC (the Brazilian-Argentina Agency for Accounting and Control of Nuclear Materials) apply their own safeguards.

Third, because the objective of safeguards is to provide assurance and create confidence, the degree of intrusiveness required may vary with the degree of trust or distrust existing in different areas. In some regions, and in the relations between some countries where hostility and fear have reigned, more intrusive safeguards may be needed to create confidence. A case in point is the Middle East. The Director General of the IAEA has been requested by the Agency's General Conference to prepare a model safeguards agreement that could apply to that region, and preliminary contacts indicate a need for considerably more far-reaching verification and control measures than those practised under existing comprehensive safeguards, possibly including mutual inspections by the parties themselves, in addition to the IAEA safeguards.

Fourth, safeguards are not on infringement of the state's sovereignty. States accept safeguards, as they do other international obligations, because they perceive them to be in their national interest. Opening up installations for international inspection, waiving or relaxing visa requirements for inspectors and providing a transparent flow of information on nuclear activities do not diminish a state's sovereignty, but rather help create the conditions necessary for peace, in which sovereignty can be enjoyed.

Fifth, safeguards cost money, and money has to be made available and be assured if the safeguards system is to work effectively and without interruption. Regrettably, the financing of safeguards, like the financing of so many other activities of international organisations, is today inadequate and in jeopardy.

Developments in the recent past suggest that a universal non-proliferation regime could become a reality in the not-too-distant future. It is, therefore, important to ensure that adequate machinery for verifying such a universal commitment is ready. The process of taking a hard, fresh look at safeguards has began. To complete it, imagination, resolve and resources are required.

II

With the ending of the Cold War, there has been a definite acceleration in the pace of nuclear weapons reduction worldwide, and simple bilateral discourse on the subject seems to be moving gradually towards a broader, multilateral process. The actual control of nuclear weapons has ceased to be the sacrosanct issue it once was.

This subject, now frequently addressed in the mass media, has become one of vital concern to all. What has happened, or what is likely to happen, to the many strategic and tactical nuclear weapons in the hands of what used to be the military infrastructure of the former Soviet Union? This is a matter of global concern. People in many countries are discussing the control of these weapons, or lack thereof, in the hands of independent republics, members of the new Commonwealth. It is entirely possible that, in spite of the years of effort given to the NPT work, the number of states with nuclear weapons might have doubled instantly on August 19 , 1991, the date of the aborted Soviet coup. The manner in which this issue is handled internationally had profound effects on the outcome of the NPT Review Conference held in 1995. The outcome was indefinite extension of NPT – no amendment was made to the Treaty.

In the 1990s, the situation in Iraq raised a number of issues which, till then, had managed to escape full-blown public attention. The IAEA safeguards are intended to deter proliferation by imposing a considerable risk of detection of the diversion of significant quantities of nuclear material. In Iraq, the international community confronted a state party to the NPT which was not deterred by a probability statement of diversion and which in the end had to be physically stopped from carrying out weapons-oriented programmes. Clandestine material and clandestine facilities became the new focus of attention.

These issues present complicated legal questions involving interpretations of both the NPT and the safeguards agreement. An even more serious problem is the determination of what may justifiably trigger the mechanisms for forced inspection regarding either clandestine material or facilities. When the suspicion results from a use of national technical means (NTM), there may arguably be a case for international action in view of precedents in US-USSR nuclear-arms control agreements. If less comprehensive and less well established charges can trigger a mechanism, there is serious danger of abuse. There should be, in any case, well-defined procedures before an international organisation undertakes an operation which constitutes a challenge to national sovereignty. One cannot expect a text such as Security Council Resolution 687 to be always available to back up action against a violator.[4] One should also remember that the IAEA safeguards went through a period of being suspect as an instrument for industrial espionage, and it would not be desirable for the IAEA to try to operate its own CIA at KGB. In any event, output from the inspection system is extremely sensitive and needs to be handled with the utmost care because it could implicate a sovereign state as possibly being in violation of treaty obligations.

The NPT verification process needs to be revamped to strengthen the inspection authority so that undeclared facilities and undeclared material may be subject to international control. It is necessary to be able to define clearly the legally acceptable triggering mechanism for such forced inspection. Challenge inspections allowing inspectors to carry out their work in any location when a certain set of conditions are satisfied (as is contemplated in a chemical weapons treaty) are extreme cases. In the opinion of those who originally drafted this document, the special inspection referred to in paragraph 73(b) in Information Circular/153 (INFCIRC) has been interpreted too narrowly. It is a matter of striking a correct balance between effectiveness and non-intrusiveness, and paragraph 73(b) may need further clarification in writing in order to avoid confusion.

There will be an increasing need to agree upon, and arrange for, the orderly international transfer of sensitive technologies. Multilateral NTM requires the transfer of, or cooperation in, satellite-based information gathering and transmission as well as the processing of such information. In order to avoid the unrestrained transfer of weapons-related technologies, a new regime has to be worked out to supplement the "London Guidelines", which apply to NPT-related technologies or components. Work along these lines is already under way. This will entail making very difficult and sensitive decisions which require the drawing of an imaginary dividing line between the proliferation of weapons and freedom of international transfer of scientific and industrial knowledge and hardware.

In order to clarify the problems, it is useful to examine the NPT safeguards. When the Safeguards Committee met in Vienna in 1970, Article III of the NPT presented some difficulties, because paragraph I spoke of "diversion of nuclear energy" and separately of "source or special fissionable material". The Committee decided that those who had drafted the NPT did not really understand what was meant by nuclear energy, because it might be construed to mean, for example, that electricity generated in nuclear power stations should not be diverted for use in military or weapons facilities. The same type of problem exists today in the prohibition of a military attack on peaceful nuclear facilities. The statements about material are very clear, and, therefore, INFCIRC/153 has had, more or less, to slip in facility inspectors through the back door with such devices as subsidiary arrangements and facility attachments. This has led to some inevitable ambiguities regarding treaty obligations to inform the IAEA of nuclear facilities under construction (paragraph 42 of INFCIRC/153 stipulates "as early as possible" and not "within 180 days", as some seem to believe). Clandestine construction of uranium enrichment, plutonium separation, or weapons fabrication facilities may not be a violation of the letter of any obligation unless nuclear material (source or special fissionable) is placed inside them.

A scenario often described by Committee members during the 1970 meetings may explain the difficulties. Suppose an inspector observes a large number of plutonium metal hemispheres being machined under the pretext that they are new and commercially secret breeder reactor fuel. The material balance of plutonium shows nothing worn or missing (that is, no diversion) and the inspector is not at liberty to disclose information about commercially sensitive technologies, therefore, the inspector has nothing to report to the headquarters. He also observes that next door to the plutonium plant is a long workshop where people are building high explosive lenses. The inspector becomes very suspicious, but has no basis for airing any concerns because high explosives are not nuclear material, and he is prohibited from mentioning any non-nuclear commercial activities he may, by chance, have observed. The reported nuclear activity in the Democratic People's Republic of Korea which so seriously concerned those gathered in Vienna may not be very different from this hypothetical cases.

Another point realised by the Committee's technical people, but which they failed to communicate fully to their non-technical colleagues, was the tricky nature of the probability statement. The Director General of the IAEA would report to the Board of Governors that with 80 per cent confidence level, he could not confirm that there had not been a diversion by a state party. The Board would very likely ask: "What in plain language does that confidence level mean?" The Director General would have to refer the matter to his technical staff, who would explain that this was a statistical statement, which more or less meant there was a 20 per cent chance that diversion had not taken place. Can an international body take action against a sovereign state when there is a 20 per cent chance that it has not violated treaty obligations?

Many Committee members were confident that this type of accounting of material would act as a deterrent. Obviously, they foresaw very little chance of ever having actually to call such a Board meeting.

In actual practice, with the increasing throughput of nuclear material in varieties of nuclear fuel cycles, it became obvious that accumulating measurement errors over time would leave more than a significant quantity of plutonium or highly enriched uranium unaccounted for. [5] Mathematically, there is no way other than to be satisfied that the material balance is closed independently every six months or so in every material balance area (MBA). The MBA may be a reactor core, oxide fuel palletising room, or an irradiated fuel-cooling pond. Put cynically, the amount of material unaccounted for could total ten to fifty bombs every six months, depending on the number of MBAs in a country.

There is no question that those in charge of the implementation of safeguards in the IAEA have been working seriously to carry out what they believe to be their mandate and to structure a workable safeguards system. There have been some comments that inherent difficulties mentioned above were already well appreciated at the time of the drafting of INFCIRC/153, but had somehow failed to receive sufficient attention through the implementation stages. Accumulated safeguards efforts and the allocation of safeguards resources according to the amount of nuclear material in the various nuclear fuel cycles (that is, without any other consideration of assigning different weights) undoubtedly reach a saturation point when it is understood that safeguards resources, in both human and monetary terms, have a limit. In fact, already in Vienna in 1970, there were considerable calls for the financing of safeguards to be related to the benefits countries were expected to reap from the extensive exercises. The points mentioned above serve to emphasise the importance of the deterrent nature of this instrument. There is nothing in the document to restrain those in charge in the IAEA from devising methods which are less nuclear-material measurement focussed than is the current practice.

Immediately after the adoption of INFCIRC/153, Japan took the initiative in the creation of the Standing Advisory Group on

Safeguards Implementation (SAGSI) and tried to point out the importance of this consideration to the IAEA member states. It can be claimed that efforts have continued to build on the imaginative approach of the initial period, with the result that the safeguards activities do not get buried under the heavy burden of routine work.

III

The IAEA was established in 1957 by an international statute through a major policy initiative of the United States. While it did not assume the exact role visualised by President Eisenhower and became a supplier of nuclear materials, it did take on the more important function of verifying through a combination of international and national systems for safeguards that nuclear materials supplied would not go into nuclear weapons. In particular, IAEA safeguards soon provided the United States with an alternative to direct US inspection of US-supplied nuclear items, as required by bilateral and multilateral agreements for cooperation authorised by the Atomic Energy Act of 1954.

The first agreement to delegate US inspection rights to the Agency was put into affect with Japan in 1958. However, it was not until 1965 that a uniform safeguards system was established by the Agency. Known colloquially by the number of the document which described this system, INFCIRC/66, the IAEA safeguards system established the general conditions, criteria, and procedures to be employed by the Agency and its inspectors in overseeing surveillance, containment, and accounting for nuclear materials in each state subject to an agreement with the Agency. INFCIRC/ 66 in its present form reflects amendments made in 1966 and 1968 and is given the additional designation "Rev. 2". [6]

As far as plutonium was concerned, INFCIRC/66 provided that a state subject to the IAEA safeguards was to be exempt from those safeguards upon its request if it held less than one kilogram of separated plutonium, or if it operated a nuclear reactor which produced less than 100 grams of plutonium annually in its fuel. The frequency of the IAEA inspection for a given nuclear facility was to be determined by the amount of fissionable material in inventory, annually flowing through the facility, or annually produced, which ever was greatest. In determining these amounts, the Agency employed the concept of "effective kilograms". For plutonium, an effective kilogram was exactly a kilogram in weight. For enriched uranium, it was the weight in kilogram multiplied by the square of the enrichment. Thus, a kilogram of 90 per cent (0.90) enriched uranium would considered to be 0.81 effective kilogram. When a reactor contained as much as 60 effective kilograms of fissionable material, the Agency had a right of access for inspection at all times. However, in practice, the Agency could not perform unannounced inspections. At the lower end of the scale, only one routine inspection per year could be conducted at a reactor containing from one to five effective kilograms.

At reprocessing plants and other facilities handling fissionable materials in bulk form, where these materials are more accessible and more difficult to contain and measure, an annual throughput of five effective kilograms or more required that the plant be accessible to inspection at all times.

It is significant to note that the IAEA safeguards system gave no credit to the denaturing of plutonium-239 by its heavier isotopes, although diluted uranium-235 was treated favourably in this regard. This reflected the common judgement of the world nuclear community that all plutonium, regardless of its isotopic composition, should be treated as being equally dangerous from the viewpoint of its utility in weapons. According to Prawitz, the issue of how to handle the isotopic content of plutonium in a safeguards context was first discussed by an IAEA committee in 1964. [7]

Although INFCIRC/66 is an old document, it retains its vitality because it governs safeguards for those states which are not parties to the NPT. States party to the Treaty are covered by another IAEA safeguards systems documented as INFCIRC/153, which became effective after the Treaty entered into force in 1970. [8] The NPT commits non-weapon states to accept IAEA safeguards for all of their nuclear activities, and all members to require IAEA safeguards for their nuclear exports. As for the weapon states, the USA, the UK and France have voluntarily opened some of their civil nuclear facilities to IAEA inspections. The Soviet Union negotiated a comparable voluntary inspection agreement with the IAEA in 1985.

INFCIRC/153 takes a more subtle approach to safeguards because it applies to states which have committed themselves not to develop, possess, or use nuclear explosives.[9] However, it is an evolution of INFCIRC/66 and contains most of the same provisions concerning plutonium. The exempt quantity remains the same, although gram quantities without limit are also exempted if they are used as sensing components in measuring instruments. Also, plutonium with an isotopic composition greater than 80 per cent plutonium-239 is exempted from safeguards. This provision was added to reflect the development of plutonium-238 as a heat source for use in thermoelectric power supplies. Such power supplies have been used in a broad range of applications, from cardiac pacemakers to space satellites. Although plutonium-238 is fissionable and has a relatively small critical mass, it is also intensely radioactive – it quickly becomes hot if not cooled. This characteristic makes the probability of it being employed as an explosive too marginal to be of safeguards concern. Pu-238 also is not commonplace because it is made by a different nuclear process than that for plutonium-239 and is very high in cost.

The formulas for inspection frequency in INFCIRC/153 also are modified in that if a facility has an inventory or annual throughput of more than five effective kilograms, the maximum number of man-days of routine inspections permitted per year is thirty times the square root of the number of effective kilograms, but not less than 1.5 man-years of inspection per year. The amount of material that would require continuous inspection, on this basis, would be 1,332 effective kilograms. The rule is different for reactors, and the INFCIRC/66 exemption for small reactors has been removed.

Implementation of safeguards under INFCIRC/153 is for the purpose of detecting on a timely basis the diversion of "significant quantities" of nuclear materials. For plutonium, the significant quantity was set initially at eight kilograms of plutonium containing 95 per cent plutonium-239, but subsequently this amount of plutonium of any isotopic composition (except plutonium containing more than 80 per cent plutonium-238) was defined as the significant quantity. This amount is deemed to be the minimum needed to fabricate a nuclear explosive, assuming that a working stock substantially larger than the amount of material ultimately to be contained in the explosive is required.

After the IAEA safeguards system was developed and became operational, it became apparent to the USA that there was a severe deficiency in the ways to prevent diversion of fissionable materials. The safeguards system was designed to detect diversion after it had occurred. What was missing was a system of physical protection, or security, to deter diversion before the fact. After several years of discussion and negotiation, the IAEA adopted a voluntary guideline for physical protection measures in 1975, which was updated and codified in 1977 as INFCIRC/225/Rev.1.[10] The IAEA had no authority to specify security measures because security is the internal responsibility of sovereign states, and because the charter for the IAEA gave it no authority for security. In the IAEA's guidelines, the recommended level of security depends upon the amount and weapons utility of the fissionable material involved. Maximum security is specified for two kilograms or more of plutonium of any isotopic composition (except if it contains more than 80 per cent plutonium-238), or of uranium-233, and five kilograms or more of uranium enriched to more than 20 per cent. These threshold quantities are considered to be less than required to fabricate a nuclear explosive. The trigger amount for security purposes is only 25 per cent of the significant quantity for safeguards purposes, so that an additional factor of safety is obtained.

After years of negotiation resulting from inadequacies seen in controls for transfers of nuclear materials and technology from suppliers to recipient nations, the NPT was opened for signature in 1968. It went into force in 1970. Much like the establishment of the IAEA, negotiation of the Treaty was a high policy objective of the United States.

The NPT is a political statement, not a technical regulation. Nothing can be found in it which either refers directly to plutonium or its use in nuclear explosives. What is more important, however, is that the NPT set the stage for the major revision of international safeguards for plutonium. It also put no barrier in the way of non-weapons NPT states that might wish to embark large-scale nuclear power programmes, including acquisition of sensitive facilities needed to complete or "close" the nuclear fuel cycle. Sensitive facilities are defined as those for uranium enrichment and spent fuel reprocessing. In the early 1970s, the United States and most other advanced nations engaged in the development of civilian nuclear power believed that a complete fuel cycle was necessary in order to ultimately take full advantage of the latent energy stored in uranium. Pressures from the emerging nuclear power countries to acquire reprocessing technology mounted, since their accession to the NPT and their relinquishment of nuclear explosives led them to believe that the Treaty entitled them to receive and use this fuel cycle technology.[11] However, US agreements for nuclear cooperation did not provide for US supply of reprocessing technology. Indeed, US agreements retained US control over reprocessing of spent fuel that contained uranium originally enriched in the United States, and over subsequent retransfer of the plutonium recovered from it. The issue of technical assistance for reprocessing was further complicated by those states which did not accede to the Treaty. In some cases, it seemed that they wished to retain the option to develop and use nuclear explosives for peaceful purposes, and wished to keep open the option of reprocessing as the easiest route to fissionable material for explosive use. None of the nuclear weapons states party to the Treaty (the USA, the USSR and the UK) were inclined to furnish reprocessing technology either to NPT nations or to those who had not joined, believing that although much information on reprocessing was already in the public domain, proprietary information and specialised equipment still should be controlled if the potential for explosive, use of plutonium was to be restrained. Nonetheless, several NPT states went ahead and developed their own reprocessing technology. Likewise, a few nations not party to the Treaty were able to acquire the capability as well. US agreements for cooperation, either before or after the NPT went into effect, did not differentiate plutonium by its grade following the precept established by the Atomic Energy Act of 1954.

IV

The worst fears of those engaged in nuclear politics were realised in April 1974 when the United States and Sweden and perhaps the Soviet Union detected an underground nuclear explosion in India. The Government of India confirmed that it had conducted a test of a nuclear explosive device, which it said was not for military applications but for the development of nuclear explosives for peaceful applications such as earth moving. India had refused to accede to the NPT on the grounds that it was discriminatory and would prohibit India from exploiting the full range of nuclear applications such as "peaceful nuclear explosives" or PNEs. In her statement in the UN General Assembly on October 14, 1968, Prime Minister Indira Gandhi said: "It is by restricting, reducing and eventually eliminating the growing nuclear menace that firm foundations of peace can be laid. The limited achievement of the Partial Test Ban Treaty has been offset by the refusal of states to halt the testing of nuclear weapons. The problems of insecurity cannot be solved by imposing arbitrary restrictions on those who do not possess nuclear weapons, without any corresponding steps to deal with the basic problem of limiting stockpiles in the hands of a few powers. How can the urge to acquire nuclear status be controlled so long as this imbalance persists? Unless the powers who possess these weapons are prepared to exercise some self-restraint, collective efforts to rid the world of the nuclear menace cannot bear fruit." [12]

In due course it became apparent that India's test had used plutonium, and that this material had been produced in a test reactor from natural uranium. Reprocessing had occurred in a small facility of indigenous design. The reactor had been supplied by Canada under an agreement which limited its use to peaceful application of nuclear energy. The US was also implicated because it had supplied Canada with some of the heavy water used in the

Indian reactor. Since India was not a party to the NPT, it was not subject to international safeguards on all of its nuclear facilities, although a US-supplied nuclear power plant in India was under the IAEA safeguards at the time through a trilateral agreement with the Agency. In retrospect, it appears that the plutonium used in India's test was of high isotopic quality specially suited for the purpose; and did not come from either the US-supplied power plant or from a safeguard facility. [13]

What was more important in the world's eye was that India had been able to master the technology of producing a nuclear explosion with plutonium. It was from this time that efforts were redoubled to restrict the supply of reprocessing technology from the advanced nations to the less advanced. For some reason the revelation that China had embarked on a full-scale nuclear armament programme ten years earlier had failed to arouse the same public concern over the proliferation of nuclear weapons, even though China in some ways was not as technologically sophisticated as India.

With the escalation of sensitivity over, and interest in, plutonium that resulted from the Indian test explosion, attention in the United States and in several other countries was soon focussed on a draft report published a few months later in August 1974, by the US Atomic Energy Commission (AEC). Entitled "Generic Environmental Statement on Mixed Oxide Fuel" – dubbed with the acronym "Gesmo" – the draft had been prepared to meet the requirements of the National Environmental Policy Act (NEPA) of 1969. It recommended that the AEC should approve the widespread use of plutonium/uranium oxide fuels for the purpose of plutonium recovered from spent fuel. The report met with strong opposition from the environmental and anti-nuclear movements. In January 1975, the newly formed Nuclear Regulatory Commission took over the licensing and safeguards responsibility of the AEC. It continued to evaluate the draft report, which had been faulted by the Council on Environmental Quality and by the Environmental Protection Agency because it did not address these subjects before any Commission decision was reached on the use of mixed oxide fuels. However, when the final report was published in 1976, it did not include any findings on the diversion and safeguards issues. It did conclude that the economic safety, and environmental aspects of the plutonium recycle were favourable and that there was no reason to disapprove the use of plutonium for the stated purpose.[14] During this period, opposition by certain public interest groups to civilian nuclear power continued to mount, largely for environmental and non-proliferation reasons.

Changes in the US nuclear policy, particularly with respect to plutonium, were in the offing and the Nuclear Regulatory Commission (NRC) never approved the use of mixed fuels in light water reactors on a commercial scale. The impetus for performing a safeguards analysis of the mixed oxide recycle concept remained, and in 1978, the NRC published an informative report linked to the Gesmo study which addressed the plutonium question in more detail than had been customary in other government reports.[15] The report placed plutonium bearing materials into three categories of sensitivity according to their "attractiveness to a malefactor" for manufacturing illicit nuclear explosives. Type I materials were defined as those which were suitable, either directly or with minor processing, for use in explosives. Type II materials would require more elaborate processing and greater amounts of starting material. Type III materials required major facilities and processing efforts to convert them to Type I. It is to be noted that Type II materials included "plutonium spiked to degrade weapons performance," that is, plutonium which has been denatured by one means or another but not by merely reducing the isotopic concentration of plutonium-239. The NRC report made the following points: "Reactor-grade recycled plutonium is somewhat less desirable for use in an explosive device than weapons-grade plutonium, which has substantially higher fraction of plutonium-239... The isotopes plutonium-239 and plutonium-241 have similar fission cross-sections.[16] The isotopes plutonium-240 and plutonium-242 are similar in that both have poorer fission cross-sections for fission spectrum neutrons and are thus less reactive than plutonium-239 and plutonium-241. Therefore, the amount of material required for an explosive device will increase as the plutonium-240 and plutonium-242 concentration increases.

Nevertheless, the critical mass of even fourth generation recycled plutonium is smaller than the critical mass of high enriched uranium."

The report continued:

Weapons fabrication using reactor-grade plutonium is further complicated by the increased neutron background due primarily to the spontaneous fission of isotopes plutonium-238, plutonium-240 and plutonium-242 and to alpha-neutron reactions when an oxide form is present. This increased neutron background causes handling problems, and it could cause premature detonation of weapons, resulting in substantially reduced yield. Nevertheless, since nuclear explosives can be constructed using reactor-grade plutonium, appropriate safeguards measures would be necessary.

Unfortunately (probably for reasons of secrecy), the NRC report did not further explain or cite references for the last sentence of the above quotation. The probable background may be found in events occurring about the time the report was written.

An illuminating discussion then ensued on the fabrication of nuclear explosives by terrorist groups. This section of the NRC report is recommended because of its authoritative nature, but it is too long to reproduce here. Nonetheless, the following excerpts will give some idea of what the report said about prospects for terrorist use of plutonium taken illicitly from a nuclear fuel cycle. It said: "... there is essentially no likelihood that terrorist group could fabricate an efficient bomb such as those in military inventories. There is, however, a low but credible probability that such a group could assemble a crude device which would produce a fission yield. It is this possibility that must be minimized by industry safeguards."

V

Here the cases of North Korea and Iraq merit some discussion. The problem with North Korea is obvious: it was only on January 30, 1992, after several years of delay, that it signed a safeguards agreement as called for in Article III of the NPT. Although many states parties to the NPT have not yet concluded safeguards agreements with the IAEA, they are countries with little or no nuclear research activity. Even though an agreement has now been signed by North Korea and a pledge made to place all its peaceful nuclear activities under full-scope safeguards, there is still the problem of ratification, and that of the amount of time that may be required under North Korean law, about which few claim to be knowledgeable. Even after the agreement has entered into effect, the North Koreans are under no clear obligation to report, much less to place under safeguards, the large thermal output reactor and what is suspected to be a plutonium extraction plant nearby. According to intelligence reports in the world press, these two facilities were expected to be completed by 1995, and, as mentioned above, a country is under no clear obligation to report its nuclear facilities when there is no nuclear material housed within it. At most, it is required to provide design information "as early as possible".

Given the implication of possible nuclear arms in the northern half of the Korean peninsula for security considerations in the region, and the way in which various experts have underestimated the work of Saddam Hussein's regime, this is hardly a satisfactory situation. Not many countries would be against the mandatory "voluntary submission" of design information at the inception of the development of a nuclear facility, or against reporting such benchmarks as the start of construction and the granting of operating permits from time to time. Such cooperating countries could be placed in one category; let us call it "category A". In fact, in most countries, this is open information, available in government annual reports and in trade journals. Unwillingness to enter into such agreements may be taken as an indication of possible non-compliance, and the IAEA may be justified in placing countries in a second category, "category B", where extra attention could be directed to possible unannounced nuclear activities.

The situation of inspecting Iraq in the early 1990s would be somewhat complicated if there were no such extraordinary authorisation as Security Council Resolution 687 (1991). Iraq is one of the original signatories of the NPT and has been under IAEA safeguards from the beginning. It has not yet manufactured nuclear weapons or other nuclear explosive devices. Article III of the NPT states that safeguards arrangements should be applied to all source or special fissionable material in all peaceful nuclear activities. If, as reported, Iraq was producing its own natural uranium and using it in a very large calutron plant in Tarmiya to produce 465 gram of 4 per cent enriched uranium, the only way for the Iraqi regime to claim non-violation of paragraph 2 of the safeguards agreement (which is a repetition of Article III of the NPT regarding all source or special fissionable material) would be for it to claim that it was for non-peaceful activities. In order for that to be effective, Iraq should have identified the material and informed the IAEA according to paragraph 14, which it did not. Even if the IAEA had known of wide-ranging activities in preparation for nuclear weapons in Iraq, it could not have done anything in particular under the current practice. As clearly stipulated, the IAEA Board may take major action only when it "finds that the Agency is not able to verify that there has been no diversion", and this, as mentioned earlier, refers to each MBA for a significant quantity with something like an 80 per cent confidence level. In the case of highly enriched uranium, the current significant quantity is 25 kilograms, which is far more than 465 grams of 4 per cent enriched uranium.

If the story of advanced G-2 centrifuge machines in Iraq is true, this alone does not place the country in violation of NPT or the safeguards agreement, because no fissionable material had been placed in the enrichment test facilities. Extraction of 3 grams of plutonium was also reported, and one is not quite sure how this was carried out. The significant quantity for plutonium is 7 kilograms and 3 grams is a minute amount. One only notices that the plutonium extraction exercise has been performed without notifying the IAEA of the intention. This implies a very serious problem because plutonium extraction is a far more commonplace route, indeed, it is an expected one, for nuclear weapons diversion in the Third World.

There are several lessons to be drawn from the cases of North Korea and Iraq. First, provision for voluntary submission of design information and construction schedules of nuclear facilities should be included in the safeguards agreement. Those that comply should be placed in category A. Others should be placed in category B, and will be subject to extra attention by the parties to the NPT for any indication of possible nuclear fuel cycle activities.

Second, export control of fuel-cycle technology and components, including software, should be agreed on very carefully, and any suppliers found to be in violation of, or in insufficient exercise of, the agreements should be duly reprimanded, including those who may be named responsible for supplying information and component to Iraq's projects.

Third, a multilateral international mechanism should be worked out to establish a depositary of information gathered through NTM and other non-routine means of detecting possible violation of treaty obligations. The violators, as in the case of Iraq, would be dealt with by this means to make sure that only well-founded suspicion could pass through this filter. Only when this mechanism has determined that a particular suspicion is well founded, may the IAEA be authorised to take action. A single organisation such as the IAEA should not have the right to collect covert information and/or to determine suspicion on its own unless presented with sufficient evidence and unless the Board of Governors has determined to act, and has so directed the secretariat.

Last the IAEA needs to reallocate safeguards resources with less of a focus on the category A countries, which already possess an open national system of accounting for, and control of, all nuclear material (INFCIRC/153, para 31). Deterrence effects of inspection activities can be achieved with a very low level of confidence statistically, thus, requiring the deployment of considerably fewer inspectors in the field. Exercise of this sort of judgement, given due reference to criteria, should be within the terms given to organisations such as the IAEA as specifically spelt out in paragraph 81 of INFCIRC/153. Insufficient consideration seems to have been given in the past to application of criteria of this type.

The IAEA is, in fact, the only international mechanism entrusted with verification of arms control arrangements, namely those relating to Article III of the NPT. The provision of safeguards was only one of the reasons why the IAEA was established. While at the time it was found convenient in Article II of the NPT to make use of the IAEA, neither the 18-nation Committee on Disarmament, which drafted the original text of the NPT, nor the IAEA was aware of the extent and magnitude of the task that was to be undertaken. In fact, the safeguards document had to be rewritten in 1970 to accommodate NPT requirements. This also explains why the 1970 amendments were intended to be flexible enough to accommodate new situations as they arose. The events of 1991 have made evident the need for further clarification of the safeguards system in accordance with the original intention of the 1970 safeguards understanding. This Article is an effort to indicate the direction to be followed. It is of fundamental importance that the credibility of the safeguards system be strengthened as we looked at the NPT Review Conference of 1995. It was hoped to present a worthwhile precedent when one contemplates the structure and content of further international verification regimes, such as the use of multilaterally owned and operated satellites to cover such a variety of technologies as those relating to chemical weapons and long-range ballistic missiles.

The revelation, in the aftermath of the cold war, of an extensive and previously unknown Iraqi nuclear-weapons programme has raised hard questions about the efficacy of the non-proliferation regime and its supporting international safeguards system. What happened in the case of Iraq revealed a systemic failure of the non-proliferation regime: national intelligence failed to detect on-going clandestine activity; national export-control policies largely failed to close down the possibility of exporting components that could contribute to a nuclear weapons programme; and the safeguards system of the IAEA was not only not focussed and implemented in such a way as to reduce the likelihood of detecting a range of unauthorised activities, but also lacked some of the capabilities necessary for dealing with clandestine activity.

Strengthening the effectiveness and credibility of the IAEA safeguards and restoring international confidence in them are central concerns. The imbroglio is the proximate cause for such an inquiry, but the inquiry is also dictated by the sea change in international relations. The domination of the international political-security agenda by the United States-Soviet relations also meant a diminished involvement of the two nuclear superpowers in conflicts and a commensurate lessening of their capacity to exert influence over the security policies of these countries. And it has meant higher priority on the international agenda for regional and even locally based conflicts and confrontations and an increase in the relevance of these situations to international stability and security.

A number of factors have led to an increased risk of proliferation in the Third World: the spread of technology knowledge, an increase in the source of nuclear supply, the perception in some quarters that nuclear weapons can serve to bolster hegemonic ambitions and deter outside interference or compensate for the diminished role of the major nuclear states in providing security assurance.

The focus of concern is the possibility of clandestine programmes even more than diversion of nuclear material from nuclear fuel cycles dedicated to peaceful use. For states with relatively limited nuclear power reactor programmes, facing a substantial probability of the detection of diversion of nuclear material from declared peaceful activities, and having relatively modest nuclear military requirements, clandestine programmes seem to offer a preferred route to the acquisition of nuclear weapons. This, in turn, raises new questions and new challenges for traditional non-proliferation safeguards. These safeguards were largely predicated on the idea that states voluntarily undertaking solemn non-proliferation commitments were not significant risks as regards proliferation. Nevertheless, their peaceful commitments had to be effectively and independently verified. In fact, the IAEA has approached its safeguards responsibilities on the assumption that the existence of clandestine facilities could not *a priori* be excluded, and that there existed a risk of non-compliance with undertakings.

Until recently, the IAEA safeguards enjoyed a substantial degree of confidence. Important political statements to this effect were made in the 1985 and 1990 Review Conference of the NPT.

The final declaration of the 1985 Conference expressed "the conviction that the IAEA safeguards provide assurance that states are complying with their undertakings and assist states in demonstrating this compliance. They thereby promote confidence among states and ... help to strengthen their collective security. The IAEA safeguards play a key role in preventing the proliferation of nuclear weapons and other nuclear explosive devices.[17]

The draft-final document of the 1990 Conference reiterated these views,[18] but added "the possible scope, application and procedures" of special inspections to deal with the contingency of states not fulfilling their non-proliferation commitments to place under safeguards all sources or special fissionable materials, thus indicating an emerging concern about clandestine activity.

Supplier states have relied on an effective international safeguards system as a condition for doing international nuclear business. It is generally acknowledged that without safeguards, there would be little if any international nuclear cooperation, but also that this would not mean an end to nuclear activity, only a sharply increased uncertainty about the nature of the nuclear activity that was going on and an inevitable rise in insecurity and instability resulting from the dynamics of the security dilemma.

On the other hand, it was largely understood in the beginning that safeguards were not panaceas and did have limitations, although thinking about this has tended to become blurred as the notion that safeguards do, or should, *prevent* proliferation has taken hold. At the dawn of the nuclear age, the Acheson-Lilienthal Report concluded that "a system of inspection superimposed on an otherwise uncontrolled exploitation of atomic energy by a national government will not be an adequate safeguard," [19] and that "systems of inspection cannot by *themselves* be made effective safeguards ... to protect complying states and the hazards of violations and evasion. (Emphasis added. The words emphasised make clear that from the outset safeguards were seen as essential but not conclusive measures in foreclosing the risk of proliferation). This formed the basis of the proposal in the Baruch Plan that all nuclear activities that were potentially dangerous to world security be placed under the ownership and control of an international agency.[20]

Rejection of the Baruch Plan was followed by a period of secrecy which, failing to forestall continued dispersion of nuclear knowledge and development, led to a policy of controlled nuclear cooperation spearheaded by the United States with its Atoms for Peace initiative. In this context, control meant the application of a system of international safeguards on nationally owned and operated nuclear programmes to verify that nuclear activity was not diverted from peaceful to military use. Safeguards were applied, as a condition of cooperation, on any equipment, plant or material that was provided. On-site inspection was made an integral part of this approach.

The NPT, which came into force in 1970, introduced the concept of comprehensive or full-scope safeguards meaning that safeguards were to apply to all nuclear material in peaceful use in all non-nuclear weapons state parties to the Treaty.[21] Parties were required to declare *all* nuclear material in all peaceful nuclear activity. If all nuclear materials subject to safeguards could be accounted for through IAEA inspection, it could be concluded that there was no reason to suspect any diversion from peaceful to proscribed uses. It is this system, based on material accountancy and the auditing of records and reports through on-site inspections involving independent verifications, that has been the mainstay of non-proliferation verification. It is probable that the notion that safeguards prevent proliferation is derived from this linkage.

Although the IAEA safeguards under the NPT generate the confidence described in the final declarations or documents of the NPT Review Conferences, there have also been some questions and concerns about them. India's nuclear tests in 1974 not only dramatised the fact that the technical capability to design and fabricate nuclear explosives successfully was spreading, but also raised the question of the adequacy of safeguards for dealing with separated plutonium. Although measures were taken through national policies and multilateral understandings, such as the Nuclear Supplier Guidelines (NSG), to minimise the opportunity for the spread of reprocessing capabilities that would lead to plutonium stockpiles under national control, there has been, since the mid-1970s, a continuing debate concerning the adequacy of safeguards of any kind in dealing with plutonium. A vocal segment of the interested public contends not only that separated plutonium cannot be safeguarded, but that in large-scale nuclear facilities such as reprocessing plants, material accountancy, even accomplished by containment and surveillance, cannot detect the diversion of quantities of material large enough to make one or more nuclear weapons, and that plutonium separation should, therefore, be banned. It must be noted, however, that the IAEA has demonstrated considerable, if not infallible, capabilities for dealing with reprocessing facilities. What it cannot do is to assure that a government will not suddenly alter its peaceful-use-only policy and seize nuclear material for proscribed military use. It is well known that Pakistan's nuclear programme is intended for manufacturing nuclear weapons, but the IAEA has not been able to do anything to inspect, contain or control its nuclear activities. Pakistan's success in manufacturing what is called the "Islamic Bomb", has brought about a dramatic change in the entire security perspective of South Asia and the Middle East.

The Pakistani nuclear capability over the longer run is likely to have a greater impact on the West Asian situation than on the subcontinent itself. One of the underlying reasons for the conflicts in the subcontinent was Pakistan's quest for parity with the much larger India. It could not achieve parity in conventional terms. When Prime Minister Z.A. Bhutto initiated the Pakistani nuclear weapon programme in 1972, his aim was to set Pakistan on a new course, free it from the shackles of the subcontinent and align it with West Asia, with a view to finding a leadership role for Pakistan in the Islamic world. This developed military relationships extensively with West Asian countries and thereby among developing nations. Pakistan deploys the largest number of military manpower outside its borders. Bhutto became the chairman of the Organisation of Islamic States (OIS), and argued that Pakistan alone among Islamic countries had enough brain power to provide Islam the nuclear capability. Given this background and the Pakistani leaders' fervour towards Islamic fundamentalism and involvement with Arab states, it is very likely that Pakistan will use its nuclear weapon capability politically to claim leadership in the Islamic world and use its prestige gained through this achievement to expand and intensify its military interaction with the Arab states. Unfortunately, in the Western strategic literature, this aspect of Pakistani foreign policy has not attracted much attention.

At the heart of the 1981 Israeli attack on the Iraqi research reactor, Osirak, lay the concern that, however accurately international safeguards may account for nuclear material at a given time, they cannot anticipate or control future conduct. As expressed by a senior member of the Israeli nuclear establishment, "The mechanism of safeguards is good and reasonable as long as it is respected. The problem is that it can be abrogated unilaterally." It should be recalled that under Article X of the NPT, a state has the right to withdraw from Treaty commitments when its supreme national interests have been jeopardised, although it is required to provide justification and three months' notice, thus giving the international community time to address the alleged reasons and make an effort to accommodate them. At a minimum, this means that to be legitimate, withdrawal cannot be frivolous. While withdrawal would not release the state from obligations it had undertaken bilaterally to suppliers regarding the use of nuclear material or facilities they had provided, it would release it from its obligations with respect to indigenous nuclear assets.

Other limitations or constraints on international safeguards have shown up in operational experience. Some are more important than others, but all affect either how the system is perceived or how efficiently it is implemented. In normal circumstances involving routine inspections, there are limits on the access rights of inspectors, on where they can go, as well as on the frequency and intensity of inspection effort. The document underlying the NPT full-scope safeguards system was drafted to provide the secretariat with flexibility in negotiating safeguards agreements, but the politics of the situation have led to restrictive rather than liberal interpretations, in individual agreements, of what the IAEA can do. This does mean that safeguards cannot be effective, but it does impose *de facto* limits on the implementing of safeguards agreements.

States have the right to accept or reject inspectors proposed to them by the Agency. Some states will not accept as inspectors nationals of states which are not parties to the NPT, or with whom they do not have diplomatic relations, or persons who do not speak the native language. This has an impact on the efficient use of staff. Other states set limits on the number of inspectors that can be designated for assignment to them, again affecting the optimal distribution of personnel. Only a few states have waived visa requirements for inspectors and this has meant curtailment of the opportunity to conduct unannounced inspections.

Nevertheless, at the last two Review Conferences, the parties to the NPT strongly affirmed the credibility of the IAEA safeguards system and their confidence in it. Safeguards have, by and large, done what was expected of them *with regard to declared nuclear material.* It has been understood that they are evolutionary in nature, that actual experience is the ultimate testing-ground, and that adjustment, adaptation and change are inevitable features of safeguards. The political judgement was that the system provided the necessary confidence that nuclear activities under safeguards were being used only for peaceful purposes, the limitations and problems noted above notwithstanding. It is the judgement of political authorities that ultimately determines the fate of international agreements.

The Iraqi situation and the discoveries made by the IAEA-UNSCOM (United Nations Special Commission) inspection teams have had both negative and positive effects on the safeguards system. On the negative side, they showed that even ratification of the NPT and acceptance of full-scope safeguards were not a guarantee against clandestine nuclear activity; and they brought to light the fact that the IAEA safeguards system, keyed as it was to declared nuclear material, could not, as matters stood, provides assurances that undeclared nuclear materials or plants did not exist in states under NPT safeguards. In this respect, the revelations undermined confidence in the regime and the safeguards system. Put simply, the nature of the threat or risk to be protected against had changed and so did the expectations. The existing system as practised at present, could not meet those expectations and provide that degree of confidence.

On the positive sides, however, the very fact of undermining confidence has resulted in more sustained and higher level political attention to non-proliferation and safeguards than has been evident for a long time, and in more concentration on improving both non-proliferation and the verification system. Governments wish to ensure that the contribution the regime has made to stability and security can be perpetuated, and to that end, are exploring not only what new authority might be needed, but how their own past policies and behaviour might have contributed to the limitations of the present system and how that could be changed.

Iraq was the first case of deliberate and substantial cheating on the NPT and safeguards obligations in the more than two decades they have been in place. Until then, there had been no situation indicating the presence of undeclared facilities in a country subject to full-scope safeguards, no known case of deliberate failure by a state to report a facility it was obliged to report, and no confirmed diversion of nuclear material. The inability of the current system to cover all contingencies did not nullify the effectiveness of the current system for the situations it was designed to address. As discussed earlier, this comes at a time when international political change more generally dictates the need for assessing what would be required to sustain non-proliferation in the post-Cold War world.

One of the most significant effects of the Iraq experience is that it has shifted emphasis with respect to assessing the confidence that safeguards provide. Before the violations by Iraq, the question was how adequately the IAEA was carrying out its assigned responsibility of verifying that all material in all peaceful activity under safeguards could be accounted for, and to what extent it provided confidence that the activities submitted to safeguards were being used for peaceful purposes only. Because of the discoveries made, pursuant to United Nations Security Council Resolution 687 (1991), of an extensive clandestine nuclear programme in an NPT state, concern is now focussed on ensuring that countries are not secretly engaged in nuclear weapons development.

The question now is, therefore, whether the safeguards system provides the necessary confidence that no unauthorised activities are under way and no undeclared facilities or material are present in a safeguarded country. The first part of this concern is a broader question than that for which the IAEA was assigned safeguards responsibility under the NPT. While in its Article II, the NPT requires all non-nuclear weapons state parties not to "receive the transfer ... of nuclear weapons or other nuclear explosive devices or of control over such weapons ...; not to manufacture or otherwise acquire nuclear weapons ...; and not to seek or receive any assistance in the manufacture of nuclear weapons ...," the Agency was charged in Article III, paragraph I – only with verification of obligations assumed under the Treaty "with a view to preventing diversion of nuclear energy from peaceful uses to nuclear weapons or other nuclear explosive devices". This is not to say that the IAEA could not be called upon to verify other NPT obligations, but that the specific mandate relates only to the use of nuclear material subject to safeguards. How even this responsibility is implemented, however, could uncover evidence of the pursuit of alternative paths to nuclear weapons, and to this extent the Agency could contribute to bringing the existence of such activities to public attention.

There are really two issues here. One is whether the actual scope of safeguards responsibility could (or should) be expanded beyond verification of the end-use of nuclear materials and facilities to cover other routes to nuclear weapons. The other issue is the extent to which changes in the implementation of safeguards under existing authority can contribute to meeting the new expectations. Three points are relevant here. First, it is clear that inspection of declared nuclear materials and facilities only is not enough to verify compliance with non-proliferation pledges, and that the system needs to be oriented also towards the problem of undeclared nuclear activity. Second, emphasis in the present system on material accountability places a premium on quantitative measures, sometimes at the expenses of other more qualitative attributes of safeguards such as observation of activities at, or around, a safeguarded site. Third, the proliferation risk is not proportionate to the size of a nuclear programme. In fact, if one considers the three or four largest and most advanced nuclear programmes and the three or four highest-risk states in the NPT regime, there would, if anything, seem to be an inverse relationship between size and risk. This is obviously a matter of political judgement, but it is inescapable that where states are located (for example, in stable or volatile regions) and the character of their nuclear activities (such as Iraq's research reactors or sensitive fuel-cycle facilities in a programme lacking any nuclear power projects) have some bearing on how the risk of proliferation may be judged.

The case of Iraq is relevant to all of these points: it involved extensive undeclared nuclear activity leading to the only two condemnations of safeguards violations ever issued by the Board of Governors of the IAEA; the focus on material balance diverted the attention of Agency inspectors from significant nuclear activity in the vicinity of the safeguarded facilities; and the continued interest of Iraq in reconstructing Osirak as well as considerable reporting of equipment and components that made since only if nuclear weapons were the end goal were never treated as a basis for close inquiry.

The Iraqi situation also underscored the problems that arise from defining the frequency of inspection by the quantity of nuclear material in each facility as distinguished from the quantity in the country as a whole. A country basis for inspection frequency in the case of Iraq would have led to monthly instead of semi-annual on-site inspections and could well have resulted in detecting the diversion of a qualitatively very small, but symbolically very important, amount of nuclear material at its safeguarded reactor. It could have eliminated the possibility of successful diversion at the site. In the same vein, Iraq raises questions about the advisability of the Agency's continuing use of the values for significant quantities of nuclear materials that it does (for example, 8 kg plutonium, 25 kg highly enriched uranium), since they are relevant to frequency of inspection. Lowered values could increase inspection frequency in all safeguarded states under the present regime and thereby reduce the chance that a country with a partially clandestine fuel cycle (for example, a hidden reprocessing plant that depended for fuel on a safeguarded research or power reactor) might be able to divert nuclear material without being detected. Lesser values would have resulted in more frequent inspections of the small Iraqi research facility.

In considering the steps that might be taken to extend existing confidence in safeguards with respect to declared nuclear material to undeclared activities and related problems, it is essential to keep in mind that they comprise only one element, albeit a critical one, of a broader non-proliferation regime. Safeguards are not panaceas. They cannot prevent proliferation by a determined state, but they can provide the international community with early warning of the risk of proliferation and, fully implemented, they can play an important deterrent role or, at the very least, complicate the life of a would-be proliferator and increase the probability of detecting anomalous events that might suggest the possibility of illicit activity.

Since the exposure of Iraq's non-proliferation and safeguards violations, many suggestions have been made as to what to do about verifying non-proliferation. These range from abandoning the IAEA in favour of some as yet undefined alternative organisation, to adding to the Agency's authority through amendment of underlying NPT and equivalent conventions and of the safeguards system, to focussing on existing authority and taking appropriate steps to ensure its full implementation. This last approach, at least as a first step, has the merit of avoiding the need to negotiate new agreements or to modify existing ones. There is also reason to believe that it can carry the system reasonably far towards meeting public concerns about clandestine nuclear activity in safeguarded states. This does not rule out the possible need for additions to existing authority as was done, for example, by the mandate assigned to the IAEA under Security Council Resolution 687.

Rather than listing and discussing the range of proposals already in the public domain for strengthening existing IAEA safeguards authority, it is proposed to focus on two themes: transparency and political will.

In the idiom of IAEA safeguards, transparency usually refers to the system and its results. It can refer also to transparency of the activities being inspected. Both uses apply here. Transparency is extremely important to safeguards credibility. The safeguards document relating to the NPT, IAEA information circular INFCIRC/153 was drafted with the advanced industrial states primarily in mind.[22] These states were keenly sensitive to any further discrimination beyond that already imposed by the NPT division of nuclear-weapon and non-nuclear-weapon states, and the obligation of the latter to accept safeguards on all nuclear activity. The many provisions in the safeguards document regarding limiting intrusion on sovereignty, protecting commercial and proprietary interests, and specifying the obligations of the Agency and its inspectorate reflect the sensitivity of the participating weapons states to these concerns. Many of these states have been equally sensitive about publishing the results of the secretariat's annual Safeguards Implementation Report, which reviews accomplishments and problems experienced in implementing safeguards and draws conclusions with respect to the diversion or non-diversion of nuclear material. Many of these states have emphasised the service aspect of safeguards, and have rejected the notion that safeguards somehow serve to deter them from doing what they have in good faith forsworn in signing the NPT.

But safeguards are not just a service to the state wishing to demonstrate its bonafides; they are also a service to other states that seek credible and convincing evidence that their safeguarded neighbours are indeed living up to their non-proliferation undertakings and engaging in exclusively peaceful uses of nuclear energy. They do not want to take declarations of benign intent by non-NPT neighbours for granted, and want independent verification of the fulfillment by NPT neighbours of their pledges. The more transparency there is in this process and in the nuclear activities of fullscope safeguards states, the more credible the affirmations of peaceful intent become. Therefore, the more transparency, the better. However, one must understand the need for some balance between transparency, on the one hand, and legitimate commercial industrial and proprietary concern of the non-nuclear-weapon states parties, on the other. There is no inherent reason why a reasonable balance cannot be achieved.

What does transparency involve? Four key elements may be mentioned although there are others.

The first is as full and open a book on the nuclear fuel cycle in the safeguarded country as possible. This means that states will voluntarily release even information on their nuclear activities that is not required if that information can help to dispel suspicions.

The second is adoption of a system of reporting all transactions involving nuclear material (already required for NPT parties and adopted as a matter of policy by some non-parties, such as Argentina) and plants, equipment or components that can be used for nuclear purposes (not required for transactions between NPT parties because of the focus of safeguards on nuclear material and the assumption that any facility that has any nuclear material in it will automatically be under safeguards).

The third is acceptance of a liberal implementation of right of access by verification authorities even beyond agreed key measurements points, if such access would serve to circumvent the need for the Agency to pursue procedures related to anomalies in order to reach a conclusion on the accountability of nuclear material under safeguards. This would exceed any routine inspection rights that the IAEA now has, effectively broaden the concept of routine inspection, and reinstate rights that the Agency may have agreed to curtail in negotiating the subsidiary arrangements which activate safeguards agreements.

The fourth is an adoption of reporting system that publicises the findings of verification activities country by country. This could be troublesome in that inspection activities are in some respect incomplete or the results contain certain ambiguities, either or both of which could be construed as reason for suspicion when the facts are completely otherwise. However, the principle of open reporting of results in some manner would seem to be in the interest of the credibility of the safeguards system, especially if the other measures for transparency that have been mentioned were adopted.

Certain measures already under active consideration or discussion in the IAEA either support or implement the notion of transparency. Three deserve mention here: design notification procedures, universal reporting and special inspections.

States accepting full-scope safeguards are obliged to provide the Agency with *design information* for any nuclear facilities "as early as possible before nuclear material is introduced" (INFCIRC/ 153, para 42). The practice has evolved of interpreting this to mean no less than 180 days before material is introduced. It is clear that unreported construction of nuclear facilities raises concern and suspicion when other states learn of it, and that notification no later than the time that construction begins is important. The Director General has already recommended to the Board of Governors the adoption of new time-lines for notification and their formal incorporation in subsidiary arrangements to safeguards agreements, thereby providing a legal basis for the obligation. Among other things, although not technically involving an inspection, this would enable the Agency inspectors to visit construction sites periodically. This could be further strengthened if supplier states would require that any facilities, equipment or components provided to *any* state be notified to the IAEA and submitted to the Agency safeguards. This is not currently required under the NPT safeguards system; and safeguards can, of course, be applied only where there exists an underlying obligation. Requirements by supplier states would provide that basis.

There is now a strong interest in encouraging a system of *universal reporting* of all exports of nuclear material even when it is destined for non-nuclear purposes. Non-nuclear-weapon states parties to the NPT are required to report exports of nuclear material unless it is to a nuclear-weapon state. Subject to certain exceptions, nuclear-weapon states are under a similar obligation with respect to exports to non-nuclear weapon states, while states without safeguards agreements have no legal obligation to report nuclear exports. Universal reporting would obviously support the principle of transparency discussed above. As mentioned in discussing design information, obligatory reporting of exports of any nuclear related items could be considered and placed on the agenda for strengthening non-proliferation and international safeguards.

Special inspections have received considerable attention in both official and non-official circles and are the subject of a paper communicated to the Board of Governors by the Director General of the IAEA. The right of special inspection already exists but has been used almost exclusively to clarify situations arising from routine inspection where, despite discussion and investigation, certain questions remained unresolved. They have never been carried out at locations other than those under safeguards. However, exercise of the right to investigate the possibility of undeclared nuclear material and to call for inspection at undeclared locations is now widely regarded as an important means of implementing non-proliferation safeguards. It is instructive to note that the IAEA Statute provides for access at all times to all places, data and persons involving material, equipment or facilities required to be safeguarded, but that this sweeping authority was quickly circumscribed as states were unprepared to accept the implications such rights would have for national sovereignty.[23] The case of Iraq has given rise to second thoughts, and more extensive use of this right is now seen as a critical feature of credible international safeguards. The conditions for effective use of this right have been spelt out by Hans Blix, Director General of the IAEA: access to information indicating the existence and location of clandestine activity, access to suspected sites that are identified, and support by the United Nations Security Council of this access.

Effective use of existing safeguards-derived and other readily available information may suffice to establish a basis for calling for a special inspection, but, in some cases, information from outside sources, including national intelligence, may be required, and it is this additional information to which the Director General referred. As the Agency is not a police or military body, it cannot force its way into a state. It must be admitted voluntarily. Assured access is an obligation of states under safeguards, however, and their failure to comply with their obligation is a violation subject to actions built into the IAEA system, namely reporting non-compliance to the United Nations for appropriate action. Security Council support speaks for itself. But a Security Council resolution declaring that violations of the NPT and international safeguards undertaking would be considered *ipso facto* a threat to international peace and security could provide a powerful deterrent to violations and could induce compliance on the part of a state. This would be all the more effective if the Security Council and leading powers of the world were to be constructively responsive to the legitimate security concerns of states that might otherwise be induced to seek their security in nuclear arms.

Political will is essential to the success of non-proliferation and the effective implementation of international safeguards. International organisations are creatures of their client sovereign states, not independent political entities with political constituencies independent of their state members upon whom they can call for the support necessary for their effective operation. If the states of the international system want a strong non-proliferation regime and credible verification in which they can place confidence, they must provide the international secretariats to which they assign responsibilities with the necessary authority, resources and political support.

VI

In considering the credibility and effectiveness of the IAEA safeguards systems, it is necessary for everyone concerned to learn from the implications of the accidents that took place at Chernobyl and Three Mile Island. The accident in April 1986 at the Chernobyl nuclear power plant demonstrates that planning conducted at a national level alone cannot eliminate the risks posed to all nations by nuclear energy. In the aftermath of the Chernobyl accident, an attitude of "business as usual" will not sustain the atomic power industry worldwide.

The scope of the challenge to make nuclear energy production safer is even greater than that shown by the well-known accidents at Chernobyl and the Three Mile Island plant in the United States. Between 1971 and 1984, two "significant" and 149 "potentially significant" mishaps occurred in 14 industrial nations outside the two superpowers.[24] Even aside from the danger of accidents, the normal operation of nuclear power plants presents problems. These include the management of materials – plutonium and weapons-grade enriched uranium – which could be diverted for non-peaceful use by nations and terrorists, and the possibility of sabotage and military attacks on power plants. The potential damage from such actions includes radiological consequences far worse than those witnessed in the aftermath of the Chernobyl accident.

International institutions have not been oblivious to the challenges posed by the 382 commercial reactors presently operating in twenty-six countries. Emerging today are worldwide nuclear standards, albeit imperfectly applied, that attempt to treat each risk in a distinct manner. The accident at Chernobyl and the international response it generated make this an opportune time to consider the consequences of such accidents.

Had Chernobyl contaminated large populations with hundreds of rems (a unit for measuring the biological impact of radiation), projections of the ultimate extent of the accident's human costs might be relatively easy to define, given the present state of medical knowledge. But beyond the exclusionary zone within which some residents absorbed tens of rems, 75 million Soviet citizens and tens of millions of other Europeans residing in contaminated regions and eating radioactive food produced in contaminated soil will be exposed to well below five rems over a lifetime as a result of the Chernobyl explosion. No expert consensus about the physiological impact of exposure at this low level has been reached. Scientists express an extraordinary range of calculations about the long-term effects of Chernobyl, the low being 80,000 deaths and the high, one million deaths. To the extent that there is a consensus – and it is a quite shaky one – deaths are predicted in the range of 1000,000 to 500,000 within the Soviet Union, with substantial numbers outside.[25] Whatever the figure, non-fatal cancers will be of a similar magnitude and genetic effects may appear in future generations.

What accounts for these diverse estimates? What is the significance of the precise magnitude of the final casualty figure? The latter question may be easier to answer, political considerations being the "bottom line" in assessing a disaster with as many possible ramifications as Chernobyl. If the low figures prove correct, nuclear energy proponents will argue, indeed some already have argued, that atomic power poses problems not entirely distinguishable from those presented by other energy sources and toxic waste-producing industries with which we have learned to live. After all, following the Bhopal accident we have not abandoned the pesticide industry, nor have we tried to shut down coal-powered electricity-generating stations that emit sulphur dioxide and thus contribute to widespread respiratory problems for millions of people worldwide and threaten the stability of the earth's climate by creating a "greenhouse effect".

On the other hand, if the moderate or higher casualty figures are correct, opponents will make a stronger case that nuclear energy creates an unacceptable risk. Sweden adopted this position even before Chernobyl; the incident only served to harden Swedish nuclear opponents in their opinions. Sweden intends to eliminate its use of atomic power by 2010. Several years ago, Austria decided not to license a newly constructed reactor, in effect discontinuing the country's nuclear power programme. Given the global nuclear energy policy debate, it is important to strive for better estimates of the human costs of Chernobyl.

Doing so will be difficult. Scientists are deeply divided on the biological impact of low-level radiation; they base their beliefs on vastly different assumptions, due to an absence of definitive data for the effects of low doses of radioactivity. We know that exposure to radiation from natural sources, such as uranium and thorium in the earth and cosmic rays in the atmosphere, is inevitable. Certain radioactive substances occur in the body. This "background" radiation, which is not necessarily harmless, varies at different points around the globe, but it is usually on the order of 100 millirems per year. This figure is used as the baseline for setting standards of man-made radiation. There is considerable controversy among scientists over the level at which man-induced radiation results in significant biological effects. Some argue that there is no threshold below which man-made radiation exposure is harmless, that the consequences are not reparable by the body's defences, that radiation accumulated over time has the same effects as a single, acute dose and the effect of low doses are proportionate to higher ones. Another school holds that the biological risk is less below a certain threshold, because cells are able to repair sub-lethal damage.

To form hypotheses, scientists rely on studies of Japanese atom bomb survivors, Marshall Islanders irradiated by weapons-test fallout in 1954, uranium miners exposed to radon, doctors and patients using radio-therapy, and the results of animal experiments. Despite large study samples, researchers face difficulties in accurately measuring radioactive dosages and creating exactly equivalent control populations; they cannot always isolate radiation effects from those of other chemical or physical agents. They cannot easily establish a cause-and-effect relationship when there is a long period, perhaps thirty years or more, between the exposure and manifestation of the effect, particularly in the light of the fact that cancer "naturally" kills 20 per cent of the West's population. Scientists are groping for conclusions because the myriad of variables produce remarkably different results based on different interpretations of the risk level. The Soviets suggested that casualties from Chernobyl could at worst amount to two cancer fatalities per 10,000 people exposed to at least one rem of radiation, while IAEA officials estimated fatalities at half that rate.[27] Complicating matters will be the difficult assessment of measures taken to minimise exposure to radiation. Controlling the consumption of irradiated produce and scraping away affected soils or treating them with potassium fertilisers and calcium compounds to minimise caesium and strontium contamination may help ameliorate later health problems, but to varying and uncertain degrees.

The Soviets promised to study intensively the 135,000 evacuees from the exclusionary zone around the Chernobyl plant and to share the information with specialists in the United States and elsewhere. This information, if tangible – a big "if" considering that precise dosimetry may not be available – may help resolve the disputes that have risen over the human costs of Chernobyl.

Along with the human costs are still uncertain economic ones. The Soviets placed the direct costs near $ three billion. This includes lost electrical generation which, although mitigated in October 1986 by the resumption of generation at Chernobyl Units

1 and 2, will result in a 5 per cent reduction in Soviet energy generation in 1986-87, as similar RBMK* (Reactor Built for Multiple Kinetic-energy) plants are shut down for remedial improvements to be undertaken as a result of the accident. Also involved in assessing costs is the expense of relocating 135,000 people from the exclusionary zone and reimbursing them for their personal belongings.

The clean-up work was massive. To contain further releases, a concrete and metal "sarcophagus" now entombs the reactor. It will be in place for centuries and will require monitoring and continual reinforcement. To conduct heat away from the still-simmering core during the months after the accident, engineers pumped nitrogen into a basement vault now underlaid with a concrete slab to prevent groundwater contamination. However, the danger of a lateral spread of radiation into the Dneiper River remains.

The human and economic costs of the accident will take years to compute, during which time policy-makers around the world will be forced to make difficult decisions about the future of nuclear energy in their respective countries. The benefits of atomic power will have to be weighed against the availability of other energy options, the risks of nuclear energy and the experience of other countries with reactors.

Even before Chernobyl, the nuclear industry worldwide was in a serious slump. Forecasts made in the 1970s of installed nuclear capacity in OECD (Organisation for Economic Corporation and Development) countries through the 1990s reduced by 75 per cent. Hopes for a burgeoning nuclear power market in developing countries failed to materialise due to the unavailability of capital and hard currency, rising construction costs, falling oil prices, slackening demand in industrial countries for electricity, and grassroots anti-nuclear sentiment. Still, by 1990, 118 new plants in seventeen countries went into operation. At the moment, it does not appear that Chernobyl by itself has affected these plans markedly. What the accident may do is discourage countries from

* RBMK is a type of reactor that is graphite moderated and uses a direct cycle, boiling water process for generating electricity. A variety of neutronic experiments can be carried out in such a reactor.

laying further plans for construction. Other considerations will include demand for electricity, the state of capital markets and the ability of reactor vendors to reassure consumers that atomic power facilities can be built safely and with features that avoid other strategic nuclear energy risks as well.

Clearly, Chernobyl is the most serious civil nuclear energy accident to date. It demonstrates that major accidents like this are possible in nuclear weapons-producing facilities because of inadequate reactor design and incompetent management. It also illustrates that such accidents require heroic measures to combat them.

Notwithstanding more rigorous safety standards, reactors manufactured in the West have also experienced serious mishaps. In 1984, for example, at one French reactor at Le Bugey, the failure of an electrical component and an emergency diesel generator, coupled with operator error, almost led to a major accident. In the US, there was Three Mile Island; no early deaths resulted and, given the low amounts of radioactivity released, late-developing cancers, if there are any, will probably be limited to fewer than four cases, but the event highlighted the fragility of nuclear facilities. There were also several near-misses: the partial core melt in 1966 at the Enrico Fermi demonstration breeder reactor 30 miles from Detroit; the electrical cable fire at Browns Ferry, Alabama; and the mishap at Toledo Edison's Davis-Besse plant in 1985, caused by equipment failure and human error, which started a sequence similar to that at Three Mile Island.[28] Whether any of these and other accidents could have progressed to a point of becoming a Chernobyl-like disaster in the absence of remedial measures, given dissimilar reactor designs, negative void coefficients and different containments, is debatable, but there is growing concern.[29]

Serious questions have been raised about the safety of one American graphite-moderated plant that has no containment features: the "N" reactor at the Hanford nuclear reservation in Washington State, a dual-purpose facility producing plutonium for the Defence Department's weapons programme and electricity for the northwestern US power grid.[30]

Four other small plutonium production reactors at Savannah River, South Carolina, also have no containment features at all.

Besides reporting the 151 nuclear safety incidents, the General Accounting Office has suggested that the outlook is questionable for assuring the safety of 73 plants either already in operation or on order, in seventeen developing nations, because most of these countries "lacked trained personnel to draft nuclear safety personnel".[31] Assuring adequate safety standards will become more complex as South Korea, China, India, Argentina and other countries increasingly manufacture their own nuclear hardware and components rather than rely on imports. Developing countries as well as many developed nations commonly recognise that they are unprepared to address a major nuclear mishap alone.

But accidents are not the only problem for the nuclear industry. Since 1970, as many as 292 acts or threats of sabotage or diversion of nuclear materials took place worldwide. These incidents – including some bombings and arson – involved nuclear power installations, transport and personnel, and were perpetrated by terrorists, criminals and hostile employees. Recently, the number of such incidents has declined. Still, as a recent RAND Corporation report notes, "This should not lead policy-makers into a false sense of security".[32] Underscoring this admonition was the saboteur disabling three of four offsite power lines feeding the Palo Verde, Arizona, nuclear energy complex in May 1986. Power reactors, therefore, are required to have sufficient guards. In the US, though most facilities employ about five guards, recent Congressional investigation found that security around military production reactors and other sensitive defence establishments is a "shambles".[33]

By the end of the 1990s, 350 to 400 metric tons of plutonium was separated from spent fuel in the West. If history is any guide, we are sure to find that, as this material enters nuclear commerce, the opportunity for nations and terrorists to divert poorly safeguarded stocks will increase. In the US alone, 9,000 pounds of plutonium are already missing from the books.[34] Although a large fraction may have been lost due to accounting errors or the manufacturing process, the lack of accountability portends a troubled future.

Through the mid-1960s, the IAEA was an ineffectual policing organisation. Moscow, its allies and some developing nations strongly opposed its regulatory functions. The Soviet Union repeatedly denounced the concept of safeguards as a "spider's web, which would catch in its threads all the science and scientists in the world".[35] India also opposed the Agency "If safeguards are applied by the Agency to those states which cannot further their atomic development without the receipt of aid from the Agency or other member states, the operations of the Agency will have the effect of dividing member states into two categories, the smaller and less powerful states being subject to safeguards, while the greater powers are above them. This will increase, rather than decrease, international tension." [36]

By 1959, the Soviet Union was reevaluating its own position, spurred by China's nuclear development, which the Soviets supported until they recognised its threat to themselves. The Soviet Union then became both a supporter and innovator of nuclear safeguards; its limited exports to only light water reactors that did not use weapons-grade material; it required all spent fuel to be returned to the Soviet Union to minimise the danger of plutonium diversion by importers; and it forbade East European recipients to build their own enrichment and plutonium reprocessing installations.

The tightening Soviet export criteria did not initially include a role for the IAEA, but as the United States increasingly surrendered safeguard responsibilities to the Agency and as West European nations overcame their own concern that the organisation would be used for industrial intelligence, the Soviets became more supportive. The IAEA expanded its safeguards to cover reactors of all sizes in 1964 and to reprocessing and fuel fabrication plants in 1966 and 1968. The IAEA enforcement staff has grown from three inspectors in 1960 to 276 in 2002. The agency now devotes over one-third of its budget to more than 2,000 inspections conducted each year, compared to less than 4 per cent of total expenditures devoted to safeguards in 1962.

The willingness of nations to allow extra-national entities to scrutinise a most sensitive industry is remarkable indeed. Warren Donnelly, a senior analyst of nuclear affairs for the Congressional Research Service, noted: "IAEA safeguards are unique. It is the first time in history that sovereign states have invited an international organization to perform inspections on important installations within their territories." [37]

Before Chernobyl, attention was focussed on minimising the dangers of nuclear weapons proliferation. Some suggested ways to discourage states from acquiring nuclear weapons, including expanded sales of conventional arms, strengthening alliances, creating nuclear-free zones and establishing multilateral fuel banks, reprocessing plants and spent-fuel storage facilities. To address safety questions, calls were also heard for the development of a new generation of inherently safer reactors, which could come on line in a decade or two.

But in the wake of Chernobyl, pessimism seems to dominate. The principal IAEA remedies enacted in the aftermath of the accident are two conventions: one mandates that states suffering accidents which may result in "an international transboundary release" notify nations that "are or may be physically affected," either directly or through the IAEA. [38] The second agreement encourages international assistance for nations suffering nuclear power accidents.[39] Although valuable and negotiated remarkably quickly – the impetus of Chernobyl overcoming earlier opposition – these agreements are inadequate, akin to closing the barn door after the horse has escaped. They will not prevent future Chernobyls. The IAEA is mindful of this fact. It is looking to enhance safety through a modest increase in its budget, creation of study groups to examine such matters as the interface of nuclear operators and their machines and the expansion of expert committees that can advise nations about safety. But even this would not be enough, a fact acknowledged when former West German Chancellor Helmut Kohl called for an international institution to prescribe safety standards and verify implementation, and when Hans Blix, Director General of the IAEA suggested binding, minimum safety standards.[40] This suggestion would be consistent with the call of Morris Rosen, IAEA Director of Safety, for "development of a clear and universally acceptable approach to safety guided by an international body composed of prominent exporters that could alleviate national and international safety concerns and also positively influence public opinion". [41] In the most ambitious form of International Nuclear Reviews (INR), the IAEA would license all nuclear facilities, whether imported or domestically produced. [42]

Would such an incremental but comprehensive approach work? Certainly all the stages of INRs are more comprehensive, and most are more authoritative than the institutions addressing nuclear risks today. In Chernobyl, the most powerful INR might have prevented the accident by, at a minimum, requiring installation of quick starting emergency diesel generators, thereby eliminating the rationale for the ill-fated "safety" test in the first place. Efforts of this sort are not cost-free. Nations would have to accept greater international scrutiny of their nuclear programmes. But this burden is not entirely foreign to today's nuclear regime, which embraces IAEA and NPT nuclear safeguards. Considering the dangers now evident, it is reasonable to argue that the cost involved is nominal compared to the consequences of another Chernobyl – or worse.

Notes

1. See *The United Nations and Disarmament, 1945-1970*, United Nations Publication, Sales No. 70, IX, 1; p. 50.

2. On July 3, 1990, the Agency for the Prohibition of Nuclear Weapons in Latin America decided to add to the legal title of the Treaty the term "and the Caribbean", in conformity with Article 7 of the Treaty.

3. See verbatim record of the 602 meeting of the Conference on Disarmament, held on August 15, 1991 (CD/PV 602), p. 40.

4. Security Council Resolution 687 (1991) adopted during the Gulf War, set the terms for termination of the conflict. It clearly specified the term "nuclear weapons – usable" materials which has so far not appeared in any nuclear or other international arrangements.

5. A "significant quantity" is the quantity estimated to be sufficient to make one atomic bomb.

6. "The Agency's Safeguards System" (1965, as provisionally extended in 1966 and 1968); Document INFCIRC/66/ Rev. 2, Vienna; International Atomic Energy Agency (1968).

7. Prawitz, J., "Arguments for NPT Safeguards" in *Nuclear Proliferation Problems*, Stockholm International Peace Research Institute, (SIPRI), Cambridge and London, The MIT Press, p. 164.

8. "The Structure and Content of Agreement Between the Agency and States Required in Connection With the Treaty on the Non-Proliferation of Nuclear Weapons," Vienna, International Atomic Energy Agency, Document INFCIRC/153 (corrected), June, 1972.

9. Other provisions of the Treaty apply to weapons party to the Treaty. In addition, the USA and the UK voluntarily have placed some of their peaceful nuclear facilities under IAEA safeguards equal to those provided by INFCIRC/ 153 for non-nuclear weapons States.

10. "The Physical Protection of Nuclear Material", Document INFCIRC/225/Rev. 1; Vienna, International Atomic Energy Agency, (1977).

11. Treaty on the Non-Proliferation of Nuclear Weapons. Reproduced in "Arms Control and Disarmament Agreements", US Arms Control and Disarmament Agency (1980), pp. 90-4.

12. UN Document A/PV, 1693, p. 63.

13. It became clear after the test occurred that neither the USA nor Canada had obtained sufficiently explicit assurances from India that the materials and equipment supplied by them would not be used to develop, manufacture, or test nuclear explosives of any kind - whether for peaceful or military purposes.

14. "Final Generic Environmental Impact Statement On the Use of Recycle Plutonium in Mixed Oxide Fuel in Light

Water Cooled Reactor," Report NUREC - 002, US Nuclear Regulatory Commission, August, 1976.

15. "Safeguarding a Domestic Mixed Oxide Industry Against a Hypothetical Subnational Threat", Report NUREC - 0414, US Nuclear Regulatory Commission, May, 1978.

16. The term "cross section" is used by scientists to define the probability with which an induced nuclear reaction may occur. It can be expressed in qualitative terms based on measurement or theoretical calculations.

17. *Final Document of the Review Conference of the Parties to the Treaty on the Non-Proliferation of Nuclear Weapons,* Part I, (Geneva, 1985); NPT/CONF-III/64/1, annex i, para 2.

18. *Draft Final Document of the Fourth Review Conference of the Parties to the Treaty on the Non-Proliferation of Nuclear Weapons,* 1990; NPT/CONF-IV/LI/Rev I ADD. i and ADD 2/Rev. 1.

19. "A Report on the International Control of Atomic Energy", prepared for the Secretary of State's Committee on Atomic Energy, known as Acheson-Lilienthal Report, reproduced in part in *Nuclear Safeguards: A Reader* (Library of Congress).

20. "The Baruch Plan: Statement by the US Representative (Baruch) to the UN Atomic Energy Commission, 14 June, 1946," in *Documents on Disarmament,* 1945-1959; Pub. No. 7008, 2 vols. Washington D.C. US Government Printing Office, 1960, vol. 1.

21. The Text of the Treaty is reproduced in *Status of Multilateral Arms Regulation and Disarmament Agreements,* 3rd Ed., 1987, UN Publication, Sales No. E. 88. IX. 5.; pp. 71 ff.

22. The IAEA model NPT safeguard agreement of 1971 (Information Circular INFCIRC/153). "The structure and content of agreements between the Agency and States required in connection with the Treaty on the Non-Proliferation of Nuclear Weapons."

23. *Statute of the International Atomic Energy Agency,* Art. II, A, para 6.

24. United States General Accounting Office, *International Response to the Nuclear Power Reactor Safety Concerns*, GAO/NSIAD 85-128; Washington, D.C.; USGAO, September 30, 1985; *International Nuclear Safety Concerns*, Senate Committee on Government Affairs, Subcommittee on Energy, Nuclear Proliferation, and Government Processes, 99th Congress, 2nd Session, Washington D.C., Government Printing Office, 1986; *The New York Times*, May 7, 1986, p. 9.

25. The low figure comes from Richard Wilson of the Department of Physics, Harvard (*Assessing the Issues of Science and Technology*, Fall, 1986, p. 25); the high figure from E.J. Sternglass of the Department of Radiology, the University of Pittsburgh "The Implications of Chernobyl for Human Health", *International Journal of Bioscience Research*, July 1986, pp. 7-36). Also see Colin Norman and David Dickson, "The Aftermath of Chernobyl", *Science*, September 12, 1986, pp. 1041-1043, *The Wall Street Journal*, August 25, 1986, *International Atomic Energy Agency Press Release*, Vienna, IAEA Press Release 86/22, August 26, 1986.

26. Richard Wilson, op. cit, p. 28.

27. Norman and Dickson, op. cit.

28. Daniel Ford, *The Cult of the Atom*, New York, Simon & Schuster, 1982. The Le Bugey accident is reported in *Nature*, May 9, 1986, p. 462.

29. Gordon Thompson, "What Happened in Reactor Four", *Bulletin of Atomic Scientists*, op. cit. pp. 28-31. See also *The New York Times*, Oct. 27, 1986, pp. 1, 8.

30. *Nucleonics Week*, May 8, 1986, p. 7. See also the testimony of Dan Hirsch, James Warf and W. Jackson Davis, General Oversight Sub-committee, House Interior Committee, 99th Congress, 2nd Session, May 19, 1986, Washington, D. C. Government Printing Office, 1986.

31. United States General Accounting Office, op. cit., p. 4.

32. Burce Hoffman, et al, "A Reassessment of Potential Adversaries to US Programs", RAND Corporation Report, R-3363-DOE, p. 7. For different perspectives on the vulnerability of nuclear plans to sabotage, see Paul Leventhal and Yonneh Alexander, eds, *Nuclear Terrorism: Defining the Threat*, Washington D.C., Perganon-Brassey, 1986.

33. Peter Stockton in Leventhal and Alexander, op. cit., p. 89.

34. Thomas D. Davies, "What Nuclear Means and Targets Might Terrorists Find Attractive", in Leventhal and Alexander, op. cit., p. 55. See also David Albright, "World Inventories of Plutonium", also in Leventhal and Alexander, op. cit., pp. 159-192.

35. Quoted in Pierre Lellouche, *Internationalization of the Nuclear Fuel Cycle and Non-Proliferation Strategy: Lessons and Prospects*, Cambridge; Harvard Law School, November, 1979, p. 161.

36. Ibid, p. 162.

37. *SIPRI Year Book 1983*, New York, Taylor and Francis, 1983, p. 72.

38. IAEA Publication, "Convention on Early Notification of a Nuclear Accident," Vienna, August 15, 1986.

39. IAEA Publication, "Convention on Assistance in the Case of a Nuclear Accident or Radiological Emergency," Vienna, August 15, 1986.

40. *The Christian Science Monitor*, May 23, 1986, pp. 1, 12.

41. Morris. Rosen, "Establishment of an International Nuclear Safety Body", *International Atomic Energy Agency Bulletin*, September 1983, p. 3.

42. For elaboration of the INRs, see Bennett Ramberg, *Global Nuclear Energy Risks: The Search For Preventive Medicine*, Boulder, Colo, Westview Press, 1986.

6

POST-SOVIET NUCLEAR POLITICS

On December 25, 1991, the red flag was lowered from the Kremlin and by the end of the month, the Soviet Union had passed into history. As many as fifteen new independent republics now stood where one mighty superpower had held sway. Many people sarcastically remarked: "This is exactly what Marx meant by 'the withering away' of the state".

With the dismemberment of the Soviet Union, the Cold War between Moscow and Washington and the allies of both sides certainly came to a close, but many also believed that the era of Nuclear weapons was also over. In an article in *The Bulletin of Atomic Scientists*, George Lee Butler, the former commander-in-chief of all US Strategic Nuclear Forces, said that as one of the two nuclear superpowers had "gone with the wind", nuclear weapons no longer served any useful purpose, the era of the nukes was over and they should be scrapped.

Butler wrote: "Building of nuclear arsenals, rekindling of the nuclear arms race and reawakening of the spectre of nuclear war, cannot be the moral legacy of the Cold War. And it is our responsibility to ensure that it will not be. We have won, through Herculean courage and sacrifice, the opportunity to reset mankind's moral compass, to renew belief in the world free from fear and deprivation, to win global affirmation for the sanctity of life, the right to liberty, and the opportunity to pursue a joyous existence."[1]

Butler's statement is on target – and all the more powerful because of his unique experience. Nevertheless, his core idea that a world free of the threat of nuclear weapons is by necessity a world devoid of nuclear weapons, is not likely to find universal support among groups as diverse as arms controllers, government policy-makers, think-tank pundits and columnists. No matter how one may slice it, they all seem trapped in the same line of reasoning, and old circular conundrum that may be described as the following.

What are the targets of nuclear weapons? Nuclear weapons. What provocations could bring about the use of nuclear weapons? Nuclear weapons. What is the defence against nuclear weapons? Nuclear weapons. How do we prevent the use of nuclear weapons? By threatening to use nuclear weapons. Why does a country refuse to scrap nuclear weapons? Because others have nuclear weapons.

The reason Butler says he is compelled to speak out now is that despite the disappearance of the Soviet Union and the end of the Cold War, supporters of Nuclear weapons cling to the circular formation. Although nearly everyone admits that the threat of global nuclear war has virtually gone, the spectre of nuclear proliferation and terrorism and an evil world keep people spooked. It is a crisis of international climate, not supported by facts.

These facts may be summed up as follows. The number of weapons that are now operational is less than half of the number just ten years ago. Only a handful of warheads are being produced worldwide. Contrast that with a 5,000-plus annual production rate merely a decade ago. Hardly any serious research on new systems is under way. US standing military forces – naval, ground and tactical air – have been largely denuclearised. Fewer than a dozen nuclear storage sites remain outside the homelands of the nuclear powers. The roster of nations that have formally renounced nuclear capability, or have been pushed out of the nuclear business, continues to grow. Since the break-up of the Soviet Union and end of the Cold War, there have been enormous advances in the web of treaties, controls, exchange, and safeguards that discourage renewal and proliferation. And lastly, the possibility of nuclear terrorism remains more fancy than fact though it is the most favourite bogeyman of the threat-mongers.[2]

Today, nuclear professionals find themselves in a perilous balancing act. The problems associated with nuclear weapons are, of courage, grave enough for the public to surrender control to the custodians. Yet the impression can never be conveyed that things are completely out of control. That would catch the public's full attention, cause great alarm, and perhaps disrupt the gloom-and-more-gloom cycle by forcing real change as far as nuclear politics is concerned.

Arms controllers and anti-nuclear advocates inadvertently sustain this same cycle; though they spar with government custodians and unrepentant boosters, they are so wedded to the habit of declaring things forever on the brink that they come off as like-minded supporters of the relevance and utility of nuclear weapons. To them, nuclear politics means that nuclear weapons should no longer be considered as weapons of mass destruction, but as one of the most effective weapons of diplomacy, because nuclear weapons are regarded not only as currency of state power but also as a status symbol in the comity of nations.

This odd devil's alliance between opposing camps bolsters the steady impression that a lot needs to be done And yet, it is an unequal contest. The public and the anti-nuclear community have every right, if not duty, to expose the government's sluggishness or deceit, to complain that this or that facility is not enough, or this or that warhead is not safe enough, or this or that weapon is too expensive, or this or that plan is not well thought out or executed efficiently enough. But invariably, after the complaints are lodged, there is the usual back and forth and committee inquiries and blue-ribbon panels, and the bomb boosters win. This see-saw game is nothing but politics, nuclear politics to be precise. The Soviet Union or the Cold War may not be there, but nuclear politics remains a very potent factor influencing the equation of power in international relations.

For more than half a century, nuclear midnight meant just this: the end of it all. Today, that definition is fuzzy, for there is life after midnight. Because the public no longer frets much about nuclear war and the "arms race", there is enormous and simultaneous competition from pro- and anti-nuclear forces, both to prolong the public slumber and to capture the public's attention. Through it all, the two communities thrive on bad news. On one side are the anonymous colonels, bureaucrats, and scientists at nuclear agencies, laboratories and strategic commands that populate study groups and committees. On the other, are arms controllers, diplomats, peaceniks, lobbyists and busybodies who also populate study groups and committees.

These otherwise disparate actor have never had more common ground than today. They may battle for the public's heart and mind, and disagree about policy alternatives and the velocity of change, but they remain equally addicted to a climate of disaster, particularly the spectre of a nuclear crisis triggered by rampant proliferation.

The never-ending impulse to cry wolf – whether in the name of disarmament, stewardship, or renewal – creates the self-fulfilling reality of crisis and danger. Inflated demand and undermining work towards reducing the "danger". The constant ticking of the clock contributes to a sense of doom, one that naturally conveys the message that the problems are so massive as to be unsolvable.

Here one may ask: who are the faceless and too-powerful covert decision-makers who continue to nurture and safeguard their blessed weapon? In choosing not to criticise the nuclear establishment, Butler allows pro-nuclear forces to hide behind service, hardly ever facing up to their spellbound dedication to the bomb, never having to acknowledge their corrosive role in ultimately undermining the universal task of bringing the bomb under control.

On the top of the we-need-nukes- because-nukes exist conundrum, there is the self-interest of organisations and industries wedded to the bomb. Moreover, any commitment to abolition is rejected on the basis of technical impossibility. Which is to say that the very scientists and engineers who constructed and controlled tens of thousands of warheads for more than fifty years seemingly cannot put heir minds to undoing it all. Their modesty is increasingly transparent.[3]

Of all the issues at stake, the most important is national security and military planners of many countries are dead-on in saying that national security can never be ensured without at least "minimum nuclear deterrence". It is, thus, just fanciful to think that the nuclear era is over. Hasn't Butler come very late to the abolition mission?

II

Throughout the Cold War period, two contrasting views of nuclear deterrence stood centre-stage. The first view, originally espoused by Bernard Brodie, and codified in such American nuclear strategies as "Massive Retaliation" in the 1950s and "Mutually Assured Destruction" (MAD) in the 1950s and 60s, suggested that nuclear weapons deter aggression through their capacity to visit enormous destruction through retaliation. Brodie argued that because the actual use of nuclear weapons could not be harnessed for any meaningful military objective, the primary purpose of nuclear weapons would be to deter other nuclear weapons.

This notion, which would come to be called deterrence through punishment, was challenged by an opposing view that suggested that nuclear deterrence can work only if nuclear weapons are mated with a strategy that seeks victory in such a war. This latter view, called deterrence through denial, had a small but vocal band of advocates.[4] William Borden, the earliest proponent of this view, argued that while these weapons were "revolutionary" in their destructive potential and would change the way wars were fought, they were, nevertheless, ultimately, weapons of war, and if they differed from other weapons, this was a difference of degrees rather than of kind.[5] Borden's views, filtered through the American strategic debate in the 1970s, became official American nuclear strategy in the 1980s under the Reagan Administration.

As the debate on "deterrence" and "strategy of denial" was going on unabated, another view surfaced pushing the debate to the shadows. The advocates of this view started with the premise that since the Soviet Union had withered away, it did not pose any threat to the USA and, therefore, the question of deterrence or strategy of denial did not arise at all. Their argument is based on the basis that nuclear weapons have no military use and the military factors comes into play essentially to provide credibility to the posture and as a reminder of the possibility that they could be used, resulting in a horrendous scale of destruction. In reality, nuclear weapons serve as powerful political, particularly diplomatic, instruments of coercion and demonstration of power, which are enhanced by the probability and use of nuclear weapons.[6]

In fact, the total "abolition" of nuclear weapons has been in the minds of many strategists, policy-makers and leaders ever since the devastating effects of nuclear weapons became known more than five decades ago, with the bombing of Hiroshima and Nagasaki in August 1945. How has this ideal of "abolition of nukes" been practised over the years – by arms controllers and theorists – and does the new strategic concept of NATO, which was mooted at the Washington Summit on the occasion of the 50th anniversary of the founding of NATO contribute to, or take away from, a world bristling with nuclear weapons? Since NATO was founded as a shield against the now non-existent Soviet Union, the significance of its "new concept" regarding nuclear weapons cannot be exaggerated.

Rational humans recognise that nuclear weapons are not sensible as they have no utility although they have the capacity to destroy the human civilisation. Recognising this, the Pugwash Conference on Science and World Affairs, founded in 1957 by scientists who sought to build bridges between East and West and eventually to outlaw nuclear weapons, believe that if humankind acts rationally, sooner or later it will abolish nuclear weapons. *A Nuclear-Weapons Free World* (NWFW), a Pugwash book, explores, in 14 chapters by 26 authors who contributed, individually or collectively, how the dream of a NWFW can be transposed to reality. The book's preface notes that the only possible function of nuclear weapons is to deter their use by another state, but that argument becomes invalid if satisfactory guarantees are given by states that they do not posses them. The desirability and feasibility of an NWFW as an alternative, provided it is found possible to establish an effective verification system, is examined.[7]

As late as 1993, the five acknowledged nuclear powers possessed nearly 50,000 nuclear warheads. Between 1945-1993, the total warheads built by the five nuclear countries totalled a staggering 127,545.[8]

Three of the original nuclear-weapon states (NWS) — the USA, the UK and France — are also members of NATO which was established on September 17, 1949, by action of the North Atlantic Council pursuant to the North Atlantic Treaty signed at Washington DC, on April 4, 1949, by the Foreign Ministers of twelve countries — Belgium, Canada, Denmark, France, Iceland, Italy, Luxembourg, the Netherlands, Norway, Portugal, the UK and the USA. While Greece and Turkey acceded to the treaty in 1952, the Federal Republic of Germany became a member in 1955 and Spain became a signatory in 1982. In early 1999, the Czech Republic, Hungary and Poland became members, thus, increasing NATO membership to the present nineteen countries.

The Preamble to the Treaty reads:

"The Parties to this Treaty reaffirm their faith in the purposes and principles of the Charter of the United Nations and their desire to live in peace with all peoples and governments.

"They are determined to safeguard the freedom, common heritage and civilization of their peoples, founded on the principles of democracy, individual liberty and the rule of law.

"They seek to promote stability and well-being in the North Atlantic area and they are resolved to unite their efforts to collective defence and for the preservation of peace and security."

It is interesting to note that NATO was established just four years after the USA detonated two atom bombs — "Little Boy" over Hiroshima on August 6, 1945, and "Fat Man" over Nagasaki on August 9, 1945.

Washington DC was the venue for NATO's 50th anniversary celebrations which were held from April 23-25, 1999. It was during this period that a new "Strategic Concept" was adopted by the member states. The document formally recast the Alliance's Cold War era mission from one of "collective defence" to one that in the former NATO Secretary General's words would guarantee European security and uphold democratic values "within and beyond our borders".[9] The new strategy, particularly that of nuclear weapons policy, departed little from the language found in the strategic concept which had been approved in 1991 at the summit meeting held in Rome on November 7 and 8, 1991, when the

Soviet Union still existed. The two points of departure for the new strategic concept vis-a-vis that issued in 1991 are those of "out of area action" and "open door policy".[10] While "out of area" is officially sanctioned, an instance is NATO's air campaign against Yugoslavia, NATO's "open door policy" for new member countries was reaffirmed.

The introduction to NATO's new Strategic Concept states in paragraph two, "The dramatic changes in the Euro-Atlantic strategic landscape brought by the end of the Cold War were reflected in the Alliance's 1991 Strategic Concept. There have, however, been further profound political and security developments since then". While NATO has tried to lessen the role of nuclear weapons — though it had an opportunity at the summit to bring its outdated nuclear weapons first-use policy into alignment with its stated objectives and commitments — it is still stuck at the "flexible response" mode, a policy which it has been maintaining for the past three decades which allows it to introduce nuclear weapons into a conflict in reply to an attack with conventional weapons.

As the security environment in Europe changed fundamentally, NATO announced in July 1990 in its London Declaration a review of its political and military strategy to reflect "a reduced reliance on nuclear weapons" which would led to the adoption of "a new NATO strategy making nuclear forces truly weapons of last resort".

NATO's European-based nuclear arsenal stood at approximately 4,000 tactical warheads in early 1991. After President Bush announced a major unilateral withdrawal of US tactical nuclear weapons worldwide in September of the same year and Gorbachev announced reciprocal Soviet withdrawals the next month, all US ground-based and sea-based tactical weapons were affected. This left around 400 air-delivered gravity bombs in NATO's European-based nuclear arsenal, which was still the case at the end of the decade as France and Britain had subsequently decided to phase their tactical nuclear weapons.[11]

NATO's 1991 Strategic Concept noted that "the fundamental purpose of the nuclear forces of the Allies is political: to preserve peace and prevent coercion and any kind of war. It specifically stated that "the circumstances in which any use of nuclear weapons might have to be contemplated by it are remote". The Allies can, therefore, significantly reduce their sub-strategic nuclear forces. After NATO began moving towards expanding membership in countries in Eastern and Southern Europe, it issued its Enlargement Study in September 1995 which stated explicitly that the "new members will be expected to support the concept of deterrence and the essential role nuclear weapons play in the Alliance's strategy of war prevention as set forth in the Strategic Concept".[12]

In the so-called Founding Act of May 1997, NATO allies explicitly stated that "they have no intention, no plan and no reason to deploy nuclear weapons on the territory of new members", but indicated in the same document that they did not see "any need to change any aspect of NATO's nuclear posture or nuclear policy – and do not see any future need to do so".[13]

The NATO Strategic Concept adopted at the Washington Summit did not adopt a non-first use or even discuss it. However, the Concept continues to point out that "the fundamental purpose of the nuclear forces of the Allies is political" [14] and acknowledge that "with radical changes in the security situation, including reduced conventional forces in Europe and increased reaction times, NATO's ability to defuse a crisis through diplomatic and other means or, should it be necessary, to mount a successful conventional defence has significantly improved. The circumstances in which any use of nuclear weapons might have to be contemplated by them are extremely remote".

The statement found in paragraph sixty-four, goes on to point out the series of steps the allies have taken since the break-up of the Soviet Union which reflect the post-Cold War security environment, and include a reduction of the types and numbers of NATO's sub-strategic forces, including the elimination of all nuclear artillery and ground-launched, short-range nuclear missiles; a relaxation of the readiness criteria of 'nuclear-roled' forces; and the termination of standing peace time nuclear contingency plans. It adds that NATO's nuclear forces no longer target any particular country – an obvious reference to Russia — but that it would maintain "at the minimum level consistent with the prevailing security environment, adequate sub-strategic forces based in Europe which provide an essential link with strategic nuclear forces, reinforcing the transatlantic link". These will consist of dual capable aircraft and a small number of Trident warheads. Sub-strategic nuclear weapons will, however, not be deployed in "normal circumstances" on surface vessels and attack submarines.

While paragraph nineteen of the Concept states that the stability, transparency, predictability, lower levels of armaments, and verification which can be provided by arms control and non-proliferation agreements support NATO's political and military efforts to achieve its strategic objectives, it goes on to add how the Allies have played a role in this field, which, among others, includes reductions in nuclear weapons provided for in the START Treaties; the signing of the CTBT; the indefinite and unconditional extension of the NPT; and the accession to it of Belarus, Kazakhstan and Ukraine as non-nuclear-weapon states.

Significantly, paragraph sixty-three of the Strategic Concept states that the key NATO strategic rationale for nuclear forces based in Europe and committed to NATO is that they "provide an essential political and military link between the European and North American members of the Alliance". While linkage to US strategic retaliatory forces was an integral part of NATO's strategy during the Cold War, with the collapse of the Soviet Union and the Warsaw Pact, and the change in NATO's most likely mission from territorial defence to out-of-area crisis management, linkage to US strategic retaliatory forces is far less critical and less relevant. As pointed out by Jack Mendelsohn, in any case, a no-first use (NFU) policy impacts on the circumstances surrounding the decision to use nuclear weapons and not on the choice of nuclear weapons – tactical, strategic or both – that will be used once the decision is taken.[15]

Given the serious misgivings some Alliance members like Germany and Greece had over the extent of the destruction wrought in Kosovo by NATO's conventional bombing, it is highly improbable that the Alliance would ever reach a consensus to employ nuclear weapons in an out-of-area intervention and even less likely to support US interests in other areas of the world. This argument is borne out by the fact that when US-UK coalition forces attacked Iraq to overthrow the regime of Saddam Hussein, the Alliance refused to join the coalition forces.

Of the five original nuclear weapon states, it is ironic that only the two non-NATO powers, China and Russia, have declared nuclear-use policies that do not run counter to the July 1996 International Court of Justice advisory opinion on the legality of nuclear weapons in which ten of its fourteen judges determined that the use or threatened use of nuclear weapons is illegal in all but one possible circumstance i.e., a threat to the very existence of the state. China has a no-first-use policy and Russia reserves the right to use all available forces and means, including nuclear weapons, if as a result of military aggression, there is a threat to the existence of the Russian Federation as a sovereign state. Incidentally, Article 2.4 of India's Draft Nuclear Doctrine sets out India's no-first-use in unambiguous terms. [16]

While the revision of the Strategic Concept was being prepared for adoption by the members of NATO at the 50th anniversary of the Alliance, the months leading up to it saw the governments of Germany, Canada and the Netherlands take steps to urge that the Alliance consider a no-first-use policy. To cite an example, on December 10, 1998, the Canadian Parliament's Standing Committee for Foreign Affairs and International Trade released a report entitled "Canada and the Nuclear Challenge: Reducing the Political Value of Nuclear Weapons for the 21st Century" which included a recommendation that Canada urge NATO to review its nuclear weapons policy. The Washington Communique at the summit agreed that NATO, in the light of overall strategic developments and the reduced salience of nuclear weapons, "would consider options for confidence and security-building measures, verification, non-proliferation and arms control and disarmament. The Council in Permanent Session will propose a process to Ministers in December for considering such options". [17]

Were NATO to change its policy to that of NFU in the meeting, the Alliance could reduce the political acceptability and military attractiveness of nuclear weapons, strengthen the nuclear non-proliferation regime, enhance the credibility of its deterrence policy and help to ease some of the tension in the NATO-Russian relationship. Otherwise, the inescapable conclusion about NATO's new Strategic Concept will be viewed by "those outside the NATO areas as being offensive, out-of-area, unilateralist and sovereignty-transgressing. It is hard to see how some states could find this collection of attributes unattractive, if not threatening". [18]

Professor Ryukichi Imai, a key member of both the Canberra Commission and the Tokyo Forum which prescribe steps for the abolishing of nuclear weapons had stated that the Canberra Commission has "achieved a status of sort, in providing general knowledge about nuclear weapons". [19] It is to be hoped that it moves from this status. Imai concluded by noting that it had taken the world about four decades to build up the nuclear warheads, delivery system, and their command and control and that the proposal for their final elimination has to be firmly structured and described into final details. This proposal should, apart from making vague calls for elimination of nuclear weapons in some unspecified remote future, also pay careful attention to details, including the problem of human psychology in putting the genie back into the bottle. The question is: can the genie be put back?

The circular conundrum described at the very outset of this chapter with reference to George Lee Butler, clearly shows that as long as the nuclear-weapon states continue to possess nuclear weapons, non-nuclear-weapon states that have the capability, resources, technical skill and knowhow will have the urge to go nuclear, resulting in a state of nuclear proliferation, and the abolishing of nuclear weapons will then slowly but surely recede into the background and become a utopian dream.

III

Complete elimination of nuclear weapons, a cherished objective for many, has, nevertheless, been treated with much scepticism by many others who have doubted not only its feasibility but also its desirability. Arguments against universal nuclear disarmament have been made on several grounds. For instance, that it would not be possible to disinvent the weapon; that it would not be a technically feasible proposition given the difficulties involved in dismantling the weapons, arranging for their safe storage and the eventual dilution of the fissile material extracted therefrom; and that it might not even be a very desirable objective to aspire for in the first place because it might end up making the world more prone to war and instability.

Such traditional ways of thinking have been responsible for creating an atmosphere in which nuclear disarmament is still not believed to be a realistic goal. There are not a few people in the world who still argue that abolition is fine as a long-term aspiration – something to be kept in mind, but not yet to be taken in practical terms as a sensible policy goal. Not surprisingly, then, those arguing in favour of nuclear disarmament are impatiently suffered as wishful thinkers or utopian fools and summarily dismissed by the practitioners of *realpolitik*.

In order to counter such allegations and the concomitant belief systems, one can basically take two approaches: one, work on making abolition practically possible by delineating a clear pathway leading to the goal. This would entail an identification of some tangible milestones such as reducing nuclear weapons, dealerting those that exist, dismantling those that have been removed, and doing so under a well monitored verification regime, etc.

A second approach, however, could be one that is more abstract since it would attempt to target the mindset and beliefs of those against nuclear weapons abolition. While the first approach appears to be the more practical and essential one, the latter cannot afford to be ignored. In fact, the two are not mutually exclusive because the steps outlined by the first would only become possible when one's beliefs and attitudes towards nuclear weapons change. Therefore, the latter must be the starting point.

The power of the mind cannot be underestimated. In the ultimate analysis, it is his beliefs and value systems that make a man act the way he does. It has been said several times over that technology by itself is neutral. It is neither good nor bad. It is the purpose to which it is put that makes all the difference. And, the purpose is decided by a "thinking" man whose values and beliefs determine his behaviour and actions.

By the same logic, nuclear technology too can be used for peaceful generation of electricity or in medicine or food preservation. And yet, with equal, if not more ease, it could also be used to make nuclear weapons. Therefore, it is the man putting the technology to use who determines its purpose based on his beliefs and value systems. Since we have believed in the utility of harnessing nuclear energy to produce lethal WMD, so it has been. If we could change this belief in the utility of nuclear weapons, then their abolition might not seem so difficult a proposition. Therefore, the belief systems need to be strategically "attacked" or addressed to make them more favourable to nuclear abolition.

History testifies to the fact that institutions whose abolition was once thought to be unthinkable have broken down under the pressure of changed belief systems. One need only point to the case of slavery to further drive home this point. In fact, when a few had started demanding the abolition of slavery, there were many others who argued against it on the grounds that the economic system and society would not be able to survive the drastic change! It was at this time, on December 1, 1862, that President Abraham Lincoln, in his famous address to the US Congress, had said: "The dogmas of the quiet past are inadequate to the stormy present ... As our case is new, so we must think anew and act anew. We must disenthrall ourselves". [20]

This advice has come in useful whenever radical transformations have taken place – the breakdown of apartheid, the abolition of colonialism, etc. It is most relevant today in the case of nuclear weapons. We have to disenthrall ourselves from their hold and if anything can do that, it is the force of new ideas. As Victor Hugo once said: "Nothing else in the world – not all the armies – is so powerful as an idea whose time has come."

At a very basic level, countries aspire for nuclear weapons for two reasons: security and status, and not necessarily in that order. With the possession of nuclear weapons, security is deemed to be enhanced because the use of these weapons threatens such disastrous consequences that the adversary is deterred against making any move that might invite their use. It is as if nuclear weapons provide an insurance cover against the worst possible development by ensuring a retaliatory strike capable of inflicting unacceptable damage. From this, it has been surmised that deterrence provides stability to the international order and during the Cold War it was responsible for keeping World War III at bay. By inverse logic then, it has been propagated that in the absence of the stabilising effect of nuclear weapons, countries would turn trigger-happy and provoke conventional wars. This belief has over the years contributed to the inertia against any move in favour of nuclear disarmament.

When subjected to close scrutiny, however, the belief reveals itself as an untested and non-testable hypothesis. It cannot be said for sure whether wars were actually deterred by the use of nuclear weapons. But their presence did nothing to stop conventional conflagrations. Conventional wars still did take place and it cannot be taken for granted that the presence of nuclear weapons deters the very act of aggression. Wars have been, and will continue to be, a means of engagement among nations. Man killed man even in the Stone Age and he will continue to do so into the future. However, what makes a difference are the tools that he employs in a war and the acceptability of the collateral damage caused thereby. With nuclear weapons, destruction of life would occur on a massive scale and with relative ease. [21] In fact, the destruction so wrought cannot be measured only in terms of the number of casualties, but goes much further in time and space. The heat, storms, electro-magnetic pulse and radioactivity so generated would result in instantaneous death for several thousand, besides immense pain and anguish to many others who might be lucky enough to survive death but sadly unfortunate in having to suffer its damages in mutations and congenital malformations. A nuclear war would also bring on ecological disasters of unimaginable magnitude, causing long-term devastation of life and matter. All this remains a possibility as long as nuclear weapons exist. The world till then is compelled to live in the fear of every war escalating into a nuclear one. And, therefore, the belief in the desirability of retaining nuclear weapons for the sake of maintaining international stability is more than a little misplaced. In fact, it is ironical that we seem to be counting upon our potential agents of extinction a means of maintaining our security. It needs little reiteration then that an NWFW will definitely be a safer world and to that extent, it shall be a more desirable one.

The second major belief attached to nuclear weapons is that their possession enhances national status and international prestige. This is because these weapons are still the preserve of a select few and the technology involved in their production is deemed to be a frontier technology capable of being mastered by only the very scientifically advanced. Nuclear weapons are believed to confer an exalted position on the possessor state, ensuring that its policies and postures on national and international issues are taken more seriously. For the same reason, nuclear weapons are taken as great equalisers that can help even a small nation stand up to the might of a large one. The French position vis-`a-vis the erstwhile USSR demonstrated this fact.

This role of nuclear weapons as status enhancers is responsible for the nuclear-weapon states not wishing to give them up, as also for the non-nuclear weapon states desiring to attain them. Related to this is the added benefit of being able to sustain independent decision-making, especially on matters of foreign policy. French Prime Minister, Alain Juppe, had himself admitted in September 1995, "By acquiring nuclear capability, France was able to play, on the world scene, a role well above that justified by its mere quantitative significance."[22] Hence, they can serve as powerful political instruments of coercion.

This belief is no easier to crack than the one related to security. However, it can be changed if one can begin to measure national status from a new perspective. At present, it is gauged in terms of military capacity and economic power. This belief needs to be supplanted by one that considers national status from the threshold of human security. Or, in terms of equality of life index. It would imply the extent to which a state can guard its citizens against such seemingly mundane afflictions as sickness hunger, persecution, ecological disasters, poverty, unemployment and other basic human needs. In fact, in this regard, it might even be said that if people are released from the worries of everyday living, their levels of concern for global issues would proportionately rise, and in the bargain, support for nuclear disarmament would grow.

For the present, however, how does one address the kind of entrenched belief systems detailed above? The task, in fact, is further complicated by the presence of an extremely powerful military-industrial organisation in every nuclear-weapon state whose very existence depends on obtaining huge amounts of public money to maintain and update nuclear arsenals. Political leaders who might be in favour of abolition get caught under the combined pressures from the military, industry, veterans organisations, and even, journals, and are left with little option but to perpetuate the existing beliefs and attitudes.

These, nevertheless, do need to be changed if a NWFW is to be made possible. For this purpose, certain target areas will have to be identified and prescribed a syndromic change that could promote the realisation of an environment in which nuclear disarmament would seem less undesirable and more feasible. It briefly sketches four possible scenarios in which nuclear-weapon states agree to renounce their nuclear weapons. The availability of these fortuitous circumstances would automatically mean a change in not only our nuclear belief systems but also in our concepts of security, thereby, making the attainment of a NWFW more plausible.

First, common sense dictates that no nuclear-weapon state nor any state desirous of becoming one, would want to renounce its nuclear capability or ambitions until it is convinced that some other more reliable means providing for its security are firmly in place. This sense of security, in turn could be installed in two ways: one, by effecting an intrinsic change in the international security environment through the conclusion of a variety of confidence-building measures (CBMs); and secondly, by attaining a clear superiority with conventional weapons. At one level, these two prerequisites of more secure international order might appear to be mutually exclusive because amassing conventional weapons could rather vitiate the international security environment. However, it needs to be remembered that in this case, the conventional weapons would actually be replacing WMD and the likely spurt in their accumulation might prove to be transitional, occurring only soon after the actual abolition of nuclear weapons and more to serve a psychological rather than a military purpose.

The Vietnam War, the Arab-Israeli War, the civil war in the Balkans, the Afghan Wars and the Gulf Wars demonstrated the potential effectiveness of smart conventional weapons when used in a strategic role just as much as they underlined the futility of nuclear weapons. Several analysts have been making the case for choosing strategic, high precision conventional weapons over their nuclear counterparts, especially because "they are safer, cause less collateral damage, and pose less threat of escalation than do nuclear weapons".[23] In fact, conventional weapons would offer flexibility in a variety of situations where the use of nuclear weapons would be politically or militarily impractical. Moreover, their efficacy is enhanced by the fact that the enemy cannot discount the possibility of their use, unlike in the case of the nuclear weapons. Once this belief is accepted, then as extrapolated by the Committee on International Security and Arms Control (CISAC): "The active and conspicuous role given to nuclear weapons during the Cold War can be greatly reduced without significant adverse effect on the probability of major war ...".[24]

As a second prerequisite, states can be expected to renounce their nuclear option only when enough technical expertise is available to ensure adequate verification of the commitments undertaken by them to abandon their nuclear arsenals. One of the major reasons why nuclear disarmament has been considered unfeasible until now is the lack of an adequate mechanism, institutional as well as technological, to oversee the process of disarmament. The inability to decide on what to do with the dismantled warheads and how to ensure their safe and secure storage has proved to be a handicap.

History illustrates that often systems change only when it becomes technically possible to prove something. For centuries, man continued to believe that the sun revolves around the earth. Those who disputed this belief were ridiculed or persecuted. Copernicus in his lifetime could not find acceptance for his theory. The belief changed only after the invention of the telescope and other astronomical instruments that could technically prove that the sun was actually at the centre of the universe. Applying the same logic to the issue of nuclear disarmament, it may be said that advancements in the field of surveillance and monitoring technologies coupled with the ongoing research on how to deal with the nuclear materials obtained from dismantled warheads would help to change the belief systems surrounding the nuclear weapons.

Thirdly, movement towards a NWFW could be propelled if there is an accumulation of enough risks from the continued possession of these weapons. If the dangers surmount and keep on doing so, then states might see sense in doing away with these weapons. Some of these risks, in palpable proportions are already becoming evident. For instance, we are living in times when ethnic conflicts, religious fundamentalism, proliferation of a terrorist ethos, "loose nukes", illegal trafficking in nuclear weapons or materials, etc is on an upward swing. The reasons for conflict are also increasing as competition becomes as fierce for scarce renewable resources, water and fertile land, as for non-renewable resources, oil and minerals, even as the planet becomes dangerously overpopulated.

At the same time, the modern international system is experiencing a technology push in which more and more increasingly sophisticated technology is available from an ever growing number of suppliers. The collapse of the centralised Soviet control and the turmoil in Eastern Europe increased the opportunity for states or groups to acquire nuclear technology, weapons, components or expertise. This erodes the effectiveness of technology export control and heightens the risk of nuclear proliferation. In fact, even more ominous than the flow of components and technology may prove to be the transformation of nuclear weapons experts – designers, engineers, etc – from an elite core confined in space to an unemployed, floating population.[25]

In such an emerging scenario, holding onto their obsolete belief systems is placing the nuclear-weapons states in a Catch-22 situation. As new risks and challenges to international security emerge, they raise their reliance on nuclear weapons. But such moves make the other non-nuclear-weapons states suspect their sincerity to eventually commit themselves to nuclear disarmament. This, in turn, make them review their own security requirements factoring in the presence of nuclear weapons for all times to come.

These factors are sure to fuel further nuclear proliferation and the danger of such an eventuality can be awesome considering the increasing tendency among states to view nuclear weapons not as weapons of last resort, but as "weapons of the weak against the strong, as the only weapons that can counter the conventional superiority of the West".[26] However, as the risks mount, the nuclear-weapons states might see sense in renouncing nuclear weapons.

Fourthly, and most importantly, the prospects of nuclear disarmament would be brighter, if based on the above three factors, enough pressure is mounted on the governments by the international intelligentsia. Fortunately, to some extent this is already happening. At the individual level, security analysts and even former military high-ups such as Gen. George Lee Butler, Gen. Paul K. Murrow and Gen. Henry R. Christopher, have started to question the rationale behind the continuance of nuclear weapons. Cold War theologians such as Paul Nitze and Fred Ikle have expressed themselves in favour of nuclear disarmament. All of them have questioned how the American nation has "put at the service of our national survival a weapon whose sheer destructiveness was antithetical to the very values upon which our society was based"?[27] While such opinions have not yet filtered down into government policies, they do influence beliefs worldwide. In fact, nuclear beliefs, theologies, and doctrines have largely emanated from the West and if the change starts at the source, it could trigger off a chain reaction elsewhere too.

At the national level too, one can point to the efforts by some of the smaller states to distance themselves from nuclearism. For instance, New Zealand and Greece have taken strong stands against allowing their ports to be used by naval vessels carrying nuclear warheads. While such national initiatives are few and far between, at the multilateral level, such strains are more evident. For instance, in 1995, the Canberra Commission appointed by the Australian Prime Minister, proposed practical steps towards an NWFW. It also considered the related problem of maintaining stability and security during the transitional period and after the goal of complete disarmament had been achieved. The commission enumerated several "immediate" and reinforcing steps in this direction. It called upon the nuclear weapon states to commit themselves "unequivocally to the elimination of nuclear weapons" and advised the non-nuclear weapons states to support this commitment by joining in cooperative international action to implement. It also reminded all nations of the verdict of the International Court of Justice pronounced in July 1996 declaring the use of nuclear weapons as unlawful and against the principles of humanitarian law except possibly in extreme circumstances of self-defence where the survival of a state is at stake. The court concluded that "there exists an obligation to pursue in good faith and bring to a conclusion negotiations leading to nuclear disarmament in all aspects under strict international control."[28] The judgement is not binding and its violation cannot be treated with any punitive action, but it does play a role in raising the consciousness of the informed public opinion. For nations that claim to uphold the rule of law and humanitarian principles, it imposes a moral, if not a legally enforceable imperative to abolish nuclear weapons.

A build-up of pressure in favour of disarmament is also evident from the fact that the Conference on Disarmament, meeting over the sessions spread between January to September 1999, concluded without conducting any business. So much so that, it could not even decide upon a programme of work because a number of countries insisted upon some tangible movement in the direction of nuclear disarmament, a demand that the Western nuclear powers, including Russia, were not willing to concede. A few months earlier, the NPT Preparatory Committee meeting had also witnessed a clear rift among the ranks of the member states over the issue of disarmament. All these developments do point to a mounting pressure on those resisting the demand for universal nuclear disarmament.

Over a period of time, a cumulative effect of these pressures could contribute to breaking the traditional beliefs about nuclear weapons. In fact, nuclear weapons can be abolished only when the belief systems behind their use and utility change. Initially, it shall all have to begin in the mind and thereafter the possibilities would grow. Of course, one cannot set a time-frame for the realisation of these latent possibilities. Every revolution in history has taken its leaders by surprise because as long as the order exists, it tends to hide its fragility through elaborate measures. Its control then seems total and impregnable. But ideas can still sneak in and slowly snowball into a force capable of bringing about a profound change. Similarly, the present nuclear order can be broken down under the weight of more enlightened and humane beliefs and value systems.

In this context, a brief mention can be made of the concept of no-first-use as an alternative doctrine. India has upheld this principle, thereby opening up an alternative to the prevailing conventional wisdom of first use as espoused by Western nuclear powers, and even Russia. Of the P-5, China is the only other nation that has adopted a similar commitment, though it has attached conditionalities to it over the years. In any case, a counter-view to the traditional aggressive and arms race inducing doctrines is now available and it could engender a new belief system to slowly undercut the rationale of nuclear weapons. If all nuclear weapons states were to accept this precept, then none would ever initiate a nuclear strike. Naturally, therefore, over the years, the utility of nuclear weapons would decline, and so would the value attached to them as a means to security.

More such alternate belief systems will have to be put forth to replace the existing ones. But, of course, all this will have to start from the conviction that abolition of nuclear weapons is not only desirable and feasible, but also imperative. Acceptance of this belief will create the necessary climate in which other, more tangible actions can become possible.

IV

Perhaps a day will come in the remote future when a revolutionary change will come about in the mind of man, breaking down the traditional belief systems, and nuclear weapons will pass into history. Or, it is also quite possible that from the pile of rubble left by the disintegration of the Soviet Union there may yet emerge a new "belief system" which may facilitate the perpetuation of warfare – or just a massive nuclear war – which may result in the demise of human civilisation, that is, the doom of the human race for many thousands years to come.

But the reality of the day is that following the almost simultaneous end of the Cold War and the dissolution of the Soviet Union, dramatic changes have come about in the international security system. These two events had raised expectations of benign international security environment, and a "peace dividends" was perceived, though by different people in different terms. Although more than a decade has gone by since these events took place, the "peace dividends" are not yet in sight. Instead, what mankind is now witness to is breakdown of the international balance of power and the transformation of the bipolar world into a unipolar world where the United States is asserting its domination with a kind of vengeance never seen before. President George W. Bush and his "poodle", as a London newspaper described Prime Minister Tony Blair, went to war against Iraq in April 2003, building up then forces to over 2,50,000, arrogantly defying the UNO, the international community, other allies of the US and even the people of the USA and Britain. If this is the "peace dividend" one expected after the end of the Cold War and the fall of the Soviet Union, it does not augur well for the existing and forthcoming international security system.

The end of the Cold War marks the third fundamental change in the international political architecture and the driving spirit of geo-politics and geo-economics in this century. The first two resulted from the two World Wars. The arrangements for war-termination in the first case left the seeds for the second; and the cumulative effect of the two and the Russian Revolution spawned the Cold War. The first fundamental change marked the end of the European balance of power which had existed for over a century. During that century of peace, European competition, rivalry and conflict for control of resources were played out in other regions of the world. The second fundamental change arising out of World War II shifted the balance of power to essential non-European states. The third change promises to shift the central locus of the international strategic framework under the diktat of the United States.

Bush and his "poodle" launched an attack against Iraq because they had no doubt that Saddam Hussein possessed (WMD). It was their belief, but there was no concrete evidence and whatever evidence was given by David Kelly, the British government's arms expert, was "sexed up" by Blair's officials – so that the Prime Minister could justify the war against Iraq. A few days later, just when Blair went to Washington to receive the Congressional prize for his "historic loyalty" to the US, Kelly was found dead in the garden of his house. From Washington, Blair went to Tokyo and at his first press conference when he had just taken the podium, a reporter shot the opening question: "Mr. Prime Minister, do you have blood in your hands?" The British Prime Minister stood silent for five long minutes and then walked out of the press conference.

Not long after assuming office, President Bush branded four countries – Iraq, Iran, Libya and North Korea – as "rogue states". He threatened that these states were anti- American and they would soon realise what anti-Americanism meant. After having decided to attack Iraq, he said that Saddam Hussein had (WMD) and "he must pay the price for possessing them". When somebody at a press conference pointed out that both the US and its coalition partner, the UK, had enormous stocks of these weapons, Secretary of State, Colin Powell said : "So what? Yes, we have them. But why should Saddam Hussein have them? He is not only a ruthless dictator but he also has links with Al-Qaeda and the President is bent upon liberating the oppressed people of Iraq." Here Bush assumed the role of a liberator. Then, in his State of the Union address, he declared that his ultimate mission in West Asia was to reform the Islamic states and establish democracy in the countries of the region in line with the Wilsonian ideals. Here Bush assumed the role of a Reformer, a Missionary and a Champion of Democracy.

The reaction of the international community to this new American role was stunning. In a speech at Harlem, New York, the celebrated Indian writer, Arundhati Roy, burst out: "The Empire is on the move, and democracy is its sly new war cry. Democracy is the Free World's whore." Referring to US Attorney General John Ashcroft's statement that US freedoms were not the grant of any government or document, but "our endowment from God", Roy averred:

"I speak as a subject of the Empire. I speak as a slave who presumes to criticise her king. Public support in the US for the war against Iraq was founded on a multi-tiered edifice of falsehood and deceit, coordinated by the US government and faithfully amplified by the corporate media.

"Apart from the invented links between Iraq and Al-Qaeda, we had the manufactured frenzy about Iraq's Weapons of Mass Destruction. George Bush the Lesser went to the extent of saying it would be 'suicidal' for the US *not* to attack Iraq. We once again witnessed the paranoia that a starved, bombed, besieged country was about to annihilate almighty America. Iraq was only the latest in a succession of countries – earlier there was Cuba, Nicaragua, Libya, Grenada and Panama. But this time it wasn't just your ordinary brand of friendly neighbourhood frenzy. It was Frenzy with a Purpose. It ushered in an old doctrine in a new bottle: the Doctrine of Pre-emptive Strike, *aka* The United States Can Do Whatever The Hell It Wants, And That's Official. Why bother with the United Nations when God Himself is on hand?

"In these times when we have to race to keep abreast of the speed at which our freedoms are being snatched from us, and when few can afford the luxury of retreating from the streets for a while in order to return with an exquisite, fully formed political thesis replete with footnotes and references, what profound gift can I offer you tonight? As we lurch from crisis to crisis, beamed directly into our brains by satellite TV, we have to think on our feet. On the move. We enter histories through the rubble of war. Ruined cities, parched fields, shrinking forests and dying rivers are our archives. Craters left by daisy-cutters, our libraries. So what can I offer you tonight? Some uncomfortable thoughts about money, war, empire, racism and democracy. Some worries that flit around my brain like a family of persistent moths that keep me awake at night.

"Some of you will think it bad manners for a person like me, officially entered in the Big Book of Modern Nations as an 'Indian citizen', to come here and criticise the US government. Speaking for myself, I'm no flag-waver, no patriot, and am fully aware that venality, brutality, and hypocrisy are imprinted on the leaden soul of every state. But when a country ceases to be merely a country and becomes an empire, then the scale of operations changes dramatically. Since lectures must be called something, mine tonight is called: INSTANT-MIX IMPERIAL DEMOCRACY – BUY ONE, GET ONE FREE.

"So here we are, the people of the world, confronted with an Empire armed with a mandate from heaven and, as added insurance, the most formidable arsenal of weapons of mass destruction in history. Here we are, confronted with an Empire that has conferred upon itself the right to go to war at will, and the right to deliver people from corrupting ideologies, from religious fundamentalists, dictators, sexism and poverty by the age-old, tried-and-tested practice of extermination. Empire is on the move, and Democracy is its sly new war cry. Democracy, home-delivered to your doorstep by daisy-cutters. Death is a small price for people to pay for the privilege of sampling this new product : Instant-Mix Imperial Democracy bring to a boil, add oil, then bomb. But then perhaps Chinks, Negroes, dinks, gooks and wogs don't really qualify as real people. Perhaps our deaths don't really qualify as real deaths. Our histories don't qualify as history. They never have.

"Speaking of history, in these past months, while the world watched, the US invasion and occupation of Iraq was broadcast on live TV. Like Osama bin Laden and the Taliban in Afghanistan, the regime of Saddam Hussein simply disappeared. This was followed by what analysts called a 'power vacuum'. Cities that had been under siege, without food, water and electricity for days, cities that had been bombed relentlessly, people who had been starved and systematically impoverished by the UN sanctions regime for more than a decade, were suddenly left with no semblance of urban administration. A 7,000-year-old civilization slid into anarchy. On live TV.

"Before the war on Iraq began, the Office of Reconstruction and Humanitarian Assistance (ORHA) sent the Pentagon a list of sixteen crucial sites to protect. The National Museum was second on that list. Yet the Museum was not just looted, it was desecrated. It was a repository of an ancient cultural heritage. Iraq as we know it today was part of the river valley of Mesopotamia. The civilisation that grew along the banks of the Tigris and the Euphrates produced the world's first writing, first calendar, first library, first city, and yes, the world's first democracy. King Hammurabi of Babylon was the first to codify laws governing the social life of citizens. It was a code in which abandoned women, prostitutes, slaves, and even animals had rights. The Hammurabi code acknowledged not just as the birth of legality, but the beginning of an understanding of the concept of social justice. The US government could not have chosen a more inappropriate land in which to state its illegal war and display of its grotesque disregard for justice.

"So here it is – the World's Greatest Democracy, led by a man who was not legally elected. America's Supreme Court gifted him his job. What price have American people paid for this spurious presidency? In the three years of George Bush the Lesser's term, the American economy has lost more than two million jobs. Outlandish military expenses, corporate welfare and tax giveaway to the rich have created a financial crisis for the US educational system. According to a survey by the National Council of State Legislatures, US states cut $49 billion in public services, health, welfare benefits and education in 2002. They plan to cut another $25.7 billion in 2003. That makes a total of $75 billion. Bush's initial budget request to Congress to finance the war in Iraq was $80 billion.

"So who's paying for the war? America's poor. Its students, its unemployed, its single mothers, its hospitals and home-care patients, its teachers and health workers. And who's actually fighting the war?"[29]

Not America's rich, but America's poor. And once again under Bush the Lesser, America is poor. What is worse, America's yellow-belly President is a sick man, afflicted with paranoid schizophrenia. He has already displayed in no uncertain terms the range and extent of his capability for paranoid aggression. In human psychology, paranoid aggression is usually a symptom of nervous insecurity. It could be argued that it is no different in the case of the psychology of nations. Empire is paranoid because it has a soft underbelly. It is only a paranoid Emperor who could say: "Operation Iraqi freedom? Not really. It is more like – let's run a race, but first let me break your knees." Now that the Soviet Union is no more, you cannot directly confront the US Empire. You can isolate its working parts and disable them one by one.

V

The vulgar manner in which Bush and Blair ignored the UN and demonstrated power and arrogance stunned not only many of USA's close allies, but also the international community as a whole. And it is in this context that Russian President Vladimir Putin has renewed calls for a Moscow-Beijing-New Delhi triangle, a potential alliance of three nuclear armed countries of some 2.5 billion people, that might be able to balance US power in coming years.

"Russia will continue interaction with its partners in the Moscow-Beijing-New Delhi triangle," Foreign Minister Igor Ivanov declared on June 18, 2003, at an Association of Southeast Asian Nations (ASEAN) meeting held in Phnom Penh. "This interaction is important for international stability in general. The dialogue between Moscow, Beijing and New Delhi, the three nations which have shared interests in a multipolar and just world will continue," he added.[30]

The concept of a "strategic triangle" among the nuclear powers – Russia, China and India – was first mooted by former Russian Premier Yevgeny Primakov in 1999. But the idea failed to serve its immediate purpose of preventing the US-led NATO air strike against former Yugoslavia. It was also dismissed by Beijing and New Delhi.

However, in December 2002, President Putin visited China and India, and in high-level talks, the need for greater strategic cooperation among the three countries was emphasised. Putin called for a "multipolar world", Moscow's *mantra* for counterbalancing the USA's global dominance. Hence, speculation resurfaced about the three countries coming to an agreement to form an "axis" due to a perceived sense among all three that US power must somehow be checked. This time, both Beijing and New Delhi showed interest in Putin's proposal.

Although the concept of a "strategic triangle" is yet to take a concrete shape, Russia, China and India are believed to have a number of converging interests that could add substance to axis talks. All three were terribly perturbed by the US invasion on Iraq and protested in vain against what they viewed as a rejection not only of the UN but also the universally accepted rules of the international game of politics. They still firmly believe in the primacy of the UN in solving crises, and support the principle of non-intervention in the internal affairs of sovereign states. Apart from shared concerns about US dominance and the "imperial mindset" of the Bush Administration, the three have many other common interests and mutually reinforcing needs. All three are weary of militant Islamic groups, and want stability in Central Eurasia.

Many critics, however, point out that the idea that the Eastern axis may be the only answer to "US imperial design" is nothing but a mere by-product of the Cold War-era mindset. It has also been argued that the trilateral axis could hardly be feasible because the Indian nuclear and missile programme is not so much aimed at Pakistan, being, in fact, a deterrent against Chinese nuclear warheads installed in Tibet. The would-be triangle is also seen as implausible because India and China also happen to be competing economies. More important, although Russia and China have already solved their border problem, China and India are still divided by a mere chunk of barren terrain, and the grant of asylum to the Dalai Lama and thousands of his followers is still a sore point in Indo-Chinese relations. However, it is significant to note here that during Prime Minister Atal Behari Vajpayee's visit to Beijing in June 2003, a spokesman of the Chinese External Affairs Ministry said that the two sides agreed that the border issue should be resolved as early as possible in the interest of security of the entire region. The stand-office between South and North Korea over the latter's nuclear programme, he added, poses a real threat to this region.

Given the polarising effect of Iraq, some sort of strategic unity among Russia, China and India is not beyond the realm of feasibility. Therefore, the *nyet-bu-nahi* triangle – formal or informal – may finally get some substance in the near future. Is the nuclear factor a hindrance to Sino-Indian rapprochement? Since strategic analysts have been furiously debating this question, it needs to be examined in some detail. The Indian nuclear tests conducted in May 1998 have, to some extent, hindered the ongoing process of improving ties between the two countries, which had been stalled due to various reasons. The Cold War world order, based on the artificial geo-strategic divisions, started crumbling in the late 1980s. Around this period, India and China also started enhancing their efforts to revive and revitalise the age-old ties between these two great civilisations.

The visit of the then Indian Foreign Minister Jaswant Singh to China in June 1999, accompanied by a senior official delegation, including the officer in charge of disarmament issues, was very significant. It began to thaw the otherwise vastly chilled Sino - Indian relations since India declared itself as a nuclear power. Further, that this visit took place during the tense situation on the Indo-Pak border as a result of the intrusion by Pakistani regular troops and the mercenaries funded by them, was significant. China, traditionally known as a close ally and supporter of Pakistan, found it difficult to side with it this time. A senior spokesman of the Chinese Ministry of Foreign Affairs admitted that the ready acceptance by the Chinese leaders of the Indian proposal for a security dialogue mechanism at this juncture added significance to the Indian leader's visit and its importance for the ongoing process of further betterment of relations between these two great Asian powers.[31]

The Chinese, being the true disciples of the master strategist like Sun Tzu, generally follow a long-term gameplan entrenched in real politik. Here one should not forget this realpolitik is amply mixed with deception as well as diplomatic jugglery, perfected over a long time, to gain the desired goal with an air of China's "a Middle Kingdom" mentality.

India's claim that it was a nuclear power resulted in a lot of soul-searching in Beijing about its future role in future global nuclear diplomacy. India's nuclear tests and its emphatic assertion of having become a nuclear power compelled the Chinese authorities to go overboard and declare their nuclear position as a "status quoist nuclear powers".[32] This position left no one in any doubt that India's nuclear power upset China's calculations on two major counts. First, it saw a challenge in India going overt as a nuclear power – it thought this would considerably weaken its position as the sole leader of the developing world in the global arena. Secondly, India's nuclear programme compelled the Chinese leaders to rethink about their strategic perceptions. However, this did not mean any escalation in the military activity by either side on their positions on their borders as indicated by some high-profile analysts who raised the alarm bell, by pointing out that that the two Asian nuclear powers are bound to be enemies. But some others who were not so alarmist, observed that nuclear India will compel China to take a fresh look at its options along its borders as well as in other spheres in dealing with New Delhi.

Another reason for China's alarmist reaction to India going nuclear was the now famous letter written by the Indian Prime Minister to the US President immediately after the Pokhran II series of tests. In the context of this fact, there was enough reason to understand this aspect of the Chinese reaction. Even though China may never openly admit it, after the collapse of the erstwhile Soviet Union, it views the USA as not only the single important peer competitor in the international power game, but also as the one powerful nation which could create impediments in its path to become a really significant pole in the emerging new world order.

The Kosovo crisis and the adoption of a "New Strategy" for world dominance by the US-led NATO military combine had tremendously changed China's outlook. Intensive studies about these changes were underway; therefore, it would be in India's interest to closely follow these changes and adopt a flexible stance to understand the nuances, and take full advantage, of the emerging power scenarios. To a large extent, it would be better for India to go back to the merits of the genuine non-aligned approach and form its strategies accordingly.

After India went nuclear, the Chinese media had been awash with their assessment and reassessment of the concept of "hegemonism", this was a typical term used by the Chinese Communist Party as well as the intelligentsia to describe the growing dominance of the USA in international relations. Ever since the collapse of the erstwhile Soviet Union, the meaning and interpretation of this word has undergone changes from time to time. After President Clinton's visit to China in June 1998, it was felt that this word might be used in a new tone and tenor and might even disappear eventually. But the embassy bombing incident in Belgrade as well as the NATO doctrine changed all this and it seemed now that this word would be used more aggressively in the coming years. One thing that was clear was that China's efforts to establish a multipolar global power structure would gain further momentum in the future.

Ever since it signed and joined the NPT in 1992, China started seeing itself as an established status quo nuclear power. This became more visible since it became a willing party to the indefinite extension of the highly discriminatory and unequal NPT regime in 1995.[33] China went along with the other major powers to reiterate its position as a world power and a member of the exclusive P-5 and N-5 clubs.

With India becoming a declared nuclear power, the number of articles by Chinese strategic analysts explicitly pointing out these non-proliferation measures linked to global nuclear issues had gone up considerably. Some of the writings that had mildness vanished totally. And with the leakage of the Indian Prime Minister's letter to President Clinton, the reactions became almost a shrill campaign against the Indian nuclear programme. The Chinese were now arguing for nothing less than a complete rollback.[34]

At least one analyst of India's nuclear policy working with an official think-tank, wanted India to be treated at par with Iraq of the 1990s.: "What India is playing at present seems to be the risky game that Germany, Japan and Italy played in the 1930s and 1940s and Iraq played in the 1980s and 1990s. On the issue of India's nuclear tests and hegemonic behaviour in South Asia, the West seems to be repeating the mistake they made in the 1930s when they pursued an 'appeasement policy' and tried to shift the peril eastward. If the fact that Japan's starting the 18 September incident in 1931, Germany's sending troops into the non-military zone of the Rhine in 1936, and Italy's annexing Ethiopia were actions not contained by an international effort and marked the beginning of the end of Versailles-Washington Treaty System, then the mushroom cloud rising once again above South Asia is an open challenge to the forces that try to maintain the system of international treaties in the age of peace and development.[35]" This seems to be a case of either lack of knowledge about world history or a wilful effort to twist history to suit one's own purpose. There were, of course, other sane reactions. However, if one analyses a number of Chinese reactions to India going nuclear, they all end with a status quoist view on global nuclear politics.

China clearly intended to preserve the existing hegemonic nuclear order in which only the P-5 powers could keep their nuclear weapons. In other words, it intended to keep the current "nuclear apartheid" regime intact. On the flip side, this seemed to be a bizarre situation wherein the junior-most member of the exclusive club, who gate-crashed into it by sheer will and persistence, now acted as its gate and conscience keeper. When China carried out its first nuclear test in the open atmosphere in the Lop Nor test ranges, it violated the then "nuclear apartheid" regime based on PTBT. In India's case, however, the country had not violated any existing international treaty or convention, as it had consistently avoided signing any such unequal and unjustified regime.

In the current circumstances, it may not be easy to initiate a dialogue between India and China on the nuclear issue. In the verbal diatribes in the aftermath of the Indian tests, the normal bilateral relations deteriorated to such an extent that even the existing Joint Working Group (JWG) meeting could not take place in time. However, this position has changed and not only has the JWG met formally, the visit by the Indian Foreign Minister to China, as referred to earlier and his meeting with his counterpart in the ASEAN Regional Forum (ARF) meeting at Singapore have been described as highly successful.

One reality seems to be that China may not turn around and immediately agree to a dialogue on the nuclear issues, even under the existing framework. Secondly, according to the traditional Chinese psyche of "power play" and respect for power, even if it is willing to talk at a future date, it will not be keen to include the nuclear aspect as a strategic edge in favour of India. However, both these Asian giants have to come to grips with their respective nuclear capabilities and prowess at a future date. In order to attain such a state, India will have to calculate boldly and develop its nuclear capabilities to the extent where China will have to take note of its capabilities from the strategic perspective too. To achieve this, India has to develop a missile capability either matching or superior to that of China's existing arsenal. This development in no way suggests an escalation cycle followed in the Cold War era between the USA and the erstwhile Soviet Union. Essentially, the capabilities must be mutually deterrent to each other at any given time in the future.

On the other hand, India will have to play its nuclear card at the international level deftly to finally get the status and equal treatment as the sixth nuclear power in the world. To some, this may appear an unattainable goal. Here one must bear in mind that when China tested its first nuclear device at Lop Nor, it was also more or less in India's present-day state. But adroit diplomatic handling of the situation by the Chinese leadership played a key role in this regard. India also has to learn this lesson and influence the global system in its favour. Continuing with the dialogue at appropriate levels is an imperative need for this, and yet India's nuclear status cannot be a negotiable point at any future date. In short, India needs patience and a long-term strategic perspective.

Any meaningful dialogue between India and China at any future date has to take into account the nuclear reality of Pakistan. In this regard, first of all, the Pakistani nuclear capability has to be assessed and addressed properly. Further, this has also to be linked to the border issue, especially the area ceded to China by Pakistan, beyond Siachen. This area still belongs to India, even if one follows the 1949 India-Pakistan agreement; the term used in it is that the cease-fire line will be extended to the terminal point, NJ-9842, and "thence north to the glaciers".

Following India's nuclear tests, Pakistan also tested its own weapons; this, in a way, has established a certain parity; therefore, a dialogue can be initiated with Pakistan also. However, the ground realities do not tally with this superficial equation. It is necessary for the international community to ascertain the real capabilities and politico-strategic equations behind Pakistan's nuclear capabilities. In this regard, it is necessary to properly take stock of not only the Sino-Pak nuclear cooperation but also to verify the clandestine assistance it received from various other NPT signatories in the 1980s. Secondly, the aid provided by China, especially since 1992, when it formally became a part of the NPT, must be accounted for, and the legal status of such aid must be verified before considering the legal implications of Pakistan's nuclear status.

India must launch a diplomatic and media offensive to project that its nuclear capability and status are certainly not only superior to, but also substantially different from, those of Pakistan. Pakistan's nuclear capability and programme are linked entirely to one nation, that is, India. Whereas when India launched its nuclear research, even before independence, it was with a view not only to gain strategic depth but also a sustainable scientific role to improve its economic well-being and the living standards of its people. But the Pakistani leaders made no secret of the act that the sole purpose of their going nuclear was to establish a power parity with India so that their "struggle for freedom in Kashmir" could be strengthened. Immediately after the talks between US Deputy Secretary of State, Strobe Talbott, and Pakistan's Secretary Shamshad Ahmad, the Pakistani Prime Minister Nawaz Sharif stated, "Nobody can now stop Kashmir's freedom struggle. Now that Pakistan is a nuclear power, the sooner Indian understands this, the better. We are not only an atomic power but Ghauri and Shaheen missiles are also evidence of our impregnable defence in the world." After coming to power by overthrowing Sharif in a bloodless coup, President Pervez Musharraf missed no opportunity to express the same sentiment.

The diplomatic and external rubric of Pakistan's nuclear strategy included the roles played by: (a) the Islamic factor; (b) the USA; (c) China; and (d) India. It may be recalled that it was Gen. Zia ul Haq who first called for a close study of the meaning and implication of the term "Islamic Bomb". He said the US, Israel, the erstwhile Soviet Union and India have atomic bombs and asked why they were not called the "Christian Bomb", the "Communist Bomb" or "Hindu Bomb". In a press conference,

A.Q. Khan, widely known as the "father of the Pakistani Bomb" described the term "Islamic Bomb" as "a figment of the Zionist mind which has been use in full force by anti-Islamic Western countries". [36]

Gen. Zia and Khan would have done well to remember that the concept of "Islamic Bomb" was mooted by none other than Zia's predecessor, Zulfiquar Ali Bhutto. In his last testament, he said: "We know that Israel and South Africa have the full nuclear capability. The Christian, Jewish and Hindu civilisations have the capability. Only the Islamic civilisation is without it, and this position must change". [37]

Bhutto's identification with the Islamic world was mainly strategic. He exploited the Arab quest for a deterrent against the Zionist bomb as those states witnessed an oil boom and the consequent unprecedented rise in wealth. Technology-wise also, Pakistan was the most advanced country in the Islamic world. It is, therefore, not surprising that money flow, including aid and assistance, to Pakistan rose manifold.

A new Islamic dimension that has gained currency is the linkage between the nuclear weapon and the Kashmir issue. The state of Jammu and Kashmir has been witnessing low-intensity conflict or proxy war since 1998. Almost a decade ago, in July 1993, Ghulam Ishaq Khan said that a Pakistani nuclear capability was imperative to offset India's conventional superiority, adding that as long as Kashmir and other disputes remained, there was urgent need for a strong defence capability.[38] Subsequently, Moeen Qureshi, the caretaker Prime Minister reiterated the same theory. In January 1994, the Pakistani Foreign Minister, Assef Ahmad Ali said in Uzbekistan, "The concern of the world, the concern of the South Asian countries is that if a war takes place in Asia, it will inevitably become a nuclear confrontation".[39]

The US learned of Pakistan's attempts to put together the enrichment plant in 1978. Armed with the relevant legislation, Section 669 of the Foreign Assistance Act, 1979, the US announced the cut in aid to Pakistan. Despite diplomatic activity, including Gen. Zia's visit to the US in September 1979, Pakistan failed to resolve the nuclear dispute with the US.

The Soviet invasion of Afghanistan changed things for Pakistan. The US decided to aid Pakistan in a big way. The Symington Amendment was duly amended in December 1981 to enable the US to provide economic and military assistance to Pakistan if the President was satisfied that it was in the national interest of the US. Gen. Zia, realising fully well the stakes the US would now have in Pakistan, rejected the initial offer of $400 million as "peanuts". After hectic diplomatic consultations between the two countries, Deputy Secretary of State, Warren Chirstopher and National Security adviser, Zbigniew Brezezinski visited Islamabad in February 1980, and the issue was resolved in June 1981 when agreement was reached on a $3.2 billion aid package.

In 1985, another modification directed specifically at Pakistan was made to the Foreign Assistance Act. Under the Pressler Amendment, the President was required to certify annually that Pakistan did not possess a nuclear explosive device and that the US assistance to Pakistan would significantly reduce the risk of Pakistan acquiring the nuclear device. The waiver under the Pressler Amendment was granted till mid-1990 – initially till 1987, then till April 1990 and then till mid-1990.

Despite increasingly accumulating evidence on Pakistan's clandestine programme to acquire the enrichment technology, the US did nothing to prevent it. To quote from a Carnegie Endowment report prepared by sixteen specialists: "In sum, on several occasions, the United States had backed away from enforcing the sanction of an aid cut off against Pakistan, permitting the waiver of the Symington Amendment in 1981, and again in 1987; waiving the Glenn Amendment by Presidential Action in 1987; declining to react to production of highly enriched uranium in 1986 and 1987 to avoid suspension of assistance even though Pakistan had acquired the wherewithal for its first nuclear device, and waiving the Solarz Amendment in early 1988, despite finding that Pakistan had attempted to smuggle material out of the United States to be used in the manufacture of a nuclear explosive device".[40]

In October 1990, the Bush Administration did not ask Congress for a waiver to the Pressler Amendment and US aid to Pakistan remained suspended. After initial reports in 1993 that the new Foreign Assistance Act would not be country specific, the US has now decided that the Pressler Amendment has come to stay. Pakistan's nuclear strategy suffered another blow after Deputy Secretary of State Strobe Talbott's visit to Islamabad in April 1994 when he clarified that "the issue of non-proliferation is so complex that it needs to be addressed very much in its own terms".[41] This is in sharp contrast to the Clinton Administration's earlier policy review on South Asia in which Kashmir was called a "core issue" which needed to be resolved as part of the non-proliferation measures.

The least publicised aspect of Pakistan's nuclear programme is the role played by China. While there is talk of a Sino-Pak axis amidst reports of transfer of nuclear design, training, or even conducting a nuclear test at Lop Nor, no confirmation has been made. China has obviously denied these reports.

After the 1974 detonation by India, the Chinese pledged support to Pakistan against "nuclear threat and nuclear blackmail". Z.A. Bhutto said that in 1976 he arrived at an agreement with China, "the single most important achievement" of his later years. He visited China with a delegation which included, among others, A.Q. Khan. Two agreements were concluded during the visit and in terms of these agreements, China agreed to provide Pakistan with nuclear weapon design information, test data, setting up of an enrichment plant, supply of heavy water, etc. According to David Hart, a well-known Pakistan observer, China provided technical assistance to the Kahuta nuclear plant in 1979.[42]

Reports of Sino-Pak nuclear collaboration were ripe in 1980 when Gen. Zia visited Beijing in August that year. China had reportedly responded positively to a Pakistani request for a nuclear test in China A June 1984 report indicated that China had actually given Pakistan the design for the weapons used in China's fourth nuclear test.[43] In 1992, the two countries signed an accord on a 300 MW research reactor to be placed under IAEA safeguards. In September 1993, the US imposed sanctions on Pakistan and China for the reported transfer of components of M-11 missiles to the former from the latter.

Apart from direct assistance, China has played a very significant role in the Pakistani regional nuclear strategy. Realising fully well that India would never be a party to any regional denuclearisation move that excludes China, Pakistan has, year after year since 1974, put forward proposals to India seeking a bilateral nuclear dialogue and arms control. New Delhi rejected these proposals but, at the same time, put forward, one after another, a number of counter-proposals it knew Islamabad would never accept. Here nuclear politics became a new playground for India and Pakistan to score brownie points over each other.

In 1974, Pakistan brought to the UN General Assembly the proposal for a Nuclear Weapon Free Zone (NWFZ) in south Asia. India, as expected, rejected the proposal on the grounds that south Asia is a sub-region and not a region and that such a proposal should come from the countries of the region. Obviously, the reasons looked flimsy. Pakistan's gains were temporary – till its own intentions came to light. This, however, was not a gain for India – the nuclear game is not a zero-sum one. The proposal has been reduced to an annual ritual at the UN General Assembly.

In December 1985, India proposed a bilateral agreement on non-attack on each other's nuclear installations. This was finally signed in December 1988 although it took another five years before the lists of installations could be exchanged between the two countries. Interestingly, the proposal by India to extend this agreement to cover economic and population centre has been rejected by Pakistan. Curiously, Pakistan argued that the no-first use of nuclear weapons would be tantamount to accepting a nuclear weapon capability! Again, in September 1987, Pakistani Prime Minister Mohammad Khan Junejo, put froward a regional test ban proposal in the UN General Assembly. The proposal was obviously given much attention. Firstly because India's approach to the issue is global and, secondly the Chinese had not made any statement indicating their acceptance of such a test ban.

Most curious of all these has been Pakistan's approach to the arms control treaties. It acceded to the PTBT in 1963 but ratified it only in 1987 by which time the treaty had lost its relevance. As for NPT, while initially it voted for the resolution commending the treaty, it did not accede to it since India had not done so. As it developed its nuclear capability, it started talking in terms of the rights of the nuclear have-nots and no acceptance of safeguards on indigenous facilities, that is, indirectly talking against the treaty provisions, and yet it has made the signing of the NPT conditional on India's doing so.[44]

Pakistan's nuclear "doctrine", if it can at all be termed as such, is simply to gain a power-parity with India so that it can intensify its "struggle for freedom" in Kashmir by offsetting India's superiority in regard to conventional military prowess. In sharp contrast to this, India has nuclear "doctrine" in the true sense of the term. Here it must be borne in mind that a "doctrine" is expected to define the principles and concepts for the guidance of policy-makers after it has been approved by duly constituted authorities. It must not be confused with policy, strategy or even posture which no doubt may be expected to flow form it.

On August 17, 1999, the Government of India released the draft nuclear doctrine for India to encourage public debate. The document would be considered by the government in due course for a final decision. The draft has naturally attracted a great deal of comment which was the stated purpose of releasing it to the public. Thus, this is not the doctrine accepted or endorsed by the government as yet. It is, as the document clearly says, a draft proposal of the National Security Advisory Board. Much of the critique of the document has arisen form two factors. The first is the rather unique approach of making the proposal public for discussion and debate. Unlike conventional weapons whose development, deployment and employment would remain restricted to military and defence establishments, nuclear weapons concern all citizens. In a democracy, the people have the right to know what principles will govern the nation's nuclear policy. The second factor is even more important. The doctrine does not adopt the conventional wisdom of other nuclear weapon states. To that extent, this is not only in contrast to the acknowledged wisdom of the major nuclear powers but seeks to chart a new path.

The salient features of the doctrine are built on five essential principles:

(a) India's nuclear weapons are meant only to deter nuclear weapons' threat or use. Needless to say, this principle severely limits the potential development, deployment and employment of the nuclear arsenal of the country.

(b) The doctrine rests on the principle of "no-first-use" even against nuclear threat or use. The only country to adopt a similar commitment is China although uncertainties remain about whether China's commitment constitutes a political statement or is a doctrinal precept.

(c) It is based on the defensive doctrine of no-first-use and limiting the use of nuclear weapons to retaliation only. India's draft doctrine is in total harmony with the Article 51 of the UN Charter which endorses "the inherent right of individual or collective self-defence if an armed attack occurs against a member of the United Nations".

(d) The doctrine emphasises that global, verifiable and non-discriminatory nuclear disarmament is a national security objective.

(e) The doctrine is based on the concept that the nuclear policy, strategy and posture would be based on the minimalist principle. The emphasis on "minimum" deterrence clearly defines this principle in relation to the capability sought, the size of the arsenal, the costs involved, the level of retaliation required and the nuclear posture in peacetime and in times of crisis and real threat to the sovereignty and territorial integrity of the nation.

There is no doubt that India's nuclear doctrine poses a serious challenge to the prevailing doctrines of offensive orientation and first strike strategic doctrines of the US, NATO and Russia. China has been demanding a treaty on no-first-use among the weapon states. The Chinese and Indian doctrines now indicate a counter-view to the traditional aggressive doctrines of other nuclear weapon states who visualise use of nuclear weapons against non-nuclear threats. It is not surprising, therefore, that the US responded to the draft doctrine by saying that India is "moving in the wrong direction".[45] But since the State Department spokesman acknowledged that the US had yet to examine the document, this appears to have a reflex reaction to a doctrine which reflected thinking in total contrast to the US' doctrine and belief system.

VI

History usually makes a mockery of our hopes and expectations. The events that led to the break-up of the Soviet Union are perhaps more sensational than any other since 1945. The break-up of the Soviet Union was perplexing to analysts and much of what they anticipate for the post-Soviet world order is uncertain. Nevertheless, it is clear that we are entering a new world, and three lines of argument about it may be examined here.

The first question to be examined is why predication is so difficult in a world order where nuclear weapons are the currency of power. Among the reasons: multiple factors are usually at work, actors and their policies change, small events can affect the course of international relations, and most importantly in this context, many well-established generalisations about world politics may no longer hold. This leads to the second question of the ways and areas in which the future is likely to resemble the past, and the sources, areas and implications of change. It appears that while international politics in much of the world will follow patterns that are familiar in outline, although unpredictable in detail, among the nuclear powers we are likely to see new forms of relations. In this new context, the third argument goes, the USA will face an extraordinarily wide range of policy choices and must, therefore, address fundamental questions that were submerged during the Cold War. Freed from the previous constraints, Washington has many goals it can seek, but there are many hurdles than are sometimes realised. This implies that "uncertainty" is the buzz-word in the post-Soviet International world order.

The post-Soviet global environment is one characterised by a great degree of uncertainty and geo-political flux and the stability the "peace-dividend" was supposed to usher in has been elusive. As in the past when seminal historical events were unfolding, the immediate aftermath is better described as "turbulent times" and it will be a long time before some degree of clarity emerges in the wider geo-political context.

It is largely because of these turbulent times that it has become difficult to predict the course of international politics in the new equations of power all over the world.[46] The reason why prediction is difficult brings us closer to the question of how different the new world will be. Even if we knew what generalisations held in the past and even if they were not sensitive to details and idiosyncrasies, this knowledge would not provide a sure guide for the future if the generalisations themselves were no longer valid. In *Time's Arrow, Time's Cycle*, Stephen Jay Gould discusses schools of thought about geology in terms of their basic orienting metaphors. One school sees the large-scale history of the earth in terms of cycles in which there is change from one phase to another but the phase themselves recur through regular cycles; the other sees geology as revealing constant unidirectional change.[47] Each perspective can have an element of truth, as Gould argues, is the case for the earth's history, and we should be suspicious of any unqualified answer. But the question of the extent to which, and the way in which, international politics resembles a cycle or an arrow is a useful one.

If our laws are not timeless – if history resembles an arrow – some of what we have learned will not help us understand the future course of international politics. For example, many analysts have pointed out that since alliances last as long as there is a common enemy, NATO will dissolve after the break-up of the Soviet Union. But even if the historical generalisations are correct, their projection into the future may not be so, if the roles and motivations for alliances have changed.

For instance, the North Korean impasse over its nuclear programme and violation of the IAEA commitments is an illustrative example of what action a non-nuclear weapon signatory to the NPT may be compelled to take if it perceives that its core national interests are threatened. Now that North Korea, the "rogue state" as it was described by President Bush, has openly declared that it has gone nuclear, the storm-centre has obviously shifted from West Asia to the Asia Pacific. If the Korean flash-point leads to an all-out war, it is impossible to predict that nuclear weapons will not be used. In the current turbulent times, nothing can be ruled out. True, nuclear weapons were not used either in Vietnam or Iraq; but that does not guarantee that they will not be used in the event of a conflagration between the US and North Korea, given the present mood of the Bush Administration.

Thus, in some cases, generalisations will no longer hold even though the basic laws that generated them remain valid. Statesmen presumably will continue to be guided primarily by considerations of national security, but their behaviour will be different if there are change in the problems they face and the solutions they see. It probably is still true that states are more likely to be pushed into war by the expectation that they will suffer grave losses unless they fight than they are pulled into war by the attraction of opportunity and expected gains.[48]

But this law will work itself out differently if there are change in the magnitude and kinds of threats states confront. It is also possible that the import of a pattern may change as conditions do; for example, it may have been the case that liberal democracies did not fight each other, but now this generalisation yields a much more peaceful world than was true in the past because so many of the powerful states are democratic. More extreme changes are possible, although less likely; that is, the nature of the basic connections between variables, i.e., the laws themselves could change. Thus, statesmen might no longer place as high a priority on security as they did in the past.

Cyclical thinking suggests that, freed from the constraints of the Cold War and the non-existence of the Soviet Union, world politics will return to earlier patterns of relative peace and stability.[49] Many of the basic generalisations of international politics remain unaltered; it is still anarchic in the sense that there is no international sovereign that can enforce laws, treaties and agreements.[50] To put it more generally, both aggression and spirals of insecurity and tension can still disturb the peace. But in the aftermath of the break-up of the Soviet Union, are the conditions that call these forces into being as prevalent as they were when the Soviet Union posed the greatest threat to the USA? Are the forces that restrain violence now as strong, or stronger, than they were?

Consider in this connection the reaction of the US to the collapse of the Soviet Union. At long last, when the forty-year struggle to encircle, weaken and ultimately dismember the Soviet

Union ended, for many in the US who had devoted a lifetime to orchestrating the "containment" of Soviet power, this was a moment to be cheered and savoured. Cheer as they might, however, these high level officials could not entirely conceal from themselves the fact that the Soviet collapse spelled significant hardship for the American military establishment.

Throughout the Cold War era, the US war machine had been trained and equipped for one all-consuming mission; to deter Soviet aggression in Europe while blocking Soviet inroads into contested Third World areas. To sustain this mission, a bipartisan consensus in Congress had allocated some $ 15.5 trillion in military appropriations between 1947 and 1989, plus billions of dollars on such related activities as nuclear weapons fabrication, foreign military assistance, intelligence collection, civil defence preparation, and nuclear weapon research. In further support, Congress had approved a "peacetime draft", the formation of numerous military alliances, and the permanent deployment of thousands of nuclear weapons and hundreds of thousands of American troops at base and garrisons abroad.

Furthemore, the collapse of the Soviet Union provided a mental map for US military strategists – a cognitive system for dividing the world into friends and foes, shaping a response to overseas crises, and providing a rationale for periodic intervention abroad. American leaders during this period were confident that they had discovered a grand historical pattern that showed what the role of the US in the world must be. No matter what the nature of the challenge to America's global interests, these leaders determined their response by defining their role in terms of their country's unrivalled supremacy in the world.

The high-level Pentagon officials concluded that this role would require the maintenance of a powerful, high-tech military establishment equipped with a full range of modern combat systems, including nuclear weapons and ballistic missiles. This establishment, said a Pentagon spokesman, would not be smaller than that fielded during the peak years of the Cold War; it must be similar to it in its basic structure and capabilities.

The US strategists began to identify those Third World countries which could be major enemies of the US and concluded that they would have to establish a new basis on which to calculate the threat they posed. The 1990s had witnessed the emergence of a new class of regional Third World powers – states with nuclear capabilities and with large military forces and the inclination to dominate other weaker states in their immediate vicinity. It was this class of rising Third World powers that was chosen to replace the faded Soviet Empire in the Pentagon's analysis of the global threat environment. Form this point on, US leaders increasingly employed "rogue", "outlaw" and "renegade" imagery when speaking of "hostile" Third World countries.

The Pentagon strategists pointed out that states that support and sponsor terrorist actions had managed in recent year to co-opt and manipulate the phenomenon in pursuit of their own strategic goals. These states sought to use terrorism to shake America's self-confidence and sap its will to resist aggression and intimidation. These states were seeking to undermine not only America's power and national interests in the world but also its foreign policy objectives.

This imagery, although hastily manufactured in response to the sudden collapse of Soviet power, proved surprisingly effective, tapping into American fears of nuclear weapons and malevolent Third World leaders. The "Rogue Doctrine" played particularly well on Capitol Hill, where several prominent Senators, including Sam Nunn of Georgia and Willam Roth of Delaware, had already began describing nuclear weapons-seeking states in the Third World as an emerging peril. By the spring of 1994, senior Pentagon officials and many members of Congress had began using common analysis and terminology to describe the threat posed by the new type of enemy. It was just at this time that the newly appointed Chairman of the Joint Chiefs of Staff, General Colin Powell warned, "We have to put a shingle outside our door saying, 'The World's Only Superpower Lives Here', no matter who is the enemy and where it comes from and how powerful it might be".[51]

It was earlier contended that although the Soviet Union has become non-existent and does not pose any threat to the USA, both aggression and spirals of insecurity and tension can disturb international peace. The reaction of the US to the collapse of the Soviet Union, as outlined above, is illustrative of this point. The question that many would like to ask here may not require much detail: is the demise of the Soviet Union and the Cold War likely to increase or decrease global or regional conflict that may eventually engulf large areas of the world? The answer to this question has been provided by the Iraq War of 2003 and one can expect more of such conflicts in future. What could be the outcome of these conflicts is not easy to predict. But it is quite clear that the two Gulf Wars might not have taken place in the earlier era. The United States could not have afforded to act as it did had the Soviet Union been Iraq's ally and a threat in Europe.

During the Cold War era, the two superpowers offered the security umbrella to their Third World clients as well as restrained them. Now unless other forces and mechanisms that would serve these functions develop, aggression will be less difficult to restrain and partly for this reason, status quo states in the Third World will worry more about their self-protection. Their worry is all the more serious because quite a few Third World countries have gone nuclear while some others are on the "threshold" of nuclear capability. Even "absent aggressive motives" conflict will often result through the security dilemma: states' efforts to make themselves more secure will threaten others. The traditional sources of international conflict will work themselves out in a context that for at least several years will be changing rapidly as the states seek to adjust to the rapid nuclearisation of some states. Indeed, in some cases, weak clients will collapse or be overthrown, heightening the possibilities for regional disturbances.

Despite all that has been discussed above, nobody should overlook two glaring facts: although the Soviet Union had disintegrated, Russia remains a superpower – militarily at least; and secondly, a little more after the fiftieth year of the age of fission, nuclear weapons abound. Together the US and Russia today have more than 50,000 warheads. Small parts of these two forces could bring ruin to both nations. Britain, France and China may have a thousand or two among the three of them; comparatively, these forces are small, but the gross destructive power in British, French and Chinese hands is hundreds of times greater than anything ever found in a peacetime arsenal before the atom was split.

In terms of what each of these three forces could do to any enemy in an all-out nuclear conflict, they are much more like the superpower arsenals than they are like the capabilities of merely conventional forces of any age. At least two more countries are as close to a nuclear arsenal as they want to be. India had a series of nuclear tests in May 1998 but may not have yet made significant warheads. The missiles that India has developed only show that it is likely to become a full-fledged nuclear power. Israel has had no evident explosions, but it would be a most imprudent government which do not take into account the fact that if the Israelis should ever decide to use nuclear weapons, they would be right at hand. However, Pakistan has still a long way to go to become a nuclear power to be reckoned with.

It is impossible to predict the future course of international relations and the shape of nuclear danger that may confront mankind, the collapse of the Soviet Union notwithstanding. It must also be recognised that the possibility of nuclear war has not been eliminated with the events that have taken place in the Soviet Union after the fall of Gorbachev. Although nuclear realities cannot be wished away, there are now still good reasons to hope that the world will be a much safer place to live in. The survival of mankind in the first fifty years of danger offers encouragement to renew pursuit of truth, resolute practice of courage, and persistence of lively hope.

Obviously, hope alone does not of itself produce safety. Real reduction of risk comes only from real choices. Moreover, technological and political change, from one decade to another, will always require new choices. No one can tell today whether the risk of catastrophe will go up or down in the future, and still less can anyone predict the wisdom or folly of future decision-makers.

If we judge by history, it is right to expect that our progress away from nuclear danger will be slow and not always steady. It is wrong to hope for an immediate twenty-foot jump when ten is the best on record. Yet it is also true, as men like Bohr and Oppenheimer understood at the beginning, that the terrible power inside the nucleus offers hope as well as peril.

Notes

1. George Lee Butler, "The Nuclear Era is Over", *The Bulletin of Atomic Scientists* Spring, 1993, vol. XXV, no. 14, pp. 32-41.

2. S. Burrows and H. Schaffer, *Cold War and Its Aftermath*, Rothman Books, Washington, 1993, p. 63.

3. See Paul Branigin, *Boosting Nuclear Arsenal*, Westworth Books, London 1993, Chapter IV.

4. Lews A Postal, "Deterrence by Denial, IISS, *Strategic Survey: 1991-92*, London, pp. 38-60.

5. Ibid.

6. *Defense and Foreign Affairs Handbook*, New York, 1994, p. 59.

7. Ibid, p. 26.

8. *Jane's Defense Weekly*, July 1, 1994.

9. *Milavnews*, April, 1991.

10. Ibid.

11. Ibid, March, 1991.

12. *Jane's Defense Weekly*, October 2, 1995

13. Ibid, 8 June, 1997.

14. *Defense and Foreign Affairs Weekly*, July 15, 1991.

15. Jeffrey N. Sullivan, *Parameters*, Autumn, 1993, p. 9.

16. *Jane's Defense Weekly*, August 8, 1996

17. *Milavnews*, January, 1999.

18. *Handbook of Current Affairs*, January, 1998

19. Samuel B. Locsher, *The Conduct of Nuclear War*, Blackewell Books, New York, 1994, p. 116.

20. Alison H. Payne, *In Quest of Peace*, Adelphi Publications, London, 1997, pp. 70-71.

21. Samuel B. Locsher, op. cit. p. 83.

22. David Primer, *NATO and the Security of Europe*, SIPRI Year Book, 1998, pp. 93-95.

23. Malcolm Rogers, *Problems of Arms Control*, Mosbach (Germany) 1994, p. 69.

24. Ibid. p. 93.

25. Richard P. Speir, *Technology Revolution and Disarmament*, (monograph), The Brookings Institution, Washington DC., 1998, p. 46.

26. Ibid. p. 58

27. Thomas S. Dowler, "Post-Cold War Nuclear Strategy", *Strategic Review*, Fall, 1995, p. 24

28. Don F. Snider, "Are Nukes Legal?" *Arms Control Today*, September, 1996, pp. 24-30.

29. For the full text of Arundhati Roy's Speech at Harlem, New York, see *Journal of Peace Research*, June, 2003, pp. 15-26.

30. *Washington Post*, June 17, 2003.

31. *The Times of India*, July 7, 2003 and *The Times*, London, July, 2003.

32. Karin Axell, "Nuclear Factor in Sino-Indian Relations" *Eastern World*, London, April 6, 2003

33. Chris Greenwell, "China's Nuclear Strategy", *Arms Control Today*, March-April, 2003, pp. 30-47.

34. John Rothjens, "China's Nuclear Ambitions", *Survival* 30:3, 1998, pp. 331-46.

35. George P. Reed, "China and Non-Proliferation" *Eastern World*, London, August, 2002, pp. 24-36.

36. Savita Pande, "Pakistan's Nuclear Strategy", *Asian Strategic Review: 1993-94*, Institute for Defence Studies and Analyses (IDSA), New Delhi, pp 324-44.

37. Ibid.

38. Ibid.

39. Ibid.

40. Jasjit Singh, "India's Nuclear Doctrine", *Asian Strategic Review*: 1998-99, IDSA, New Delhi, pp. 9-23.

41. Ibid.

42. Ibid.

43. See *India Abroad News Service*, August 19, 1999.

44. Savita Pande, op. cit.

45. Jasjit Singh, op. cit.

46. The literature on this subject is very large. See the summary in Nazil Chaucri and Thomas Robinson (eds), *Forecasting in International Relations*, Freeman, San Francisco, 1978.

47. Stephen J. Gould, *Time's Arrow, Time's Cycle*, Cambridge, Harvard University Press, 1978, pp. 65-71.

48. Robert Jervis, "Loss Aversion in International Politics", *Political Psychology*, May, 1998, pp. 34-36.

49. A good example is John Mearsheimer, "Back to the Future" Instability in Europe after the Cold War, *International Security*, vol. 15, no. 1. Summer, 1990.

50. See Helen Milner, "The Assumption of Anarchy in International Relations", *Review of International Studies*, vol. 17, no. 1, January, 1991, pp. 67-86.

51. Michael Klare, *Rogue States and Nuclear Outlaws (America's Search for a New Foreign Policy)*, Universal Book Traders, New Delhi, pp. 27-30.

7

EPILOGUE

The events of 1989, perhaps more sensational than those of any year since 1945, were unforeseen. Much of what analysts anticipated for the 1990s were unpleasant. Nevertheless, it is clear that we are entering a new world, and three lines of argument about it will be presented here. The first question to be discussed is why prediction is so difficult in world politics. Among the reasons: multiple factors are usually at work, actors learn, small events can affect the course of history and, most importantly in this context, many well-established generalisations about world politics may no longer hold. This leads to the second question of the ways and areas, in which the future is likely to resemble the past, and the sources, areas, and implications of change. It appears that while international politics in much of the world will follow patterns that are familiar in outline although unpredictable in detail, among the developed states we are likely to see new forms of relations. In this new context, the third argument goes, the United States will face an extraordinarily wide range of policy choices and must, therefore, address fundamental questions that were submerged during the Cold War. Freed from the previous constraints, the United States has many goals it can seek, but there are more conflicts among them that are sometimes realised.

We all know that it is difficult to predict the course of international politics.[1] Nevertheless, it is useful to note eight reasons why this is so.[2] First, social scientists have only a limited stock of knowledge to rely on and there are few laws whose validity is uncontested. Take, for example, the polarity of the international system, which different scholars define differently. For some, pre-World War I Europe was bipolar, in the eyes of others it was multipolar. Following Kenneth Waltz, John Mearsheimer argues that bipolar systems are more stable than multipolar ones; this provides the foundation for his pessimistic predictions about the future of Europe.[3] But the logic of Waltz's position is open to dispute; indeed, it suffers from internal contradictions.[4] Furthermore, even if the arguments for or against this position were more compelling, they might not be true. Politics has the nasty habit of not always behaving as even the most plausible and rigorous theories suggest it should.

Second, only rarely does a single factor determine the way politics will work out. Even the best propositions are couched in terms of conditions and probabilities. Thus, it is doubtful that we would ever learn that either bipolarity or multipolarity is always more stable than the other. So even if multipolar systems usually are less stable than bipolar ones, this does not mean that the future will be less stable than the past. Other factors could cancel out this effect or interact with polarity in a way that makes an overall judgement about the influence of the latter impossible. The most obvious factor, as Mearsheimer and Waltz note, is the presence of nuclear weapons; perhaps in the non-nuclear era, multipolar systems were less stable than bipolar ones, but today the reverse could be true.

Third, learning about international politics can act as a self-denying prophecy. Although we should not exaggerate the influence of scholarship on world politics, actors may pay attention to academic theories and alter their behaviour in ways that render them incorrect. For example, if scholars find that actors who make their threats in public rather than in private are rarely bluffing, then bluffers can choose to make public threats. Or, if theorists convince statesmen that regional integration is characterised by spillover processes in which small steps towards economic coordination lead to much greater integration than was originally envisioned, then those who do not want to reach this end may refuse to take the initial steps. Furthermore, when actors are seeking advantages over others, generalisations may be particularly short-lived as each uses any new knowledge to estimate how others will behave and to outwit them.[5]

Fourth, unless national behaviour and international outcomes are entirely determined by the external environment, there is significant room for choice by the public and the statesmen. Since the United States is the most influential power in the world, after the disintegration of the Soviet Union, to predict the future of world politics requires us to predict the future of American foreign policy. To the extent that the latter will be strongly influenced by the values, preferences, and beliefs of particular presidents, the enterprise is particularly questionable. To the extent that broader but still changeable domestic sources shape American foreign policy, the task is not much easier.

Even if the external environment is dominant, there now is a fifth obstacle to prediction: the current world situation is unprecedented. While each era appears unique to those living through it, it can be reasonably guessed that even later generations will view the 1990s as unique. World politics has rarely been reordered without a major war. In fact, looking at the behaviour and condition of the Soviet Union, one could infer that it had just lost a war. And the enormous domestic failure is the equivalent of a major military defeat. But this is a war without another country or coalition that acts like a winner, ready to move into the power vacuum and structure a new set of rules to guide international behaviour. Although the United States remains the most powerful country in the world, its mood – and perhaps its economy – do not fit this position, even after the triumph of the Gulf War.

The future is also unprecedented because while the Soviet Union is economically and politically weak and geographically disintegrated, Russia still remains the only country that could possibly destroy the United States. Other states that are America's economic rivals (as well as its economic partners) are its close allies (and even its friends). This configuration is so odd that we cannot easily determine the system's polarity. Is it unipolar because the

United States is so much stronger than the nearest competitor, bipolar because of the distribution of military resources, tripolar because of an emerging United Europe, or multipolar because of the general dispersion of power? Thus, even if polarity were a major determinant of world politics, it would be hard to tell what we should expect.

To the extent that external forces are not only important, but truly constitute a system, there is a sixth difficulty in making predictions. When elements are tightly interconnected, as they are in international politics, changes in one part of the system produce ramifications in other elements and feedback loops. Thus, international politics is characterised by unintended consequences, interaction effects, and patterns that cannot be understood by breaking the system into bilateral relations. For example, a stable (if bloody) balance of power can be produced by a system in which all the major actors want to dominate or in which the relations among many pairs of countries are very bad.[6] With complex interaction and feedback, not only can small causes have large effects, but prediction is inherently problematic as the multiple pathways through which the system will respond to a stimulus are difficult to trace after the fact, let alone estimate ahead of time.[7]

It is tempting but a mistake to imagine that world politics will continue on its current trajectory, with the obvious and large exception of the drastic diminution of former Soviet-American tensions. Proceeding this way is tempting because, although still very difficult, it is relatively manageable. It is an error, however, because in a system, the alteration of one element will lead to multiple changes as states react. If some of the anticipated consequences of the end of the Cold War are undesired, actors will try to counteract them, although, of course, such efforts may produce results that are very different from the intentions. For example, it is possible that the developed countries, believing that the end of the Soviet threat will increase tensions among them, will redouble their efforts to work together and minimise frictions. But, of course, if any one state realises that this is what the others are doing, it can seek to turn their reasonableness to unilateral advantage.

The final two arguments as to why prediction is so difficult are more controversial. The flow of international politics is, in significant measure, contingent or path-dependent.[8] History matters. Particular events can send world politics down quite different paths.[9]

Stephen Jay Gould makes a similar argument for evolution. The operation of natural selection does not preclude a large role for chance and accidents. Had certain life forms been destroyed or others survived eons ago – and there are no general principles or scientific laws that precluded this – life would have evolved very differently.[10]

If international politics fits this pattern, then in order to know what the world will be like twenty years from now, we would have to know what will happen next year, an extremely difficult requirement. While proof is, of course, impossible, several actual or hypothetical events can illustrate the plausibility of this claim. For example, the history of the world after 1918 was crucially affected not only by the fact that World War I occurred, but that it was a war that took place at a particular time with certain countries on each side. Even if some sort of world war was inevitable during that decade, it is hard to argue that there had to be a war in the summer of 1914. And had it occurred earlier or later, much else about it could have been different in a way that would have produced a different post-war world. The aftermath of the war was also influenced by accidents. The United States might have joined the League of Nations had Wilson's personality been different or had his judgement not been impaired by his stroke.[11] Without the Korean War, many of the characteristics we associate with the Cold War – high defence budgets, a militarised NATO, great Sino-American hostility, and American security commitments throughout the world – probably would not have developed.[12]

Looking to the future, the war in the Persian Gulf may similarly influence aspects of the post-Cold War era. Turning the clock back to August 1990, or even to October 1990 or January 1991, one can imagine a variety of policies and outcomes, each of which would have produced quite a different world. A world in which Iraq's aggression was allowed to stand would have been quite different from one in which economic sanctions forced a retraction, which in turn would have been different from the world that emerged in the aftermath of the Gulf War. Even more clearly, the future of world politics would have been different if the Soviet Union could stay together or was shattered by a civil war. But the Soviet Union dissolved peacefully, and it might have influenced the events in Yugoslavia if that country's civil war intensified before events in the Soviet Union were determined, the object-lesson might decrease the chance of large-scale violence among the successor republics.[13] Less dramatically, the long-run state of US-Japanese relations may be permanently influenced by the way in which the next trade crisis arises and is worked out. Furthermore, the way in which the US-Japan trading relationship develops will strongly influence the worldwide international economic system.

It can be argued that these claims exaggerate the role of contingency because they underestimate the power of the structure of the international system and other deeply imbedded influences. While events like the Gulf War cannot be predicted, neither do they send the world along radically different paths. Instead, politics resembles roads that intersect rather than diverge.[14] Shocks may push the world in one direction or another, but eventually the underlying factors will exert themselves and return the world to something like what it would have been without the earlier "deviant" events. In international politics, however, such an argument seems plausible only if the international structure determines most behaviours. One can perhaps claim that this was the case during the more competitive years of the Cold War; it is not likely to be true for many aspects of world politics in the current era.

The final reason why prediction is difficult brings us closer to the question of how different the new world will be. Even if we knew what generalisations held in the past and even if they were not sensitive to details and idiosyncrasies, this knowledge would not provide a sure guide for the future if the generalisations themselves were no longer valid. In *Time's Arrow, Time's Cycle*, Stephen Jay Gould discusses schools of thought about geology in terms of their basic orienting metaphors. One school sees the large-scale history of the earth in terms of cycles in which there is change from one phase to another but the phases themselves recur through regular cycles; the other sees geology as revealing constant unidirectional change.[15] Each perspective can have an element of truth, as Gould argues is the case for the earth's history, and we should be suspicious of any unqualified answer. But the question of the extent to which, and the ways in which, international history resembles a cycle or an arrow is a useful one.

If our laws are not timeless, if history resembles an arrow, some of what we have learned will not help us understand the future. For example, many commentators have pointed out that alliances last only as long as there is a common enemy and so they have concluded that NATO will soon dissolve. But even if the historical generalisation is correct, the projection of it into the future may not be, if the roles and motivations for alliances have changed. Similarly, even if previous eras of multipolarity were characterised by instability, a future multipolar world might not be. We need to understand why certain generalisations held true in the past and see whether basic impulses of international politics may work themselves out differently in a changed environment.

In some cases, generalisations will no longer hold even though the basic laws that generated them remain valid. Statesmen presumably will continue to be guided primarily by considerations of national security, but their behaviour will be different if there are changes in the problems they face and the solutions they see. It probably is still true that states are more likely to be pushed into war by the expectation that they will suffer grave losses unless they fight than by the attraction of opportunity and expected gains. [16] But this law will work itself out differently if there are changes in the magnitude and kinds of threats that states confront. It is also possible that the import of a pattern may change as conditions do; for example, it may always have been the case that liberal democracies did not fight each other, but now this generalisation yields a much more peaceful world than was true in the past because so many of the powerful states are democratic.

More extreme changes are also possible, although less likely; that is, the nature of the basic connections between variables i.e., the laws themselves could change. Thus, statesmen might no longer place as high a priority on security as they did in the past. Of course, if we make our theories sufficiently general – e.g., people seek to maximise their expected utilities – we may find they have not changed, but this will not be particularly significant if the utilities and beliefs about how to reach them have changed.

Cyclical thinking suggests that, freed from the constraints of the Cold War, world politics will return to earlier patterns.[17] Many of the basic generalisations of international politics remain unaltered; it is still anarchic in the sense that there is no international sovereign that can make and enforce laws and agreements.[18] The security dilemma remains as well, with the problems it creates for states which would like to cooperate but whose security requirements do not mesh. Many specific causes of conflict also remain, including the desires for greater prestige, economic rivalries, hostile nationalisms, divergent perspectives on and incompatible standards of legitimacy, religious animosities, and territorial ambitions. To put it more generally, both aggression and spirals of insecurity and tension can still disturb the peace. But are the conditions that call these forces into being as prevalent as they were in the past? Are the forces that restrain violence now as strong, or stronger, than they were?

The answers may be different for different regions of the world. Even where fundamental changes have not occurred, the first seven impediments to prediction remain in place; but there we can at least say that the variables and relationships that acted in the past should continue. Where time's arrow predominates, on the other hand, our first task may be negative: to argue that some familiar patterns are not likely to reappear. On some questions we may be able to discern at least the outlines of the new arrangements; on others, what will emerge may not yet be determined.

Time's arrow is most strikingly at work in the developed world; it is hard to see how a war could occur among the United States, Western Europe, and Japan, at least in the absence of revolutionary domestic changes, presumably linked to severe economic depression. Indeed, peace among these countries is over-determined; there are many reasons, each of which is probably sufficient, why they should remain at peace.[19] One indication of the profound change is that although Britain's primary aim always was to prevent any power from dominating the continent of Europe, even those Britons who opposed joining the European Community or who remain opposed to seeing it develop political sovereignty would laugh at the idea of going to war to prevent its formation. The United States, too, fought to prevent Germany from dominating Europe, but sponsored European integration during the Cold War and still looks on it with favour, even though Germany is its leader.[20]

Similarly, if international politics in the West had not changed, in the absence of bipolarity it would be hard to understand how the United States would not now fear the French and British nuclear forces which, after all, could obliterate it. A test of whether the standard logic of international politics will continue to apply among the developed states will be whether this fear will emerge. A parallel – and more disturbing – test will be whether Germany and Japan, freed from the security and constraints of the Cold War, will seek nuclear weapons, following the previous rule that Great Powers seek the most prestigious and powerful military weapons available even in the absence of a clear threat. A decision to "go nuclear" would not prove the point, however, if it was motivated by fear of Russia or China.

These dramatic breaks from the past and the general peacefulness of the West are to be explained by increases in the costs of war, decreases in its benefits and, linked to this, changes in domestic regimes and values. Earlier it was argued that specific events sometimes send history into different path. But these changes in the developed world are so deep, powerful, and interlocked that they cannot readily be reversed by any foreseeable event.

The costs of war among developed states probably would be enormous even if there were no nuclear weapons.[21] But such weapons do exist, and by increasing still more the costs of war, they also increase the chances of peace. This much is generally agreed upon. Many analysts believe that mutual deterrence means not only that each nuclear power can deter a direct attack, but also that nothing else can be deterred, i.e., that allies cannot be sheltered under the nuclear umbrella and that "extended deterrence" is a fiction. As argued elsewhere, however, both logic and the historical record indicate that this position is not true. [22] Because inadvertent escalation is always a possibility, a conventional war that involves a nuclear power – or that could draw in a nuclear power – could lead to nuclear devastation.

During the Cold War, the risks of escalation meant that the United States could protect Western Europe even if the West had neither a first-strike capability nor an adequate conventional defence; in the current era, it means that the European states gain some of the deterrent advantages of nuclear weapons even if they do not own them. Because statesman realise that any European war could lead to a nuclear conflagration, aggression and even crises will be discouraged. This sharply decreases the incentives for proliferation; nuclear weapons are not necessary to ensure the security of European states like Germany that lack them, and would not greatly help such countries realise expansionist aims if they should develop them. Because the French and British nuclear forces increase the chance that any fighting in Europe could escalate, they decrease the likelihood of war and so, far from threatening the United States, should continue to be welcomed by it.

Because the expected costs of armed conflict among the developed countries are so high, only the strongest pressures for war could produce such an outcome. Yet it is hard to conjure up any significant impulses towards war. The high level of economic interdependence among the developed states increases not only the costs of war, but the benefits of peace as well. Even in the case that shows the greatest strain – US-Japan relations – no one has explained how a war could serve either country's interest.[23] The claim that a high degree of integration prevents war by making it prohibitively costly for states to fight each other has often been incorrectly attributed to Norman Angell's *The Great Illusion*, and the outbreak of World War I, a few years after this book was published, is cited as proof of the error of the position. But the title of Angell's book gives its actual argument: it is an illusion to believe that war will provide economic gain.[24] The argument was as much prescription as description; the former would not have been necessary had the latter been self-evident. The implications for today are obvious; while the objective facts of interdependence are important, one must also ask how they are viewed by the general public, elites, and statesmen.

Not only the degree but also the kinds of interdependence matter. If statesmen examine the situation with any sophistication, they will be concerned not about the size of the flows of trade and capital, but rather with what will happen to their states' welfare if these flows are halted.[25] Thus, the fact that levels of trade are higher among the developed countries today than they were in 1914 may be less significant than the fact that direct foreign investment is greater and that many firms, even if they are not formally multinational, have important international ties.[26] It would be harder for states and firms to arrange for substitutes if conflict or war severed these financial ties than would be the case if it were only goods that were being exchanged.

The other side of this coin is that continued high levels of economic intercourse may significantly increase each state's wealth. This, of course, is the foundation of the argument for the advantage of open international economic systems, and the post-war history of the developed world is strongly consistent with it. Even those who call for some protection do not doubt that trade is necessary for prosperity. Most importantly for a consideration of the political relations among the developed countries, no one in any of these states believes that his or her country can grow richer by conquering any of the others than it can by trading with it, in part because the techniques of controlling an occupied country are not compatible with making a post-industrial economy function well.[27] People in each country can believe, sometimes with good reason, that their own fortunes would improve more if others do less well or may attribute their difficulties to extreme and unfair economic competition, but this does not mean that they believe that they are likely to thrive if their partners suffer significant economic misfortune.

The belief that one's economic well being is linked to that of others is not sufficient to bring peace, however. Many values are more important to people than wealth. High levels of economic interdependence have not prevented civil wars, although it may have inhibited them; perhaps more internal conflicts would have occurred had countries not been fairly well integrated. This could help explain why modern countries rarely experience these bloody disturbances. Alternate explanations are possible, however, and the Spanish Civil War and the unrest in Yugoslavia, Czechoslovakia, and the Soviet Union at the minimum show that a higher level of economic integration than that which characterises the current international system does not prevent armed conflict.

In international politics, it is particularly true that wealth is not the primary national goal. Not only will states pay high prices to maintain their security, autonomy, and the spread of their values, but the calculus of economic benefit is affected by the international context. While economic theory argues that the actor should care only about how the outcome of an economic choice affects him, those who fear that they may have to fight need to worry about relative advantages as well as absolute gains.[28] Furthermore, states that become more dependent on others than others are on them will be vulnerable to pressure, as the Balkan states discovered before World War II. [29]

Both the fear of dependence and concern about relative gains are less when states expect to remain at peace with each other. Indeed, expectations of peaceful relations were a necessary condition for the formation of the European Common Market; the growth of interdependence in the developed world is as much a symptom as a cause of the basic change in international politics. Had the Europeans thought there was a significant chance that they would come to blows, they would not have permitted their economies to grow so interdependent. The price of greater wealth would have been excessive if they felt their security would be endangered, and so it is not surprising that other regions have not imitated the successful European experience.

When states fear each other, interdependence can increase conflict.[30] Thus there is at least an element of reinforcing feedback in the current situation: interdependence has developed in part because of the expectations of peace, and the economic benefits of close economic relations in turn make peace more likely. The political implications of the economic situation were very different in the early 20th century when Britain and Germany, although trading heavily with each other, each feared that economic endeavours that strengthened the other would eventually weaken its own security. As one British observer put it after an extended tour of Germany: "Every one of these new factory chimneys is a gun pointed at England". [31] The growth of another state's political and economic power now is worrisome only if it causes harm to the first in some direct way; it is no longer automatically seen as decreasing the first state's ability to protect its interests in the next war. Samuel Huntington argues that the answer to the question of why Americans are so concerned about the Japanese challenge is straightforward: "The United States is obsessed with Japan for the same reason that it was once obsessed with the Soviet Union. It sees that country as a major threat to its primacy in a crucial arena of power."[32] But it is far from clear that one state's economic progress constitutes a threat to another unless the two are likely to fight, the former's relative advantage will diminish the other's absolute wealth, or the former will gain leverage it can use in important political disputes. The first condition does not hold in the US-Japan case, and it is certainly debatable whether either of the other two do. Rivalry is different in its meaning and implications when it is conducted with an eye to future fighting than when the interactions are expected to be peaceful. .

The change in relations among the developed states is partly a result of a shift in basic outlook and values. As John Mueller has noted, war is no longer seen as good, or even as honourable, in anything less than desperate circumstances. [33] No Western leader would speak, or even think, in terms like those expressed by Chief of the German General Staff Helmuth von Moltke in a letter to his wife during the 1911 Moroccan crisis: "If we again slip away from the affair with our tail between our legs and if we cannot, bring ourselves to put forward a determined claim which we are prepared to force through with the sword, I shall despair of the future of the German Empire. I shall then resign. But before handing in my resignation, I shall move to abolish the Army and to place ourselves under Japanese protectorate; we shall then be in a position to make money without interference and to develop into ninnies."[34] These sentiments seem archaic; we may now be seeing, among developed states, the triumph of interests over passions, as Angell and Joseph Schumpeter foresaw.[35]

As the Gulf War reminds us, it is not as though developed states do not feel a sense of pride, or even self-identity, in asserting themselves abroad. But the impulse is more episodic than it once was; it is not directed against other democracies, and is more often exercised in the service of economic values than counterposed to them. Part of the explanation for this change is the naming of nationalism, perhaps in the sense of pride, in the achievements of one's nation, and certainly in the sense of a belief that one's country is superior to others and should dominate them. The progress towards West European unification both facilitated, and is made possible by, a weakening of the attachment to one's nation as a source of identity and personal satisfaction. The residual feelings may be sufficient to prevent Europe from completely unifying, but the process never could have moved this far had nationalism remained even at the level of the fairly benign late 1920s, let alone in any other era. It is doubtful if we will see a return of these periods; reduced nationalism is now closely associated with economic and political gains and has been embodied in institutions that have become the focus of power and perhaps loyalty. Nationalism was discredited in some European states (although not Germany) after 1918, but this was because it had brought failure, not that being less nationalistic had produced success.

Change in values is also evident from the absence of territorial disputes. Germans no longer seem to care that Alsace and Lorraine are French. The French, who permitted the Saar to return to Germany in a plebiscite, are not bothered by this loss, and indeed do not see it as a loss at all. The Germans did feel sufficient Germanness to seek the unification of their country, but the desire to regain the "lost territories" to the east seems extremely low. Furthermore, unification was not accomplished against the will of any other country and, unlike manifestations of more disturbing nationalism, did not involve the assertion of the rightful domination of one country over another.

Equally important, the developed states are now democratic and it appears that liberal democracies rarely, if ever, fight each other.[36] Here too values play a large role. What would one democracy gain by conquering another? The United States could conquer Canada, for example, but why would it want to do so when much of what it would want to see there is already in place? Neither security considerations nor the desire to improve the world would impel one liberal democracy to attack another.

In summary, war among the developed states is extremely unlikely because its costs have greatly increased, the gains it could bring have decreased especially compared to the alternative routes to those goals, and the values states seek have altered. Four qualities of these changes are particularly important. First, they are powerful determinations of behaviour; compared to these factors, the influence of the polarity of the international system is slight. Even if multipolar systems are less stable than bipolar ones and even if the future world will be multipolar, it is hard to see how the overall result could be dangerous. The forces of peace among the developed countries are so overwhelming that impulses which under other circumstances would be destabilising will not lead to violence.

Second, the three kinds of changes interact and reinforce each other. The high costs of war permit economic interdependence by reducing each state's fear of armed conflict with others. The joining of economic fates reciprocally gives each state a positive stake in the others' well being, thus, limiting political conflict. But these developments would not have had the same impact were it not for the spread of democracy and the shift of values. These changes in turn support the perceived advantages of peace. If hyper-nationalism and the belief that one's country was destined to rule over others were rampant, then violence would be the only way to reach state goals. If statesmen thought expansion brought national honour, they might risk the high costs of war as an instrument of coercion. So focussing on any one of these elements in isolation from the others misunderstands how and why the world has changed.

Third, many of the changes in West European politics and values were caused in part by the Cold War. The conflict with the Soviet Union generated an unprecedented sense of unity and gave each state an important stake in the welfare of the others. To the extent that each was contributing to the anti-Soviet coalition, each reaped political benefit from the others' economic growth and strength.[37] Since the coalition could be undermined by social unrest or political instability, each country also sought to see that the others were well off, that social problems were adequately managed, and that sources of discontent were minimised. It would then have been costly for any country to have tried to solve its own domestic problems by exporting them to its neighbours. Indeed, since the coalition would have been disrupted if any country had developed strong grievances against others in the coalition, each had incentives to moderate its own potentially disturbing demands and to mediate if conflicts developed between others.

But the end of the Cold War will not bring a return to the older patterns. Rather, the changes are irreversible, especially if the developed countries remain democratic, which is likely. The ties of mutual interest and identification, the altered psychology, whereby individuals identify less deeply with their nations and more with broader entities, values, and causes, the new supranational institutions, and the general sense that there is no reason for the developed countries to fight each other will remain.

Finally, these changes represent time's arrow; international politics among the developed nations will be qualitatively different from what history has made familiar. War and the fear of war have comprised the dominant motor of politics among nations. The end of war does not mean the end of conflict, of course. Developed states will continue to be rivals in some respects, to jockey for position, and to bargain with each other. Disputes and frictions are likely to be considerable; indeed the shared expectation that they will not lead to fighting will remove some restraints on vituperation. But with no disputes meriting the use of force and with such instruments being inappropriate to the issues at hand, we are in unmapped territory; statesmen and publics will require new perspectives if not new concepts; scholars will have to develop new variables and new theories. Although Karl Deutsch and his colleagues explored some of the paths that could lead to the formation of what they called a pluralistic security community – a group of states among whom war was unthinkable[38] – there are few systematic treatments of how countries in such a configuration might conduct themselves.[39]

In other areas of the world, however, we are likely to see time's cycle. The resurgent ethnic disputes in what was once Eastern Europe and the Soviet Union appear much as they were when they were suppressed by Soviet power forty-five and seventy years ago. It is almost as though we had simply turned back the clock or, to change the analogy, as though they were the patients described by Oliver Sacks who came back to life after medication had released them from the strange disease that had frozen them.[40] The prospects for international politics in this region are likely to remain worrisome for quite some time to come – despite the far-reaching changes that have come about in this region.

Most of the arguments made in the preceding pages about the prospects for peace in Western Europe do not apply to the Eastern part of the continent. The latter is not filled with stable governments that have learned to cooperate and have developed a stake in each other's well being. Nationalism and militarism are dangerous, and grievances abound, especially those rooted in ethnic and border disputes — even if Stephen Van Evera is correct to argue that the decrease in social stratification will remove one of the causes of hyper-nationalism.[41] The traditional sources of international strife are sufficient to lead the relations among these states to be permeated by the fear of war.

War is not inevitable, however. Statesmen realise that the costs of fighting are likely to be high, even if the likelihood of Soviet intervention is no longer there. Also powerful will be the new factor of East Europeans' knowledge that economic prosperity depends on access to the markets of the European Community and that such success is not likely to be granted to unstable, authoritarian, or aggressive regimes. Thus, the very existence of the European Community should encourage peace and stability in the East. [42] The West can also support democracy and moderation in Eastern Europe and Russia by seeking to build appropriate institutions, habits, and processes, although the extent of this influence is difficult to determine now that the countries of Eastern Europe have broken away from the former Soviet empire. [43]

Much is likely to depend on internal developments within each country of the region and the way one country develops may influence what happens in others as well. If the forces of nationalism and militarism are kept under control, the chances for peace will be increased. [44] This, in turn, depends in part on the success of the countries' economic programmes. But whether the results are peaceful or violent, the general determinants of international politics in this region are likely to be fairly traditional ones, such as the presence or absence of aggressive regimes, the offence/defence balance in military strategy and technology, and the level of political and diplomatic skill of the national leaders. Our inability to predict the results stems from the fact that we cannot be certain about the values of a number of the key variables. But, with the exception of the pacifying influence of the hope for acceptance by West Europe, the variables at work and the ways they relate to each other should be quite familiar.

Because Eastern Europe is not alone on its continent, the optimism that was expressed earlier about the developed countries needs to be qualified. Probably the greater danger, but still slight, to the peace and stability of Western Europe, and by extension to the United States, is large-scale violence – either international or civil – in Eastern Europe and the republics that once formed the Soviet Union. The power, location, and history of Germany implies that the most disturbing scenarios involve that country, now unified, which could easily be drawn into the East by strife, generating fears that the result, if not the intention, would be German dominance of the continent.

This chain of events seems unlikely, however. Offensive motivations are not strong; neither the West in general nor Germany in particular is likely to see a great deal to be gained by using force against any country in the East which once remained within the Soviet empire. More troublesome would be the threat that unrest in the East could pose to established Western interests. This problem would be greater if and when the West has extensive economic ties to the East, but even under these conditions the costs of using force probably would outweigh the expected benefits. Security could be a more potent motivator in the face of extensive violence. But quarantine probably would be a more effective response than intervention. Violence in the East could also set in motion large flows of refugees that would create an economic and political menace, but there too military force would not be the most appropriate remedy. Ideology might pull the West in; the urge to protect a newly democratic regime could be a strong one. But while active diplomacy would certainly be expected in this situation, force would only be a last resort. In all of these possible cases what would be crucial for the West would be the extent of its solidarity. The danger would be least if any intervention were joint, greater if any one country, especially Germany, proceeded on its own, and greatest if different Western states were linked to opposing factions or countries in the East. To a large extent, then, the West can contain the consequences of violence in Eastern Europe even if it fails to prevent it. Indeed, maintaining Western unity is perhaps the most important function of NATO, and the 1991 discussions of a joint NATO force for potential use in Eastern Europe seem to have been motivated largely by the shared desire to avoid unilateral interventions.

To include all of Africa, Asia, and Latin America under one rubric is to wield an even broader brush than we have employed so far. The crudeness of this residual category is indicated by the name "Third World", which is surely a confession of intellectual failure. That being neither economically developed nor Communist give these countries much in common is to be doubted; the pattern of politics is likely to be different in different regions. Also perhaps, for better and for worse, international politics in Central and South America will continue to be strongly influenced by the United States. International politics among the states of sub-Saharan Africa are likely to continue to show at least some restraint because the lack of legitimacy of borders makes them all vulnerable and, thus, gives them powerful incentives to avoid fighting each other.[47] Furthermore, most African countries have quite weak states; a characteristic that will continue to influence both their domestic and foreign policies by limiting both the resources that leaders can extract and the extent to which national as opposed to personal and societal interests can be expected to prevail.[48]

The question that many would like to ask here may not require much detail: is the end of the Cold War likely to increase or decrease international conflict in the Third World? To put this another way, did the Cold War dampen or exacerbate conflict? It probably did both; dampened it in some areas of the globe, exacerbated it in others, dampened it under some circumstances, exacerbated in under others. In the net, however, it generally dampened conflict and we can, therefore, expect more rather than less conflict in the future. [49]

Many analysts argued that superpower competition spread conflict to the Third World. On some occasions, strife might not have developed at all had not a superpower sought out, or been receptive to, the pleas of a local actor to undermine or at least to preoccupy the other superpower's client. In other cases, conflict would have been less bloody and prolonged had the states or factions not expected that they could compensate for local weakness by garnering increased aid from abroad. Furthermore, the aid itself, especially financial and military, made these conflicts more intense and destructive. The civil war in Angola epitomises these processes, although traces can be found in many other countries as well.

This is only the most visible part of the story, however. The extent to which superpower involvement dampened Third World conflicts is more difficult to discern because it resulted in non-events. But it is at least as important. Each superpower had an interest in seeing that the other did not make significant gains in the Third World, and also realised that the other had a parallel interest. Each knew that under most circumstances, to succeed too well, or to permit its clients to do so, would invite a forceful response. Of course, the Soviet Union in its desire to change the status quo welcomed and assisted disruptive movements and sought clients who, in part because of the nature of their domestic regimes, challenged their neighbours. But often it was indigenous forces that created violence and were restrained from abroad. The civil strife in Sri Lanka and Punjab shows that even without superpower involvement, internal conflict can be prolonged and become bloody. Furthermore, it is no accident that the only protracted armed conflicts in the Middle East were those that did not engage the superpower rivalry (the Iran-Iraq War and Egypt's intervention in Yemen). The Arab-Israeli Wars were short because they were dangerous not only to the local actors, but also to the superpowers who, therefore, had an interest in seeing that they did not get out of hand. In some cases, such as Angola and Afghanistan, extensive superpower involvement was compatible with a lengthy conflict, and indeed may have prolonged it. But when the superpower stakes were great, the area volatile, and the Third World actors not completely under control, the superpowers could not be content to fuel the conflict by indiscriminate assistance but also had to see that it did not lead them to a dangerous confrontation.

The 1991 Gulf War, the first case of major post-Cold War violence, might not have afforded to act as it did had the Soviet Union been Iraq's ally and a threat in Europe. The latter factor would have made the United States unable to deploy such a large military force; the former would have made it fear that a military response could call in the Soviet Union. On the other hand, aggression by a client of the Soviet Union would have been more of a threat than was Iraq's action in the actual event. So the United States would have realised this and might have restrained its client. Iraq's behaviour also would have been different. With Soviet assistance, its need for Kuwait's wealth would have been slightly diminished. Furthermore, to the extent that it acted out of fear of isolation or the hope that the new international constellation provided it with a "window of opportunity", a continuation of the Cold War would have made the aggression less likely.[50]

The superpowers offered security to the Third World clients as well as restraining them. Unless other forces and mechanisms that would serve these functions develop, aggression will be less difficult and, partly for this reason, status-quo states in the Third World will worry more about self-protection. Even in the absence of absent aggressive motives, conflict will often result through the security dilemma: states' efforts to make themselves more secure will threaten others. These traditional sources of international conflict will work themselves out in a context that for at least several years will be changing rapidly as the states seek to adjust to the decreased superpower presence. Indeed, in some cases, weak clients will collapse or be overthrown (e.g., Ethiopia), heightening the possibilities for regional disturbance.

The Third World may not necessarily recapitulate the international history of developed states. What Alexander Gerschenkron showed about domestic politics is true for international relations as well – the countries that go first, change the environment so that the paths of latecomers are different.[51] Even without their Cold War hyper-involvement the superpowers and European states will continue to exert some influence. Third World leaders may also seek to emulate the First, in part in the hope of thereby earning greater aid, investment, and access to markets. Nevertheless, as in Eastern Europe, a decrease in superpower influence will permit more of the display of aggression and mutual insecurity that constitute the standard patterns of international conflict. Nationalism, ethnic disputes, and regional rivalries are likely to be prominent. Undoubtedly, there will be surprises in the details, and specific predictions are beyond reach, but there is no reason to think that the basic contours of international politics will be unfamiliar.

II

Whether or not the new era turns out to be more violent than the Cold War, it will present the United States with a wider range of choices. While the Soviet-American rivalry did not entirely dictate American policy – witness the past forty-five years of vigorous political and academic debates – Americans agreed on crucial questions most of the time; the United States' security needs were the core of its national interest; the Soviet Union was the greatest threat; the United States had no choice but to be actively engaged in the world to protect itself. Even when the answers differed sharply, for example, over whether the Third World mattered to the United States, almost everyone agreed that the question was what policy would bolster American national security.[52] This is no longer the case; the realm of compulsion has contracted and that of freedom of choice has expanded. The reason is not only the collapse of the Soviet Union but also the changes in world politics among the developed countries discussed earlier. If the standard rules of international relations were still to apply, the Soviet Union would be replaced as an American adversary by one of the other most powerful states in the system. But it is hard to believe this will occur in the near future.

Some threats to American security remain: nuclear weapons in the hands of Russia and other states, scarcity of economic resources, and non-traditional menaces such as migration and pollution. While they call for serious attention, they are not likely to narrow the range of American choice nearly as severely as the Cold War.

Although the Soviet Union has disintegrated, Russia will still have a nuclear stockpile that could destroy the United States. Nevertheless, the threat is much reduced even if one concentrates on capabilities and puts aside the enormous change in intentions (which, some argue, can easily revert to hostility, especially as Russian domestic politics changes).[53] With the Soviet withdrawal from Eastern Europe, not only is there little threat to Western Europe, but it is difficult to see how a Russo-American nuclear confrontation could develop. During the Cold War, most analysts did not doubt the American ability to deter a direct attack; they feared a nuclear war resulting from NATO's inability to stop an invasion of Western Europe.

A second threat is the spread of nuclear weapons. Americans used to take comfort in the fact that most potential proliferators were enemies of the Soviet Union - e.g., Taiwan, Pakistan. But with the diminution of the Soviet threat and the increasing awareness that countries like Iraq and North Korea could acquire nuclear weapons, the menace to the United States has increased, at least relative to other threats. Former Soviet clients may at once be more desperate (lacking a powerful superpower patron) and more autonomous (lacking a superpower to restrain them). Even though they are many years away from being able to threaten the United States directly, the day is much nearer when they could menace American allies or present a potent deterrent to American intervention in their region.[54] If Iraq had possessed nuclear weapons, for example, US policy in the 1991 Persian Gulf crisis and war would have been more complicated, to say the least.

The heightened danger of proliferation still provides a great deal of room for freedom of choice, however. The United States can seek to minimise the risk of having to fight a regional nuclear power by minimising its involvement with that country and its neighbours. Alternatively, it can pursue an active foreign policy aimed at discouraging proliferation and deterring the outbreak of dangerous regional conflicts. During the Cold War, the first option was seen as unacceptable because it would permit unhindered (at least by the United States) Soviet access to the region, a concern that is no longer relevant. The Cold War also inhibited a vigorous non-proliferation policy because the United States felt it could not afford to alienate its regional allies, a consideration that is also now less constraining.

Is access to raw materials a central security concern? With the possible exception of oil, it is hard to see how a hostile power could deny any raw materials to the United States. Even oil is dispersed throughout many areas of the world and the ability of a cartel to drive the price up – let alone withhold sales to the West – is limited by the potential availability of alternative energy sources. Thus, even if Saddam Hussein had retained control of Kuwait and gained slightly great influence over Saudi Arabia, the United States would not have been at his mercy. To the extent that dependence on Middle Eastern oil is worrisome, conservation and the development of alternative energy sources would probably be cheaper than maintaining and using military force. During the Cold War, one could reply that America's strong position was simply irrelevant because Europe and Japan were very vulnerable. Now, even if this is true, there are no immediate security reasons for oil to be an American concern, although a major price increase would still be economically disruptive. Furthermore, Western oil exploitation techniques applied to the Russian oilfields should greatly increase the global supply, barring a prolonged civil war in that country or among the successor republics.

New threats to American security may still emerge. A revolution or widespread civil unrest in Mexico could send large numbers of refugees across the border. Although such an event represents the highest combination of likelihood and danger, it is doubtful whether traditional security policies can have much influence on whether this will occur or how the United States could cope with it. This menace, thus, cannot be the premise for many of the guidelines for general foreign policy.

Non-traditional security threats such as global warming, ozone-depletion, and other forms of environmental degradation are also of concern. But the dangers are too far off, the scientific evidence is too ambiguous, the domestic interests involved are too conflicting, and the alternative approaches are too many for these issues to dominate American foreign policy and provide an agreed-upon basis for action as containment did previously.

Even with the new dangers, the United States is now free – and indeed is required – to think much more seriously about how to define its interests. Old questions of both ends and means which the Cold War answered or put in abeyance have returned. What does the United States want? What does it value, what does it seek, what costs is it willing to pay, and what methods are likely to be efficacious? If possible, Americans would like to see the world resemble them or, to put it alightly differently, embody their values.

Thus, the United States seeks a world composed of states that are liberal, democratic, prosperous, and peaceful, both internally and in their foreign policies. In such a world, the United States would probably prosper as well and would have little cause for concern if others grew even richer, since this would neither threaten its security or its self-image. Indeed, Americans desire such a world less for the direct benefits it would bring to the United States than because they believe that it would serve the best interests of all people.[55]

But these generalities do not tell us how active a foreign policy the United States should adopt. Should the United States attempt to influence others by intervention (not limiting this to the military sense) or by example? The latter tradition, overwhelmed and abandoned by the exigencies of the Cold War, has deep roots in American institutions, values, and politics. The desire to be "like a city upon the Hill" is a strong one, having been embraced by liberals and conservatives in different periods of history. That complete isolation is impossible does not rule out a significant retraction of American involvement abroad.[56]

With security concerns no longer pressing, other values must determine how deeply and in what ways the United States should pursue an activist foreign policy. Human rights is a prime example. When the House of Representatives voted to renew China's most-favoured-nation status for tariffs in the fall of 1990, it not only said that this concession would not be granted unless China eliminated major human rights violation within six months, but also permitted the President to waive this requirement if doing so would further encourage China to improve human rights.[57] Compare the Cold War, when it was routine for Congress to attach various conditions to foreign aid bills with the proviso that they could be waived if doing so was in the American national security interest. At least some Americans would like to elevate human rights to this privileged status. Although enhancing its status is not presently national policy, during the Cold War would the American ambassador to Kenya have so publicly criticised that government for its human rights abuses?[58] Even more strikingly, the United States temporarily halted aid to Yugoslavia in May 1991 because of the "pattern of systematic gross violations of human rights" in that country, which in the past had a privileged position as a crucial bulwark against Soviet expansionism.[59]

The United States could also use its new flexibility to promote democracy abroad. To some extent it did this during the Cold War; the "Reagan Doctrine" included support for guerrillas in Afghanistan, Angola, and Nicaragua. But for Reagan, the promotion of democracy meant supporting any non-Communist forces. More often, seeking democracy was seen as too dangerous; the fear of communism meant that the United States supported right-wing dictatorships out of the fear that if they were undermined, the victors would not be democratic reformers but the hardcore left-wing.[60] As President Kennedy said after the assassination of the Dominican Republic's Dictator, Rafael Trujillo: "Here are three possibilities in descending order of preference; a decent democratic regime, a continuation of the Trujillo regime, or a Castro regime. We ought to aim at the first, but we can't renounce the second until we are sure that we can avoid the third".[61] Although the third possibility is still disturbing because it would oppress the people in the country involved, the demise of the Cold War has sapped much of the force of the dilemma Kennedy articulated and allows American Presidents to support democratic movements if they so choose.[62]

The United States could also seek to protect – or more accurately minimise the damage to – the environment. This would have high economic costs, at least as measured by the standard – and perhaps misleading – indicators of well being. Most obviously, curbing the emission of greenhouse gases would slow economic growth. The effort would have to be an international one, and could strain relations with other developed states and require economic concessions to developing ones. But the end of the Cold War makes it possible to give more consideration to such policies. Not only have some resources been liberated by the decline in military spending, that the end of the Russian threat permits, but part of the previous necessity for high economic growth was security in the form of staying ahead of the Soviet Union. Diplomatic capital that was previously required for anti-Soviet policies could also now be employed for environmental issues.

Encouraging domestic economic growth remains an important goal. Foreign policy may need to play an even larger role here than in the past as the pressures on the open international economic system increase due to the diminution of the shared Western interest in maintaining common strength against the Soviet Union. There is now a greater danger of the world breaking into trading blocks, damaging the American economy and increasing political friction.[63] To prevent this, foreign political involvement and even security guarantees may be called for, as Robert Art and Stephen Van Evera argue.[64] But these measures may be neither necessary nor sufficient for the objective. Protectionist impulses have proved weaker than many analysts expected and may not be able to dominate even though proponents of free trade now lack the Cold War rationale. An activist foreign policy in the form of support for and close ties to, trading partners would not reduce domestic pressures for protection unless it produced significant concessions from them, a bargain these countries might reject. Furthermore, concessions to the United States granted in return for security support might contradict the non-discriminatory principles of an open system. Thus while supporting the American (and the world) economy will continue to be an important objective, it is not likely to provide agreed-upon guidelines for US foreign policy or to readily gain pride of place over other values.

An additional continuing American goal could be the prevention of the spread of nuclear weapons, less for narrow concerns about US security than for the desire to spare other countries the horrors of nuclear war. If the former were all that were at stake, the United States could react to Pakistan's nuclear programme by disengaging from the subcontinent. A nuclear war between India and Pakistan would not menace America. Indeed, if it turned out badly for both countries – which probably would be the case – it might discourage proliferation in areas of more direct concern to the United States. But security is not the only value at stake – nuclear war is an evil that is worth a significant price to suppress.

Perhaps the most ambitious goal the United States could seek is curbing, if not eliminating, war. However much this might have accorded with America's deepest hopes, it was out of the question during the Cold War; the intrinsic evil of war had to yield to a consideration of how the American stance towards a particular conflict could affect the worldwide rivalry with the Soviet Union.[65] As the conflict in the Gulf reminds us, the decline in the Soviet power means that the United States need not fear that military interventions could trigger undesired Soviet responses, and it vastly increases the possibilities for collective security. Even before Iraq's invasion of Kuwait, President Bush called for the United States to build such a system: "As the world's most powerful democracy, we are inescapably the leader, the connecting link in a global alliance of democracies. The pivotal responsibility for ensuring the stability of the international balance remains ours."[66]

If collective security is desirable and even feasible, how much should the United States contribute to it? To the extent that the United States takes the lead, it is likely to demand primacy in setting the policy, as it did in the Persian Gulf. But it is far from clear whether other states would tolerate having as little influence as they did in that case. The alternative is a smaller American contribution and truly multilateral decision-making. But how often has the United States been willing to take a very active part in an international venture without playing the leading role? Little of the talk of a new world order asks the United States to bend its conception of the common good to that of other members of the international community. Furthermore, the collective good problem would be harder to surmount if the American contribution was less than dominant. If a sizeable number of states are asked to take relatively equal shares in the venture, each will feel that it can shirk and pass more of the burden to its partners, thereby increasing both friction and the chance that the enterprise will collapse.

The Cold War has freed America from the overriding concern with security and has presented it with a wide range of possibilities. This poses a "necessity of choice" – to borrow the title of a book written in an era when there was actually little room for choice [67]

– because the goals and values are not entirely consistent with each other. Some can be pursued only by slighting others; when the foreign regimes engage in many practices of which the United States disapproves, it will have to choose which of them to most vigorously oppose. For example, if a country seeks nuclear weapons, violates civil rights, and tolerates aggression, the United States and others will have to order its priorities and decide which is the greatest evil. Perhaps in some cases, the United States can help a new regime come to power that will cease all these practices. But this is not to be counted on. Indeed, free elections can produce a regime that follows unfriendly foreign policy and distasteful domestic practices.[68] The problem is illustrated by President Bush's proposal on foreign aid in 1991 which sets forth "five objectives: promoting democratic values, strengthening United States competitiveness, promoting peace, protecting against transnational threats, and meeting humanitarian needs".[69] But the proposed legislation does not prioritise these objectives or explain how to make trade-offs among them.

Many specific conflicts between American goals are possible. The United States may have to choose between protecting some parts of the environment and maintaining good relations with Japan. Continuing friction over fishing, whaling, and importation of ivory may be followed by the need for the United States to decide whether to spend its political capital opposing the extensive Japanese logging of the rain forests of Southeast Asia. In the security area, encouraging European unity would further the chances of peace as well as more deeply embed Germany in a supranational structure. But a United Europe would be a more effective competitor for global influence and economic advantage. The goal of non-proliferation could be furthered at the cost of offering political support to authoritarian and oppressive regimes.[70] Security guarantees could be a potent tool against proliferation, but they would bolster undesirable regimes and unjust borders as also increase the danger that America would be drawn into any war that did break out. In other cases, such as North Korea, the United States might emulate Israel and destroy the nuclear facilities of a would be proliferator. But acting in this way could undermine a collective security system by convincing others that their participation was not necessary, or that the United States was too reckless to provide acceptable leadership. A collective security system, in turn, would freeze the status quo and protect tyrants unless it were supplemented by a method for producing peaceful change and curbing outrageous internal practices.

Collective security was represented and perhaps furthered by the war against Iraq. Maintaining an inclusive coalition displayed great American skill; however, it also came at the price of other American values. Thus, the United States had to alter its stance toward Iran and, even more, Syria, regimes that do not fully abide by the norms of proper international, let alone domestic, behaviour. Furthermore, Syria took the opportunity to consolidate its control over Lebanon, an act of aggression that the United States could not in those circumstances oppose or even protest. Other states with less direct interests in opposing Iraq also may have required significant inducements. Thus, apparently to gain Chinese cooperation in the Security Council, the United States reduced its pressure on the human rights issue.

The Gulf War also elevated overall expectations of what the United States can and should do. As Bush himself said, "Never before has the world looked more to the American people. What makes us Americans is our allegiance to an idea that all people everywhere must be free." Such rhetoric may lay a trap for policy.[71] Just as twenty years ago people asked: "If the United States can put a man on the moon, why can it not end poverty, produce racial harmony, etc?" So now others and American public opinion as well, expect the United States to protect the Kurds, democratise Kuwait, and perhaps bring peace and security to much of the globe. Dashing these expectations may create disappointment and bitterness that will be obstacles to a more modest policy; trying to live up to them would lead the United States to overreach itself.

The costs of leading this coalition will be particularly high if the war – and the way it was conducted – increases anti-Americanism in the Third World, especially in Muslim countries. Such a reaction would destabilise friendly regimes, set back moderate political movements, and decrease support for other American interventions in the Third World.[72] Indeed, if this proves to be the case, this exercise of collective security, far from deterring future aggressors and laying the foundations for a moderate world order, will have increased instability and violence.

During the Cold War, American security policy was marked by what was sometimes known as "the great trade-off" – a deterrence policy that relied on the threat that an all-out war increased the probability of peace, but at the price of risking total destruction if it failed. In the current era, the great trade-off is between America's security and non-security interests. The reduced urgency of the former allows greater attention to the latter. Moreover, while the pursuit of many values would require US foreign policy to be as active as it was during the Cold War, American security could be well-served by minimising military and even political involvement abroad. It is hard to see how the American homeland could be threatened except through commitments and entangling alliances. Furthering the other values discussed above requires promises, threats, and a variety of close political ties abroad, and these may come at some cost to American security.

More specifically, policies that seek to keep the peace in various areas of the world (especially Eastern Europe, and in the Third World as well) incur the cost of increasing the chance that the United States will be drawn into these conflicts if they occur. If the United States cared only about promoting democracy and peaceful intercourse in Eastern Europe, it would become deeply involved in that region, offering aid and investment, seeking to build liberal domestic and international institutions, and even offering security guarantees. But if these policies were to fail and violence were to break out in the region, there would be greater pressure on the United States to intervene, with force if necessary. This would be costly and dangerous. Indeed, the only plausible path to a Russo-American nuclear war is through the United States resisting the reimposition of Russian rule over Eastern Europe or the breakaway republics of the former Soviet Union. Such Russian actions can hardly be seen as threats to American security, however; this war would depend on a drastic extension of American interests.[73] In fact, the NATO recently declared that "coercion or intimidation" of states in Eastern and Central Europe would be a "direct and material concern" to the alliance, although officials also announced that this was not intended as a challenge to Russia.[74] Whether the United States and its European partners will make this a real commitment is not yet clear. Of course, the United States could get the worst of both possible worlds: it could fail to involve itself in efforts that might prevent strife and yet be unable to remain aloof when conflict broke out.[75] After all, President Bush announced that the United States would not intervene to protect the Kurds, but political, and perhaps personal, pressures overcame this stance of self-control.[76]

In sum, the end of the Cold War bears witness both to time's cycle and to time's arrow. Politics among the developed countries will not return to what it was before 1939. The costs of war have drastically increased while the benefits, especially compared with those available from alternative means, have decreased. Part of the reason for the latter change, in turn, is that the values of states and the individuals that compose them have changed. Although such constant factors as rivalry, the security dilemma, and the desire for advantage over others will continue, they are not likely to produce violence. And without the recurring threat of war, the pattern of international politics in the developed world cannot be the same. This is not true elsewhere on the globe. While Eastern Europe and the Third World are not likely to simply recapitulate the West's history from which so many of our theories of international politics are derived, neither should we expect a basic change from the familiar ways in which nations relate to each other.

The combination of the end of traditional threats to American security and the continuation of violence in many parts of the world confronts the United States with a wide range of choice. Without the clear framework that constituted the Cold War, there will be conflicts between security interests and other interests. New possibilities arise but not all of them can be pursued simultaneously. While the new era will be a less constrained one for the developed states in general and the United States in particular, by the same token the intellectual and political tasks are considerably increased. How involved America should be in world politics and what values it should seek to foster – and at what cost and risk – are questions that however, do no longer remain open, unanswered and unaddressed. The answers to these questions are to be found, at least partially, in President George W. Bush's reaction to the terrorist attack on the Twin Towers of the World Trade Center on September 11, 2001 and the subsequent "War on Terror" and the Anglo-US invasion of Iraq in March 2003. These events have been discussed in detail in the previous chapter–"Post Soviet Nuclear Politics".

III

Despite all that has been discussed above, we should not overlook two glaring facts: first, although the Soviet Union has disintegrated, Russia remains a superpower, militarily at least; and second, in the fiftieth year of the age of fission, nuclear bombs abound. Together, the two superpowers have more than 50,000 warheads. Small parts of these two forces could bring ruin to both nations. Britain, France, and China may have a thousand or two among the three of them; comparatively, these forces are small, but the gross destructive power in British, French, and Chinese hands is hundreds of times greater than anything ever found in a peace time arsenal before the atom was split. In terms of what each of these three forces could do to any enemy in an all-out nuclear conflict, they are much more like the superpower arsenals than they are like the capabilities of merely conventional forces in any age. At least two more countries are as close to a bomb as they want to be. India has had an explosion but may not have made significant warheads. The missiles that India has developed only show that it is very likely to become a full-fledged nuclear power. Israel has had no evident explosion, but it would be a most imprudent government which did not assume that if the Israelis should ever decide to use bombs, they would be right at hand.

The forces that have driven governments to have the bomb, and then to have it in large quantities, are not trivial. In each of the first five causes, the national decision to have this weapon was essentially unchallenged. It would take a great revision of basic policy and purpose to change the decisions of Roosevelt, Stalin, and Attlee, to reverse the process of development that governed successive French Prime Ministers through the 1950s, or to change the judgement of Mao that for nuclear deterrence China must be dependent on no one but herself. The decision to have the bomb rests primarily on the deep conviction that it is intolerable to accept a future in which others have this weapon and we do not, where "we" in every case means the responsible leaders and scientists of a nation that will not willingly accept a second rank. Even for Stalin it was not "I" but "we". For the Indians and the Israelis it is different. The bomb for India remains a doubtful prize in that something about this apocalyptically destructive standard of greatness is not truly Indian. The bomb for the Israelis is something they have decided they must have at hand not merely to match or outmatch some nuclear competitor, and not for prestige, but as protection against a continuing and presently non-nuclear threat of national extinction.

To have the bomb was the initial imperative, but soon after having it came the need to have enough. The need has been greatest for the two former superpowers, each concerned with what the other might have or come to have, and each drawn by fear and hope to the pursuit of technological and military "advances", some of them impressive in their raw capabilities and others disappointing. The hydrogen bomb certainly "worked", but effective air defence has been always out of reach for both sides. Bombers are followed by ballistic missiles; MIRVs are added; accuracy improved. Missile defences are planned, then held back by agreement, and then dreamed of again. The complexities of the sets of systems have multiplied, and so have the numbers of warheads.

Both governments found it a heavy task to have what they think is enough. Only intermittently has either side felt that its nuclear position and prospects were satisfactorily sufficient. The Americans felt that way in the first years after Hiroshima, until the rude shock of the first Soviet test. The two sides then competed all through the 1950s, to get the H-bombs and then ballistic missiles. After 1962, the Americans had another few years, perhaps as many as ten, when the Khrushchev-Eisenhower-Kennedy triad seemed safely in place, and enough was enough. But what was enough for the Americans was more than enough to stir a strong Soviet response. The decade between 1965 and 1975 was marked by a massive Soviet build-up, which eventually produced renewed American fear. Since the mid-seventies, Moscow had been less uneasy about the strategic balance than Washington, but neither side had been truly comfortable. In the early eighties, the pace of technological competition and of new deployments had quickened in both countries. Meanwhile, MIRVs on both sides have multiplied the numbers of warheads on strategic ballistic missiles. In the 1970s, a time when the prophets of present danger saw the United States as standing still or even sliding back, the numbers of such American warheads went from 2,000 to 7,000. Only in raw megatonnage has there been even modest restraint on either side. The two mammoth sets of offensive systems now have fewer warheads in the multimegaton class and less total explosive power than they once had. But these reductions tell us more about the irrational megatonnage of earlier years than about present arsenals, which remain excessive on both sides.

The decisions leading to massive and varied deployments have been dominated by the conviction in each government that it could not tolerate the nuclear superiority of the other. In their initial decision to have the bomb, the British and French certainly, and the Chinese perhaps, had a similar conviction that they must not be "behind". But soon all three were forced to understand that it would be hard enough to have a force that no hostile superpower could wholly destroy, so that its survivable reply must be respected. The nuclear powers of the second rank have been governed not by any search for parity, but by their sense of what will allow them self-confidence in their dealings with the superpowers. Their calculations have regularly included the question of the value of these weapons for their relations with friendly nations as well as with the not so friendly Russians.

The competition to develop and deploy nuclear weapons, and fragmentary defences against them, is far less arresting, at the end of the first half-century of fission, than the fact that since the first two bombs were dropped in August 1945, no government has used a single warhead against an enemy. In fact, no government has ever come close. Plans for use and war-fighting doctrines have existed. Moments of danger have occurred, but such moments have been few, and the real risk has been more in what might have gone out of control than in the intentions or desires of responsible leaders. Open atomic threats have been generally ineffective, and their value – even their existence – often exaggerated; in retrospect we have found an instructive difference between doctrine and behaviour, theory and practice, in the time of Dwight Eisenhower. The weapons were secretly asserted to be "as available for use" as any other, and both the President and his Secretary of State, in many ways so different from each other, were agreed on the value of readiness to threaten use. But the real choices of this careful and experienced President tell us a different story – one of respect for the opinions of Asian adversaries and European friends, of steady understanding that nuclear weapons are different, and of close control that was recognised and accepted by all subordinate commanders. In the age of Radford and Lemay, the doctrines in which they deeply believed – that nuclear weapons should be used whenever needed, even in small wars – were disregarded at every moment of choice. A tradition of non-use took over and grew strong, proving itself most conspicuously in the Vietnam War, where the use of nuclear weapons was the one solution that had no serious advocate. The best consequence of that war is that it reinforced the tradition of non-use.

The Soviets did not use the bomb either, and while estimates of Soviet decision making must be made without access to Soviet archives, the public record makes clear the great distance between Soviet nuclear bluster and Soviet nuclear action. There is no evidence that the Soviet Government had ever come close to using even one of its warheads, and no evidence that Soviet bomb rattling had any large effect anywhere. The most dangerous moments might also be the most revealing – moments of confrontation with the United States over Berlin and Cuba, and at a much lower level with China over a long common border. In these moments what is most visible in retrospect is Soviet caution, as clear when the immediate opponent had only a small supply of nuclear warheads, China in 1969, as in facing an evidently superior United States in 1962. The Soviets had faced nothing as painfully unsuccessful as the American effort in Vietnam, but they had encountered reverses at least as large politically: the "loss" of Yugoslavia, the "loss" of Egypt, and the largest of all, the "loss" of China. For the Soviet leaders too, the non-use of nuclear weapons was a strong tradition, and as far as anyone in the West could tell, that shared tradition was as welcome on one side of the Iron Curtain as on the other.

What Thomas Schelling in 1960 first called the "tradition" of non-use is the most important single legacy of the first half-century of fission.[77] Its power was visible in the behaviour of the superpowers, lesser nuclear powers, and non-nuclear nations. No government that has nuclear weapons is now unaware of the enormous political cost of using them for any but the gravest and most obviously defensive reasons. No government without such weapons needs to be easily coerced by nuclear threats from others, because both history and logic make it clear that no government would resort to nuclear weapons over a less than mortal question. Having and not having nuclear weapons are not now a part of the ordinary daily currency of international politics.

The tradition of non-use has strengthened with each decade. It is a long distance from the untroubled choice of Harry Truman in 1945 to the politically compelled decision of Richard Nixon in 1969, that he simply could not make the nuclear threat in Vietnam that he believed he had seen Eisenhower use successfully in Korea. The forces arrayed against breaking the tradition were overwhelming to Nixon in 1969, and they were stronger during the Gulf War.

The existence of the weapons and the absence of their use have their roots in the same enormous fact that nuclear explosions are vastly more deadly than any ever known before. Fear of what these weapons can do in the hands of an enemy has been the driving force in the creation of nearly every nuclear arsenal, and the same fear has been decisive at moments of crisis in producing caution among decision makers.

The United States and the Soviet Union threatened not only each other's existence, but the whole of human future. Only these two governments had moments of direct confrontation in which nuclear danger became a visible reality to all the world. It has been and is still a matter of the greatest importance that these two arsenals should never be engaged against each other.

The double reality is that the arsenals cannot be abolished and that neither country can now build an effective defence of its homeland. For both governments, whatever their leaders may claim to hope, it is impossible to suppose that nuclear weaponry can be altogether abandoned. These two countries possess such numbers of warheads that their abolition could never be verified for sure in either country; they will not let go of the one protection they have found against the warheads of the other. Each arsenal may get larger or smaller, but there had never been any prospect that either side would give up its ability to reply to a first strike by the other. Reagan's personal vision of a space shield that blocks the missiles as a root keeps out the rain is a dream with no basis in technical possibility. Technology makes it possible and mutual fear makes it inescapable that the two great offensive deterrents will remain for a long time to come.

When political leaders in Moscow and Washington thought about nuclear war, what they thought about first was what such a war could mean for their own country, and they understood for more than forty years that this war must not happen. No one in either government could hope to know what the full effect of a nuclear attack on the homeland would be. The "literature" on the physical effects of nuclear explosions is enormous, and in so far as it is honest, it recognises that the subject is surrounded by enormous uncertainty. Only two primitive weapons have ever been used in war, and those two events do not begin to tell us what could happen to a whole society under large-scale assault. Uncertainties about targeting policy and levels of operational effectiveness are equally inescapable. Who knows what kind of attack or response would in fact be ordered at the terrible moment of choice, and who can tell in advance just how many of what weapons would work as their designers intended? The "fog of war" was familiar to Tolstoy in the nineteenth century and to generals and statesmen on all sides in the two great world wars of the twentieth century. But the fog that shrouds the unknown realities of a nuclear war between the two superpowers has wholly new dimensions.

Leaders cannot see through this fog, but they still know all they need to know: that they do not want to bring on their country a nuclear strike. Given the warheads deployed, just one incoming strategic warhead on just one strictly military target – a missile silo perhaps, or a submarine base – would be the worst event for either government since World War II. Ten warheads on ten such targets would be much more than ten times worse, presenting not only immediate and hideous devastation, but questions of the utmost urgency and foreboding about the next decisions of both sides. A hundred warheads, on no-matter-what targets, would be an instant disaster. Still more terrible, a thousand warheads would be a catastrophe beyond all human experience. And all of these things could happen with an expenditure of only a fraction of the weapons ready in each country.

There could be only two situations in which the deterrent power of these appalling possibilities might be overcome. One was the prospect of some defeat or disaster so large and so unacceptable that the hazards of nuclear war would seem preferable. The other was the possibility of a disarming attack on the nuclear systems of the adversary. Let us call one the fear of conventional disaster, and the other the hope of nuclear victory, where both the disaster and the victory were very large indeed. We can dismiss the hope of nuclear victory, because, as we have seen, both sides have ceased to believe in such a prospect, both have been amply deterred in fact. There was no reason for either side to allow any such prospect to the other.

Nor has either superpower ever faced the prospect of any conventional disaster even remotely large enough to provoke the use of nuclear weapons. Each side has carefully avoided that kind of challenge to the other. When we looked at Khrushchev's Berlin crisis of 1958-62, we found that the existence of this nuclear danger, this real possibility, was in itself fully deterrent to Khrushchev himself. We do not have to know just what Eisenhower and Kennedy would have done to know that their Soviet adversary had no desire to find out. A parallel caution on the American side has been so visible as not to require detailed study.[78]

It has become common practice in the nuclear decades not to run such risks. Exceptional cases like the attempt to take West Berlin and the placement of missiles in Cuba are now assessed on both sides as unsuccessful and imprudently dangerous. Nothing could do more for the recognised reduction of nuclear danger than strengthening the conditions that will discourage such adventures. In this connection, it is not trivial that Mikhail Gorbachev made a sweeping and categorical denial of any Soviet desire to challenge the West by force, either in Europe or in the Middle East.[79]

Depriving the other power of any rational hope of nuclear victory has so far proved relatively easy for both governments. We have seen this "second-strike capability" challenged by technological change, and we have seen its sturdiness debated hotly in the years in which many Americans perceived a window of vulnerability. But we have also found no moment since the 1950s when either government could see any prospect of nuclear victory at acceptable cost. From the Geneva summit of 1955 to the time of Reagan and Gorbachev in the late 1980s, political leaders have agreed that a Soviet-American nuclear war would be a shared disaster.

We have seen that early in his Presidency, Eisenhower recognised the importance of second-strike survivability in deterring surprise attack. In his years, the groundwork was laid for the survivable triad-bombers, submarines, and land-based missiles. In the Kennedy years, attention shifted to the next question: "How much is enough?" We have seen how crudely that question was answered by the criterion of survivable second-strike forces sufficient to produce "assured destruction" even after absorbing the strongest possible Soviet first strike. Mathematical estimates of this kind of enoughness changed from time to time that beyond a certain point, when thousands of the most important targets had been hit, the value of additional warheads would be affected by the law of diminishing returns. It was in this brutal sense, that enough was considered enough in 1965. This crude criterion was reinforced by the recognition that there was no way to get and keep a satisfactory capability for limiting damage to ourselves. There was survivable overkill on both sides.

We can make a simpler and still more brutal estimate now when the number of warheads that can survive for a second strike may be five times more larger than twenty years ago, before the multiple-warhead submarine missile. American second-strike forces have been, to put it mildly, ample. By any measure of Soviet appetite for self-destruction, the Kremlin was deterred from getting into a general nuclear war.

So was the United States. Even when the United States had a monopoly, no American political leader was tempted to start a nuclear war with the Soviet Union, and once the Soviet Union had survivable weapons of its own, it was plain that "preventive war" was impossible. There had been an enduring belief that massive Soviet conventional aggression might require a nuclear response, and since 1949, American policy has been to use nuclear weapons, if necessary, in reply to Soviet aggression in Europe. There had been a similar appearance of readiness in relation to Korea since 1953, and in relation to the Middle East since 1979. None of these undertakings reflects a desire to pick a nuclear quarrel with the Soviet Union. From Eisenhower onward, American leaders have understood that any American choice that brought even a small number of nuclear warheads on targets in the United States would be a disaster. Eisenhower and Kennedy accepted the reality of two-way deterrence in years when others with less understanding and less responsibility thought they saw an American superiority with great strategic and political weight. What Eisenhower and Kennedy found conclusive was what could, and must not, happen to the United States.

It is sometimes argued that democracies are more readily deterred than dictatorships, and it is certainly true that under Stalin, there was a Soviet ruthlessness about human life that has no American parallel. But if historically there has been an imbalance in ruthlessness, there is a second imbalance that runs the other way. The people of the Soviet Union – emphatically including their leaders – remember a "merely conventional" war, between 1941 and 1945, that has no match in the American memory. Those who have known the worst of the conventional World War II are the most wary of any World War III. It is an error of the most insensitive sort (and one that is frequent among right-wing analysts) to suppose that this Soviet experience weighs on the side of belligerence and not caution.

The stalemate that kept nuclear peace between the superpowers was so deep and strong that it was not affected by the relative ruthlessness of the two societies or their different experiences of twentieth-century war. What each could do to the other, whoever went first, was more than enough to stay every hand that did not belong to a madman. Leaders on both sides had been sane, and they had also been watched by sane associates.

The imperative of avoiding nuclear war imposed great caution on both governments. In the words of Raymond Aron in 1966, there was a "solidarity of Great Powers against the total war of which they would be the first victims". They remained determined "not to interdestroy themselves".[80]

This mutual deterrence had been steady through more than three decades of dramatic variations in the relative numbers of warhead, in the explosive power of arsenals, in the accuracy and reliability of delivery systems, and in the degree of vulnerability of particular systems on each side. The record makes it clear that the sturdiness of the balance does not rest on having as much of this or that system as the other side. Such partial enumerations are not a good guide to the basic strategic assessments of the political decision-makers on both sides. What each side had always seen in the other was a capability for strategic reply that made it wholly unacceptable to run any avoidable risk of nuclear war. It was, to repeat, what could happen to your own side that counted most. We have found uninterrupted awareness of that danger on both sides, and what demonstrated it most clearly was what each side did not do at moments of real crisis – it did not make any move that could end its own control over nuclear danger. That was the caution we have seen in Berlin from 1958 to 1963, in Cuba in the autumn of 1962, and on the Soviet-Chinese border in 1969. There was no visible correlation between any numerical advantage and this caution.

There was a parallel lack of correlation, throughout this period, between merely numerical measures of strength and what the leaders of the two powers believed about nuclear war. On the American side, the pattern was intrinsically unchanging from Eisenhower to Reagan: there would be only losers in any general nuclear war. On the Soviet side, there was change, but it was not what believers in the importance of numerical superiority would expect. It was Khrushchev, with his forces outweighed and outnumbered, who tried nuclear blackmail, and his generals who wrote of socialist victory in any general war. In 1968, when hundreds of big Soviet missiles were coming on line, it was the military leader, Marshal V.D. Sokolovsky, who warned that the losses of a nuclear world war would be suffered by both sides. In the age of excessive Soviet throw-weight that had followed, the Soviet Government had continually strengthened its assertions on this point, until Gorbachev could say in 1987 that "a nuclear tornado will sweep away socialists and capitalists, the just and sinners alike".[81]

Thus, the leaders of both the United States and the Soviet Union realised that the most important thing that they could do to stay clear of the "nuclear tornado" was to see to it that they had no war of any kind with each other. Here too we have a good historical record to build on. Each government had been extremely cautious about the use of military force against the other. Stalin's blockade of Berlin, and Kennedy's blockade of Cuba, were limited, and neither led to open confrontation. Nonetheless, these examples ought not to be repeated; the real lesson of the crisis over Berlin and Cuba was that neither side should take such risks again.

The avoidance of war meant the avoidance of all steps that could bring the two powers into open conflict with one another.

This left room for contests in which each of the superpowers supported some other combatant, and even for conflicts in which one side was directly engaged against forces, supported by the other, as in Korea, Vietnam, and Afghanistan. But each side had an interest in avoiding a direct military challenge to the other, and the reality of nuclear danger made that interest very large indeed.

This is not to argue that a single battle between regiments or cruisers or fighter aircraft would inevitably mean nuclear war. The interest in avoiding such a war would not end with the first exchange of shots, and both sides would come back to the war-ending problem. Nonetheless, it is easier to avoid escalation before combat than after and the prudence historically displayed by the leaders of both countries in the avoidance of open combat deserves attention and imitation by their successors.

In Europe, this constraint held both sides back behind the borders set at the end of World War II. Each side knew that the other would fight if those lines are crossed, and neither side could have any certainty that the resulting conflict would be contained below the nuclear level. The danger here was not primarily a matter of doctrine or of specific deployments, and there was a certain unreality in debates among "experts" about the precise weapons systems and doctrines that would deter. Deterrence was inherent in what any nuclear power could do if it wanted, and also in the possibility that open warfare might drive one side or both to permit in anger what it would never consider in peace. However, much one may hope and pray that such a war could be kept limited, the danger of unlimited escalation was inescapable.

What has actually happened should not blind us to the significance of what has not. Even more instructive is that the crises over Berlin and Cuba are the military challenges that have not been made in the nuclear years. The Americans made no military response to repeated Soviet acts of repression in areas that mattered more to Moscow than to Washington, and although Moscow continually sought to separate the United States from its friends and allies, most conspicuously in Western Europe, there had been no resort to warfare in the area. Even in Berlin, where

Khrushchev tried atomic diplomacy, the attempt was in the end exposed as a bluff.

The avoidance of war implies the acceptance of coexistence. This proposition had been emotionally hard for many in both countries, but since it was only by war that either one could hope to bring an end to the power of the other, it followed that each must accept the other's existence. Internal change was bound to come – had actually come – to one or both, but change imposed by external force was excluded.

The word "coexistence" was suspect to some Americans because it had sometimes been used to mask Soviet policies that were not benign. Nonetheless, the word itself was straightforward, and it should be remembered that the first man to use it in the National Security Council was George Humphrey, no friend of Communism. What led Humphrey to advocate "a policy of coexistence" in 1954 was the imperative that there should not be nuclear war with the Soviet Union.[82] Both sides had, in fact, been practising coexistence in the nuclear decades, and the prospect that they would continue could be greatly improved by more explicit recognition of what they have gained from the avoidance of war.

The defence of the two Koreas from one another was best assured by the visible unwillingness of either superpower to support hostilities begun by its Korean ally. The Soviets made that mistake once, and their behaviour over a thirty-five-year period argues that they had no intention of making it again. Nor would the United States support South Korea if it should begin a war. The situation was not comfortable, but it was stable, and an American nuclear threat was not the indispensable stiffener that the Eisenhower Administration believed it to be in 1953. So there was no hurry in any formal revision of a long-standing declaratory policy, but it would be right for every American president to examine with care his own view of what kind of policy it would ever be wise to follow in Korea.

A similar inquiry is needed in the still more important case of Japan. In the strategic situation of Japan, so plainly defensive and so clearly defined by the surrounding seas, there was no reason to believe that there need ever be a situation in which only a first use of nuclear weapon could ward off defeat. Japan's self-confidence was never shaken because there were no Soviet invaders in prospect. With good sense on both sides, the Americans and Japanese together could keep nuclear danger out of the Japanese future.

The Middle East was a good place for a firm and early American decision that the United States would not be the first to use nuclear weapons. We have seen wars of many kinds in that region in the last forty years, but none in which there was any call for American warheads. The American alert of 1973, as its authors have acknowledged, was no more than a diplomatic signal in a situation in which there was no desire by either superpower for any direct encounter. In early 1980, after the Soviet invasion of Afghanistan, American fear of further Soviet advance led to the announcement of the so-called Carter Doctrine, which seemed to promise a first use if necessary, but no one had ever presented a persuasive argument that such a use could lead to a good result. The nation which was first to use nuclear weapons in the Middle East ran an overwhelming risk of becoming the long-term loser in the area simply because it would inevitably be held responsible for whatever happened next. The strategic detente of the Middle East required less apocalyptic kinds of strength. Here, as elsewhere in the developing world, it was the political and social stability of the countries of each region that mattered most, and American nuclear weapons could make no contribution to that.

This negative judgement obviously did not constitute a policy. It did not tell us how to discourage Soviet trouble-making of the sort that helped to make Ethiopia a disaster area. Neither détente nor confrontation offered a sovereign remedy in such cases. Many believed that over time it would turn out that neither superpower could hope to bring much of the Third World under its durable control. All sorts of forces – demographic, economic, ideological, and nationalistic – were arrayed against any such result. Otherwise, the study of nuclear danger could tell us very little about such hard areas for American policy-makers as the Middle East or Central America or the Philippines, just as it could not tell the Politburo how to handle its over-extension in Afghanistan and in Africa.

The superpowers did share one great common interest in all countries without nuclear weapons: that such countries should steer clear of nuclear danger by not seeking warheads for themselves. It was realised that it would take much careful work, and a new level of mutual trust, to find ways to advance this common interest more effectively, but the challenge was clear and the rewards would be great. The United States and the Soviet Union cooperated to some degree in the effort to constrain nuclear weapons development in South Africa. The leaders of both superpowers realised that there would be both need and opportunity for further cooperation in pursuing a clear common interest.

As the tradition of non-use grew stronger, the role of atomic diplomacy necessarily shrank. What you could do only at very great risk to yourself, you could not plausibly threaten for any ordinary political purpose. When we add up the achievements of atomic diplomacy, we find a thin record. Khrushchev's bluster won no rewards. Boasts of the power of nuclear warning, as by Truman in his old age to Senator Jackson about Iran, proved to be only imagined war stories, understandable but not credible. We have seen that there must be doubt about the effect of Eisenhower's signals in Korea, and still more doubt about the recollections of Richard Nixon. In the real record the Nixon threats never materialised. Only in the cases of Quemoy and Matsu was there a significant likelihood that a nuclear threat was decisive, a small harvest. The legends of atomic diplomacy had been appealing to those who believed that whoever was "ahead" in nuclear strength would dominate whoever was "behind".

The ineffectiveness of atomic diplomacy was certainly not predicted at the beginning. In 1945, at the end of an enormous war, it was only too natural to suppose that a weapon vastly more powerful than any before it would confer a new level of influence. It would have been astonishing if some Americans had not had that expectation. But the expectation was quickly disappointed, and the same thing happened repeatedly in later years. Both in Killian's report of 1954 and in Gaither's of 1957 there were urgent recommendations for the conduct of a diplomatic campaign designed to bring about a durable settlement with Moscow while the United States still had a clear upper hand in nuclear strength, on the theory that this upper hand could be translated into a diplomatic success. Nothing came of these recommendations. Neither Eisenhower nor Dulles ever showed any political interest in such diplomacy. On the Soviet side the evidence was not so clear, but in the 1970s there was enough Soviet talk about improvements in the correlation of forces to suggest that some Soviet leaders expected political rewards from nuclear strength. But the fact that atomic diplomacy attracted advocates only made the absence of its effective practice all the more impressive.

It was a long way from Khrushchev's nuclear threats to the calm and collected Soviet posture in years of undoubted Soviet strategic strength. Only Gromyko, in the 1980s, was still including nuclear threats in his diplomatic repertoire, trying to frighten Western Europe away from new deployments. In this respect, as in others, Gromyko was a voice from the past. He was also ineffective.

The successful coexistence of these extravagantly overequipped nuclear powers had been possible because there was literally nothing at all – no place, no ally, no "sphere of influence" – where dominance was a truly vital interest to both at once. The Soviet establishment of Communist regimes in Eastern Europe was a basic cause of the Cold War, because it was so sharply at odds with the expectation of the West that victory would mean freedom for all the people Hitler had overrun, but the resulting oppression had not been a cause of real war. Since 1945, there had been many grim happenings in Eastern Europe, and some had gravely affected relations between the superpowers, but there had been, no moment of nuclear danger in this harsh history, because the interest of the United States in these countries was not, and never had been a war-fighting interest. The tension between the sentiment of Americans with ties to Eastern Europe and their national unwillingness to make that part of the world a fighting interest had been a recurrent embarrassment to political leaders who had used words about American concern for "captive nations" that were much stronger than any actions that country had ever been ready to take.

This is not to suggest that it was nuclear danger as such that limited the American interest in Eastern Europe. There is no reason to believe that the United States would have acted more strongly over Hungary or Czechoslovakia or Poland if there were no bomb. Quite aside from the nuclear stalemate, there was no American stake in those countries that compared to the interest of the Soviet Union in maintaining untroublesome regimes in the countries along her Western border, across which invaders had been coming for centuries. This Soviet interest greatly outweighed the strong human feelings of individual Americans with and without ancestral ties to those countries. What happened in Eastern Europe could have a great effect on Soviet-American relations, but it carried no danger of open conflict and, therefore, none of nuclear war.

There was a parallel absence of danger in Western Europe, as long as the countries of that region were self-confident and the tradition of mutual trust between them and the United States was maintained. While the Atlantic Alliance held together, the Russians were not coming. There was need for armed forces and need for nuclear deterrence, but these requirements did not have to pass the tests imposed by defence analysts professionally preoccupied by the possible outcomes of an extended war. The Soviet Union wanted no war of any kind in Western Europe – easy pickings yes, but open warfare no. The Americans needed the Atlantic Alliance to make it clear to them and to themselves that there were no easy pickings. NATO had never been as strong in military terms as its professional commanders would like, but it had never come close to failure.

It is not easy to understand the role of nuclear weapons in Europe. The primary nuclear deterrent was American, while the primary exposure was not. It was the countries nearest to the Russians that most needed protection, and none of them had its own nuclear weapons. There had also been a mistaken belief that the American nuclear umbrella could be protective only if the Americans continued to have strategic superiority. That notion was both a natural historical inheritance and a misleading export of politically naive American strategic analysis. We have seen that for statesmen there had been a basic strategic standoff since the

1950s. It had been recognition of nuclear danger and not respect for American nuclear advantage that had ensured prudence in Moscow.

What established this deterrent danger was not American doctrine, and not American nuclear warheads in particular locations, but the American military presence there and the American political commitment which it represented and reinforced. The decision to use nuclear weapons would never be easier in Western Europe than anywhere else, and that theatre offered no more promising outcome for any first use of these weapons than any other. But where there was a serious American engagement, there was inescapable nuclear danger in any Soviet aggression – more than enough to deter. The American engagement that was enough to defend West Berlin in 1958-63 was enough to defend Western Europe later.

A defence based on nuclear weapons alone would not sustain the self confidence of Western Europe: it would not persuade those nearest to the Soviet Union that no Kremlin leader would be tempted to try for easy pickings. Conventional forces were indispensable. There was a continuing need to keep them respectably modern and well trained, and in the future as in the past, governments would do less than their military commanders would like. But these forces were no mere trip wire. They were a guarantee that aggression against Western Europe would mean war between the superpowers, with all the risks that were inherent in that.

It was sufficient to recognise this nuclear danger as a reality, and better not to attempt judgement in advance as to where or how a president might ever give the nuclear command. In fact, different presidents had different doctrinal preferences, and every president had been careful. There were vulnerabilities in every clear-cut doctrine. It was argued by some that it would be much better if NATO would provide itself with conventional strength so great that it could formally and confidently adopt a policy of no first use of nuclear weapons.[83] However, it had become plain that America's European allies would not make the balancing conventional investment because they did not think it necessary.

They did not think that Soviet conventional strength was evidence of Soviet intent to make war against the West, and on the record they were right. In this situation, it was well that awareness of nuclear danger should persist on both sides, as indeed it would even if there had been a full exchange of pledges on no-first-use.

An important less-than-nuclear deterrent in Europe was the enduring cost to the Soviet Union of any move to change a border by force, even if large scale war should be avoided. Even such a limited grab would have the effect that Acheson foresaw in a successful Soviet coup at Berlin. It would galvanise the West and impose on the Soviet Union the increased danger to her own security that her policy in Europe was designed to fend off.

The most important purpose of the Western alliance was to underpin the political independence and self-confidence of its own members over the long run. The Soviets hoped for gains in Europe, but the gains they sought were political. In the words of Sir Michael Howard, the American military presence was needed in the first place "not just in the negative role of a deterrent to Soviet aggression, but in the positive role of a reassurance to the West Europeans". Initially it was feared in Europe that there might be no general recovery of war-torn societies. But recovery came, and Western Europe had never had a better forty years. Yet the American role persisted to make deterrence credible and reassurance strong. In this situation, it was both unseemly and destructive for American leaders to parade a feat of aggressive eight-foot Russians as so many had done in the past. Michael Howard made his classic statement when this rhetoric was at its worst, and he made the point with painful clarity. American propaganda on the Soviet threat and the need for massive rearmament was spreading more fear than encouragement, until in 1982 it was "against the prospect of nuclear war itself" that the Europeans required reassurance. That reassurance could come only from the President of the United States, and the basic message was as simple as this: "We are here, and the Russians are not coming".[84]

American leaders could also reassure Europe by reaffirming the reality and the value to the West of détente in Europe. We have seen that détente was the first line of defence for West Berlin, and the American Government had been uncharacteristically modest in not claiming credit for its own contribution to that result. Détente in Europe was not yet as strong as it should have been, and what happened in 1980 to Solidarity in Poland had an inescapably chilling effect on East-West relations. But in Berlin and in the two Germanys, détente endured, and even the wall began to look out of date. The Soviet Union could destroy European détente in a day, but only at great cost to itself. In the hands of the self-confident, détente was an important deterrent.

There was one further element of great potential importance in the security of Europe: the nuclear weapons of the British and French. We have seen how these weapons were developed for reasons of national self-esteem, and we have seen also that their day-to-day political utility had been small. But it is wrong to suppose that they had no bearing on the possibility of a crisis caused by open Soviet aggression in Europe. There had been no such crisis since 1945, and indeed no hint of Soviet aggressive action since the pressure on West Berlin was relaxed in 1963. The relatively low importance of British and French weapons in the Berlin crisis does not tell us much about the future, because these forces, especially that of France, were then small, and also because that crisis was by its very nature a test of American political will. It would be another matter if the Soviets should threaten open armed aggression against any part of NATO. The Soviet Government would then have to ask itself what it would say about peace and war, not only to Washington, but also to London and Paris, and it was a clear probability that it would wish to offer peace and immunity from attack to all three. Any such offer would be potentially divisive, but it would also be a demonstration of the deterrent value of all three Western nuclear forces. It would, therefore, constitute a reminder to the three governments that their weapons could be daunting to Moscow just as far as the will of each government could believably reach.

Like other possessors of nuclear weapons, the British and French decided to have them long before they considered the design of delivery systems or the possible choice of possible targets or even the question of the occasion that might justify the use of the weapon. Neither the promoters of these forces nor their critics had a notable record of analytic foresight as to what they would be good for. To men like Churchill and De Gaulle, such analytic questions were trivial compared to the basic point that their great nations must not be absent from this rank of power. But the simplicities of the early years might not be good enough for the future, as indeed they were not for the Americans either. The British and French nuclear forces were facing a requirement for modernisation with costs and complexities that required a new attention to questions about their value and especially their connection to deterrence in Europe. The balance of opinion was not the same in the two countries, and the channel remained politically wide. Western Europe had not developed the political coherence that great men sought in the first post-war decades. Moreover, nuclear weapons could easily breed inter-allied mistrust. Ingenious nuclear "solutions" like the multilateral force had not always been helpful.

The growing community among former enemies suggested how much shared concern there was among Britain and France and their West European allies. The choices ahead in the two nuclear weapon countries were choices for leaders in London and Paris, and the historical record did not encourage unsolicited advice from the Americans. The United States had sensibly learned to accept what it could not prevent. There was a long-standing public partnership with Britain, and the connections between the United States and France on these matters had been closer than either government had chosen to say. It would be better for all these countries and for their friends if they would tell the truth about their relationships. The general security of the West could be considerably reinforced if it turned out that there were affordable solutions to the open question of the future of British and French weapons. Such solutions could reinforce both national and European self-confidence. To put it modestly, the nuclear protection of Western Europe was no longer dependent only on the political will of the American president.

Yet the American connection remained essential, and it was unlikely that European nuclear weapons alone would make it sensible for the Americans to disengage. There was a particularly strong connection between the American deterrent and the political stability of West Germany. There had been recurrent shocks in relations between Bonn and Washington, most of them caused by American insensitivity. An American government which put reassurance and détente ahead of fear and confrontation had no great trouble repairing such temporary damage. As long as Western Europe was politically self-confident, respectable in conventional strength, and properly reassured by British, French and American presence, or even American presence alone, the Atlantic Alliance was sure of peace.

IV

A closely related but neglected proposition was that even if a nuclear war began, no matter how or by whose choice, the ending of that war would become an enormously important objective for both sides. One reason for this neglect was reluctance to confront the reality that since Ronald Reagan was entirely right when he said that "a nuclear war cannot be won", any nuclear war would have to end without victory for either side – by some joint decision of the contestants, both of whom would be losers. The prospect was deeply unattractive to many Americans in and out of uniform – and probably to many Soviets too. In the relatively marginal case of Vietnam, American acceptance of failure came with the greatest reluctance and only after great national suffering. Bias against peace without victory was deep-seated, so deep-seated that many analysts were unaware of their own subjection to it and therefore, unable to confront the fact that once a nuclear war began it would be disastrous for both sides to let the exchange get worse. Nuclear escalation could lead only to a shared and expanding disaster. It follows that the least bad thing that the combatants could do was to stop. Their chances of achieving this result would be uncertain at best – which was, of course, why neither one would ever have got into this terrible situation on purpose – but those chances would be better if there continued to be leaders on both sides who could communicate with each other and with their own nuclear forces.

Consider the case of ending a nuclear war begun by the Soviet Union. What response or lack of response had the best chance of bringing such a war to an end? Nobody could be confident of the right answer to this question, but there could be no doubt that the question itself was the right one. Once a nuclear war had begun, it was literally a vital interest for both combatants that it should, and before it got totally out of control.[85]

One way to think about the right answer was to try to see what answers would probably be wrong, and the most obvious answers of this sort would turn out to be ones routinely suggested by analysts of nuclear escalation. Given that each side had enormously redundant capabilities for destruction of all kinds, the one plainly suicidal course was to go on raising the stakes. The better choice then might be to reply at a level more moderate than that of the initial attack. It is even conceivable that there could be an attack that should receive no nuclear reply at all. The president who chose not to reply with nuclear weapons to a single limited nuclear strike – a single warhead, perhaps, at a single strictly military target – might well be both wise and brave. It is well to remember that when Kennedy held back from instant reaction to the unauthorised Soviet attack on Rudolf Anderson's U-2, he turned out to be right.

But let us turn to the question of the shape of a second strike designed for war ending; that would be the response that required nuclear plans and capabilities prepared in advance. This subject engaged the serious attention of many analysts, and, complaints against plans for excessively destructive retaliation came as often from believers in nuclear victory as from disbelievers in nuclear deterrence. A strong argument made by many was that there was a compelling difference between having a survivable capacity for assured destruction, a powerful deterrent to war of any kind between the superpowers, and a decision to inflict that destruction after deterrence failed. The chance that a full retaliatory strike would be an act of national suicide was appallingly high. But it is hard to suppose that a large-scale nuclear attack on Americans or their allies could wisely be left with no reply at all.

For illustration, let us assume an attack in which twenty or thirty warheads, aimed at military targets at home or abroad, had killed two hundred thousand people – the numbers are deliberately arbitrary. In nuclear terms, this would be a small event, but in ordinary and human terms it would be enormous. What response could be the best chance of ending the war?

Many would certainly believe that the answer to this question might lie in recognition of the most important underlying political reality of any nuclear exchange, that each side must be vastly more distressed by the warheads it received than pleased by the warheads it delivered. For this reason, the nuclear strike in our example could be made a dreadful disaster for the enemy by a response that was clearly and visibly smaller than the initial attack. Let us suppose that the victim made a reply with half as many warheads – ten or fifteen, also aimed at military targets, preferably lower in yield, and designed to kill fewer people, indeed just as few as possible. Such a reply should be entirely sufficient to demonstrate the urgency of an immediate cease-fire, and such an immediate cease-fire, no matter who had gained or lost what before the nuclear exchange began, would be the best available next step for both sides. Further use of nuclear weapons by either side could only lead on to further replies in which both sides would have further terrible losses.

In any situation in which nuclear weapons were being used by the two superpowers, no matter how it started and no matter how small the first use, the notion of victory in the traditional sense would be an illusion. In a world with thousands of survivable weapons on both sides, there could be no such victory. In this situation, a strategy that was visibly not one of escalation presented a clear-cut invitation to stop. No one could guarantee that the invitation would be accepted; any nuclear war would have among its hazards the possibility that one side or the other or both, once the horror began, might be unable to recognise the commanding shared interest in a cease-fire. Therefore, it may be stated that a less-than-equal reply would have a better chance of eliciting a rational response than any reply that would enlarge the scale of destruction.

The less-than-equal reply has one further advantage: it fits the requirement that one's own arsenal must never be exhausted. In a war of full-scale retaliation, there is a real danger of early exhaustion. Strategic planners are familiar with the traditional double requirement that a second strike must be as effective as possible against enemy strategic power and that ample reserve must be held back. They also know that no single strike, first or second, could disarm the enemy; effective damage limitation is beyond their reach. So they are led to plan very large attacks that will not bring victory. Planners can try to escape this difficulty by calling for more procurement, but the trouble is that even if their calls should be answered even more abundantly, both the number of targets and the unknown location of many of them will always outrun the planners' capabilities. In the world of strategic parity, the planners have always had enough for deterrence, but never enough for victory. In that situation, the attempt to win is the way to suicide.

Strategic stability between the superpowers, as we have seen, did not depend on a closely calibrated equality of their nuclear forces. We have not bedeviled our discussion with extended statistics on weapon systems, but we have seen that ever since each side had a substantial second-strike force, neither had ever believed that it had a usable nuclear superiority, and neither had any significant success with atomic diplomacy. It had been clear to both governments that in a general strategic exchange, the result must be Aron's "interdestruction" of both countries. Given survivable overkill on both sides, there was a parity of moral danger that was not sensitive to this or that specific difference in numbers of warheads or megatons. At the strategic level, what McNamara called "the band of parity" was wide.[86]

To understand this reality was also to understand that it was not sensible to allow decisions on strategic forces to be governed by the false perception that measures of marginal advantage had the kind of weight that we assume when we count the pawns in chess games of the tanks and battleships in conventional arms races. Only too often responsible men had allowed themselves to be persuaded that such perceptions were a good argument for new deployments not otherwise required. But the demands on the national budget were such that it was foolish to let false perceptions cost the country tens of billions of dollars; it was cheaper and better to correct the false perceptions. It was obviously essential to maintain sufficient survivable strength, but beyond that level, no matter what the other side did, the right thing to do was to talk sense and save money.

This is not to suggest that there was no case for nuclear modernisation. Strategic survivability itself could require change – as in the move away from MIRVs in silos that had been so intensely resisted by the friends of the vulnerable MX-In-Minuteman. There was also a need for capabilities much more discriminating than those designed primarily for large-scale use. The President, in search of the right reply to a small nuclear attack – not a likely event in the historical record, but entirely possible – would not wish to fire large salvos, whether or not he saw value in a less-than-equal strike. The nuclear forces of the United States should have a modest number of single warhead weapons of low yield and high accuracy, precisely to encourage nuclear war ending. Quite possibly, such forces could be designated from among the systems already on hand or on order. In modest numbers, such weapons would not change the stable strategic balance of the superpowers, but they could well provide the right answer to any "small" first use by anyone. There was also great promise in highly accurate conventional weapons, and the importance of the tradition of non-use gave them a special importance for use against all kinds of less-than-nuclear aggression.

American understanding of the strange realities of nuclear strategy was strongest among military professionals. There were great difficulties in their way, and, of course, there were military strategists as wrong-headed as any civilian. The problems of analysis were forbidding, and so were the problems of tradition. The targeting priorities of the 1950s rested on convictions deeply rooted in air force experience and a balance of forces very different from later reality; plans were designed for the knockout victory that would be wholly out of reach, say, in the seventies and eighties. But military professionals had not missed the new realities of the age of bilateral overkill. They were the ones who now knew best the limitations of existing plans, and they had long recognised that communication, in the widest sense of the word, was more important even than accuracy. They also understood that nothing in the continuing technological revolution lessened the vital deterrent role of strategic nuclear forces. Even when earlier commanders thought they could win strategic victory, the political purpose of that ability was always deterrence – that the war should never happen. The requirements for professional dedication, skill, and integrity were if anything greater then ever. It is difficult to improve on a comment that President Kennedy made to air force cadets in 1963. He was dealing with the notion that air force officers of the future would be "nothing more than silent silo sitters", and he was assuring them that "nothing could be further from the truth". He commented:

> The fact that the greatest value of all of the weapons of massive retaliation lies in their ability to deter war does not diminish their importance, nor will national security in the years ahead be achieved simply by piling up bigger bombs or burying our missiles under bigger loads of concrete. For, in an imperfect world, where human folly has been the rule and not the exception, the surest way to bring on the war that can never happen is to sit back and assure ourselves it will not happen. The existence of mutual nuclear deterrents (*sic*) cannot be shrugged off as stalemate, for our national security in a period of rapid change will depend on constant reappraisal of our present doctrines, on alertness to new developments, on imagination and resourcefulness, and new ideas. Stalemate is a static term and not one of you would be here today if you believed you were entering an outmoded service requiring only custodial duties in a period of nuclear stalemate.[87]

Yet military men could not have sole responsibility for nuclear weapons policy. From the very beginning, this subject had been presidential. Congress has also had a great role, but nuclear doctrine, assessment of nuclear danger, and above all decisions on use or threat of use have always been presidential. In this situation, nothing was more important than sustained understanding between the president and the decision-makers in the Pentagon, and nothing had been harder to achieve.

Let us look again at the hard question of the nature and purpose of any American use of nuclear weapons if nuclear war did come, "if deterrence fails", in the deceptively cool phrase of the experts. On this hard matter, there had been no clear understanding

between presidents and planners. Such understanding was not easy
to get when targets were given sharply different values or when
officials disagreed about when the United States itself should begin
nuclear warfare. It is well to remember how Eisenhower and
Radford, united in warm mutual respect, treated each other as
allies within the government on this subject. Nonetheless, they
had different priorities when they were faced by choices in
Indochina or on the offshore islands. We have seen that when
Robert McNamara set up the criterion of "assured destruction" as
a measure of what was enough, neither he nor the two Presidents
he served ever succeeded in tackling the next question: just which
strategic attack should be ordered in this or that situation?
McNamara instead reached the conclusion that the United States
must never go first and that the Soviet Union was amply deterred.
He shared his second judgement with the world and his first only
with the two Presidents.

In later administrations there were new efforts to refine strategic
nuclear doctrine, but a gap remained between presidents and planners.
The doctrinal adjustments approved by later presidents were the result
of serious analytic efforts, especially under Defence Secretaries James
Schlesinger, in the Administrations of Nixon and Ford, and Harold
Brown, in the Administration of Carter, but there was still much
distance between all these conceptual adjustments and the world in
which strategic planners tried to translate doctrine into operational
plans. There had been fault at both ends of this line of communications
– too much possessiveness at the Strategic Air Command, and not
enough sustained attention from commanders in chief. But fault was
not the point

The question was how to do better. Here it was thought by
many that the starting point must be in a new effort to connect
the political objective of avoiding nuclear war with the military
ways and means of maintaining effective deterrence. The crude
control that all American presidents had retained, both over broad
levels of procurement and over final decision on use, was not in
itself sufficient for long-term safety. Both strategic plans and crisis
management, when technology imposed complexity, and rapid
choice might be imperative, required a better connection between

political authority and military choice than there had been in any administration so far, and the necessary attention and effort must come from all concerned, especially the president himself.

There were three specific situations in which the role of the president could be critical. First, only the president had the standing to make choices that affected the balance of responsibilities and resources among the military services, and such choices were necessary as technology affected what could survive. A strong secretary could make recommendations, but only the president could make them stick and had them respected. Second, only the president could explain with authority what nuclear options he did, and did not, want in the event of a desperate need for choices. The distance between strategic plans and real presidential needs could be a convenience for both sides in ordinary times, but it could be catastrophic at a time of necessary choice. Third, it was important that in any crisis there should be firm presidential control over all actions that could lead an adversary to fear an imminent attack. Sometimes such measures were important to ensure survivability – one example was the aircraft on air alert – but no president would want any command to make its own decisions, as the Strategic Air Command did in the missile crisis, about the signals it wanted Moscow to get.

It had not been easy to get the truth told clearly in nuclear matters, and failure on this front had led to mistakes and danger. Advocates of this or that preferred policy had often been careless with the truth, but the best place for truth telling and the worst place for its absence had been the White House.

Roosevelt made two central decisions: to make the weapon and if possible, not to consider what to do with it until later. The first decision was better than the second. It is not easy to see what would have been gained by a public discussion of the Manhattan project before the time of Roosevelt's death, but what was also missing here was any internal process by which there could be serious consideration of the choices that were so incompletely studied in the short time between Roosevelt's death and Truman's decision. That internal process was wholly blocked in Roosevelt's last months by the interaction of his established policy of secrecy, his insistence that policy decisions must be his alone, and the weariness that he and Stimson shared. What we know of his own state of mind is too little to tell us what would have happened if he and his advisers had addressed the nuclear question as they addressed other strategic choices, but we know enough to regret this empty page of history.

The presidents of the nuclear age have a mixed record in seeking and telling the truth about the United States' nuclear predicament. They have all understood nuclear danger, and the attacks on Hiroshima and Nagasaki have remained exceptional. The tradition of non-use owes much to American presidents, and it is striking that in all the nuclear debates there has been no serious interest in proposals to shift the final responsibility for the command and control of these weapons away from the president. Yet we must note the mixed record of American presidents, in both public exposition and assuring the careful analysis of choices within the government.

Roosevelt kept it all too much to himself. Truman was too quick in his judgements. Eisenhower's theory and practice were different in ways that confused both citizens and commanders, and later he failed to make it clear why he was right about the absence of a missile gap. Kennedy understood the danger better than he explained it, and missed a chance to make it clear that no one could be "number one" in this field. Johnson recognised as well as any political leader what nuclear weapons were not good for, but both in choices and in explanation of them, he and his lieutenants were less effective. Nixon recognised that sufficiency was a much better term than superiority, but he was genuinely confused about atomic diplomacy, and neither he nor Kissinger was even remotely straightforward. Ford understood nuclear danger, but he had too little time, and he did not seize his one big chance to lead in finishing SALT II and taking it to the country. Carter understood nuclear danger in both human and technical terms, and his Secretary of Defence was honest and intelligent, but the decisions of his Administration were constrained both by excessive secrecy and by imperfections in such inherited undertakings as the SALT II Treaty and the MX missile. Reagan understood one big thing – that a nuclear war must never be fought – but he failed to understand many other things that were not small, and he left to his successor a record of internal confusion and public misinformation which was the worst Americans had so far.

This inheritance offered the next president an opportunity to reestablish a truly presidential capability for analysis and decision. This means, among other things, that he should seek the kind of technical counsel that Eisenhower and Kennedy got from the President's Science Advisory Committee, although he should certainly not replace one set of precommitted advocates by another, or imitate Reagan by appointing biased advisory committees to give surface respectability to positions already uncritically adopted. He could connect the presidency to military advisers in a way that no president has yet done in nuclear matters, and here the best model may be Franklin Roosevelt as a "conventional" commander-in-chief.[88] The President as commander-in-chief had been missing all too often in the planning, the procurement, and the doctrinal guidance of nuclear defence policy.

One wide-open opportunity was the chance to discard the process of selective truth telling that became a national disgrace under Reagan and Weinberger. The country and the world needed good data on the complex realities of nuclear weapons, and it was a scandal that the fearful official propaganda of the 1980s had required regular and authoritative correction from analysts outside the administration. Nothing would do more for confidence and understanding than a determined official effort to tell the truth, for example with respect to SDI – the Strategic Defence Initiative.

The presidents of the United States would have done well to realise that truth telling would help in dealing with Congress, with allies, and with the Kremlin. The United States had repeated troubles on all three lines, and we have also seen moments of clarity and renewed understanding. It, however, need not be supposed that all the difficulties could be resolved by improved communication, but neither should the costs of failure be forgotten.

There was obviously a parallel value in straightforward communication from the other end of the line. There had been folly as well as wisdom in the work of Congress. There had been weakness in the communication from the allies to the United States, as from Washington to them. American communication with the Soviet Union had been gravely hampered by the Soviet belief that the less any adversary knew about Soviet capabilities, the better for the Soviet Union, a dangerous illusion which tied a persistently negative effect on nuclear stability in general and arms control negotiations in particular.

The historical record does not show us that arms control could be expected to remove all nuclear danger, but it does show us that it could help. Acheson and Lilienthal and Oppenheimer were right in their conclusion of 1946 that the elimination of nuclear weapons would require an international authority with reliable monopoly over the ways and means of making them. Unfortunately, their proposal was wholly incompatible with the political reality of the time. One great state had a temporary monopoly that it would not surrender except on conditions that a second great state was wholly determined not to accept. We have also seen that none of the states now having clear access to nuclear warheads had been held back by any outside influence. But these sweeping conclusions do not tell us that arms control was a failure, only that its success must be measured by less absolute standards. Has the effort for arms control helped the two superpowers toward stable coexistence? Has the effort to limit the spread of nuclear weapons helped in some countries to prevent a decision to have warheads? The answers of some analysts would be cautiously affirmative. The superpowers have been helped by their agreements, and the world as a whole has been less dangerous than it would be if there were not a serious and growing awareness, worldwide, that there was both danger and cost in seeking national nuclear arsenals.

Arms control agreements have been hard to get, politically vulnerable, and, so far, limited in scope. For both superpowers, the acceptance of agreement had always required assurance that the basic deterrent balance would be preserved, and it was no accident that limits on atmospheric testing and on strategic defence had been easier to get than limits on offensive deterrent forces. There had also been grave issues of confidence – especially the American fear of cheating by the Soviets, and the Soviet fear of technological breakout by the Americans.

It remains possible to establish a stronger and more sustained process for doing what the Americans had done only episodically in the past – identifying and reaching agreements that were helpful to both sides in reducing danger. The greatest of these dangers was that changes in deployment might weaken the common confidence that neither side had any interest in resorting to nuclear war. The threat to this shared confidence presented first by the excessive deployment of large Soviet silo-based missiles and then by the possibility of American space-based strategic defence was precisely what gave attraction to the grand compromise that seemed attainable. [89]

Arms control of this sort could never be a substitute for the attention to nuclear danger and nuclear reality that was required of presidents and their subordinates, but as the imperative of coexistence became more clearly understood in both governments, the role of careful and substantial arms agreements could be enlarged.

Nor should the two sides have limited themselves to the formal treaties. Treaties were not the only way to get ahead, and the treaty process in the United States allowed a minority of the Senate to block progress. Given the wide band of parity, there was room on each side for unilateral moderation. It could save money and leave real parity intact. Each side could make choices of this sort that were at once advantageous to itself and encouraging to the other. This was what Kennedy did in 1963 when he decided not to match the second set of Soviet tests, and it was what Gorbachev did in the field of conventional arms. A process of this sort could go a long way to undo the damage their strategic competition had done to the political relations between the two superpowers. Gorbachev had it right when he said that the arms race was the most important obstacle to good Soviet-American relations.[90]

It cannot be taken for granted that the years of Gorbachev were a time of major progress in arms control or indeed Soviet-American relations. Nonetheless, there was good reason for hope. At the very least, it made sense for the United States Government to make progress of this sort a primary objective. The Soviets and Americans could make good progress through the recognition of the underlying realities that made stable and self-confident deterrent strong, and neither could accept less. The interest of the United States in stability had been equal. No one on either side could want mutual assured destruction to happen. Fortunately, both sides realised that they must prefer mutual assured deterrence. It was in this way that they could let MAD have that less confusing meaning, and the people everywhere could call it SANE for survivable adequate nuclear effectiveness. Best of all, the two sides could forget acronyms and simply recognise their overwhelming common interest in avoiding Aron's "inter-destruction".

We can come to the conclusion of our discussion by asserting once again that it is impossible to predict the future course of international relations and the shape of nuclear danger that may confront mankind, the collapse of the Soviet Union notwithstanding. It must also be recognised that the possibility of nuclear war has not been eliminated with the events that have taken place in the Soviet Union after the fall of Gorbachev. Although nuclear realities cannot be wished away, there are now good reasons for hope that the world will be a much safer place to live in. Our survival in the first fifty years of danger offers encouragement to renewed pursuit of truth, resolute practice of courage, and persistence in lively hope.

Obviously, hope alone does not of itself produce safety. Real reductions of risk come only from real choices. Moreover, technological and political change, from one decade to another, will always require new choices. No one can tell today whether the risk of catastrophe will go up or down in the future, and still less can anyone predict the wisdom or folly of future decision-makers.

If we judge by history, it is right to expect that our progress away from nuclear danger will be slow and not always steady. It is wrong to hope for an immediate twenty-foot jump when ten is the best on record. Yet it is also true, as men like Bohr and Oppenheimer understood at the beginning, that the terrible power inside the nucleus offers hope as well as peril.

V

In an article, published on the eve of the 1995 Review and Extension Conference of the Parties to the Treaty on the Non-Proliferation of Nuclear Weapons held in New York from April 17 to May 12, John D. Holum, who worked on arms control and foreign affairs issues at the State Department during the Carter Administration, related the apocryphal story of the young man who climbed a distant mountain to seek advice from the revered old wise man who had renounced vast riches and celebrity. When he asked the wise man what he should do, he was told, "My son avoid hedonism, do not seek fame – such things are a snare and a delusion." The younger man looked at the wise man and said: "Thank you wise one. Could I just try for a month first?"

Holum then commented that one of the problems with nuclear weapons was that nobody could just try them for a month. It was human nature to try things out, keep options open, explore new possibilities. That was often not a bad thing. But the NPT was too essential to put at risk. Nevertheless, as the NPT Review Conference approached, many voices were heard demanding that the Treaty should be "tinkered with". While some of them might be sincere, experimentation would be folly.

Holum then added that the NPT's entry into force in 1970 transformed the acquisition of nuclear weapons from an act of national pride into a violation of international law. If it crumbled – indeed, if cracks were detected – a great deal of the nuclear security architecture painstakingly constructed by the international community might collapse. He emphasised that the NPT served two mutually reinforcing aims: nuclear non-proliferation and disarmament. It did this by balancing positive and negative rights and obligations. It was at once an agreement to forego nuclear weapons; an agreement to put peaceful nuclear facilities under international safeguards; an undertaking to end the arms race and pursue nuclear disarmament; and an agreement promoting access to technical cooperation in the peaceful use of nuclear energy. And it was for all these reasons that winning the NPT's indefinite and unconditional extension was the USA's "highest priority".

Holum then underlined the fact that when the Argentines communicated their decision to join the NPT, the words they used revealed the powerful legal and moral norm at work. They said that they had long kept their nuclear options open out of a desire to add to their security. But they found that keeping the nuclear option open had the opposite effect of excluding them from the political and economic circles where, they finally realised, their true security lay. They wanted to join the NPT in order to "join the civilised world".[91]

Before dealing with the contention of Holum, it is necessary to make a few points regarding some procedural aspects of the Review Conference. The task of the Conference was to "decide whether the Treaty shall continue in force indefinitely or shall be extended for an additional fixed period or periods." The Treaty was, however, silent on the procedural aspects, even after the Preparatory Committee meeting (Prepcom), leaving room for interpretation.

The extension decision was to be taken by a majority of parties to the Treaty and not merely a majority of states attending the Conference. This raised the possibility of the circumstances under which no majority vote was forthcoming. Going strictly by the text, in case the number of states participating in the Conference was less than half the total number of parties to the NPT, it would be impossible to determine the attendance at the Conference. The attendance, of course, was not expected to be thin, considering the fact that the Prepcom was attended by as many as 123 members. Interestingly, in a situation like the fourth Review Conference which was attended by 84 out of 140 parties, a negative vote by 14 was sufficient to block a decision.

Nothing had been stipulated about the manner of voting at the Extension Conference. In the event of extremely thin attendances, would absentee voting be permitted? The proposal would be fraught with all sorts of difficulties. Postal voting and proxy voting were even more difficult options because states had not been known to let others vote in their place.

The text of the Treaty did not state whether the two Conferences, Review and Extension, should be held separately or together. The Prepcom attendances hedged the problem by calling it "The 1995 Conference of the Parties to the Treaty on Non-Proliferation of Nuclear Weapons".

It has become an international practice in conferences to avoid voting, and opt for consensus. Such attempts bog down the efforts by a small group or even a single individual to bring about a compromise. Thus, the Iran-Iraq dispute would have brought the conference to a near failure. The prospects of consensus voting do not point to a successful Extension Conference. David Fischer has, in fact, suggested that if formal or informal review of the Treaty forms a part of the extension process, it is imperative that there should be no requirement that a final document on the results of the review be approved by consensus.[92]

At the Prepcom, the issue of how to take a decision remained unsolved – whether by vote or by consensus. Several non-aligned countries criticised the proposal, calling consensus "another form of veto" and sought unambiguous language allowing for a vote if all else failed.

The Treaty empowered a conference alone to take a decision on further extension. There was no provision for an additional Extension Conference. In case the Treaty got extended for additional "fixed period", it meant termination of the Treaty after a fixed period or till a time the parties decide. The Treaty, however, said nothing about the length of the periods. Procedurally, it might be simpler to follow "equal periods" duration.

The Treaty was silent about termination. Extension for additional periods implied termination. If parties in the course of fixed periods decided to terminate the Treaty, it was not clear if it would be legal or illegal. Alternatively, withdrawal by all parties, an extremely difficult, if not impossible, situation, also implied termination. As per the Vienna Convention (Article 54), in the absence of a specific provision for termination in a treaty, it may be terminated at any time by the consent of all parties, after consultation with other contracting parties.

What about conditional extension? During the fourth Review Conference suggestions were made that extension be made subject to phased implementation of Article VI of the Comprehensive Test Ban Treaty (CTBT). The USA, however, put its foot down on not linking NPT proposals with conclusion of the CTBT. Any proposal for conditional extension was, therefore, bound to be resisted, probably by a sufficient number of parties attending the conference. Here it must be pointed out that the legality of a conditional extension was not specified in the Treaty. It might require an amendment, but the possibility of such an amendment coming through was remote.

Absence of provisions or decisions should not be taken to mean that if the conference was unable to reach a decision that reflected the will of the majority of parties, the NPT would *ipso facto* become permanent. "The absence of a decision," said Serge Sur, "would have the same effect as a positive decision. It would indeed impose a greater obligation on the parties than a positive decision that a treaty would be extended for a fixed period. The latter would not create an obligation. The assumed outcome is in conflict with the notion of extension and would nullify the provision to continue the treaty in force. In any case, in the event of failure of a decision, it would only continue 'provisionally' till further moves are made. Lastly, the decision of the conference would not constitute an amendment of the Treaty. It would require ratification by Parliament or national authorities. Prospects in this context are not conditioned by change in decisions back home between the conference and ratification." [93]

Now a few observations about India's options. The arguments of the Indian pro-bomb lobby against the NPT show that, often, the right thing can be said to maintain the status quo – in this case, keeping the Indian nuclear weapons option open.

It is well-known that the NPT is contradictory in several respects – its objective is to prevent nuclear proliferation but it allows vertical proliferation by the Haves while prohibiting horizontal proliferation to the Have-nots; it actually promotes commercial nuclear technology and materials that can be used in weapons programmes; it justifies peaceful nuclear explosions whose benefits are yet to be demonstrated but whose disastrous environmental consequences are all too apparent.

The non-nuclear nations are justified in viewing the NPT as an unequal and inadequate treaty. But while the shortcomings of the Treaty need to be publicised, the political question to be asked at this point is with what goal in mind are the defects in the NPT being pointed out. Is the perspective one of meaningful progress towards nuclear disarmament and nuclear non-proliferation or of merely occupying a high moral ground while simultaneously creating a space for maintaining a nuclear weapons option? The question is one of tendency – which way is one moving while making the right noises?

By saying that in West Asia the NPT alone cannot prevent local conflicts, Israel is only defending its undeclared nuclear status. When Pakistan says that it will join the NPT only if India does too, it is not merely emphasising its security concerns vis-a-vis India. It knows that its bluff will never be called. And when India criticises the NPT for not promoting global nuclear disarmament and for being discriminatory, it is only to keep its nuclear weapons option open.

The run-up to the NPT Review Conference produced several devious arguments in India to justify not giving up the nuclear weapons option. The use of the racial metaphor of maintaining a balance between the White and the non-White nuclear or nuclear-capable powers, the argument for achieving self-reliance and strategic autonomy through nuclear proliferation and attempting to "manage" proliferation instead of preventing it were all part of the same bag of arguments.

Yet another argument was that since some nuclear proliferation had already taken place, why not shift the focus from preventing nuclear proliferation to "managing" it. Thus, it was suggested that a supplementary agreement to the NPT be signed to create what was termed "an equal opportunity NPT" which would bring the nuclear holdouts against the Treaty into the regime without undermining it. This, it was suggested, could be followed by an arrangement prohibiting all further nuclear weapon-related activity worldwide with comprehensive verification regimes.

It is noteworthy that the West in general and the US in particular have come to accept the Indian position on the NPT and one does not come across any direct pressure on India to sign the NPT. The strategy now is to insist on confidence building and bilateralism, the plea in the Moscow Declaration being a test in case. Meanwhile, a Carnegie Endowment task force report has suggested that while recognising India's sovereign right to retain its nuclear option and its belief that the NPT is discriminatory, New Delhi should be urged to show sensitivity to this concern by making two important policy changes. Without signing the NPT, India should unilaterally make a formal pledge to abide by the NPT provisions barring the export of nuclear weapons or of military-related nuclear technology. Specifically, this would mean (a) requiring that any nuclear exports would be subject to the IAEA inspection in the recipient country to verify that military-related technology is not involved; and (b) withholding from other states any technological or other assistance related to the development of nuclear weapons. It may be mentioned here that the study cites similar pledges by Argentina in 1985 and South Africa in 1984. It, however, does not explain how these pledges benefit India or what incentives can be given to India in case it does so, except have a favourable impact on India's image as a responsible "international state" in the United States.

One of the options open to India is to rally international public opinion to pinpoint the structural and functional weaknesses of the NPT and emphasise that "it needs to be dumped, rather than beating the discriminatory drum". Moreover, India should only talk about a new treaty which takes into account the difference in levels of the nuclear capability of different countries. The new treaty should recognise the stratified structure of the nuclear regime, and the safeguards, etc can be tailored according to the capabilities of the country. The differentiation should be based on declared capabilities of the countries rather than any arbitrary or obsolete criteria like March 1, 1967, as a cut off date. Since the problem is stratified, the solution can only be seen in a stratified structure. It is in this framework of a stratified structure that solutions can be suggested, say, no-first-use pledge, reduction of nuclear armaments, fissile materials cut off, etc. Denuclearisation, like nuclearisation, does not come overnight. Therefore, the nations should get down one rung of the ladder at a time for eventually reaching the bottom. On the way, it can bring other members positioned on different rungs of the ladder, depending on their capability, down. This is the only viable option. Admitting the capability is a must for this type of model to work because nations, like individuals, benefit in a bargain only if they are doing it from a position of strength. In such a scenario, if the proposal amounts to admitting a capability, it is a good beginning.

VI

The 1995 Review and Extension Conference of the Parties to the Treaty on the Non-Proliferation of Nuclear Weapons decided that in accordance with the preamble and Article VI of the Treaty, it shall remain in force indefinitely and that conferences to review and evaluate the Treaty shall be held every five years, and that the conference held in the year 2000 had, as its first task, evaluated fulfillment of the commitments made at the 1995 conference and the steps taken to achieve the Treaty's universality.

It was further decided that to ensure their effectiveness, the conferences shall (a) retain the structure of the review meetings, by establishing three main committees which shall review how each of the Treaty's provisions has been implemented; (b) seek to establish specific objectives for attaining full compliance with each and every provision of the Treaty and its preamble including, whenever possible, the setting of goals with a specific time-frame; and (c) promote the establishment, within the context of the Treaty, of the necessary arrangements to permit the conduct of negotiations on specific issues between one conference and the next. The conviction was then reiterated that pending the entry into force of a Comprehensive Test Ban Treaty, the nuclear weapon states should suspend all nuclear tests through unilateral or agreed moratorium.[94]

India, Israel and Pakistan were rapped by the Review Conference for their unsafeguarded nuclear programmes and urged to join the twenty-five-year-old Treaty after a month-long contentious debate between the nuclear Haves and Have-nots. The censure of the three "undeclared nuclear powers", which are among the handful of nations not signatories to the NPT, came about in an indirect manner through a resolution sponsored by the three "depository governments" – the United States, Britain and Russia – who are guardians of the original Treaty. The move replaced an earlier last-minute resolution sponsored by Egypt and thirteen other Arab countries urging Israel to join the Treaty without delay and place all its nuclear activities under full-scope safeguards.[95] The United States firmly opposed what it described as "excessively isolating" Israel and insisted that if there was any naming to be done, then all countries would have to be named. The Arab countries put up a token resistance to this since they wanted the focus exclusively on Israel and the Middle East.

After hectic negotiations, the compromise arrived at was a resolution sponsored by the nuclear powers instead of the Arab countries which does not name any country directly, but makes a reference to another document which names all the countries. That document – a report of one of the main committees–calls on those remaining states not party to the Treaty to accede to it, thereby accepting an international legally binding commitment not to acquire nuclear weapons or nuclear explosive devices and to accept international safeguards on all their nuclear plants. There are 12 countries in this list of outsiders – as against 178 countries which are party to the Treaty – but "only India, Israel and Pakistan among the dozen are believed to have nuclear capabilities."[96]

The document referred to in the toned down resolution also isolated India, Israel and Pakistan from the twelve outsiders and urge these three specifically named non-parties "which operate unsafeguarded sensitive nuclear facilities" to join the Treaty while affirming the important contribution that this would make to regional and global security.[97] It is well known that India resolutely rejected joining the NPT on the grounds that it is discriminatory.

India also has the largest number of unsafeguarded nuclear facilities among the three. As a non-signatory to the Treaty, India did not participate in the conference, as also Israel and Pakistan, although the latter two had observer delegations.

"It is unfortunate, almost tragic, that nuclear disarmament has been pushed to such a low priority," says Air Commodore Jasjit Singh of the Institute for Defence Studies and Analyses, New Delhi, who was in New York as an academic observer, while maintaining that the negotiations and the outcome of the Treaty extension proved beyond doubt that power and economic clout remain the dominant factor at the cost of international cooperation.[98]

In its first comment after the New York vote for the indefinite extension of the NPT, New Delhi reiterated its stand against the discriminatory arrangement envisaged in it. Given India's consistent line, there was no question of its acceding to the Treaty and that was officially stated on May 12. According to a Foreign Office spokesman, "The indefinite extension of the NPT perpetuates the discriminatory aspects and provides legitimacy to the nuclear arsenals of the nuclear weapon states. India will not sign the NPT in its present form but will continue to work for achieving genuine non-proliferation through elimination of all nuclear weapons." [99]

Thus, India stuck to its view of the NPT that it was a discriminatory Treaty which creates a division between the nuclear Haves and Have-nots, and that its 1988 action plan called for the elimination of all nuclear weapons as the only means for achieving genuine non-proliferation. The reiteration was on expected lines. New Delhi could not have changed its stand because the NPT members, under strong US pressure, had made the Treaty permanent.

New Delhi's conduct in the new, post-extension phase, could be viewed from two angles. One, the New York vote makes no difference to it – India was against the Treaty when it had a twenty-five year life and would continue with its opposition now that it had been extended indefinitely. Two, the massive support managed by the USA and its success in ensuring the compliance of various groups of countries with its line creates a new situation, in which

India has to reckon with the possibility of increased pressure on it. Whether one likes it or not, the Treaty now gets a new moral authority, a new legality and this would make difficult India's job of resisting, as it has done so far, the exhortations to fall in line with the majority. New Delhi was already engaged in a series of bilateral dialogue with industrialised countries on the issue of non-proliferation and disarmament and these processes could acquire a new thrust, confronting India with a new situation. Whatever the future of the NPT, the pressure on India will certainly continue to mount up.

The events leading up to the final vote have several lessons, the most important being the demonstrated inability of various countries, be they the members of the Non-Aligned Movement (NAM) or the Arab bloc, to resist the pressure of the US – the only superpower in the political if not the economic context. Their resistance collapsed towards the end, as all of them fell in line. At one stage, their brave statements conveyed what turned out to be a misleading impression. The Arab League Ministers, for instance, vowed not to accept extension unless Israel was brought into the Treaty. Israel continues to be outside the NPT but the Arab nations gave up their original objection on the basis of a cosmetic, face-saving formulation offered to them. The proposal, sponsored by Indonesia, the then NAM Chairman, on behalf of ten others, visualising extension through the rolling twenty-five year period, also met the same fate. Allowing for five-year reviews, this proposal sought to set a specific time-frame for a Comprehensive Test Ban Treaty, a legally binding agreement against the use or the threat of use of nuclear weapons, a fissile material production cut off, the elimination of all nuclear weapons and the unimpeded non-discriminatory transfer of nuclear technology for peaceful purposes.

The decision in New York to extend the NPT indefinitely, implies that India will continue to pay a heavy political price for its nuclear option. As a major target of export controls on dual-use and leading edge technologies, India is also incurring significant economic costs for its independence. It may be pointed out here that barely had the NPT Review and Extension Conference ended,

China conducted yet another nuclear explosion with a yield in the 40-150 kiloton range. Even as Beijing continues to test new warheads designs barely 1,100 km from Jammu and Kashmir, build up its nuclear armoury, and covertly provide nuclear and missile assistance to Pakistan, it is not China but India that is widely viewed as a proliferator. [100]

France also resumed nuclear testing in the South Pacific to ensure the reliability and safety of the French nuclear deterrence before Paris signs a Comprehensive Test Ban Treaty outlawing all further explosions in late 1996. The French President, Jacques Chirac, said France intended to conduct eight tests at the Mururoa atoll in French Polynesia between September 1995 and May 1996, ending a French moratorium on testing that had been decreed by his predecessor, Francois Metterrand, in 1992. Chirac said France needed to carry out the tests to acquire the data experts required to switch to simulating nuclear blasts by computer and lasers. This would enable the country to continue modernising its *force de frappe* after the test ban goes into effect in 1996. French Defence Minister Charles Million said that "without new tests the French deterrent could lose all effectiveness by the year 2010." [101]

However, military sources said another major reason for the tests was to carry out vital preparatory work on two weapons systems that are to form the backbone of French nuclear defence after 2000. These are the M-5 missile that is to equip the country's fleet of SSBNs from 2010 and France's long-range air-to-surface ASLP (*air sol a longue portee*) missile which the new Rafale fighter aircraft will carry. The series of eight tests was expected to cost about FFr 3 billion. France has carried out 210 tests since it set off its first atomic bomb on February 13, 1960, in the Sahara desert. [102]

To come to the impact of the New York conference on India, the implication of the NPT extension is that India should indefinitely accept nuclear asymmetry with China and do this without even the benefit of extended deterrence guarantees enjoyed by the countries such as Canada, Germany and Australia that were in the forefront of the indefinite extension movement.

That the Pokhran test of May 18, 1974, was a momentous development with a global political fallout is well known. It implied the secret formation of the London Suppliers Club, the reshaping of the international non-proliferation regime, and the inclusion of dual-use items in Western export controls. It also had a major impact on US policy, leading to significant institutional reforms in export policy, the enactment of the 1978 Nuclear Non-Proliferation Act, the attachment of non-proliferation conditions to foreign aid, and the emergence of the sanctions approach to proliferation.

Domestically, however, the explosion was not part of any well-thought out, long-term strategy. Rather, it was treated by the Government as a mere peaceful nuclear explosion technology demonstrator whose exact timing may have been dictated by internal political considerations.

The intense international pressure the explosion triggered is one explanation why the government shied away from any further test. But had the detonation been part of an integrated, well-calculated blueprint of India's nuclear option, with different component projects already in motion, follow-up tests would have become inescapable.

In strategic terms, a credible nuclear option for India today cannot be available from a rudimentary, aircraft-deliverable capability. The perceived security concerns demand a minimal missile-based deterrent with second-strike capability.

Even in an age of computer simulation and sophisticated X-ray diagnostic techniques, nuclear testing is still required for developing compact, reliable missile-deliverable warheads. Except for low-technology systems, nuclear testing is almost mandatory for most designs, especially boosted fission weapons for missile delivery. If this was not so, China and France would not still be testing. And as long as countries such as China and France continue to develop and test nuclear weapons, the future of the NPT will remain under a big question mark.

Anyway, how the Government of India intends to safeguard India's nuclear option is not known. It is true the Pokhran device weighed only 800 kg, well within the payload capability of missile systems developed by Indian scientists, but the exploded device was not a warhead design. The deterrent value – and the reliability and safety – of untested warheads is an open question. And yet India is branded as the prime proliferator of nuclear weapons.

The other two so-called-threshold states are in a different boat than India, having received weapons-related assistance from external sources. Israel, which is believed to have advanced fission warheads boosted with deuterium-tritium gas/and or lithium hydrides, has received, directly or through espionage, French-US warhead designs as well as computer-based weapon design codes.

Pakistan, according to several Reagan, Bush and Clinton Administration sources, obtained from China the design of one missile-deliverable warhead in the early 1980s. China, in fact, in the words of CIA Chief James Woolsey, "has consistently regarded a nuclear-armed Pakistan as a crucial ally and as a vital counterweight to India's growing military capabilities. And building on a close and extensive defense cooperation effort, Beijing, prior to joining the NPT in 1992, probably provided some nuclear weapons related assistance to Islamabad that may have included training, design, and equipment. Based on China's long-standing links with Islamabad, its unclear whether Beijing has broken off contact with elements associated with Pakistan's programme."103

It may be recalled that President Nixon rejected out of hand India's plea in the mid-1960s for a Western guarantee against a possible Chinese nuclear strike or threat thereof. No doubt, Nixon did not either like China acting as "the developing world's nuclear door-to-door salesman" and even suggested that the United States "must apply discriminating pressure on China to alter those foreign policies that threaten American interests", but he warned that Washington "should not overreact and should provide rewards for changes in Chinese policy."104

Another similar instance can be traced in George Quester's argument when he believes: "Despite the often-quoted fears of an 'Islamic Bomb', one looks in vain for Pakistani references to extending deterrence to, or sharing technology with, other Islamic states in the region. If extended deterrence is not a component of

Pakistani strategic thinking, US policy and strategy in the region might be spared worrying about Pakistan as a regional proliferator of weapons of mass destruction." [105]

Actually, given its own vulnerabilities, it is unlikely that the Pakistani Government would easily give "references to extending deterrence or sharing technology with other Islamic states in the region." Pakistan is well aware of its dependence on the US, the Western view of its nuclear programme, the importance given to the Middle Eastern region in US strategic thinking and the cost of giving such references. In fact, Pakistan is more likely to strongly argue against any such analysis that would suggest Pakistan's high ambitions in the Persian Gulf or the Middle Eastern region. Furthermore, Pakistan should be expected to highlight India's nuclear capability to justify its nuclear weapons programme and wait until a suitable time when it is fully established as a credible nuclear power to play its Middle Eastern card, if any.

A subtle opinion on similar lines can be observed in Geoffery Kemp's analysis. In summing up his study on the spread of advanced military technology to the Middle East and South Asia, he noted:

> The US supports Pakistan in the furtherance of US policy to contain Soviet influence, but rather schizophrenically, threatens to cut Islamabad off because of its nuclear weapons program. Pakistan cherishes its relationship with the US as a means to acquire the equipment to deter Indian aggression, but India's intransigence on bilateral disputes and overwhelming nuclear superiority have forced Pakistani leaders to seek nuclear weapons to stay in the game. And finally, Pakistani nuclear weapons, which are not overtly threatening to the far larger and stronger India, are a constant source of annoyance to New Delhi because they spark efforts by the US to reduce India in stature to Pakistan's level, and thus interfere with India's goals of achieving parity with China and eventual great power status.[106]

Viewed against this background, the generous support extended by India to two proposals – a CTBT and a global fissile cut off – further clouded the issues surrounding its nuclear option. No doubt, these two measures would directly impact on the option, imposing a qualitative and quantitative cap on the country's nuclear capabilities.

The support, including Indian co-sponsorship of the 1993 UN resolutions on a CTBT and fissile cut-off, was originally intended to blunt Western, particularly American, pressure. In effect, however, the government had been left saying that it was ready to accept non-proliferation measures even if they circumscribed India's own nuclear capabilities, provided such measures were non-discriminatory, verifiable and applicable to all powers.

Both these proposed measures would have minimal impact on the declared nuclear-weapons states, particularly the largest two, and probably the maximum impact on India, bearing in mind that unlike Pakistan and Israel, it has had no external benefactors. If these measures came into force, India,, with its small weapons-usable fissile material stockpile and lack of nuclear testing, might never emerge with full-fledged nuclear deterrent capabilities.

The main bottleneck to an early conclusion of the CTBT was the insistence of the nuclear weapon states to retain the right to conduct hydronuclear tests and other low-yield explosions, although they disagreed over the threshold level that should be permitted. Hydro-nuclear tests release tiny or negligible amounts of fission (or fusion) energy as they are limited to subcritical or slightly supercritical neutron multiplication. If the nuclear weapons states have their way and the CTBT does permit hydronuclear tests, India as a non-signatory to the NPT would have the right to carry out such experiments to develop advanced warhead designs employing less plutonium and with smaller weights and volumes for easy missile delivery. However, in practice, the value of hydronuclear tests depends on factors that favour the nuclear weapon states, such as the availability of calibrated codes from full-scale nuclear testing and sophistication of diagnostic tools. Moreover, for reasons of safety against vaporisation and dispersal of toxic plutonium, hydronuclear tests cannot be conducted in laboratories but only underground at proper test sites. If India has not carried out the more valuable full-scale nuclear testing despite being bound by no international legal constraints, it seems unlikely it would conduct hydronuclear tests in the near future.

Dr Brahma Chellaney rightly says that it is time Parliament debated the essential elements of a nuclear option. The lack of a coordinated decision-making structure in the government on security issues impairs nuclear and disarmament policy-making. Parliament has played a weak role in influencing or overseeing this policy. The Prime Minister is saddled with a host of portfolios and a plethora of domestic problems. He has very little time for nuclear policy-making and is more apt to delay a crucial decision than to radically alter existing policy or construct a policy, where none exists. The national debate should focus on the political and economic costs of continuing the present policy versus changing to a new course. Even as the country opens up its market to Western goods and services, it faces mounting barriers to import of high technology. The proposed successor cartel to CoCom* will prohibit high-tech exports to "the Middle East and India and Pakistan as well as the four pariah states of Iran, Iraq, Libya and North Korea," according to a May 15, 1995, briefing by a US State Department official.

It is, therefore, clear that in the context of the indefinite extension of the NPT, coupled with the agreement that "universal adherence" to the Treaty is an "urgent priority", will put the spotlight on India and Israel principally. At a minimum, the decision to perpetuate the monopoly of the P-5 calls for a reappraisal of India's arms control policy. The fissile cut off and CTBT were intended to be steps towards the complete elimination of nuclear weapons. Now more than ever before they threaten to become an end in themselves. [107]

In the context of the above discussion, a fundamental question may now be posed: what is it about the NPT that should concern the citizens of the world? Is it merely the iniquitous, discriminatory aspect that should trigger alarm bells or is there more to it? To answer these questions, it is necessary to distinguish between the politico-security aspect of nuclear weapons and their possession at one level and the deeper ethno-moral plane. The NPT, as it is currently structured recognises only the privileges that accrue to

---

* CoCom is an informal abbreviation for "Coordinating Committee for Multilateral Controls"

the P-5 and does not adequately emphasise the responsibilities that they have towards their less privileged brethren. Some of the contradictions and imperative inconsistencies need to be recognised, particularly the US interpretation of these developments.

Contrary to popular view, the end of the Cold War has not devalued nuclear weapons and even now the P-5 maintain that nuclear weapons are essential for protecting their core national security interests. This is an untenable position for the P-5 have declared that none of them is a threat to the other and, thus, it may be inferred that these weapons will be used only against non-nuclear states. The US position is that it needs to "hedge" against the possibilities of the "uncertain future", including a Russian threat. In the same fashion, all the other nuclear powers justify their arsenals based on security interests. This brings us to the vital question: is the security of the P-5 more equal than the rest of the world? The answer to this question is a *sine qua non* for projecting the future of the NPT.

Interestingly, the P-5 have repeatedly watered down the security assurances that they can and should offer to the nuclear Have-nots. Thus, foolproof, binding security assurances are not part of the main text of the NPT and it was on the eve of the Review Conference that the P-5 started to address the subject. But the final resolution of the conference did not offer any categorical security assurances to the nuclear Have-nots. Even if such offers were made, they would well be a case of too-little-too-late, for the NPT has never adequately assuaged the security concerns of nation states, including, paradoxically, the heightened neurosis of the P-5 themselves. The Cold War best reflected this absurdity and in a way the world was held hostage to the reckless adventurism of the two superpowers and their acolytes.

Article VI of the NPT calls upon the P-5 to negotiate "in good faith on effective measures relating to cessation of the nuclear arms race at an early date and to nuclear disarmament." But this has been the most abused provision of the NPT. From about 10,000 warheads at the time of signing the NPT in 1970, the P-5 peaked at over 50,000 warheads when the Cold War finally ended. [108] Dispassionate analysis of the past reveals that the NPT was conceived in deceit and the major powers had no qualms in contravening all its provisions to further their interests. The point to remember here is that the monopoly of the P-5 over nuclear weapons cannot continue indefinitely and it is difficult to see how the Treaty would remain in force after, say, twenty years. As already noted, the nuclear weapons states have violated all the provisions of the NPT and it will be hardly surprising if these powers themselves say farewell to the NPT much earlier than a two-decade period.

In such a scenario, the P-5 led by a vocal USA, are exhorting the world to join the NPT "unconditionally and indefinitely" and that the world would be better off with it. This is a highly moot question for an unfettered, unqualified NPT will remove whatever leverage the non-nuclear powers have to make the P-5 acknowledge their anxieties and sensitivities. In short, the P-5 are not perceived to be the enlightened guardians they wish to be seen as.

Currently, the USA is projecting the arms reduction effected in START I and II as being indicative of the P-5 meeting disarmament obligations under Article VI of the NPT. Nothing could be further from the truth. The end of the Cold War had its own dynamics and had little to do with the NPT. What was inevitable or common practice for the major nuclear powers is being repeatedly packaged as a disarmament initiative or a shining virtue. This is as true of the reduction in the US/Russian arsenals as it is of the test ban and fissile material negotiations. Interestingly enough, the other three nuclear powers – France, Britain and China – have been non-committal about these moves and are actually investing large amounts of scarce resources in modernising their nuclear weapons. The USA has spent an average of $75 billion dollars annually for the last fifty years and plans to spend $40 billion for the next twenty-five years for its nuclear arsenal. By 2020, the USA would have spent $4,750 billion on its nuclear arsenal while espousing the cause of disarmament. [109]

On an ethical plane, the decision to extend the NPT indefinitely is fraught with grave implications. It would in effect legitimise a very unique and apocalyptic weapon in the hands of the P-5. This is an unprecedented step, for to date, the world has never legitimised weapons of mass destruction such as chemical weapons. The 1925 Geneva Convention recognised these weapons as inhuman and it took the world almost seventy years to sign a Chemical Weapons Convention, which again awaits US ratification and then these weapons will be deemed illegal.

Eventually, the NPT would go against the grain of the collective human ethic which would ban one class of weapons but selectively legitimise the more devastating lethality of nuclear arsenals. It would be a sad day if the citizens of the world allowed this to happen. Luckily, the non-governmental and anti-nuclear movement in the West, including the USA, is very vociferous and may yet save the day. Thomas Graham, the US Ambassador to the NPT justified their position saying: "Do not gamble with something you cannot afford to lose." It appears that one section of the non-nuclear world may dig their heels in and just not gamble, for they cannot afford to lose their last chance to save the world from an irrevocable nuclear apartheid.

Predictably, the French nuclear tests in the South Pacific raised a storm of protests around the world. The Pacific basin countries which kept quiet over hundreds of American, British and previous French nuclear tests and which voted to legitimise nuclear weapons at the Review Conference of the NPT, now expressed great outrage. Nine out of sixteen European countries, other than the U.K., Germany, Spain and four others also expressed their disapproval. When the US Administration released information in 1993 that they had conducted some 200 nuclear weapon tests in secret and that they had in the fifties and sixties subjected human beings to radiological experiments without the knowledge and consent of those concerned, there was no appreciable agitation. When the dropping of the atomic bombs on Hiroshima and Nagasaki was being glorified as a great achievement, none of those who are expressing grave indignation and moral outrage (except for the Japanese) aired their views. Even the Japanese, in their draft reply to the International Court of Justice, on the issue of legality of the use and threat of use of nuclear weapons on which the General Council of the World Health Organisation had made a reference, first chose to toe the US line that the use of nuclear weapons was not illegal and thereafter changed their stand towards a more neutral one because of the public outcry.

If the international community legalises the use and threat of use of nuclear weapons through the extension of the NPT, it does not appear rational to then protest against an underground nuclear test. If the nuclear weapons can be legitimately used above the ground which is what the indefinite and unconditional extension of the NPT means, what explains the hue and cry over a few underground tests? Therefore, it is logical to assume that there is more to the present agitation against the French nuclear tests than the professed concern about either stopping the tests or damage to the environment. Stopping the tests is not an end in itself if nuclear weapons are accepted for use by five nuclear weapon powers as endorsed by the members of the NPT Extension Conference.

Nuclear proliferation is no longer a major issue since 173 out of 178 countries which extended the NPT have voluntarily abjured nuclear weapons. It is no secret that there were also the three undeclared nuclear weapon capable powers – India, Israel and Pakistan. Any additions to their capabilities would not constitute any more nuclear proliferation than what the five nuclear weapons powers have been doing all these years. The international community is aware of this. The present agitations against the French and Chinese nuclear tests and the attempt to promote a CTBT and fissile materials production cut off are partly directed against the undeclared weapon powers but are more a reflection of the rivalry among the five declared nuclear weapon powers in flaunting their nuclear arsenals as a currency of power. Since the undeclared nuclear weapon powers are not thinking of further refining their nuclear arsenals, they do not flaunt their nuclear weapon capabilities. Even the crude devices and capabilities they have serve the purpose of deterrence which is perhaps the only purpose for which they have developed these capabilities.

The nuclear rivalry on today is between the USA and Russia, on the one hand, and France and China, on the other. There are to be discussions between the US and Russia about the Anti-Ballistic Missile Treaty. The Americans are keen on developing a theatre anti-missile capability and are carrying out extensive research and development. Though the US justification for such research and development is that such theatre missile defence is needed against the possibility of the emergence of "rogue states," no one is taken in by such untenable arguments. China is very worried that the development of theatre missile defence may lead to anti-ballistic missile defence which will undermine the credibility of its ICBMs which are aimed against the USA.

The credibility of the deterrent capability of the Chinese ICBMs is imperative for them if they are to emerge as the dominant Asian power, in both economic and military terms. In all probability, the Chinese may follow the American and Soviet theologies of the early seventies. They are likely to equip their mobile ICBMs with MIRVs. If this hypothesis is correct, one wonders whether the Chinese will agree to the fissile materials production cut-off at this state unless they are able to make a deal with Russia similar to the US-Russian deal which has led to the US buying huge quantities of Russian fissile materials.

The French too are engaged in enhancing the potency of their currency of power in terms of nuclear weapons. The French may agree to have a system analogous to that which the US used to have under the NATO system of double key. The main outcome of such an arrangement will be to degrade the roles of both the US and Russian nuclear forces. The former will no longer be a protective power of Europe with its extended deterrence and the Russians will be one of the four major nuclear weapons powers in the world. The French and the Chinese will thereby make the world polycentric. The nations that are protesting against the French nuclear tests prefer the continued US extended deterrence over Europe.

The CTBT in the present circumstances will not prevent major nuclear powers from continuing with computer simulation and new weapon designing. It may even become easier for some of the major nuclear weapon powers that have a history of breaching Article I of the NPT and transferring nuclear weapons technology to other non-nuclear nations to continue to do so and test the newly-proliferating nation's weapon design in their computer complex.

Therefore, it was felt that India's adherence to the CTBT and fissile materials production cut-off would have to be thought through afresh in the light of the intense nuclear rivalry among the major nuclear weapon powers in a world which has legitimised nuclear weapons and has continued to treat them as a currency of power in the international system. Since 1993, the world has undergone a radical transformation with nuclear weapons being legitimised. The co-sponsorship of the CTBT was undertaken at a time when there were hopes that the NPT Extension Conference would result in a short or medium-term extension of a Cold War arms control agreement, enabling the world to consider ways and means of advancing towards a nuclear weapons-free world. Now the NPT is no longer an arms control agreement but the legitimisation of nuclear weapons permanently and unconditionally. Therefore, India had every reason to rethink co-sponsoring any more resolutions to ban tests unless this is inextricably linked with total prohibition and elimination of nuclear weapons, immediate steps for their delegitimisation such as a no-first-use treaty and with the establishment of machinery to negotiate elimination of nuclear weapons.

On fissile materials production cut-off, India will have to watch global developments. As long as nuclear weapons are legitimately used as a currency of power, there are difficulties in verifying the transfer of fissile materials accumulated in vast quantities in the nuclear weapon powers to others and since there is no verification scheme to monitor the activities of these nuclear weapon powers, India should not commit itself to any aspect of this and other related issues. And it was for this reason that India said "no" to the CTBT.

To examine India's stand on the CTBT, it is necessary to keep the following facts in mind: (a) a move to ban nuclear testing was mooted by India in 1954; (b) India signed the Partial Test Ban Treaty (PTBT), which prohibited testing in the open in 1963;

(c) India's only peaceful nuclear test was in May 1974 and since then India has kept its nuclear option open; (d) talks on a ban on nuclear testing started at the Conference on Disarmament (CD) in Geneva in January 1994 and India and the USA were among the original co-sponsors; (e) after the permanent and indefinite extension of the NPT in May 1995, India linked the signing of the CTBT with a time-bound plan for global disarmament and this was done because the NPT failed to tackle disarmament which is one of its fundamental aims; the other two being non-proliferation and peaceful use of nuclear energy; (f) in addition to the five nuclear powers, India, Israel and Pakistan are "Threshold Countries" capable of developing nuclear weapons; (g) the CTBT seeks to achieve a total ban on nuclear testing and sixty-one countries participated in the talks to decide the political and legal basis of the treaty.

The two major unresolved issues were:

(1) *Entry into Force*: The treaty should have a legal basis so that it can be enforced by the United Nations. An approved draft by all forty-four participating nations with nuclear reactor programmes, was expected to reach the United Nations by September 18, 1996, where it should be signed by representatives of these governments. It then becomes a treaty, which will be sent to member countries for ratification. The entire procedure is expected to be completed by January 1999, when the CTBT will enter into force. According to the procedure, even if one country of the forty-four does not approve the draft, it will be considered as vetoed. The only option then is to send a detailed report, instead of an approved draft, to the UN, which is considered a politically diluted basis for a CTBT. The U.K., Russia and China demand that the five nuclear powers and three threshold nations sign as original members. India has refused both to sign CTBT in its present form, and to disengage from the talks. The USA had been pushing to get the five nuclear nations and some of the forty-four nations to sign the draft. The threshold nations, it is hoped, will sign the Treaty before 1999. Failing which, the USA has declared a need to review the ratification procedure three years after the signing of the Treaty for its Entry into Force. This procedure outlined by the USA aims to sideline India at a later date.

(2) *Verification Regime*: The member countries agreed on the procedure to penalise defaulters after the Treaty comes into force. This has two elements: who will identify a defaulter, and what physical verification is necessary for legal action? The CD will upgrade international monitoring stations costing $120 million in two years in thirty-one countries. India, Pakistan and China have already installed these facilities. It was agreed that a majority of the executive council of the CD must approve a physical inspection. This followed a compromise between the USA and China. The former earlier pushed for a simple majority of all members to enforce physical verification; the latter – aware that the USA has sophisticated satellites for detection – did not accept an easy procedure for inspection.

The USA has so far conducted 1,032 nuclear tests and has in its possession 8,711 nuclear weapons. The corresponding figures for the other four nuclear powers are as follows: Russia 715 and 6,833; France 210 and 524; Britain 45 and 200 and China 45 and 450.

On August 20, 1996, India formally vetoed the draft text of the CTBT saying it "did not serve the purpose of promoting the realization of universal disarmament goals." By rejecting the Jaap Ramekar draft, India prevented the formal adoption of the draft test ban treaty in Geneva and, thus, thwarted efforts to send the pact to the United Nations General Assembly. "The conference on disarmament has no text of a CTBT to recommend to the UNGA at this time," India's representative to the CTBT negotiations, Arundhati Ghose said. She condemned the US-China backroom deal, by which China's concerns on verification procedures were accommodated and added: "The entry into force clause has been modified at the insistence of a small number of countries with the clear aim of imposing obligations on India and placing it in a position in which it did not wish to be. Such a provision has no parallel. It is unprecedented in multilateral negotiations and international law that any sovereign country should be denied its right of voluntary consent on adherence to an international treaty." This remark came as the five nuclear powers were making moves to bypass India's veto and have the treaty text forwarded for adoption at the General Assembly anyway.

Whether or not India should sign the CTBT was a question over which opinions in India were sharply divided as a result of which the tub-thumping debate in the country tended to defog and skew the vital issues involved. According to one view, the real issues had been distorted by nuclear hawks – with their intransigent postures based on basically exogenous factors – who had been mooting the oft-repeated argument that India was being coaxed and coerced by the nuclear-Haves to compromise its security and sign an unequal treaty. This view, it was argued, ignored the core issues and conveniently reiterated a lot of misconceptions, jumbling thoughts. Little wonder, it was not realised that signing a non-discriminatory, verifiable CTBT would serve India's long-term interest, and New Delhi should go the whole hog to campaign for such a treaty without hedging it with conditions that would make its passage difficult. In fact, if the CTBT talks fell through, the nuclear disarmament agenda of which India was the most ardent votary, would suffer an irretrievable setback. There were not a few Indians who were not convinced that it was in India's long-term interest to secure a non-discriminatory, verifiable CTBT which purported to prohibit all positive-yield explosives. The "assertive urgency" for finalising the CTBT on the part of the USA had really nothing to do with a genuine desire for eliminating weapons of mass destruction from the arsenals of the countries in a non-discriminatory framework. There was no doubt that the CTBT, as it was conceived, would be another dimension of perpetuating the differences between the nuclear weapon powers and the other countries, in both military and technological terms. It was pointed out that India had committed a blunder in joining the US in sponsoring a resolution at the UN in 1993 for bringing about comprehensive test ban arrangements. However, there would be nothing wrong if India backed out of its commitment in view of the fact that it agreed to sponsor the resolution with the hope that the NPT would be reviewed or at least its indefinite extension delayed. As these expectations were not fulfilled, New Delhi was under no obligation to stick to its commitment made in 1993.

More so because of the fact that the US was using the CTBT not as an intermediate station on the way to disarmament, but as a tool for non-proliferation that could be used to cap India's nuclear option by the global route.

Apart from these reasons, it was its close linkage with the NPT that rendered the CTBT unacceptable to India. The linkage had been conclusively established ever since negotiations on nuclear arms control and disarmament began in the early 1950s. In fact, over a time, a comprehensive test ban had been a determinant of NPT performance. At the 1980 and 1990 NPT Review Conferences, the CTBT issue was responsible for the failure of these conferences to agree to a final document. Specific reference was made in the Preamble to the NPT to completion of a CTBT and the linkage was discussed frequently ever since negotiations on the NPT began. The non-implementation of the measure was seen by many countries as a major criterion for deciding whether the nuclear weapon states had fulfilled their obligations under Article VI of the treaty. Failure on this front had been interpreted as perpetuating the discrimination between the nuclear-Haves and Have-nots and defaulting of an obligation by nuclear weapon states.

Despite this linkage, the protagonists of the CTBT evoked the following arguments to make out a case for India's support for the treaty. It was contended that the case for a CTBT arose from its function as a nuclear constraint or capping measure. Although it was not by itself a disarmament measure, it could contribute significantly to disarmament. That rationale drove Jawaharlal Nehru to propose a CTBT in April 1954. Fifty years on, it still held. A CTBT would not eliminate the offensive capabilities of the nuclear weapon states or threshold states like India, Pakistan and Israel because no tests were needed to manufacture weapons of existing designs. But it would contribute to the slowing down and cessation of the nuclear arms race — an indisputably worthy goal.

For one, it was argued, it would generate both an impetus towards disarmament and pressure on the nuclear weapon states to fulfil their disarmament obligations under the NPT. It would redress one asymmetry between nuclear-weapon states and non-nucelar weapon states in today's unequal nuclear order. For another, it would make development of a new generation of weapons or refinement of existing armaments virtually impossible: such development required elaborate testing. And for a third, it would strengthen the sentiment in favour of delegitimising nuclear weapons as a currency of power, help expose the false link between nuclear arms and security, and assuage fears about instability, unpredictability and sudden crisis eruption. After the INF Treaty and START, CTBT would be the most important step towards a more secure world. As a marker of direction, it was invaluable and indispensable. Real security could only lie in a non-proliferation regime.

These arguments were specious enough. They held no water in the face of stark facts and realities of international relations. How could one hope that a CTBT would contribute significantly to disarmament by generating pressure on the nuclear weapon states to fulfil their obligations under the NPT? Plain facts did not inspire anybody to harbour any such hope. When France and China were going ahead with their nuclear tests, the US was openly planning to conduct underground hydronuclear experiments in Nevada. The Chemical Weapons Convention and START II had not yet been ratified by Washington and Moscow. Little wonder, these gave rise to a sense of deception and double-dealing, with many non-nuclear weapon states feeling that their expectation that the end of the Cold War would bring about nuclear disarmament had been dashed and they rightly held the view that political power in the world would continue, to be determined by nuclear might. While the indefinite extension of the NPT had legitimised the arsenals of the nuclear-Haves, these big powers argued before the World Court that the threat or use of nuclear weapons was permissible under international law. It was for this reason that the Australian Prime Minister, Paul Keating, expressed his deep anguish that "we have been cheated – robbed of a chance of a world free of nuclear weapons." Obviously, the prospect of a CTBT had failed to inspire Keating to hope for a world where political power would not be determined by nuclear muscle.

In fact, it was clear from the very outset that the CTBT would not be concluded without a hitch. As rightly pointed out by Air Commodore Jasjit Singh, the attitudes in India were already hardening against the coercive diplomacy of a handful of states which wished to retain nuclear weapons indefinitely, and did not actually want a CTBT, but did not display the moral courage to stand on their own feet while wanting to fire their guns on Indian shoulders. The real responsibility for blocking the treaty under such circumstances rested not on India, but on countries that insisted on making the CTBT conditional to a patently illegal and perverse clause. Ramekar's second draft, supported by the US, China, Britain and Russia, shifted the central issue from the nature and substance of the treaty to issues of sovereignty and international norms. The way these got resolved would have long-term implications on international peace and security, well beyond the CTBT.

India's "no" to the CTBT did not come as a surprise to any Indian. In India, every man in the street knew that the Deve Gowda Government was extremely fragile and would not make any foreign policy move that might bring it down. In fact, most Indians could not care less about the CTBT when social and economic issues, particularly the financial shenanigans of the country's political elite dominated the overall scene. However, there was a residual interest in "disarmament" and some groups were turning the CTBT into a vehicle for anti-Americanism.

In the context of this, the Americans would do well to keep in mind that they have a larger strategic fish to fry with the Indians. It is unfortunate that by making the CTBT the centrepiece of Indo-Americans relations, as Washington did with the NPT, the Americans make it seem as if their only interest in New Delhi is non-proliferation. Ironically, this builds up those who favour proliferation. Americans and Indians have important shared interests – their respective problems with China, the spread of terrorism, strengthening their economic ties, coping with a nuclear-capable but still unstable Pakistan. The CTBT should not disrupt the two countries' dialogue on these concerns.

In fact, the Americans need to appreciate that India has yet to recover from the end of the Cold War. They have lost their chief strategic ally, the Soviet Union, and Indian leftists are still angry with the USA for "winning the Cold War"; Pakistan, the state they could have destroyed in 1971 and 1987, has bounced back with a nuclear capability and substantial interference in Kashmir, and Chinese policy has recently become more nationalistic. Indians do not know whether to appease China (by pretending that the border dispute is settled), or to balance China (by building nuclear weapons). They do not even remember that Americans were their ally in 1962. Indian cannot figure out why Americans have rewarded North Korea for its violation of the NPT.

The Indian press, without any exception, has lauded New Delhi's stand at Geneva and the general refrain has been that the government can be justifiably proud of having kept a clear head, withstood pressure, and done what needed to be done in the interests of the country's future security. It has been pointed out that although the US and some other countries intend to take the text of the CTBT to the UN General Assembly, whatever emerges there will not be the same thing. Even if the draft treaty wins a majority vote, it will lack the kind of legitimacy that would come out of a consensus of negotiating countries at the Conference on Disarmament. India's tough stand has been welcomed as an assertion of its right to think and act independently.

But it is agreed that the game is not over. Now the Disarmament Conference has to decide what kind of report it will submit to the General Assembly. But it can be taken as given that Western negotiators are not ready to pronounce that the test ban talks have ended in failure, not after so much midnight oil has been burnt and when so many political reputations are linked to the outcome. Washington in particular will be loath to snatch defeat from the jaws of victory. The question that now concerns India is: will the five-power informal moratorium on nuclear testing hold?

Even if the text of the CTBT is accepted by the General Assembly, no one should hope that it will herald an end to the nuclear arms race. Given the expected demise of nuclear weapons testing, the UK has been planning to enhance the alternative means of maintaining a nuclear warhead capability, the Ministry of Defence told the House of Commons Defence Committee last year. It referred to "recent technical discussions with France on a number of aspects, including hydrodynamics experiments, laser, plasma physics, computer simulation, possible arrangements for peer review."

Two weeks after the end of Geneva negotiations, news leaked out from Washington that the US has agreed to supply nuclear test and other research data to France. With Britain, and now France also, having the benefit of the American test database and computer simulation techniques, an elite group has been formed within the select club of nuclear weapon states. The group is engaged in a trilateral exchange of information that makes nuclear tests redundant. Those who expected India to agree to the CTBT, had hoped New Delhi would not notice the ways of the nuclear powers and the US Energy Department's warheads "stockpile stewardship" programme with an annual budget of $3 billion. The privileged nuclear powers, therefore, can have it both ways. They can give up testing and still can make their bombs work.

The Lawrence Livermore Laboratory's National Ignition Facility, where lasers focus on heavy hydrogen to generate temperatures of a fusion bomb, is getting several million dollars more. It will have a new supercomputer, the plans for which have already been announced by President Clinton. The machine will be powerful enough to learn even more precisely the characteristics of nuclear weapons, and simulate explosions. This nuclear test simulator, a supercomputer 300 times more powerful than any existing machine, was built by IBM in 1998. It is capable of doing one trillion calculations per second and its successors will do ten trillion calculations per second by 2004.

The French have been assured of the American data, a bribe that secured the French consent for not conducting more nuclear tests after having conducted 210. And yet, the French themselves are pouring in nearly £1.3 million on Project Megajoules, some of which will be duplicating the results of the American National Ignition Facility. China may have been helped by Russia to conduct computer-simulated tests or France may have shared test data with China.

All this demonstrates that only scientists with supercomputers can enable a country to accept a ban on nuclear tests, and only countries with a credible nuclear programme can hope to share the American test data. A bill, currently before the Congress, forbids anyone, apart from Britain and France, sharing any American nuclear weapon stewardship technology. India, at that time with the record of a solitary test, does not qualify to get the US data. Why has India not won at least some appreciation for its self-imposed nuclear *brahmacharya*? Prof. William Walker of University of St. Andrews has an explanation that may upset the advocates of the policy of nuclear ambiguity. He says that in Defence Ministries elsewhere than Islamabad, India's nuclear capabilities are viewed as neither sufficient, nor sufficiently helpful, for there to be common cause with India. Paradoxically, had India already successfully established a nuclear deterrent against China, in particular, strategic analysts in Washington, Moscow and other capitals might have regarded it as another useful part of the strategic balance. Precisely because the Indian nuclear capability has so far achieved little deterrence value against China, it is discounted and there is no possible commonality of interests. On the other hand, where deterrence of sorts has been established – against Pakistan – it is regarded by foreign powers as a liability rather than an asset. The reason is, of course, that the containment of China is a geopolitical issue, whereas India's containment of Pakistan (or Pakistan's containment of India) is regarded as a local and "bounded" issue, albeit with the capacity to irritate foreign powers.

Prof. Walker says there is considerable empathy with India even though its position is not acceptable. India's critique of the nuclear weapon states has a resonance in many countries, including Germany. He says: "Rather than the threshold states, it is now the nuclear weapon states that are most guilty of practising ambiguity. In the past two years, the perception has gained ground that the nuclear weapon states are simply retrenching and modernizing."

Prof. Walker wonders what kind of pressure or punishment India will face for its refusal to agree to the CTBT. Unless India explores the path of collective security in the region, it will find it difficult to find its way out of the labyrinth. Its present posture gives it a psychological advantage but no great security, he says. Thus, instead of trying to build castles in the air, India must explore the road to collective security, without necessarily giving up the nuclear option. While exploring the road to collective security, India should stay till the end, be firm and expound its position. For, it has to be remembered that India's nuclear policy has to respond to challenges and not be restricted to reaching to the big powers. As far as pressures are concerned, there will only be a marginal difference if one is inside or outside the CTBT. And, finally, it should be recognised by all that the text of the CTBT was shaped more by the technological preferences of the nuclear weapon states rather than the imperatives of nuclear disarmament. This is not the treaty that India envisaged in 1954 nor the one it was mandated to negotiate.

Notes

1. The literature on this subject is very large. See the summary in Nazil Chaucri and Thomas Robinson (eds), *Forecasting in International Relations*, Freeman, San Francisco: 1978.

2. This is not to imply that prediction rather than understanding is the goal of social science; see Stephen Toulmin, *Foresight and Understanding: An inquiry Into the Aims of Science*, Indiana University Press Bloomington, 1961.

3. Waltz, Kenneth, *Theory of International Politics*, Reading, Mess: Addison-Wesley, 1979; Mearsheimer, John, "Back to the Future: Instability in Europe After the Cold War", *International Security*, vol. 15, no. 1, Summer, 1990, pp. 5-56.

4. Jervis, Herman, *Systems and Interactions*, Harvard Press, Cambridge, 1974, pp. 77-81.

5. Many Realist scholars develop arguments that are both descriptive and prescriptive. They claim not only to analyse the way the world works, but also to guide statesmen. However, they often pay insufficient attention to the question of whether their theories will be accurate if statesmen do not accept them (and if statesmen do, then prescription is unnecessary) and the possibility that if their truths were generally believed, the patterns of behaviour would be altered.

6. Claude, Inis, *Power and International Relations*, Random House New York:, 1962, pp. 40-51; Waltz, *Theory of International Politics*, pp. 102-128.

7. Zeckhauser, Richard, *Strategy and Choice*, MIT Press Cambridge, Mass, 1990, pp. 64-74.

8. Path-dependence is one of themes of the new institutionalism. See, for example, March, James and Olsen, Johan, *Rediscovering Institutions* ; Free Press, New York, 1989.

9. This argument has a hopeful side to it; the possibility of contingent predictions. That is, we can and should focus on saying what we expect to happen, given *various conditions*. This is worthwhile, especially for the intellectual discipline that it imposes. But if there are a large number of important variables that many states can assume and if the variables build on each other as time passes, then we cannot expect the exercise to produce many practical benefits.

10. Gould, Stephen Jay, *Wonderful Life: The Burgess Shale and the Nature of History,* Norton New York, 1989, p. 116.

11. For the more extreme argument that Wilson would have taken a different position had a bizarre incident involving a low-level British diplomat who led him to refuse to bear the advice of Sir Edward Gray, the British Special Ambassador, see Mechling Jr. Charles, "Scandal in Wartime Washington: The Craufurd-Sturat Affair of 1918," *International Journal of Intelligence and Counterintelligence*, vol. 4, no. 3, Fall, 1990, pp. 357-370.

12. For further discussion see Jervis, Robert, "The Impact of the Korean War on the Cold War", *Journal of Conflict Resolution*, vol. 24, no. 4, December, 1990, pp. 563-592.

13. Schmemann, Serge, "Report by Soviets Expresses Fears of Following the Path of Yugoslavia," *New York Times*, October 4, 1991, p. A4.

14. Elster, Jon, *Logic and Society: Contradictions and Possible Worlds*, Willey, New York, 1978, pp. 177-78; Gaddis, John, "Nuclear Weapons and International Systemic Stability", Occasional Paper No. 2, *International Security Studies Program*, AAAS, January 1990.

15. Gould, Stephen Jay, *Time's Arrow, Time's Cycle*, Harvard University Press, Cambridge, 1987.

16. See Jervis, Robert, "Loss Aversion in International Politics" *Political Psychology*, May, 1988, pp. 34-36. Kahneman and Tversky, "Choices, Values, and Frames", *American Psychologist*, vol. 39, no. 3, April, 1984, pp. 341-350; Lebow, Richard Ned and Stein, Janice, "Beyond Deterrence", *Journal of Social Issues*, vol. 43, no. 4, Winter, 1987, pp. 5-17.

17. A good example is Mearsheimer, "Back to the Future".

18. The best critique of the utility of theorizing based on the assumption of anarchy is Milner, Helen, "The Assumption of Anarchy in International Relations Theory: A Critique, "*Review of International Studies*", vol. 17, no. 1, January 1991, pp. 67-85.

19. See Evera, Stephen Van, "Primed for Peace; Europe After the Cold War", *International Security*, vol. 15, no. 3, Winter, 1990/91, pp. 7-57; Ullman, Richard H., *Securing Europe*, Princeton University Press, Princeton, N.J., 1991.

20. George Bush states that the "United States has deemed it a vital interest to prevent any hostile power or group of powers from dominating the Eurasian land mass", but in fact neither the United States nor Britain was willing to trust the benign intentions of any state that seemed likely to control the continent, Bush, George, *The National Security Strategy of the United States*, 1990-91, Washington, D.C., Brassey's 1990, p. 5.

21. This point is stressed in Mueller, John, *Retreat from Doomsday: The Obsolescence of Major War*, Basic Books, New York, 1989.

22. Jervis, Robert, *The Illogic of American Nuclear Strategy*, Cornell University Press, Ithaca, 1984, chapters 5 and 6; Jervis, *The Meaning of the Nuclear Revolution*, Cornell University Press, Ithaca, 1989, Chapter 3.

23. For an unconvincing attempt, see Friedman, George and LeBard, Meredith, *The Coming War with Japan*, St. Martin's, New York, 1990.

24. See the discussion in Miller, J.D.B., *Norman Angell and the Futility of War,* St. Martin's New York, 1986.

25. See the discussion of vulnerability and sensitivity interdependence in Cooper, Richard, *The Economics of Interdependence*, McGraw-Hill, New York, 1968; and Keohane, Robert and Nye, Joseph S. Jr., *Power and Interdependence*, Little Brown, Boston, 1977; as well as the path-breaking study by Hirschman, Albert, *National Power and the Structure of International Trade*, University of California Press, Berkeley, 1980 (originally published in 1945).

26. Rosecrance, Richard, *The Rise of the Trading State*, Basic Books, New York, 1986, Chapter 7; Milner, Helen, *Resisting Protectionism*, Princeton University Press, Princeton, N.J., 1988.

27. Evera, Stephen Van, "Why Europe Matters; Why the Third World Doesn't; America's Grand Strategy After the Cold War", *Journal of Strategic Studies*, vol. 13, no. 2, June, 1990, p. 5; Evera, *"Primed for Peace"*, pp. 14-16; Kaysen, Carl, "Is War Obsolete? A Review Essay", *International Security*, vol. 14, no. 4, Spring 1990, pp. 53-57.

28. Waltz, *Theory of International Politics*; Stein, Arthur, "The Hegemon's Dilemma: Great Britain, the United States, and the International Economic Order", *International Organization*, vol. 39. no. 2, Spring, 1984, pp. 355-386; Jervis, Robert, "Realism, Game Theory, and Cooperation", *World Politics*, vol. 40, no. 3, April, 1988, pp. 334-336: Grieco, Joseph, "Anarchy and the Limits of Cooperation: A Realist Critique of the Newest Liberal Institutionalism", *International Organization*, vol. 42, no. 3, Summer, 1988, pp. 465-507; Mastanduno, Michael, "Do Relative Gains Matter? America's Response to Japanese Industrial Policy", *International Security*, vol. 16, no. 1, Summer, 1991, pp. 73-113; For an exposition and application of strategic trade theory see Milner, Helen and Yoffie, "Between Free Trade and Protectionism: Strategic Trade Policy and a Theory of

Corporate Trade Demands", *International Organization*, vol. 43, No. 2, Spring, 1989, pp. 237-272; and Richardson, David J., "The Political Economy of Strategic Trade Theory", *International Organization* vol. 44, no. 1, Winter, 1990, pp. 107-135. The broad dynamic in which a small relative advantage leads to much greater absolute and relative gains later is the heart of the argument in *Hobsbawm*, E.J., *Industry and Empire*, New York, Pantheon, 1968; and Wallerstein, Immanuel, *The Modern World System*, vols. 3, Academic Press, New York, 1974-88.

29. Hirschman, op. cit. pp. 204-9.

30. Waltz, *Theory of International Politics*, pp. 151-160.

31. Quoted in Kennedy, Paul, *The Rise of the Anglo-German Antagonism, 1860-1914*, George Allen and Unwin, 1980, Boston, p. 315.

32. Huntington, Samuel, "America's Changing Strategic Interests", *Survival*, vol. 23, no. 1, January-February, 1991, p. 8.

33. Mueller, *Retreat From Doomsday*. For a discussion of changes in values among Europeans on matters of domestic society and ways of life, see Inglehart, Ronald, *The Silent Revolution*, Princeton University Press, Princeton, N.J., 1977; and Inglehart, *Culture Shift in Advanced Industrial Society*, Princeton University Press, Princeton, N.J., 1990. For a rebuttal, see Clarke, Harold, and Dutt, Nitish, "Measuring Value Change in Western Industrial Societies", *American Political Science Review*, vol. 85, no. 3, September 1991, pp. 905-920.

34. Quoted in Berghahn, V.R., *Germany and the Approach of War in 1914*, St., Martin's, New York, 1973, p. 97.

35. Angell, Norman, *The Great Illusion*, 4th ed. Putnam's New York, 1913; Schumpeter, Joseph, "The Sociology of Imperialism" in *Imperialism and Social Classes*, Kelley, New York, 1951. The phrase is borrowed from Albert Hirschman (although the story he tells is much more complex), in *The Passions and the Interests*, Princeton University Press, Princeton, N.J., 1977.

36. Doyle, Michael, "Kant, Liberal Legacies and Foreign Affairs", Part-I, *Philosophy and Public Affairs*, vol. 12, no. 3, Summer, 1983, pp. 205-235; and Part-II, ibid, no. 4, Fall, 1983 pp. 323-353.

37. Gowa, Joanne, "Bipolarity, Multipolarity, and Free Trade, "*American Political Science Review*, vol. 83, no. 4, December, 1989, pp. 1245-1256.

38. Deutsch, Karl, et al, *Political Community and the North Atlantic Area: International Organization in the Light of Historical Experience*, Princeton University Press, Princeton, N.J. 1957.

39. Keohane and Nye, *Power and Interdependence*, developed a model of complex interdependence that applies when force is not central, but much of the subsequent debate concerned whether the conditions for it were met, rather than elaborating and testing theories of how relations within a pluralistic security community would be conducted. Furthermore, the previous behavior was strongly influenced by the Cold War setting and so may be different, although still peaceful, in the future.

40. Sacks, Oliver, *Awakening*, Dutton, New York, 1983. The analogy should not be carried too far, however. The history of the intervening years has left strong, damaging marks: see Kennan, George, "Communism in Russian History", *Foreign Affairs*, vol. 69, no. 5, Winter, 1990/91, pp. 168-186. Alexander Motyl argues that *Perestroika* has not merely permitted the rise of ethnic nationalism in the USSR, but has made it a necessity for economic survival: Motyl, "Empire or Stability? The case for Soviet Dissolution", *World Policy, Journal*, vol. 8, no. 3, Summer, 1991, pp. 499-524.

41. Evera, Van, "Primed for Peace", pp. 9-10, 43-44.

42. The incentives of ties to the rest of Europe, in conjunction with the active assistance of European politicians, facilitated Spain's transition to democracy; see Malefakis, Edward, "Spain and Its Francist Heritage" in Herz, Johan, ed., *From Dictatorship to Democracy*, Westport, Conn., Greenwood,

1982, pp. 217-219; and Barker, Mary, "International Influences in the Transition to Democracy in Spain", Columbia University Press, Columbia, Spring, 1988.

43. Snyder Kack, "Avoiding Anarchy in the New Europe", *International Security*, vol. 14, no. 4, Spring, 1990, pp. 5-41.

44. This is central to Snyder's policy prescription in "Avoiding Anarchy." Mearsheimer also sees hyper-nationalism as "The most important domestic cause of war", but exaggerates the extent to which "its causes ... lie in the international system," Mearsheimer, "Back to the Future", p. 21.

45. For an excellent discussion of the links between migration and security, see Wiener, Myron, "Stability, and International Migration", MIT Center for international Studies Occasional Paper, December, 1990.

46. For general overviews of Third World security, see Sayigh, Yezid, *Confronting the 1990s: Security in the Development Countries*, Adelphi Paper No. 251, London, International Institute of Strategic Studies, Summer, 1990; and Ayoob, Mohammed, "The Security problematic of the Third World", *World Politics*, vol. 43, no. 2, January, 1991, pp. 257-283.

47. See, for example, Herbst, Jeffrey, "The Creation and Maintenance of National Boundaries in Africa", *International Organization*, vol. 43 no. 4, Fall, 1989, pp. 673-692.

48. Jackson, Robert and Rosberg, Carl, "Why Africa's Weak States Persist: The Empirical and the Juridical in Statehood", *World Politics*, vol. 35, no.1, October, 1982, pp. 1-24: Herbst, Jeffrey, "War and the State in Africa", *International Security*, vol. 14, no. 4, Spring, 1990, pp. 117-139. As these articles note, more wars might lead to stronger states. See also Jackson, Robert, *Quasi States: Sovereignty, International Relations and the Third World*, Cambridge University Press, Cambridge and New York, 1990.

49. It should be noted, however, that the conclusion about the future follows from the judgement of the past only if all

other things remain equal. This ignores the possibility that the end of the Cold War will trigger processes that could compensate for the removal of the superpower restraint, or on the other hand, that would alter politics in the Third World in ways that are difficult to foresee. For reasoning of this type, see Jervis, "Systems Effects".

50. See Viorst, Milton, "Report from Baghdad" *New Yorker*, June 24, 1991, pp. 67-68.

51. Gerschenkron, Alexander, *Economic Backwardness in Historical Perspective*, Belknap Press Cambridge; 1962. Also see Tilly, Charles, *Capital, Coercion and European States, AD 990-1990*, London, Blackwell, 1990, Chapter 7.

52. See, for example, the articles by Walt, Stephen, "The Case for Finite Containment: Analyzing US Grand Strategy"; David Steven, "Why the Third World Matters"; Desch, Michael, "The Keys that Lock up the World: Identifying American Interests in the Periphery" and Johnson, Robert, "The Persian Gulf in US Strategy: A Skeptical View," in *International Security*, vol. 14, no. 1, Summer 1989, pp. 5-160; and Evera, Van, "Why Europe Matters, Why the Third World Doesn't". It can also be argued that America had fewer valid security concerning during the Cold War than was generally believed see, for example, Art, Robert, "A Defensible Defense: America's Grand Strategy After the Cold War, *International Security*, vol. 15, no. 4, Spring, 1991, pp. 19-22; Nordlinger, Eric, "Prospects and Policies for Soviet-American Reconciliation", *Political Science Quarterly*, vol. 103, no. 2, Summer, 1988, pp. 197-222; Nordlinger, "America's Strategic Immunity," in Jervis, Robert and Bialer, Seweryn, eds., *Soviet-American Relations After the Cold War*, Duke University Press, Durham, N.C., 1990, pp. 239-261; Jervis, *Meaning of the Nuclear Revolution*, chap. 1; Jervis, *The Logic of Images in International Relations*, 2nd. ed, Columbia University Press, New York, 1989, pp. 244-250.

53. See, for example, Gray, Colin, "Do the Changes Within the Soviet Union Provide a Basis for Eased Soviet-American

Relations?" in Jervis and Bialer, eds, *Soviet–American Relations*, pp. 61-75.

54. For a general discussion of the danger of proliferation and possible American responses in the post-Cold War world, see Art, "Defensible Defense", pp. 24-30; and Arnett, "Choosing Nuclear Arsenals", *Journal of Strategic Studies*, vol. 13, no. 3, September, 1990, pp. 166-171.

55. Whether this is the case is an interesting question that can be dealt with only briefly here. America's vision of the good society is not universally shared either domestically or internationally. Some people, especially those who see political and social development as unidirectional, may believe that with sufficient education and exposure to the Western world all people will want to be like Americans. Perhaps this will be true in the long run, but it appears that for the foreseeable future many in the Third World will find Western liberal individualism repellant. This presents the United States with an intellectual – and emotional conundrum as well as a policy dilemma. Americans want to see their values realised throughout the world, and one of these values is self-determination in the broadest sense of the term. But should Americans rejoice or despair if others then define themselves in ways that are antithetical to Americans' values and hostile to their interests? For an argument that if America is to have a benign effect on the world and realize its deepest values, it must "recast ... its self-conception, its place in the West, and its relation to the former Leninist and 'third' worlds", see Jowitt, Kenneth, "The Leninist Extinction", in Chirot, Daniel, ed., *The Crisis of Leninism and the Decline of the Left: The Revolution of 1989*, University of Washington Press, Seattle, 1991, p. 94. Also see Hartz, Louis, *The Liberal Tradition in America*, Harcourt Brace, New York, 1955, Chapter-11.

56. See *Time*, October 7, 1991, p. 15. Also see Apple, R W. "Majority in Poll Fault Focus by Bush on Global Policy But Back New Order" *New York Times*, October 11, 1991, p. 8.

57. Krauss, Clifford, "Democratic Leaders Divided on China Trade", *New York Times,* October 9, 1990, p. 5.

58. Bonner, Raymond, "A Reporter at Large: African Democracy", *New Yorker,* September 3, 1990, pp. 93-105. Also see Perez, Jane, "Kenyan Magazine Editor Held After Articles on Opposition Party", *New York Times,* March 3, 1991. For reports of an American attack on human and political rights violation in Pakistan, see Luhan, Michael J., "Bhutto and Her Party Languish After Defeat", *New York Times,* May 6, 1991, p. 5.

59. Binder, David, "U.S., Citing Human Rights, Halts Aid to Yugoslavia", *New York Times,* May 19, 1991, p. 10. Also see the stories in the *Times* over the succeeding week.

60. The best discussion is Macdonald, Douglas, *Adventures in Chaos,* Harvard University Press, New York, 1992.

61. Quoted in Schlesinger, Arthur Jr., *A Thousand Days,* Houghton Miffin, Boston, 1965, p. 769.

62. For the case for making the spread of democracy the pivot of American foreign polity, see Fossedal, Gregory, *The Democratic Imperative: Exporting the American Revolution,* Basic Books, New York, 1989. For balanced discussions, see Snyder, "Averting Anarchy"; Art, "Defensible Defense", pp. 42-43; Van Evera, "Why Europe Matters", pp. 25-30.

63. Gilpin, Robert, *The Political Economy of International Relations,* Princeton University Press, Princeton, 1987, pp. 397-401.

64. Art, "Defensible Defense", pp. 30-41; and Van Evera, "Why Europe Matters", pp. 10-11.

65. As Arnold Wolfers put it, collective defense had primacy over collective security; Wolfers, Arnold, *Discord and Collaboration: Essays on International Politics,* John Hopkins University Press, Baltimore, 1962, Chapter 12.

66. Bush, George, *National Security Strategy of the United States,* p. 7. This is part of Bush's "new world order". For a good exposition of this concept, see Slaon, Stanley, "The U.S.

Role in a New World Order: Prospects for George Bush's Global Vision", *Congressional Research Service Report*, March 28, 1991. Also see Kupchan, Charles and Kupchan, Clifford, "Concerts, Collective Security, and the Future of Europe", *International Security*, vol. 16, no. 1, Summer, 1991, pp. 114-161.

67. Kissinger, Henry, *The Necessity for Choice*, Harper and Row, New York, 1961.

68. This would probably be true in Algeria. See Ibrahim, Youssef, "Algeria Imposes a Curfew and Promises to Use Force", *New York Times*, June 7, 1991, p. 6.

69. Battaile, Janet, "Bush Seeks Expanded Powers on Foreign Aid, *New York Times*, April 4, 1991, p. 7.

70. Betts, Richard, "Paranoids, Pygmies, Pariahs, and Nonproliferation", *Foreign Policy*, no. 26, Spring, 1977, pp. 167-168, 179-183.

71. Quoted in Maureen Dowd, "Bush Stands Firm on Military Policy in Iraqi Civil War", *New York Times*, April 14, 1991, p. 1.

72. For a related discussion, see Herrmann, Richard K., "The Middle East and the New World Order: Rethinking U.S. Political Strategy after the Gulf War", *International Security*, vol. 16, no. 2, Fall, 1991, pp. 42-75.

73. For the advocacy of this position, see Huntington, "America's Changing Strategic Interest," p. 13. Slocombe, Walter, "The Continued Need for Extended Deterrence", *Washington Quarterly*, vol. 14, Autumn, 1991, pp. 160-167.

74. Friedman, Thomas, "NATO Tries to Ease Security Concerns in Eastern Europe", *New York Times*, June 7, 1991, p. 1.

75. Knox, Peter, "U.S. Strategy in the Gulf War", *New York Times*, July 12, 1991, p. 7.

76. Secretary of State Baker apparently came to support intervention only after he visited the Kurdish refugee camps.

77. Schelling, Thomas C., *The Strategy of Conflict*, Harvard University Press, Cambridge, 1980, p. 260.

78. Bundy, McGeorge, "To Cap the Volcano", *Foreign Affairs*, October, 1969.

79. Gorbachev, Mikhail, *Perestroika: New Thinking of our Country and the World*, Harper and Row, New York, 1987, pp. 178, 202-3.

80. Aron, Raymond, *Paix et Guerre entre les nations*, 4th ed. Calmann Levy, Paris, 1966, p. 7.

81. Gorbachev to the International Forum, February 16, 1987. Reported in *Foreign Broadcast Information Service*, February 17, 1987, p. AA18.

82. *Foreign Relations of the United States*, Washington D.C., U.S. Government printing office, 1952-54, vol. II, p. 837.

83. Bundy, Kennan, McNamara and Smith, "Nuclear Weapons and the Atlantic Alliance", *Foreign Affairs*, Spring, 1982. Also see Garthoff, Raymond L., *Détente and Confrontation: American Soviet Relations from Nixon to Reagan*, The Brooking Institute, Washington D.C., 1985.

84. Howard, Michael, "Reassurance and Deterrence", *Foreign Affairs*, Winter, 1982-83, pp. 310, 318.

85. Ikle, Fred Charles, *Every War Must End*, Columbia University Press, New York, 1971.

86. McNamara, Robert, *Blundering in Disaster*, Pantheon Books, New York, 1986, pp. 44-45.

87. Kennedy, John F., *Public Papers of the President of the United States: John F. Kennedy, 1961-63*, United States Government Printing Office, Washington, 1962-64, p. 441.

88. Larrabee, Eric, *Commander in Chief*, Harper and Row, New York, 1987.

89. Gorbachev, Mikhail, *Perestroika..*, p. 219.

90. Ibid. p. 218.

91. John D. Holum, "Why Non-Proliferation?" *Washington Post*, Washington, March 12, 1995.

92. David N. Fischer, "Reviewing the NPT", *Journal of International Affairs*, New York, February, 1995, p. 36.

93. Serge Sur, "Review Conference on the NPT: Some Legal Aspects," *Journal of International Law*, Washington, March, 1995, p. 61.

94. NPT/Conf. 1995/L. 1/Rev.1. Also see General Assembly Resolution No. 2373 (XXII), Annex.

95. *Jerusalem Post*, May 11, 1995.

96. *Washington Post*, May 12, 1995.

97. Ibid.

98. *The Indian Express*, New Delhi, May 12, 1995.

99. *The Hindu*, Madras, May 13, 1995.

100. *The Indian Express*, New Delhi, May 18, 1995.

101. *Jane's Defence Weekly*, June 24, 1995.

102. Ibid.

103. Dunbar Lockwood, "On Clinton's Calendar", *The Bulletin of the Atomic Scientists*, January-February, 1993, p. 7. Also see Hearings, Senate Governmental Affairs Committee. "To examine nuclear, biological and chemical weapons proliferation threats of the 1990s," February 24, 1993.

104. Richard Nixon, *Seize the Moment: America's Challenge in a One Super-Power World*, New York, 1992, p. 180.

105. George Quester, *Nuclear Proliferation in South Asia*, New York, 1992, p. 20.

106. Geoffery Kemp, *Powderkeg: Weapons Proliferation in the Near East and South Asia: US Policy Dilemmas*, quoted in Stephen P. Cohen (ed), *Nuclear Proliferation in South Asia: The Prospects for Arms Control*, New York, 1991, p. 346.

107. Brahma Chellaney, "Pokharan and After: Caught between Thrift and Drift", *The Indian Express*, New Delhi, May 18, 1995.

108. C. Uday Bhaskar, "What is at Stake?" *The Indian Express*, New Delhi, April 14, 1995.

109. Ibid.

APPENDICES

I

A CHRONOLOGY OF US-SOVIET ARMS CONTROL AND SECURITY INITIATIVES (1946 - 1990)

A

Arms Control, Demilitarisation and Disarmament Initiatives

1946 - June 14

Baruch Plan

Bernard M. Baruch, US representative on the UN Atomic Energy Commission, submits detailed US proposals for international control of atomic energy. The "Baruch Plan" envisages "the creation of an International Atomic Energy Development Authority, to which should be entrusted all phases of the development and use of atomic energy, starting with the raw material", and including direct control of all potentially dangerous atomic activities and licensing of all other atomic activities.

The Authority would be empowered to send officials into states to conduct comprehensive inspections for violations of the treaty. Decisions of the Authority would not be subject to veto in the Security Council. The Baruch Plan emphasised the fundamental US position that establishment of international control of atomic energy should precede the prohibition of national atomic forces.

1953 - April 16
"Chance for Peace"
In his major "Chance for Peace" speech, President Dwight D. Eisenhower proposes that nations set limits on the portion of total production of strategic materials devoted to military purposes. National military and security forces might be restricted in size either by a numerical limitation or by an agreed national ratio between states. The President suggests that the resulting savings be applied to a fund for world aid and reconstruction.

1953 - December 8
"Atoms for Peace"
Speaking to the United Nations General Assembly, President Eisenhower presents his "Atoms for Peace" plan. It calls for the creation of an international atomic agency which would receive contributions for nations holding stocks of nuclear materials and would utilize them for peaceful purposes.

1954 - August 30
Atomic Energy Act
President Eisenhower signs the Atomic Energy Act of 1954, authorising the exchange of information for the peaceful use of atomic energy with other countries and supporting the development of commercial nuclear power.

1955 - May 26
US Disarmament Report
The first comprehensive report of Harold Stassen, Special Assistant to the President for disarmament, stresses the extreme importance of providing against surprise attack, the absolute necessity of stipulations for an effective inspection system in any agreement, and the crucial role of aerial surveillance, photography and scientific monitoring.

The report also notes that there is absolutely no sure method for searching out clandestine nuclear weapons. The solution is control of the atom bomb, not visionary, unenforceable "elimination". As a result, the United States should accept only rigidly reciprocal, verifiable proposals.

1957 - January 14
Comprehensive Force Limitations
Henry Cabot Lodge, US ambassador to the United Nations, presents a comprehensive proposal for nuclear and conventional arms reductions to Committee I of the UN General Assembly. Among its chief provisions:

- Future nuclear production would be restricted to peaceful purposes under adequate inspection;
- Action would be taken at a later stage to reduce existing stockpiles and to convert them to peaceful purposes;
- When future production is effectively controlled, it will be possible to limit and eventually eliminate nuclear tests;
- First-stage reductions in conventional arms would limit the United States and the Soviet Union to 2,500,000 persons and the United Kingdom and France to 750,000 persons;
- At the same time an effective inspection system, including serial reconnaissance and ground control, would be established;
- Space-missile tests would be inspected;
- An international armament agency would come into being at once; and
- Further reductions would depend on major political settlements.

1957 - August 29
Western Disarmament Plan
Following consultation among the NATO allies and other nations, the West presents a working paper entitled "Proposals for Partial Measures of Disarmament" to the UN Subcommittee, intended as "a practical, workable plan" for a start on world disarmament. The paper covers:

- The limitation and reduction of conventional and nuclear armed forces and weaponry;
- Military expenditures;
- The control of fissionable material;
- Nuclear weapons testing;
- The control of objects entering outer space;

- Safeguards against the possibility of surprise attack; and
- Establishment of an international control organisation.

With ratification of such an agreement, Western officials explain, this plan would stop all nuclear bomb testing, bring a halt in production of nuclear bomb materials, start a reduction in nuclear bomb stockpiles, reduce the dangers of surprise attack through warning systems, and start reduction in armed forces and armaments.

1958 - January 12
Peaceful Uses of Space
Replying to a letter from Soviet Premier Nikolai Bulganin that had proposed a cessation of nuclear tests, President Eisenhower proposes an agreement to use outer space for peaceful purposes and to cease nuclear weapons production. The President also says that the United States would be willing to convert a larger amount of its nuclear weapons stockpiles to peaceful uses than the Soviet Union.

1959 - May 14
European Peace Plan
At the Geneva Foreign Ministers' Conference, the Western powers – France, Britain and the United States – present a peace plan containing proposals on German reunification, European security and a final peace settlement. Its parts are all linked together and must be viewed as a whole. This plan, coordinating the timing of conventional force reductions with steps in the reunification of Germany, envisages a gradual and logical development through stages of "security" and "reunification" into a final and conclusive stage where a "final Peace Settlement" would be signed "with a Government representing all Germany".

Regarding armament levels, the three Western powers and the USSR would restrict or reduce their armed forces to agreed limits such as 2,500,000 each for the United States and the Soviet Union. In the next stage, they would limit their armed forces further, to 2,100,000 each for the United States and the Soviet Union, for example, with negotiations aimed at still further reductions.

1959 - December 1
Antarctic Treaty
The United States, the Soviet Union and ten other countries sign a treaty in Washington to internationalise and demilitarise the Antarctic continent. The treaty declares the Antarctic an area to be used exclusively for peaceful purposes and prohibits any measure of a military nature in the region such as the establishment of military bases and fortifications, the carrying out of military activities, or the testing of any type of weapons, as well as any nuclear explosion.

1960 - June 27
Arm Reduction Proposal
After a long series of proposals and counterproposals by the West and the Soviet Union, the United States introduces a new plan calling for:
- Prior notification of missile launching;
- Inspection of mutually agreed air bases and launching sites;
- A nuclear production cutoff ; and
- Initial conventional force reduction.

Second stage measures would include further reduction of nuclear stockpiles and conventional forces. In the third stage, national forces would be reduced to levels required for internal order and contingents made available for an international peace force. All armaments not required for these forces would be destroyed or converted to peaceful uses.

The programme emphasises the need for technical studies, an effective control organisation and verification of all measures. Transition from one stage to the next would require approval by the UN Security Council.

1960 - August 16
Control of Nuclear Materials
US ambassador Lodge tells the UN Disarmament Commission that the United States is ready, on a reciprocal basis, to transfer 30,000 kilograms of weapons-grade uranium for peaceful purposes if the Soviet Union agrees to a cutoff of the production of fissionable

materials for military purposes. He also says that the United States is prepared "to shut down, one by one, under international inspection, major plants producing enriched uranium and plutonium, if the Soviet Union will shut down equivalent facilities".

1960 - September 22
Peaceful Uses of Space
In an address to the UN General Assembly, President Eisenhower proposes a series of steps for the peaceful uses of space:
- Celestial bodies should not be subject to national appropriation by any claims of sovereignty;
- There should be no warlike activities on celestial bodies;
- Subject to appropriate verification, no nation should "put into orbit or station in outer space weapons of mass destruction"; and
- There should be a UN program of international cooperation in the peaceful uses of outer space.

1961 - September 20
Disarmament Guidelines
Following intermittent talks, the United States and the Soviet Union agree on a joint statement of principles to guide negotiations for general and complete disarmament. The statement recognises the need for international peacekeeping machinery and international control, and the possibility of taking partial measures before agreement can be reached on the entire disarmament program. The Soviet Union refuses to accept the US position that verification should apply to forces retained as well as forces disbanded under a disarmament agreement.

1961 - US Presents Disarmament Plan
US General Disarmament Plan
Speaking to the United Nations, President John F. Kennedy presents a new US plan for general and complete disarmament calling upon states to seek "the widest possible area of agreement at the earliest possible date ... and to continue their efforts without interruption until the whole program has been achieved." The President calls for:

- Immediate signing of a test ban treaty, independently or other disarmament negotiations;
- Ending production of nuclear weapons and preventing their transfer to non-nuclear powers;
- Preventing transfer of control of nuclear weapons to non-nuclear powers;
- Barring nuclear weapons from outer space;
- Gradually destroying existing nuclear weapons and transferring the nuclear materials to peaceful uses;
- Halting the testing and production of strategic nuclear delivery vehicles and gradually destroying existing ones; and
- Earmarking national forces for call by the United Nations to perform peacekeeping duties, and improving the operations of the UN peacekeeping machinery.

1962 - April 18
Three-Stage Disarmament Proposal
The United States introduces new disarmament proposals. Stage one provides for:

- Three-step, 30 per cent reduction of nuclear delivery vehicles and other major armaments;
- Restrictions on arms production;
- Reduction of US and Soviet forces to 2.1 million;
- Nuclear production cutoff and transfer of fissionable material to peaceful uses;
- Agreement not to transfer nuclear weapons to nations not possessing them;
- Test ban agreement;
- Advance notification of missile launching;
- Reports on military spending;
- Measures to reduce the risk of war;
- Establishment of an international disarmament organisation;
- Initial peacekeeping arrangements; and
- Study of measures to reduce and eliminate nuclear weapons stockpiles.

Stage two calls for a 50 per cent cut in the remaining nuclear delivery vehicles and armaments, as well as a similar cut of US and Soviet forces from first-stage levels, a reduction of nuclear stocks, and the dismantling or conversion of certain military bases.

Stage three provides for reduction of arms and forces to levels required for internal order, elimination of nuclear weapons from national arsenals, elimination of remaining bases (except those needed for retained forces), monitoring of military research and strengthening of the UN peace force so that no state could challenge it.

The first stage would be for three years. No time limit is specified for the other stages. Ultimate decisions on timing and other matters would rest with the Security Council.

1963 - August 5
Partial Test Ban Treaty

The treaty prohibits the carrying out of any nuclear-weapon test explosion, or any other nuclear explosion: (a) in the atmosphere, beyond its limits, including outer space, or under water, including territorial waters or high seas, or (b) in any other environment if such explosion causes radioactive debris to be present outside the territorial limits of the state under whose jurisdiction or control the explosion is conducted.

1964 - January 21
Nuclear Freeze

At disarmament talks in Geneva, the United States proposes an agreement that would:

- Freeze all nuclear delivery vehicles with effective verification;
- Halt nuclear production facilities on a plant-by-plant basis under international verification;
- Establish observation posts to help prevent surprise attack, accident or miscalculation;
- Prohibit the transfer of nuclear weapons to states not possessing them;
- Place all transfers of nuclear materials for peaceful purposes under international safeguards and inspections; and

- Ban all nuclear weapons tests (including underground tests) under effective verification and control.

1965 - April 29
Outer Space
The United States proposes negotiations to prevent the use of outer space and celestial bodies for military purposes. This proposal follows similar initiatives launched by the Western allies since 1959.

1966 - June 16
Treaty on the Peaceful uses of outer Space
The United States and the Soviet Union submit draft treaties on the peaceful uses of outer space to the United Nations. The treaty is signed on January 27, 1967 and enters into force on October 30, 1967.

1967 - January 27
Outer Space Treaty
The treaty prohibits the placing in orbit around the Earth of any objects carrying nuclear weapons or any other kinds of weapons of mass destruction, the installation of such weapons on celestial bodies, or stationing them in outer space in any manner. The establishment of military bases, installations, and fortifications, the testing of any types of weapons, and the conduct of military activities on celestial bodies are also forbidden.

1967 - February 14
Treaty of Tlatelolco
The treaty prohibits the testing, use, manufacture, production, or acquisition by any means, as well as the receipt, storage, installation, deployment, and any form of possession of any nuclear weapons by Latin American countries.

Under Additional Protocol I, annexed to the treaty, the extra-continental or continental states which de jure or de facto are internationally responsible for territories lying within the limits of the geographical zone established by the treaty undertake to apply the statute of military denuclearisation, as defined in the treaty, to such territories.

Under Additional Protocol II, annexed to the treaty, the nuclear weapon states undertake to respect the statute of military denuclearisation of Latin America as defined in the treaty, not to contribute to acts involving a violation of the treaty, and not to use or threaten to use nuclear weapons against the parties to the treaty.

The treaty enters into force for each state that has ratified it when the requirements specified in the treaty have been met.

The Additional Protocols enter into force for the states that have ratified them on the date of the deposit of their instruments of ratification.

1967 - December 2

Inspection of Nuclear Facilities

The United States announces that to help allay misgivings about its own intentions, it would place all nuclear facilities in the US under treaty safeguards of the International Atomic Energy Administration, excluding only facilities with "direct national security significance".

1968 - 1 July

Non-Proliferation Treaty (NPT)

The treaty prohibits the transfer by nuclear-weapon states to any recipient whatsoever of nuclear weapons or other explosive devices or of control over them. It prohibits the receipt by non-nuclear-weapon states from any transfer whatsoever, as well as the manufacture or other acquisition by those states, of nuclear weapons or other nuclear explosive devices. Non-nuclear-weapon states undertake to conclude safeguards agreements with the International Atomic Energy Agency (IAEA) with a view to preventing diversion of nuclear energy from peaceful uses to nuclear weapons or other nuclear explosive devices.

1969 - March 18

Seabed Weapons

President Richard Nixon instructs the US delegation to the UN Disarmament Committee to lay the groundwork for an international agreement prohibiting the emplacement of weapons of mass destruction on the seabed and ocean floor. He points out that an agreement of this kind, like the Antarctic and Outer Space treaties, "would prevent an arms race before it has a chance to start".

1969 - October 7
Seabed Weapons Treaty
After several months of negotiations and consultations with Western allies, the US drafts a treaty with the Soviet Union for the control of nuclear and other weapons of mass destruction on the seabed, which is submitted to the UN Committee on Complete Disarmament. (The treaty is the subject of prolonged discussion and revision in the United Nations, winning approval on December 7, 1970.)

1971 - September 30
"Hot Line" Modernization Agreement
The agreement establishes, for the purpose of increasing the reliability of the direct communications link set up pursuant to the memorandum of understanding of June 20, 1963, two additional circuits between the USA and the USSR each using a satellite communication system (the US circuit being arranged through Intelsat and the Soviet circuit through the Molnita II system) and a system of terminals (more than one) in the territory of each party. Matters relating to the implementation of these improvements are set forth in an annex to the agreement.

1971 - September 30
Nuclear Accidents Agreement
The agreement provides for immediate notification in the event of an accidental unauthorized incident involving a possible detonation of a nuclear weapon (the party whose nuclear weapon is involved should take necessary measures to render harmless or destroy such weapon), immediate notification in the event of detection by missile warning systems of unidentified objects, or in the event of signs of interference with these systems or with related communications facilities, as well as advance notification of planned missile launchers extending beyond the national territory in the direction of other party.

1972 - May 25

Agreement on the Prevention of Incidents on and over the High Seas

This agreement provides for measures to assure the safety of navigation of the ships of the armed forces of the USA and the USSR on the high seas and the flight of their military aircraft over the high seas which represent a danger to navigation or to aircraft in flight, as well as exchange of information concerning instances of collision or other incidents at sea between ships and aircraft of the parties.

1972 - May 26

SALT - ABM Treaty

The treaty prohibits the deployment of ABM systems for the defence of the whole territory of the USA and the USSR or of an individual region, except as expressly permitted. Permitted ABM deployment are limited to two areas in each country – one for the defence of the national capital, and the other for the defence of some intercontinental ballistic missiles (ICBMs). No more than 100 ABM launchers and 100 ABM interceptor missiles may be deployed in each ABM deployment areas. ABM radars should not exceed specific numbers and are subject to qualitative restrictions.

1972 - May 26

SALT Interim Agreement

The agreement provides for a freeze for up to five years of the aggregate number of fixed land-based intercontinental ballistic missiles (ICBMs) launchers and ballistic missile launchers on modern submarines. The parties are free to choose the mix, except that conversion of land-based launchers for light ICBMs, or for ICBMs of older types, into land-based launchers for modern "heavy" ICBM is prohibited.

   A protocol which is an integral part of the Interim Agreement specifies that the USA may have not more than 710 ballistic missile launchers on submarines and 44 modern ballistic missile submarines, while the USSR may have not more than 950 ballistic missile launchers on submarines and 62 modern ballistic missile submarines. Up to those levels, additional submarine-launched ballistic missiles (SLBMs) – in the USA over 656 ballistic missile launchers on nuclear powered submarines and in the USSR over 740 ballistic missile launchers on nuclear powered submarines, operational and under construction – may become operational as replacements for equal numbers of ballistic missile launchers of types deployed prior to 1965, or of ballistic missile launchers on older submarines.

1973 - May 22

Protocol to the Agreement on the Prevention of Incidents on and over the High Sea

The protocol provides that ships and aircraft of the parties shall not make simulated attacks by aiming guns, missile launchers, torpedo tubes, and other weapons at non-military ships of the other party, no launch nor drop any objects near non-military ships of the other party in such a manner as to be hazardous to these ships or to constitute a hazard to navigation.

1973 - June 22

Agreement on the Prevention of Nuclear War

This agreement provides that the parties will act in such a manner as to exclude the outbreak of nuclear war between them and between either of the parties and other countries. Each party will refrain from the threat of use of force against the other party, against the allies of the other party, and against other countries in circumstances which may endanger international peace and security. If at any time relations between the parties or between other party and other countries appear to involve the risk of a nuclear war or if relations between countries not parties to this agreement appear to involve the risk of nuclear war between the USSR and the USA or between either party and other countries the Soviet Union and the United States, acting in accordance with the provisions of this agreement, shall immediately enter into urgent consultations with each other and make every effort to avert this risk.

1978 - July 22
SALT ABM Treaty
This treaty provides that each party shall be limited to a single area for deployment of antiballistic missile systems instead of two such areas as permitted by the ABM Treaty. Each party will have the right to dismantle its ABM system in the area where it is deployed at the time of signing the Protocol and to deploy an ABM System in the alternative area permitted by the ABM Treaty, provided that prior to initiation of construction, notification is given during the year beginning 3 October 1977, and ending October 2, 1978, or during any year which commences at five-year intervals thereafter. This right may be exercised only once. The deployment of an ABM system within the area selected shall remain limited by the levels and other requirements established by the ABM Treaty.

1974 - July 3
Treaty on the Limitation of Underground Nuclear-Weapon Tests
This treaty prohibits the carrying out of any underground nuclear weapon test having a yield exceeding 150 kilotons, beginning March 31, 1976. Each party shall limit the number of its underground nuclear weapon tests to a minimum. A protocol which is an integral part of the treaty specifies the data that will have to be exchanged between the parties to ensure verification of compliance with the obligations, undertaken. The treaty remains in force for five years and can be extended for successive five-year periods. Underground nuclear explosions for peaceful purposes shall be governed by a separate agreement to be concluded at the earliest possible time.

1984 - September 24
"Umbrella" Arms Talks
In a speech to the UN General Assembly, President Ronald Reagan proposes a broad "umbrella" framework for talks between the United States and the Soviet Union on atom control issues. Reagan suggests that it would be mutually beneficial for the United States and the Soviet Union to consider:

- Exchanging observers at nuclear test sites;

- Exchanging the outlines of five-year plans for weapons development and the schedules for arms procurement; and
- Strengthening contacts between military personnel.

The United States, Reagan says, is committed to achieving the following results in bilateral and multilateral arms control talks:

- A complete ban on chemical weapons at the 40-nation Conference on Disarmament in Geneva;
- Real reductions to lower and equal levels in Soviet and American, Warsaw Pack and NATO conventional forces at the Mutual and Balanced Force Reduction (MBFR) talks in Vienna;
- Concrete, practical measures to enhance mutual confidence, to reduce the risk of war, and to reaffirm commitments concerning non-use of force, at the 35-nation Conference on Confidence and Security Building Measures and Disarmament in Europe (CDE);
- Improvements in verification, essential to ensure compliance with the US-Soviet Threshold Test Ban Treaty of 1974 to limit underground testing of nuclear weapons, and the Peaceful Nuclear Explosions Agreement, signed by the United States and the Soviet Union in 1976;
- Close cooperation to strengthen the international institutions and practices aimed at halting the proliferation of nuclear weapons; and
- A substantial reduction in US and Soviet nuclear arsenals.

1985 - November 21

The Geneva Summit

President Reagan and General Secretary Mikhail Gorbachev issue a Joint statement in Geneva following two days of intensive negotiations. On arms control they agree:

- To commit their two countries to early progress at the Geneva Nuclear and Space Talks, and to focus in particular on areas where there is common ground – the "principle of 50 per cent reductions in the nuclear arms of the US and USSR appropriately applied" and the "idea of an interim INF (Intermediate Range Nuclear Forces) agreement".

- To step up efforts to conclude an effective and verifiable ban on chemical weapons, and to begin discussion on preventing the proliferation of chemical weapons.
- To facilitate an early and successful completion of the work of the Conference on Disarmament in Europe (CDE) in Stockholm. They reaffirm the "need for a document which would include mutually acceptable confidence and security-building measures and give concrete expression and effect to the principle of non-use of force."
- To emphasize the importance of the multilateral NBFR talks in Vienna on reducing the conventional force levels of East and West in Central Europe.
- To study, at the level of experts, the question of "risk reduction centers".

1986 - September 22

Nuclear Weapons, Strategic Defences, Nuclear Testing

Speaking to the UN General Assembly, President Reagan describes a letter that he sent to General Secretary Gorbachev on July 25, in which he discusses "reducing nuclear arms, agreeing on strategic defenses and limiting nuclear testing." The President says the United States is seeking a "50 per cent reduction of American and Soviet arsenals – with the central focus on the reduction of ballistic missile warheads" and the total elimination of INF missiles on a global basis.

The President says that if the US and USSR can agree on radical reductions in strategic offensive weapons, the United States is prepared to sign agreement with the USSR on research, development, testing and deployment of strategic defenses based on the following:

- Both sides "would agree to confine themselves, through 1991, to research, development and testing, which is permitted by the ABM Treaty, to determine whether advanced systems of strategic defense are technically feasible;
- "If, after 1991, either side should decide to deploy such a system, that side would be obliged to offer a plan for sharing

the benefits of strategic defense and for eliminating offensive ballistic missiles; and

- "If the two sides cannot agree after two years of negotiation, either would be free to deploy an advanced strategic defensive system, after giving six months' notice to the other."

President Reagan adds that the United States is prepared to move forward on ratification of the Threshold Test Ban Treaty (TTBT) and the Peaceful Nuclear Explosions Treaty (PNET), "once agreement is reached on improved verification procedures". Upon ratification, the President says, the United States is prepared to discuss ways to implement a step-by-step parallel programme – in association with a programme to reduce and ultimately eliminate all nuclear weapons – of limiting and ultimately ending nuclear testing.

1986 - November 15-16

Reagan-Thatcher Talks

President Reagan and British Prime Minister Margaret Thatcher meet at Camp David and discuss post-Reykjavik prospects for arms control. The leaders agree that priority should be given to achieving, with effective verification:

- An INF agreement, with constraints on shorter-range missile systems;
- A 50 per cent cut over five years in US and Soviet strategic weapons; and
- A ban on chemical weapons.

The President and Prime Minister also agree on the need to press ahead with Strategic Defense Initiative (SDI) research, which is permitted by the ABM Treaty.

The leaders confirm that NATO's defense strategy would continue to require effective nuclear deterrence. They also recognize that reductions in nuclear weapons would increase the importance of eliminating NATO and Warsaw Pact disparities in conventional forces.

B

Chemical and Biological Weapons and Non-Proliferation

1969 - November 25

Chemical and Biological Weapons

President Richard Nixon declares that the United States unilaterally renounces first use of lethal or incapacitating chemical weapons (CW) and unconditionally renounces all methods of biological warfare.

Henceforth the US biological program would be confined strictly to research and defensive measures such as immunisation. The President further instructs the Department of Defense to draw up a plan for the disposal of existing stocks of biological agents and weapons.

1970 - February 14

Toxin Weapons

The United States extends its ban on biological weapons to include toxins (chemical weapons produced through biological or microbic processes).

1971 - August 5

Biological Weapons Convention

The United States and the Soviet Union submit separate but identical draft texts on international convention prohibiting the development, production and stockpiling of biological and toxin weapons, and calling for their destruction.

1972 - April 10

Biological Weapons Convention

The United States, Great Britain and the Soviet Union sign the convention against biological and toxin weapons.

1979 - July 10

Radiological Weapons

After years of negotiation, the United States and the Soviet Union present a draft treaty to ban the use of radiological weapons to the Geneva United Nations Committee on Disarmament.

1983 - February 4
Chemical Weapons Ban
At the UN committee on Disarmament, Vice-President George Bush urges the total elimination of chemical weapons.

1983 - November 14-16
Workshop on Destruction of Chemical Weapons
The US Arms Control and Disarmament Agency sponsors a workshop at Tooele, Utah, on the means of verifying the destruction of chemical weapons. Representatives from thirty member states of the UN Committee on Disarmament attend.

1984 - April 18
Draft Treaty Banning Chemical Weapons
At the Committee on Disarmament, Vice-President Bush presents a US draft treaty banning the development, production, stockpiling and use of chemical weapons. The plan calls for systematic on site-inspection of chemical weapons facilities to ensure compliance.

1986 - January 28
US-Soviet Discussions on Chemical Weapons
The United States and the Soviet Union begin the first round of intensified discussions on a comprehensive ban on chemical weapons as agreed at the November 1985 Geneva Summit.

1987 - February 5
Proposed Global Chemical Weapons Ban
At the Conference on Disarmament, Arms Control and Disarmament Agency Director Kenneth L. Adelman says that the United States gives negotiations aimed at achieving a global ban on chemical weapons "the highest priority". However, the United States "will not accept ... a ban without sound machinery of verification."

1987 - April 23
Chemical Weapons Destruction Facility
Following up on discussions between Secretary of State George Sultz and Foreign Minister Eduard Shevardnadze, the United States formally invites the Soviet Union to visit the US chemical weapons

destruction facility in Tooele, Utah, during 1987 as a means of improving confidence in an eventual chemical weapons ban.

1987 - August 6

US Statement on Chemical Weapons

The Reagan Administration welcomes new Soviet moves toward a chemical weapons ban that were announced by Foreign Minister Shevarnadze in Geneva, August 6.

US Conference on Disarmament (CD) negotiator Max Friedersdorf, US negotiator to the Conference on Disarmament (CD) says the initiatives may close the gap between the US and Soviet positions, but adds that it constitutes only one step toward a chemical weapons convention in a forum with thirty-eight other equal negotiating partners. Significant differences remain, he says.

The Soviet Foreign Minister announced that the Soviet Union would henceforth be willing to accept the principle of "mandatory challenge inspections without right to refusal" as part of the verification provisions of a chemical weapons ban. Challenge inspection, which calls for mandatory on-site inspection of suspected violators of a chemical weapons ban, was included in the US draft chemical weapons convention submitted to the CD in 1984. The Soviet Foreign Minister also invited CD participants to a Soviet military facility to observe the destruction of chemical weapons.

1988 - June 1

Moscow Summit Statement

At the Moscow Summit, President Ronald Reagan and General Secretary Mikhail Gorbachev reaffirm their commitment to a comprehensive, effectively verifiable and global ban on chemical weapons. They also express concern over the growing proliferation and use of chemical weapons.

1988 - July 28

UN Discloses CW Production Facilities

In a speech to the UN 40-nation Conference on Disarmament, US ambassador Max Friedersdorf declares the location of all US CW production facilities and outlines plans for their elimination under a CW ban. The US calls on the Soviet Union and other states with CW to do the same.

1988 - September 26
US Calls for Chemical Weapons Conference
President Reagan, in a speech to the UN General Assembly, urges the parties to the 1925 Geneva Protocol and all other concerned states to convene a conference to reverse the rapid-deterioration of respect for international norms against CW use.

1989 - January 7-11
Paris Chemical Weapons Conference
One hundred and forty-nine nations meet in Paris for a conference to restore respect for the prohibition of illegal use of chemical weapons. In a concluding document, the nations "solemnly affirm their commitments not to use chemical weapons" and stress "the necessity of concluding at an early date, a convention on the prohibition of the development, production, stockpiling, transfer and use of all chemical weapons, and on their destruction".

Participating nations also express grave concern over the spread of chemical weapons, and call on all states to exercise restraint and act responsibly. They reaffirm their commitment to the 1925 Geneva Protocol banning the use of CW in war.

1989 - January 8
Soviet Statement
Soviet Foreign Minister Shevardnadze announces at the Paris CW Conference that the Soviet Union plans to begin destruction of its CW stockpile upon completion of a destruction facility. He also states that the Soviet Union has ended production of CW and calls on other states to follow the example.

1989 - February 9
President Bush Presses for CW Ban
In a speech to the US Congress, President George Bush relates his personal commitment to a CW ban, saying that "chemical weapons must be banned from the face of the earth, never to be used again."

1989 - February 23
US Trial Inspection
The United States conducts a trial inspection of a private US chemical production plant. This is part of an experiment by the UN Conference on Disarmament to develop procedures for a routine inspection regime, which would satisfy confidence and security requirements without significantly disrupting the civilian chemical industry.

The Soviet Union and other members of the Conference on Disarmament subsequently conduct similar trial inspections of their own chemical industries.

1989 - March 6
US Initiatives
In a speech in Vienna, US Secretary of State James Baker calls for an international conference of government and industry to consider ways to curb the proliferation of chemical used to produce chemical weapons. Secretary Baker also announces that the United States will explore ways and means to accelerate the current 1992 withdrawal schedule of US CW from the Federal Republic of Germany. The United States calls upon the Soviet Union to withdraw and destroy its "excessive stocks of CW".

1989 - September 18-22
Canberra Chemical Weapons Conference
Following the US initiative of March 1989, 67 nations attend an International Government – Industry Conference Against Chemical Weapons hosted by the Australian government in Canberra.

Chemical industry participants issue an unprecedented statement:
- Expressing willingness to work for an early conclusion of a global ban on chemical weapons;
- Opposing misuse of industrial products for the dangerous proliferation of chemical weapons;
- Committing industry to continue its dialogue with governments on ways to implement a convention on chemical weapons; and
- Accepting a self-policy role.

1989 - September 23
US–Soviet Memorandum of Understanding on Chemical Weapons
At the Wyoming Ministerial, US Secretary of State Baker and Soviet Foreign Minister Shevardnadze reaffirm the objective of an early conclusion of a comprehensive, effectively verifiable and global ban on chemical weapons.

To intensify efforts towards this goal, and to enhance openness and confidence between the two countries, they sign a Memorandum of Understanding (MOU) on a bilateral verification experiment and data exchange.

The MOU provides for:

Phase I
- Exchange of general data before the end of 1989 on the chemical weapons capabilities of both sides;
- Visits to verify this data to begin by June 30, 1990, to relevant CW military and civil facilities chosen by the host country, such as production and storage facilities and industrial chemical plants.

Phase II
- To begin when the sides formally and jointly acknowledge the possibility that a CW treaty could be initiated in four months;
- Exchange of detailed data on the CE capabilities of both sides;
- On-site inspections to help verify the declared data;
- Each side to conduct up to five inspections of facilities chosen from a list of sites declared by the other, plans up to 10 "challenge" inspections at undeclared facilities;
- Of the 10 "challenge" inspections, up to five per side can take place in a four-month period before a CW treaty is initiated. Up to five additional "challenge" inspections per side can take place after the sides submit a CW treaty to their respective legislative bodies for ratification; and
- "Challenge" inspections to be conducted in accordance with the laws of the inspected country, and in the case of third countries, with their consent.

1989 - September 25

President Bush's Chemical Weapons Initiative

Speaking to the 44th UN General Assembly in New York, President Bush reaffirms the US commitment to a multilateral treaty to eliminate chemical weapons in ten years, provided all CW-capable states become parties to the treaty.

To accelerate agreement on, and implementation of, a total ban on the production, storage, transfer and use of chemical weapons, the president offers the following initiative:

- The United States will destroy more than 98 per cent of its current CW stockpile within eight years after entry into force of a multilateral CW convention, provided the Soviet Union is also a party to the treaty;
- The remaining two per cent to be destroyed in the next two years after all CW-capable states become parties to the convention;
- While working to complete a global convention on chemical weapons, the United States and the Soviet Union will destroy a major portion of their CW stockpiles to an equal interim level set at about 20 per cent of the current US level. The process of destruction would take place on mutually agreed terms and would include verification provisions;
- The United States will accelerate and significantly expand its efforts to improve verification capabilities, and resolve the technical and procedural problems associated with verifying a ban on chemical weapons.

1989 - December 2-3

Malta Summit

President Bush puts forward the following proposals during his meeting with Chairman Gorbachev:

- Speeding achievement of a CW ban by offering to and US production of binary weapons when the multilateral convention enters into force, in return for Soviet acceptance of the terms of the US September 1989 UN proposal to ban chemical weapons;

- Signing an agreement at the 1990 summit to destroy US and Soviet chemical weapons down to 20 per cent of the current US level.

1989 - December 29

US-Soviet Data Exchange on CW Stockpiles

The United States and the Soviet Union provide each other with general data on their CW stockpiles and facilities, in accordance with their MOU on CW signed on September 23, 1989. This exchange is designed to facilitate negotiations on a multilateral CW ban.

1990 - February 10

Moscow Ministerial

Following meetings between Secretary Baker and Foreign Minister Shevardnadze, the US and USSR reaffirm that chemical weapons must be eliminated worldwide. They agree on the following framework for the achievement of this high priority:

- The sides will work to expedite the negotiations on a CW convention in Geneva with a view to resolving main outstanding issues as soon as possible, and to finalise the draft convention at the earliest date.
- Pending the international convention, the sides will proceed with the objective of completing and signing a bilateral agreement at the 1990 summit on reciprocal obligations, including the destruction of the bulk of their CW stocks to equal low levels.
- When the CW convention enters into force, the sides will further reduce their CW stocks to equal levels at a very small fraction of their present holdings over the first eight years of operation of the convention. All remaining CW stocks should be eliminated over the subsequent two years. All CW-capable states must adhere to the convention.
- The sides share the view that both nations should be among the original parties to the convention, whose ratification would be necessary for its entry into force.

- The Multilateral convention shall contain the provision that all production of chemical weapons will halt upon its entry into force.

- The multilateral convention shall contain the provision that all production of chemical weapons will halt upon its entry into force.

C

Confidence-Building Measures

1955 - July 21
"Open Skies"
Meeting with the heads of France, Britain, and the Soviet Union in Geneva, President Eisenhower presents his "Open Skies" plan designed to protect nations against military build-up and surprise attack. He proposes that the Soviet Union and the United States agree immediately to exchange blueprints of their military establishments and to furnish each other facilities for aerial reconnaissance. The purpose would be to prevent surprise attack and to begin a comprehensive and effective system of inspection and disarmament.

1955 - October 11
"Open Skies" Letter
President Eisenhower, in a letter to Soviet Premier Nikolai Bulganin, asks that the Soviets study further his "Open Skies" proposal, and states the willingness of the United States to accept a Soviet proposal for ground-control teams if the Soviets accept aerial inspection.

1956 - March 21
"Open Skies" Test
The United States presents a proposal for an "Open Skies" demonstration test area to the UN Disarmament Subcommittee. The United States also proposes immediate exchanges, for a test period, of technical missions for preliminary study of methods of control and inspection.

1957 - August 2

Inspection Proposal
Secretary of State John Foster Dulles presents a Western paper proposing a combined system of aerial inspection and ground control to the UN Disarmament Subcommittee. Under its terms, all territory of the United States and the Soviet Union and Canada would be opened for inspection. The Western powers indicate, however, that they are prepared to discuss other proposals if the Soviet Union agrees to include a significant part of its own territory in a European zone of inspection.

1962 - December 12

Prevention of Accidental Conflict
At the UN disarmament talks, the United States introduces proposals to reduce the risk of war through accident, miscalculation or failure of communication and recommends informal talks. The proposals include:
- Advance notification of major military movements;
- Installation of permanent observation posts at major transportation centres;
- Exchange of military missions to promote improved understanding;
- Establishment of rapid and reliable communications links between major capitals (the "hotline"); and
- Establishment of an international commission on reduction of the risk of war.

1963 - June 20

"Hotline Agreement"
The United States and the Soviet Union sign a memorandum of understanding in Geneva to establish a direct communications links, or "hotline" between the two governments for use in crises.

1971 - September 30

Accord on Accidental Nuclear War
After months of exploratory talks and negotiations by the SALT delegations, the United States and the Soviet Union sign an

"Agreement on Measures to Reduce the Risk of Outbreak of Nuclear War". The agreement covers three main areas:
- A pledge to maintain and improve safeguards against accidental or unauthorized use of nuclear weapons;
- Immediate notification should a risk of nuclear war arise from detection of unidentified objects or any other unexplained incident involving a possible detonation of a nuclear weapons; and
- Advance notice of any planned missile launches beyond the territory of the launching party and in the direction of the other party.

1973 - June 22
Prevention of Nuclear War
The United States and the Soviet Union sign an agreement to consult each other in the time of crisis to avoid nuclear conflict.

1975 - August 1
Helsinki Final Act
The United States, the Soviet Union and thirty-three other nations participating in the Conference on Security and Cooperation in Europe (CSCE), sign a concluding document in Helsinki that provides for notification of major military activities involving more than 25,000 troops and other confidence-building measures.

1982 - June 11
Confidence-building Measures
Speaking in Berlin, President Ronald Reagan states that the United States seeks to increase understanding and communication between the United States and the Soviet Union in times of peace as well as crisis. The US will submit proposals for advance notification of strategic exercises that otherwise might be misinterpreted, advance notification of missile launches and an expanded exchange of strategic forces date.

1982 - June 17
Military Expenditures
At the UN Special Session on Disarmament, President Reagan proposes an international conference on military expenditures to

build on the work of the United Nations in developing a common system for accounting and reporting.

1984 - January 17

Conference on Disarmament in Europe (CDE)

The Conference on Confidence and Security-Building Measures and Disarmament in Europe (CDE) opens in Stockholm, Secretary of State George Shultz reiterates US willingness to resume suspended arms control talks on nuclear weapons. He says the United States is ready to negotiate concrete and verifiable measures in Stockholm that would be a significant improvement over the confidence-building measures adopted in the Helsinki Final Act of 1975.

1984 - January 24

CDE Proposals

At the Stockholm Conference on Disarmament in Europe, the United States and its NATO allies table a package of confidence and security building measures. They include:

- Exchange of information about military forces;
- Annual forecasts of military activities;
- Providing advance notice on important military activities;
- Allowing observation of important military activities;
- Providing means for verifying compliance with agreements reached; and
- If warranted by the above measures, establishing special communications among participating countries.

1984 - July 17

"Hotline" Accord

The United States and the Soviet Union initial a diplomatic note in Washington agreeing on technical improvements in the 21-year old Direct Communications Link, or "hotline" between Washington and Moscow.

1985 - March 8

CDE / Amplified Western Proposal

The United States and the fifteen other members of NATO table the full texts of the six Western confidence-and-security building measures (CSBMs) as a single, comprehensive document. They are thus the first to present the Conference on Disarmament in Europe with a fully developed negotiating position in precise, detailed language suitable for a final agreement.

1985 - May 8
Step to Reduce Military Tensions
In an address to the European Parliament in Strasbourg, President Reagan proposes steps to reduce East-West tensions, including:
- An exchange of observers at military exercises;
- The establishment of regular high-level contacts between Soviet and US military leaders; and
- A permanent military-to-military communications link.

The President also repeats his offer of June 4, 1984, to discuss Soviet proposal on non-use of force in the context of Soviet agreement to concrete confidence-building measures in the Conference on Disarmament in Europe.

1986 - May 5-6
Nuclear Risk Reduction Centers
US and Soviet negotiators meet in Geneva to discuss establishing Nuclear Risk Reduction Centers (NRRCS) in Washington and Moscow, staffed separately by US and Soviet officials, to lessen the chance of misunderstandings which could lead to accidental nuclear war.

1986 - June 30
CDE Negotiations
In an effort to accelerate progress of the Conference on Disarmament in Europe, the West offers a major five-point initiative identifying areas of Western flexibility on key issues of negotiations, observation and verification.

1986 - September 22
CDE Accord
In Stockholm, the 35-nation Conference on Confidence-and Security Building Measures and Disarmament in Europe (CDE) adopts an accord designed to reduce the risk of war in Europe.

Under the accord, NATO and Warsaw Pact agree to give each other advance notice, in some cases by as much as two years, of all major military activities from the Atlantic Ocean to the Ural Mountains. The agreement also provides for air and ground on-site challenge inspections, without the right to refusal, to verify compliance with commitments undertaken in the CDE.

President Reagan says the set of measures adopted by the Stockholm CDE conference "marks a substantial advance over those in the Helsinki Final Act. These measures will make military activities more predictable and inhibit opportunities for political intimidation.

1987 - May 4
Nuclear Risk Reduction Centers
US and Soviet negotiators in Geneva reach a referendum agreement on draft joint text to establish Nuclear Risk Reduction Centers in Washington and Moscow to lessen the chance of misunderstandings which could lead to accidental nuclear war. Staffed separately by the US and Soviet officials, the centers would be connected by a new, dedicated communications link and would play a role in exchanging information and notifications required under existing and possible future arms control and confidence-building measures agreements.

1987 - July 10
NATO CSCE Proposal
At the Third Review Meeting in Vienna of the Conference on Security and Cooperation in Europe (CSCE), the US and its NATO allies table a proposal calling for two distinct negotiations to take place within the framework of the CSCE process:

- One negotiation, involving all 35 CSCE participating states, would continue the work of the Conference on Confidence and Security Building Measures and Disarmament in Europe (CDE).
- The other negotiation, involving only NATO and Warsaw Pact members, would have as its goal strengthened stability in Europe at lower levels of conventional forces. Participants in

this autonomous negotiation would periodically exchange views with and provide information to the other 12 CSCE states.

Representatives of NATO and Warsaw Pact nations also have meeting separately in Vienna since February to reach agreement on a negotiating mandate for talks on conventional force stability covering the whole of Europe from the Atlantic to the Ural Mountains.

1987 - September 15

US–USSR Nuclear Risk Reduction Center Accord

Secretary of State George Shultz and Foreign Minister Eduard Shevardnadze sign in Washington an agreement to establish Nuclear Risk Reduction Centers in Washington and Moscow to reduce the risk of conflict between the US and the Soviet Union that might result from accidents, miscalculations or misinterpretations.

President Reagan, at the signing ceremony, says these centers would "provide a means to transmit notifications required under existing confidence-building measures and could play a key role in exchanging the information necessary for effective verification of future arms control agreements."

1988 - April 1

US Nuclear Risk Reduction Center Opens

The US Nuclear Risk Reduction Center officially opens at the Department of State.

Together with its Soviet counterpart, the centers, for example, transmit notifications related to short-notice inspections conducted under the December 1987 Intermediate-Range Nuclear Forces Treaty (IMF), and to ballistic missile launches under an agreement signed at the Moscow Summit.

1988 - May 31

Ballistic Missile Launch Notification Agreement

During the Moscow Summit, the United States and the Soviet Union sign an agreement requiring each side to notify the other at least twenty-four hours in advance of all launches of intercontinental ballistic missiles and submarine launched ballistic missiles. Both countries launch such missiles from time to time for testing and training purposes and maintaining their reliability. The agreement is designed to reduce the risk of nuclear war, in particular as a result of misinterpretation, miscalculation or accident.

1989 - January 17
CSBM Negotiations
The Concluding Document of the 35-nation Vienna follow-up meeting of the Conference on Security and Co-operation of Europe (CSCE) calls for resumed negotiations on confidence- and security building measures (CSBMs). CSBMs will focus on openness and predictability of military activities, and open access to military information.

The document directs negotiators to "build upon and expand the results already achieved at the Stockholm Conference (concluded September 19, 1986) with the aim of elaborating and adopting a new set of mutually complementary confidence-and- security-building measures designed to reduce the risk of military confrontation in Europe."

1989 - March 19
Western CSBM Proposal
On the opening day of the Vienna Negotiations on Confidence- and Security Building Measures, the 16 Western allies table a set of 12 measures:
- Exchange of military information;
- Information exchange on major conventional weapons deployment programs;
- Establishment of a system for random evaluation of information;
- Enhanced information in the annual calendar of military activities;
- Enhanced information in notification of military activities;
- Improvements to observation modalities;
- Lowering thresholds of observation;
- Improvements to thresholds of inspection;

- Lowering thresholds for longer notice of large-scale military activities;
- Improved access for accredited personnel dealing with military matters;
- Improvement of means of communication; and
- Equal treatment of media representatives at observable military activities.

In addition, the West tables a proposal for a seminar on military doctrine.

President George Bush says: "Our aim is to lift the veil of secrecy from certain military activities and thus contribute to a more stable Europe."

The Warsaw Pact also tables a proposal which focuses on, additional constraints and on extending CSBMs to naval and air activities.

1989 - May 5 - July 12

Round II of CSBM Talks

During Round II of the Vienna CSBM negotiations:

- The West amplifies its proposal;
- The East explains its proposals calling for the extension of CSBMs to air and naval activities, and for a European Risk Reduction Center;
- The neutral and non-aligned countries table a paper in an effort to bridge the gap between the Eastern and Western packages; and
- All thirty-five participants agree to hold a seminar on military doctrine and to set up a seminar-planning group.

1989 - May 12

President Bush's "Open Skies" Initiative

In remarks at Texas A&M University, President Bush renews and expands upon President Eisenhower's 1955 "Open Skies" proposal. He invites the Soviet Union and other members of the Warsaw Pact and NATO to agree to unarmed surveillance flights over their territories.

The President says that such flights, "complementing satellites, would provide regular scrutiny for both sides. He suggests that a conference of interested participants be held to work out the necessary operational details."

1989 - June 9
Western Amplified CSBM Proposal

At the CSBM negotiations, the West tables an amplified version of its March proposal. NATO seeks to expand the regime established by the 1986 Final Document of the Stockholm Conference on Confidence-and-Security-Building Measures and Disarmament in Europe to include not only military activities, but also military structure and deployment.

1989 - June 12
Agreement on Dangerous Military Activities (DMA)

The United States and the Soviet Union sign the Dangerous Military Activities (DMA) Agreement, which commits both nations to seek to prevent four kinds of dangerous military activities during peacetime:

- Unintentional or emergency entry into the national territory of the other side;
- Hazardous use of laser devices;
- Disruption of military operations in a mutually agreed upon "Special Caution Area"; and
- Interference with the command and control network of either side.

1989 - September 8 - November 10
Round III CSBM Talks / Military Doctrine Seminar

During the third round of the CSBM negotiations, the participating states agree to a Western proposal to conduct a seminar on military doctrine. The seminar will begin on January 16 and will last for three weeks. High-level military representatives of the thirty-five states will be invited to discuss their countries' military doctrines as it relates to force structure and deployment, training and military budgets. The seminar will take place in Vienna and is part of the CSBM talks.

1989 - September 22-23
USSR and "Open Skies" Proposal
At a meeting in Wyoming with US Secretary of State James Baker, Soviet Foreign Minister Shevardnadze agrees in principle to the "Open Skies" concept proposed by President Bush on May 12, 1989, and notes his willingness to attend an international conference on the subject.

The "Open Skies" proposal seeks to:
- Encourage reciprocal openness among members of the two alliances;
- Increase transparency, reduce danger and relax tensions by observing military activities and installations; and
- Allow participating states to establish flight quotas, frequency and duration on the basis of the geographic size of countries.

1990 - January 16 - February 5
Military Doctrine Seminar
Colin Powell, US Chairman of the Joint Chief of Staff, and his thirty-four counterparts meet at the CSBM talks in Vienna to discuss military doctrines. More detailed discussion among experts covers force structure, military activities and training and military budgeting and planning.

1990 - February 12-28
Ottawa "Open Skies" Conference
At the beginning of Round I of the "Open Skies" Conference, the twenty-three ministers and representatives of NATO and Warsaw Pack nations issue a communiqué agreeing that an "Open Skies" should:
- Ensure maximum possible openness and minimum restrictions for observation flights;
- Include the right to conduct, and the obligation to receive, observation flights;
- Provide for the use of unarmed observation aircraft and equipment capable of fulfilling the goals of the regime in all circumstances; and

- Allow for the possible participation of other countries, primarily the European Neutral and Nonaligned States (NNSs).

1990 - February 23

West on Military Budgets / Implementation

At the CSBM negotiations, the West tables new proposals growing out of the Military Doctrine Seminar; a measure to exchange military budgets, and a proposal for an annual CSBM implementation meeting.

1990 - April 23

"Open Skies" Conference in Budapest

Round II of the "Open Skies" Conference opens in Budapest and is scheduled to end May 10th.

D

Conventional Forces

1973 - October 30

MBFR Talks

The United States, Soviet Union, and other NATO and Warsaw Pact countries formally begin the Mutual and Balanced Force Reduction (MBFR) negotiations in Vienna to reduce conventional military forces in Central Europe to equal but significantly lower levels.

On November 22, the West presents its proposal for first phase cuts in Soviet and US personnel. In the second phase, both sides would reduce troop strength to a common ceiling of 700,000 ground forces and 900,000 ground and air forces combined. These ceilings remained the centerpiece of the NATO position throughout the lengthy negotiations.

1982 - June 9

MBFR Negotiations

In a speech to the West German Bundestag, President Ronald Reagan calls for progress in reducing conventional troop levels in

Europe, and repeats the US conviction "that a stable military balance at the lowest possible level will help further the cause of peace".

A month later, the West submits a new draft treaty at the MBFR talks in Vienna whose major change would be to bind all treaty participants to one overall agreement in reducing troop ceilings of 700,000 ground force personnel and 900,000 total ground and air force personnel. The draft treaty also calls for verification and confidence building measures.

1983 - December 15

Soviet MBFR Suspension

The 31st negotiating round of MBFR talks on reducing conventional troop strength in Central Europe ends in Vienna without Soviet and Warsaw Pact agreement on a resumption date.

1984 - March 16

Soviet Union and MBFR Talks

The West makes a new proposal at the MBFR talks aimed at breaking the deadlock over Warsaw Pact troop strength and verification. Under terms of the proposal, NATO will show flexibility and defer full agreement on the actual size of Warsaw Pact forces until the first troop reductions have taken place. In return, the Soviet Union and other East European participants will meet Western verification requirements.

1984 - September 27

MBFR "Dialogue"

In a statement at the beginning of the latest round of talks, the United States and its NATO allies call for an "in-depth dialogue on concrete issues" of the East-West talks on conventional troop cuts. The flexibility shown by the West in its April 19th proposal to break the deadlock over the number of Warsaw Pact forces stationed in Central Europe, they point out, opens the way for a "further rapprochement" between East and West.

1985 - December 5

New Western Proposal at MBFR

The United States and its NATO allies present a new proposal at the MBFR talks, and offer to negotiate, "without further delay, a

joint reduction in American-Soviet force levels in Central Europe
and a subsequent collective no-increase commitment" on Eastern
and Western forces for three years. Following are the major points
of the new Western MBFR initiative:

- To break the decade-long empasse, the West defers its
  requirement for agreement on the number of troops both sides
  field in the reductions area;
- The West offers to "work toward a time-limit, first-phase
  agreement", building on the framework proposed by the Soviet
  Union and its Warsaw allies in February;
- The United States initially to reduce its ground forces by 5,000
  and the Soviet Union by 11,500; and
- A verification regime, including a detailed exchange of data
  and thirty inspections a year, to verify troop levels on both
  sides and to confirm compliance with all the provisions of the
  agreement.

1986 - March 20
MBFR Negotiations

At the close of the 38th round of MBFR talks in Vienna, the
White House expresses disappointment that the East has not
responded constructively to NATO's December 1985 initiative
to reach an early accord.

The White House statement points out that, not only did
the West set aside its insistence that an understanding on existing
force levels, be reached before an agreement is signed, it also adopted
the East's own general approach; to negotiate a first-phase, time-
limited agreement in which initial US and Soviet reductions would
be followed by a no-increase commitment in the area of reductions
by all participating states. The Warsaw Pact, however, on February
20 "tabled a draft agreement which recycled old and unacceptable
Eastern positions and which included an utterly inadequate
verification regime ... If the Soviet Union and its allies show the
political will to match that of the West, then there is hope that
the MBFR negotiations can result in an effective and fair
agreement."

1987 - May 14

42nd Round of MBFR Talks

As the 42nd session of the MBFR talks opens, the State Department says the United States believes a verifiable agreement to reduce and limit conventional forces in Europe is achievable despite previous failures.

The State Department statement says that President Reagan has asked the US representative to seek acceptance by Eastern bloc leaders of a Western initiative for a time-limited, first-phase agreement for initial US and Soviet force reductions. Such an agreement would serve "the goal of fostering security and stability in Europe."

1987 - July 10

NATO CSCE Proposal

At the Third Review Meeting in Vienna of the Conference on Security and Cooperation in Europe (CSCE), the US and its NATO allies tabled a proposal calling for two distinct negotiations to take place within the framework of the CSCE process:

- One negotiation, involving all 35 CSCE participating states, would continue the work of the Conference on Confidence- and Security-Building Measures and Disarmament in Europe (CDE).
- The other negotiation, involving only NATO and Warsaw Pact members, would have as its goal strengthened stability in Europe at lower levels of conventional forces. Participants in this autonomous negotiation would periodically exchange views with and provide information to the other 12 CSCE states.

Representatives of NATO and Warsaw Pact nations also have been meeting separately in Vienna since February to reach agreement on a negotiating mandate for talks on conventional forces stability covering the whole of Europe from the Atlantic Ocean and the Ural Mountains.

1987 - July 27

NATO on Conventional Force Stability

The United States and the other 15 NATO countries present a draft-negotiating mandate for new conventional force stability negotiations. According to Stephen Ledogar, US representative to the Vienna discussions on a mandate for conventional stability negotiations, the new negotiations should:

- Eliminate disparities in forces that are prejudicial to stability and security.
- As a matter of high priority, seek to eliminate the capability for launching surprise attack and for initiating large-scale offensive action.

The NATO draft mandate proposes a number of arms control method, including limitations and reductions. It calls for establishment of an effective verification system, which would require exchanges of information as well as on-site inspections as a matter of right.

The Western proposal would permit the twenty-three members of the NATO and Warsaw Pact alliances to begin serious negotiations within the framework of the CSCE process.

1988 - March 2-3
Statement of NATO Heads of State

NATO's "bold new steps" on conventional arms control, first outlined at Halifax, Canada, in May 1986, are strongly endorsed in the statement, "Conventional Arms Control: The Way Ahead," issued by NATO heads of state and government meeting in Brussels. The statement says: "The Soviet Union's military presence in Europe, at a level far in excess of its needs for self-defence, directly challenges our security as well as our hopes for change in the political situation in Europe. Thus the conventional imbalance in Europe remains at the core of Europe's security concerns. The problem is to a large extent a function of the Warsaw Pact's superiority in key conventional weapon system."

1988 - May 29 - June 2
Moscow Summit

President Reagan and General Secretary Mikhail Gorbachev agree that it is important to strengthen stability and security in Europe.

1988 - November 25
NATO Force Comparison Report
NATO's report, "Conventional Forces in Europe: The Facts", demonstrates that the Soviet Union deploys a larger number of tank, artillery and armored infantry fighting vehicles in Europe than all other members of the Warsaw Pact and the Atlantic Alliance combined. Overall, the report says, the Warsaw Pact maintains a considerable advantage over NATO in virtually every category of conventional arms.

1988 - December 7
Announced Soviet Conventional Force Cuts
In an address to the United Nation, General Secretary Gorbachev announces a unilateral decision to cut within two years Soviet armed forces by 500,000 personnel. He also announces cuts of 8,500 artillery pieces, 800 aircraft and 10,300 tanks in East Germany, Hungary, Czechoslovakia and the Western Soviet Union. He says that 50,000 troops would be withdrawn from Eastern Europe within the same period.

Soviet implementation of this decision would still leave the Warsaw Pact with a significant advantage in conventional forces in Europe.

1988 - December 8
NATO Approach to Talks on Conventional Force
The North Atlantic Council outlines the Western approach to future negotiations on conventional forces, calling for:
- Substantially lower limits on holdings of tanks, artillery and armored troop carriers;
- Limits on holdings in these types of equipment by any one country;
- Limits on forces stationed outside national territory; and
- Rigorous and effective verification measures.

1989 - January 10
Mandate for Talks on Conventional Forces
The twenty-three members of NATO and the Warsaw Pact initial a mandate for the Negotiation on Conventional Armed Forces in Europe (CFE). The mandate sets out the objectives for CFE:

- Strengthen stability and security in Europe through the establishment of a stable and secure balance of conventional forces at lower levels;
- Eliminate disparities prejudicial to stability and security; and
- Eliminate the capability for launching surprise attack and for initiating large-scale offensive action.

The mandate also calls for "an effective and strict verification regime" to include on-site inspections as a matter of right.

The talks will cover the land territory of the participants in Europe from the Atlantic to the Urals (ATTU).

1989 - January 23-27
Eastern Bloc Conventional Force Cuts

Erich Honecker, the leader of the German Democratic Republic, announces future unilateral reductions in that nation's conventional forces and military budget. Within a few days, similar announcements are made by the leaders of Czechoslovakia, Bulgaria, Poland and Hungary.

The United States welcomes the announced cuts, saying that willingness to take such unilateral moves is the best evidence of the superiority of Warsaw Pact conventional forces in Europe. Implementation of these reductions would still leave the Warsaw Pact with conventional forces far superior to those of NATO and far stronger than necessary for the East's legitimate defence needs.

1989 - January 30
Warsaw Pact Force Comparison Estimates

For the first time, the Warsaw Pact publishes its own estimates of the military balance in Europe, claiming that a rough parity exists between East and West.

The Warsaw Pact's publication admits Eastern superiority in the types of weapons critical to large-scale offensive operations, such as tanks, armoured infantry fighting vehicles and artillery. The United States welcomes the publication, but does not agree with its conclusion that NATO's and the Warsaw Pact's conventional forces in Europe are equal.

1989 - March 9

Opening of CFE Talks

The twenty-three members of NATO and the Warsaw Pact formally opens the Negotiation on Conventional Armed Forces in Europe (CFE) in Vienna. NATO tables a proposal to limit:

- Main battle tanks to 20,000 for each side;
- Armoured troop carriers to 28,000 for each state; and
- Artillery pieces to 16,500 for each state.

NATO also proposes:

- A sufficiency rule to allow one country to retain no more than 30 per cent of the forces in any one category; and
- A stationing rule to allow each nation to maintain within the zone from the Atlantic to the Urals no more than a certain number of forces outside of its national territory.

In the following two months, the Warsaw Pact tables similar proposals that differ slightly in suggested numerical ceilings.

1989 - May 29-30

US Initiative at NATO Summit

At a summit celebrating NATO's 40th anniversary, Alliance heads of state and government unanimously endorse President George Bush's proposal to:

- Lock-in Eastern acceptance of NATO's proposed ceilings on main battle tanks, armoured troop carriers and artillery pieces.
- Expand NATO's original proposal of March 9 to include reductions of land-based combat aircraft and helicopters to equal ceilings 15 per cent below current NATO levels.
- Propose a cut in the manpower of US and Soviet forces stationed outside national borders in Europe, to result in equal ceilings of approximately 275,000 personnel. This would require the United States to cut about 30,000 ground and air troops and the Soviet Union about 325,000.

In addition, NATO approves President Bush's proposal to:

- Destroy withdrawal equipment and demobilise withdrawn forces; and

- Seek a CFE-agreement in 6 to 12 months and complete reductions by 1992 or 1993.

President Bush also secures the agreement of the NATO allies on a common framework to address the question of short-range nuclear missile (SNM).

A NATO report:

- Announces that once implementation of an agreement on conventional force reductions in Europe is underway, the United States, in consultation with the allies concerned, is prepared to enter into negotiations to achieve a reduction of American and Soviet land-based nuclear missile forces of shorter range to equal and verifiable levels; and
- Calls upon the Soviet Union to unilaterally reduce its short-range missile systems to current levels within NATO's integrated military structure.

1989 - July 13
NATO's Expanded Proposal at CFE
On the last day of Round II of CFE, NATO presents its enhanced proposal incorporating the president's summit initiative of May. NATO proposes to reduce land-based combat aircraft to 5,700 for each side and land-based combat helicopters to 1,900 for each side.

1989 - September 21
NATO Tables Proposals
During Round III, which opened on September 7, the West completes implementation of decisions taken on the NATO Summit in May by tabling proposals on:

- Information exchange, which provides for an exchange of information between members of NATO and the Warsaw Pact on existing forces and for regular updates of this data to facilitate verification;
- Verification, which includes on-site and aerial inspections and rights to observe the destruction of reduced equipment;
- Stabilising measures, which include provisions to supplement force cuts through such measures as monitoring of storage and constraints on certain military activities; and

- Non-circumvention, which makes explicit the inherent right of a party to withdraw from a treaty if its supreme interests are jeopardised.

1989 - September 28
Eastern Proposal on Helicopters / Aircraft
In a new proposal tabled in Vienna, the Warsaw Pact:
- Accepts NATO's proposed limit of 1,900 combat helicopters for each alliance; and
- Moves towards NATO's proposed ceiling of 5,700 combat aircraft for each alliance by suggesting a ceiling of 4,700.

Differences remain between NATO's and the Warsaw Pact's definition of combat helicopters. The East's narrow definition of combat aircraft excludes thousands of its own combat-capable aircraft.

1989 - October 5
Eastern Proposal on Troops
The East modifies its proposal on personnel by lowering the ceiling on forces stationed outside their national territory in Europe from 350,000 to 300,000 for each alliance. Unlike the NATO proposal, which covers only US-and-Soviet-stationed troops, the Eastern ceiling for such stationed forces would cover British, French, Canadian, Belgian, Dutch and US forces. All stationed Eastern forces are Soviet.

1989 - October 19
Warsaw Pact Tables Proposals
The East presents proposals on verification, stabilising measures and information exchange that, in the words of the Soviet negotiator, each of NATO's September 21st proposals on the same topics were clearly mentioned. Though differences remain to be overcome in all three areas, the Eastern verification proposal uses the same structure and some of the same language as the Western proposal on verification.

1989 - December 14
Draft Treaty Texts
Both NATO and the Warsaw Pact table draft treaty texts at the CFE negotiations.

1990 - January 31
President Bush's Initiative on Personnel
The President announces a new initiative to limit US and Soviet ground and air force personnel stationed outside national territory in Central and Eastern Europe to 195,000 for each side. In addition, the United States is allowed 30,000 such personnel in Europe outside this region.

1990 - February 8
Western Proposals in Aircraft, Personnel
NATO tables new proposals on aircraft and personnel levels.

1990 - February 13
Presidential Proposal on Personnel
In Ottawa, foreign ministers of the twenty-three nations participating in CFE endorse the initiative offered by President Bush in his January 31st State of the Nation Address.

1990 - February 22
Western Inspection Protocol
NATO proposes a detailed inspection protocol.

1990 - March 15
NATO Proposals on Destruction and Reductions
NATO tables a draft protocol on Destruction and a Treaty Article on Reductions. NATO also introduces, at the working level, a draft Protocol on Notification and Exchange of Information. The West has now made proposals covering all major elements of a CFE treaty.

1990 - April 4-6
Washington Ministerial
At a meeting in Washington between Secretary James Baker and Foreign Minister Shevardnadze, the Soviets propose limits on US-and-Soviet-stationed aircraft within the CFE area of application.

The United States rejects the proposal and emphasise the importance of including land-based naval aviation in the combat aircraft category.

1990 - April 12

Eastern Draft Inspection Protocol

On behalf of the Warsaw Pact, the German Democratic Republic tables the East's draft inspection protocol at the CFE talks as a "supplement" to the Western draft, rather than a counter proposal.

1990 - April 24

Soviet Proposal on Armoured Combat Vehicles

The Soviet make a national proposal at the CFE talks for limiting armoured combat vehicles to 30,000 for each alliance.

1990 - April 26

Soviet Draft Destruction Protocol

At the CFE talks, the Soviets table as a national proposal a draft destruction protocol, including destruction modalities.

1990 - April 26

NATO Proposal on Attack Helicopters

NATO tables a draft article on the recategorisation of attack helicopters and a protocol on procedures governing the recategorisation of attack helicopters.

E

Defence and Space

1985 - March 12

Nuclear and Space Talks (NST) Open

The United States and the Soviet Union begin NST talks in Geneva. In the Defence and Space Talks (DST), part of NST, the US seeks to:

- Discuss the possibility of both sides making a transition from deterrence based solely on the threat of nuclear retaliation toward increased reliance on non-threatening defences, whether ground or space-based, against ballistic missiles; and

- Reverse the erosion of the 1972 Anti-Ballistic Missile Treaty (ABM), caused by Soviet violations and actions inconsistent with the letter and spirit of the agreement, and achieve the promise of the ABM Treaty by reversing the continuing building up of Soviet offensive nuclear forces.

In DST, the Soviets seek to have a comprehensive ban on research, development, testing and deployment of "Space Strike Arms". With this objective, the Soviets attempt to kill the US Strategic Defence Initiative (SDI) programme while retaining their own robust research and development on advanced defences.

1985 - October 11

US Position on ABM Treaty

President Ronald Reagan determines the broader interpretation of the ABM Treaty to be fully justified. The President also directs that, as a matter of policy, the SDI programme will continue to be conducted according to a more restrictive interpretation of the ABM Treaty than the US could justifiably observe.

Under the broader interpretation of the treaty, ABM systems that are "based on other physical principles" (i.e., other than ABM interceptor missiles, ABM launchers and ABM radars), and including components capable of substituting for ABM interceptor missiles, ABM launchers or ABM radars, may be developed and tested but not deployed, regardless of their basing mode.

Under the more restrictive interpretation, development and testing of ABM systems based on other physical principles are allowed only for fixed land-based systems and components.

1985 - November 1

US Proposal

The US tables a new proposal at DST. The major points are:

- The US is committed to the SDI programme as permitted by, and in compliance with, the 1972 ABM Treaty;
- The US seeks a Soviet commitment now to jointly explore how a cooperative transition could be accomplished should new defensive technologies prove possible; and

- The US proposes that the Soviet Union join an "Open laboratories" arrangement under which both sides would provide information on each other's strategic defence research programme and provide facilities for visiting associated research organisations and laboratories.

1986 - July 25

Reagan's Letter to Gorbachev

In a letter to General Secretary Mikhail Gorbachev, President Ronald Reagan proposes that the sides agree not to deploy advanced strategic defences for a period through 1991. Thereafter, if either side wished to deploy such defences, it would present a plan for sharing the benefits of strategic defence and eliminating ballistic missiles. The plan would be subject to negotiation for two years. If, at the end of two years, the sides were unable to reach agreement, either side would be free to deploy defences after giving six months' notice.

1986 - September 22

Reagan's Proposal at the UN General Assembly

Speaking to the UN General Assembly, President Reagan says that if the US and the Soviet Union can agree on radical reductions in strategic offensive weapons, the US is prepared to sign an agreement with the Soviet Union on research, development, testing and deployment of strategic defences based on the following:

- Both sides would "agree to confine themselves" through 1991 to research, development and testing, which is permitted by the ABM Treaty to determine whether advanced systems of strategic defence are technically feasible";
- "If after 1991, each side should decide to deploy such a system, that side would be obliged to offer a plan for sharing the benefits of strategic defence and for eliminating offensive ballistic missiles; and
- "If the two sides cannot agree after two years of negotiation, either side would be free to deploy an advanced strategic defensive system, after giving six months' notice to the other."

1986 - October 11-13
Reykjavik Summit

At a meeting in Reykjavik, Iceland, President Reagan and General Secretary Gorbachev come close to an agreement for significant reductions of offensive ballistic missiles. However, Soviet efforts to cripple SDI prevent agreement.

In response to the Soviet proposal that the US provide a 10-year commitment not to withdraw from the ABM Treaty, the US offers to accept such a commitment for the 10-year period through 1996, during which research, development and testing, which are permitted by the ABM Treaty, would continue. US acceptance is contingent upon:

- A 50 per cent reduction in strategic offensive forces of the US and the Soviet Union by 1991;
- Elimination by 1996 of all US and Soviet offensive ballistic missiles; and
- Agreement that either side could deploy advanced strategic defences after 1996, unless the sides agreed otherwise.

The Soviets, however, seek in effect to amend the ABM Treaty by banning testing space-based "elements" of a missile defence system outside of laboratories. This would have killed the US SDI programme – something President Reagan could not accept.

1986 - November 5-6
Soviet Proposal on ABM Treaty

At meetings between US Secretary of State George Shultz and Soviet Foreign Minister Eduard Shevardnadze in Vienna, the Soviet Union proposes special talks to negotiate what would be permitted and prohibited under the ABM Treaty.

1987 - January 15
US Position

The US begins Round VII of the NST talks in Geneva with its DST proposals already on the table:

- Mutual commitment, through 1996, not to withdraw from the ABM Treaty for the purpose of deploying advanced strategic defences and during that period to observe all ABM

Treaty provisions while continuing research, development and testing, which are permitted by the ABM Treaty.

- Mutual commitment not to withdraw from the ABM Treaty through 1996 contingent upon 50 per cent reductions in strategic offensive arms by the end of 1991 and the total elimination of all remaining US and Soviet offensive ballistic missiles by the end of 1996.

- Acknowledgement that either side shall be free to deploy advanced strategic defences after 1996 if it so chooses, unless the parties agreed otherwise.

- The right to withdraw from the ABM Treaty for reasons of supreme national interests or material breach would not be forfeited by the above commitment.

All of the above elements are to be incorporated in a new treaty. Alternatively, the US proposal set out by President Reagan's July letter to General Secretary Gorbachev remains on the negotiating table.

1987 - April 15

US Offers New Proposal in Moscow

During meetings with General Secretary Gorbachev and Foreign Minister Shevardnadze in Moscow, Secretary Shultz makes a new US DST proposal, incorporating the following elements:

- Both the US and the Soviet Union would commit through 1994 not to withdraw from the ABM Treaty;

- This commitment would be contingent on implementation of the agreed SART (Strategic Arms Reduction Talks) reductions, i.e. 50 per cent cuts to equal levels of 1,600 strategic nuclear delivery vehicles and 6,000 warheads, with appropriate sublimits;

- The agreement would not alter the sovereign rights of the parties under customary international law to withdraw in the event of material breach of the agreement or jeopardy to their supreme interest; and

- After 1904, either side could deploy defensive systems of its choosing, unless mutually agreed otherwise.

To build mutual confidence by further enhancing predictability in the area of strategic defence, and in response to stated Soviet concerns, the United States also proposes that the US and the Soviet Union annually exchange data on their planned strategic defence activities.

In addition, the United States seeks reciprocal US and Soviet briefings on their respective strategic defence efforts and visits to associated research facilities, as proposed in the US Open Laboratories Initiative. The US also proposes establishing mutually agreed procedures for reciprocal observation of strategic defence testing.

1987 - July 29
Soviet Draft Defence and Space Agreement
The Soviets propose at Geneva a draft Defence and Space agreement limiting ABM research and development to laboratories on Earth and permitting some non-ABM research in space. The Soviets still seek to impose additional constraints on US SDI far beyond those contained in the ABM Treaty and still tie reductions of strategic offensive nuclear weapons to US acceptance of measures designed to cripple SDI.

1987 - September 12
Soviets Amend Proposal
In the Geneva DST talks, the Soviets amend their July proposal, thus acknowledging the right of the sides to conduct ABM research in space.

1987 - November 30
Soviet Admission of SDI-Type Research
In the first public admission by the Soviets that they are engaged in research similar to the US Strategic Defence initiative programme, General Secretary Gorbachev says during a televised interview: "Practically, the Soviet Union is doing all that the United States in doing, and I guess we are engaged in research, basic research, which relates to those aspects which are covered by SDI in the United States."

1987 - December 7-10
Washington Summit
At the Washington Summit, President Reagan and General Secretary Gorbachev agree to instruct their delegations at DST in Geneva to work out an agreement that would commit both nations to observe the ABM Treaty, as signed in 1972, while conducting their research, development and testing as required, which are permitted by the ABM Treaty, and not withdraw from the ABM Treaty, for a specified period of time for the purpose of deploying advanced defences.

The leaders agree that:
- Intensive discussion of strategic stability shall begin not later than three years before the end of specified period. After the specified period, in the event the sides have not agreed otherwise, each side will be free to decide its own course of action.
- Such an agreement must have the same legal status as the treaty on strategic offensive arms, the ABM Treaty and other similar legally binding agreements.
- The sides shall discuss ways to ensure predictability in the development of the US-Soviet strategic relationship under conditions of strategic stability to reduce the risk of nuclear war.

1988 - January 15
Soviet Draft Defence and Space Protocol
The Soviets table a draft START treaty protocol pertaining to defence and space issues. The draft is not consistent with the Washington Summit Joint Statement. The protocol links reductions in strategic offensive weapons to limit development and testing in the US SDI programme – a Soviet position the United States has consistently maintained as unacceptable.

1988 - January 22
US Draft Defence and Space Treaty
The United States tables a Draft Defence and Space Treaty, which is consistent with and includes language from the Washington Summit Joint Statement.

The draft treaty also includes the following additional provisions:

- Entry into force contingent upon entry into force of START treaty;
- Defence and Space treaty would be of unlimited duration with a "specified period" of non-withdrawal from the ABM Treaty to be negotiated;
- Continued observance of the ABM Treaty through that period and until either party chooses a different course of action;
- After the "specified period", either party is free to choose its own course of action, including deployment of strategic missile defences that are prohibited by the ABM Treaty, upon giving the other party six months' written notice of its intention to do so; and
- The United States proposes that confidence-building measures to provide predictability for each side regarding the strategic defence programmes of the other be included as an integral part of the Defence and Space treaty in the form of a protocol.

1988 - March 17

US Draft Predictability Protocol

The United States proposes a Draft Predictability Protocol to the Draft Defence and Space Treaty. The protocol includes:

- An annual exchange of programmatic data on planned strategic defence activities;
- Annual meetings of experts to review the data exchanged and plan further measures cited below:
- Reciprocal briefings on strategic efforts;
- Reciprocal visits to associated research facilities; and
- Reciprocal observations of strategic defence tests.

1988 - March 22-23

US Proposal on Sensors

At a Washington meeting of Secretary Shultz and Foreign Minister Shevardnadze, the United States presents a new initiative concerning sensors. The initiative seeks to avoid future, unsolvable verification problems by committing both parties to a statement that neither would object, on the basis of the ABM Treaty, to the development, testing or deployment by the other of any space-based sensors. Accordingly, each party may develop, test or deploy space-based sensors without restriction.

The United States tables a new proposal to help clarify the meaning of the phrase "research, development and testing as required, which are permitted by the ABM Treaty," in the Washington Summit Agreed Statement. The United States is prepared to carry out such permitted testing only from designated ABM test satellites in order to reassure the Soviets that permitted testing of space-based components of ABM systems does not represent the deployment of such components of ABM systems. The United States proposes that the number of designated ABM test satellites in orbit simultaneously shall not exceed a number well short of that associated with any realistic deployed capability. The United States notes that 15 such satellites would be well below that threshold.

1989 - May 12

US Goal at DST

President George Bush, in a speech at Texas A&M University, says that the US objective in the DST is to preserve the option to deploy advanced defences when they are ready.

1989 - September 22-23

Wyoming Ministerial

During two days of meetings between US Secretary of State James Baker and Foreign Minister Shevardnadze in Wyoming, progress is made in the following areas:

- LINKAGE: The Soviets say they have dropped their linkage between achieving a Defence and Space agreement and completing and implementing an agreement on START. They indicate that they might withdraw from the START treaty if the United States does not abide by the ABM Treaty, as they interpret it.

- KRASNOYARSK: The Soviets agree to eliminate their illegal radar at Krasnoyarsk without preconditions – a long-standing

US requirement for the signing of any strategic arms control treaty.

- ABM NONWITHDRAWAL: The two sides agree to drop the approach of a non-withdrawal commitment to the ABM Treaty while continuing to discuss ways to ensure predictability in the development of the US-Soviet strategic relationship under conditions of strategic stability to reduce the risk of nuclear war.

- PREDICTABILITY: Secretary Baker invites Soviet experts to visit two US laboratories involved in SDI research. The Soviets would be shown one device recovered after a successful flight into space, and another undergoing preparatory research for planned flight into space in the mid-1990s.

1989 - December 5

Revised US Draft Defence and Space Treaty

The United States tables a revised Draft Defence and Space Treaty, which preserves the central elements of the agreement reached at the Washington Summit in December 1987 and reflects the outcome of the Wyoming Ministerial in September 1989.

1989 - December 14-19

Soviets Visits SDI Labs

Accepting Secretary Baker's invitation to visit two US laboratories conducting SDI research, ten Soviet experts visit the TRW Corporation's ALPHA laser facility at San Juan Capistrano, California, and the Beam Experiment Abroad Rocket (BEAR) neutral particle beam facility at Los Alamos National Laboratory, New Mexico.

1990 - March-April

US Tables New Predictability Initiatives in Geneva

The United States proposes a freestanding executive agreement, not tied to the ABM Treaty, on predictability measures in the field of strategic missile defence. The proposal, which is designed to build confidence, would involve exchange of data, meetings of experts, briefings, visits to laboratories, observations of tests and notifications of ABM test satellites.

In addition, the US calls on the sides to conduct a pilot implementation of the US predictability measures. The initiative will require the sides to each select one of their own projects in the field of strategic ballistic measures on that project.

F

Intermediate Range and Short-Range Nuclear Forces

1977 - Early Months
Soviet SS-20 Deployment
The Soviet Union begins deployment of the SS-20 intermediate-range nuclear missiles in the European USSR. The SS-20 is a modern, mobile ballistic missile with three independently targetable warheads and a range covering all of Western Europe from bases well inside the USSR.

1979 - December 12
NATO "Dual Track" Strategy
The NATO unanimously adopts a "dual track" strategy to counter Soviet deployment of SS-20 missiles.

One track calls for arms control negotiations with the Soviet Union to restore the balance in intermediate-range nuclear forces (INF) to the lowest possible level.

In the absence of an arms control agreement, NATO's second track is to modernise its INF with the deployment in Western Europe of 464 single-warhead US ground-launched cruise missile (GLCMs) and 108 single-warhead US Pershing II ballistic missiles, beginning in December 1983.

1981 - November 18
US "Zero Option" Proposal
In a major policy address calling for a framework of negotiations on reductions in all types of arms, President Ronald Reagan proposes the "zero option", agreeing to the cancellation of planned US INF missile deployment, if the Soviet Union agrees to eliminate all its SS-4, SS-20 missiles.

1981 - November 30

INF Negotiations Open

Formal negotiations on INF begin in Geneva. The US seeks global elimination of US and Soviet longer-range intermediate nuclear forces (LRINF) missiles and collateral constraints on shorter-range intermediate nuclear force (SRINF) missiles.

1981 - December 18

Soviet INF Proposal

The Soviets propose an agreement that would establish an eventual ceiling of 300 "medium-range" missiles and nuclear-capable aircraft in Europe for each side, and that would include British and French independent nuclear forces in the US count.

1982 - June 13

US-Soviet "Walk in the Woods" Proposal

US and Soviet negotiators develop an informal package of elements to be included in a possible INF agreement.

This so-called "Walk in the Woods" proposal would:

- Set equal levels of INF missile launchers in Europe;
- Preclude deployment of US Pershing IIs; and
- Freeze Soviet SS-20 deployments in the Asian part of the USSR. Moscow subsequently rejects the package.

1983 - February 3

US Criteria for INF Agreement

The US reiterates criteria, set forth in November 1981 after consultation with approval by the allies, for reaching agreement with the Soviets in INF negotiations:

- Equality of rights and limits between the US and the USSR;
- Exclusion of independent third country, i.e. British and French nuclear deterrent forces from any agreement;
- Agreed-upon limits must be applied on a global basis; no shift of Soviet LRINF missiles from the European USSR to the Asian USSR;
- No weakening of NATO's conventional deterrent forces and
- Effective verification measures.

1983 - March 30

Reagan: Interim Agreement Acceptable

President Reagan announces publicly that the US and the allies are prepared to accept an interim agreement on INF missiles that would establish equal global levels of US and Soviet warheads on INF missile launchers at the lowest possible number, with zero still the ultimate goal.

1983 - May 19

US Draft INF Treaty

The US tables a draft treaty embodying the interim agreement proposed on March 29.

1983 - September 22

New US INF Proposals

At the Geneva negotiations, the US offers three new elements to its proposed interim agreement:

- The US would entertain the idea of not offsetting all Soviet global INF deployments by US deployments in Europe. The US would keep the right, however elsewhere to reach an equal global ceiling.
- The US is prepared to apportion its reductions of Pershing IIs and GLCMs in an appropriate manner.
- The US is prepared to consider proposals involving land-based aircraft.

1983 - October 27

NATO to Maintain Lowest Possible Nuclear Capability

At Montebello, Canada, the US and the allies agree to maintain NATO's nuclear capability at the lowest level consistent with security and deterrence. This would include withdrawing 1,400 US nuclear warheads from Europe over a period of several years. This is in addition to the 1,000 warheads withdrawn following NATO's December 1979 "dual track" decision.

1983 - November 23

US IMF Deployment/Soviets Halt Talks

Deliveries of the first US GLCM components begin in Great Britain and West Germany. This begins implementation of INF deployment in accordance with the second track of NATO's 1979 decision.

The Soviet delegation walks out of the INF negotiations.

The US offers to resume the talks whenever the Soviets are willing to return. On November 30, 1983, 360 Soviet SS-20s, with 1,080 warheads, are deployed.

1983 - November - 1985 January

INF Talks Suspended

Formal INF negotiations remain suspended in the absence of the Soviet delegation.

1984 - November 24

US, Soviets Agree to NST Talks

President Reagan announces that the US and the Soviet Union have agreed to enter into new negotiations, known as the Nuclear and Space Talks (NST), concerning nuclear offensive arms and defence and space issues.

1985 - March 12

NST Talks Open

The US and the Soviet Union begin the NST Talks in Geneva. The US seeks the elimination or reduction of INF to the lowest possible number, with global equal limits.

1985 - March-April

US Reaffirms Draft Treaty / Soviets Table Proposal

At the beginning of the new INF talks, the US reaffirms its approach and its draft treaties of 1983 on the global elimination of INF missiles, and for an interim agreement on equal INF limits at the lowest possible number.

In the new NST talks, the USSR maintains its 1983 position, opposing US INF deployment, and insisting on linkage of Soviet SS-20 with British and French strategic forces.

The Soviet delegation tables a proposal for a bilateral moratorium on INF deployments and a proposal for subsequent "reductions" that would result in zero US INF missiles, but allow Soviet INF missiles at levels equivalent to British and French strategic forces.

General Secretary Gorbachev also announces a unilateral Soviet moratorium on INF missile deployments in the USSR. Soviet deployments nonetheless continue at sites already under construction.

1985 - October 3

Soviet Counterproposal

During a visit to Paris, General Secretary Gorbachev announces elements of a counterproposal to the US proposals of March 1985 in the NST. He calls for a freeze in US and Soviet INF missile deployments, followed by the "deepest possible" reductions, and he announces that Soviet SS-4s are being phased out and some SS-20s are being removed from combat status.

1985 - November 1

US Response

The US response to the Soviet counterproposal contains the following points on INF:

- While preferring the total elimination of US and Soviet INF, the US proposes – as an interim step – limiting US INF missile launchers deployments in Europe to 140 Pershing IIs and GLCMs (each GLCM launcher has four missiles). This is the number to be deployed by December 31, 1985. This proposal also calls for reductions in the Soviet force of SS-20 missile launchers within range of NATO Europe to 140 (each SS-20 missile has three warheads).

- Within that launcher limit, the US and the Soviet Union could have an agreed equal number of warheads between 420 and 450 in Europe.

- To achieve equal global and Soviet INF warheads limits, the Soviets must reduce SS-20 launchers in Asia (that are outside the range of NATO Europe) by the same proportion as the reduction of launchers within the range of NATO Europe.

- Appropriate constraints on SRINF should be agreed, so that the Soviets cannot circumvent an agreement on LRINF with a build up of their SRINF.

1985 - November 21
Geneva Summit
At the Geneva Summit, President Reagan and General Secretary Gorbachev agree to focus on several issues in arms control, including the "idea of an interim INF agreement".

1986 - October 11-12
Reykjavik Summit: LRINF Agreement
At the Reykjavik Summit, the US and the Soviet Union agree to equal global ceilings of 100 LRINF missile warheads for each side, with none in Europe.

The Soviets also offer to freeze the SRINF missile systems, pending negotiation of reductions, but they would require US SRINF missile systems to be "frozen" at the current level of zero. They also agree in principle to some key verification elements. However, the Soviets link an INF agreement to US acceptance of constraints on its Strategic Defence Initiative (SDI). These constraints go beyond, those of the 1972 Anti-Ballistic Missile (ABM) Treaty.

1987 - January 15
US INF Proposal
The US proposes at the INF Talks in Geneva:
- Phased reduction of LRINF warheads to a global ceiling of 100 LRINF warheads for each side by the end of 1991, with remaining Soviet LRINF warheads permitted in Soviet Asia, and US LRINF warheads permitted in US territory, including Alaska;
- Reduction of US and Soviet LRINF warheads in Europe to zero by the end of 1991;
- Agreement on INF reductions not contingent on the resolution of other issues outside of the INF negotiations, as agreed at the November 1985 Geneva Summit;

- Global constraints limiting US and Soviet SRINF within the range band of the Soviet SS-23 to SS-12 (Scale-board) missiles to the current Soviet global level;
- Ban on development and deployment of SRINF missiles in the range between the US Pershing II (the shortest-range LRINF missile) and the Soviet Scale-board (the longest-range SRINF missile);
- Subsequent negotiations on additional SRINF constraints or reductions would begin within six months after an initial INF agreement is reached;
- Exchange of data before and after reductions take place;
- On-site observation of elimination of weapons and an effective monitoring arrangements for facilities, including on-site inspection, following elimination of weapons; and
- Negotiations on the details of verification to take place in parallel with negotiations on reduction of weapons.

1987 - March 4

US Draft INF Treaty

The United States presents its draft US-Soviet INF treaty, which provides for the reduction of LRINF missile warheads on each side to 100 globally, with zero in Europe, as agreed to by US and Soviet leaders at Reykjavik. The US makes clear, however, that global elimination of US and Soviet INF missiles remains its preference.

1987 - March 12

US Approach to INF Verification

At the INF negotiations in Geneva, the US presents a treaty articles providing for a comprehensive approach to verification of an INF agreement. The basic elements of the US approach to verification are:

- Provision for the use of and non-interference with National Technical Means (NTM), a requirement for the broadcast of engineering measurements on missile flights, a ban on encryption and a ban on concealment measures that impede verification;

- Specification of areas and facilities where treaty-limited systems must be located and prohibition against having them elsewhere;
- Reciprocal exchange of a specified comprehensive set of data on related treaty-limited systems and their support facilities and equipment;
- Reciprocal updating of this data;
- Specialised procedures for destruction, dismantlement and conversion of LRINF systems, including on-site inspection; and
- On-site inspection and monitoring initially when the treaty goes into effect, and subsequently to ensure compliance with the treaty limitations.

1987 - April 27
Soviet Draft INF Treaty
The Soviet Union presents a draft INF treaty, which reflects basic agreements on land-based LRINF missiles reached at Reykjavik.

The Soviet proposal would reduce each side's LRINF in Europe to zero by the end of five years, and would limit Soviet LRINF missile warheads in Soviet Asia to 100 warheads deployed beyond a striking distance of the United States. It also would limit US LRINF missile warheads in US territory to 100 missile warheads deployed beyond a striking distance of the Soviet Union, thus precluding deployments in Alaska.

1987 - June 12
NATO Support For INF Elimination
In a communiqué issued following a meeting in Reykjavik of NATO's North Atlantic Council, the foreign ministers express support for global and effectively verifiable elimination of all US and Soviet land-based SRINF missiles with a range of 500 to 1,000 kilometers as an integral part of an INF agreement.

The communiqué calls on the Soviet Union to drop its demand to retain a portion of its SS-20 capability and reiterates the wish to see 411 US and Soviet longer-ranges, land-based INF missiles eliminated in accordance with NATO's long-standing objective.

1987 - June 16

US Calls for SRINF Elimination

The United States formally presents its position on SRINF missile systems of the INF talks in Geneva. The position calls for the global elimination of all US and Soviet SRINF missile systems.

1987 - July 23

Soviets Accept "Double Global Zero"

Secretary General Gorbachev announces a change in the Soviet position on INF. The Soviets essentially accept the "double global zero" proposal indicating:

- Readiness, as part of an agreement with the US, to eliminate all "medium-range missiles" in Soviet Asia, including the 100 LRINF warheads of such missiles, provided the US also gives up all such missiles and warheads; and
- Readiness to eliminate "operational and tactical-missiles (SRINF), if the United States does the same.

1987 - August 3

Bilateral Arms Accord Affecting US Allies Unacceptable

Soviet arms negotiator Aleksei A. Obukhov says the USSR will consider a compromise to resolve US-Soviet differences over West Germany's Pershing IA missiles. The Soviets had called the missiles "the main barrier" to an INF agreement and had demanded elimination of these missiles.

US arms negotiator Max Kampelman says: "We will not, in a bilateral relationship between the United States and the Soviet Union, have a provision in that agreement which affects our allies."

1987 - August 26

Federal Republic of Germany Announces IMF Proposal

Chancellor Helmut Kohl of the Federal Republic of Germany announces that West Germany will dismantle its 72 shorter-range INF Pershing IA missiles, and will not replace them with more modern, weapons, if the United States and the Soviet Union:

- Eliminate all of their own LRINF and SRINF missiles as foreseen under the proposed INF treaty;

- Adhere to whatever schedule is agreed to for eliminating their missiles; and
- Comply with the terms of the treaty.

1987 - September 14
US Inspection Protocol

At the INF negotiations in Geneva, the US presents an Inspection Protocol detailing the procedures it considers necessary to effectively verify compliance with an INF treaty that provides for the elimination of all US and Soviet INF missiles.

The new US proposals call for the most stringent verification regime in armed control history. Key elements of the proposal include:

- The requirement that all INF missiles and launchers be geographically fixed in agreed areas or in announced transit between such areas during the reduction period;
- A detailed exchange of data, updated as necessary, on the location of missile support facilities and missile operating bases, the number of missiles and launchers at those facilities and bases, and technical parameters of those missile systems;
- Notification of movement of missiles and launchers between declared facilities;
- A baseline on-site inspection to verify the number of missiles and launchers at declared missile support facilities and missile operating bases prior to elimination;
- On-site inspection to verify the destruction of missiles and launchers;
- Follow-on inspection at short notice of declared facilities during the reductions period to verify residual levels until all missiles are eliminated;
- Short-notice, mandatory challenge inspection of certain facilities in the US and the USSR at which banned missile activity could be carried out; and
- A requirement for a separate "close out" inspection to ensure that when a site is deactivated and removed from the list of declared facilities, it has indeed ended MF-associated activity.

1987 – December 8

INF Treaty

President Reagan and General Secretary Gorbachev sign in Washington the Treaty between the United States and the Soviet Union "on the elimination of their intermediate-Range and Shorter-Range Missiles".

1987 – December 1

Basing Country Agreements

The United States signs agreements with Belgium, the FRG, Italy, the Netherlands and Great Britain concerning INF Treaty inspections between the United States and the Soviet Union.

On December 18 and 23, 1987, the United States acknowledges notes from Czechoslovakia and the German Democratic Republic agreeing to inspections on their territories.

1988 – May 12

Agreed Minute to the INF Treaty

The United States and the Soviet Union sign the Agreed Minute, which provides clarifications for certain inspection procedures.

1988 – May 27

Senate Ratification

The US Senate passes a resolution giving advice and consent to the ratification of the INF Treaty.

1988 – June 1

Entry into Force / MOU Update

The INF Treaty enters into force.

The Memorandum of Understanding (MOU) of the INF Treaty containing data compiled as of November 1, 1987, is updated in accordance with the treaty, which calls for updates every six months.

The second and third MOU updates are completed on December 1, 1988 and June 1, 1989.

1988 - June 6 - July 15
Special Verification Commission (SVC)
The United States and the Soviet Union hold the first session of the Special Verification Commission of the INF Treaty in Geneva. Three more sessions of the SVC are held between September 12, 1988 and June 9, 1989.

1988 - July 2
Continuous Monitoring
The United States begins continuous monitoring at the Soviet Votkinsk Machine Building Plant, and the Soviet Union begins continuous monitoring at Hercules Plant Number 1 at Magna, Utah.

1988 - July 22
Soviet INF Eliminations
The Soviet Union begins eliminations under the INF Treaty at Kapustin Yar with the explosion of one SS-22 missile and launcher canister. Between August 25 and November 24, 1988, the Soviets launch 72 SS-20s for destruction at Kansk and Chita.

1988 - September 8
US INF Eliminations
The United States begins eliminations under the INF Treaty at Longhorn Army Ammunition Plant with the burning of a Pershing IA first-stage missile and Pershing II first-stage missile.

1988 - October 4
Soviet INF System Eliminated
The Soviet Union completes the elimination of the SSC-X-4, a GLCM of intermediate range which was never deployed.

1989 - July 6
US SRINF Systems Eliminated
The United States completes the elimination of SRINF system almost five months ahead of schedule with the destruction of its Pershing IA missile.

1989 - July 26
Elimination of Soviet SRINF System
The Soviet Union completes the elimination of the SS-12, one of
its SRINF systems.

1989 - August 9
Elimination of Soviet SS-5
The Soviet Union completes the elimination of the intermediate
range SS-5 missile.

1989 - October 27
Elimination of Soviet SS-23
The Soviet Union eliminates its last SS-23 SRINF missile.

1990 - May 1
Status of US and Soviet INF Inspections / Eliminations

Inspections:

	Soviet Inspections at US Sites	US Inspections at Soviet Sites
Elimination	62	100
Quota	37	37
Closeout	7	82
Baseline	31	117
Total	**137**	**336**

Completed Eliminations:

	Missiles Subject to Elimination	Missiles Eliminated
US Systems:		
Pershing IA	169	169
Pershing II	234	97
Ground-Launched Cruise Missiles	443	220
Total	**846**	**486**

	Missiles Subject to Elimination	Missiles Eliminated
Soviet Systems:		
SS - 20	654	430
SS - 12	718	718
SS - 23	239	239
SS - 4	149	142
SS - 5	6	6
SSC-X - 4	80	80
Total	**1,846**	**1,615**

1990 - May 3

President on Short-range Nuclear Force (SNF)

President Bush announces his decision to cancel:

- The US Follow-on-to-Lance ground-launched, short-range missile programme in Europe;
- Any further modernisation of US nuclear artillery shells deployed in Europe.

The President says there is less need for nuclear systems of the shortest range in Europe "as democracy comes to Eastern Europe and Soviet troops return home".

He adds that a NATO summit in June or July should agree broad objectives for future negotiations between the United States and the Soviet Union on the current short-range nuclear missile forces in Europe. These negotiations should begin shortly after a treaty on Conventional Armed Forces in Europe (CFE) has been signed.

G

Nuclear and Missile Non-Proliferation

1965 - August 17

Nuclear Non-Proliferation

The United States submits a draft non-proliferation treaty to the UN Disarmament Committee. The draft would oblige the nuclear weapons powers not to transfer nuclear weapons to the national control of any country not having them. Non-nuclear nations would undertake to apply International Atomic Energy Agency or equivalent safeguards to their peaceful nuclear activities.

1967 - August 24

Draft Treaty on Nuclear Non-Proliferation

The United States and the Soviet Union submit separate but identical texts of a draft treaty on nuclear non-proliferation for extensive debate in the United Nations.

1968 - July 2

Nuclear Non-Proliferation Treaty (NPT)

The United States, United Kingdom, Soviet Union and fifty-nine other countries sign the Nuclear Non-Proliferation Treaty (NPT). On July 9 President Lyndon Johnson submits the treaty to the US Senate for its advice and consent to ratification.

The Soviet invasion of Czechoslovakia, however, slows ratification of the treaty until President Richard Nixon asks for Senate agreement in February 1969. The President ratifies the treaty in November.

1977 - May 26

Treaty of Tlatelolco

The United States signs Protocol I of the Treaty of Tlatelolco, which prohibits nuclear weapons in Latin America and strengthens the principle of nuclear non-proliferation. Under its provisions, the US pledges not to test, produce or deploy nuclear weapons anywhere within the zone of the Latin American treaty.

1981 - July 16

Presidential Statement on Non-Proliferation

President Ronald Reagan lists the following basic guidelines for US nuclear non-proliferation policy:

- The US will seek to prevent the spread of nuclear explosives to additional countries as a fundamental national security and foreign policy objective.

- The US will strive to reduce the motivation for acquiring nuclear explosives by working to improve regional and global stability and to promote understanding of the legitimate security concerns of other states.

- The US will continue to support adherence to the Treaty on the Non-Proliferation of Nuclear Weapons and to the Treaty for the Prohibition of Nuclear Weapons in Latin America by countries that have not accepted these treaties.

- The US will view a material violation of these treaties or an international safeguards agreement as having profound consequences for international order and US bilateral relations, and also view any nuclear explosion by a non-nuclear weapons state with grave concern.

- The US will strongly support and continue to work with other nations to strengthen the International Atomic Energy Agency (IAEA) to provide for an improved international safeguards regime.

- The US will seek to work more effectively with other countries to forge agreement on measures for combating the risk of proliferation.

- The US will continue to inhibit the transfer of sensitive nuclear material, equipment and technology, particularly where the danger of proliferation demands, and to seek agreement on requiring IAEA safeguards on all nuclear activities in a non-nuclear-weapon state as a condition for any significant new nuclear supply commitment.

1983 - March 31
Nuclear Safeguards
President Reagan urges US allies to join the United States in
following a common policy of requiring comprehensive safeguards
from all non-nuclear-weapon states before giving new
commitments to supply them with significant amounts of nuclear
materials.

1984 - November 1
Nuclear Non-Proliferation
In an address to the United Nations Association of the United
States, Secretary George Shultz outlines the US approach to
nuclear non-proliferation:

- The US remains firmly committed to strengthening
  international safeguards against the spread of nuclear weapons;
- The US has improved export controls on nuclear material,
  equipment and technology;
- The US supports peaceful uses of nuclear energy for economic
  development and energy security, and will not ignore the
  legitimate needs of the developing world;
- The US makes "rational distinctions between close friends and
  allies who pose no great proliferation risk, and those areas of
  the world where we have real concerns about the spread of
  nuclear weapons";
- The US recognises a clear need to "restrict sensitive nuclear
  activities in regions of instability and proliferation concern"
  such as the Middle East and South Asia;
- The US strives to reduce the motivation of some states to
  acquire nuclear explosives by working with them to improve
  regional and global stability;
- The US seeks consultation and cooperation with other nations
  to advance its non-proliferation policy, and to give its closest
  nuclear trading partners a "firmer and more predictable basis
  in which to plan their vital energy programmes";
- The US believes nuclear cooperation with China will advance
  global non-proliferation objectives;

- The US and the Soviet Union have "broad common interests" in non-proliferation, and hold bilateral discussions on the subject; and
- The US seeks to expand the non-proliferation dialogue, and has resumed talks with rapidly industrializing countries such as Brazil, Argentina and South Africa.

1985 - August 28
NPT Review Conference
In a message to the Third Review Conference of the 1968 Treaty on the Non-Proliferation of Nuclear Weapons meeting in Geneva, President Reagan addresses three major arms control issues:

- Nuclear Weapons: "The United States has proposed in Geneva radical reductions in the number of existing nuclear weapons. This, I believe, is the most direct and best course to pursue if we are to eliminate the danger of nuclear war."
- Verification of Nuclear Tests: "At the same time, I believe that verifiable limitations on nuclear testing can play a useful, although more modest role ... We have invited the Soviet Union to send observers, with any instrumentation devices they wish to bring, to measure a nuclear test at our site. This invitation has no conditions."
- Treaty on the Non-Proliferation of Nuclear Weapons: "The United States remains firmly committed to the objectives embodied in this treaty, and to its vision of a more stable and secure world for all nations."

1987 - April 16
Missile Technology Control Regime (MTCR)
President Reagan announces that the United States and six nations – Canada, France, West Germany, Italy, Japan, and the United Kingdom – have agreed to common "guidelines to control the transfer of equipment and technology that could contribute to nuclear-capable missiles". The President adds that "it is the continuing aim of the United States government to encourage international cooperation in the peaceful use of modern technology,"

including the peaceful use of technology in space in ways that are fully consistent with non-proliferation policies.

1988 - June 13

Shultz on Challenges of Proliferation

In a speech before the Third Special Session of the UN on Disarmament, Secretary Shultz says the spread of nuclear and chemical weapons capabilities, of ballistic missiles technology and biotechnology is a global problem.

Shultz makes the following major points:

- The proliferation of ballistic missiles is a "new and urgent challenge – a worldwide threat."
- The US is especially concerned about the introduction of advanced missiles into the Persian Gulf War, and believes mutual restraint to be a "better way for the nations of that troubled area to see to their security".
- There is no good reason why every nation should not make a binding commitment to the NPT. Nuclear proliferation is one of the most direct and serious threats to regional and global stability. The danger today is most acute in South Asia, and the US is "prepared to work with countries inside and outside the region to find a lasting solution to the danger of proliferation that satisfies all parties".

1989 - April 20

Presidential Statement on Tlatelolco Treaty

President Bush says the Treaty of Tlatelolco:

"Continues to stand as an important barrier to the spread of weapons of mass destruction in the Western Hemisphere; its contributions to regional and hemispheric security are substantial. The treaty strengthens international legal restrictions on the proliferation of nuclear weapons, protecting the peace and the security interests of every nation. Increasing concern about the spread of nuclear arms around the world is a compelling reminder that we must continue to pursue the goals set by the authors of the Tlatelolco Treaty."

1989 - September 25
Presidential Statement on the IAEA
Recognising the International Atomic Energy Agency's "vital role in preventing the spread of nuclear weapons, and in promoting cooperation in peaceful nuclear technologies among states," President Bush reaffirms the US commitment to strengthen the Agency.

1990 - February 7-9
Moscow Ministerial: Non-Proliferation
In a Joint statement, Secretary James Baker and Foreign Minister Eduard Shevardnadze, agree to "prepare a document for consideration by their leaders covering both principles and concrete steps of cooperation in all areas of non-proliferation – chemical, missile and nuclear."

The two sides also note that they both adhere to the export guidelines of the existing regime relating to missiles, which applies to missiles capable of delivering at least 500 kilograms of payload to a range of at least 300 kilometers.

1990 - March 5
President Bush on the 20th Anniversary of NPT
In a statement on the 20th anniversary of the entry into force of the Nuclear Non-Proliferation Treaty, President Bush says:

"One hundred and forty states have joined the treaty, making it the most widely accepted arms control instrument in history. The NPT represents the primary legal barrier to nuclear proliferation and thus constitutes a principal foundation of international security. I call upon all states party to the Treaty to join our effort to secure the integrity of the NPT, which benefits all countries."

H

Nuclear Testing

1957 - August 21

Nuclear Testing Proposal

President Dwight D. Eisenhower announces that the United States would be willing, as part of the US Proposal for a first-step disarmament agreement, to suspend testing of nuclear weapons for a period of up to two years under certain conditions and safeguards. These include Soviet acceptance of the US call for a permanent cessation of production of fissionable materials for weapons purposes and installation of inspection systems to ensure compliance. The President also states that until such a first-step arms control agreement comes into force, the United States will conduct such nuclear testing as the security of the United States requires.

1958 - August 22

Statement on US Nuclear Testing Proposal

President Eisenhower announces that the United States is prepared "to negotiate an agreement with other nations which have tested nuclear weapons for the suspension of nuclear weapons tests and the establishment of an international control system."

If this proposal is accepted in principle by other nations which have tested nuclear weapons, the President's statement continues, "then in order to facilitate the detailed negotiations the United States is prepared, unless testing resumed by the Soviet Union, to withhold further testing on its part of atomic and hydrogen weapons for a period of one year from the beginning of the negotiations." As a part of the agreement, and on a basis of reciprocity, "the United States would be further prepared to suspend the testing of nuclear weapons on a year-by-year basis subject to a determination at the beginning of each year that:

- The agreed inspection system is installed and working effectively;

- Satisfactory progress is being made in reaching agreement on and implementing major and substantial arms control measures."

1958 - October 25
Suspension of Nuclear Testing

President Eisenhower reaffirms US willingness to withhold testing of atomic and hydrogen weapons for a period of one year from the beginning of the negotiations on October 31, 1958. The US objective, he says, is to facilitate negotiations for the suspension of nuclear weapons tests and the establishment of an international control system.

1959 - April 13
Nuclear Test Ban Proposal

In a letter to Premier Nikita Khrushchev, President Eisenhower offers an alternative approach to a nuclear test ban. He proposes that, if the Soviet Union still insists on a veto over an on-site control system to monitor underground detonations, the two sides could implement a test ban in phases, starting with a prohibition of nuclear weapons tests in the atmosphere up to 50 kilometers. Meanwhile, the negotiations could continue to resolve the political and technical problems associated with control of underground and outer space tests.

1959 - May 5
Nuclear Test Ban

A letter from President Eisenhower to Premier Khrushchev urges technical discussions on the possibility of banning nuclear tests to a greater atmospheric height than that mentioned in his April 13 letter. The president again urges the Soviet Union either to accept the control measures that would make possible a complete ban on nuclear weapons tests, or to agree to the US proposal for a partial ban.

The President states that the United States is prepared to explore Khrushchev's proposal for a predetermined number of inspections in the territory of the United States, the United Kingdom and the Soviet Union at Geneva, but adds that the number should be replaced to scientific facts and detection capabilities.

1959 - August 26
Suspension of Nuclear Tests
President Eisenhower directs that the voluntary suspension of nuclear weapons testing by the United States, which began on October 31, 1958, for one year, be extended to December 31, 1959.

1961 - September 3
Atmospheric Test Ban Proposal
In response to Soviet resumption of nuclear tests in the atmosphere on September 1, 1961, President John F. Kennedy and British Prime Minister Harold Macmillan urge the Soviet Union to agree immediately to a ban on atmospheric tests. On September 5, President Kennedy announces the resumption of nuclear testing "in the laboratory and underground, with no fallout."

1962 - August 27
Draft Test Ban Treaties
The United States and the United Kingdom introduce two new draft test ban treaties. The first calls for a comprehensive ban on tests, enforced by nationally manned control posts under international supervision and obligatory on-site inspection. The second, offered as an alternative calls for a limited ban ending testing in all environments except underground, monitored by national means without the need to establish any international verification machinery.

1963 - June 10
Test Ban Talks
The United States, the United Kingdom and the Soviet Union announce that high-level talks will be held in Moscow in July to seek agreement on a test ban. In a speech on settlement of Cold War problems, President Kennedy says the United States would voluntarily suspend nuclear tests in the atmosphere pending negotiation of test ban agreement, provided other countries would follow suit.

1963 - August 5
Limited Test Ban Treaty
The United States, the United Kingdom and the Soviet Union sign a treaty outlawing nuclear tests in the atmosphere, in outer space and underwater. Underground tests are also outlawed if they result in spreading radioactive debris outside the territorial limits of the state where the explosion is conducted.

1974 - July 3
Threshold Test Ban Treaty (TTBT)
The United States and the Soviet Union sign the Treaty on the Limitation of Underground Nuclear Weapon Tests. This treaty bans underground nuclear weapon tests having a yield exceeding 150 kilotons.

1974 - October 7
Peaceful Underground Tests
Negotiations begin between the United States and the Soviet Union on an agreement concerning underground nuclear explosions for peaceful purposes.

1976 - May 28
Peaceful Nuclear Explosions Treaty (PNET)
In simultaneous ceremonies in Moscow and Washington, Soviet General Secretary Leonid Brezhnev and President General Ford sign the Treaty on Underground Nuclear Explosions for Peaceful Purposes, which sets a ceiling of 150 kilotons on such explosions, equal to that established in the Threshold Test Ban Treaty.

1985 - July 29
Measuring Nuclear Tests
President Ronald Reagan invites Soviet experts to the US test site in Nevada to measure the yield of a US nuclear test with any instrumentation devices they think necessary.

1985 - December 19
Comprehensive Test Ban
The White House issues a statement saying: "A comprehensive test ban ... is a long-term objective of the United States in the context of

achieving broad, deep and verifiable arms reductions, substantially improved verification capabilities, expanded confidence-building measures, greater balance in conventional forces, and at a time when a nuclear deterrent is no longer as essential an element as currently for international security and stability."

1986 - March 14

On-site Monitoring of Nuclear Tests with Corrtex

President Reagan announces as new, specific proposal for on-site monitoring of nuclear tests that could be implemented immediately and strengthen the verification provisions of the Threshold Test Ban Treaty (TTBT) and Peaceful Nuclear Explosions Treaty (PNET). The President identifies a new hydrodynamic yield measurement method, known as CORRTEX, that could improve verification of compliance with the 150-kiloton threshold on underground tests. CORRTEX, which uses a coaxial cable placed in a hole parallel to that of the nuclear device, measures the propagation of the underground shock wave from a nuclear explosion.

The President also invites Soviet scientists to inspect the CORRTEX system more fully at the US test site in Nevada during the third week of April 1986, and monitor a planned nuclear weapons test. He notes that he told General Secretary Mikhail Gorbachev: "If we could reach agreement in the use of an effective verification system incorporating such a method to verify the TTBT, I would be prepared to move forward on ratification" of both the Threshold Test Ban and Peaceful Nuclear Explosion treaties.

1986 - July 25

Geneva Talks on Nuclear Testing

The US and Soviet experts begin the first round of discussions in Geneva on nuclear testing issues – a direct result of President Reagan's offer.

1986 - October 10

Proposed Ratification of TTBT/PNET Treaties

The White House announces that President Reagan will inform General Secretary Gorbachev at their October 11-12 Reykjavik meeting that, if the Soviet Union will agree to essential verification procedures for the TTBT and PNET treaties prior to the start of ratification proceedings in the US Senate in 1987, the President will ask the Senate for advice and consent on ratification of the treaties. If the Soviet Union does not meet these criteria, however, the President will still seek Senate advice and consent, but with an appropriate reservation to the treatise, ensuring that they would not take effect until they are effectively verifiable.

According to the White House statement, "Once out TTBT/PNET verification concerns have been satisfied and the treaties have been ratified, the president will propose that the United States and the Soviet Union immediately engage in negotiations on ways to implement a step-by-step parallel programme – in association with a programme to reduce and ultimately eliminate all nuclear weapons – of limiting and ultimately ending nuclear testing."

1987 - January 13
Verifying Nuclear Testing Treaties
President Reagan sends a message to the US Senate requesting advice and consent on ratification of the TTBT and PNET with a reservation that would ensure they would not take effect until they are effectively verifiable.

1987 - March 11
Violation of Limited Test Ban Treaty
The United States conveys its concern to the Soviet Union regarding the Soviet nuclear test of February 25, 1987, which violated the Limited Test Ban Treaty by causing radioactive debris to be present in the atmosphere outside the Soviet territorial limits.

1987 - August 12
Limited Nuclear Test Ban Treaty Violation
The United States conveys its concern to the Soviet Union regarding the Soviet nuclear test of August 2, 1987, which violated the Limited Test Ban Treaty causing radioactive debris to be present in the atmosphere outside the USSR's territorial limits.

1987 - September 17

Washington Ministerial

Secretary of State George Shultz and Foreign Minister Eduard Shevardnadze issue a joint statement:

"The US and Soviet sides have agreed to begin before December 1, 1987, full-scale stage-by-stage negotiations which will be conducted in a single forum. In these negotiations, the sides, as the first step, will agree upon effective verification measures which will make it possible to ratify the US-USSR Threshold Test Ban Treaty of 1974 and Peaceful Nuclear Explosions Treaty of 1976, and proceed to negotiating further intermediate limitations on nuclear testing leading to the ultimate objective of the complete cessation of nuclear testing as part of an effective disarmament process. This process, among other things, would pursue, as the first priority, the goal of the reduction of nuclear weapons and, ultimately, their elimination. For the purpose of the elaboration of improved verification measures for the US-USSR treaties of 1974 and 1976, the sides intend to design and conduct joint verification experiments at each other's test sites. These verification measures will, to the extent appropriate, be used further for nuclear test limitation agreements which may subsequently be reached."

1987 - November 9

US-Soviet Talks

The first round of the Nuclear Testing Talks (NTT) between the United States and the Soviet Union opens in Geneva. The sides agree that, as a first step, they will find effective verification measures for the Threshold Test Ban Treaty (TTBT) of 1974 and the Peaceful Nuclear Explosions Treaty (PNET) of 1976, making ratification of these treaties possible in the United States.

1987 - December 9

Joint Verification Experiment (JVE)

During the Washington Summit, the United States and the Soviet Union agree to design and conduct a Joint Verification Experiment at each other's test site. The JVE will be conducted in such a way as to address the concerns identified by both sides regarding the methods proposed by the other for verification of the Threshold Test Ban Treaty and the Peaceful Nuclear Explosions Treaty.

1988 - January 8-15
Semipalatinsk Test Site

US nuclear testing experts visit the Soviet nuclear test site in Semipalatinsk. The purpose of the visit – the first by any foreign group to the site – is to familiarise US experts with the Organisation and operation of the Soviet test site.

1988 - January 24-30
Nevada Test Site

Soviet nuclear testing experts visit the US nuclear test site in Nevada. The purpose of the visit – the first by the Soviets – is to familiarise Soviet experts with the Organisation and operation of the US test site.

1988 - May 29 - June 1
Moscow Summit

During the summit in Moscow, US Secretary of State George Shultz and Soviet Foreign Minister Eduard Shevardnadze initial the JVE agreement which lays down the procedures for conducting the experiment and analysing its results.

1988 - August 17
JVE-Kearsage

The US portion of the Joint Verification experiment – the nuclear test SHAGAN – is conducted at the Soviet test site at Semipalatinsk. Soviet and US scientists, technicians and observers are present to measure the yield of the explosion and discuss the results of the test.

1988 - November 16
US-Soviet AD Referendum Agreement

The United States and the Soviet Union reach ad referendum agreement on a new verification protocol for the PNET.

1988 - December 14
Joint Draft Text on TTBT Protocol
At the end of Round III of the Nuclear Testing Talks in Geneva, the United States and the Soviet Union reach agreement on a joint draft text of a new TTBT verification protocol.

1989 - September 22-23
Wyoming Ministerial
US Secretary of State James Baker and Soviet Foreign Minister Shevardnadze reach agreements that provide a framework for conclusion of the verification protocols for the PNET and the TTBT. They agree that:

- Hydrodynamic and seismic monitoring, as well as on-site inspection, will be incorporated into the verification protocol for the 1974 Threshold Test Ban Treaty; and

- To obtain a statistically significant number of data points to improve the national technical means of each side, each side will guarantee the other the right to make on-site hydrodynamic yield measurements of at least two tests per year during the first five years following ratification of the TTBT, and once per year thereafter unless otherwise agreed by the two sides.

1990 - January 9
Presidential Statement on Nuclear Testing
President George Bush issues a comprehensive US policy statement on nuclear testing, which includes the following major points:

- The United States has a step-by-step approach to further limits on nuclear testing;

- The first step is to agree on effective verification provisions for the TTBT and the PNET, thereby allowing their ratification;

- In view of the new and complex techniques necessary for effective verification of the TTBT and the PNET protocols, it is necessary to observe implementation of the ratified treaties;

- After a period of observation, the United States will be better able to assess the verification lessons learned, and also to determine the additional moves that would make sense from a national security standpoint;

- Nuclear weapons will continue to play a critical role in US national security strategy;
- As long as this is the case, the United States must be free to conduct nuclear tests to ensure the credibility, safety and security of its nuclear forces;
- The United States has not identified any further limitations on nuclear testing beyond those now contained in the TTBT that would be in the US national security interest;
- A comprehensive test ban remains a US long-term objective; and
- The United States believes that a comprehensive test ban must be viewed in the context of a time when we do not need to depend on nuclear deterrence to ensure international security and stability, and when we have achieved broad, deep and effectively verifiable arms reductions, substantially improved verification capabilities, expanded confidence-building measures, and greater balance in conventional forces.

1990 - February 8-9
Moscow Ministerial
During meetings between Secretary James Baker and Foreign Minister Shevardnadze, the sides reach agreement on several remaining TTBT issues, including:

- The right to simultaneous use of the hydrodynamic yield measurement method and use of the in-country seismic method;
- A number of issues related to implementation of the hydrodynamic method; and
- The sides reaffirm their adherence to the agreement reached in September 1987 with regard to the negotiations on nuclear testing.

I

Soviet Noncompliance

1984 - January 23

Reagan's First Report on Soviet Noncompliance

President Reagan's first Report to Congress on "Soviet Noncompliance with Arms Control Agreements", analyses seven specific cases of certain, probable, or likely violations by the USSR of arms control obligations and commitments.

1985 - February 1

Report Questions Compliance with SALT Interim Agreement

In the administration's second annual report requested by the Congress on Soviet arms control compliance, the President says the unclassified report updates information on the seven issues reported in January 1984 and adds six other compliance issues. "The six cases involve questions of Soviet compliance with provisions of the SALT I Interim Agreement, the Limited Test Ban Treaty, and the Anti-Ballistic Missile Treaty (ABM).

1985 - December 23

Soviet Noncompliance Allows Military Gains

In his third report to the US Congress, President Reagan describes a continuing pattern of Soviet noncompliance with existing arms control agreements, which has allowed the Soviet Union to make military gains in strategic offensive arms as well as in chemical, biological and toxin weapons.

The report states: "As violations of legal obligations or political commitments, they cause grave concern regarding Soviet commitment to arms control, and they darken the atmosphere in which current negotiations are being conducted in Geneva and elsewhere."

1987 - March 10

Despite US Efforts, Soviet Noncompliance Uncorrected

In a Report to Congress, President Reagan says that despite intensive US efforts, the Soviet Union "has failed to correct its noncompliance with illegal activities" . The report analyses ten cases of certain, probable or likely Soviet violations of arms control obligations and commitments. Due to the President's May 1986 decision to end US observance of the SALT I Interim Agreement, and SALT II, the report does not cover the SALT Treaties.

1987 - December 2

Soviet Violations Continue Despite Critical Arms Talks

In an annual Report to Congress, President Reagan cites instances of Soviet noncompliance. He notes that despite continuing intensive US efforts and the "critical stage we have entered in negotiation of arms reductions of historic proportion, the Soviet Union has failed to correct its noncompliance activities". He also reports that the Soviets have not provided explanations sufficient to alleviate our concerns on other compliance issues. Indeed, recent Soviet activities at an electronics facility at Gomel have raised an additional compliance issue with regard to the ABM Treaty.

1988 - August 8

White House on Soviet Violations of ABM Treaty

The United States defines its principal objectives at the ABM Treaty Review Conference in Geneva August 24-31 to be:

"To obtain the Soviet Union's agreement to correct its violations of the ABM Treaty and to satisfy other US concerns regarding Soviet noncompliance with its obligations under the treaty ..." In preparation for the upcoming review, the president has issued guidance that the US delegation should continue to make it clear that the existence of the Krasnoyarsk radar violation calls into question the viability of the ABM Treaty and, therefore, it should be dismantled without further delay and without condition. Unless resolved, the radar violation will force the United States to consider the exercise of its rights under international law to take appropriate and proportionate responses. In this context, the United States will also have to consider whether to declare the Krasnoyarsk radar to be a material breach of the ABM Treaty.

"The President has also directed that the Department of Defense, working with other executive branch agencies and the Congress, take the lead in developing a range of appropriate and proportionate responses for consideration if the Soviet Union continues to refuse to correct the Krasnoyarsk violation."

1988 - August 31

US Unilateral Statement Following ABM Review

In a unilateral statement following the Third US-Soviet Review Conference of the ABM Treaty, the United States says:

"Since the Soviet Union was not prepared to satisfy US concerns with respect to the Krasnoyarsk radar violation ... the United States will have to consider declaring this continuing violation a material breach of the treaty. In this connection, the United States reserves all its rights, consistent with international law, to take appropriate and proportionate responses in the future.

"During the ABM Treaty Review, the United States also discussed the violation of the ABM Treaty involving the illegally deployed radars at Gomel ... and a number of ABM-related compliance concerns, the totality of which suggests that the Soviet Union may be preparing a prohibited ABM territorial defense ...

"The United States will not accept Soviet violations of double standard of treaty compliance, and reserves the right to take appropriate and proportionate responses in the future."

1988 - December 2

President's Report on Soviet Noncompliance

In his last annual Report to Congress, President Reagan says the Soviet Union "has not corrected the noncompliance activities" cited in his report of December 1987. In particular, the President emphasises that the Krasnoyarsk radar is a "significant violation of a central element of the ABM Treaty and makes it impossible to conclude future arms control agreements in the START or Defense and Space areas. "This violation", he adds, "will continue to raise the issues of material breach and proportionate responses until it is resolved."

The report also summarises the Soviet implementation of the Intermediate Range Nuclear Force (INF) Treaty and finds:

"Issues and questions regarding noncompliance which have been discussed with the Soviets have been resolved to the US' satisfaction or are in the process of resolution."

1989 - Spring
Soviets Dismantle Gomel Radars
The Soviet Union dismantles the illegally deployed radars near Gomel. The United States tells the Soviet Union that although all procedures that were undertaken by the Soviets have not been fulfilled, the violation has been corrected.

1989 - August 23
KRASNOYARSK Radar
The Soviets announce that they will "completely eliminate the Krasnoyarsk radar," a significant violation of a central element of the ABM Treaty.

1989 - September 4
Soviets Admit ABM Violation
Soviet Foreign Minister Shevardnadze acknowledge that the Krasnoyarsk radar violates the ABM Treaty.

1990 - February 23
US Report on Soviet Noncompliance
The United States issues its annual Report to Congress, "Soviet Noncompliance with Arms Control Agreements". The report notes certain constructive steps the Soviets have taken, such as the destruction of the radars illegally deployed at Gomel and Soviet Foreign Minister Shevardnadze's commitment to correct the Krasnoyarsk radar violation of the ABM Treaty.

At the same time, the report also lists several issues that continue to concern the United States, including some related to the ABM Treaty, the 1972 Biological and Toxin Weapons Convention and the 1963 Limited Test Ban Treaty.

The report discusses Soviet violation of the 1978 INF Treaty, but notes that violations have been corrected after discussion between the United States and the Soviet Union.

J

Strategic Defence Initiative

1982 - March 23

Reagan Address on Strategic Defence Initiative (SDI)

In an address to the nation, President Reagan announces his intention to commit the United States to a research programme, consistent with the 1972 ABM Treaty, that will study the feasibility of defensive measures against ballistic missiles to maintain the peace:

"What if free people could live secure in the knowledge that their security did not rest upon the threat of instant US retaliation to deter a Soviet attack, that we could intercept and destroy strategic ballistic missiles before they reached our own soil or that of our allies?

"I call upon the scientific community in our country, those who gave us nuclear weapons, to turn their great talents now to the cause of mankind and world peace, to give us the means of rendering these nuclear weapons impotent and obsolete ... I am directing a comprehensive and intensive effort to define a long-term research and development program to begin to achieve our ultimate goal of eliminating the threat posed by strategic nuclear missiles."

1983 - April 22

Soviet Scientists Denounce US SDI Programme

One letter to *The New York Times* denouncing SDI is signed by more than 200 senior Soviet scientists, a number of whom have been instrumental in the development of Soviet advanced ballistic missile defensive systems.

1983 - October 22

Recommendations of Three SDI Studies

The findings and recommendations of three studies ordered by the president are delivered. The Defense Technology Study, focusing on the technical feasibility of a defence, concludes that "powerful new technologies are becoming available that justify a major technology development effort offering future technical options to implement a defensive strategy." The study recommends a five-year programme to determine the technical feasibility of future ballistic missile defences and proposes 26,000 million dollars for this study.

The two Future Security Strategy studies conclude that effective US defence systems can offer a new, more stable and secure basis for managing long-term US relations with the Soviet Union.

1984 - January 4
Organisation for SDI Programme Created
The Strategic Defence Initiative Organization (SDIO) is created to undertake a "comprehensive programme to develop the key technologies associated with concepts for defence against ballistic missiles". The SDIO charter notes that the technology plan identified by the Defence Technology Study and the policy approach derived from the Future Security Strategy Studies will "serve as general guides" for the programme.

1984 - February 14
SDI Budget, Programme Submitted to Congress
The first SDI budget and programme are submitted to Congress.

1984 - March 3
Objective of US SDI Programme
The US Department of Defense booklet, "Defense Against Ballistic Missiles" makes clear that the "essential objective" of SDI is to "diminish the risk of nuclear destruction and provide for a safer, less menacing way of preventing nuclear war in the decades to come."

1984 - April 15
Abrahamson Becomes SDI Director
Lt. General James A. Abrahamson becomes the director of the Strategic Defense Initiative Organization (SDIO).

1984 - June 10
Homing Overlay Experiment
The Homing Overlay Experiment (HOE) successfully intercepts and destroys a mock ballistic missile warhead in the mid-course

phase of its flight. This non-nuclear intercept is the first such experiment, demonstrating the homing guidance system and the potential of kinetic simply by colliding with them at great speed.

1985 - January 4

Meaning and Objectives of US SDI Programme

A White House publication, "The President's Strategic Defense Initiative" explains the meaning and objectives of the SDI Programme:

- The SDI is a programme of intensive research into advanced defensive technologies, with the aim of eventually eliminating the threat posed by ballistic missiles, of all ranges and armaments. The SDI is consistent with all US treaty obligations, including the 1972 US-Soviet ABM Treaty;
- The purposes of the SDI are to: strengthen deterrence and stability; fashion an environment that serves the security interests of the United States, its allies and the Soviet Union; and lower the level of nuclear weapons;
- Ballistic missile defences would enhance deterrence by significantly increasing the uncertainty facing an aggressor and by reducing or eliminating the incentive for launching a first strike;
- Any effective strategic defensive system must be survivable and cost-effective;
- Together with air defences, effective defences against ballistic missiles would substantially lower the possibility of nuclear war. They would also provide protection against the accidental launch of such weapons, or deliberate attacks by irrational leaders;
- Should it prove possible to develop a highly capable defence against ballistic missiles, the United States would envision parallel US and Soviet deployments with the outcome being enhanced mutual security and international stability;
- Unlike the current deterrent doctrine of nuclear retaliation, greater reliance on defensive systems would threaten no one;
- There are three major reasons why it is necessary to pursue the SDI: the Soviet Union's offensive and defensive buildup, which has upset the military balance in the areas of greatest

importance during crises; the awesome destructive potential of nuclear weapons; and new technologies that may make effective non-nuclear defenses against ballistic missiles possible;

- The SDI research programme is also a prudent response to the Soviet Union's activities in both traditional and advanced technologies for ballistic missile defence, including the world's only operational ABM system; activities which violate or potentially violate the ABM Treaty, and which together suggest that the Soviet Union may be preparing an ABM defence on its national territory; and active research and development into advanced technologies; such as lasers and neutral particle beams (NPBs), for ballistic missile defence;

- A unilateral Soviet deployment of advanced defences against ballistic missiles, together with massive Soviet offensive forces and impressive air and passive defence capabilities, would destroy the foundation upon which deterrence has rested.

1985 - March 18
US Invites Allied Participation in SDI
Secretary of Defence Casper Weinberger invites eighteen allied governments to participate in the SDI programme so that both SDI and Western security as a whole can be strengthened by taking advantage of allied excellence in research areas relevant to SDI.

1985 - June 17
Major Features of SDI Programme
A US Department of State Special Report on the SDI, based on a key presidential policy directive, outlines major features of the programme:

- The aim of SDI is not to seek superiority, but to maintain the strategic balance and thereby assure stable deterrence. The SDI represents no change in the US commitment to deterring war and enhancing stability.

- The SDI is designed to enhance allied security as well as US security. The United States will continue to work closely with its allies to ensure that, as SDI research progresses, allied views are carefully considered.

- Research will last for some years. The United States seeks to adhere strictly to the ABM Treaty and insists that the Soviets do so as well.

- The purpose of the defensive options that United States seeks is to find a means to destroy attacking ballistic missiles before they can reach any of their potential targets.

- The United States has no preconceived notions about the defensive options the research may generate. The United States will not proceed to development and deployment unless the research indicates that defenses will meet strict criteria of military effectiveness, survivability and cost-effectiveness at the margin.

- If and when US research criteria are met, and following close consultations with US allies, the United States intends to consult and negotiate, as appropriate, with the Soviets pursuant to the terms of the ABM Treaty, on how deterrence could be enhanced through a greater reliance by both sides on new defensive systems. It is the US intention and hope that, if new defensive technologies prove feasible, the United States (in close and continuing consultation with its allies) and the Soviets will jointly manage a transition to a more defence-reliant balance.

- For a foreseeable future, offensive nuclear forces and the prospect of nuclear retaliation will remain a key element of deterrence. Therefore, the United States must maintain modern, flexible and credible strategic nuclear forces.

- America's ultimate goal is to eliminate nuclear weapons entirely by necessity, this is a very long-term goal which requires, as the United States pursues its SDI research, equally energetic efforts to diminish the threat posed by conventional arms imbalances, through both conventional force improvements and negotiation of arms reductions and confidence-building measures.

1985 - September 6

MID-Infrared Advanced Chemical Laser Experiment

A ground-based, directed energy experiment using the Mid-Infrared Advanced Chemical Laser (MIRACL) device is conducted at the White Sands Missile Range in New Mexico.

The target, a Tital booster rigged to simulate a thrusting booster, is successfully destroyed by the laser.

1985 - September 27
Demonstration of Tracking with Laser
The SDIO conducts the first successful demonstration of the ability to track a sounding rocket in space with a low-power, ground-based laser after adjusting the beam for atmospheric distortion.

1985 - October 4
US Documents Soviet Strategic Defence Activities
The Department of State and Defense pointedly issue a report, "Soviet Strategic Defense Programme", which documents the extent of Soviet activities in all aspects of strategic defence, including passive defence, air defence, and both traditional and advanced technologies for defence against ballistic missiles. The report points out that Soviet efforts in most aspects of strategic defence have long been far more extensive than those of the United States.

1985 - October 11
Reagan on the ABM Treaty and the SDI Program
President Reagan determines the broader interpretation of the ABM Treaty to be fully justified. The President also directs that, as a matter of policy, the SDI program will continue to be conducted according to a more restrictive interpretation of the ABM Treaty than the United States could justifiably observe.

Under the broader interpretation of the treaty, ADM system that are "based on other physical principles" (i.e. other than ABM interceptor missiles, ABM launchers and ABM radars) and including components capable of substituting for ABM interceptor missiles, ABM launchers or ABM radars, may be developed and tested but not deployed, regardless of their basing mode.

Under the more restrictive interpretation, development and testing of ABM systems based on other physical principles are allowed only for fixed land-based systems and components.

1985 - December 12

SDI Recommendations of East Port Group

The East port Study Group, formed "to devise an appropriate computational/communications response to the (strategic defence battle management) problem and make recommendations for a research and technology development programme to implement the response", issues its report to General Abrahamson.

The report concludes that "computing resources and battle management software for strategic defence systems are within the capabilities of the hardware and software technologies that could be developed within the next several years."

1985 - December 6

US, Great Britain Sign Memorandum of Understanding on SDI Research

The United States and Great Britain sign a Memorandum of Understanding (MOU) on British Participation in SDI research.

1986 - February 26

SDI Destroy Missile, Not People

In an address to the nation, President Reagan says, "We're pushing forward our highly promising Strategic Defence Initiative – a security shield that may one day protect us and our allies from nuclear attack, whether launched by deliberate calculation, freak accident or the isolated impulse of a madman. Isn't it better to use our talents and technology to build systems that destroy missiles, not people?"

1986 - March 27

US, West Germany Sign Memorandum of Understanding on SDI Research

The United States and the Federal Republic of Germany sign a Memorandum of Understanding on the terms of West German participation in SDI research.

1986 - April-June

Flexible Lightweight Agile Guided Experiments

A series of Flexible Lightweight Agile Guided Experiments (FLAGE) are conducted. These kinetic energy experiments demonstrate the guidance technology necessary to intercept a warhead both in and beyond the Earth's atmosphere.

1986 - May 6
US, Israel Sign Memorandum of Understanding on SDI Research
The governments of the United States and Israel sign a Memorandum of Understanding on the terms of Israeli participation in SDI research.

1986 - July 6
Particle Beam Experiment
SDI's first Particle Beam Experiment irradiates a miniature reentry vehicle with a high-intensity proton beam. The results indicate that the explosive contained in the reentry vehicle is highly vulnerable to the particle beam.

1986 - August 2
US Report Explains Soviet Anti-SDI Campaign
"The Soviet Propaganda Campaign Against the US Strategic Defence Initiative," is published by the US Arms Control and Disarmament Agency.

It explains the methods of the Soviet anti-SDI campaign: to flood the West with statements from high Soviet officials; with interviews with Soviet spokesmen on Western broadcast media; and with newspaper articles, press release, pamphlets, and petitions from front organisations and state-controlled Soviet scientific groups.

It also explains the goals of this campaign: to "stimulate opposition to SDI in the United States and other allied countries, inhibiting Western research and development into defences – even as the Soviet Union forges ahead with its own ABM programmes, including research and development in advanced ballistic missile defence technologies."

1986 - August 6
SDI Not a Bargaining Chip
In remarks at a Washington briefing on SDI, President Reagan says: "SDI is no bargaining chip, it is the path to a safe and more

secure future ... It's the number of offensive missiles that needs to be reduced, not efforts to find a way to defend mankind against these deadly weapons."

1986 - September 5
Delta 180 Experiment
The Delta 180 experiment obtains data for characterising rocket plumes during the boost phase; studies rocket signatures during the close-in phase of a space intercept and validates guidance laws using actual accelerating vehicles in space. The mission's results provide data critical to the development of small space based interceptors.

The experiment utilises an SDI satellite carrying a radar tracker and a rocket modified to carry advanced infrared sensors, the first laser radar ever flown in space, a Maverick air-to-ground missile infrared imaging system and two cameras. The Target is intercepted at a closing speed of 10,459 kilometers (6,500 miles) per hour.

1986 - September 19
US, Italy Sign Memorandum of Understanding on SDI Research
The United States and Italy sign a Memorandum of Understanding on the terms of Italian participation in SDI research.

1987 - May 21
Flage Follow-on Test
A FLAGE follow-on test is conducted at the White Sands Missile Range. The successful intercept demonstrates guidance technologies and accuracy required for the interception and destruction of a tactical ballistic missile within the atmosphere.

1987 - July 21
US, Japan Sign Memorandum of Understanding on SDI Research
The United States and Japan sign a Memorandum of Understanding on the terms of Japanese participation in SDI research.

1987 - September 18
First Milestone Review
Secretary Weinberger approves the recommendations of the Defence Acquisition Board (DAB) that selected SDI concepts

and technologies enter the Demonstration and Validation phase of the defence acquisition process.

1987 - November 30
Soviet Admission of SDI-Type Research
In the first public admission by the Soviets that they are engaged in research similar to the US Strategic Defence Initiative programme, General Secretary Gorbachev says during a televised interview:

"Practically, the Soviet Union is doing all that the United States is doing, and I guess we are engaged in research, basic research, which relates to those aspects which are covered by SDI in the United States."

1988 - January - December
Light Exo-atmospheric Projectile (LEAP)/Space-Based Interceptor (SBI) Miniaturisation
This research demonstrates the ability to:
- Develop lightweight, low-cost, exo-atmospheric interceptors for a Strategic Defence System; and
- Integrate advanced interceptor technologies developed in technology based programmes.

1988 - February 8
Delta 181 Experiment
A Delta rocket is launched from Cape Canaveral, Florida, with a payload of sensors and test objects. The sensor module deploys fourteen test objects and, using an assortment of active and passive sensing instruments, characterises the objects in a variety of space environments. Sensors also observe the launching of research rockets to collect data on rocket plumes.

The data gathered from this unmanned, orbital space mission will help in the design of sensors for a Strategic Defence System. The Delta 181 experiment also helps demonstrate that it is possible to discriminate between reentry vehicles and decoys with passive sensors.

1988 - March 23

Anniversary SDI Speech/National Test Facility

The fifth anniversary of President Reagan's address to the nation announcing his intention of committing the United States to an SDI research program is observed.

The official groundbreaking for the construction of SDI's National Test Facility (NTF) is held. The NTF will serve as the 'accordinating' point and hub for the various geographically remote facilities that will be linked electronically. These experiment and simulation facilities together constitute the National Test Bed (NTB).

The NTB programme will provide the capability to compare, evaluate and text the alternative architectures proposed for a layered defence and its associated battle management and command, control and communications. The NTB will represent the major simulating activity for the SDI programme.

1989 - January 31

Monahan Becomes SDIO Director

Lt. General George L. Monahan Jr. becomes the second director of the SDIO, succeeding Lt. General Abrahamson.

1989 - February 2

Janus Flight Experiment

The Janus flight experiment succeeds in obtaining the first high-resolution imagery of a post-boost vehicle (PBV) in space.

1989 - February 9

President Bush on SDI

President George Bush announces in an address to a Joint Session of Congress that he will "vigorously pursue the Strategic Defence Initiative."

1989 - March 24

Delta 183 (Delta Star)

The Delta Star spacecraft carries aloft a laser radar and seven imaging sensors. Several sounding rockets are launched during the course of the experiment, enabling Delta Star's sensors to collect data characterising their plumes.

Data collected by Delta Star will be valuable in designing and engineering a broad range of systems for a strategic defence, particularly space-based sensors and seekers on board kinetic energy weapons such as Space-Based Interceptors (SBI).

1989 - April 10
Alpha Chemical Laser
The Alpha Chemical Laser for the first time produces a high-power beam when fired in its ground test facility. This milestone in the space-based, chemical laser programme will be used to validate the technology, computational methods, and fabrication processes necessary for scaling chemical lasers to power levels required for strategic defence. Chemical space-based lasers are candidates for follow-on phases of a Strategic Defence System.

1989 - April 25
No Change in US Goal for SDI
Secretary of Defence Richard Cheney testifies before the House Armed Services Committee:

"The goals of the Strategic Defence Initiative remains unchanged. We will continue to pursue the general framework of both space-and-ground-based defences while providing the flexibility to adjust the specific deployment schedule as evolving technology is tested and proven. A restructured programme would continue toward deployment of a system that will meet the requirements of Phase I by focusing on evaluating the potential of the most rapidly advancing technologies such as Brilliant Pebbles."

1989 - April 27
SBI Hover Test
The first full-length laboratory flight test to demonstrate the technologies for a space-based interceptor projectile is successful.

1989 - June 14
Thunderbolt Electromagnetic Launcher
Several concept validation tests on the Thunderbolt Electromagnetic Launcher are successfully conducted. Of the 12 shots launched on this system, one projectile weighing 110 grams is propelled to a speed of 4.3 kilometers per second.

1989 - July 13
Beam Experiment Abroad Rockets (BEAR)
SDIO successfully conducts the first test in space of a neutral particle beam (NPB) accelerator. An NPB system is a candidate for follow-on phases of a Strategic Defence System, either to facilitate discrimination between targets and decoys, or as a weapon to destroy attacking ballistic missiles and their reentry vehicles.

1989 - August 3
SBI On-Target Test
Another increment in the laboratory flight tests demonstrating technologies for the Space-Based Interceptor projectile is successfully completed. The test vehicle hovers at a height of 9 meters (30 feet) while tracking its target: a solid fuel rocket motor simulating a thrusting missile, operated in a stationary mode on the Edwards Air Force Base range.

1989 - September 12
SBI On-Target Test
The final test in a series of laboratory flight tests demonstrating technologies for a Space-Based Interceptor projectile uses a new, super high speed computer to demonstrate the detection and tracking capabilities of the test projectile.

1989 - September 14
Jason Report On Brilliant Pebbles
The Jason study group's report on Brilliant Pebbles endorses continued research on the concept of small, lightweight, smart interceptors for defence against ballistic missiles.

1989 - September 20
DSB Study On Brilliant Pebbles
In a study of the Brilliant Pebbles concept, the Defense Science Board (DSB) finds no fundamental flaws and pronounces the idea innovative. It predicts that two years of continued research would resolve remaining technical issues.

1989 - September 22-23
Wyoming Ministerial
In an effort to facilitate negotiation of confidence-building predictability measures in the field of ballistic missile defence, Secretary of State James Baker invites Foreign Minister Eduard Shevardnadze to send a team of Soviet experts to visit two US laboratories conducting SDI research.

1989 - December 14
Soviets Visit SDI Labs
Ten Soviet experts, led by Ambassador Yuri Nazarkin, head of the delegation to the Nuclear and Space Talks, visit the TRW Corporation's ALPHA laser facility at San Juan Capistrano in California, and the Beam Experiment Abroad Rockets (BEAR) neutral particle beam facility at Los Alamos National Laboratory in New Mexico.

The Soviets see both the ALPHA laser, which will be launched into space as part of the Zenith Star space-based chemical laser experiment, and the BEAR neutral particle beam payload, which was launched into space and recovered in July 1989.

1990 - January 26
Hedi Kite I Test Flight
The US Army Strategic Defense Command and the SDIO successfully conduct the first in a series of tests of the High Endoatmospheric Defense Interceptor Kinetic Kill Vehicle Integrated Technology Experiment (HEDIKITE) at White Sands Missile Range, New Mexico. The Kite tests are designed to resolve critical technology issues related to the non-nuclear intercept of reentry vehicles within the Earth's atmosphere.

1990 - January 31
US, France Sign MOU On SDI Research
The US Department of Defense and the French Ministry of Defense sign a Memorandum of Understanding promoting Cooperative Programmes on Free Electron Laser Technology.

1990 - February 7

President Bush On Strategic Defences

In remarks at the Lawrence Livermore National Laboratory in California, President Bush says: "Together with strategic modernisation and arms control, programmes like SDI – the Strategic Defence Initiative – and one of its most promising concepts, Brilliant Pebbles, complement our ability to preserve the peace into the 1990s and beyond ... Even as we work to reduce arsenals and reduce tensions, we understand the continuing, crucial role of strategic defenses. Beyond their contributions to deterrence, they underline effective arms control by diminishing the advantages of cheating. They can also defend us against accidental launches or attacks from the many other countries that, regrettably, are acquiring ballistic missile capabilities. In the 1990s, strategic defense makes more sense than ever before."

1990 - February 14

LACE/RME Space Experiments

The first SDI long-term directed energy space experiments are launched from Cape Canaveral. The 30-month Low-Power Atmospheric Compensation Experiment (LACE) will measure the distorting effects of the Earth's atmosphere on low-power laser beams. The one-year Relay Mirror Experiment (RME) will demonstrate the relay element of a Ground-Based Laser (GBL) system and measure the accuracy of the system in pointing a laser beam uplinked from the ground to a space platform.

1990 - March 29

Firefly Experiment

SDIO conducts a successful test of the Firepond Laser Radar near Westford, Massachusetts. The test involves the tracking of a sounding rocket launched from Wallops Island on Virginia's Atlantic coast, and of a specially designed payload carried abroad the rocket.

This is the first time laser radar has demonstrated the precision tracking and imaging techniques needed for midcourse discrimination between decoys and warheads.

K

Strategic Nuclear Arms

1969 - November 17
SALT Talks

Preliminary Strategic Arms Limitation Talks (SALT) between the United States and the Soviet Union begin in Helsinki and continue until December 22.

1970 - April 16
SALT Talks

Formal SALT negotiations open in Vienna. The Soviets at first insist on including all US "forward-based systems" intended to protect Europe from Soviet attack, but capable of reaching the western portion of the USSR. The United States points out the inequity of an approach that ignores the varied Soviet intermediate-range air and missile systems directed at Europe. The lack of symmetry in the weapons systems and strategies of the two powers also complicate the negotiations.

1972 - May 26
SALT I Treaty

The United States and the Soviet Union, represented by President Richard Nixon and Soviet Communist Party Secretary Leonid Brezhnev, sign the basic-documents of SALT I:

- An ABM Treaty limiting anti-ballistic missile systems to two ABM deployment areas so restricted that they cannot provide a nation-wide ABM defense or become the basis for developing one.

- An Interim Agreement limiting competition in offensive strategic arms and providing further time for negotiations. The agreement essentially freezes the number of ballistic missile launchers at existing levels, whether operational or under construction, and permits an increase in submarine-launched missile launchers up to an agreed level only with the dismantling or destruction of a corresponding number of intercontinental ballistic missiles (ICBMs) or submarine-launched ballistic missiles (SLBMs).

1974 - July 3
SALT I ABM Protocol
The United States and the Soviet Union sign a protocol limiting deployment of strategic defensive weapons to one anti-ballistic missile site for each country.

1974 - November 24
Vladivostok Agreement
Meeting at Vladivostok, President Gerald Ford and Soviet Communist Party Secretary Brezhnev announce agreement on a formula for the limitation of strategic offensive arms. The leaders agree that:

- The new agreement will incorporate the relevant provisions of the Interim Agreement of May 26, 1972, which will remain in force until October 1977;
- The new agreement will cover the period from October 1977 through December 31, 1985;
- Based on the principle of equality and equal security, the new agreement will include the following limitations: Both sides will be entitled to have an agreed aggregate number of strategic delivery vehicles, and both sides will be entitled to have an agreed aggregate number of ICBMs and SLBMs equipped with multiple independently targetable reentry vehicles (MIRVs);
- The new agreement will include a provision for further negotiations beginning no later than 1980-1981 on the question of further limitations and possible reductions of strategic arms in the period after 1985; and
- Negotiations to work out the new agreement incorporating the foregoing points will resume in Geneva in January 1975.

1977 - March 30
Strategic Arms Reductions
In Moscow, Secretary of State Cyrus Vance proposes that the two powers agree to substantial reductions of, and qualitative constraints

on, strategic arms. At the same time, the United States presents an alternative proposal for a SALT II agreement similar to the framework agreed to at Vladivostok in 1974.

1979 - June 18

SALT II Treaty

President Jimmy Carter and Soviet Communist Party Secretary Brezhnev end their Vienna summit meeting with the signing of the second Strategic Arms Limitation Treaty (SALT II) between the United States and the Soviet Union. Its major provisions are:

- A ceiling of 2,400 strategic missiles and bombers for both sides to be reached within six months after the treaty enters into force, and a further reduction to 2,250 by 1981;

- Within this ceiling, no more than 1,320 strategic missiles or bombers to be equipped with multiple warheads or cruise missiles; of those, no more than 1,200 land-based, sea-based or air-to-surface ballistic missiles to have multiple warheads; and of those land-based ICBMs no more than 820 to have multiple warheads;

- The Soviet Union to dismantle 270 missiles to reach the 2,250 ceiling;

- The Soviets to stop production and deployment of the SS-16 missiles;

- Both sides may build and deploy a single new type of ICBM;

- No more than 20 warheads on the new ICBM, and no more than 14 warheads on SLBMs;

- The 1972 ABM Treaty remains in effect;

- A three-year protocol provides some temporary constraints on mobile ICBMs and cruise missiles;

- Compliance to be monitored by satellites and other "national" intelligence means; and

- An exchange of letters in which the Soviets agree not to increase the production rate of the Backfire bomber.

SALT II is not ratified following the Soviet invasion of Afghanistan on December 27, 1979; however, the United States announces that, on reciprocal basis, it will not "undercut" the treaty's provisions.

1981 - August 13
US Position On Strategic Forces
Following an in-depth review of US security, arms control and compliance policies, President Ronald Reagan decides to seek significant reductions in strategic forces rather than limitations on future growth.

1982 - May 9
US Proposal
In a speech at Eureka College in Illinois, President Reagan outlines the US proposal, which emphasises reductions in the most destabilising systems, particularly intercontinental ballistic missiles. The basic US objective is a verifiable agreement that enhances stability, reduces the risk of war, and achieves deep reductions in the strategic nuclear weapons of both sides.

1982 - June 29
START/US Proposal For Phased Reductions
The Strategic Arms Reductions Talks (START) with the Soviet Union open in Geneva. Shortly thereafter, the US presents a proposal for strategic reductions to be implemented in two phases. The proposal includes:

- Reductions in the number of deployed strategic ballistic missile warheads to 5,000 for each side with a sublimit of 2,500 on land-based ICBMs.
- A limit of 850 deployed strategic ballistic missiles with a sublimit of no more than 210 heavy and medium ICBMs of which no more than 110 could be heavy ICBMs. The sublimits are to ensure substantial cuts in the most destabilising missile systems – ballistic missiles, especially large ICBMs with multiple independently targetable reentry vehicles.
- A ban on new heavy missiles.
- Substantial reductions in ballistic missile destructive capability and potential throw-weight.
- An equal ceiling on heavy bombers below the US level in SALT II.
- Equitable limits and constraints on other strategic systems.

1983 - March 29
Soviet Draft START Treaty
The Soviets table a draft START treaty which would result in 25 per cent reduction in the number of strategic nuclear delivery vehicles (ballistic missiles and bombers). The proposal bans all ground and sea launched cruise missiles (GLCMs, SLCMs) and limits air-launched cruise missiles (ALCMs) with a range in excess 600 kilometers.

The Soviet proposal provides modest reductions of the most destabilising systems – fast, accurate ballistic missiles with multiple warheads – and, in fact, would permit substantial growth in the number of ballistic missile warheads about current levels.

The Soviets charge that the US proposal discriminates against the Soviet Union and would force them to restructure their strategic forces.

1983 - April 6
SCOWCROFT Commission Report
The Commission on Strategic Forces (Scowcroft Commission), appointed by President Reagan, publishes its report. The report underscores the need to modernise US strategic weapons, and to undertake negotiations leading to balanced arms control agreements that would promote stability in times of crisis and result in meaningful, verifiable reductions. The President endorses this report.

1983 - July 7
US Draft START Treaty
The US presents its first draft START treaty. The draft text reflects the central elements of the US START proposal, while also taking into consideration several Soviet concerns about the original US proposal. The US relaxes its proposed limit of 850 deployed ballistic missiles and its insistence that no more than half of the warheads on ballistic missiles be land-based. The proposal would give both sides the option of restructuring their forces more flexibly, including moving in the direction of smaller and less threatening single-warhead ICBMs.

1983 - October 6
US on Strategic Weapons' Build-down
President Reagan adds to the US START position the principle
of mutual, guaranteed build-down of strategic weapons, whereby
a ratio of older weapons would be reduced as certain new ones are
deployed. Variable ratios are designed to channel modernisation
of strategic forces toward more stabilising systems.

1983 - December 7
Soviets Suspend START
The START talks come to a halt when the Soviets refuse to set a
date for their resumption. They allege a "change in the strategic
air situation" following NATO deployment of intermediate-range
nuclear missiles in response to Soviet deployment of SS-20 missiles,
which threaten Western security.

      The US offers to return to the talks whenever the Soviets are
ready.

1984 - September 24
US Proposal for "Umbrella" Arms Talks
In a speech to the United Nations General Assembly, President
Reagan proposed a broad "umbrella" framework for talks between
the United States and the Soviet Union on arms control issues.
Reagan makes clear that the US is committed to achieving, among
other objectives, a substantial reduction in US Soviet nuclear
arsenals.

1985 - January 7-8
Shultz, Gromyko Set Agenda for NST
US Secretary of State George Shultz and Soviet Foreign Minister
Andre Gromyko meet in Geneva to set an agenda for new Nuclear
and Space Talks (NST) to cover strategic nuclear arms,
intermediate-range nuclear forces, and defence and space.

1985 - March 12
NST Opens/US Objectives/Soviet Linkage
The United States and the Soviet Union begin new negotiations
in the Nuclear and Space Talks. Among other objectives, the US

seeks radical reductions in the number of destructive power of offensive strategic arms. The US draft START treaty of 1983 remains on the table. The Soviet side makes no specific proposal.

Progress in the talks is slowed by Soviet insistence on placing unacceptable limits on the US Strategic Defence Initiative (SDI) as a precondition for progress in the strategic arms area.

1985 - September 30
Soviet START Proposal

The Soviet Union presents its START proposal, which contains a number of unacceptable elements, such as counting certain US systems as "strategic", while excluding an even greater number of comparable Soviet systems. The Soviets, however, accept for the first time the principle, long advocated by the US, of deep reductions in strategic offensive forces.

1985 - November 1
US START Proposal

The US presents a new proposal at the negotiating table, including the following major elements:

- A limit of 4,500 reentry vehicles (RVs) on ICBMs and SLBMs – about 50 per cent below current levels.
- A sublimit of 3,000 RVs carried by ICBMs – about 50 per cent below the current Soviet level.
- A sublimit of 1,500 RVs carried on permitted ICBMs except those on silo-based light and medium ICBMs with six or fewer warheads.
- A 50 per cent reduction in the highest overall strategic ballistic missile throw-weight of either side – that is, from the Soviet level of over 5.4 million kilos (The US has fewer than 1.9 million kilos).
- Contingent upon Soviet acceptance of these RV and throw-weight limits, the US would accept an equal limit of 1,500 on the number of long-range ALCMs carried by US and Soviet heavy bombers – about 50 per cent below planned US deployment levels.

- A limit of 1,250 - 1,450 on strategic ballistic missiles (ICBMs and SLBMs) – about 40 to 50 per cent below the current higher Soviet level.
- In the context of an appropriate agreement on strategic ballistic missiles, the US could accept a limit of 350 on heavy bombers – roughly a 40 per cent reduction from US SALT-accountable levels.
- A ban on all new heavy strategic ballistic missiles and the modernisation of existing heavy missiles – the most destabilising weapons.
- A ban on all mobile ICBMs because of difficulties in verification.

1985 - November 21
Geneva Summit
President Reagan and General Secretary Mikhail Gorbachev issue a joint statement in Geneva. At the Geneva NST talks, they agree to focus on areas where there is common ground, including the "principle of 50 per cent reductions in the nuclear arms of the US and Soviet Union appropriately applied".

1986 - January 15
Soviet Proposal to Eliminate Nuclear Weapons
General Secretary Gorbachev proposes the elimination of nuclear weapons over 15 years, Gorbachev's plan rests on several Soviet proposals, including:
- The elimination of nuclear weapons contingent upon US acceptances of measures which would cripple the US SDI programme; and
- A 50 per cent reduction in each side's nuclear arms capable of reaching the other's territory, which would include many US intermediate-range systems while excluding comparable Soviet systems.

1986 - May 21
US Position on SALT
Because of continued Soviet noncompliance with major arms control commitments, the continued build-up of Soviet strategic

forces, and Soviet failure to follow through on its commitment to achieve early progress in the Geneva negotiations, President Reagan announces that in the future, the US will base decisions regarding its strategic force structure on the nature and magnitude of the threat posed by Soviet strategic forces, not on standards contained in SALT. He points out the inappropriateness of continuing US unilateral compliance with the SALT II Treaty, which the Soviet Union has repeatedly violated, which has never been ratified, and which would have expired had it been ratified.

The US will continue to exercise the utmost restraint in the future, seeking to meet US strategic needs, given the Soviet buildup, by means that minimise incentives for continuing Soviet offensive force growth.

1986 - June 2
Soviet Interim START Proposal
The Soviets present a new "interim" proposal, which calls for less than the 50 per cent reductions agreed to at the 1985 Geneva Summit.

1986 - July 27
Revised US START Proposals
The US presents substantial revisions of its proposals to accommodate the Soviet idea of taking interim steps of 50 per cent reductions. The US makes clear, however, that its 50 per cent reduction proposal remains on the table and is preferred.

1986 - October 11-12
Reykjavik Summit
President Reagan and General Secretary Gorbachev agree reductions in strategic nuclear delivery vehicles (SNDVs) to 1,600 for each side, with no more than 6,000 warheads on these delivery vehicles. The Soviets recognise the need for significant cuts in heavy ICBMs, and there is agreement on counting rules for bomber weapons. The Soviet Union, however, demands that US accepts all Soviet proposals as a package, including measures that would have crippled SDI. The President refuses.

1986 - October 22
New US START Proposal

The US presents a new START proposal in Geneva, which incorporates areas of agreement reached at Reykjavik and proposes new solutions in areas where differences remain. Major elements of the proposal include:

- Fifty per cent reduction to equal levels in strategic offensive arms, carried out in a phased manner. As agreed by General Secretary Gorbachev at the November 1985 Geneva Summit, agreement would not be contingent upon resolution of other issues outside START negotiations.
- A ceiling of 1,600 on strategic nuclear delivery vehicles, including ICBMs, SLBMs and heavy bombers.
- A ceiling of 6,000 warheads, to include ICBM and SLBM warheads and long-range ALCMs. Each heavy bomber carrying gravity bombs and short-range attach missiles (SRAMs) would count as a warhead in the 6,000 limit. Each ALCM carried on a heavy bomber would count as one warhead in the 6,000 ceiling.
- Sublimits of 4,800 ballistic missile warheads, 3,300 ICBM warheads, and 1,650 warheads on permitted ICBMs except those on silo-based light and medium ICBMs with six or fewer warheads.
- Substantial reductions (50 per cent) in heavy ICBMs. Heavy ICBM warheads would be included in the 1,650 warhead limit.
- Fifty per cent reduction from the current Soviet throw-weight level, to be codified by direct or indirect limits.
- A ban on mobile ICBMs.
- Commitment to find a mutually acceptable solution to limiting long-range nuclear-armed SLCMs outside the 1,600/6,000 limits.
- Verification of compliance to include an exchange of comprehensive and accurate data both before and after the reductions take place, on-site observation of weapon reduction, and effective monitoring of remaining inventories and associated facilities, including on-site inspection.

- Negotiations on verification details should take place in parallel with negotiations on reduction of weapons.

1986 - November 7
Soviet START Proposals
The Soviets present proposals which only partially reflect the headway made at Reykjavik and which, in part, backtrack on certain issues. The Soviets continue to insist that progress in all three of the NST negotiating forums be tied to US acceptance of the unacceptable Soviet position on strategic defences.

1987 - Early 1987
Joint Working Document
The US seeks to narrow further the differences between the two sides, proposing that areas of agreement reached at Reykjavik should serve as the basis for a START agreement.

The sides develop a joint working document which specifies the points of agreement and disagreement on key issues.

1987 - May 8
US Draft START Treaty
The US presents a draft START treaty in Geneva, reflecting basic areas of agreement reached by President Reagan and General Secretary Gorbachev at Reykjavik in October 1986:

- A ceiling of 1,600 strategic nuclear delivery vehicles;
- A ceiling of 6,000 warheads on these delivery vehicles;
- Bombers and their weapons would be counted as agreed at the Reykjavik Summit.

Other elements of the US Draft treaty includes:

Sublimits of 4,800 ballistic missiles warheads, 3,300 ICBM warheads and 1,650 warheads on permitted ICBMs except those on silo-based, light or medium ICBMs with six or fewer warheads;

A reduction of 50 per cent from the current Soviet throw-weight level to be codified by direct or indirect limits;

A ban on mobile missiles; and

Reductions to be phased in over seven years period, rather than five years, to permit additional time for the sides to make adjustments in strategic forces required by the reductions.

1987 - July 31
Soviet Draft START Treaty
The Soviet Union presents a draft treaty, which includes:
- A 50 per cent reduction in each side's strategic offensive arms;
- A ceiling of 1,600 on strategic nuclear delivery vehicles, including ICBM and SLBM launchers and heavy bombers;
- A 50 per cent reduction in heavy ICBM launchers, which would mean 1,540 warheads; and
- A ceiling of 6,000 nuclear warheads.

The Soviet proposal differs from the US initiative in several important ways, including:
- It would limit launchers of ICBMs and SLBMs and not the missiles themselves as called for in the US proposal;
- It does not include specific sublimits on warheads;
- It would not record in a legally binding form 50 per cent reductions in throw-weight;
- It would permit mobile ICBMs;
- It would create a ceiling of 400 on long-range SLCMs and permit their deployment on submarines only; and
- It would require that the 50 per cent cuts be taken over five years rather than seven years.

Under the Soviet proposal, the 50 per cent reduction in strategic offensive arms is contingent upon achievement of a US-Soviet accord to limit the testing and deployment of space-based missile defence systems.

1987 - October 14
US Draft Protocol
At the Geneva talks, the US presents a draft Protocol on Conversion or Elimination, a key element of a START treaty.

1987 - December 7-10
Washington Summit
President Reagan and General Secretary Gorbachev agree that their START negotiators should build upon the areas of agreement on 50 per cent reductions as reflected in the joint draft START treaty text being developed in Geneva. These include:

- A ceiling of 1,600 strategic nuclear delivery systems with 6,000 warheads;
- A ceiling of 1,540 warheads on 154 heavy missiles;
- Agreed counting rules for heavy bombers and their nuclear armament;
- Agreed counting rules for ballistic missile warheads;
- Agreement that as a result of the reductions the aggregate throw-weight of Soviet ICBMs and SLBMs will be reduced to a level approximately 50 per cent below the existing level, and this level will not be exceeded by either side. The agreement is to be recorded in a mutually satisfactory manner.

During the summit, the two leaders make further progress on START, including agreement on a sublimit of 4,900 for the total number of ballistic missile warheads, declaration of the number of warheads on existing ballistic missiles and, building on the verification provisions of the INF Treaty, guidelines, for effective verification of a START treaty. Important differences remain, including such issues as mobile intercontinental ballistic missiles, additional warhead sublimits on ICBMs, SLBMs and the details of an effective verification regime.

1988 - February 12
US Draft Protocol
At the Geneva talks, the US presents Draft Protocol on the Inspection and Monitoring, a key element in a START treaty.

1988 - February 21-23
Shultz - Shevardnadze Meeting/Verification
Meeting in Moscow, Secretary Shultz and Foreign Minister Eduard Shevardnadze reaffirm the Washington summit commitment to an intensive effort to complete a START treaty. They direct their negotiators to develop joint drafts of three key verification documents before the next ministerial in March:

- Protocol on Inspection;
- Protocol on Conversion or Elimination of strategic nuclear delivery systems; and
- Memorandum of Understanding on data exchange.

1988 - Mid-March
Joint Draft Verification Document
Negotiators develop joint draft texts of the three verification documents.

1988 - November 16
Round X Ends/Status of SRART
At the end of Round X of the Nuclear and Space Talks, the United States and the Soviet Union agree on the following elements:

- Deep reductions in deployed strategic forces, to a ceiling of 6,000 warheads on 16,000 strategic nuclear delivery vehicles, sublimits of 4,900 ballistic missile warheads, and 1,540 warheads on 154 heavy missiles;
- Approximately 50 per cent reduction in throw-weight for Soviet ballistic missiles, to equal ceilings for both sides;
- The number of warheads attributed to each existing type of ballistic missile, and some of the counting rules for heavy bomber armaments; and
- The outlines of a verification regime, including several kinds of on-site inspection, data exchange and measures to reduce the possibility of cheating.

Major areas of disagreement are:

- Mobile ICBMs;
- Sea-launched cruise missiles;
- Rules accounting for ALCMs;
- Sublimits of ICBM warheads;
- Modernisation of heavy ICBMs; and
- Soviet attempts to link a SRART treaty to provisions that would cripple the US SDI programme.

1989 - May 10-11
Baker-Shevardnadze Meeting/US START Position
Meeting in Moscow, US Secretary of State James Baker and Foreign Minister Shevardnadze reaffirm the desire of both sides to reach a START agreement and also set dates for the resumption of the Nuclear and Space Talks in Geneva.

The new US administration of President George Bush says that work done on START under the previous administration will be an excellent foundation upon which to build, but it reserves the right to change and modify some US positions.

1989 - June 19

Round XI/US Verification and Stability Initiative

Round XI of the Nuclear and Space Talks opens in Geneva. President Bush announces a Verification and Stability Initiative, designed to build confidence, enhance stability and accelerate resolution of outstanding verification issues, and provide both sides practical verification experience, thereby facilitating efforts to conclude a START treaty.

The US initiative includes:

- Immediate establishment of on-site perimeter/portal monitoring of certain missile production facilities;
- Exchange of data on each side's strategic nuclear forces;
- Prohibition of encryption of telemetry on ICBMs and SLBMs;
- Familiarisation with procedures for inspection to monitor the number of warheads on ballistic missiles;
- Addressing the problem of short-time-of-flight SLBMs;
- Notification of strategic exercises; and
- Demonstration of techniques for identifying missiles.

1989 - September 19

US Position on Mobile ICBMs

Secretary Baker announces the President's decision that the United States will withdraw its proposal at START to ban mobile ICBMs contingent upon US Congressional approval of funding for US mobile ICBM programme.

1989 - September 22-23

Wyoming Ministerial

During the two days of meetings between Secretary Baker and Foreign Minister Shevardnadze, progress is made in the following areas:

- LINKAGE: The Soviets say they have dropped their linkage between achieving a Defence and Space agreement and complementing and implementing an agreement on START. They indicate that they might withdraw from a START treaty if the United States does not abide by the ABM treaty as they interpret it.

- KRASNOYARSK: The Soviets agree to eliminate their illegal radar at Krasnoyarsk without preconditions – a long-standing US requirement for concluding any strategic arms control treaty.

- SLCMs: The Soviets raise the possibility of dealing with sea-launched cruise missiles in a broader naval arms context, and say that in the context of verification system for SLCMs these weapons could be limited outside of the text of a START treaty on the basis of reciprocal obligations. While willing to study these Soviet ideas on SLCMs, the United States emphasises its:

(i) Long-standing view that any discussion on limiting naval arms presents serious problems; and

(ii) Doubts that a viable verification system for SLCMs is feasible.

- UNIT OF ACCOUNT: The United States and the Soviet Union agree that the unit of account for ballistic missiles will be an "ICBM and its associated launcher" and an "SLBM and its associated launcher".

- VERIFICATION AND STABILITY: Following President Bush's June 19 initiative on verification and stability measures, Secretary Baker and Foreign Minister Shevardnadze sign the "Agreement on principles of implementing Trial Verification and Stability Measures that would be carried out pending the conclusion of the US-Soviet Treaty on the Reduction and Limitation of Strategic Offensive Arms."

- STRATEGIC EXERCISES: Secretary Baker and Foreign Minister Shevardnadze sign an agreement on Reciprocal Advance Notice of Major Strategic Exercises, which provide that:

(i) Each side notify the other no less than fourteen days in advance of one of its major strategic exercises involving heavy bombers to be held during that calendar year; and

(ii) Notifications be provided through the Nuclear Risk Reduction Centers of each side.

- VERIFICATION OF MOBILE ICBMs: The Soviets agree to the US proposals on the following elements of verification for mobile ICBMs:

(i) Upon return to garrison following a dispersal, rail-mobile ICBMs would be subject to enhanced National Technical Means (NTM) measures whose nature, scope and procedures are to be agreed upon by the two sides;

(ii) No more than 10 road-mobile launchers of ICBMs may be based or located in a restricted area;

(iii) NTM enhancement measures would involve either moving road-mobile launchers halfway out of their structures, or displaying such launchers next to their structures with the roofs of the structures open at the option of the inspecting side; and

(iv) Agreement is reached in principle that rail garrisons would be limited in size.

1989 - November 26 - December 4
US-Soviet Tagging Demonstration
The United States and the Soviet Union conduct reciprocal demonstrations of techniques for identifying, or "tagging" ballistic missiles.

1989 - December 6
Bush-Gorbachev Meeting in Malta
President Bush proposes to General Secretary Gorbachev that the START negotiations in Geneva be accelerated to resolve all substantive issues and to conclude a treaty, if possible, by a 1990 US-Soviet Summit.

1989 - December 8
US-USSR Agree On Heavy Bomber Inspections
The United States and the Soviet Union agree to conduct reciprocal exhibitions of strategic (or heavy) bombers. The exhibitions will demonstrate those features which distinguish bombers equipped to carry nuclear-armed ALCMs from bombers not so equipped.

The Soviet Union will first exhibit two versions of the Tupolev-95, followed by a US exhibition of two variants of the B-1B.

1990 - January 22

US–USSR Agree On RV Demonstrations
The United States and the Soviet Union sign an agreement providing for reciprocal demonstrations of each side's proposed procedures for verifying that the number of RVs, or warheads, on a ballistic missile does not exceed the number assigned to it in a START treaty.

The United States will first demonstrate procedures for the peacekeeper ICBM and the Trident II SLBM, and the Soviet Union will demonstrate procedures for its SS-18 ICBM and SS-N-23 SLBM.

1990 - February 7-9

Moscow Ministerial
Following meetings between Secretary Baker and Foreign Minister Shevardnadze, a Joint Statement records agreement on all ALCM issues accept the range threshold above which ALCMs would be limited. It also states that the sides agree that SLCMs should be dealt with by parallel, politically binding declarations for the duration of a START treaty. Agreement is also reached on limits on non-deployed ballistic missiles and on non-denial of telemetry data during flight tests of START accountable ballistic missiles.

1990 - April 4-6

Washington Ministerial
The Soviets indicate that, notwithstanding the February Joint Statement in Moscow, major differences may remain on ALCMs and SLCMs.

1990 - April 18

Inspection of Soviet Heavy Bombers
Implementing an agreement reached at the end of Round XII, a team of US experts travels to the Soviet Union to inspect two versions of the Tupolev-95 heavy bomber. The exhibition is

designed to demonstrate features which distinguish bombers equipped to carry nuclear-armed ALCMs from bombers not so equipped and to demonstrate maximum equipage. A reciprocal exhibition will take place in the United States on May 11, 1990.

1990 - April 25-26
Demonstration of US Procedures for RV Verification
Implementing an agreement reached at the beginning of Round XII, Soviet experts visit the United States to observe a demonstration of US-proposed procedures for verifying the number of reentry vehicles (RVs), or warheads, on the US Peacekeeper ICBM. A reciprocal demonstration on an SS-18 will take place in the Soviet Union on May 11, 1990. The United States will demonstrate its RV procedures on the D-5 SLBM between May 29-31. The Soviets will demonstrate their RV on-site inspection procedures on the SS-N-23 between June 12-13, 1990.

II

TREATY ON THE NON-PROLIFERATION OF NUCLEAR WEAPONS: SIGNED ON JULY 1, 1968 AND CAME INTO FORCE ON MARCH 5, 1970

The States concluding this Treaty, hereinafter referred to as the "Parties to the Treaty":
- *Considering* the devastation that would be visited upon all mankind by a nuclear war and the consequent need to make every effort to avert the danger of such a war and to take measures to safeguard the security of peoples;
- *Believing* that the proliferation of nuclear weapons would seriously enhance the danger of nuclear war;
- *In conformity with* resolutions of the United Nations General Assembly calling for the conclusion of an agreement on the prevention of wider dissemination of nuclear weapons;
- *Undertaking* to cooperate in facilitating the application of International Atomic Energy Agency safeguards on peaceful nuclear activities;

- *Expressing* their support for research, development and other efforts to further the application, within the framework of the International Atomic Energy Agency safeguards system, of the principle of safeguarding effectively the flow of source and special fissionable materials by use of instruments and other techniques at certain strategic points;

- *Affirming* the principle that the benefits of peaceful applications of nuclear technology, including any technological by-products which may be derived by nuclear-weapon States from the development of nuclear explosive devices, should be available for peaceful purposes to all Parties to the Treaty, whether nuclear-weapon or non-nuclear states;

- *Convinced* that, in furtherance of this principle, all Parties to the Treaty are entitled to participate in the fullest possible exchange of scientific information for, and to contribute alone or in cooperation with other States to, the further development of the applications of atomic energy for peaceful purposes;

- *Declaring* their intention to achieve at the earliest possible date the cessation of the nuclear arms race and to undertake effective measures in the direction of nuclear disarmament;

- *Urging* the co-operation of all States in the attainment of this objective;

- *Realising* the determination expressed by the Parties to the 1963 Treaty banning nuclear weapon tests in the atmosphere, in outer space and under water in its Preamble to seek to achieve the discontinuance to all test explosions of nuclear weapons for all-time and to continue negotiations to this end;

- *Desiring* to further the easing of international tension and the strengthening of trust between States in order to facilitate the cessation of the manufacture of nuclear weapons, the liquidation of all their existing stockpiles, and the elimination from national arsenals of nuclear weapons and the means of their delivery pursuit to a treaty on general and complete disarmament under the strict and effective international control;

- *Recalling* that, in accordance with the Charter of the United Nations, states must refrain in the international relations from the threat or use of force against the territorial integrity or political independence of any State, or in any other manner inconsistent with the purposes of the United Nations, and that the establishment and maintenance of international peace and security are to be promoted with the least diversion of armaments of the world's human and economic resources;

Have agreed as follows:

Article I

Each nuclear-weapon State Party to the Treaty undertakes not to transfer to any recipient whatsoever nuclear weapons or other nuclear explosive devices or control over such weapons or explosives devices directly, or indirectly; and not in any way to assist, encourage, or induce any non-nuclear-weapon State to manufacture or otherwise acquire nuclear weapons or other nuclear explosive devices, or control over such weapons or explosive devices.

Article II

Each non-nuclear-weapon State Party to the Treaty undertakes not to receive the transfer from any transferee whatsoever of nuclear weapons or other nuclear explosive device or of control over such weapons or explosive devices directly, or indirectly; not to manufacture or otherwise acquire nuclear weapons or other nuclear explosive devices; and not to seek or receive any assistance in the manufacture of nuclear weapons or other nuclear devices.

Article III

1. Each non-nuclear-weapon State Party to the Treaty undertakes to accept safeguards, as set forth in an agreement to be negotiated and concluded with the International Atomic Energy Agency and the Agency's safeguards system, for the exclusive purpose of verification of the fulfillment of its obligations assumed under this Treaty with a view to preventing diversion of nuclear energy from peaceful uses to nuclear weapons or other nuclear explosive devices. Procedures

for the safeguards required by this article shall be followed with respect to source or special fissionable material whether it is being produced, processed or used in any principal nuclear facility or is outside any such facility. The safeguards required by this article shall be applied on all source or special fissionable material in all peaceful nuclear activities with the territory of such State, under its jurisdiction, or carried out under its control anywhere.

2. Each State Party to the Treaty undertakes not to provide (a) source or special fissionable material, or (b) equipment or material especially designed or prepared for the processing, use or production of special fissionable material, to any non-nuclear-weapon State for peaceful purposes, unless the source or special fissionable material shall be subject to the safeguards required by this article.

3. The safeguards required by this article shall be implemented in a manner designed to comply with Article IV of this Treaty, and to avoid hampering the economic and technological development of the Parties or international cooperation in the field of peaceful nuclear activities, including the international exchange of nuclear material and equipment for the processing, use or production of nuclear material for peaceful purposes in accordance with the provisions of this article and the principle of safeguarding set forth in the Preamble of the Treaty.

4. Non-nuclear-weapon States Party to the Treaty shall conclude agreements with the International Atomic Energy Agency to meet the requirements of this article either individually or together with other States in accordance with the States of the International Atomic Energy Agency. Negotiation of such agreement shall commence within 180 days from the original entry into force of this Treaty. For States depositing their instruments of ratification or accession after the 180-day period, negotiation of such agreements shall commence not later than the date of such deposit. Such agreements shall enter into force not later than 18 months after the date of initiation of negotiations.

Article IV

1. Nothing in this Treaty shall be interpreted as affecting the inalienable right of all the Parties to the Treaty to develop research, production and use of nuclear energy for peaceful purposes without discrimination and in conformity with Article I and II of this Treaty.

2. All the Parties to the Treaty undertake to facilitate, and have the right to participate in, the fullest possible exchange of equipment, materials and scientific and technological information for the peaceful uses of nuclear energy. Parties to the Treaty in a position to do so shall also co-operate in contributing alone or together with other States or international organisations to the further development of the applications of nuclear energy for peaceful purposes, especially in the territories of non-nuclear-weapon States Party to the Treaty, with due consideration for the needs of the developing areas of the world.

Article V

Each Party to the Treaty undertakes to take appropriate measures to ensure that, in accordance with this Treaty, under appropriate international observation and through appropriate international procedures, potential benefits from any peaceful applications of nuclear explosions will be made available to non-nuclear-weapon State Party to the Treaty on a non-discriminatory basis and that the charge to such Parties for the explosive devices used will be as low as possible and exclude any charge for research and development. Non-nuclear-weapon States Party to the Treaty shall be able to obtain such benefits, pursuant in a special international agreement or agreements, through an appropriate international body with adequate representation of non-nuclear weapon States. Negotiations on this subject shall commence as soon as possible after the Treaty enters into force. Non-nuclear-weapon States Party to the Treaty so desiring may also obtain such benefits pursuant to bilateral agreements.

Article VI

Each of the Parties to the Treaty undertakes to pursue negotiations in good faith on effective measures relating to cessation of the nuclear arms race at an early date and to nuclear disarmament, and on a treaty on general and complete disarmament under strict and effective international control.

Article VII

Nothing in this Treaty affects the right of any group of States to conclude regional treaties in order to ensure the total absence of nuclear weapons in their respective territories.

Article VIII

1. Any Party to the Treaty may propose amendments to this Treaty. The text of any proposed amendment shall be submitted to the Depositary Governments which shall circulate it to all Parties to the Treaty. Thereupon, if requested to   do   so   by one-third or more of the Parties to the Treaty, the Depositary Governments shall convene a conference, to which they shall invite all the Parties to the Treaty, to consider such an amendment.

2. Any amendment to this Treaty must be approved by a majority of the votes of all the Parties to the Treaty, including the votes of all nuclear-weapon States Party to the Treaty and all other Parties, which on the date of the amendment is circulated, are members of the Board of Governors of the International Atomic Energy Agency. The amendment shall enter into force for each Party that deposits of such instruments of ratification by a majority of all the Parties, including the instruments of ratification of all nuclear-weapon States Party to the Treaty and all other Parties which, on the date the amendment is circulated, are members of the Board of Governors of the International Atomic Energy Agency. Thereafter, it shall enter into force for any other Party upon the deposit of its instrument of ratification of the amendment.

3. Five years after the entry into force of this Treaty, a conference of the Parties to the Treaty shall be held in Geneva, Switzerland, in order to review the operation of this Treaty with a view to assuring that the purposes of the Preamble and the provisions of the Treaty are being realised. At intervals of five years thereafter, a majority of the Parties to the Treaty may obtain, by submitting a proposal to this effect to the Depositary Governments, the convening of further conferences with the same objectives of reviewing the operation of the Treaty.

Article IX

1. This Treaty shall be open to all States for signature. Any State which does not sign the Treaty before its entry into force in accordance with paragraph 3 of this article may accede to it at any time.

2. This Treaty shall be subject to ratification by signatory States. Instruments of ratification and instruments of accession shall be deposited with the Governments of the Union of Soviet Socialist Republics, The United Kingdom of Great Britain and Northern Ireland and the United States of America, which are hereby designated the Depositary Governments.

3. This Treaty shall enter into force after its ratification by the States, the Governments of which are designated Depositaries of the Treaty, and forty other States signatory to this Treaty and the deposit of their instruments of ratification. For the purposes of this Treaty, a nuclear-weapon State is one which had manufactured and exploded a nuclear weapon or other nuclear explosive device prior to January 1, 1967.

4. For States whose instruments of ratification or accession are deposited subsequent to the entry into force of this Treaty, it shall enter into force on the date of the deposit of their instruments of ratification or accession.

5. The Depositary Governments shall promptly inform all signatory and acceding States of the date of each signature, the date of deposit of each instrument of ratification or of

accession, the date of the entry into force of this Treaty, and the date of receipt of any requests for convening a conference or other notices.

6. This Treaty shall be registered by the Depositary Governments pursuant to article 102 of the Charter of the United Nations.

Article X

1. Each Party shall in exercising its national sovereignty have the right to withdraw from the Treaty if it decides that extraordinary events, related to the subject matter of this Treaty, have jeopardised the supreme interests of its country. It shall give notice of such withdrawal to all other Parties to the Treaty and to the United Nations Security Council three months in advance. Such notice shall include a statement of the extraordinary events it regards as having jeopardised its supreme interests.

2. Twenty-five years after the entry into force of the Treaty, a conference shall be convened to decide whether the Treaty shall continue in force indefinitely, or shall be extended for an additional fixed period or periods. This decision shall be taken by a majority of the Parties to the Treaty.

Article XI

This Treaty, the Chinese, English, French, Russian and Spanish texts of which are equally authentic, shall be deposited in the archives of the Depositary Governments. Duly certified copies of this Treaty shall be transmitted by the Depositary Governments to the Governments of the signatory and acceding States.

IN WITNESS WHEREOF the undersigned, duly authorised, have signed this Treaty.

Done in triplicate, at the cities of London, Moscow and Washington, the first day of July one thousand nine hundred and sixty-eight.

Source: *UN General Assembly Resolution 2373 (XXII): June 12, 1968.*

GLOSSARY

Counterforce Strategy: A Strategy of using nuclear weapons to destroy the opponent's nuclear and general military forces. The main consequences of adopting such a strategy is the need for large number of extremely accurate nuclear weapons.

Countervalue Strategy : A strategy of targeting nuclear weapons on the opponent's cities and industrial areas. When compared with a counterforce strategy, this strategy requires fewer and less accurate nuclear weapons.

Damage Limitation : A term used in nuclear strategy debates to indicate a situation in which one side, feeling that an attack is imminent, launches a preemptive strike with the objective of reducing the opponent's nuclear forces and therefore the severity of the expected attack.

Deterrence : A measure or set of measures designed to narrow an opponent's freedom of choice among possible policies by raising the cost of them to levels thought to be unacceptable. At least until recently, US and, it is assumed, Soviet nuclear weapon policies have been based on the principle of deterrence. Their mutual ability to mount an unacceptably severe nuclear attack under all conceivable circumstances is referred to as a Mutual Assured Destruction.

First Strike Strategy : A strategy adopted perforce by a country which possesses nuclear weapons that are vulnerable to an attack and must therefore be used before such an attack is made. The term first strike *capability* has a different meaning, namely the ability to destroy all, or very nearly all, of the enemies' strategic forces in a pre-emptive nuclear attack.

Nuclear Parity : Rough equivalence between the nuclear forces of opposing countries. Equivalence can be defined in a number of ways: number of launchers; number of individually deliverable warheads; total deliverable explosive power, so-called "throw-weight". At a time, when both the United States and the Soviet Union possessed nuclear arsenals in excess of those required for deterrence nuclear parity has essentially become a political matter.

Overkill: A destructive capacity in excess of that required to achieve stated objectives. For example, the Soviet Union might consider that an assured ability to deliver 200 nuclear warheads would deter the United States. If, after a hypothetical US first strike it is calculated that some 600 deliverable warheads would remain, this would constitute overkill, of magnitude 400 warheads, insofar as the strategy of deterrence is concerned.

Second Strike Capability : The ability to mount a nuclear attack after a first strike by the opponents for a strategy of deterrence; the object is to convince the enemy that no matter what he does (in a first strike), you will retain the capability to deliver an unacceptable severe second strike.

Surgical Strike : A US term used to indicate a selective attack with nuclear weapons in contrast to an all-out first strike or retaliatory second strike. The desirability of being able to carry out a surgical strike is being used to justify the development and procurement of nuclear weapons with counterforce capabilities.

Antiballistic Missile System : A missile system specifically designed to detect, intercept, and destroy incoming nuclear warheads. The US safeguard ABM system employs two missiles with associated radars. For long-range interception a mammoth radar called the Perimeter Acquisition Radar detects and tracks attacking missiles above the atmosphere at ranges up to 4,000 kilometers and dispatches Spartan missiles to destroy them. A second line of defence consists of the rapidly accelerating and highly maneuverable Sprint missile and the Missile Site Radar. The Sprint missile would attempt to intercept incoming warheads after they re-enter the atmosphere.

Airborne Warning and Control System : A US programme to install detection and tracking equipment for defence against air attack in an aircraft. AWACS will carry radars and navigation and communications equipment to direct US interceptor aircraft.

B-1 : A new US strategic bomber with a 34,000 kilogram payload capable of flying intercontinental missions without refueling. The B-1 will be capable of high subsonic speeds at treetop level (to penetrate radar defences) and supersonic speeds (Mach 2.2) at high altitudes. This aircraft is in an advanced stage of twenty-four nuclear-tipped short-range attack missiles (SRAM) and free-fall nuclear bombs.

Ballistic Missile : A missile which follows a ballistic trajectory (part of which may be outside the earth's atmosphere) when thrust is terminated.

Captor : A US antisubmarine weapon system consisting of a homing torpedo inserted into a mine casing and a sonar device. If a submarine passes within some 3 kilometers of the mine it releases the torpedo which then seeks out the target. This weapon, which can be deployed at great depths (some 800 meters), is in an advanced state of development.

F-14 Tomcat : A highly sophisticated variable-sweep wing all-weather interceptor first deployed operationally in 1974 on a US aircraft carrier. It is armed with a machine-gun and short, medium, and long-range air-to-air missiles. The fire control system for the long-range Phoenix missile is capable of simultaneously tracking and engaging six targets.

Fractional Orbital Bombardment System (FOBS) : A technique of delivering nuclear warheads on a low orbital trajectory in contrast to the high parabolic path followed by a typical ICBM. A FOBS warhead descends to the target relatively quickly thus cutting radar warning time, but there are penalties in the form of a loss of accuracy and payload. The "fractional orbit" is a consequence of the Outer Space Treaty which prohibits the emplacement of nuclear weapons into full orbit around the earth.

Launcher : Equipment which launches a missile. ICBM launchers are land-based launchers which can be either fixed or mobile. SLBM launchers are missile tubes on submarines.

Minuteman III : Principal US intercontinental ballistic missile, introduced in 1970. Range 7,020 nautical miles and a payload consisting of three 160-kiloton independently targetable warheads.

Multiple Warhead Systems; MRV Multiple Re-entry Vehicle : The simplest multiple warhead system in which the warheads are caused to fall in a fixed pattern around the aim point. In the Multiple Independently Targetable Re-entry Vehicle (MIRV) system each warhead can be directed towards an individually selected target. The warheads are mounted on a "bus" which is guided through a series of predetermined velocity changes, releasing a warhead after each change. In MIRV Manoeuvrable Re-entry Vehicle system warhead will be provided with the capability to manoeuvre in the terminal states of its trajectory. Warheads with this capability can evade ballistic missile defences or, together with equipment for terminal guidance, achieve pinpoint accuracy.

Mya-4 : Soviet four-jet long-range strategic bomber introduced in the late 1950s. It has an estimated payload of 4,500 kilograms, a maximum speed of 560 miles per hour, and a typical range of 7,000 miles.

Polaris : US submarine-launched ballistic missile in three versions: A-1, first deployed in 1960 with a range of 1,200 nautical miles and one megaton nuclear warhead, no longer operational; A-2, first deployed in 1962 with a range of 1,500 nautical miles and an 800 kiloton nuclear warhead, no longer operational; A-3, first deployed in 1964 with a range of 2,500 nautical miles and three 200 kiloton warheads (not independently targetable), operational on 14 strategic submarines.

Poseidon : US submarine-launched ballistic missile first deployed in 1971. Range 2,500 nautical miles and a payload consisting of ten to fourteen 40-kiloton independently targetable warheads. Now deployed on 27 strategic submarines.

SAM-D : A US land-mobile antiaircraft missile currently under deployment. The fire-control system for the missile includes a phased-array radar that searches for, acquired, tracks, and engages the target. The missile is supersonic with either a nuclear or high explosive warhead.

Short Range Attack Missile - SRAM : An air-to-ground missile with a nuclear warhead deployed on US strategic bombers (FB-111 and B-52) since 1972. Its main purpose is to attack enemy aircraft defence (for example, anti-aircraft missile sites) to enable the bombers to penetrate to their primary targets. Maximum range 160 kilometres.

SS-N-6 : US designation for Soviet submarine-launched ballistic missiles introduced in 1967. Range 1,520 nautical miles and believed to have multiple, but not independently targetable, warheads. Currently deployed on 33 strategic submarines.

SS-N-8 : US designation for Soviet submarine-launched ballistic missile introduced in 1972. Range 4,200 nautical miles and believed to have acquired multiple warheads.

SS-11 mod. 1 : US designation for the most numerous Soviet ICBM. Introduced in 1965. This missile has a range of 5,650 nautical miles and a single one-megaton warhead.

SS-11 mod. 3 : A development of SS-11 mod. 1, introduced in 1973 with a payload consisting of three 300-kiloton warheads (not independently targetable).

Trident C-4 : A new US SLBM currently under improvement programme. Range 4,000 nautical miles and multiple-independently targetable warheads.

Conference on Disarmament (CD) : Multilateral arms control negotiating body, based in Geneva, which is composed of 40 states, including all the nuclear weapon powers. The CD reports to the UN General Assembly.

Conference on Security and Cooperation in Europe (CSCE) : Conference of 33 European NATO, WTO and neutral and non-aligned states plus the USA and Canada, which began in 1972 and in 1975 adopted a Final Act (also called Helsinki Declaration), containing, among others, a document on confidence-building measures and disarmament. Follow-up meetings were held in Belgrade (1977-78), Madrid (1980-83) and Vienna (1986-89).

Cruise Missile : Unmanned, self-propelled, guided weapon-delivery vehicle which sustains flight through aerodynamic lift, generally flying at very low altitudes to avoid radar detection, sometimes following the contours of the terrain, it can be air, ground or sea launched and deliver a conventional or nuclear warhead.

Flexible Response : The NATO doctrine for reaction to an attack with a full range of military options, including the use of nuclear weapons.

Intercontinental Ballistic Missile (ICBM) : Ground-launched ballistic missile with a range in excess of 5,500 km.

Kiloton (Kt) : Measure of the explosive yield of a nuclear weapon equivalent to 1,000 tons of trinitrotoluene (TNT) high explosive. The bomb detonated at Hiroshima had a yield of about 12-15 kilotons.

Megaton (Mt) : Measure of the explosive yield of a nuclear weapon equivalent to one million tons of TNT high explosive.

Mutual Assured Destruction (MAD) : Concept of reciprocal deterrence which rests on the ability of the nuclear weapon powers to inflict intolerable damage on one another after receiving a nuclear attack. It implies what it called "Second-strike capability", that is, the ability to receive a nuclear attack and launch a retaliatory blow large enough to inflict intolerable damage on the opponent.

Strategic Arms Reduction Talks (START) : Negotiations between the Soviet Union and the United States, initiated in 1982, which seeks to reduce the strategic nuclear forces of both sides. Suspended in December 1983 but resumed under the Nuclear and Space Talks that opened in Geneva in March 1985.

Strategic Nuclear Weapons : ICBMs, SLBMs and bomber aircraft carrying nuclear weapons of intercontinental range (over 5,500 km), which can reach the territories of the other strategic nuclear weapon powers.

Terminal Guidance : Guidance provided in the final, near-target phase of the flight of a missile.

Theatre Nuclear Forces (TNF) : Nuclear weapons with ranges of up to and including 5,500 km. In the 1987 INF Treaty, missiles are divided into intermediate-range (over 1,000 km) and shorter-range (500-1,000 km). Also called non-strategic forces. Nuclear weapons with range up to 500 km are sometimes called short-range.

Throw-Weight : The sum of the weight of a ballistic missile's re-entry vehicle(s), dispensing mechanisms, penetration aids, and targeting and separation devices.

Warhead : That part of a weapon which contains the explosive or other material intended to inflict damage.

ABBREVIATIONS

ABM	: Anti-Ballistic Missile
ABRES	: Advanced Ballistic Re-entry System
ACDA	: Arms Control and Disarmament Agency
ADA	: Atomic Development Authority
AIRTAS	: Airborne Toward Array System
ASW	: Anti-submarine Warfare
ATTU	: Atlantics to the Urals
AWACS	: Airborne Warning and Control System
BEAR	: Beam Experiment Abroad Rocket
BMLN	: Ballistic Missile Launch Notification
CAC	: Conventional Arms Control
CACW	: Conference Against Chemical Weapons
CASS	: Command Activated Sonobuoy System
CBU	: Cluster Bomb Unit
CD	: Conference on Disarmament
CDE	: Conference on Disarmament Europe
CEP	: Circular Error Probability
CFE	: Conventional Armed Forces in Europe
CSBM	: Confidence and Security-Building Measures

CSCE	: Conference on Security and Cooperation in Europe
CW	: Chemical Weapons
DAB	: Defense Acquisition Board
DEW	: Directed-Energy Weapon
DIMUS	: Digital Multibeam Steering System
DIRID	: Directional Infrared Intrusion Detector
DMA	: Dangerous Military Activities
DSB	: Defense Science Board
DST	: Defense and Space Talks
EPA	: Environmental Protection Agency
EW	: Electronic Warfare
FAE	: Fuel Air Explosive
FLAGE	: Flexible Lightweight Agile Guided Experiments
GBL	: Ground-Based Laser
GESMO	: Generic Environmental Statement on Mixed Oxide Fuel
GLCM	: Ground-Launched Cruise Missile
HOE	: Homing Overlay Experiment
IAEA	: International Atomic Energy Agency
ICBM	: Intercontinental Ballistic Missile
INF	: Intermediate-Range Nuclear Force
INR	: International Nuclear Review
JVE	: Joint Verification Experiment
MAD	: Mutual Assured Destruction
MBA	: Material Balance Area

MBFR	: Mutual and Balanced Force Reduction
MIRACL	: Mid-Infrared Advanced Chemical Laser
MIRV	: Multiple Independently Targetable Re-entry Vehicle
MOU	: Memorandum of Understanding
MRBM	: Medium-Range Ballistic Missile
MSS	: Moored Surveillance System
MTCR	: Missile Technology Control Regime
NEPA	: National Environmental Policy Act
NNAS	: Neutral and Nonaligned States
NPB	: Neutral Particle Beam
NPT	: Nuclear Non-Proliferation Treaty
NRC	: Nuclear Regulatory Commission
NRRC	: Nuclear Risk Reduction Centres
NSG	: Nuclear Supplier Guidelines
NST	: Nuclear and Space Talks
NTB	: National Test Bed
NTF	: National Test Facility
NTM	: National Technical Means
OECD	: Organisation for Economic Cooperation and Development
OIS	: Organisation of Islamic States
PAIR	: Performance and Integration Retrofit
PBV	: Post-Boost Vehicle
PNET	: Peaceful Nuclear Explosions Treaty
PWR	: Pressurised Water Reactor

RME	: Relay Mirror Experiment
RPV	: Remotely Piloted Vehicle
SAC	: Strategic Air Command
SALT	: Strategic Arms Limitation Talks
SAS	: Suspended Array System
SBI	: Spaced-Bases Interceptors
SDI	: Strategic Defence Initiative
SDIO	: Strategic Defence Initiative Organisation
SLBM	: Submarine-Launched Ballistic Missile
SLCM	: Submarine-Launched Cruise Missile
SNDV	: Strategic Nuclear Delivery Vehicle
SRAM	: Short-Range Attack Missile
SRBM	: Short-Range Ballistic Missile
SRINF	: Shorter-Range Intermediate Nuclear Force
START	: Strategic Arms Reduction Talks
SVC	: Special Verification Commission
TNF	: Theatre Nuclear Force
TTBT	: Threshold Test Ban Treaty
UNAEC	: United Nations Atomic Energy Commission
UNCD	: United Nations Committee on Disarmament
UNSCOM	: United Nations Special Commission
WTO	: Warsaw Treaty Organisation

BIBLIOGRAPHY

Documents, Journals and Newspapers

Alsop, Joseph, "Nuclear Grand Strategy", *Peace and Change*, 4, Spring, 1974.

Apple, R.W., "Majority in Poll Fault Focus by Bush on Global Policy But Back New Order," *New York Times*, October 9, 1990.

Arms Control and Disarmament Agreement, US Arms Control and Disarmament Agency, Washington D.C., US Government Printing Office, 1980.

Arneson, R. Gordon, "Balance of Armaments," *Saturday Evening Post*, December 1, 1979.

Arnett, Charles T., "Choosing Nuclear Arsenals", *Journal of Strategic Studies*, vol. 13, no. 3., September 1990.

Art, Robert, "A Defensive Defense: America's Grand Strategy After the Cold War," *International Security*, vol. 15, no. 4., Spring, 1991.

Ayoob, Mohammed, "The Security Problem of the Third World," *World Politics*, vol. 43, no. 2, January, 1991.

Backgrounder, no.48, Asian Study Center, Washington D.C., July 24, 1986.

Bernstein, Barton J., "The Atomic Bomb and American Foreign Policy, 1941-45; A Historiographical Controversy", *Peace and Change*, no. 2., Spring, 1974.

Betts, Richard, "Paranoids, Pariahs, and Non-Proliferation?", *Foreign Policy*, no. 26, Spring, 1977.

Binder, David, "US Citing Human Rights, Halts Aid to Yugoslavia," *New York Times*, May 19, 1991.

Blechman, Robert R., "What is the Strategic Superiority?", *International Organization*, no. 19., Summer, 1982.

Bonner, Raymond, "A Reporter at Large: African Democracy", *New Yorker*, September 3, 1990.

Brick, Andrew P., "The Failure of Nuclear Balance?", *World Policy Journal*, vol. 4, no. 2. Fall, 1976.

Brodie, Bernard, "The Development of Nuclear Strategy", *International Security*, Spring, 1978.

Bullard, Mont, R., "Defining China's Nuclear Role", *Asian Survey*, August, 1971.

Bulletin of the Atomic Scientists, Washington D.C., May 1, 1946.

Bundy, Kennan, McNamara and Smith, "Nuclear Weapons and the Atlantic Alliance," *Foreign Affairs*, Spring, 1982.

Bundy, McGeorge, "To Cap the Volcano", *Foreign Affairs*, October, 1969.

Bundy, McGeorge, "The Bishops and the Bomb", *The New York Review of Books*, June 10, 1983.

Buwie, Robert R., "Nuclear Strategy and Atlantic Alliance," *International Security*, no. 9, Summer, 1984.

Christian Science Monitor, May 23, 1986.

Clarke, Harold and Dutt, Nitish, "Measuring Value Change in Western Industrial Societies", *American Political Science Review*, vol. 85, no. 3, September 1991.

Convention On Assistance in the CSCE of a Nuclear Accident or Radiological Emergency, IAEA Publication, Vienna, 1986.

David, Steven, "Why the Third World Matters", *International Security*, vol. 14, no. 1, Summer, 1989.

Department of State Document, No. 2498, Washington D.C., US Government Printing Office, 1987.

Department of State Bulletin, Washington D.C., US Government Printing Office, December 15, 1958.

Department of State Bulletin, Washington D.C., US Government Printing Office, January 19, 1959.

Department of State Bulletin, Washington D.C., US Government Printing Office, December 30, 1945.

Deutsch, Karl, et al, "Strategic Change in the Atlantic Area," *Orbis*, vol. 23, Summer, no. 4, 1965.

Desch, Michael, "The Keys that Look Up the World: Identifying American Interests in the Periphery," *International Security*, vol. 14, no. 1, Summer, 1989.

Document on Disarmament: 1945-1959; "The Baruch Plan: Statement by the US Representative to the UN Atomic Energy Commission", June 14, 1946; Publication no. 7008, 2 vols., Washington D.C., US Government Printing Office, 1960, vol. 1.

Document INFCIRC/225/Rev. 1., "The Physical Protection of Nuclear Material," IAEA Publication, Vienna, 1977.

Document INFCIRC/66/Rev. 2.; IAEA Publication, Vienna, 1968.

Documents on American Foreign Relations, Washington D.C., US Government Printing Office, 1954.

Doyle, Michael, "Kant, Liberal Legacies and Foreign Affairs", Part I, *Philosophy and Public Affairs*, vol. 12, no. 3, Summer, 1983.

Draft Final Document of the Fourth Review Conference of the Parties to the Treaty on the Non-Proliferation of Nuclear Weapons, NPT/Conf-IV/DC/LI/Rev. 1 and ADD 1 and 2/Rev. 1.

Draft Third Report of the UN Atomic Energy Commission, UN Publication, Washington D.C., May 1948.

Draper, Theodore, "Nuclear Temptations", *The New York Review of Books,* January 19, 1984.

Evera, Stephen Van, "Why Europe Matters; Why the Third World Doesn't: America's Grand Strategy After the Cold War," *Journal of Strategic Studies*, vol. 13, no. 2., June, 1990.

Evera, Stephen Van, "Primed for Peace: Europe After the Cold War", *International Security*, vol. 15, no. 3, Winter, 1990-91.

Final Document of the Review Conference of the Parties to the Treaty on the Non-Proliferation of Nuclear Weapons, Part I, NPT/CONF-III/64/1 - annex 1; Geneva, 1985.

Foreign Relations of the United States: 1952-54, vol. II, Washington D.C., US Government Printing Office, 1956.

Friedman, Thomas, "NATO Tries to Ease Security Concerns in Eastern Europe", *New York Times*, June 7, 1991.

Gaddis, John, "Nuclear Weapons and International Systemic Stability", Occasional Paper No. 2, *International Security Studies Program*, AAAS, January, 1990.

Gelb, Leslie H., "Is the Nuclear Threat Manageable?" *New York Times*, March 4, 1984.

Gordon, Bernard K., "National Security Strategy", *International Herald Tribune*, May 16, 1974.

Gordon, Thompson, "What Happened in Reactor Four," *Bulletin of Atomic Scientists*, Washington D.C., September, 1986.

Gowe, Joanne, "Bipolarity, Multipolarity, and Free Trade", *American Political Science Review*, vol. 83, no. 4., December, 1989.

Grieco, Joseph, "Anarchy and the Limits of Cooperation: A Realist Critique of the Newest Liberalism Institutionalism," *International Organization*, vol. 42, no. 3, Summer, 1988.

Gwertzman, Bernard, "President Says US Should Not Waver in Backing Studies," *New York Times*, October 18, 1981.

Halloran, Richard, "Pentagon Draws Up First Strategy For Fighting a Long Nuclear War" *New York Times*, May 30, 1982.

Herbst, Jeffrey, "War and State in Africa", *International Security,* vol. 14, no. 4. Spring, 1990.

Herbst, Jeffrey, "The Creation and Maintenance of National Boundaries in Africa," *International Organization,* vol. 43, no. 4, Fall, 1989.

Herrmann, Richard K., "The Middle East and the New World Order: Rethinking US Political Strategy After the Gulf War", *International Security,* vol. 16, no. 2, Fall, 1991.

Hoffman, Bruce et al, "A Reassessment of Potential Adversaries to US Programs," *RAND Corporation Report,* R-3363-DOE, August, 1986.

Hollingsworth, Claire, "China and the Bomb", *Wall Street Journal,* June, 1978.

Howard, Charles R., "Nuclear Strategy Today", *New Yorker,* June 26, 1974.

Howard, Michael, "Reassurance and Deterrence," *Foreign Affairs,* Winter, 1982-83.

Huntington, Samuel, "America's Changing Strategic Interests," *Survival,* vol. 23, no.1, January-February, 1991.

IAEA Model Safeguard Agreement, 1971, Information Circular, INFCIRC/153, Vienna, 1971.

Ibrahim, Youssef, "Algeria Imposes a Curfew and Promises to Use Force," *New York Times,* June 7, 1991.

Ikle, Fred Charles, "Nuclear Arms Race," *Atlantic Monthly,* March, 1978.

International Atomic Energy Agency Bulletin, "Establishment of an International Nuclear Safety Body", Vienna, September, 1983.

International Atomic Energy Agency Press Release, IAEA Press Release, 86/22, August 26, 1986.

International Nuclear Safety Concerns, USGPO, Washington D.C., 1986.

International Response to the Nuclear Power Reactor Safety Concerns, GAO/NSIAD, Washington D.C., USGPO, September 30, 1985.

Jackson, Robert and Rosberg, Carl, "Why Africa's Weak States Persist: The Empirical and the Juridical in Statehood," *World Politics,* vol. 35, no. 1, October, 1982.

Jervis, Robert, "Realism, Game Theory, and Cooperation," *World Politics,* vol. 40, no. 3, April, 1988.

Jervis, Robert, "Loss Aversion in International Politics", *Political Psychology,* May, 1988.

Jervis, Robert, "The Impact of the Korean War on the Cold War," *Journal of Conflict Resolution,* vol. 24, no. 4, December, 1980.

Johnson, Robert, "The Persian Gulf in US Strategy: A Skeptical View," *International Security,* vol. 14, no. 1, Summer, 1989.

Kahneman, David and Tversky, P., "Choices, Values, and Frames", *American Psychologist,* vol. 39, no. 3, April, 1984.

Kaysen, Carl, "Is War Obsolete?: A Review Essay", *International Security,* vol. 14, no. 4, Spring, 1990.

Kennan, George, "Communism in Russian History," *Foreign Affairs,* vol. 69, no. 5, Winter, 1990-91.

Knox, Peter, "US Strategy in the Gulf War," *New York Times,* July 12, 1991.

Krauss, Clifford, "Democratic Leaders Divided on China Trade", *New York Times,* October 9, 1990.

Kupchan, Charles and Kupchan, Clifford, "Concerts, Collective Security and the Future of Europe", *International Security,* vol. 16, no. 1, Summer, 1991.

Lebow, Richard N., "International Security", *New Yorker,* June 12, 1975.

Lippmann, Walter, *Washington Post,* June 20, 1946.

Luhan, Michael J., "Bhutto and Her Party Languish After Defeat", *New York Times,* May 6, 1991.

Mastanduno, Michael, "Do Relative Gains Matter?: America's Response to Japanese Industrial Policy", *International Security,* vol. 16, no. 1, Summer 1991.

Maureen, Dowd, "Bush Stands Firm on Military Policy in Iraqi Civil War," *New York Times,* April 4, 1991.

McNamara, Robert S., "The Military Role of Nuclear Weapons: Perceptions and Misperceptions", *Foreign Affairs,* Fall, 1983.

Mearsheimer, John, "Back to the Future: Instability in Europe After the Cold War," *International Security;* vol. 15, no. 1, Summer, 1990.

Mechling, Charles Jr., "Scaldal in Wartime Washington: The Craufurd-Stuart Affair of 1918," *International Journal of Intelligence and Counterintelligence,* vol. 4, December, 1980.

Milner, Helen and Yoffic, M., "Between Free Trade and Protentionism: Strategic Trade Policy and a Theory of Corporate Trade Demands," *International Organization,* vol. 43, no. 2, Spring, 1989.

Milner, Helen, "The Assumption of Anarchy in International Relations Theory: A Critique", *Review of International Studies,* vol. 17, no. 1, January 1991.

Mohr, Charles, "Carter Orders Steps to Increase Ability to Meet War Threats", *New York Times,* August 26, 1977.

Motyl, Alexander, "Empire Or Stability? The Case for Soviet Dissolution," *World Policy Journal,* vol. 8, no. 3, Summer, 1991.

Nature, May 9, 1986.

New Times (Moscow), March 20, 1946.

New York Times, April 13-15, 25, 1945.

New York Times, December 7, 1945.

New York Times, July 28, 1949.

New York Times, June 15, 1946.

New York Times, January 24, 1982.

New York Times, May 7, 1986.

New York Times, August 17, 1945.

New York Herald Tribune, March 28, 1948.

New York Herald Tribune, September 9, 1946.

Nitze, Paul, "Assuring Strategic Stability", *Foreign Affairs,* vol. 54, no. 2, January, 1976.

Nordlinger, Eric, "Prospects and Policies for Soviet-American Reconciliation," *Political Science Quarterly,* vol. 103, no. 2, Summer, 1982.

Norman, Colin, and Dickson, David, "The Aftermath of Chernobyl", *Science,* September 12, 1986.

Nover, Barnet, *Chicago Daily News,* February 2, 1948.

Nover, Barnet, *Denver Post,* February 2, 1948.

Nucleonics Week, May 8, 1986.

Oberdorfer, Don, "US Analyzes Gorbachev's Bid to China," *The Washington Post,* July 30, 1986.

Phipps, John, "What Kind of Stability?" *Pacific Review,* vol. 12, no. 5, March, 1982.

Perez, Jane, "Kenyan Magazine Editor Held After Articles On Opposition Party," *New York Times,* March 3, 1991.

Prawitz, J., "Argument for NPT Safeguards", *Nuclear Proliferation Problems,* SIPRI Publication, Cambridge and London, The MIT Press, 1968.

Records of the 602nd Meeting of the Conference on Disarmament, CD/PV/602/1991, United Nations Publication, New York, 1991.

Records of the UN Atomic Energy Commission: International Conciliation; UN Publication; Pamphlet No. 430, New York, April, 1947.

Report NUREG - 002: "Final Generic Environmental Impact Statement on the Use of Recycle Plutonium in Mixed Oxide Fuel in Light Water Cooled Reactor", US Nuclear Regulatory Commission, August, 1976.

Report NUREG - 0414, "Safeguarding a Domestic Mixed Oxide Industry Against a Hypothetical Subnational Threat," US Nuclear Regulatory Commission, May, 1978.

Report of the General Oversight Subcommittee, House Interior Committee, 99th Congress, Second Session, May 19, 1986, Washington D.C., US Government Printing Office, 1986.

Reston, James, *New York Times,* November 11, 1945.

Richardson, David K., "The Political Economy of Strategic Trade Theory," *International Organization,* vol. 44, no. 1, Winter, 1990.

Ross, Robert S., "International Bargaining and Domestic Politics: US-China Relations Since 1972," *World Politics,* vol. 38, January, 1986.

Sayigh, Yezid, *Confronting the 1990s: Security in the Developing Countries,* Adelphi Paper No. 251, London, IISS, Summer, 1990.

Second Report of the UN Atomic Energy Commission, UN Publication, September 11, 1947.

Schell, Jonathan, "Reflections: The Abolition," *The New Yorker,* January 2, 1984.

Schlesinger, Arthur Jr., "Foreign Policy and the American Character," *Foreign Affairs,* Fall, 1983.

Secretary of Defense, *Annual Report to the Congress,* 1982, US Department of Defense, January 19, 1981, Washington D.C., 1981.

Schmemann, Serge, "Report by Soviets Expresses Fears of Following the Path of Yugoslavia," *New York Times,* October 4, 1991.

Singh, Jasjit, "India's Nuclear Policy": A Perspective", *Strategic Analysis,* Institute for Defence Studies and Analyses (IDSA), New Delhi, November, 1989, vol. XII, no. VIII.

Slaon, Stanley, "The US Role in a New World Order: Prospects for George Bush's Global Vision," *Congressional Research Service Report,* March 28, 1991.

Slocombe, Walter, "The Continued Need for Extended Deterrence", *Washington Quarterly,* vol. 14, Autumn, 1991.

Snow, C.P., "The Moral Un-Neutrality of Science," *Science,* January 27, 1961.

Snow, Edgar, "Stalin Must Have Peace," *Saturday Evening Post,* March 1, 1947.

Snyder, Kock, "Avoiding Anarchy in the New Europe", *International Security,* vol. 14, no. 4, Spring, 1990.

Southerland, Daniel S., "Chinese Leaders' Offer to Gorbachev," *The Washington Post,* September 7, 1986.

Status of Multilateral Arms Regulation and Disarmament Agreements, 3rd Ed., 1987, UN Publication, Sales No. F-88, IX, 5.

Stein, Arthur, "The Hegemon's Dilemma: Great Britain, the United States and the International Economic Order," *International Organization,* vol. 38, no. 2, Spring, 1984.

Stein, Janice, "Beyond Deterrence," *Journal of Social Issues,* vol. 43, no. 4, Winter, 1987.

Sternglass, E.J., "The Implications of Chernobyl for Human Health", *International Journal of Bioscience Research,* July, 1986.

Stimson, Henry L., "The Decision to Use the Atomic Bomb," *Harper's Magazine,* February, 1947.

Teller, Hans, "Superpower Nuclear Stability," *International Security*, no. 12, Winter, 1987-88.

"The Challenge of Peace: God's Promise and Our Response," *Origins*, May 19, 1983.

The Hindu, January 1, 1982.

The Military Balance: 1976-77; IISS, London, 1977.

The Monthly Review, March 19, 1959.

The Times of India, January 25, 1982.

The United States Strategic Bombing Survey: The Effects of Atomic Bombs on Hiroshima and Nagasaki, Washington, D.C., 1946.

Time, October 7, 1991.

Times (London), April 16, 1945.

Times (London), July 21 1949.

Ullman, Richard H., "No First Use of Nuclear Weapons", *Foreign Affairs*.

United Nations Document A/PV/1963; New York, 1987.

United Nations and Disarmament: 1945-1970; United Nations Publications, Sales No. 70, IX, i. New York, 1971.

US Strategic Bombing Survey No. 4: The Summary Report on the Pacific War, Washington D.C., 1946.

Viorst, Milton, "Report from Baghdad," *New Yorker*, June 24, 1991.

Wall Street Journal, August 25, 1986.

Walt, Stephen, "The Case for Finite Containment: Analyzing US Grand Strategy", *International Security*, vol. 14, no. 1, Summer, 1989.

Weinberger, Casper W., "Why Offense Needs Defense", *Foreign Policy*, vol. 68, Fall, 1982.

Weiner, Myron, "Stability and International Migration", *MIT Center for International Studies;* Occasional Paper, December, 1990.

Books

Adams, Graham, *American Defense Policy,* Rutherford, N.J. Fairleigh Dickenson Press, 1984.

Adomeit, Hannes, *Soviet Risk-Taking and Crisis Behavior: A Theoretical and Empirical Analysis,* London: George Allen and Unwin, 1982.

Allison, Joseph, *The Essence of Decision,* London: George Allen and Unwin, 1981.

Ambrose, Stephen F., *Eisenhower,* 2 vols., Simon & Schuster, 1983.

Aron, Raymond, *Paix et querre entre les nations,* 4th ed. Paris: Calmann Levy, 1966.

Bailey, Sydney R., *The Strategic Arms,* New York: Stein & Day, 1978.

Bajpai, U.S. (ed.), *India's Security: The Politico-Strategic Environment,* New Delhi: Lancers Publishers, 1982.

Ball, George W., *Nuclear Diplomacy,* Boston: Little, Brown & Co., 1981.

Barker, Mary, *International Influences in the Transition to Democracy in Spain,* Columbia: Columbia University Press, 1988.

Barnaby, Frank (ed.), *SIPRI Year Book,* Stockholm, Almgvist & Wiksell, 1977.

Barnaby, Frank (ed.), *World Armament Report,* SIPRI Publication, Stockholm, Almgvist & Wiksell, 1977.

Barnaby, Frank and Huisken, Ronald, *Arms Uncontrolled,* SIPRI Publication, Cambridge, Harvard University Press, 1975.

Barnaby, Frank and Huisken, *Trade in Arms,* SIPRI Publication, Stockholm, Almgvist and Wiksell, 1978.

Barnett, Doak A., *The Making of Foreign Policy in China,* Boulder and London: Westview Press, 1985.

Beaton, Leonard, *Must Arms Spread?* London: Allen Lane, 1978.

Bell, Coral, *Survey of International Affairs: 1954,* Edited by Benham, F.C., London: Oxford University Press, 1957.

Bell, Coral, *Nuclear Strategy: Crucial Issues,* Athens, Ohio, Ohio University Press, 1972.

Bennet, Ramberg, *Global Nuclear Energy Risks: The Search* for *Preventive Medicine,* Boulder, Colo, Westview Press, 1986.

Berghahn, V.R., *Germany and the Approach of War in 1914,* New York: St. Martin's Press, 1973.

Blackett, P.M.S., *Fear, War, and the Bomb: Military and Political Consequences of Atomic Energy,* New York: McGraw Hill, 1948.

Bottmme, James F., *A World of Nuclear Powers,* Wye Plantation, AIHS, 1981.

Bracken, Paul, *The Command and Control of Nuclear Forces,* New Haven: Yale University Press, 1983.

Brodie, Bernard, *War and Politics,* New York: Macmillan Co., 1973.

Brodie, Steil P. *Nuclear Arms and Stability,* London: Kegan Paul & Co., 1979.

Brown, Harold, *Thinking About National Security: Defense and Foreign Policy in a Dangerous World,* Westview Press, 1983.

Brown, Peter M., *Why the SALT Failed,* London: Pall Mall Press, 1978.

Buchan, Alastair (ed.), *A World of Nuclear Powers?* Prentice Hall, Englewood Cliffs, N.J., 1966.

Bundy, McGeorge, *Danger and Survival: Choices About the Bomb in the First Fifty Years,* New Delhi: Affiliated East-West Press, 1989.

Burnes, Peter, *Nuclear Balance*, Washington D.C., The Brookings Institution, 1984.

Burns, James MacGregor, *Roosevelt: The Soldier of Freedom*, New York: Harcourt Brace Jovanovich, 1970.

Bush, George, *The National Security Strategy of the United States: 1990-91;* Washington D.C., Brassey's, 1990.

Butow, Robert J., *Japan's Decision to Surrender*, Stanford: Stanford University Press, 1954.

Byrnes, James F., *Speaking Frankly*, New York: Harper and Brothers, 1947.

Campbell, Jonathan H., *Nuclear Proliferation*, Washington D.C., Ballinger Books, 1982.

Carrell, Henry F., *Future of SALT,* London: Casseil & Co., 1979.

Carter, Field, *Bernard Baruch: Park Bench Statesman*, New York: McGraw Hill, 1944.

Chaucri, Nazil and Robinson, Thomas (eds.), *Forecasting in International Relations*, San Francisco: Freeman, 1978.

Clarke, Robin, *Defense and Development*, London: Jonathan Cape, 1981.

Claude, Inis, *Power and International Relations*, New York: Random House, 1962.

Cooper, Richard, *The Economies of Interdependence*, New York: McGraw Hill, 1968.

Dawer, John W., *Future of SALT,* Chicago: University of Chicago Press, 1978.

Deniel, Ford, *The Cult of the Atom*, New York: Simon & Schuster, 1982.

Deutsch, Karl, et al, *Political Community and the North Atlantic Area: International Organization in the Light of Historical Experience*, Princeton, N.J., Princeton University Press, 1957.

Diehl, Paul F., *China and the Bomb,* Athens, Ga: The University of Georgia Press, 1981.

Divine, Robert A., *War Without Mercy,* New York: Harper's & Brothers, 1976.

Dower, Herbert S., *Arms Control: Issues and Prospects,* New York: W.W. Norton & Co., 1982.

Drell, Anthony, *Nuclear Strategy Planning,* Baltimore: The John Hopkins University Press, 1981.

Drell, Sydney D., *Weapons and Hope,* New York: View Points, 1977.

Dreyr, June Teufl, *Nuclear China,* Stanford, Ca: Stanford University Press, 1972.

Duffy, Gloris, *Future of Arms Control,* Cambridge: Ballinger Books, 1988.

Dyson, John, *Weapons and Hope,* Garden City, N.Y.: Doubleday & Co., 1978.

Earle, Robert L., *Nature of US Nuclear Strategy,* New York: Doubleday Press, 1980.

Eisenhower, Dwight D., *Crusade in Europe,* Garden City, New York: Doubleday & Co., 1948.

Elster, John, *Logic and Society: Contradiction and Possible Words,* New York: Wiley, 1978.

Erickson John, *Evolution of the Nuclear Strategy,* Handen, Conn., The ShoeString Press, 1979.

Feis, Herbert, *End of SALT?* Athens, Ga, The University of Georgia Press, 1977.

Feis, Otto, *Shaping the Defense Program,* New York: St. Martin's Press, 1981.

Fleming, D.F., *The Cold War And Its Origins (1917-1960);* 2 vols., London: George Allen and Unwin, 1968.

Forsberg, Randall, "Call to Halt the Nuclear Arms Race", in Forsberg et al, *Seeds of Promise: The First Real Hearing on the Nuclear Arms Freeze*, Andover: Mass., Bank House Publishing, 1983.

Fossedal, Gregory, *The Democratic Imperative: Exporting the American Revolution*, New York: Basic Books, 1989.

Freedman, Lawrence, *The Evolution of Nuclear Strategy*, New York: St. Martin's Press, 1983.

Friedman, George and Lebard, Meredith, *The Coming War with Japan*, New York: St. Martin's Press, 1990.

Fuller, J.F.G., *The Grand Strategy*, London: Nicholson & Watson, 1979.

Furniss, Edgar S., *US Nuclear Strategy*, Ithaca: Cornell University Press, 1979.

Galanter, M., *The Pattern of the Arms Race*, Boston: Little, Brown & Co., 1979.

Garthoff, Raymond L., *Détente and Confrontation: American-Soviet Relations from Nixon to Reagan*, Washington D.C., The Brooking Institute, 1985.

Garthoff, Robert L., *Deterrence: Theory and Practice*, New York: Simon and Schuster, 1971.

George, Alexander L., and Smoke, Richard, *Deterrence in American Foreign Policy: Theory and Practice*, New York: Columbia University Press, 1974.

Gerschenkron, Alexander, *Economic Backwardness in Historical Perspective*, Cambridge: Belknap Press, 1962.

Gilpin, Robert, *The Political Economy of International Relations*, Princeton, Princeton University Press, 1987.

Gorbachev, Mikhail, *Perestroika: New Thinking of Our Country and the World*, New York: Harper and Row, 1987.

Gould, Stephen Jay, *Time's Arrow: Time's Cycle*, Cambridge: Harvard University Press, 1987.

Gould, Stephen Jay, *Wonderful Life: The Burgess Shale and the Nature* of History, New York: Norton, 1989.

Gompert, David C., Mandelbaum, Michael, Garwin, Richard L., and Barton, John H., (Eds.), *Nuclear Weapons and World Politics*, New York: McGraw-Hill Book Co., 1984.

Gray, Colin, "Do the Changes With the Soviet Union Provide a Basis for Eased Soviet-American Relations?" in Jervis and Bialer (eds.), *Soviet-American Relation*, New York: St. Martin's Press, 1990.

Grew, Joseph G., *Political Strategy and Nuclear Arms Race*, Boston: New Books, Beacon Press, 1978.

Groves, Ted, *The Ends of Nuclear Power*, New York: Herder and Herder, 1978.

Halparin, Morton H., *The Nuclear Fallacy*, Bloomington: Indiana University Press, 1978.

Hamilton, Lee, *Superpower Rivalry*, New York: Basic Books, 1964.

Harderman, Samuel, *Nuclear Weapons in a Changing World*, New York: Harper & Row, 1981.

Harper, Edgar L., *The Balance of Power*, Boston: Little & Brown, 1978.

Hartz, Louis, *The Liberal Tradition in America*, New York: Harcourt Brace, 1955.

Hermoot, Peters, *The World Without the Bomb*, New York: Martin Press, 1948.

Herz, John (ed.), *From Dictatorship to Democracy*, Westport, Conn.: Greenwood, 1982.

Hewlett, John W., *The Great Crusade*, Baltimore: The John Hopkins University Press, 1978.

Hirschman, Albert, *The Passions and the Interests*, Princeton: Princeton University Press, 1977.

Hirschman, Albert, *National Power and the Structure, of International Trade*, Berkeley: University of California Press, 1980. (Originally Published in 1945).

Hobsbawn, E.J., *Industry and Empire*, New York: Pantheon, 1968.

Hollowway, Michael R., *US Nuclear Strategy*, New York: Basic Books, 1983.

Hull, Cordell, *The Memoirs of Cordell Hull*, vol. II, New York: Macmillan, 1948.

Ikle, Fred Charles, *Every War Must End*, New York: Columbia University Press, 1971.

Inglehart, Ronald, *The Silent Revolution*, Princeton, NJ: Princeton University Press, 1977.

Inglehart, Ronald, *Culture Shift in Advanced Industrial Society*, Princeton NJ: Princeton University Press, 1990.

Jackson, Robert, *Quasi-States: Sovereignty, International Relations and the Third World*, Cambridge and New York: Cambridge University Press, 1990.

Jervis, David, *The Illogic of American Nuclear Strategy*, Ithaca, NY: Cornell University Press, 1984.

Jervis, Herman, *Systems and Internations*, Cambridge: Harvard University Press, 1974.

Jervis, Robert, *The Logic of Images in International Relations*, 2nd Ed., New York: Columbia University Press, 1989.

Jervis, Robert, *Meaning of Nuclear Revolution*, New York: Columbia University Press, 1989.

Jervis, Robert, *Soviet-American Relations After the Cold War*, Durham, NC: Duke University Press, 1990.

Jones, Herbert, *World Without Arms* ? Toronto: Macmillan Co., 1979.

Jowitt, Kenneth, "The Leninist Extinction" in Chirst, Daniel (ed.), *The Crisis of Leninism and the Decline of the Left: The Revolution of 1989,* Seattle: University of Washington Press, 1991.

Kahn, Herman, *On Escalation: Metaphors and Scenarios,* New York: Frederick A. Praeger, 1965.

Kaplan, Fred, *The Wizards of Armageddon,* New York: Simon & Schuster, 1983.

Kase, Robert F., *The Strategy of Peace,* New York: Vintage Books, 1971.

Kaufman, John S., *India and the Bomb,* New York: Harcourt Brace, 1979.

Kennan, George, *The Nuclear Delusion,* New York: Pantheon Books, 1983.

Kennedy, John F., *Public Papers of the President of the United States: John F. Kennedy, 1961-63,* Washington D.C.: USGP, 1964.

Kennedy, Paul, *The Rise of the Anglo-German Antagonism, 1860-1914,* Boston: George Allen & Unwin, 1980.

Keohane, Robert and Nye, Joseph S. Jr., *Power and Interdependence,* Boston: Little, Brown, 1977.

Kevles, George S., *Years of Upheaval,* New York: Harper & Brothers, 1978.

Killian, George, *Nuclear Weapons and Foreign Policy,* Boston: Little, Brown & Co., 1980.

Killian, James R., *Diplomacy of Power,* Washington D.C.: The Brookings Institution, 1981.

Kinnard, Douglas, *A Study in Defense Politics,* Kentucky: Kentucky University Press, 1977.

Kissinger, Henry A., *Nuclear Weapons and Foreign Policy,* New York: Harper & Brothers, 1957.

Kissinger, Henry A., *The Necessity for Choice,* New York: Harper & Row, 1961.

Kissinger, Henry A., *Years of Upheaval,* Boston: Little, Brown & Co., 1982.

Kox, Robert L., *American-Soviet Strategic Relations,* New York: Herder and Herder, 1972.

Kraft, Harold, *Nuclear Diplomacy,* Boston : Little, Brown & Co., 1972.

Kull, Steven, *Minds of War: Nuclear Reality,* New York: Basic Books, 1988.

Lapp, Ralph Eugene, *Containing the Arms Race,* Cambridge: Mass, MIT Press, 1976.

Lamont, Eric, *Diplomacy of Power,* Princeton: Princeton University Press, 1975.

Larrabee, Eric, *Commander-in-Chief,* New York: Harper and Row, 1987.

Larson, Daniel, *Nuclear Reality,* New York: Harper & Row, 1976.

Larson, Daniel, *Nuclear Unreality,* New York: Harper & Row, 1980.

Larson, Derek K., *The Strategic Design,* New York: Funk & Wagnalls, 1968.

Laurence, William L., *The Hell Bomb,* New York: Knopf, 1951.

Lellouche, Pierre, *Internationalization of the Nuclear Fuel Cycle and Non-Proliferation Strategy: Lessons and Prospects,* Cambridge: Harvard Law School, 1979.

Leventhal, Paul and Yonneh, Alexander, eds., *Nuclear Terrorism: Defining the Threat,* Washington D.C.: Perganon-Brassey, 1986.

Lewis, Wilson K., *Nuclear Deterrence,* Stanford: Stanford University Press, 1973.

Lowell, Harold, *Patterns of Soviet-American Strategic Relations,* New York: Stein & Day, 1982.

Lowell, Joseph N., *US-Soviet Nuclear Strategy,* Notre Dame, Ind.: University of Notre Dame Press, 1979.

Lowell, Stephen, *Whether SALT?*, Washington D.C.: National Defense University Press, 1974.

MacDonald, Doublas, *Adventures in Chaos,* Cambridge: Harvard University Press, 1992.

March, James, and Olsen, Johan, *Rediscovering Institutions,* New York: Free Press, 1989.

Martin, Graham, *Arms Uncontrolled* ?, Boston: Little, Brown & Co., 1978.

Martin, John Barlow, *Our Nuclear Dilemma,* New York: McGraw Hill, 1977.

Masters, Dexter and Way, Katharine, eds., *One World Or None,* New York: McGraw Hill, 1946.

McNamara, Robert, *Blundering into Disaster,* New York: Pantheon Books, 1986.

Miller, Normal B., *The Essence of Security,* Westport: Greenwood Press, 1976.

Miller, Ronald B., *The Missile Race,* New York: Stein & Day, 1977.

Milner, Helen, *Resisting Protectionism,* Princeton: NJ., Princeton University Press, 1988.

Morrison, Herald, *The Arms Race,* Notre Dame, Ind.: University of Notre Dame Press, 1977.

Morrison, Leonard R., *Nuclear Arms Race,* Baltimore: The John Hopkins University Press, 1979.

Morrison, Norman, *Strategic Thought in the Nuclear Age,* Notre Dame, Ind.: University of Notre Dame Press, 1980.

Mueller, John, *Retreat from Doomsday: The Obsolescence of Major War,* New York: Basic Books, 1989.

Nicholas, Ronald R., *Decade of Decision,* New York: St. Martin's Press, 1983.

Nicholas, Steven D., *The Strategy of War and Peace*, Boston: Little Brown & Co., 1979.

Potter, James R., *SALT I and After*, Ithaca, NY: Cornell University Press, 1974.

Poulose, T.T. (ed.), *Perspectives of India's Nuclear Policy*, New Delhi: Young Asia Publishers, 1978.

Puller, David R., *The Arms Race*, Stanford: Stanford University Press, 1979.

Rees, Andrew J., *Myth and Reality in Nuclear Age*, Baltimore: The John Hopkin's University Press, 1979.

Roosevelt, Franklin D., *The Public Papers and Addresses of Franklin D. Roosevelt, 1944-1945*, New York: Random House, 1946.

Roosevelt, James with Libby, Bill, *My Parents: A Differing View*, Chicago: Playboy Press, 1976.

Rosecrance, Richard, *The Rise of the Trading State*, New York: Basic Books, 1986.

Rostow, W.W., *Nuclear Weapons - Strategy and Politics*, Berkeley: University of California Press, 1978.

Rovere, Hugh, *The Nuclear Balance*, Urbana: University of Illionis Press, 1975.

Rovere, Warner R., *Nuclear Options Today*, Cambridge, MIT Press, 1979.

Sacks, Oliver, *Awakening*, New York: Dutton, 1983.

Schell, Jonathan, *The Time of Illusion*, New York: Alfred A. Knopf, 1976.

Schelling, Robert N., *India's Nuclear Choice*, Princeton: Princeton University Press, 1981.

Schelling, Thomas C., *The Strategy of Conflict*, Cambridge: Harvard University Press, 1980.

Schlesinger, Arthur Jr., *A Thousand Days,* Boston: Houghton Miffin, 1965.

Schuman, Frederick L., *International Politics,* New York: McGraw Hill, 1958.

Schumpeter, Joseph, *Imperialism and Social Classes,* New York: Kelley, 1951.

Sen Gupta, Bhabani, *Nuclear Options: Policy Options for India,* New Delhi: Sage Publications, 1983.

Shea, Glenn T., *Nuclear Politics Today,* Boston: D. Reidel Publishing Co., 1981.

Sidey, Henry F., *Fighting to the Finish,* New York: Harper & Brothers, 1978.

SIPRI Year Book, New York: Taylor and Francis, 1983.

Smith, Alice Kimball, *A Peril and A Hope: The Scientists' Movement In America, 1945-47,* Chicago: University of Chicago Press.

Speer, Albert, *Politics of Arms Race,* Toronto: Macmillan Co., 1979.

Stern, Theodore, *Nuclear Power Today,* New York: Vintage Books, 1977.

Stimson, Henry L., and Bundy, McGeorge, *On Active Service in Peace and War,* New York: Harper & Brothers, 1948.

Stone, Jeremy K., *Containing the Arms Race,* Cambridge: Mass, MIT Press, 1979.

Subramanian, R.R., *Nuclear Pakistan: Atomic Threat to South Asia,* Vision Books, 1980.

Sutter, Robert G., *China's Nuclear Policy,* New York: St. Martin's Press, 1982.

Talbot, Lewis L., *Nuclear Strategy Today and Tomorrow,* New York: Alfred A. Knopf, 1984.

Tatu, Michael, *Power of Kremlin,* New York: The Viking Press, 1969.

Toland, Henry A., *Men Who Play God*, Cambridge: Harvard University Press, 1986.

Toland, John, *The Rising Sun: The Decline and Fall of the Japanese Empire, 1936-1945;* New York: Random House, 1970.

Toulmin, Stephen, *Foresight and Understanding: An Inquiry into the Aims of Science*, Bloomington: Indiana University Press, 1961.

Truman, Harry S., *Public Papers of the President of the United States: Harry S. Truman: 1946-1950;* Washington D.C.: UGPO, 1950.

Tyroler, Ferrell, *The World in Crisis*, Chicago: University of Chicago Press, 1973.

Ullman, Richard H., *Securing Europe*, Princeton, NJ: Princeton University Press, 1991.

Walker, Richard L., *Strategic Planning*, Washington D.C.: National Defense University Press 1983.

Wallance, Paul, *Just Or Unjust Nuclear War,* Cambridge: Harvard University Press, 1982.

Wallerstein, Immanuel, *The Modern World System*, 3 vols. New York: Academic Press, 1974-88.

Waltz, Kenneth, *Theory of International Politics*, Reading, Mass: Addision-Wesley, 1979.

Watkins, Herman, *Problems of Security,* Washington D.C.: National Defense University, 1979.

Weiner, Richard, *The United States in World Affairs*, New York: The Viking Press, 1973.

Welch, David A., *Foreign Policy in the Nuclear Age*, Boston: Little, Brown & Co., 1979.

Wilson, Richard, *Assessing the Issues of Science and Technology*, New York: St. Martin's Press, 1986.

Wolfers, Arnold, *Discord and Collaboration: Essays on International Politics,* Baltimore: John Hopkin's University Press, 1962.

World Armament and Disarmament, SIPRI Year Book, 1974, Stockholm: Almgvist and Wiksell, 1974.

Yager, Joseph A., *Nuclear Stability,* London: Macmillan, 1983.

York, Robert K., *Making Weapons, Talking Peace,* Boston: Houghton Miffin Co., 1971.

Zeckhauser, Richard, *Strategy and Choice,* Cambridge: Mass, MIT Press, 1990.

INDEX

ABACC (Brazilian-Argentina Agency for Accounting and Control of Nuclear Materials), 274

ABM systems (Anti-Ballistic Missile system) (*see also* Missiles), 41, 118, 124-125, 188-189, 206, 208, 209
: ABM Treaty, 459
: ABM Treaty (1972), 163-164, 210
: ABM Treaty (1974), 131

ABRES (Advanced Ballistic Re-entry System), 129-130

ASEAN (Association of Southeast Asian Nations, 348
: ASEAN Regional Forum (ARF), 353

ASLBMZ, 127

Abu Dhabi, 144

Acheson, 59, 64, 79, 81, 423, 436
: Acheson-Lilienthal Plan, 217, 225
: Acheson-Lilienthal Report, 60, 294
: Acheson-Lilienthal Proposals, 59

Afghan wars, 338

Afghanistan, 392, 398, 416, 418
: Soviet Union's invasion of 96, 357
: Taliban in, 346

Africa (*see also* South Africa), 10, 83, 91, 142, 183, 196-197, 390, 391, 418
: Sub-Saharan, 391

Ahmad Ali, Asraf, 356

Air Power
: Strategic, 30

Airborne Warning and Control System (AWACS), 124, 133

Alamogordo Desert, New Mexico, 74, 83, 84
: first over nuclear explosion at (July 1945), 113

Albania, 268

Algeria, 268

Allies, 11, 65, 79, 172, 211, 314, 328-329, 425, 435,
: Allied Control Commission, 55
: Allied victory in World War II, 20

Al-Qaeda, 344, 345

Ambrose, Stephen, 86

America (*see also* USA), 26, 56
: American-Soviet bilateral agreements (1971, 1972, 1973), 43-44
: Anglo-American alliance, 11, 56, 60, 71
: Central, 391, 418
: Civil war, 226
: Island Powers (Britain and America), 11
: Latin, 40, 142, 266, 390
: North, 182, 330
: Policy-makers, 13
: Security, 376 (*see also* USA)
: South 391

Anderson, Rudolf, 427

Angell, Norman, 381-382, 385

Anglo-American alliance (front; leaders; officialdom) against Soviet Union, 11, 56, 60, 71

Anglo-US invasion of Iraq (2003), 330-331, 343-344, 346, 349, 367, 405 (*see also* Britain; Iraq; USA)

Angola, 392, 398
: Civil war in, 391

Antarctica, 39, 40
: Antarctica Treaty (1959), 39-40 (*see also* Disarmament)

Arab States (nations), 165, 296-297, 356, 446, 448
: Arab bloc, 448
: Arab-Israeli war (conflict), 229, 338, 392
: Arab League, 448

Argentina, 40, 144, 239, 265, 274, 304, 313, 444
: ABACC, 274 (*see also* Nuclear materials)
: Argentina-Brazil Agreement for Exclusively Peaceful Uses of Nuclear Energy (1991), 266, 267

Arms Control (*see also* Disarmament), 44, 149-172, 227, 230, 254, 323, 359
: agreements, 436-437
: bilateral arms control, 157-158
: Committee on International Security and Arms Control (CISAC), 338
: literature, 178

Arms race (competition) (atomic race; nuclear weapons race) (*see also* Atomic; Soviet Union; USA;), 37, 56, 62, 99, 113-117, 145-146, 148, 193-194, 199, 342

Arms trade, international, 143

Arnold, Henry H, 66

Aron, Raymond, 414, 429, 438

Art, Robert, 399

Ashcroft, John, 344

Asia (Asians), 10, 13, 83, 86, 142, 350, 353-354, 356, 359, 390, 408, 459
: Asia-Europe-Africa and
: Heartland (World Island), 10, 11
: Asia Pacific, 363
: Central, 114
: East, 210
: Greater East, 10
: North, 241
: Nuclear Powers, 350, 351
: South, 239, 240, 241, 296, 352, 353, 356, 358, 452
: Southeast, 183, 401; ASEAN, 348, 353
: West, 296, 344, 363, 443 Atlantic, 8, 10
: Atlantic alliance, 425, 426
: Atlantic powers, 8
: Atlantic Union, 5
: North Atlantic Council, 327
: North Atlantic Treaty, 327
: North Atlantic Treaty Organisation (NATO) (*see* NATO)

Atlas (missile), 115

Atomic arms (weapons) (*see also* Nuclear), 13-14, 62
: atomic arms race (*see* Arms race)

Atomic bomb(s) (Atom bomb), 30, 327, 449 (*see also* Bombs)

Atomic diplomacy (atom diplomacy), 89, 419-420, 434

Atomic energy, 57-60, 62-68, 81
: Atomic Energy Act (1954), 280, 285
: Atomic Energy Commission, 57-60, 61, 63, 81
: Congressional Joint Committee on Atomic Energy, 78-79
: EURATOM, 274
: International Atomic Energy Agency (IAEA), 140, 225, 237,

246, 247, 265-316, 358, 363, 444 : activities, 265-316; commitments, 363; Relationship Agreement between IAEA and UN, 272; Safeguards System of (agreements), 264-316, 358 (categories and elements), 267-270

: Joint Committee on Atomic Energy, 81
: State's committee on Atomic Energy, 59
: Report on International Control of Atomic Energy, 59
: Statute and Relationship Agreement with United Nations, 272, 273
: UN Atomic Development Authority (ADA), 59-60, 61, 64
: UN Commission on Atomic Energy, 57-60, 61, 63, 64, 81

Atomic Scientists
: Emergency Committee of Atomic Scientists, 63
Atoms for Peace, 264, 295
Attlee, 56-57, 58, 406
Austin, Warren R, 63
Australia, 145, 449, 465
Austria, 145, 309
Azilard, Leo, 72

Balkan States (Balkans), 60, 71, 383
: Civil war in, 338
Bard, Ralph A, 69, 77
Barnard, Chester 9, 59, 62
Bartkyt, Walter, 69
Baruch, Bernard, 9, 59, 61, 62, 63
: Baruch Plan, 294, 295
Bastogne and Dresden, 184
Beijing, 88, 348, 349, 350, 358, 449, 451
Belarus, 330
Belgium, 46, 139, 145, 327

Berlin, 11, 20, 81, 90, 182, 409, 415, 416, 423
: Berlin crisis, 88, 89, 412, 424
: West, 88, 89, 90, 91, 412, 424
Bhutto, Zulfiquar Ali, 296, 356, 358
Bidault, Georges, 86
Big Book of Modern Nations, 345
Big Three, 58
Bikini Atoll, 87, 114
bin Laden, Osama (*see* Osama)
Binary weapons, 42
Biological weapons, 41-42
Blair, Tony, 343, 344, 348
Blix, Hans, 306, 315
Bohr, 439
Bomb (A) (nuclear bombs), 30-31, 49, 56-57, 60, 62, 64-71, 73, 74, 80-81, 82, 87, 114, 117, 135, 136, 212, 324, 405-407
: atom bombs (atomic bombs), 30, 56-57, 60-74, 80-82, 327, 449
: Fat Man bomb, 327
: hydrogen bomb (H-bombs), 30, 80, 81, 406-407
: Little Boy bomb, 327
: neutron, 135
: super bomb, 80
: Zionist bomb, 356
Bombers, 189, 406
: long-range, 189
Borden, William, 325
Bourgeois decadence, 8
Brazil, 40, 144, 239, 265, 274
: ABACC, 274 (*see also* Nuclear materials)
: Argentina-Brazil Agreement for Exclusively Peaceful Uses of Nuclear Energy (1991), 266, 267
Brezezinski, Zbigniew, 357
Brezhnev, 161
: Brezhnev- Ford accord, 119
: Brezhnev-Nixon Summit (talks), 42, 118

Britain (British empire) (*see also* Anglo;
     England; UK), 11, 16, 19, 56, 64,
     70, 71, 87, 88, 89, 138, 139, 140,
     159, 181, 328, 343-344, 367, 368,
     380, 381, 384, 405, 407, 424-425,
     426, 446, 456, 462, 466, 468, 469
   :   Anglo-US invasion of Iraq
       (US-Britain coalition forces
       attacked Iraq-2003), 330-331,
       343-344, 346, 349, 367, 405
       (*see also* Iraq)
   :   British Isles, 65
   :   Island Powers (Britain and
       America), 11
Brodie, Bernard, 94-95, 325
Brown, Harold, 101, 432
Brown, Harrison, 79
Browns Ferry, Alabama, 312
Buchan, Alastair, 201
Bulgaria, 58
Bundy, McGeorge, 72, 73, 77, 89-90,
     94-95
Bush, George W, 75, 80, 328, 343-349,
     357, 363, 364, 400, 401, 402, 404,
     405, 451
Bush, Vannevar, 59, 73
Business activity
   :   governmental control of, 9
Butler, George Lee, 321-322, 325, 332,
     340
Byrnes, James F, 58, 59, 67, 69, 72, 74,
     81
   :   Byrnes-Bevin Doctrine, 60

Canada, 59, 78, 139, 145, 285, 327, 331,
     386, 449
   :   "Canada and the Nuclear
       Challenge: Reducing Political
       Value of Nuclear Weapons for
       21st Century", report, 331
Canberra Committee, 332, 340-341
Capitalism
   :   anti-capitalism, 8
   :   capital explotation, 8
Capital Hill, 366

Caribbean, 40, 91, 191
Carlyle, 5
Carnegie Endowment task force report,
     357, 444
Carr, E.H, 28-29
Carter, Jimmy, 16, 100, 101-102, 139,
     168, 432, 434, 439
   :   Carter-Brown PD-59, 101
   :   Carter Doctrine, 418
Castro, 398
Catch-22 situation, 339
Chellancy, Bahma, 454
Chemical weapons, 42, 146
   :   Chemical Weapons
       Connection, 457, 465
   :   Chemical weapons treaty, 277
Chernobyl, accident (explosion) (1986)
     at, 307-312, 315, 316
Chile, 144
China, 11, 19, 44, 58, 68, 70, 81, 87,
     89, 117, 134, 140, 142, 145, 147,
     160, 176, 182, 185, 195, 209, 210,
     238, 240, 243, 256, 264, 286, 313,
     314, 331, 342, 348, 349-351, 353-
     354, 355, 358, 359, 361, 367, 368,
     380, 397, 402, 405, 406, 407, 409,
     449, 450, 451, 452, 456, 458, 459,
     461, 462, 465, 466, 467, 468, 469
   :   Chinese-Soviet borders, 415
   :   first nuclear test in open
       atmosphere in Lop Nor test
       ranges, 353, 354
   :   Heartland Powers (Russia and
       China), 11
   :   nuclear doctrine, 361
   :   nuclear tests, 353, 354, 358
   :   nuclear warheads in Tibet, 349
   :   psyche of power play, 353-354
   :   US-China backroom deal, 462
Chinks, 346
Chirac, Jacques, 449
Christopher, Henry R, 340
Christopher, Warren, 357
Christian bomb, 355

Churchill, Winston, 48, 54, 56, 60, 64, 71, 73, 74, 87, 425

Citizen, private
: influence of in national policy-making, 20-22, 28

Clinton, 352, 358, 451, 468

CoCom (Coordinating Committee for Multilateral Controls), 454

Coexistence, 417, 420

Cold War, 13, 15, 16, 39, 55, 103, 179, 242, 264, 275, 292, 299, 321, 322, 325, 327, 328, 329, 330, 335, 340, 349, 350, 354, 362, 364, 365, 366, 372, 375, 376, 377, 379, 380, 381, 387, 391, 392, 393, 394-395, 396, 397, 398, 399, 400, 403, 404, 407-410, 420, 455, 456, 460, 465, 466

Columbia, 60, 144

Committee on Social and Political Implications, 68

Commonwealth, 275

Communication, 431

Communism, 5, 16, 229, 417
: anti-communism, 8
: Communist bomb, 355
: Communist power-holders, 13
: Communists, 89

Comprehensive Test Ban Treaty (CTBT), 41, 147, 330, 442, 445, 448, 452-470
: entry into force, 461-462
: UN resolution on CTBT (1993), 453, 463
: verification regime-462

Conant, James B, 59

Confidence building measures (CBMs), 337

Conflict resolution, 18-20
: compromise form of 20

Congressional Research Service, 315

Continental US-Over-The-Horizon Backscatter Radar (CONUSOTHB), 124

Conventional arms, 223-234, 235

Conventional wars, 233, 335 (*see also* War)

Copernicus, 338

Cousins, Horman, 26

Cuba, 40, 90, 91, 98, 144, 168, 182, 191, 252, 268, 345, 409, 412, 415
: Cuban missile crises of (1962), 19, 27, 43, 90, 92, 96, 103-104, 191, 416

Curtis, H. J, 56

Cutler, Robert, 86

Czechoslovakia, 145, 164, 183, 327, 383, 421
: Czechoslovakia uprising of (1968), 20

Dachau, 11

Dalai Lama, 349

Dartmouth conference, 26-28

Davis, Forrest, 55

de Gaulle, Charles, 9, 176, 425

de Jouvenel, Frenchman Bertrand, 30

de Leon, Ponce, 3

de Seversky, Alexander, 9

Delaware, 366

Delhi (New Delhi), 200, 348, 351, 359, 444, 447-448, 452, 463, 466, 467, 468

Democracy, 5, 28-29, 344, 346, 360, 398, 413
: European democracies, 8

Denmark, 145, 327

Denuclearisation (denuclearised world), 220-233 (*passim*), 445

Deterrence, nuclear (*see* Nuclear deterrence)

Detroit, 312

Deutsch, Karl, 388

Development
: International Development Strategy, 146
: link between disarmament and, 145-146

Dewey, Thomas, 81

Dictatorship of Proletariat, 5

Diplomacy (diplomatic conflict; diplomatic war), 12, 18, 231, 232, 233, 234, 236
:   atomic diplomacy, 89, 419-420, 434
:   tacit, 18

Disarmament (nuclear), 39-45, 47, 119, 134-135, 136, 171, 265, 292, 332-342, 350, 462, 470 (*see also* Arms Control)
:   18- nation committee on, 292
:   Antarctic Treaty (1959), 39-40
:   Committee on International Security and Arms Control (CISAC), 338
:   Conference of Committee on Disarmament (CCD), 39, 44, 146-147, 341, 461, 462, 467
:   general and complete (GCD), 39
:   link between development and, 145-146
:   Partial Test Ban Treaty (1963), 40-41
:   UN Special Session on Disarmament, 145, 147, 148

Donnelly, Warren, 315

Doomsday Machine, 106

Douhet, Giulio, 9

Dresden, 46

Dulles, Joh Foster, 84, 85-86, 87, 88, 420

Dum Dum bullets, 45, 46

East (Eastern world), 326, 389, 390
:   East-West relations (tension) (bridges between), 96, 326, 424

Eberstadt, Ferninand, 59

Economy (Economic)
:   competition, 382-383
:   growth, 398-399
:   interdependence, 381-386
:   national, 9
:   New International Economic Order, 5

:   planning, 9

Eden, Anthony, 58

Egypt, 20, 144, 409, 446
:   Egypt Third Army, 252
:   Egyptian-Syrian attack on Israel (1973), 20
:   intervention in Yemen, 392

Einstein, 56

Eisenhower, Dwight, 14, 26, 84-88, 280, 407, 408, 409, 412, 413, 415, 417, 419, 420, 432, 434, 435
:   Eisenhower-Khurshev Summit (1959), 26

England, 113, 224, 384 (*see also* Britain; UK)

Eniwetok Atoll, 83, 114

Enrico Fermi demonstration, 312

Environment
:   Council on Environmental Quality, 286
:   Environmental Protection Agency, 286
:   Genetic Environmental Statement on Mixed Oxide Fuel, 286
:   Gesmo, 286, 287
:   National Environmental Policy Act (NEPA) (1969), 286

Equality, numerical (strategic), 189-192

Ethiopia, 352, 393, 418

Ethnic conflicts (disputes), 339, 388, 393

Euphrates, 346

Eurafrica, 8

Eurasia, 8, 10, 11
:   Central, 349

Europe (Europeans), 10, 16, 17, 30, 35, 40, 44, 49, 55, 67, 84, 89, 104, 117, 135, 138, 178, 180, 182, 184, 189-190, 196, 197, 210, 211, 212, 213, 308, 328, 329-330, 343, 365, 373, 375, 380, 381, 384, 388, 392, 393, 396, 401, 408, 412, 413, 416, 421, 423, 424, 426, 457, 459

: allies, 211
: Central, 240, 254, 404
: democracies, 8
: East, 10, 55, 71, 102, 134, 212, 314, 329, 339, 388, 389, 390, 393, 403, 404, 420, 421
: EURATOM (European Atomic Energy Community), 274
: European Common Market, 383
: European Community, 380, 389
: European detente, 424
: South, 329
: United Europe, 5
: West, 13, 16, 30, 64, 65, 83, 91, 102, 211, 314, 379, 381, 385, 387, 388, 389, 394, 395, 416, 420, 421, 422, 425, 426
: Western State System in, 8
Explorer (satellite), 115

Far East, 10, 66, 67, 113, 239, 240
Fascism, 5
: fascist totalitarianism, 8
Fatman atom bomb, 327
Fertile Crescent, 10
Feudalism, 224
Finland, 145
Fischer, David, 441
Fleming, 55, 70
Foch, Ferdinand, 9
Force-building (nuclear forces), 148-172
Ford, President, 118, 432-434
: Ford-Brezhnev accord, 119
Foreign Assistance Act (1979), 356, 357, 358
Formosa, 88
France (French), 16, 19, 20, 29, 35, 40, 46, 64, 86, 87, 88, 89, 117, 138, 139, 140, 143, 144, 145, 147, 159, 176, 181, 182, 195, 264, 312, 327, 328, 336, 367, 368, 380, 381, 385,

405, 406, 407, 424-425, 426, 450, 456, 457, 458, 459, 462, 465, 467, 468, 469
: ASLP missile, 449
: atomic bomb, 449
: French deterrent, 449
: French Polynsia, 449
: French Revolution (1789), 29
: French-US warhead designs, 451
: missiles of, 449
: nuclear tests, 449, 457, 458
: SSBNs, 449
Franck, James, 68, 77
: Franck Committee, 68, 69, 75
: Franck Report, 68
Free Enterprise, 5
Free world, 5
Freedman, Lawrence, 106
Frenzy, 345
Fuel-air-explosive (FAE), 135-136
Fuel-cycle technology, 291
Fultong, 60
Fundamentalism
: religious, 339

GDP (Gross Domestic Product), 141, 142
Gabon, 144
Gaither's report (1957), 419
Gamelin, 9
Gandhi, Indira, 285
Garwin, Richard, 216
Geneva, 467, 468
: Conference on Disarmament (CD) (1994), 461, 462, 467
: Geneva Convention (Protocol) (1925), 45, 457
: Geneva Summit (1955), 412
Geopoliticians, 9-10
Germany, 10-11, 19, 20, 46, 55, 65, 70, 88, 330, 331, 352, 366, 380, 381, 384, 385, 386, 389, 390, 401, 449, 457, 469

: anti-communist West Germans, 89
: Democratic Republic of, 145
: East, 88, 89, 424
: Federal Republic, 138-139, 141, 145, 327
: German-Russian-Japanese bloc, 11
: Pan-German expansionist ambitions of Nazi leaders, 11
: West, 164, 315, 424, 426
Gerschenkron, Alexander, 393
Ghose, Arundhati, 462
Glenn Amendment, 357
Global Positioning System (GPS), 131
Godlessness, 8
Gorbachev, Mikhail, 17, 328, 368, 412, 415, 437, 438
Gould, Stephen Jay, 363, 376, 377-378
Government(s), 6-7, 24-25
Gowda, Deve, 466
Graham, Thomas, 457
Grand Alliance, 53
Great Britain, 70 (*see also* Britain; England; UK)
Great Design, 55
Great Gamble, 55
Great powers, 144, 148, 189, 192, 198, 199, 380, 414 (*see also* Superpowers)
Great war, 49 (*see also* War)
Greece, 327, 330, 340
Grenada, 345
Gromyko, Andrei, 62, 63, 420
Groves, Leslie R, 56, 59, 69, 72
Guerrillas, 398
Gulf war(s), 338, 367, 374, 377, 385, 392, 400, 402, 409

Hague Convention (1899), 45
Halford, Sir, 11
Hamilton, Alexander, 9
Hammurabi of Babylon, 347
Hancock, John, 59
Hanford nuclear reservation,

Washington, 312
Happenstances, 12
Harriman, Averill, 52
Hart, David, 358
Hart, Liddle, 9
Hasey Jr., William F, 66
Haushofer, Karl, 10-11
Heartland Powers (Russia and China), 10, 11
Hegemonism, concept of, 351
Heinz, 11
Hemisphere
: northern, 21, 33-34, 147
: southern, 34
Hess, Rudolf, 10
Hichenlooper, Bouke B, 79
Hiroshima and Nagasaki
: atomic bombardment of, 30, 46, 56, 65, 66, 71, 72, 74-75, 76, 77, 81, 82, 113, 147, 184, 189, 197, 326, 327, 355, 406, 434, 457
Hitler, 10, 11
Holloway, Bruce K, 37
Holum, John D, 439-440
Howard, Michael, 423
Hugo, Victor, 334
Hull, Cordell, 53, 54
Human rights, 397-398
Humburg, 31
Humphrey, George, 417
Hungary, 145, 183, 327, 421
: Hungarian rebellion (1956), 20
Huntington, Samuel, 384
Hutchins, Chancellor, 56
Hyde Park, 73, 74
Hydro-nuclear tests, 453
Hydrogen bomb, 30, 80, 81, 406-407 (*see also* Bombs)

IAEA (*see* Atomic energy)
IBM, 468
ICBM (ICBMs), 115, 116, 120, 122, 125, 126, 127, 128, 129, 130,

131, 136, 137, 204, 205, 206, 207, 209, 210, 212, 459 (*see also* Missiles)
: launchers, 118
IMF Treaty (agreement), 16, 17, 465 (*see also* Nuclear)
INFCIRC/66, 280-282
INFCIRC/153, 277-278, 279, 281, 282, 291, 303, 305
INFCIRC/225/Rev.1, 283
IRBM, 115-117, 210, 211, 212 (*see also* Missiles)
Iceland, 327
Ikle, Fred, 340
Imai, Ryukichi, 332
Imperialism
: imperialistic sin, 8
India, 40, 87, 139, 144, 195, 200, 238, 240, 268, 285-286, 296, 313, 314, 345, 348, 349-351, 353-354, 358, 359, 368, 399, 405, 406, 443, 444, 446, 452, 454, 458, 460, 466-467, 469, 470
: bilateral agreement on non-attack on each other's nuclear installations, proposal of, 359
: CTBT, stand on (view of), 452, 460-464, 466: formally vetoed draft text of, 462-463
: Draft Nuclear Doctrine of, 331, 360-361
: Indo-Chinese relations, 349, 354
: Indo-Pakistan border, 350
: NPT, views on, 443-444, 446-451
: no-first-use of nuclear weapons concept of, 342
: nuclear capabilities, 452-453, 464
: nuclear doctrine, 331, 360-361
: nuclear doctrine, draft of (1999): salient features of, 360-361
: nuclear option for, 450-452
: nuclear policy of, 352-353
: nuclear programme, 349, 351
: nuclear research launched, 355
: nuclear tests of, 350, 352-353, 354
: Partial Test Ban Treaty (PTBT) signed by, 460-461
: Pokhran test (1974), 450
: Pokhran II, 351
: Sino-Indian relations, 349, 350
: went nuclear, 351
Indian summer, 48
Indo-Pacific sphere, 10
Indochina, 45, 46, 86, 87, 432
Indonesia, 144, 448
Industrial Revolution, 30
Industralisation, 48
Information
: international, 247-248
Inspection(s) of nuclear material (international control of nuclear industry), 233-236, 298-302
: Iraq : IAEA-UNSCOM inspection teams in, 298-302
: on-site, 269-270
: special, 269-270, 271, 305-306
Instant-Mix Imperial Democracy, 346
Institute of USA/ Canada Affairs, 27
Interdependence, economic, 381-386
International Court of Justice, 331, 341, 457
International Nuclear Reviews (INR), 316
International relations (international politics) (power politics) relations among nations; (world affairs) 1-6, 7, 22-24, 28, 35, 48, 381-386
: interdepartmental discipline, 6
: interdependence, 381-386
Internationalised System (World order) (internationalisation) (international inspection of nuclear industry), 233-236
Iran, 60, 144, 239, 344, 402, 454

Iraq, 144, 265, 271, 272, 276-277, 290, 292, 298-302, 343-344, 345, 347, 349, 352, 364, 376-377, 395, 400, 402, 454
: G-2 centrifuge machines in, 290
: Iran-Iraq war, 392
: Israeli attack on research reactor of, 297
: nuclear weapons programme, 292
: Operation Iraqi freedom, 347
: situation and discoveries made by IAEA-UNSCOM inspection teams, 298-302
: US-UK coalition forces attack on (Anglo-US invasions of) (war of 2003), 330-331, 343-344, 346, 349, 367, 405
: weaponisation programme of, 271
: weapons of mass destruction, 345
Islam, 296
Islamabad, 358, 359, 451, 469
Islamic bomb, 296, 355, 356, 451
Islamic factor, 355
Islamic fundamentalism, 296-297
Islamic states, 451-452
: Organisation of Islamic States (OIS), 296
Islamic world, 296-297, 356
Island Powers (Britain and America), 1
Israel, 46, 144, 164, 268, 355, 356, 368, 406, 443, 446, 447, 448, 451, 458, 461
: Arab-Israeli war, 338, 392
: attack on Iraqi research reactor, 297
: Egyptian-Syrian attack on (1973), 20
Italy, 10, 20, 46, 58, 139, 145, 327, 352
Ivanov, Igor, 348
Ivory Coast, 144
Jackson, 419

Jammu and Kashmir, 356, 449 (*see also* Kashmir)
Japan, 10, 11, 20, 38, 41, 56, 58, 65-67, 69, 70, 71, 72, 73, 74, 102, 139, 141, 142, 145, 182, 280, 310, 352, 379, 380, 384, 385, 396, 401, 417-418, 457
: US-Japan trading relations, 377
Jasjit Singh, 447, 465-466
Jaswant Singh, 350
Jerusalem, 9-10
Johnson, 434
Joint Working Group (JWG), 353
Jordan, 144
Junejo, Mohammad Khan, 359
Jupiter (missile), 115
Juppe, Alain, 336

Kahuta nuclear plant, 358
Kantaro, Suzuki, 75
Kashmir issue, 355, 356, 358, 360, 467
Kazakhstan, 330
Keating, Paul, 465
Kelly, David, 344
Kemp, Geoffery, 452
Kennan, George, 95, 96
Kennedy, President, 20, 88, 90, 91, 100, 243, 398, 407, 412, 413, 415, 427, 431, 434, 435, 437
Kenya, 397
Kettering Foundation, 27
Khan, A.Q (father of Pakistani bomb), 355-356, 358
Khan, Ghulam Ishaq, 356
Khrushchev, Nikita, 33, 88-91, 168, 407, 412, 415, 416-417, 420
: Khrushchev-Eisenhower-Kennedy triad, 407
: Khruschev's crisis, 88-89
: Killian's report (1954), 419
: Kissinger, Henry, 35, 243, 434
Kjellen, Rudolf, 10
Knowland, 78, 79
Kohl, Helmut, 315

Korea, 19, 45, 58, 81, 82, 83, 84, 409, 413, 416, 419
: Democratic People's Republic of, 278
: Korean flash-point, 363
: Korean peninsula, 183
: Korean war, 19, 46, 376
: north, 144, 288-290, 344, 349, 363, 364, 395, 401, 417, 454, 467
: south, 144, 313, 349, 417
Kosovo, 330
: cirsis, 351
Kremlin, 83, 160, 321, 413, 422, 435
Kurds, 402
Kuwait, 392, 396, 400, 402

LORD options, 205-206
Latin America (*see also* America) 40, 142, 390
: Treaty of Tlatelolco (1967), 40, 266, 267
Le Bugey, 312
League of Nations, 376
Lebanon, 229, 402
Lemay, 408
Liberalism
: anti-liberalism, 8
Libya, 144, 344, 345, 454
Lie, Trygve, 64
Lilienthal, David E, 59, 62, 63, 436
: Lilienthal-Acheson plan, 217, 225
: Lilienthal-Acheson proposals, 59
: Lilienthal-Acheson report, 60, 294
Limited counter force, 187
Limited retaliation, 187, 188
Limited Test Ban Treaty, 197
Lincoln, Abraham, 334
Lippmann, Walter, 3-4
List, Friedrich, 9
Little Boy, atom bomb, 327
London, 60, 86, 424

: London Club, 139-140
: London Declaration, 328
: London Guidelines, 277
: London Suppliers Club, 450
Loose nukes, 339
Lop Nor, 353, 354, 358
Luxemburg, 327

MAD (Mutually Assured Destruction), 176, 188, 189, 190, 203, 214, 325, 438
MBA (material balance area), 279
MFR (Mutural Force Reduction), 44, 254
MIRV (MIRVs), 41, 116, 118, 119, 121, 122, 129, 130, 131, 137, 204, 208, 406, 407, 430, 459
MIRVed, 119, 126, 128, 133, 136, 137, 204
MRV, 121
MX-in-Minuteman, 430
MX missile, 435
MW research reactor, 358
Mackeller, 62
Mackenzie, 57
Mackinder, Halford J, 10, 11
Magonot, 9
Mahan, Alford Thayer, 9
Malaysia, 144
Manhattan project, 74, 433
Mao, 243, 406
Marshall, George, 72, 75, 81
: Marshall plan, 81
Marshall Islanders, 310
Marx, 321
Marxland, 65
Mathews, David, 27
Matsu, 87, 88, 419
McCloy, John D, 59, 75
McNamara, Robert, 429, 432
Mearsheimer, John, 373
Mendelsohn, Jack, 330
Mercantilism, 9
Mesopotamia, 346
Metterrand, Francois, 449

Mexico, 396
  : New Mexico : first ever nuclear
     explosion (July 1945) at
     Alamogordo, 65, 113
Middle East, 9, 142, 144, 183, 239, 241,
     274, 296, 392, 396, 412, 413, 418,
     446, 452, 454,
  : crisis, 43
  : peace talks, 265
  : war (1967), 43, 44
Militarism, 388
Military
  : alliances, 264
  : capabilities, 219-220
  : laboratories, 156
  : power, 219-220
  : research and development
     (R & D), 47
  : satellite missions (satellites),
     140 (*see* Satellites)
  : science, 7-8
  : technology, 30, 47, 49
  : worldwide expenditure on
     activities of, 141-145
Million, Charles, 449
Missiles, 15-17, 74, 89, 94, 115-133,
     136-138, 143, 152, 154, 155, 162,
     163, 168, 182, 187, 205, 206, 241,
     355, 368, 413, 415,
  : ASLP missiles, 449
  : Air Launched Cruise Missile
     (ALCM), 133
  : air-to-surface, 117
  : anti-ballistic missiles (ABM),
     41, 118, 124-125, 188-189,
     206, 208, 209
  : Anti-Ballistic Missile Treaties,
     131, 163-164, 210, 459
  : ballistic, 115, 136, 155, 168,
     406, 407
  : cruise, 133, 138, 155, 204, 212
  : Cuban missile crisis, 19, 27, 43,
     90, 92, 96, 103-104, 191, 416
  : depressed-trajectory ballistic,
     117

  : Ghauri, 355
  : international ballistic missiles
     (ICBMs), 115, 116, 120, 122,
     124, 125, 126, 127, 128, 129,
     130, 131, 136, 137, 204, 205,
     206, 207, 209, 210, 212, 459
  : intermediate range ballistic
     missiles (IRBMs), 115, 117,
     210, 211, 212
  : land-based, 156, 172, 189
  : long-range strategic, 115
  : M-5, 449
  : M-II (Minuteman II), 121, 358
  : M-III (Minuteman III), 116,
     121
  : MPMS (Missile Performance
     Measurement System) 130
  : MX, 435
  : MX-in-Minuteman, 430
  : mobile, 155
  : nuclear-tipped, 189
  : Polaris submarine-launched
     ballistic missiles
     (SLBMs), 115, 116, 117
  : SAM-D air defence surface-
     to-air-missile system, 124, 133
  : Shaheen, 355
  : Spartan, 209
  : SRAM (Short-Range Attack
     Missile), 123, 132
  : submarine-launched ballistic,
     115, 116, 117
  : Thor, 115
  : Titan, 115, 116
  : Trident I, 204
Mitchell, William, 9
Modernisation (nuclear modernisa-
     tion), 425, 430
Molotov, Vyacheslav, 51, 79
Moroccan crises, 384
Moscow, 16-17, 26-27, 43, 51, 52, 58,
     60, 62, 64, 70, 73, 118, 131, 176,
     190, 208, 254, 256, 314, 321, 348,
     407, 410, 416, 420, 424, 433, 465,
     469

: Moscow Accord (agreements) (1972), 104-105
: Moscow agreements (1973), 172
: Moscow-Beijing-New Delhi triangle, 348
: Moscow Conference (1943), 70
: Moscow Declaration, 59, 444

Mueller, John, 384

Multipolar world, 348

Munich, II
: Munich settlement (1938), 19

Murrow, Paul K, 340

Musharraf, Pervez, 355

N-5 Club, 352

NATO (North Atlantic Treaty Organisation), 13, 16, 44, 135, 138, 140, 160, 170-171, 210-211, 212, 326, 327, 328-332, 348, 351, 352, 361, 363, 376, 378, 390, 395, 404, 421, 422, 424, 459
: NATO-Russian relations, 331-332
: strategic concept, 328-332

NFU policy, 330, 331

NJ-9842, 354

NTM (national technical means), 276, 277, 291

NWFW, 336, 337, 339, 341

Nagasaki (*see also* Hiroshima)
: atomic bombardment on, 30, 46, 56, 65, 66, 71, 72, 74-75, 76, 77, 81, 82, 113, 147, 184, 189, 197, 326, 327, 355, 434, 457

Nationalism, 29, 30, 48, 385, 386, 388, 389, 393

Nawaz Sharif, 355

Near East, 11

Negroes, 346

Neomercantilism, 9

Netherlands, 145, 327, 331

Nevada, 465

New International Economic Order, 5

New Zealand, 145, 340

Nicaragua, 345, 398

Nitze, Paul, 340

Nixon, Richard, 104, 409, 419, 432, 434, 451
: Nixon-Brezhnev talks, 42, 118

Noel-Baker, Philip, 39-40

Non-Aligned Movement (NAM), 448

Non-nuclear-weapon, states, 305
: agreements with, 266-268

Non-proliferation commitments (obligations), 265-268, 270, 275, 307, 352
: Nuclear Non-Proliferation Act (1978), 450

Non-Proliferation Treaty (NPT) (1970), 40, 41, 139-140, 195, 197, 199-200, 238, 245, 246, 266, 267, 268, 270, 275, 276, 277, 283-284, 285, 286, 288, 289, 290, 291, 292, 295, 297, 298, 299, 300, 301-306, 316, 352, 355, 359-360, 363, 439-467
: Prefatory Committee, 341, 440, 441
: Review Conference (1985), 293-294, 295, 298
: Review and extension conference (1995), 275, 292, 439-449, 455, 456, 457, 458, 460, 464
: Review Conference of Parties to NPT (2000), 270

Norway, 145, 327

Nuclear age, 14, 434

Nuclear anarchy, 180, 185, 194

Nuclear: anti-nuclear movement, 92, 95

Nuclear apartheid, 353

Nuclear arms (*see* Arms control; Arms race; Disarmament; weapons)

Nuclear blackmail, 358, 415

Nuclear bombs (*see* Bombs)

Nuclear club, 199, 200

Nuclear deterrence, 92-106, 176, 217-219, 228, 252-253, 406, 414, 416,

421, 423, 424, 426, 431, 432, 449, 452, 459
Nuclear disarmament (*see* Disarmament)
Nuclear energy
: accidents, 307-313
: peaceful uses of, 264-265
Nuclear equilibrium, 181, 185, 188, 194, 195, 196, 198
Nuclear escalation, 422, 426, 427, 428
Nuclear explosion (s), 31, 32, 33
: first ever (July 1945), 113
: peaceful, 43, 147
Nuclear explosives, 189
Nuclear free zones, 134
Nuclear freeze movement, 96-97
Nuclear fuel cycle, 301, 304
Nuclear hierarchy, 181, 185, 194, 195, 196, 198
Nuclear intermediate nuclear forces (INF), 15-16
: INF Treaty, 16, 17, 465
Nuclear intervention of nuclear industry, 227-236
Nuclear materials
: ABACC (Brazilian -Argentina Agency for Accounting and Control of Nuclear Materials, 274
: accountancy, 269
: three elements designed to verify, 269
Nuclear missiles (*see* Missiles)
Nuclear peace, 245-246, 414-439
: efforts between superpowers (US and Soviet Union) (nuclear debates, 414-439
Nuclear power plants, 264
Nuclear programmes
: peaceful nature of, 264-266
Nuclear proliferation, 135, 172, 197-200, 203, 215, 224, 229, 232, 238-239, 240-244, 248, 264, 277, 300-301, 339, 458

Nuclear regimes
: first, 179-201, 202, 207
: second, 179, 201-216
: third, 179, 180, 216
: fourth, 179-180
Nuclear Regulatory Commission (NRC), 286, 287, 288
Nuclear relationships, 239-240, 245, 248
Nuclear strategy, 100-106
Nuclear Supplier Guidelines (NSG), 295-296
Nuclear surveillance and containment measures, 269-270
Nuclear technology, 36-37, 222, 334, (*see also* technology)
: competition, 405-428
Nuclear terrorism, 217 (*see also* Terrorism)
Nuclear thermonuclear war, 35 (*see also* Thermonuclear arms)
Nuclear Threat, 358
Nuclear war (*see also* War), 32-38, 43-44, 48, 49, 83, 92,-93, 95, 96, 99, 101, 106, 188, 423
Nuclear Warheads (*see* warheads),
Nuclear Weapon Free Zone (NWFZ) 359
Nuclear weapon powers, 38-39
Nuclear weapon states, (NWS), 264, 327
Nuclear weapons (arms) (*passim* throughout text) (*see also* Arms; Atomic Energy; Bombs; Disarmament; Missiles; Weapons)
: atomic bombs (*see* Bombs)
: competition of, 405-428
: complete elimination of 326, 332-342
: control literature, 178
: existence of, 176-177
: incendiary, 45
: management of, 177-179
: meaning of, 179
: significance of, 175-177

: targetable re-entry vehicle (MIRV) (*see* MIRV)
: thermonuclear, 41
: total abolition of, 326, 332-342
Nuclear-Weapons Free World (NWFW), 326, 336, 337, 339, 341
Nuclear Winter, 48, 106
Nuclearisation, 445
Nuclearism, 340
Nunn, Sam, 366
Nyet-bu-nahi triangle, 349

OECD (Organisation for Economic Cooperation and Development), 311
ORHA (Office of Reconstruction and Humanitarians Assistance), 346
OTEB radar, 124
Oak Ridge project, 78
Oil exploitation, 396
Oppenheimer, J.R. 56, 59, 369, 436, 439
Osama bin Laden, 346
Osborn, Frederick H, 63

P-5 Club, 342, 352, 454, 455, 456, 457
Pacific, 8, 10, 41, 82, 114, 457
: Asia Pacific, 363
: Pacific Ocean, 32
: South, 457
: South Pacific Nuclear Weapon Free Zone Treaty (Treaty of Rarotonga) (1985), 266
: Thermonuclear test (1952) at Eniwetok Island, 82
: war, 71
Pakistan, 139, 200, 240, 268, 296-297, 349, 356, 357-359, 368, 395, 399, 443, 446, 447, 449, 451, 452, 454, 458, 461, 466, 469
: clandestine programme, 357
: nuclear capabilities of, 354-355, 356

: nuclear doctrine of, 360
: nuclear programme of, 358
: nuclear reality of, 354
: nuclear strategy, 355-356
: nuclear status, 355
: US aid to, 357
: US-Pak relations, 452
Palestine, 10
Palo Verde, Arizona, 313
Panama, 345
Paris, 424, 425, 449
Partial Test Ban Treaty (PTBT), 40-41, 42, 92, 285, 353, 359, 460-461
Peace, 12, 14, 36, 37, 51, 56, 67, 79, 82, 141, 217, 236, 245, 246, 364, 383, 389, 426, 466 (*see also* Nuclear Peace)
: peace dividends 343
Peaceful nuclear activities (explosions), 43, 147, 268, 285
Peaceful uses of nuclear energy, 264-266
: Atoms for peace, 264, 295
Pearl Harbour, 52
Pentagon, 132, 172, 346, 365, 366
Persian Gulf, 10, 102, 241, 376, 395, 400, 452
Philippines, 418
Plato, 3-4
Pokhran test (1974), 450
: Pokhran II, 351
Poland, 63, 145, 327, 421
: Polish question, 54
Politburo, 418
Politics, international (foreign), 1-6
Portugal, 327
Potsdam Conference, 66, 70, 71, 74, 76, 84
Powell, Colin, 344, 366
Power politics (Great powers, 1-6, 7-13, 14
: superpowers (*see* Super-powers) (*see also* Soviet Union; USA)
Pressler Amendment, 357, 358
Primakov, Yevgeny, 348

Proliferation (*see* Nuclear proliferation)

Prussia, 224

Pugwash Conference on Science and World Affairs, 326

Punjab
: civil strife in, 392

Putin, Vladimir, 348

Quemoy, 87, 88, 419

Qureshi, Moeen, 356

Quester, George, 451

RAND Corporation, 313

RBMK (Reactor Built for Multi Kinetic-energy), 311

Radford, Arthur 86, 87, 408, 432

Radiation weapons, 135

Radiological weapons, 146

Ramekar, Jaap, 462
: draft of, 466

Rathenau, Walter, 9

Ratzel, Friedrich, 10

Reactors, 312-313

Reagan, Ronald, 15, 16, 17, 18, 92, 99-100, 101, 102, 103, 325, 398, 412, 415, 426, 435, 451
: Reagan doctrine, 398
: Reagan-Weinberger Defence Guidance document, 101

Red Army, 71

Red Cross
: International Committee of Red Cross, 45

Regional rivalries, 393

Reich, 11

Religious fundamentalism, 339

Renuclearisation (nuclear rearmament), 232, 234

Research and Development (R&D), 143

Rhine, 352

Rimlands, 11, 12

Rogue doctrine, 366

Roman Catholic Church, 29

Romania, 58, 145

Roosevelt, Franklin, 51-56, 69, 73, 74, 75, 80, 406, 433-434, 435

Rosen, Morris, 315-316

Roth, William, 366

Roy, Arundhati, 344

Russia (*see also* Soviet Union; USSR), 11, 52, 54, 55, 56, 57, 66, 67, 68, 70-71, 72, 75, 79, 80, 87, 161, 176, 236, 248, 252, 329, 331, 341, 342, 348, 349, 361, 367, 374, 380, 389, 394, 398, 404, 405, 407, 421, 446, 456, 459, 461, 462, 466, 468
: Heartland Powers (Russia and China), 11
: New Russia, 8
: Oilfields, 396
: Russian Federation, 331
: Russian Revolution, 343
: Russo - American arms control, 254
: Russo - American nuclear confrontation, 394-395
: Russo - American nuclear war, 403

SAGSI (Standing Advisory Group on Safeguards Implementation), 279-280

SALT (Strategic Arms Limitation Talks) agreements, 38, 42, 43, 104, 118, 120, 140, 149, 161, 168, 170, 190, 195, 198, 237, 254,
: SALT-I, 119, 120, 122, 123, 125, 126, 127, 129, 131, 161, 168, 169, 188, 189, 206, 209-210
: SALT-II, 118, 119, 133, 136, 137-138, 206, 434, 435

SANE, 438

SCAD (Subsonic Cruise Armed Decoy) programmes, 132-133

SIPRI, 143

SIPRI (Stockholm International Peace Research Institute), 141

Index

667

SLBMs, 118, 120, 126, 127, 130-131, 133, 136, 137, 204, 207, 210
START Treaties, 330
: START-I, 456, 465
: START-II, 456, 465
Sacks, Oliver, 388
Saddam Hussein, 331, 343-344, 346, 396
Safeguards Committee, Vienna, 277-279
Sakharov, Andrey, 80
Salisbury, Harrison, 79
Satellites, 60, 115, 123, 124, 125, 140-141, 154-155, 162-163, 205
: artificial earth satellites, 140
: satellite observation, advent of, 154-155, 162-163
: system, 131
Saudi Arabia, 144, 239, 396
Saunders, Harold H, 28
Savannah River, South Carolina, 313
Schell, Jonathan, 95, 96
Schelling, Thomas, 409
Schlesinger, James, 187, 432
Schuman, Frederick L, 65
Schumpeter, Joseph, 385
Science and technology, 83 (see also Technology)
: scientific knowledge: exchange for peaceful purposes of, 57-58, 62
Seabed Treaty (1971), 40
Searles, Fred, 59
Security (international), 37, 51, 56, 140, 225, 229, 239, 240, 283, 294, 337, 376, 383, 390, 393, 394-405, 443, 446, 466
: collective, 6-7, 402, 469-470
: Committee on International Security and Arms Control (CISAC), 338
Semipalatinsk, 114
Shamshad Ahmad, 355
Siachen, 354
Singapore, 144, 353

Sino-American hostility, 376
Sino-Indian relations, 349, 350
Sino-Pak nuclear collaboration, 355, 358
Slavery, 8
: abolition of, 334
Snow, Edgar, 54-55
Snow, C.P., 96
Socialist system of society, 79
Sokolovsky, V.D. 415
Solarz Amendment, 357
South Africa, 141, 144, 164, 239, 241, 265, 356, 419, 444 (see also Africa)
Southeast Asia (see Asia)
South Pacific (see Pacific)
Soviet Union (see also Russia; USSR), 8, 15-16, 20, 26, 28, 32, 37-43 (passim), 51-69 (passim), 72, 79, 80, 83, 85, 88-104 (passim), 113-172, 181-257(passim), 264, 285, 308, 310, 311, 314, 321-328 (passim), 330, 331, 342, 343, 347, 351, 354, 355, 362-368 (passim), 374, 377, 383-428 (passim), 452, 466
: ABM (anti-ballistic missile), 116, 163-164
: ASW, 130
: built-up nuclear weapons by, 407-425
: competition with USA for building-up nuclear weapons by, 143, 148, 405-428
: components of mobile ABM systems, 163-164
: disintegration of (dissolution of), 343, 405
: Eisenhower-Khrushchev Summit, 26
: expansionism, 398
: explosion of first nuclear weapon near Semipalatinsk, Central Asia, 114

: explosion in atmosphere at Hovaya Zemlja, 41
: first long-range flight, 115
: first test, 406
: Fractional Orbital Bombardment System (FOBS), 122, 163
: interventions to crush Hungarian rebellion, 20
: invasion of Afghanistan, 96, 357
: KGB, 160-276
: MIRV warheads, 42
: metal eaters, 160, 166
: negotiating style (negotiators), 158-172
: nuclear balance between USA and, 189-192
: nuclear debates for nuclear peace, 414-439
: nuclear missiles, 15-16, 17
: nuclear peace efforts between USA and, 414-439
: nuclear politics of, 160-172
: satellites : Sputnik I and II, 115; weapon satellites, 163
: sea-based strategic force, 126, 131
: secrecy, passion for 161-162, 166-167
: Soviet American (USA) accord, 59
: Soviet-American (USA) nuclear arms race, 143, 148, 405-428
: Soviet-American (USA) nuclear relationship (conflict rivalry; tension), 19, 143, 148-172, 217, 249, 349, 405-428
: Soviet-American (USA) relations, 19, 27-28, 92-93, 143, 148-172, 217, 249, 293, 394, 407-439 : mutual assured destruction (MAD), 19, 28
: strategic competition between USA and, 148-172

: strategic nuclear forces, 118, 126, 131
: thermonuclear bomb (1955), 114
: US-USSR nuclear arms control agreements, 276
: weapon satellites, 163
Space
: Outer Space Treaty, 40, 140, 163
Spain , 145, 327, 457
: Spanish civil war, 383
Sputnik I , 115
Sputnik II, 115
Spykman, Nicholas, 11
SriLanka
: civil strife in, 392
Stability, 235, 364, 389, 429
Stalin, Marshal, 51, 52, 54, 60, 71, 80, 83, 159, 406, 413, 415
Stimson, Henry, 56, 69, 70, 72, 84, 434
Strategic (strategy), 207, 414, 421, 430, 450
: Air command, 432, 433
: competition between US and Soviet Union, 148-172
: concept of, 328-332
: conditions, 251-252
: disparities (inequalities), 190-193, 255-257, 430
: new, 351
: nuclear arms, 116, 219
: nuclear forces, 187, 188, 190, 192, 193, 208-209
: planners, 429
: programmes, 215
: relationships, 178
: SALT (*see* SALT)
: SDI (Strategic Defence Initiative), 435
: Situation, world's) 236
: stability, 429
: thinking, 452
: triangle, concept of, 348
Submarines, 127, 130, 133, 168, 189, 204, 207, 208, 413

Subsonic Cruise Armed Decoys (SCAD), 123

Super bomb, 80

Superpowers (*see also* Soviet Union; USA), 8-9, 43, 60, 103, 104, 154, 172, 179, 183, 188, 192, 194, 196, 198, 199, 230, 239, 240, 245, 248, 249, 293, 393, 405, 406, 419, 428, 429, 436
: strategic relationship; three factors, 148-172, 240-241

Sur, Serge, 442

Surface-to-air missile (SAM-D), 124, 133

Sweden, 139, 145, 285, 309

Switzerland, 46, 145

Swope, Herbert Bayard, 59

Szilard, Leo, 69, 76, 77

Symington Amendment, 357

Syria, 20, 402
: Egyptian-Syrian attack on Israel (1973), 20

TNT, 136, 189

Taiwan, 144, 395

Talbott, Strobe, 355, 358

Taliban
: in Afghanistan, 346

Technology (nuclear), 98, 122, 126, 127, 131, 134, 154, 222, 231-232, 237-239, 249, 264-265, 266, 291, 334, 336, 339, 356, 357, 410, 450
: MIRV, 126
: new, 97
: revolution, 431
: science and, 83

Terrorism
: non-nuclear, 231-232
: nuclear, 231
: popular movements of terrorist attacks, 230
: terrorist attack on Twin Towers of World Trade Center (USA), 405
: terrorist ethos, 339
: terrorists, 231, 405

Thermonuclear
: age, 14
: bomb, first, 114
: devices, 114
: explosion, 80
: test (1952) at Eniwetok Island, Pacific, 82
: war, 35
: warheads, 121
: weapons, 41, 114

Third World, 44, 138, 142, 143-144, 145, 244, 290, 293, 365, 366, 367, 390, 391, 392, 393, 394, 402-403, 404, 414, 418

Thomas, Charles A, 59

Thor (missile), 115

Three Mile Island Plant
: accident at (explosion), 307, 312

Threshold stages, 265, 461

Thurmond, Strom, 81

Tiananmen, 21

Tibet: Chinese nuclear warheads installed in 349

Tigris, 346

Timisoara, 21

Titan (missile), 115, 116

Tlatelolco
: Treaty of Tlatelolco (1967), 40, 266, 267

Tokyo, 46
: Tokyo Forum, 332

Toledo Edison's Davis-Besse plant, 312

Tolstoy, 411

Trafficking
: illegal, 339

Treaty (1968), 266

Treaty for Prohibition of Nuclear Weapon (1967) in Latin America (Treaty of Tlatelolco), 40, 266, 267

Treaty of Rarotonga (1985), 266, 267

Trujillo, Rafael, 398

Truman, Harry S, 51, 56, 57, 59, 60, 66, 69, 70, 71, 72, 74, 76, 79, 80-81, 82, 83, 114, 409, 433, 434
: doctrine of, 81

Tully, Grace, 74
Turkey, 145, 191, 327
Tyranny, 8
Tzu, Sun, 350

UK (United Kingdom) (*see also* Anglo;
    Britain; England), 11, 40, 41, 46,
    117, 143, 144, 145, 146, 264, 284,
    327, 344, 457, 461, 467
    : US-UK coalition forces attack
      on Iraq, 330-331, 343-344,
      346, 349, 367, 405
UNO (United Nations Organisation),
    8, 44, 45, 53, 58, 60, 63, 68, 68,
    91, 113, 134-135, 197, 227, 268,
    272, 273, 306, 327, 343, 345, 349,
    361, 461
    : Atomic   Development
      Authority (ADA), 59-60, 61,
      64
    : Atomic Energy Commission
      (UNAEC), 57-60, 61, 63, 64,
      81
    : Charter, 61, 361
    : General Assembly, 38, 59, 134-
      135, 196, 285, 359, 462, 463,
      467 : special session on
      disarmament, 145, 148
    : sanctions, 346
    : Security Council, 57, 59, 60,
      61, 62, 266, 273, 306, 307, 402
    : resolution 687, (1991), 272,
      276, 289, 299, 302; resolution
      (1993) on CTBT, 453, 463
    : UNSCOM (United Nations
      Special Commission), 298-299
USA (United States of America) *see also*
    America), 8, 11, 16, 18, 20, 21,
    28, 32, 33, 37-46 (*passim*), 53, 56,
    60, 63-70 (*passim*) 79, 80, 83-90
    (*passion*), 95, 99-103, 113-172,
    176, 181-257 (*passim*), 264, 280,
    283-286 (*passim*), 295, 307-314
    (*passim*), 321, 322, 325, 327, 328,
    334-348 (*passim*), 354-410
    (*passim*), 440, 442, 444, 446, 448,
    450, 451, 452, 455, 456, 457, 458,
    459, 461-468 (*passim*)
    : 15-megaton test at Bikini, 87
    : ASW operations, 127
    : aid to Pakistan, 357
    : allies, 211 (*see also* Allies)
    : Anglo-US invasion of Iraq
      (2003) (*see* Iraq)
    : anti-ballistic missile (ABM)
      system, 116
    : anti-nuclear freeze movements,
      16
    : Arms   Control   Impact
      Statement, 135
    : arms controllers, 160
    : Atomic Energy Commission
      (AEC), 286
    : CIA, 164, 166, 276
    : Competition with Soviet
      Union for building-up nuclear
      weapons by, 405-428
    : Defence Guidance (1982),
      100, 101
    : Energy Department War-
      heads, 468
    : foreign policy, 403
    : Golden Grail of strategic
      superiority, 101
    : inspection of US-supplied
      nuclear items, 280
    : intermediate nuclear forces
      (INF), 15-16, 17
    : Lawrence   Livermore
      Laboratory's National Ignition
      Facility, 468
    : long-range strategic missiles,
      115
    : MAD (*see* MAD)
    : MIRVED (*see* MIRVED)
    : MIRV (*see* MIRV)
    : MRVs (*see* MRVs)
    : Minuteman (*see* Minuteman)
    : missiles, 16, 17; programmes,
      115
    : National Security Council, 13,
      85, 135

: Navstar, 212
: New Look, 84, 85
: nuclear arsenal, 117-118
: nuclear balance between Soviet Union and, 189-192
: nuclear negotiators, 160-172
: nuclear peace efforts between Soviet Union and (nuclear debates), 414-439
: nuclear politics of, 160-172
: Organisation of American States (OAS), 91
: Pentagon, 13, 72, 346, 365, 366
: Pershing II, 17
: Polaris, 115, 116, 120, 121, 127, 130
: Presidential Directive 59 (1980), 100
: SAC, 114, 115, 116
: satellite, first, 115
: security, 394-405
: Strategic Air Command, 13, 30, 37, 113, 123, 206
: strategic competition between Soviet Union and, 148-172
: Strategic Defence Initiative (SDI), 17, 18
: strategic nuclear forces, 116
: thermonuclear first bomb (1954), 114
: thermonuclear explosion (1954), 41, 114
: thermonuclear reaction, first, 114
: Undersea Long-Range Missile System (ULMS), 121
: US-Britain coalition forces war against Iraq (*see* Iraq)
: US-China backroom deal, 462
: US-Japanese relations, 377
: US-Russian deal, 459
: US - Soviet nuclear relationship (conflict; rivalry; tension *see* Soviet Union)

: US - Soviet relations (*see* Soviet Union)
: US - USSR nuclear - arms control agreements, 276
: World Trade Center, Twin Towers of, terrorist attack on, 405

USSR (*see also* Russia; Soviet Union), 11, 13, 61, 63, 64, 85, 117, 284, 336
: Supreme Soviet of, 52
Ukraine, 330
Ustinov, 166
Uzbekistan, 356

Vajpayee, Atal Behari, 349
Van Evera, Stephen, 388, 399
Venezuela, 144
Versailles-Washington Treaty System, 352
Vladivostok, 118 protocol (1974), 118, 189
Vienna
: Congress of Vienna (1815), 29
: MFR negotiations in, 44
: Safeguards Committee in, 277-279
: Vienna Convention, 441-442
Vietnam, 19, 86, 104, 135, 183, 364, 409, 416, 426
: north, 18, 19, 20
: south, 18, 20
: US intervened in, 18
: Vietnamese Communists' defeat of France, (1954), 20
: war, 338, 408
Violence, 36-37, 390
von Moltke, Helmuth, 9, 384
von Schlieffen, Alfred, 9

WMD, 334, 337, 343, 344
Walker, William, 469
Wallace, Henry A, 56, 62, 81
Waltz, Kenneth, 373
Walzer, Michael, 75, 76-77

War (*see also* atomic war; nuclear war), 12, 14, 28-29, 35-36, 37, 48, 49, 51, 65, 67, 73-74, 83, 92-93, 95, 96, 97, 186, 194, 218, 226, 232, 236, 335, 380, 381, 387-389, 399, 408, 410, 411, 426, 428, 431, 432, 437
: Agreement on Prevention of Nuclear War (June 1973), 165
: avoidance of: US-Soviet effort, 414-439
: conventional, 233, 335
: Great War, 49
: limited war, old concept of, 14,
: World War I, 10, 14, 35, 48, 49, 226, 234, 343, 373, 376, 381
: World War II, 8, 11, 14, 20, 30, 32, 35, 45-46, 49, 55, 82, 113, 114, 117, 141, 143, 177, 182, 184, 224, 234, 242, 335, 343, 383, 411, 414, 416
: World War III, 184, 414
Warheads (nuclear), 118, 119, 121, 122, 125, 126, 128, 130, 163, 249, 250, 326, 330, 405, 407, 410, 411, 422, 428, 436, 468
Warlordism, 224
Warsaw Pact, 211, 212, 215, 330
Warsaw Treaty Organisation (WTO), 44, 46
Washington, 13, 16, 18, 43, 57, 60, 62, 70, 71, 75, 80, 88, 176, 190, 208, 213, 254, 256, 321, 344, 362, 407, 410, 416, 424, 426, 436, 451, 465, 466, 468, 469
: Versailles-Washington Treaty System, 352
: Washington Summit, 326, 329
Weapons (nuclear) (arms) (*passim* throughout text) (*see also* Arms; Atomic Energy; Bombs; Disarmaments; Missiles)
: binary, 42
: biological, 41-42
: Chemical, 42, 146, 277, 457, 465
: modern weapon systems, 45
: weapons-building plans, 148-172
: weapons technology, 193
Weinberger, 101, 435
West (Western Countries), 15, 53, 178, 310, 312, 313, 340, 341, 352, 380, 381, 389, 390, 396, 399, 409, 423, 425, 452, 453, 454, 457
: alliance, 423
: diplomatic practice (negotiators), 159-160
: East-West relations (bridges between), 96, 326, 424
: nuclear powers, 341, 342
: oil exploitation, 396
: state system, 12
West Asia (*see* Asia)
Wilson, Robert, 56, 376
Wilsonian ideals, 344
Winne, Harry A, 59
Woolsey, James, 451
World affairs (*see* International relations)
World Court, 465
World Health Organisation
: General Council of, 458
World Island (Asia-Europe-Africa and Heartland), 10, 11,
World Trade Centre, Twin Towers of
: terrorist attack on, 405

Yalta Agreement, 55, 70
Yeman
: Egypt's interventions in, 392
Yugoslavia, 145, 328, 348, 377, 383, 397, 409

Zaire, 141
Zia ul Haq, 355, 356, 357, 358
Zionist bomb, 356
Zionist mind, 356